Anonymus

Annual Report of the Comptroller of the Currency to the second session of the fifty-third Congress of the United States

December 4, 1803

Anonymus

Annual Report of the Comptroller of the Currency to the second session of the fifty-third Congress of the United States
December 4, 1803

ISBN/EAN: 9783742814302

Manufactured in Europe, USA, Canada, Australia, Japa

Cover: Foto ©Suzi / pixelio.de

Manufactured and distributed by brebook publishing software
(www.brebook.com)

Anonymus

Annual Report of the Comptroller of the Currency to the second session of the fifty-third Congress of the United States

ANNUAL REPORT

OF THE

COMPTROLLER OF THE CURRENCY

TO THE

SECOND SESSION OF THE FIFTY-THIRD CONGRESS

OF

THE UNITED STATES.

DECEMBER 4, 1893.

IN TWO VOLUMES.

VOLUME I.

WASHINGTON:
GOVERNMENT PRINTING OFFICE.
1893.

TABLE OF CONTENTS.

CONTENTS.

REPORT

OF

THE COMPTROLLER OF THE CURRENCY.

TREASURY DEPARTMENT,
OFFICE OF THE COMPTROLLER OF THE CURRENCY,
Washington, December 4, 1893.

SIR: In compliance with law I have the honor to herewith submit for the consideration of Congress the annual report of the Comptroller of the Currency. It covers the year which ended October 31, 1893, and is the thirty-first report made since the organization of the Bureau.

The records of the Bureau show that at the close of the year the total number of national banks in active operation was 3,796, with an authorized capital stock of $683,598,120, represented by 7,450,000 shares, held by 300,000 shareholders.

On October 3, the date of their last report of condition, the total resources of the 3,781 banks then in operation was $3,109,563,284.36, of which their loans and discounts aggregated $1,843,634,167.51, and money of all kinds in bank $369,862,636.97. Of their liabilities $1,451,-124,330.50 represented individual deposits, $339,153,447.54 surplus and net undivided profits, and $182,959,725.90 circulating notes outstanding.

The total amount of circulation of national banks, October 31, as shown by the books of the office, was $209,311,993, a net increase during the year of $36,886,972 and a gross increase of $40,775,165 on circulation secured by a deposit of bonds.

During the year 119 banks were organized in thirty-two States and Territories, with a capital stock of $11,230,000. Of these 44, with a capital stock of $5,135,000, are located in the Eastern States, 41 west of the Mississippi River, with a capital stock of $2,340,000, and 34 in the Central and Southern States, with a capital stock of $3,755,000.

The number of banks whose charters were extended was 40, distributed throughout twenty-five States, with a capital stock of $5,046,000, and circulation to the amount of $1,585,925. The charters of 4 expired, but in each instance the banks were succeeded by new associations.

Within the same period 158 banks suspended, with a capital stock of $30,350,000. Of this number, however, 86, with a capital stock of $18,205,000, resumed business. The number which passed into the hands of receivers was 65, with a capital stock of $10,935,000. On October 31 seven remained in the charge of examiners, with prospects of speedy resumption. Forty-six banks, with a capital stock of $5,735,000, went into voluntary liquidation.

By comparing the foregoing synopsis of the history of the banks for the year ended October 31, 1893, with that of the year ended October 31, 1892, as the same is set forth in the Comptroller's Report for that year, the following changes are noted: The number of banks organized decreased 44, receiverships increased 48, voluntary liquidations

3

decreased 7, corporate extensions decreased 47, and expirations of corporate existence decreased 7. The total gain in the number of active banks was 8.

The varying condition of the banks throughout the year appears from the following abstract of the reports of condition, made in response to the five calls required by law.

SUMMARY OF THE STATE AND CONDITION OF EVERY NATIONAL BANK REPORTING DURING THE YEAR ENDED OCTOBER 3, 1893.

	Dec. 9, 1892.	Mar. 6, 1893.	May 4, 1893.	July 12, 1893.	Oct. 3, 1893.
	3,784 banks.	3,806 banks.	3,830 banks.	3,807 banks.	3,781 banks.
RESOURCES.					
Loans and discounts.	$2,166,615,720. 28	$2,159,614,092. 48	$2,161,401,858. 50	$2,020,483,671. 04	$1,843,634,167. 51
U. S. bonds to secure circulation	166,449,250. 00	170,096,550. 00	172,412,550. 00	176,588,050. 00	206,463,850. 00
U. S. bonds to secure deposits	15,321,000. 00	15,351,000. 00	15,261,000. 00	15,256,000. 00	14,816,000. 00
U. S. bonds on hand	4,148,600. 00	4,372,600. 00	3,519,550. 00	3,078,050. 00	2,760,950. 00
Stocks, securities, etc	153,648,180. 71	153,420,770. 68	150,747,862. 86	149,690,701. 61	148,569,950. 46
Due from reserve agents	204,948,159. 79	202,612,051. 30	174,312,119. 44	159,352,677. 33	158,499,644. 28
Due from national banks	142,623,106. 36	124,384,884. 35	121,673,794. 24	111,956,506. 81	94,740,014. 97
Due from State banks and bankers	34,403,231. 75	30,126,300. 21	32,681,708. 90	27,211,234. 32	24,220,106. 82
Banking house, furniture, and fixtures	72,294,364. 78	72,680,344. 23	73,386,921. 79	72,750,830. 15	72,322,826. 68
Other real estate and mortgages owned	15,926,687. 47	17,030,064. 31	16,646,853. 69	16,632,446. 13	16,828,949. 40
Current expenses and taxes paid	14,204,970. 25	10,992,932. 60	11,746,470. 23	4,892,772. 88	11,071,996. 65
Premiums on U. S. bonds	13,913,289. 71	13,270,691. 10	12,935,077. 74	11,933,004. 69	13,981,867. 44
Checks and other cash items	16,755,332. 09	18,755,010. 52	17,546,973. 93	16,707,680. 61	15,359,764. 56
Exchanges for clearing house	110,522,668. 49	125,142,839. 74	114,977,271. 08	107,765,890. 44	106,181,394. 59
Bills of other national banks	20,488,761. 00	18,248,706. 00	20,085,688. 00	20,135,054. 00	22,402,611. 00
Fractional currency, nickels, and cents	893,909. 82	915,532. 50	952,810. 90	952,632. 48	1,026,813. 90
Specie	209,895,260. 76	208,341,816. 42	207,222,141. 81	186,761,173. 31	224,703,869. 07
Legal-tender notes	102,276,335. 00	90,935,774. 00	103,511,163. 00	95,833,677. 00	114,799,352. 00
U. S. certifs. of deposit	6,470,000. 00	14,675,000. 00	12,130,000. 00	6,600,000. 00	7,020,000. 00
Five percent redemption fund	7,282,413. 90	7,401,830. 74	7,467,989. 77	7,600,604. 72	8,977,414. 18
Due from Treasurer other than 5 per cent fund	1,268,405. 03	1,322,444. 60	1,556,801. 28	1,019,074. 42	1,262,749. 85
Total	3,480,349,667. 19	3,459,721,235. 78	3,432,176,697. 25	3,213,261,731. 94	3,109,563,284. 36
LIABILITIES.					
Capital stock paid in	689,698,017. 50	688,642,876. 00	688,701,200. 00	685,786,718. 50	678,540,338. 93
Surplus fund	239,931,932. 08	245,478,362. 77	246,139,133. 32	249,135,300. 30	246,750,781. 32
Undivided profits	114,603,884. 52	103,067,550. 15	106,060,733. 57	93,944,649. 73	103,474,662. 87
National-bank notes outstanding	145,669,490. 00	149,124,818. 00	151,694,110. 00	155,070,821. 50	182,959,725. 90
State-bank notes outstanding	74,176. 50	75,075. 50	75,075. 50	75,072. 50	75,069. 50
Dividends unpaid	1,308,137. 97	1,350,392. 10	2,579,556. 38	3,879,073. 50	2,874,607. 59
Individual deposits	1,764,456,177. 11	1,751,439,374. 14	1,749,930,817. 51	1,556,761,230. 17	1,451,324,330. 55
U. S. deposits	9,073,349. 92	9,813,762. 17	9,657,243. 49	10,379,842. 66	10,546,135. 51
Deposits of U. S. disbursing officers	4,034,240. 37	3,927,760. 44	4,293,739. 93	3,321,271. 84	3,776,438. 21
Due to other national banks	323,339,449. 03	304,785,336. 62	275,127,229. 28	238,913,573. 51	226,423,979. 06
Due to State banks and bankers	160,778,117. 18	166,901,054. 78	153,500,923. 94	125,079,422. 16	122,891,098. 21
Notes and bills rediscounted	15,775,618. 63	14,021,506. 43	18,953,306. 98	20,940,438. 50	21,066,737. 01
Bills payable	9,318,249. 82	18,180,228. 71	21,506,247. 53	31,381,451. 27	27,426,907. 54
Liabilities, other	1,688,817. 56	2,013,047. 88	3,051,379. 82	28,689,265. 08	31,632,352. 16
Total	3,480,349,667. 19	3,459,721,235. 78	3,432,176,697. 25	3,213,261,731. 94	3,109,563,284. 36

A comparison of the figures of 1893 with those of 1892 in the foregoing table will indicate to what extent and in what respect the national-banking interests of the country suffered from the severe and unusual monetary stringency which characterized the greater portion of the past year. Comparing their aggregate resources or liabilities on October 3, 1893, with those of September 30, 1892, it is found they were $400,531,613 less, being but $3,109,563,284 on the former date as against $3,510,094,897 on the latter, the highest point ever reached in the history of the national-bank system. This unparalleled shrinkage in liabilities is accounted for by a decrease between the dates mentioned in the following items, viz: Capital stock $8,032,677, individual deposits $314,298,653, and bank and bankers' deposits $181,338,125. An increase is shown in circulation outstanding to the amount of $39,536,428, in liabilities of all kinds for money borrowed $54,464,628, and in surplus and undivided profits $9,701,265.

Not less marked is the decrease in the items making up the resources of the banks. It shows as follows: Loans and discounts, $327,406,926; stocks, securities, etc., $5,965,564, and due from banks and bankers, $132,054,654. Cash of all kinds on hand increased $21,991,191, including $8,410,815 in gold, and United States bonds held for all purposes increased $40,601,250. These figures illustrate the far-reaching effect of the year's financial depression and show that when panic-stricken depositors withdrew their money the banks of necessity, to meet the sudden and extraordinary demands made upon them, called in their loans and discounts, supplementing such amounts by borrowed money and the additional circulation which they were able to procure from the Government through a deposit of bonds.

A closer examination of the figures contained in the reports of condition made to the Comptroller shows this shrinkage to have occurred chiefly between May 4 and October 3, 1893. Within this period of five months $298,806,487 of individual deposits and $79,313,076 of bank deposits, a total sum of $378,119,563 was withdrawn from the banks. To meet this withdrawal loans and discounts were reduced to the amount of $318,767,691; amounts due from banks and bankers, $51,198,856, and stocks, securities, etc., $2,177,912, and to provide against further danger of withdrawals of deposits, which strongly menaced them, the banks between the same dates increased their liabilities for money borrowed in various ways $36,615,092, and through the taking out of additional circulation $31,265,616, of which amount $27,888,905 was taken out between July 12 and October 3, 1893.

The cash resources of the banks, which on May 4, 1893, amounted to $343,901,803, were $32,559,267 less on July 12, but between that date and October 3 increased $59,520,1'0, amounting at the last-named date to $369,862,637, the largest sum ever held by them. This was accumulated in the face of continued heavy withdrawals of deposits and is the most practical demonstration that could be had of the solvency of the banks as a whole and their ability in an emergency to rapidly convert their assets into cash.

It is unnecessary to here enter upon a further or more specific analysis of these tables. They comply in detail with the requirements of the law, and show " a summary of the state and condition of every association from which reports have been received the preceding year, at the several dates to which said reports refer, with an abstract of the whole amount of banking capital returned by them, of the whole amount of their debts and liabilities, the amount of circulating notes outstanding, and the total amount of means and resources, specifying the amount of lawful money held by them at the times of their several returns."

The careful and unbiased student of the facts shown in this summary must inevitably reach the conclusion that the cause which more than all others contributed to bringing about the stagnation of the past months in commercial business, the suspension of manufacturing and the closing of mills, was this unprecedented demand on the part of depositors for money which the banks had distributed through the channels of trade and which, to meet this demand, they were obliged to withdraw.

The situation made so dangerous for the banks by the action of depositors caused a sudden contraction of the volume of money needed and already employed for business wants, prevented the making of new loans and rendered it hazardous on the part of the banks to grant renewals of credit, already extended. It is to be said, however, that despite the dangers threatening them, the banks contributed in the largest measure by a wise, judicious and, under all the circumstances, generous course, to the prevention of a general commercial panic. In evidence of this is the fact that at no time throughout the prolonged monetary stringency was there complaint made to the Comptroller by any depositor, creditor, or patron of a national bank on account of the treatment accorded him, either as to cash payments of indebtedness, or for any other reason.

So, too, it is worthy of remark that, when there is taken into consideration the widespread feeling of distrust so prevalent throughout these months, the fact most deserving of comment is not that so many banks closed their doors, but that so many were able to continue in operation. No stronger evidence can be had of the honesty, conservatism, and ability of those active in the management of the banks than the comparatively few failures which occurred, and no greater tribute can be paid to the principles upon which the system as a whole is based and administered.

Supplementary to the information which has already been given should be added that which bears upon the corporate existence of the banks of the system. The table on page 73 shows the title, capital, and circulation of associations whose corporate existence expired by limitation during the year, and of the associations which succeeded them, the new associations showing an increase in capital of $5,000 and an increase in circulation of $30,250.

The table on page 73 shows by States the number, capital stock, and circulation of the forty banks whose corporate existence was extended during the year. Their aggregate capital stock was $5,046,000, and their circulation $1,585,925.

The table on page 74 shows the charter numbers, title, location, date of expiration, capital, bonds, and circulation of the forty-nine associations whose corporate existence will expire during the year ending October 31, 1894. These associations are located in twenty different States, with an aggregate capital of $6,708,000, and circulation amounting to $2,006,950.

The table on page 73 shows by States the number, capital, and circulation of associations whose corporate existence will expire during the period from 1894 to 1903. Of these there are 777, with an aggregate capital of $117,275,850, and circulation of $32,467,992.

The table on page 72 shows by States the number and capital of the 1,466 banks, whose corporate existence has been extended since the beginning of the system, located in forty States and Territories, with an aggregate capital of $375,945,005. Of these, New York has 225, with a capital of $72,872,460, Massachusetts 209, with a capital of $88,612,500, and Pennsylvania 174, with a capital of $45,954,000.

Of the 119 banks organized, as shown in the table on page 71, Pennsylvania is first, with 25 banks, having a capital stock of $2,375,000, New York next, with 11 banks, with a capital stock of $2,050,000, Texas and Iowa have 10 each, with capital of $610,000 and $500,000, respectively. Wisconsin follows New York in amount of capital stock of newly organized banks, having $1,750,000, although the number of banks organized was but 5.

The marked difference in the number of banks organized during the year ended October 31, 1893, as compared with the preceding year, arises largely from the changed monetary conditions, but is also due in a measure to the very rigid rules now enforced in the granting of charters. It has become the policy of this Bureau to more carefully scrutinize all applications for authority to organize new banks, as the Comptroller appreciates the necessity of discrimination to protect the system from the entrance of associations whose weakness would be an injury. To this end the Comptroller before approving an application for authority to organize, satisfies himself in detail as to the business experience and financial responsibility of each of the applicants, by information obtained through inquiries from sources believed to be reliable.

BANKS OTHER THAN NATIONAL.

That the general statement of the resources, liabilities, and condition of banks and banking companies other than national, namely, State, savings, private banks, and loan and trust companies, may be presented to Congress, as is required by law, the Comptroller, through the courtesy of State officers having supervision of these institutions, has obtained official returns from each State and Territory, excepting Delaware, Maryland, South Carolina, Arkansas, Tennessee, Kansas, Nevada, Oregon, Idaho, Montana, Arizona, and Oklahoma. A summary of this information is here given to complete a résumé of the various banking interests of the country throughout the past year. It will be found in detail in the tables which appear in the appendix.

At the close of the fiscal year ended June 30, 1893, there were in operation in the United States 5,024 incorporated banks, banking institutions, and savings banks, and from 4,837, or 96 per cent, reports of conditions were received, an increase of 419 over the number reporting last year. The number of private banks from which reports were received is 313 less than last year, but the net increase is 106.

In view of the fact that the returns from banks other than national show their condition in most of the States prior to the financial stringency of 1893, the effect of that depression does not appear in these statistics with respect to banks organized under State authority.

The total resources of the 4,837 incorporated and 848 private banks, as shown by the returns from both official and unofficial sources, amount to $3,979,008,533, of which loans and overdrafts are $2,348,193,077; United States bonds, $149,952,221; State, county, etc., bonds, $407,709,961; railroad bonds and stocks, $133,729,231; bank stocks, $45,752,014; all other bonds, stocks, and securities, $272,430,923; due from banks and cash on hand, $250,700,719 and $205,645,203, respectively.

Of the liabilities the capital reported is $406,007,240: surplus and undivided profits, $346,206,287; individual deposits, $1,285,311,723; savings deposits, $1,785,150,957. The capital employed by the 3,579 State banks is $250,767,700, and their deposits $706,865,643. The reported capital of the 228 loan and trust companies is $94,867,268, and deposits $486,244,079.

The capital of the private banks is $26,943,075 and deposits $68,552,696. Nearly 51 per cent of the resources of the 5,685 banks is reported by the 1,030 savings banks, of which 614 are mutual and 381 stock savings institutions; the resources of the former, however, are over 84 per cent of those of both classes. With the exception of two banks in the Southern and 10 in the Western States, mutual savings banks are confined to the Eastern and Middle States. Excepting 17 in the Eastern and 7 in the Middle States, stock savings banks are located in the Southern, Western, and Pacific States and Territories.

It also appears that while the entire deposits in mutual savings institutions are "savings," the reports show that over 10 per cent of the deposits in the other class are not of that nature, and the presumption is that the percentage is much greater, as it is known that stock savings banks in certain States make no classification of deposits, and yet transact a commercial as well as a savings bank business.

In the table on page 226 is shown the resources and liabilities of both classes by States and geographical divisions, to which is appended a statement of the number of depositors and the average amount due each, by States, etc.

The table on page 237 is a consolidated statement of both classes, showing the aggregate number of depositors, amount of savings deposits, and the average amount due each in each State. The average savings deposit in the Eastern States is $359.48; in the Middle States, $362.21; in the Southern States, $168.21; in the Western States, $328.11; in the Pacific States and Territories, $661.22. The large average in the latter division is due to the fact that the average amount due depositors in the savings banks of California is $771.28; the average amount due depositors in that division, exclusive of California, being but $163.07.

On page 238 a table appears showing the growth of savings banks from 1820 to 1893, the interesting features of which are the average annual savings deposit and per capita deposit in each census year from 1820 to 1890, and annually since the latter date. The per capita deposit in 1820 was but 12 cents; in 1830, 54 cents; 1840, 82 cents; 1850, $1.87; 1860, $4.75; 1870, $14.26; 1880, $16.33; 1890, $24.35; and in 1891, 1892, and 1893, $25.29, $26.11, and $26.63, respectively. The number of savings banks in 1820 was 10; the number of depositors, 8,635; the amount of deposits, $1,138,576; and the average deposit, $131.86; the number of banks this year is 1,030; depositors, 4,830,599; deposits, $1,785,150,957; the average deposit $369.55; and per capita deposit, based on the estimated population on June 1, last, $26.63.

The aggregate loans of savings banks amount to $1,047,270,478, of which $763,579,985 are secured by real estate, $74,179,877 by collateral other than real estate, and the remainder, principally, by personal security. The stock and bond investments amount to $799,372,476, of which $129,610,783 are United States bonds, $398,606,298 State, county, and municipal bonds, $121,519,071 railroad bonds and stocks, $44,466,725 bank stocks, and $105,169,599 other stocks, bonds, and securities.

The capital stock of national banks on July 12 last, and of other banks, at date of latest returns to this Bureau, in each State and geographical division, is shown in the table on page 241. This table also shows the amount of capital stock per capita of population in each State. The total capital reported is $1,091,793,959, and the average per capita $16.29. By comparison with similar returns for 1892, it appears that there has been a shrinkage of capital to the extent of about $20,000,000, the average per capita at that time being $16.33.

In this connection data appearing in the table on page 242 showing the total amount of banking funds at the command of national and other banks, namely, capital, surplus, undivided profits and deposits, will be of interest, for, while as heretofore stated, their total capital is but $1,091,793,950, their aggregate banking funds amount to $6,412,939,954, and is an increase of $22,845,826 over the amount held on the same date in 1892. The estimated population of the United States on June 1 last was 67,021,000, making an average, per capita, of these funds of $95.68, as against an average of $97.42 in 1892.

The table referred to gives the average of these funds per capita of population and the per capita averages in each class of banks, and in all. The averages in each class are: National banks, $38.64; State banks, $15.83; loan and trust companies, $9.73; savings and private banks, $29.93 and $1.55, respectively.

The amount of coin, paper currency, etc., held by national banks on July 12, last, and by all other banks on or about the same date is shown in detail in the table to be found on page 240.

The aggregate reported is $515,987,740, of which $310,342,537 was reported by national banks and $205,645,203 by other banks; the total holdings were: Gold coin, $103,417,876; silver coin, $15,315,656; specie not classified, $15,093,221; paper currency, $264,602,355; fractional currency and cash not classified, $117,558,632.

In the appendix, pp. 219-251, will be found tables showing the condition at the date of latest returns of State banks, loan and trust companies, savings banks and private banks; State banks from 1872-'73 to 1892-'93; loan and trust companies, 1888-'89 to 1892-'93; savings banks, 1888-'89 to 1892-'93; number of depositors, amount of savings deposits, and average amount due each depositor in savings banks by States 1891-'92 and 1892-'93; growth of savings banks from 1820 to 1893; condition of private banks in 1889-'93; condensed statement showing the aggregate resources and liabilities of each and all classes of banks in 1892-'93; the capital of national banks on July 12, 1893, and of all other banks on or about the same date, and average per capita of population by States; the population of the United States by States, the capital, surplus, undivided profits, and deposits of national and other banks, the average of these funds per capita, and the per capita averages in each and all classes of banks; the cash holdings of national and other banks on or about July 12, 1893; the number, assets, and liabilities of State banks, etc., which suspended during the first eight months of 1893; the number, assets, and liabilities of suspended State banks, etc., which resumed business during the first eight months of 1893; the condition of the loan and trust companies of the District of Columbia on October 3, 1893, and the condition of the Canadian banks on August 31, 1893.

A condensation of the foregoing for the sake of comparison with national banks shows the principal items of resources and liabilities, and the total resources of banks other than national, as indicated by the latest returns to the Comptroller, to be as follows:

Items.	State banks.	Loan and trust companies.	Savings banks.	Private banks.
Loans	$763,051,774	$462,823,514	$1,047,270,478	$75,047,311
United States bonds	412,654	18,486,696	129,610,783	1,472,148
Other bonds	76,143,722	110,338,265	669,761,693	3,378,449
Capital	250,767,709	94,867,268	33,429,183	26,943,075
Surplus and undivided profits	103,137,836	70,771,477	163,473,173	8,823,801
Deposits	706,865,643	486,244,079	1,808,800,262	68,552,696
Total resources	1,130,725,537	726,664,506	2,013,775,147	107,843,343

That comparison is herewith made:

	National banks.	All other banks.
Loans, etc	$1,843,634,168	$2,348,193,077
United States bonds	224,040,800	149,982,221
All other bonds	148,569,950	859,622,129
Capital stock	678,540,339	406,007,210
Surplus and profits	350,225,444	346,206,287
Deposits	1,465,446,904	3,070,462,680
Total resources	3,109,563,284	3,979,008,533

SUSPENSIONS OF NATIONAL BANKS.

In the introductory pages of this report is indicated the number of associations " whose business has been closed during the year." In the appendix will be found tables giving in detail names, location, circulation redeemed and outstanding, voluntary liquidations, failures, and temporary suspensions of banks as is required by the statute to be furnished to Congress, together with such other facts as are necessary.

It does not seem essential, nor would it be possible to enter into a minute statement of all the circumstances attendant upon the closing of the banks during the past year. It is sufficient to say that the cause which brought about the large proportion of such suspensions was the action of depositors who, becoming doubtful of the solvency of the banking institutions of the country, withdrew their deposits. The result was that many banks after paying out on the one hand all the money in their vaults and failing to collect their loans on the other, suspended and passed into the hands of the Comptroller. With a full knowledge of the general solvency of these institutions and the cause which brought about their suspension, the policy was inaugurated of giving all banks, which, under ordinary circumstances would not have closed, and whose management had been honest, an opportunity to resume business. This policy was one which seemed to commend itself to the Comptroller as proper to pursue under the circumstances, and it is believed the results have justified the experiment of its adoption.

In no instance has any bank been permitted to resume on money borrowed or for which as an association it has become liable. Whenever those active in the management of the banks resuming, either as executive officers or directors, have been debtors to such banks, their indebtedness has been paid or secured, and whenever impairment of capital stock has been found, such impairment has been made good, either by voluntary or enforced assessment on the shareholders. In a number of instances changes have been made in the directory and official corps of resuming banks. The criticism to be made upon the management of these banks was the improper distribution of their loans, a circumstance which greatly retarded the conversion of such loans into money at a time when it was needed to avoid suspension.

Of the banks which failed to resume many had long been under the continual criticism of this Bureau for violations of law and imprudent methods of banking, and the closing of them was only hastened by the general condition of financial affairs. Some failed because of criminal acts on the part of the officials in charge, and others because of a lack of proper appreciation of the purposes of a bank.

An analysis of the suspensions and failures which occurred shows that during the year 158 national banking associations, as heretofore stated, were compelled to suspend business, being 4.09 per cent of the number of existing associations. Their capital stock aggregated $30,350,000, or approximately 4.3 per cent of the paid-in capital stock of all the banks in the system.

Of the banks which suspended 65, or 41.14 per cent, with a total capital stock of $10,935,000, were insolvent, and required the appointment of receivers; 86, or 54.43 per cent, with a capital stock aggregating $18,205,000, were able to resume business and 7, or 4.43 per cent, with a capital stock of $1,210,000, were placed in charge of examiners in the expectation of resumption. Of the suspended banks two were located in the New England States, both in New Hampshire, with a total capital stock of $250,000, for each of which a receiver was appointed.

In the Middle States there were three suspensions—two in New York, with a total capital stock of $500,000, and one in Pennsylvania, with a capital stock of $50,000. Those in New York were placed in the hands of receivers, and the one in Pennsylvania in charge of an examiner pending proposed resumption.

There were 38 suspensions in the Southern States, the capital stock involved aggregating $8,815,000. Of these 19, with a total capital stock of $5,630,000, resumed business, and the same number, with a total capital stock of $3,185,000, failed. In this geographical division, Texas furnished the greatest number of suspensions, namely 12, with a total capital stock of $1,480,000, of which 6, with a total capital stock of $430,000, resumed business, and the remainder, capitalized to the amount of $1,050,000, failed. There were 6 suspensions in Kentucky and the same number in Tennessee. The total capital stock of those in Kentucky was $2,300,000 and of those in Tennessee $2,750,000. In Kentucky all the banks that suspended, except one, with a capital stock of $50,000, were permitted to resume business. Two of the banks in Tennessee, with a total capital stock of $2,000,000, resumed business and 4 were placed in the hands of receivers. Four banks in Georgia suspended and the same number in Alabama, with a total capital stock of $675,000 and $550,000 respectively. Of these, 1 bank in Georgia, with a capital stock of $250,000, and 3 in Alabama, with a total capital stock of $400,000, resumed business. Two banks in North Carolina suspended, with a total capital stock of $300,000, both of which were able to resume business, but the two which suspended in Florida, with a total capital stock of $200,000, required the appointment of receivers, as did also the one in Mississippi, which had a capital stock of $60,000, and the one in Arkansas, with a capital stock of $500,000.

The Western States furnished 49 suspensions, with an aggregate capital stock of $10,125,000. Of these 31 resumed business, 17 failed, and 1 was placed in the charge of an examiner pending resumption or the appointment of a receiver. The capital stock of the banks which resumed aggregated $6,275,000, and of those which failed $3,750,000. The greatest number of suspensions which occurred in this section was in Kansas, namely, 8, although the capital stock involved, $880,000, was less than that of the banks in four other States. Four of the banks in Kansas, with a total capital stock of $480,000, resumed, and three, with a capital stock of $300,000, failed. Of the 7 banks in Indiana which suspended, 4, with a total capital stock of $450,000, resumed, and 3, with a total capital stock of $550,000, were placed in the hands of receivers. In Iowa 6 banks suspended, with a total capital stock of $575,000, of which number but one failed, with a capital stock of $50,000. The same number of banks in Nebraska suspended, three of which, with a total capital stock of $350,000, resumed business, and receivers were appointed for the remaining three, the total capital stock of which was $450,000. Five banks suspended in Wisconsin, with a total capital stock of $625,000, all of which resumed business, while in Illinois there were 4 suspensions, with a capital stock aggregating $2,150,000. All of these were placed in the hands of receivers. In Missouri 3 banks suspended, with a total capital stock of $1,300,000, all of which resumed. In Michigan there were the same number of suspensions as in Missouri, but the capital stock involved aggregated only $215,000. But one of these banks resumed, the capital stock of which was $65,000. The fewest suspensions which occurred in any State in this division was in Ohio, there being but 2, the aggregate capital stock of which was $180,000. One of these banks, with a capital stock of $80,000, resumed business and the other failed.

Sixty-six banks suspended in the Pacific States and Territories, being nearly 42 per cent of the total suspensions which occurred and represent capital stock amounting to 35 per cent of the total capital involved. Of these, 36 banks, with a capital of $6,300,000, were solvent and resumed business; 25, with a capital stock of $3,250,000, were placed in the hands of receivers, and 5, with a total capital of $1,060,-000, in charge of examiners pending resumption. The greatest number of suspensions was in Colorado, involving the largest amount of capital stock of suspended banks of any State in the Union, the number being 16 and the capital $3,600,000. All of these banks resumed, except two, the capital stock of which was $300,000. The second greatest number of suspensions occurred in the State of Washington, 14 banks, with an aggregate capital stock of $1,735,000. Of this number 4, with a capital stock of $425,000, resumed; 3, with a capital stock of $510,000, were placed in charge of examiners pending resumption, and 7 failed. The suspensions in Montana numbered 10, and their capital stock amounted to $1,875,000. Of these, 2, with a capital stock of $300,000, resumed, and 7, with a capital stock of $1,075,000, were placed in the charge of receivers. Six suspensions occurred in Oregon, and the same number in California, the aggregate capital stock represented being $800,000 and $1,200,000, respectively. There was but one failure in each State, the capital stock in the case of the Oregon bank being $100,000, and that of the California bank $250,000. There were 3 suspensions in Utah, 3 in North Dakota, and 3 in South Dakota. The three banks in Utah, with a capital stock aggregating $250,000, resumed business, while the three in North Dakota, with a total capital stock of $400,000, failed. Two of the banks in South Dakota, with a total capital stock of $100,000, were placed in the hands of receivers, and one, with a capital stock of $125,000, resumed. Two suspensions occurred in Wyoming, and the same number in New Mexico. One bank in Wyoming, with a capital stock of $200,000, resumed, and one, the capital stock of which was $50,000, failed. Of the banks in New Mexico, one, with a capital stock of $175,000, failed, and the other, with a capital stock of $50,000, was placed in the hands of an examiner pending resumption or the appointment of a receiver. The only other suspension in this geographical division occurred in Oklahoma, being that of a bank with a capital stock of $50,000, which, being solvent, resumed.

In the appendix, page 80, will be found the information above referred to in tabular form.

The official records show that of 4,930 national banks organized since February, 1863, 246, or about 5 per cent, have been placed in the hands of receivers. In this number are included 9 banks which had previously gone into voluntary liquidation, but upon failing to pay depositors the Comptroller appointed receivers to wind up their affairs. Of the 246 failed banks, 39 have paid their creditors, principal and interest in full, 7 have paid principal and a part of the interest, and 16 have paid the principal only. The affairs of 115 of the 246 banks have been finally closed, leaving 131 in process of settlement, of which 16 are virtually closed, with the exception of undetermined litigation. There are 115 receiverships in active operation. In four instances prior to October 31, 1893, the receiverships were terminated and the banks permitted to resume business.

The total amount thus far paid to creditors of insolvent national banks is $50,943,147, upon approved claims aggregating $81,963,207. The amount paid during the year was $3,041,134.90. Assessments under the provisions of section 5151 of the Revised Statutes of the United States aggregating $20,118,350 have been made upon shareholders of insolvent national banks. From this source the gross collections have been $8,035,931, of which there was received during the past year $462,171. The affairs of but five banks have been closed during the year and final dividends paid to creditors, while the titles of four on the inactive list in 1892 have disappeared.

It is a source of regret that no better exhibit is made of dividends paid to the creditors of failed national banks during the past year, but the same conditions which produced so many failures seriously retarded the ability of receivers to collect the assets of their trusts, and consequently large dividends could not be declared. However, when are taken into consideration the many embarrassments of the year, the general average is good. In the appendix will be found a tabular statement of all dividends, expenses, and kindred matters connected with the trusts which are yet in process of liquidation.

SUSPENSION OF BANKS OTHER THAN NATIONAL.

The same causes which so seriously affected the national banks affected in like manner State, savings, and private banks, and loan and trust companies.

During the year ended June 30, 1892, there were 69 failures of private banks and of those incorporated under State authority, with liabilities amounting to $11,024,628 and assets to $6,125,189. The failures included 24 State banks, with $3,177,529 liabilities; 6 savings banks, with $917,000 liabilities; 36 private banks, with $6,505,099 liabilities; and 3 loan and trust companies, with $425,000 liabilities.

The number of failures of this class during the last six months of 1892 was 35, of which 18 were State banks, 16 private banks, and 1 a loan and trust company. During the first eight months of the current calendar year the failures and suspensions, as reported by the Bradstreet Agency, numbered 415, the assets aggregating $94,291,348 and the liabilities $97,193,530. Of these institutions 79, or 19 per cent, with liabilities amounting to 14 per cent of the total liabilities of the suspended banks, resumed business.

The number, assets, and liabilities, by classes, of banks which suspended and of those which resumed, from January 1 to September 1, 1893, are shown in the following table:

Class.	Suspended.			Resumed.		
	Number.	Assets.	Liabilities.	Number.	Assets.	Liabilities.
State banks............	172	$41,281,848	$36,903,266	44	$10,828,088	$7,255,885
Savings banks.........	47	17,673,938	16,830,809	10	3,657,013	2,541,936
Loan and trust companies	13	14,337,500	22,354,000	2	1,850,000	1,215,000
Mortgage companies....	6	760,803	1,790,000	....	....	....
Private banks	177	20,237,259	19,315,455	23	4,680,875	2,903,200
Total	415	94,291,348	97,193,530	79	21,015,976	13,916,021

For purposes of comparison the following statement is given, showing the number of national, State, and other banks, in existence on July 1, 1893; the number and per cent of resumptions, failures, etc., of national banks during the year ended October 31, and of other banks during the first eight months of the current calendar year:

Class.	Number in existence July 1, 1893.	Suspensions.		Resumptions.		Failures.		In charge of national bank examiners.	
		No.	Per cent.	No.	Per cent.	No.	Per cent.	No.	Per cent.
National banks............	*3,857	158	4.09	86	2.23	65	1.68	7	.18
State and savings	5,024	219	4.36	54	1.07	......	......	......	......
Loan and trust companies.	(?)	19	(?)	2	(?)	......	......	......	......
Private	3,950	177	4.48	23	.58	......	......	......	......
Total...................	12,831	573	....	165	....	65	....	7	....

* June 1, 1893.

In the appendix, pp. 244-246, will be found tables showing, by classes, States, and geographical divisions, the suspensions and resumptions of State banks, etc., from January to September, 1893. It appears from the first table that of the total suspensions 172 were State banks, 47 savings banks, 177 private banks, 13 loan and trust companies, and 6 mortgage companies. Of the ten suspensions in the Eastern States, 6 occurred in New Hampshire, 3 in Vermont, and 1 in Rhode Island. In the Middle States 15 suspensions occurred in New York, 8 in Pennsylvania, 1 in New Jersey, and 1 in Delaware. The Southern States had 61 suspensions, of which 12 were in Texas, 10 in Tennessee, 8 in Virginia, 6 in Georgia, 6 in Florida, 4 in Alabama, 4 in Kentucky, 3 in Arkansas, 2 in West Virginia, 2 in North Carolina, 2 in South Carolina, and 1 in Louisiana. The most severe effects were felt in the Western States, both in the number of suspensions, which were 232, and the amount of liabilities, which were $51,777,665, or 56 per cent and 53 per cent, respectively. In Kansas, the largest number (32) occurred, though the liabilities were but 3 per cent of the total; Wisconsin, with 30 suspensions, followed, but the liabilities were over 14 per cent of the total; in Ohio 27 were reported, Minnesota 26, Illinois 24, Indiana 23, Iowa 22, Missouri 21, Nebraska 16, and Michigan 11. The number occurring in the Pacific States and Territories was 87, of which California furnished 21, with liabilities amounting to nearly 8 per cent of the aggregate of all the banks. Colorado followed California in number (20), although the liabilities were less than half of those of the banks in California. Oregon furnished 13 suspensions, Washington 11, Montana 8, Idaho 4, Wyoming 3, North Dakota 3, and Utah, New Mexico, Arizona, and Oklahoma 1 each.

The second table referred to gives similar information in detail with respect to banks which have resumed. Of the 79 resumptions, 44 were State banks, or 25+ per cent of the total suspensions; 10 savings banks, or 21 per cent; 2 loan and trust companies, or 15 per cent, and 23 private banks, or 13 per cent. Of the suspensions in the New England States, there was but one resumption, that of a private bank in Vermont. One savings and 2 State banks resumed in New York. Of the 61 banks which closed in the Southern States, 8 reopened: 2 in West Virginia and one each in South Carolina, Georgia, Florida, Alabama, Louisiana, and Texas. As the suspensions in the Western States were the most numerous, so also were the resumptions, 58 per cent of the total resumptions being reported from that division. In Minnesota, 10 occurred; in Ohio, Wisconsin, and Iowa, 6 each; in Missouri, 5; Indiana and Kansas, 4 each; in Michigan, 3, and Nebraska, 2. The resumptions in the Pacific States and Territories were confined to California (13), Colorado (7), and Montana (1).

The fright among depositors of the present year appears to have affected all classes of banking institutions alike. The shrinkage of deposits of national banks from May 4 to July 12 last exceeded $190,000,000. In order to ascertain the extent of the shrinkage in banks other than national, the Comptroller requested each State officer charged with the supervision of banks organized under State authority to submit a statement showing similar information with respect to that class of banks. Replies were received from the officers of 23 States and 2 Territories indicating that the loss to banks of this character corresponded with that shown by the returns from national banks. Generally no information was given with respect to savings banks and much less regarding private banks.

CLEARING-HOUSE LOAN CERTIFICATES.

The unprecedented condition of the money market from June to September called for extraordinary remedies, not only to avert general disaster to the banks but to prevent commercial ruin. This remedy was the issuing of clearing-house loan certificates, which were brought into use as in 1873, 1884, 1890–'91, by the associated banks of New York, Boston, Philadelphia, Baltimore, and other cities where needed. The service rendered by them was invaluable, and to their timely issuance by the associated banks of the cities named is due the fact that the year's record of suspensions and failures is not greatly augmented.

The form of these certificates, with the conditions under which they were issued in 1890–'91 (the form and conditions being the same during the late issuance of them as then), is described at length in the Comptroller's Annual Report for 1891. The subject is alluded to again only because it constitutes a very important part of the year's banking history, and for the additional reason that here and there are to be found those who entertain an entirely erroneous idea of the purpose for which these certificates were issued and what was accomplished by their issuance. Briefly stated, they were temporary loans made by the banks associated together as a clearing-house association, to the members of such association, and were available to such banks only for the purpose of settling balances due from and to each other, these balances under normal conditions of business being always settled in coin or currency. Each clearing-house association selected a committee charged with the issuing of the certificates to each bank desiring the same, such bank being required before receiving them to deposit with the committee its bills receivable, or other securities, as collateral for the loan. The amount of certificates issued to each bank was limited to 75 per cent of the value of the securities deposited. They bore interest at rates varying from 6 to $7\frac{3}{10}$ per cent. Immediately upon their surrender to the committee they were canceled and the securities held as collateral were returned to the bank depositing the same.

At a time when vast sums of coin and currency were being withdrawn from the banks, to be hoarded, these loan certificates, by performing the functions of the currency or coin customarily required for settling daily balances at the clearing house, released so much currency or coin to the legitimate and current demands of business and unquestionably placed it within the power of the banks in the cities named to extend to outside banks the aid needed on the one hand and liberally granted on the other. In no instance were these certificates designed to nor did they circulate as money. They were but due-bills and their sole function consisted in discharging the single obligation at the clearing house. An attempt on the part of a bank in any of the associations issuing these certificates to use them otherwise would have incurred a fine and other penalties provided in the rules governing such associations. Their issuance at so early a date in the financial derangement of the country was most opportune in not only preventing an acute panic, but in tending to restore public confidence, such action demonstrating that by mutual agreement of all, the weak banks of the association would be, so far as depositors and other creditors were concerned, as strong as the strongest.

In inaugurating the issuing of certificates so promptly and in issuing them to so large an amount the Clearing-house Association of New York, in particular, rendered the country great service, and the associated banks of that city are entitled to the credit which the public generally accords them.

The following figures, showing the movement and amount of the issue of loan certificates in 1893 in the cities named, will indicate the measure of relief afforded by them:

	Date of issue of first certificate.	Date of largest amount outstanding.	Largest amount outstanding.	Date of surrender of last certificate.	Amount outstanding Oct. 31.
New York	June 21	Aug. 29 to Sept. 6	$38,280,000	Nov. 1	
Philadelphia	June 16	Aug. 15	10,905,000		$3,835,000
Boston	June 27	Aug. 23 to Sept. 1	11,445,000	Oct. 20	
Baltimore	do	Aug. 24 to Sept. 9	1,475,000		815,000
Pittsburg	Aug. 11	Sept. 15	987,000		332,000
Total			63,152,000		

The issue of loan certificates in 1893 greatly exceeded that of previous years. In 1873 and 1884 they were issued only by the New York Clearing House Association, the total amount issued in 1873 being $26,565,000 and in 1884 $24,915,000.

In 1890-'91 they were issued in New York, Boston, and Philadelphia, the largest amounts outstanding at any time being as follows:

	Date of first issue.	Largest amount outstanding at any one time and date of same.
New York	Nov. 12, 1890	$15,205,000, Dec. 13, 1890.
Boston	Nov. 19, 1890	5,065,000, Dec. 6, 1890.
Philadelphia	Nov. 19, 1890	29,140,000, Jan. 9, 1891.
Total		49,410,000

LAWFUL MONEY RESERVE.

Not less attention has been attracted during the present year, and particularly during the closing months of the year, to the subject of lawful-money reserve to be held by the banks, than to that of clearing-house loan certificates, and the discussion provoked has been quite as widespread.

As the law now stands all national banks, outside of certain designated "reserve cities," are required to maintain a reserve fund equal to 15 per cent of the net deposits made with such banks by individuals and by other banks and bankers. They are permitted by law to deposit not over three-fifths of this 15 per cent (or 9 per cent) with such national banks located in the "reserve cities" as the outside banks may with the Comptroller's approval select. The remaining two-fifths (or 6 per cent) must be kept in bank in lawful money, or more, if less than three fifths is kept with reserve agents. The national banks located in reserve cities are divided into two classes: (1) Those in the "central" reserve cities of New York, Chicago, and St. Louis being required to keep 25 per cent of their net deposits in bank in *lawful money*, with the privilege of acting as the reserve agents of any national banks located outside of these three cities. (2) Those located in the reserve cities, other than New York, Chicago, and St. Louis, being required to keep 25 per cent of their net deposits on hand, not over one-half of which may be deposited with any national bank or banks located in any of the three central reserve cities, while the remainder must be actually on hand in lawful money. The banks in the reserve cities of this class have the privilege of holding a part of the reserve of any bank or banks located outside of all reserve cities, viz, banks of the 15 per cent class.

In effect these requirements are not as onerous as they appear, for a national bank in New York City holding $100,000 of the reserve of any other bank or banks on deposit must keep only $25,000 of the amount on hand in money, while it is at liberty to lend or otherwise invest the remaining $75,000. So a bank in a reserve city of the second class holding $100,000 on deposit for other national banks may loan out or invest $75,000 of the amount, and of the remaining $25,000 must keep $12,500 in bank in money and may deposit $12,500 with its reserve agents, receiving a low rate of interest (usually 2 per cent) on the same. A bank of the 15 per cent class must keep only 6 per cent of its depositors' money actually on hand in bank, and is at liberty to deposit not over 9 per cent with its reserve agents, on which it usually receives a low rate of interest. To illustrate the operation of the law it will be found that with normal conditions of business the banks in reserve

10665 CUR——2

cities (not central) held on December 9, 1892, net deposits amounting to $495,196,952, against which they held $77,869,593 cash in bank, or about 16 per cent, and the 15 per cent banks held net deposits of $975,622,088, and against these $108,012,546 cash in bank, or about 11 per cent. Again, a large portion of the reserve actually held by the banks can not be considered as taken out of circulation, or as hoarded through operation of the law, for much of it is paid out during each business day, other money coming in through deposits to take the place of that paid out.

In any view of the matter, however, the intent of the law is to compel a bank to retain always on hand a very moderate proportion of the money deposited with it for safe keeping by the depositor, who practically makes a loan to the bank payable on demand, for the use of which he ordinarily receives no interest. The entire effect is to exercise a wholesome restraint upon a tendency to an undue extension of business by a bank, and that this intent is recognized as an underlying principle of safe and conservative commercial banking is evidenced by the fact that those banks which are compelled by law to maintain but 15 per cent reserve have voluntarily for years past held an average of over 25 per cent, the proportion required for banks located in reserve cities.

The evident theory of the law is that a bank shall always have on hand such an amount of lawful money as will enable it under normal conditions of business to meet the current demands of its depositors. A careful examination of section 5191, United States Revised Statutes, as amended, will show that it is expected that emergencies will arise under which this fund will fall below the legal requirements. This contingency is distinctly recognized by the plain provisions contained in the section named, prescribing what shall be done " whenever the lawful money reserve of any association shall be below the amount" of the required percentage of its deposits. The provisions referred to are that the bank shall make no new loans or discounts, except the discount of bills of exchange payable at sight, nor make any dividend of its profits until the required amount of reserve has been again accumulated. The reason for this is obvious. The depletion of a bank's reserve occurs either because the bank has loaned out or otherwise invested too great a proportion of the funds it has received on deposit, or that its depositors have withdrawn their money to an extent which produces a similar result. In either case the only safe and prudent course for the bank to pursue is to cease paying out money in any direction except to depositors until either through the collection of demand or maturing loans on the one hand, or the receipt of deposits on the other, the required proportion has been restored. The discount of sight bills of exchange is excepted because money invested in this way will be repaid immediately, and in this branch of its business the bank's customers will be caused no inconvenience and the commercial interests of the country be thus protected from loss which otherwise might ensue.

The provision of law governing the time allowed a bank to make good a depleted reserve is most lenient. It provides that the Comptroller *may* notify the bank to make good its reserve, and further that if it fails for thirty days thereafter to do this the Comptroller, with the concurrence of the Secretary of the Treasury, *may* appoint a receiver for the bank. However, before the Comptroller can send notice to any bank he must have reliable information that its reserve is deficient, and as the source of such information is either the report of its examination heretofore made once a year, but hereafter to be made twice, or its sworn report of condition made five times a year, some time may intervene before such condition becomes known to him. Again, when he is officially informed, the use of the word *may* both as to his sending notice and as to his appointing a receiver in a case of noncompliance with such notice, plainly leaves the enforcement of the law to the discretion of the Comptroller in either or both of these particulars. This power thus conferred upon the Comptroller is one that ought to be used with great prudence and caution. It would be not only unwise but would work great injury to the business interests of individual communities and the general public to exercise the authority thus vested in him at a time when arbitrary action must necessarily result in general disaster, and therefore in the interest of the public the discretion given to the Comptroller has always been used with moderation. It is this moderation which in an emergency has in numerous instances contributed in no small degree to averting widespread financial ruin. In this view there can be no question as to the legality and propriety of a bank's exhausting its entire reserve, if necessary, in an emergency, to pay its depositors, but for no other purpose, except to discount or buy sight bills of exchange, and where the withdrawal of deposits continues or is likely to continue no careful bank manager needs to be informed that not only must he cease to make new loans and discounts, but must replenish his exhausted stock of lawful money by converting his resources into cash through collections of loans and discounts or selling securities, or where this is not possible by using these assets to borrow the money needed to enable him to meet his liabilities.

Tabular statements showing deposits, reserve required, and reserve held, classification of reserve, and average percentage of same on or about October 1 of each year from 1874 to 1893, both inclusive, will be found on pages 130–131 of the appendix, also a table, page 134, showing similar information at the date of each report of condition from December 9, 1892, to October 3, 1893. This last-named table is inserted to show the movement of the reserve during the financial stringency of the present year, both as to volume and average percentage of deposits. An inspection of these figures will show that the average percentage of reserve to deposits from December 9, 18 2, to July 12, 1893, varied only between 26.42 per cent and 27.24 per cent, and that on October 3, 1893, the average increased to 32.66 per cent. In volume the amount of lawful money actually held by the banks was $318,641,595 on December 9, 1892, decreased to $289,244,850 on July 12, 1893, but increased by October 3, 1893, to $346,433,212, an amount approximating $57,000,000 greater than on July 12, 1893, when the panic was at its height, and almost $27,000,000 greater than on December 9, 1892, when business was in a normal condition.

AMENDMENTS RECOMMENDED.

By provision of law it is made incumbent upon the Comptroller of the Currency to call the attention of Congress to "any amendment to the laws relative to banking by which the system may be improved and the security of the holder of its notes and other creditors may be increased." There are certain amendments which it is obvious ought to be made, and which, in their operation, would make the present system more nearly serve the purpose for which it was designed, and to a measurable extent give an increase in the volume of circulation, if such is desirable. The following amendments to the law as it now stands **are recommended to be made.**

(1) That every association be authorized to issue circulating notes equal to the par value of the bonds deposited.

No good reason can possibly exist at present for depriving the banks or the business interests of the country of the additional circulation which would be added by such amendment. Whatever reason may have existed at the time of the enactment of the present provision does not now exist and its effect is to make circulation unprofitable and to lock up in bond investments the difference between 90 per cent and 100 per cent of this par value which, under the amendment suggested, would be adding to active circulation, under the present deposit of bonds, $20,941,635.

(2) That the semi-annual duty on circulation be so reduced as to equal one-fourth of 1 per cent per annum.

In support of this proposed amendment it is respectfully suggested that the present rate of tax takes from the banks a very large sum of money which is not used by the Government to meet the expenses for which the tax was originally laid. Its bearing upon the question of an increased circulation on the part of the banks is important, as the additional cost entailed by it of necessity so largely reduces the profits of circulation and adds to the cost of taking it out that banks will not, except under other circumstances, increase their issue.

Unwillingness on their part to add to the volume of currency, coupled with a tendency some years since to decrease the same, has subjected the banks to criticism. Such criticism, however, is unjust in this, that it is based on the idea that the banks are simply indifferent to the matter and are content to be banks of deposit and discount rather than banks of issue. The fact is banks ceased taking out circulation simply because until recently there was no profit in it. The high price of Government bonds necessary to be deposited, coupled with the tax upon circulation, and the refusal to grant more than 90 per cent of the par value of the bonds in currency return, has rendered circulation either without profit or profitable to so slight an extent as to offer no inducement to banks to take out circulation.

The Government can not relieve the banks of the additional expense to them by reason of the premium on bonds to be deposited, but it can materially lessen the cost of their circulation by enacting the amendments suggested, and in this manner offer an inducement, which is now wholly wanting, to the banks to add to the volume of bank-note circulation. The whole question is one of a business character. Banks are but business institutions, conducted upon the same lines and for the same purpose as other business undertakings. It can not be expected that they will do that which either entails a positive loss or warrants little or no profit, and if relief is to come through an expansion of the national-bank currency, Congress must remove rather than erect unnecessary barriers.

The following amendments pertaining to the administration and conduct of banks are recommended :

(3) That the Comptroller of the Currency, with the approval of the Secretary of the Treasury, be empowered to remove officers and directors of a bank for violations of law, first giving such officers and directors an opportunity to be heard, leaving the vacancy so created to be filled in the usual way.

It is respectfully suggested that the powers now vested in the Comptroller do not accomplish the result that they otherwise would if the law permitted the removal of officers and directors for misconduct in office. Many banks would be saved from embarrassment, creditors from loss, and shareholders from assessments if the Comptroller, upon learning of the misconduct of those charged with the management of a bank, could take positive action in the premises.

(4) That no executive officer of a bank or employé thereof be permitted to borrow funds of such bank in any manner, except upon application to and approval by the board of direction.

This amendment is recommended with the knowledge that the House of Representatives, at the late special session of Congress, passed a bill (H. R. 2344), entitled "An act for the better control of and to promote the safety of national banks," which bears upon the same subject-matter, but differs in that it embraces in its provisions all directors of a bank, instead of confining them to the executive officers and employés only.

At the best the question as to what extent loans and discounts should be made by a bank to its directors and executive officers by reason of the various circumstances under which these are granted is a difficult one to satisfactorily legislate upon, and an equally difficult one upon which to make specific recommendations. Where money is borrowed directly by any such officer or director to an amount exceeding the limit prescribed by section 5200 of the Revised Statutes of the United States, the Comptroller's duty is as plain as in any other case where the law is violated, but the limit to which discounts should be granted them is a question involving consideration of safety and prudence. Holding this view, the Comptroller has, in cases where the aggregate of loans and discounts to executive officers and directors appeared to be out of proportion to the total loans and discounts made by the bank, addressed the following form of letter to the bank, with the request that all directors unite in a reply:

TREASURY DEPARTMENT,
OFFICE OF COMPTROLLER OF THE CURRENCY,
Washington, D. C., ——, 189 .

————,
Cashier, —— ——,
—— —— :

SIR: Upon examination of your report of condition on ——, it is found that the "loans and discounts upon which officers and directors are liable" amount to $——, out of total loans and discounts of $——.

While recognizing the right of directors and officers to borrow within the limitations of law and safety, the Comptroller must insist most rigidly that directors and others connected with the bank in this fiduciary relation shall not avail themselves of the easy opportunity afforded them to borrow beyond this limit, either directly or indirectly, the funds intrusted to their keeping, in order to carry on enterprises outside of the banks with which they are connected.

Officers and directors should remember that the funds held by banks are in a large measure funds of others held in trust for the safe-keeping thereof, and, as trust funds, ought not to be loaned to the trustees of such funds, except upon the very best collateral or other security.

In the matter of accommodations to them, directors and officers should be placed upon the same footing as other customers of the bank, except that their financial ability and standing should be the more rigidly scrutinized, for the reason that they act in the dual capacity of lenders as well as borrowers.

The continued experience of this office is that such loans in many instances result disastrously to all concerned, and therefore the danger attending upon such a course ought not to be risked. The Comptroller must insist that this condition of affairs be remedied with the least possible delay, by reducing the amount of these accommodations to safer and more reasonable limits.

Please bring this communication to the immediate attention of your board of directors for consideration, and request them to unite in making a prompt reply over their individual signatures.

Respectfully, yours,

—— ——,
Comptroller.

The information upon which this letter is based is found in the reports of condition made under oath to the Comptroller, in which appear the indebtedness of every kind and character of each director and officer of the bank.

Accompanying this letter is sent to directors a copy of such sections of the National Bank Act as prescribe their duties and the penalties attaching for the nonperformance of them.

Beyond the substance of the amendment above set forth the Comptroller is not prepared to recommend any legislation upon this subject.

It seems that a difference should be made between loans to and overdrawn accounts of directors, who are simply directors, and of those who are the executive officers of a bank, and as such have and receive adequate compensation for the active management of its affairs. The abuse of the easy privilege of loaning to themselves is generally on the part of the managing officers, and not on the part of directors who are only members of the board of direction, and hence the distinction which is drawn between the recommendation here made and the bill referred to.

So far as loans, through drafts or otherwise, to directors who are not executive officers of the bank, are concerned, there are strong reasons against the advisability of such legislation. Any positive restriction imposed by direct law might have the effect of deterring honest, intelligent, and substantial men from serving as directors. As a rule, men of this class are sought for these positions in order to obtain the benefit of their judgment and business capacity in managing the affairs of the bank, and to secure their own business for the bank. This business does not consist alone of deposits, but is largely made up of loans and discounts, by means of which the profits are chiefly earned. As a rule these directors receive no compensation for their services, which are rendered largely through motives of interest as shareholders, or of pride in holding a position supposed to give a certain prominence in business circles.

An inquiry as to the practice of banks paying directors for attendance upon meetings showed that in some cities this is in vogue. It would be better for all concerned if all banks adopted such policy. However small the compensation, it could not but result in benefit to the shareholders and more than compensate for the expense involved. The general criticism to be passed upon directors is their failure in so many instances to give to the business of the bank the attention their oaths and duties require. The successful administration of a bank's affairs depends upon the watchfulness and fidelity of the board of directors. When such conduct is wanting bank failures ensue, or if failures do not follow great loss to shareholders is entailed through want of profits or assessment to make good the impairment of capital stock caused by imprudent loans. The administration of the Comptroller, if supplemented by the watchful care of directors, would minimize even the comparatively few failures which occur.

(5) That the assistant cashier, in the absence or inability of the cashier of a national bank to act, be authorized and empowered to sign the circulating notes of such bank.

This amendment is suggested in order to meet a difficulty which has arisen in numerous instances during the past months, there being no provision in the law for any one to sign currency for the cashier in his absence or inability to act, and banks are frequently put to serious inconvenience on this account.

(6) That the law be amended by appropriate legislation so as to empower some class of public officers to administer the general oaths required by the provisions of the National Bank Act.

The necessity for this amendment is occasioned by the fact that the authority of officers empowered to administer oaths is now restricted under the Federal statutes to certain specific cases, and with the exception of the acknowledgment of the organization certificate and the verification of reports of condition, required by section 5211 of the Revised Statutes of the United States, no provision is made for administering the oaths required of the officers of national banks.

The following amendments bearing upon the subject of bank examiners would, the Comptroller believes, result in benefit, and are therefore recommended:

(7) That bank examiners be required to take an oath of office before entering upon the discharge of their duties, and to give bond with proper conditions in such amount and with such sureties as the Comptroller of the Currency may require.

An anomoly is presented in the case of bank examiners, which does not appear in that of any other public official. No position under the Government is more responsible in the duties attaching to it, and none requires a higher degree of integrity in the incumbent. The exception is rare where dishonesty has been found in examiners, but it is the opinion of the Comptroller that an oath, such as is required of other officers under the Government, should be taken and a bond given.

(8) That the Comptroller of the Currency, with the approval of the Secretary of the Treasury, be empowered to appoint two general examiners of conspicuous ability and experience to be paid out of the reimbursable funds, whose duty it shall be to visit, assist, and supervise the various examiners in their several districts, in order to secure uniformity in method and greater efficiency in work.

This amendment has been heretofore recommended by former Comptrollers, and the reasons for it suggested. It would aid in uniformity of method and give to the office of the Comptroller at all times officers who could do special and confidential work, which can not be done at present, because no compensation is provided.

(9) That the law be so amended as to provide that the compensation of all bank examiners be fixed by the Comptroller of the Currency, with the approval of the Secretary of the Treasury.

This amendment is suggested in the interest of better examinations. Thoroughness in bank examinations is not to be expected under a system in which compensation is provided for and ascertained by a method that furnishes a constant temptation to the examiners to neglect their duty. Under the law as it now stands the compensation for bank examinations made outside of reserve cities, and the States of Oregon, California, and Nevada, and the Territories, is fixed at various amounts, ranging from $20 in the case of a bank having a capital of less than $100,000 to $75 in the case of a bank having a capital of $600,000 and over. As the earnings of the examiner are thus made dependent upon the number of examinations he makes, without regard to the amount of work he actually performs, it is obvious that he has a pecuniary interest in increasing the number of examinations by neglecting his duty to make them thorough.

Again, the law requires a bank which is properly conducted, and the examination of which involves but little time, to pay the same compensation therefor that is paid by a bank which is not properly conducted and which by reason thereof requires a much longer time for its examination. These objectionable features could be remedied if the law were so amended as to provide that the compensation for all bank examinations be fixed by the Comptroller, with the approval of the Secretary of the Treasury.

Many other amendments have been suggested to the Comptroller as proper ones to be made to Congress for action, but it is not deemed best to submit them. The foregoing are presented, with the earnest request that they receive consideration. Some of these amendments have been recommended by former Comptrollers in the belief based upon knowledge gained from experience in the Bureau that they would "improve the system and add to the security of the holders of bank notes and other creditors," but no action has been taken upon them. It is respectfully submitted that as the national banks are under the supervision of the general government, and as Congress is vested with the power to legislate upon all matters pertaining to their control and conduct, it should be the constant aim of Congress to so legislate as to enable them to meet the public needs.

CURRENCY LEGISLATION.

The Comptroller has been urged to make some specific recommendation with respect to a revision of the law so far as it pertains to the issuing of currency. After a careful consideration of the question the Comptroller is of the opinion that, aside from the amendments heretofore suggested, allowing banks to issue circulating notes to an amount equal to the par value of the bonds held to secure circulation, and abolishing a portion of the tax on national-bank circulation, the public good will be best subserved at this time by making no radical change in the provisions of the law.

The financial situation of the past months was not the result of either a lack in the volume of currency, of which there is now a plethora, or a want of elasticity in the present system of issuing it, but arose from a loss of confidence on the part of the people in the solvency of the distinctively monetary institutions of the country. It is worthy of note and of serious consideration that at the very time the scarcity of currency for business purposes was at its height, the country's volume of currency was increasing the most rapidly, and the amount per capita was much larger than in any recent years. Under the same peculiar condition of affairs which marked the monetary situation from May to September, no system, no matter how elastic, or volume of currency however large, could afford relief. As long as confidence is destroyed and credit wanting, money hoarding will go on and additional issues but add to the hoardings and give but little, if any, actual relief. On the other hand, when confidence and credit abound there exists little need for an abundant circulating medium, because under such a condition of affairs the amount of actual money required to transact the daily business affairs of life is reduced to a minimum.

The statistics show that the volume of business carried on through cash transactions is on an average but 8.7 per cent, and as the monetary conditions of the country become more fixed and confidence in them established, cash transactions will decrease and credit transactions correspondingly increase. This fact is to be considered in connection with all plans having as their sole object an increase of the volume of banknote or other paper currency, and coupled with this is the further fact that no issue is so dangerous to a people's prosperity as a large paper issue, unless such paper rests upon a proper foundation, is absolutely redeemable and convertible into coin upon the demand of the note-holder, and surrounded with every safeguard as to supervision of issue and redemption.

In view of the fact that there is now a very great abundance of unemployed currency in the country, as shown by the daily money returns from the commercial centers, it would seem that whatever need appeared some months since for enlarging to any marked extent the circulating medium has now ceased to exist; and therefore Congress is afforded an opportunity of giving to the whole subject that careful research and investigation which its importance in all of its bearings demands. It will not do to place upon the statute books any experimental legislation upon this subject, but whenever a new law governing bank issues is enacted it must be one that immediately upon going into operation shall command in every respect the confidence of the whole people and insure to them a currency as safe in every respect as the present one, but with none of its defects.

In the meantime it is respectfully suggested that Congress, either through a monetary commission created for such purpose or through the appropriate committees, obtain detailed information of the various systems of banks of issue now in operation, and also such information as is to be ascertained from skilled students of finance and practical financiers, that it may be able to formulate a system complete and harmonious.

CONCLUSION.

In concluding this report the Comptroller desires to bear testimony to the general efficiency of the employés in the Bureau, to the examiners in the field, and to the work accomplished by the receivers in relation to the trusts in their charge.

An extraordinary amount of work has been placed upon the employés of the Bureau, but it has been performed promptly and intelligently.

In the appendix will be found in detail the usual tables, together with a digest of legal decisions rendered by the various courts of the country involving questions affecting national banks.

In the second volume of this report will be found a detailed statement of the condition of all the national banks as shown by the report of condition of October 3, 1893, alphabetically arranged by States, and properly indexed.

JAMES H. ECKELS,
Comptroller of the Currency.

The SPEAKER OF THE HOUSE OF REPRESENTATIVES.

APPENDIX.

Name.	Grade.	Salary.
James H. Eckels	Comptroller	$5,000
Oliver P. Tucker	Deputy comptroller	2,800
Charles J. Stoddard	Chief clerk	2,500
George M. Coffin	Chief of division	2,200
Watson W. Eldridge	....do	2,200
Abram R. Serveu	....do	2,200
George W. Robertson	Superintendent	2,200
Amos Webster	Teller	2,000
Theodore O. Ebaugh	Bookkeeper	2,000
Willis J. Fowler	Assistant bookkeeper	2,000
Edward A. Demaray	Clerk class 4	1,800
John A. Hebrew	....do	1,800
Endicott King	....do	1,800
George T. May	....do	1,800
Edmund E. Schreiner	....do	1,800
Charles A. Stewart	....do	1,800
Charles McC. Taylor	....do	1,800
Walter Taylor	....do	1,800
Thomas P. Kane	Stenographer	1,600
Harriet M. Black	Clerk class 3	1,600
Willard E. Buell	....do	1,600
William E. Colladay	....do	1,600
George W. Collison	....do	1,600
Washington K. McCoy	....do	1,600
Isaac C. Miller	....do	1,600
Joseph K. Miller	....do	1,600
Ebenezer Southall	....do	1,600
William D. Swan *	....do	1,600
Ephram S. Wilcox	....do	1,600
George H. Wood	....do	1,600
Eliza R. Hyde	Clerk class 2	1,400
Robert Leroy Livingston	....do	1,400
Mary L. McCormick	....do	1,400
Loren H. Milliken	....do	1,400
Franklin L. Mitchell	....do	1,400
Morris M. Ogden	....do	1,400
Carrie L. Pennock	....do	1,400
Margaret L. Simpson	....do	1,400
Arthur M. Wheeler	....do	1,400
Anna M. Whiteside	....do	1,400
Eliza M. Barker	Clerk class 1	1,200
Eveline C. Bates	....do	1,200
Margaret L. Brown	....do	1,200
Philo L. Bush	....do	1,200
Sarah M. Cartwright	....do	1,200
Mary L. Conrad	....do	1,200
Anna E. Rhodes	....do	1,200
Marie Richardson	....do	1,200
Eliza A. Saunders	....do	1,200
Warren E. Sullivan	....do	1,200
Louisa Campbell	Clerk class E	1,000
Virginia H. Clarke	....do	1,000
Sarah G. Clemens	....do	1,000
William S. Davenport	....do	1,000
Frank T. Israel	....do	1,000
Arthur L. Hitchcock	....do	1,000
Alice M. Kennedy	....do	1,000
Emma Lafayette	....do	1,000
William A. Nestler	....do	1,000
Adelia M. Stewart	....do	1,000
Clara L. Willard	....do	1,000
Henry F. Loveaire	Engineer	1,000
Thomas H. Austin	Clerk, class D	900
David C. Baugs	....do	900
Benjamin F. Blye, jr	....do	900
John E. Briggs	....do	900
Ellen Carey	....do	900
Geraldine Clifford	....do	900
Harry Dresbach	....do	900

* Additional to bond clerk, $200.

NAMES AND COMPENSATION OF OFFICERS AND CLERKS IN THE OFFICE OF THE COMP-
TROLLER OF THE CURRENCY, OCTOBER 31, 1893—Continued.

Name.	Grade.	Salary.
James W. Farrar	Clerk, class D	$900
Margaret E. Gooding	do	900
Mary B. Harvell	do	900
Charles S. Hyde	do	900
Mary A. Martin	do	900
William W. Matthews	do	900
Mary E. Oliver	do	900
Julia A. Snell	do	900
Emma W. Stokes	do	900
Julia C. Towusend	do	900
William J. Tucker	do	900
William Griffiths	Messenger	840
Joseph O. Broadfoot	Assistant messenger	720
Silas Holmes	do	720
John F. Robertson	do	720
John Earle	Watchman	720
Daniel H. Mason	do	720
Samuel M. Freeman	Fireman	720
Rochard Corcoran	Laborer	650
Peyton B. Kent	do	660
William D. Peck	do	660
Percy H. Towson	do	660
Herbert F. Walker	do	660

EXPENSES OF THE OFFICE OF COMPTROLLER OF THE CURRENCY FOR THE YEAR
ENDED JUNE 30, 1893.

For special dies, plates, printing, etc	$73,211.37
For salaries	102,319.56
For salaries, reimbursable by national banks	16,533.77

Total expenses of the office of the Comptroller of the Currency from its organization,
May, 1863, to June 30, 1893 .... 7,339,994.24

The contingent expenses of the Bureau are not paid by the Comptroller but from
the general appropriation for contingent expenses of the Treasury Department; no
separate account of them is kept.

DIGEST OF NATIONAL-BANK DECISIONS.

INDEX.

ABATEMENT:

An action brought by the creditor of a national bank is abated by a decree of a district or circuit court dissolving the corporation and forfeiting its franchises *First National Bank of Selma v. Colby, 21 Wall., 609.*

ACCOMMODATION PAPER:

1. A national-banking association can not guarantee the paper of a customer *for his accommodation. Seligman v. Charlottesville National Bank, 3 Hughes 647.*
2. The accommodation paper of a national-banking association is void in the hands of one who takes it with knowledge of its character. *Johnson v. Charlottesville National Bank, 3 Hughes, 657.*
3. A national bank can not become an accommodation indorser. *National Bank of Commerce v. Atkinson, 55 Fed. Rep., 465.*

31

ACTIONS: *See* Jurisdiction.

1. Suit may be brought against a national-banking association though it is in the hands of a receiver. *Bank of Bethel* v. *Pahquioque Bank, 14 Wall., 383; Security National Bank* v. *National Bank of the Commonwealth, 2 Hun., 287; Green* v. *The Wallkill National Bank, 7 Hun., 63.*

2. A national-banking association is a foreign corporation within the meaning of a State statute requiring corporations created by the laws of any other State or country to give security for costs before prosecuting a suit in the courts of the State. *National Park Bank* v. *Gunst, 1 Abb. N. C., 292.*

3. As a national-banking association can acquire no title to *negotiable* paper purchased by it, it can maintain no action thereon in a State where the person suing must be owner of the paper. *First National Bank of Rochester* v. *Pierson, 24 Minn., 140.*

4. A shareholder of a national-banking association can not maintain an action against the directors to recover damages sustained for neglect and mismanagement of the affairs of the association whereby it became insolvent and its stock was rendered worthless. Such an action can be brought only by the corporation itself. *Conway* v. *Halsey, 15 Vroom, 462; Heme* v. *Barney, 45 Fed. Rep., 668.*

5. But where the receiver refuses to bring an action against negligent directors to recover the amount which the shareholders have been compelled to contribute to pay the debts of the association, an action against such directors may be brought by a shareholder on behalf of himself and the other shareholders. *Nelson* v. *Burrows, 9 Abb. N. C., 280.*

6. And when the receiver is a director, and one of the parties charged with misconduct and against whom a remedy is sought, the action may be brought by a shareholder on behalf of himself and the other shareholders. *Brinckerhoff* v. *Bostwick, 88 N. Y., 52.*

7. A stockholder in a national bank can not maintain an action at law against the officers and directors thereof to recover damages for willful waste of the assets whereby the value of his shares was decreased and he became liable to an assessment thereon. His remedy must be sought in equity. *Hirsh* v. *Jones et al., 56 Fed. Rep., 137.*

8. A receiver may sue either in his own name or the name of the bank. *National Bank* v. *Kennedy, 17 Wall., 19.*

9. Suits and proceedings under the act in which the United States or their officers or agents are parties, whether commenced before or after the appointment of a receiver are to be conducted by the district attorney under the direction of the Solicitor of the Treasury. *Bank of Bethel* v. *Pahquioque Bank, 14 Wall., 383.*

10. But section 380, Revised Statutes, is directory merely, and the employment of private counsel by the receiver can not be made a ground of defense to a suit brought by him. *Ib.*

11. Receivers may sue in the courts of the United States by virtue of the act, without reference to the locality of their personal citizenship. *Ib.*

12. The provisions of the codes that every action must be brought in the name of the real party in interest, except in the case of the trustee of an express trust or of a person authorized by a statute to sue, does not apply to the receiver of a national-banking association suing in a Federal court held in a State which has adopted the code procedure; for the right of the receiver to sue is derived from the national-banking law. *Stanton* v. *Wilkeson, 8 Ben., 357.*

13. Under section 1001 of the Revised Statutes, no bond for the prosecution of the suit, or to answer in damages or costs, is required on writs of error or appeals issuing from or brought to the Supreme Court of the United States by direction of the Comptroller of the Currency in suits by or against insolvent national-banking associations or the receivers thereof. *Pacific National Bank* v. *Mixter, 114 U. S., 463.*

14. The State statute of limitations applies to a suit brought by the receiver of a national bank against a shareholder to recover an assessment upon his stock to pay the debts of the bank. *Butler* v. *Poole, 44 Fed. Rep., 586.*

15. When the full personal liability of shareholders is to be enforced the action must be at law. *Kennedy* v. *Gibson, 8 Wall., 505; Casey* v. *Galli, 94 U. S., 673.*

16. And it may be at law, though the assessment is not for the full value of the shares; for, since the sum each shareholder must contribute is a certain exact sum, there is no necessity for invoking the aid of a court of equity. *Bailey* v. *Sawyer, 4 Dill., 463.*

17. But the suit may be in equity. *Kennedy* v. *Gibson, supra.*

ACTIONS—Continued.

18. The provision of the banking law, section 5198, Revised Statutes, which requires that actions brought against national-banking associations in State courts shall be brought in the county or city in which the association is located, applies only to transitory actions; it was not intended to apply to actions local in their character. *Casey* v. *Adams*, 102 U. S., 66.

19. Whether a suit against a director for negligent performance of his duties, as required by the statutes of the United States and the by-laws of the association, will survive against the executor or administrator depends upon State laws. *Witters* v. *Foster*, 25 Fed. Rep., 737.

20. A specific performance of a contract to sell the stock of a national-banking association will not be enforced in favor of a purchaser who places his claim for equitable relief upon the ground that he desires to obtain control of the association. Such an object is contrary to public policy. *Foll's Appeal*, 81 Penn. St., 434.

21. Under section 57 of act of 1864, suits may be brought by, as well as against, any association. *Kennedy* v. *Gibson*, 8 Wall., 498.

22. Actions, local in their nature, may be maintained in the proper State court in a county or city other than that where it is established. *Casey* v. *Adams*, 102 U. S., 66.

23. A national bank may be sued in any State, county, or municipal court in county or city where located. *Bank of Bethel* v. *Pahquioque Bank*, 14 Wall., 383.

24. Such action is not prescribed by the limitation of one year in Louisiana. *Case* v. *Bank*, 100 U. S., 446.

25. It is no objection to a bill against stockholders within the jurisdiction of the court, that other stockholders, not within such jurisdiction, are not co-defendants. *Ib.*

26. Under the original act respecting national banks, and before the act of June 30, 1876, a court of equity had jurisdiction of suit to prevent or redress maladministration or fraud against creditors, in voluntary liquidation of such bank, whether contemplated or executed; and such suit by one creditor must be for all. *Richmond* v. *Irons*, 121 U. S., 27.

ASSESSMENT :   *See* Insolvent banks; Receiver.

1. Where national-banking association is insolvent, order of Comptroller of Currency, declaring to what extent the individual liability of stockholders shall be enforced, is conclusive. *Kennedy* v. *Gibson*, 8 Wall. 498; *Casey* v. *Galli* v. 94 U. S., 673; *National Bank* v. *Case*, 99 U. S., 628.

2. Payments of assessments by stockholder in national bank on increased stock can not be applied, in law or in equity, to discharge assessments by Comptroller in final liquidation of the bank. *Pacific National Bank* v. *Eaton*, 141 U. S., 227; *Thayer* v. *Butler*, 141 U. S., 234; *Butler* v. *Eaton*, 141 U. S., 240.

3. The assessments made by the Comptroller upon the shareholders of an insolvent association bear interest from the date of the order. *Casey* v. *Galli*, 94 U. S., 673.

4. Where shareholders have assessed themselves to the amount of the par value of the stock for the purpose of restoring impaired capital, the contributions made in pursuance of such assessment, though all used in paying the debts of the association, will not so operate as to discharge the shareholders from their individual liability. *Delano* v. *Butler*, 118 U. S., 634.

5. Where a married woman is by the State law capable of holding stock in a national bank in her own right, she is liable to an assessment upon her shares, though the law of the State does not authorize married women to bind themselves by contracts for the payment of money. The law annexes her obligations by its own force; no act or capacity to act on her part is required. *Witters* v. *Sowles*, 35 Fed. Rep., 640; 33 Fed. Rep. 767.

6. Married women, who are permitted by the laws of the State in which they reside to become shareholders in national banks, are liable to assessments under the national-banking laws. *In re First National Bank of St. Albans*, 49 Fed. Rep., 120.

7. The coverture of a married woman, who is a shareholder in a national bank, does not prevent the receiver of the bank from recovering judgment against her for the amount of an assessment levied upon the shareholders equally and ratably under the statute. *Keyser* v. *Hitz*, 133 U. S., 138.

8. It is not essential, in an action to enforce the individual liability of the shareholders of an insolvent national-banking association, to aver and prove that the assessment was necessary; for the decision of the Comptroller on this point is conclusive. *Strong* v. *Southworth*, 8 Ben., 331; *Kennedy* v. *Gibson*, 8 Wall., 505; *Casey* v. *Galli*, 94 U. S., 673.

ASSESSMENT—Continued.

9. And the fact that the title to the stock of a deceased shareholder vests in his administrator does not relieve the estate from the burden of an assessment. *Davis* v. *Weed, 44 Conn., 569.*

10. Nor will the fact that the administration is complete, and all the assets have been distributed, defeat an action brought to recover the assessment. *Ib.* But see *Witters* v. *Sowles, 32 Fed. Rep., 30.*

11. A decision rescinding sale, so as to restore to the purchaser the proceeds of stock fraudulently sold, does not necessarily involve a decision that the purchaser is not liable to an assessment upon the stock, if necessary to pay debts. *Florida Land & Imp. Co.* v. *Merrill, 52 Fed. Rep., 77.*

12. The question whether there is a deficiency of assets, and when it is necessary to enforce the individual liability of shareholders, it is for the Comptroller to determine; and his decision in this matter is final and conclusive. *Kennedy* v. *Gibson, 8 Wall., 498; National Bank* v. *Case, 99 U. S., 628; Casey* v. *Galli, 94 U. S., 673.*

13. The amount contributed by each shareholder should bear the same proportion to the whole amount of the deficit as his own stock bears to the whole amount of the capital stock at its par value. And the solvent shareholders can not be made to contribute more than their proportion to make good the deficiency caused by the insolvency of other shareholders. *United States* v. *Knox, 102 U. S., 422.*

14. Where, to discharge liabilities of an insolvent bank, Comptroller assessed against shareholders a sufficient per cent on par value of stock held by each, some being insolvent, he can not provide for deficiency by new assessment. *Ib.*

ATTACHMENT:

1. When a creditor attaches the property of an insolvent bank he can not hold such property against the claim of a receiver appointed after the attachment suit was commenced. Such creditor must share pro rata with all others. *First National Bank of Selma* v. *Colby, 21 Wall., 609; Harvey* v. *Allen, 16 Blatch, 29.*

2. The stock of a shareholder indebted to it may be attached by the association and sold on execution. *Hager* v. *Union National Bank, 63 Me., 509.*

3. No State court can issue an attachment against the funds of a national bank. Although the provision forbidding attachments was evidently made to secure equality among the general creditors in the division of the proceeds of the property of an insolvent bank, its operation is by no means confined to cases of actual or contemplated insolvency; but the remedy is taken away altogether and can not be used under any circumstances. The effect of the provision in section 5242, Revised Statutes, is to write into all State attachment laws an exception in favor of national banks, and all such laws must be read as if they contained an exception in favor of national banks. *Pacific National Bank* v. *Mixter, 124 U. S., 721.*

4. No attachment can issue from United States circuit court in an action against a national bank before final judgment in the cause, and a bond given on such attachment is illegal. *Ib.*

5. Sureties on attachment bond against national bank who have received assets of the bank to secure them from loss thereon, the obligation being illegal, will be discharged in equity and be compelled to transfer their collateral to the receiver of the bank. *Ib.*

BONDS OF OFFICERS:

1. It is not necessary that national-banking associations shall signify their approval of the official bonds of their officers by memoranda entered upon the journals or minutes of the directors. The acceptance is to be presumed from the retention of the bond, and from the fact that the officer is permitted to enter upon or continue in the discharge of his duties. *Grover* v. *The Lebanon National Bank, 10 Bush., 23.*

2. Where the sureties of an officer can reasonably be presumed to have been deceived by the statement of the condition of the bank published just prior to the execution of the bond, and to have been led to think that there was no deficit, whereas there had been a misapplication of a large part of the funds by the officer whose bondsmen they became, which fact would have been ascertained had the directors exercised ordinary diligence, the sureties are discharged from their liability. *Ib.*

BOOKS, INSPECTION OF: See Taxation.

1. Code of Alabama, 1886, section 1677, which provides that stockholders of all corporations have the right to have access to and inspection and examina-

BOOKS, INSPECTION OF—Continued.

tion of the books, records, and papers of the corporation at all reasonable and proper times, applies to national banks located within the State; and *mandamus* will lie against the officer having custody of the books to enforce the right. *Winter* v. *Baldwin, 7 So., Rep., 731.*

2. The rights of stockholders are not curtailed nor the statute in conflict with Revised Statutes, United States, which provide that national banks shall not be subject to visitorial powers other than those authorized by Congress or vested in the courts of justice. *Ib.*

BRANCH BANKS:

Under Revised Statutes, section 5190, providing that "the usual business of each national-banking association shall be transacted at an office or banking-house located in the place specified in its organization certificate," a national bank can not make a valid contract for the cashing of checks upon it at a different place from that of its residence, through the agency of another bank. *Armstrong* v. *National Bank of Springfield, 38 Fed. Rep., 883.*

BROKER: *See* Government securities.

A national-banking association is not authorized to act as a broker or agent in the purchase of bonds and stocks. *First National Bank of Allentown* v. *Hoch, 89 Penn. St., 324; Weckler* v. *The First National Bank of Hagerstown, 42 Md., 581.*

CAPITAL STOCK: *See* Transfer of stock; Increase of; Reduction of.

Where a national-banking association purchases shares of its own stock, and divides them among its directors, to whom the shares are transferred upon the stock books, the transaction is void, and no title passes. *Meyers* v. *Valley National Bank, 13 National Bankruptcy Register, 34.*

CERTIFICATE OF DEPOSIT:

1. National-banking associations may issue certificates of deposit. *Hunt, Appellant, 141 Mass., 515; Riddle* v. *First National Bank, 27 Fed. Rep., 503.*

2. Certain persons, directors of a savings and of a national bank, procured money from the former on notes made by a third person to them for the payment of stock of the national bank, issued in the name of such third person for their benefit. These persons were behind in their accounts with the national bank, and the savings bank allowed them to overdraw their accounts with it to a large amount, which was used in settling their accounts with the national bank. Thereafter the savings bank delivered the notes and the check to the national bank, which issued to it a certificate of deposit for an amount covering the whole amount represented by them. *Held,* that this certificate of deposit was without consideration and void, and any loss accruing to the savings bank by virtue of the transactions was due to the fraud or incompetency of its own officers. *Murray* v. *Pauly, 56 Fed. Rep., 962.*

CERTIFICATION OF CHECKS:

1. A national-banking association may "certify" a check. *Merchants' National Bank* v. *State National Bank, 10 Wall., 604.*

2. A broker received coupon railroad mortgage bonds to cover future margins of a customer and pledged them to a bank as collateral security for any indebtedness he might owe to it. Afterward the bank advanced money and certified checks on the faith of these bonds, when broker did not have money on deposit equal in amount to the checks. *Held,* under section 5208, that although the certifications were unlawful the checks certified were good and valid obligations against the bank. *Thompson* v. *St. Nicholas National Bank, 146 U. S., 240.*

CIRCULATION: *See* Post-notes; Taxation.

1. The circulating notes of a national-banking association are valid though they do not bear the imprint of the seal of the Treasury. Such imprint was intended to be simply evidence of the contract, and forms no part of the contract itself. *United States* v. *Bennett, 17 Blatch., 357.*

2. The State can not tax the circulating notes of national-banking associations. *Horne* v. *Greene, 25 Miss., 452;* contra, *Board of Commissioners* v. *Elston 32 Ind., 27;* see also *Ruffin* v. *Board of Commissioners, 69 N. C., 498; Lily* v. *The Commissioners, 69 N. C., 300.*

3. The circulating notes of national-banking associations are included in the phrase "United States Currency" when used in a penal statute. *State* v. *Gasling, 23 La. Ann., 1609.*

COLLATERAL SECURITIES:

1. A national-banking association may take stock of a corporation as collateral security for a loan. *Shoemaker* v. *The National Mechanics' Bank, 2 Abb. U. S., 416; Canfield* v. *The State National Bank of Minneapolis, Thomp. Nat. Bank Cas., 312.*
2. And it may take for such purpose the stock of another national-banking association. *National Bank* v. *Case, 99 U. S., 628.*
3. A national-banking association may take a pledge of personal chattels as security for a loan. *Pittsburg Locomotive and Car Works* v. *State National Bank of Keokuk, 2 Cent. L. J., 692; 1 New York Weekly Digest, 332.*
4. A national-banking association may take as collateral security for a loan a warehouse receipt for merchandise. *Cleveland, Brown & Co.,* v. *Shoeman, 40 Ohio St., 176.*
5. Where stockholder borrows money from bank and gives as security certificate of his shares of its stock, he is not entitled to recover when, on nonpayment of loan, the bank sold his stock and applied proceeds to his credit. *National Bank of Xenia* v. *Stewart, 107 U. S., 676.*
6. Creditor of insolvent bank has the right to prove and have dividends upon his entire claim, irrespective of collateral security he may hold. *Peoples* v. *Remington, 121 N. Y., 328.*
7. The property which a creditor holds as collateral to the indebtedness of his debtor secures him to that extent in case his debt is not paid in full by the debtor, or by his estate. *Everton* v. *Booth, 19 Johns., 485.*
8. It is the duty of a receiver if a secured debt is so reduced by dividends that the security will more than pay it, to redeem the security for the benefit of his trust. *West* v. *Bank of Rutland, 19 Vermont, 403. Miller's Estate, 82; Penn. St., 113; Bates* v. *Paddock, 7 Western Reporter, 222.*
9. A secured creditor is entitled to dividends upon his claim as it existed at the time of proving. *Chemical National Bank* v. *Armstrong, 50 Fed. Rep., 798.*

CONSTITUTIONALITY:

1. Congress has the constitutional power to incorporate banks. *McCulloch* v. *Maryland, 4 Wheat., 316; Osborne* v. *Bank of the United States, 9 Wheat., 738.*
2. Congress has power to clothe national-banking associations, as to their contracts and dealings with the world, with any special immunities and privileges exempting them, in their trade and intercourse with others, from the laws and remedies applicable in like cases to other citizens. *The Chesapeake Bank* v. *The First National Bank of Baltimore, 40 Md., 269.*
3. Thus, the provision of the banking law that no attachment, injunction, or execution shall issue against a national-banking association before final judgment in any suit, action, or proceeding in a State court is constitutional. *Ib.*
4. Congress having, in the exercise of undisputed constitutional powers, undertaken to provide a currency for the whole country, may secure the benefit of it to the people by appropriate legislation. *Veazie Bank* v. *Fenno, 8 Wall., 533.*
5. Congress has the power to divest the United States courts of their jurisdiction of suits by or against national banking associations. *National Bank of Jefferson* v. *Fare et al., 25 Fed. Rep., 209.*
6. National-banking associations, being instruments designed to aid the Government in the administration of a branch of the public service, can not be controlled by the States, except in so far as Congress may see proper to permit. *Farmers and Mechanics' Bank* v. *Dearing, 91 U. S., 29.*
7. A State law prohibiting the establishment of banking companies in the State without the authority of the legislature was not intended to apply to banking corporations created by authority of Congress, since such corporations may be legally established in the State without the consent of the legislature. *Stetson* v. *City of Bangor, 56 Me., 274.*

CONVERSION OF BANK: *See Oath of director.*

1. Where a State bank has been converted into a national-banking association it may enforce all contracts made with it while a State corporation. *City National Bank* v. *Phelps, 97 N. Y., 44.*
2. And it is liable, after the conversion, for all the obligations of the old institution. *Coffee.* v. *The National Bank of Missouri, 46 Mo., 140; Kelsey* v. *The National Bank of Crawford, 69 Penn. St., 426.*
3. A national-banking association, organized as the successor of a State bank, may take and hold the assets of the bank whose place it takes, though there was not in form a conversion from a State to a national corporation but the organization of a new corporation. *Bank* v. *McIntyre, 40 Ohio St., 528.*

CONVERSION OF BANK—Continued.

4. And such association will be liable to the depositors of the former bank. *Eans* v. *Exchange Bank, 79 Mo., 182.*

5. A State law authorizing national banking associations which have been converted from State banks to use the name of the original corporation for the purpose of prosecuting and defending suits is not in conflict with the national-banking law, and therefore proceedings based upon a judgment obtained before the conversion may be instituted by such association in its former corporate name. *Thomas* v. *Farmers' Bank of Maryland, 46 Md., 43.*

6. The conversion of a State bank into a national bank, with a change of name, under the national-bank act does not affect its identity or its right to sue upon liabilities incurred to it by its former name. *Michigan Insurance Bank* v. *Eldred, 143 U. S., 293.*

7. No authority other than that conferred by act of Congress is necessary to enable any State bank to become a national-banking association. *Casey* v. *Galli, 94 U. S., 673.*

8. When a State bank is converted into a national-banking association all of the directors at the time will continue to be directors of the association until others are appointed or elected, though some of them may not have joined in the execution of the articles of association and organization certificate. *Lockwood* v. *The American National Bank, 9 R. I., 308.*

9. But even were the oath required, a majority of all who were directors at the time of the conversion, and not merely a majority of those who take the oath, are necessary to constitute a quorum. *Ib.*

CRIMINAL LAW: *See* False entries; Indictment.

1. The willful misapplication of the moneys and funds of a national-banking association, made an offense by section 5209, Revised Statutes, must be for the use or benefit of the party charged or of some person or company other than the association. *United States* v. *Britton, 107 U. S., 655.*

2. The exercise of official discretion in good faith, without fraud, for the advantage or the supposed advantage of the association, is not punishable; but if official action be taken in bad faith, for personal advantage and with fraudulent intent, it is punishable. *United States* v. *Fish, 24 Fed. Rep., 585.*

3. It is not necessary that the officer should personally misapply the funds of the association. He will be guilty as a principal offender though he merely procures or causes the misapplication. *Ib.*

4. A loan in bad faith, with intent to defraud the association, is a willful misapplication within the meaning of the statute. *Ib.*

5. It is no defense to a charge of embezzlement, abstraction, or misapplication of the funds of a national-banking association that the funds were used with the knowledge and consent of the president and some of the directors. The intent to defraud is to be conclusively presumed from the commission of the offense. *United States* v. *Taintor, 11 Blatch., 374.*

6. Where the president, charged as a trustee with the administration of the funds of the bank in his hands, converts them to his own use without authority for so doing, he embezzles and abstracts them within the meaning of section 5209, Revised Statutes. *In the matter of Van Campen, 2 Ben., 419.*

7. If, with intent to defraud the association, an officer allows a firm in which he is a member to overdraw its account, he will be guilty of misapplying the funds of the association. *Ib.*

8. Allowing the withdrawal of the deposit of one indebted to the association can not be charged as a misapplication of the money of the association. *United States* v. *Britton, 108 U. S., 193.*

9. It is not a willful misapplication of the moneys of the association within the meaning of section 5209, Revised Statutes, for a president who is insolvent to procure the discounting by the association of his note not well secured. *Ib.*

10. To constitute the offense of a willful misapplication of the moneys, funds, or credits of the association within section 5209, Revised Statutes, it is not necessary that the person charged with the offense should have been previously in the actual possession of such moneys, funds, and credits under or by virtue of any trust, duty, or employment committed to him. Nor is it necessary to the commission of this offense that the officer making the willful misapplication should derive any personal benefit therefrom. When the funds or assets of the bank are unlawfully taken from its possession, and afterward willfully misapplied by converting them to

CRIMINAL LAW—Continued.

the use of any person other than the bank, with intent to injure and defraud, the offense as described in the statute is committed. *United States* v. *Harper, 33 Fed. Rep., 471.*

11. This criminal act may be done directly and personally, or it may be done indirectly through the agency of another. If the officer charged with it has such control, direction, and power of management by virtue of his relation to the bank as to direct an application of its funds in such manner and under such circumstances as to constitute the offense of willful misapplication, and actually makes such direction or causes such misapplication to be made, he is equally as guilty as if it was done by his own hands. *Ib.*

12. To constitute the offense of willful abstraction by an officer, defined by the statute, it is necessary that the money or funds of the association should be withdrawn by the officer or by his direction; that such taking or withdrawing should be without the knowledge or consent of the bank, or of its board of directors; that the money or funds so taken or withdrawn should be converted to the officer's own use, or for the benefit and advantage of some person other than the association, and that this should be done with intent to injure and defraud the association. *Ib.*

13. It is competent for a State by penal enactments to protect its citizens in their dealings with national-banking associations located within the State. *State* v. *Fuller, 34 Conn., 280.*

14. An officer of a national-banking association can not be punished under State laws for embezzling the funds of the association. *Commonwealth ex rel. Torrey* v. *Ketner, 92 Penn. St., 372; Commonwealth* v. *Felton, 101 Mass., 204.*

15. But where the offense committed by an officer is properly a larceny of the funds, and not an embezzlement, he may be indicted under a State law. *Commonwealth* v. *Barry, 116 Mass., 1.*

16. And an officer may be punished under State laws for making false entries in the books of the association with intent to defraud it. *Luberg* v. *Commonwealth, 94 Penn. St., 85.*

17. The officers of a national-banking association may be prosecuted under State statutes for fraudulent conversion of the property of individuals deposited with, and in the custody of, the association. *Commonwealth* v. *Tenney, 97 Mass., 50: State* v. *Fuller, 34 Conn., 280.*

18. As the national-banking law makes the embezzlement, abstraction, or willful misapplication of the funds of a national-banking association merely a misdemeanor, a person who procures such an offense to be committed can not be punished under a State statute which provides that a person who procures a felony to be committed may be indicted and convicted of a substantive felony. *Commonwealth* v. *Felton, 101 Mass., 204.*

19. The procuring by two or more directors of the declaration of a dividend at a time when there are no net profits to pay it, is not a willful misappropriation of money of bank within section 5204, Revised Statutes. *United States* v. *Britton, 108 U. S., 199.*

20. It is not a willful misapplication of bank money by the president, under section 5209, for him to procure the discount by bank for his own benefit of an unsecured note on which both maker and indorser are insolvent to his knowledge. *Ib., 193.*

21. Nor is president liable for a criminal violation of that section solely by reason of permitting a depositor who is largely indebted to bank to withdraw his deposits without first paying such indebtedness. *Ib.*

22. It is not a conspiracy against United States, under section 5440, Revised Statutes, nor a willful misapplication of money of bank, under section 5209, for president and director of bank to cause shares of its stock to be purchased with its money and held on trust. *Ib., 192.*

23. Purchase of stock in violation of section 5201, Revised Statutes, made with intent to defraud, and by officers named in section 5209, is not punishable under latter section. *United States* v. *Britton, 107 U. S., 655.*

DIRECTORS: *See* Officers.

DISTRICT ATTORNEY:

1. For services performed by the district attorney in bringing a suit against a national bank, and obtaining a forfeiture of its charter, he is not entitled to more than $10, the fees prescribed by section 824, there being no other law in the United States giving a compensation to a district attorney for such services. *Bashaw* v. *United States, 47 Fed. Rep., 40.*

DISTRICT ATTORNEY—Continued.

2. The 56th (now 153rd) section of the act providing that suits under it, in which the officers of the United States are parties, shall be conducted by the district attorney of the district, is directory only. *Kennedy* v. *Gibson, 8 Wall., 498.*

3. District attorney can not recover compensation for services in conducting suit arising out of the provisions of the national-banking law in which the United States or any of its agents or officers are parties. *Gibson* v. *Peters, Receiver, U. S. S. C., October, 1893.*

4. The expenses of a receivership can not be held to include compensation of district attorney for conducting a suit in which the receiver is party, and he can not receive any compensation for services so rendered or offered to be rendered. *Ib.*

DISTRICT OF COLUMBIA:

After the act of June 30, 1876 (19 Stat., 63), savings banks organized in the District of Columbia under an act of Congress, and having a capital stock paid up in whole or in part, were entitled to become national banking associations in the mode prescribed by Revised Statutes, Sec. 5151. *Keyser* v. *Hitz, 133 U. S., 138.*

ESTOPPEL:

1. Where an officer of a bank loaned money for his individual benefit upon pretended collateral security of the bank, held, that his bank was estopped to deny the loan and is liable therefor, as the lender dealt with him solely in his official capacity. *Stewart* v. *Armstrong, 56 Fed. Rep., 167.*

2. Vice-president of bank, also manager of a commercial house, substituted as collateral, notes to order of his house, and indorsed by them without consideration. Held, that as against holders of collateral, the house was estopped to deny that these notes were properly pledged as security for a loan to his bank. *Ib.*

3. The estoppel upon his bank exists only in favor of lender. Hence, his house has no remedy against it for any liability enforced by the lender on account of its endorsed notes so pledged. *Ib.*

4. A shareholder who has held himself out to the world as such is estopped to deny that the association was legally incorporated. *Casey* v. *Galli, 94 U. S., 673; Wheelock* v. *Kost, 77 Ill., 296.*

5. Where one sued by a national bank is accustomed to deal with it as such, and does so deal with it in respect to the matter in suit, he is estopped from denying its incorporation. *National Bank of Fairhaven* v. *The Phœnix Warehousing Company, 6 Hun., 71.*

6. A person who received dividends on shares of stock standing in his name on the books of a national bank is estopped from denying his liability on the ground that he returned the same by check to an officer of the bank. He is presumed to be the owner of the stock when his name appears upon the books of the bank and the burden of proof is upon him to show that he is not in fact the owner. *Finn* v. *Brown, 142 U. S., 56.*

7. A shareholder against whom suit is brought to recover the assessment made upon him by the Comptroller will not be permitted to deny the existence of the association, or that it was legally incorporated. *Casey* v. *Galli, 94 U. S., 673.*

8. A director is not, by reason of his position, estopped from setting up the defense of usury in an action brought against him by the association. *Bank of Cadiz* v. *Slemons, 34 Ohio St., 142.*

9. The legality of the appointment of the receiver can not be questioned by the debtors of the bank when sued by him. The bank may move to have the appointment set aside, but the debtors can not. *Cadle* v. *Baker, 20 Wall., 650; Platt* v. *Beebe, 57 N. Y., 339.*

10. Where a national-banking association has entered into a contract which it is not authorized to make, a party who has enjoyed the benefit of such contract can not question its validity. *Casey* v. *La Société de Crédit Mobilier, 2 Woods, 77; German National Bank* v. *Meadowcroft, 95 Ill., 124.*

11. Debtors of national banks, when sued by person whom Comptroller has appointed receiver under section 50, can not question the legality of his appointment. *Cadle* v. *Baker, 20 Wall., 650.*

12. Where officer of a bank guaranteed payment in name of bank and sold the note, the bank by retention and enjoyment of the proceeds is estopped to deny officer's act. *People's Bank* v. *National Bank, 101 U. S., 181.*

13. In such suit stockholder is estopped to deny existence or validity of corporation. *Casey* v. *Galli, 94 U. S., 673.*

EVIDENCE :

1. The certificate of the Comptroller of the Currency that an association has complied with all the provisions required to be complied with before commencing the business of banking is admissible in evidence upon a plea of *nul tiel corporation*; and such certificate, together with proof that the association has been acting as a national-banking association for a long time, is amply sufficient evidence to establish, at least prima facie, the existence of the corporation. *Mix v. The National Bank of Bloomington, 91 Ill., 20; Merchants' National Bank of Bangor v. Glendon, 120 Mass., 97.*

2. The certificate of the Comptroller that the association has complied with all the provisions of law touching the organization of associations removes any objection which might otherwise have been made to the evidence upon which he acted. *Casey v. Galli, 94 U. S., 673; Thatcher v. West River National Bank, 10 Mich., 196.*

3. And in a suit against the association or its shareholders such certificate of the Comptroller is conclusive as to the completeness of the organization. *Casey v. Galli, supra.*

4. A letter from the Comptroller directing the receiver to institute suit, if not objected to at the time, is sufficient evidence that the Comptroller has decided that the enforcement of the individual liability of the shareholders is necessary. *Bowden v. Johnson, 107 U. S., 251.*

5. A certificate signed by the Deputy Comptroller of the Currency as "Acting Comptroller of the Currency," is a sufficient certificate by the Comptroller of the Currency within the requirements of Revised Statutes, Sec. 5154. *Aspinwall v. Butler, 133 U. S., 595.*

EXECUTION:

A judgment against a national bank in the hands of a receiver only establishes the validity of the claim; the plaintiff can have no execution on such judgment, but must wait pro rata distribution. *Bank of Bethel v. Pahquioque Bank, 14 Wall., 383.*

FALSE ENTRIES:

1. The only remedy for the making of a false return to the auditor by the cashier of a bank, of the resources and liabilities of the bank for the purposes of taxation, is afforded by revised statutes of Ohio, section 2679, which provides that the auditor may examine the books of the bank, and any officer or agent of it under oath, and make out the statement; and any officer of the bank may be fined not exceeding $100 for failing to make the statement, or for willfully making a false one. *Miller v. First National Bank, 21 N. E. Rep., 860.*

2. Any entry on the books of the bank which is intentionally made to represent what is not true or what does not exist, with intent either to deceive its officers or defraud the association, is a false entry within the meaning of the statute. *United States v. Harper, 33 Fed. Rep., 471.*

3. It may be made personally or by direction. *Ib.*

4. The erasure of figures already written in the books of a national bank and the substitution of other figures which falsify the state of the account constitute a "false entry" within the meaning of section 5209, Revised Statutes, by which it is declared to be a misdemeanor to make "any false entry in any book, report, or statement of the association, with intent to injure or defraud," etc. *United States v. Crecelius, 34 Fed. Rep., 30.*

5. Where false entries are made by a clerk at the direction of the president, the latter is a principal. *In the matter of Van Campen, 2 Ben., 419; United States v. Fish, 24 Fed. Rep., 585.*

6. A report of condition of a national bank, whether called for by the Comptroller of the Currency or not, which is a report in the usual form made by an officer of the bank in his official capacity, if it contains a false entry made with intent to deceive, is within Revised Statutes, United States, section 5209, which declared such false entries to be a misdemeanor. *United States v. Hugbitt, 45 Fed. Rep., 47.*

7. Where false entries were made by a bookkeeper in a statement requested by a national-bank examiner purporting to give the balance due to depositors, which statement it was the duty of the examiner to make and not the bookkeeper, an indictment for making "false entries in a statement of the association" will not be sustained. *United States v. Eqe, 49 Fed Rep., 852.*

8. In an indictment of an officer of a national bank under section 5209, Revised Statutes, United States, for making false entries in a report to the Comptroller of the Currency, it is no defense that such entries were made by a

FALSE ENTRIES—Continued.

clerk and verified by the officer without actual knowledge of their truth, since it was his duty to inform himself. *United States* v. *Allen, 47 Fed. Rep., 696.*

9. A "false entry" in a report by a national-bank officer or a director to Comptroller of the Currency within the meaning of section 5209, is not merely an incorrect entry made through inadvertent negligence or mistake, but is an entry known to the maker to be untrue and incorrect and by him ·intentionally entered while so knowing its false and untrue character. *United States* v. *Graves, 53 Fed. Rep., 634.*

10. In determining whether a certain false entry, made by a national-bank officer in a report to the Comptroller, was made with intent to deceive or defraud, etc., within the meaning of the statute, the jury are authorized to infer the intent if the natural and legitimate result of such false entry would be to deceive any other officer or officers of the bank or any agent appointed to examine into its affairs. *Ib.*

11. In determining whether defendant made a "false entry" within the meaning of the statute, when he included in such report, as "Loans and discounts" of the bank, amounts which were being carried on the books of the bank as "overdrafts," the jury will not consider whether other national banks followed the same practice; but the jury, in determining whether such entry, if a "false entry," was made with intent to deceive and defraud, may consider whatever knowledge defendant is shown to have had as to practice of any other national bank in this respect. *Ib.*

12. It is not necessary to complete the offense of making a "false entry" in a report to the Comptroller of the Treasury of the condition of a national bank, with intent to deceive or defraud, that any person shall have been in fact actually deceived or defrauded; for the making of such a "false entry" with the intent to deceive or defraud is sufficient. *Ib.*

13. Under section 5209 of the national-bank act, it is an indictable offense to make a false entry in a report to the Comptroller of the Currency, or to aid and abet the making of such entry. *United States* v. *French et. al., 57 Fed. Rep., 382.*

14. It is not a "false entry" to enter under heading of "Loans and discounts," items which, on books of the bank, and for convenience of its officers, have been temporarily withdrawn from that heading, and which are, from day to day carried on books of the bank under heading of "Suspended loans" while awaiting action of directors as to same being withdrawn from character of loans and entered up as a loss on profit and loss account. *United States* v. *Graves, 53 Fed. Rep., 634.*

FORFEITURE OF CHARTER:

1. Under Revised Statutes, United States, section 5239, providing that if the directors of a national bank shall violate any of the provisions of the title relating to the organization and management of banks, the franchises of the bank shall be forfeited, such violation, however, to be determined by a proper court of the United States in a suit therefor by the Comptroller, and that in cases of such violation every.director participating therein shall be personally liable for all damages which the bank, its shareholders, or any other person shall have sustained in consequence thereof, the Comptroller can not authorize the receiver to bring suit, under section 5231, to enforce such personal liability, until it has been adjudged by a proper court that such acts have been done as authorize a forfeiture of the charter. *Welles* v. *Graves, 41 Fed. Rep., 459.*

2. The right to maintain an action under Revised Statutes, United States, section 5239, to recover from a bank director the damages sustained by his bank in consequence of excessive loans made by him while serving in the capacity of director, is not affected by the fact that the Comptroller has or has not procured a forfeiture of the bank's charter. *Stephens* v. *Overstolz, 43 Fed. Rep., 771.*

GOVERNMENT SECURITIES:

National-banking associations can engage in the business of dealing in and exchanging Government securities. *Van Leuven* v. *First National Bank, 54 N. Y., 671; Yerkes* v. *National Bank of Port Jervis, 69 N. Y., 383; Leach* v. *Hale, 31 Iowa, 69.*

GUARANTY:

A personal guaranty, given by stockholders and directors to another bank in consideration of loans, discounts, or other advances to be made, for the repayment of any indebtedness thus created, imposes a liability on the

GUARANTY—Continued.

> guarantors when acted on by the guarantee though no notice of the accept-
> ance of the guarantee was given, for the contract shows a personal interest
> of the guarantors in the advances constituting a consideration moving to
> them. *Doud et. al. v. National Park Bank, 54 Fed. Rep., 846.*

INCREASE OF CAPITAL STOCK:

1. National banks have no authority to increase their capital stock except as
provided by Revised Statutes, section 5142, and act of Congress, May 1, 1886;
and where an increase is attempted to be made without obtaining the consent of two-thirds of the stock, the payment in full of the amount of such
increase, and the certificate and approval of the Comptroller of the Currency, as required by those statutes, the proceedings are invalid, and preliminary subscriptions to such increase can not be enforced. *Armstrong v.
Stanage et al., 37 Fed. Rep., 508.*

2. Where one subscribes for shares in the increase of the capital of a national-
banking association in a certain amount, such subscription and payment
are upon the implied condition that the increase shall be in the exact
amount so fixed; and if such amount is changed, the subscriber may avoid
the subscription and recover the amount paid in. *Eaton v. Pacific Bank,
144 Mass., 260.*

3. And the certificate of the Comptroller of the Currency that the amount of
the increase in another sum has been paid in, which amount includes what
was paid by the dissenting subscriber, will not be conclusive upon such
subscriber. *Ib.*

4. But if such subscriber has assented to or ratified the change he will be held a
shareholder. *Delano v. Butler, 118 U. S., 634.*

5. When the previous proceedings looking to an increase in the capital stock
of a national bank have been regular and all that are requisite, and a
stockholder subscribes to his proportionate part of the increase and pays
his subscription, the law does not attach to the subscription a condition
that it is to be void if the whole increase authorized be not subscribed;
although there may be cases in which equity would interfere to protect
him in case of a material deficiency. *Aspinwall v. Butler, 133 U. S., 595.*

6. The Comptroller of the Currency has power by law to assent to an increase
in the capital stock of a national bank less than that originally voted by
the directors, but equal to the amount actually subscribed and paid for by
the shareholders under that vote. *Ib.*

7. Where one subscribes for shares in an increase of capital stock of a national
bank and pays for the same without waiting to see whether the whole
amount of the increase is taken, he is bound by such subscription and
payment, though the amount of the increase is afterward reduced by the
bank and the Comptroller of the Currency. *Butler v. Eaton, 141 U. S., 240.*

8. The conditions imposed by Revised Statutes, Sec. 5142, to the validity of
increase of national-bank capital were intended to secure actual cash
payment of subscriptions and to prevent watering stock, not to invalidate
bona fide subscriptions actually made and paid. *Aspinwall v. Butler, 133
U. S., 595.*

9. Stockholder in national bank who, with knowledge of its insolvent condition and of all material facts, subscribes for increased stock to same
amount as his original stock, and amount of proposed increase is afterward reduced, can not question validity of proceedings for such increase
to annul such subscription and payment. *Delano v. Butler, 118 U. S.,
634; Pacific National Bank v. Eaton, 141 ib., 227; Thayer v. Butler, ib.,
234; Butler v. Eaton, ib., 240.*

INDICTMENT:

1. An indictment charging defendants with aiding and abetting a director in a
willful misapplication of the money of an association must state facts to
show that there has been such misapplication committed by the director.
United States v. Warner, 26 Fed. Rep., 616.

2. An indictment under act of July 12, 1882, amending section 5208, making it a
misdemeanor to "certify any check" drawn by a person not then having
on deposit sufficient money to meet same need not allege delivery of check
by bank after certification. *United States v. Potter, 56 Fed. Rep., 83.*

3. When indictment alleges certification as accomplished, authentication will
not be presumed as an essential part thereof, and hence it is unnecessary
to allege absence of required credit or deposit at time of authentication.
Ib.

INDICTMENT—Continued.

4. The indictment in charging in the language of section 5208 that the drawer of the check had not on deposit, at the time it was certified, "an amount of money equal to that specified" in the check is sufficient. *Ib.*

5. The indictment does not charge two offenses in the same count because it alleges therein that the check was certified "before the amount thereof had been entered to the credit of the drawer on the books of the bank," and also at a time when the drawer did not "have on deposit an amount of money equal to" the amount of the check. *Ib.*

6. An indictment against the president for "aiding and abetting" cashier in certifying check under prohibition can not be sustained. *Ib.*

7. An indictment charging directors of a national banking association with making false entries in a report of condition to the Comptroller of the Currency can not be sustained under section 5209. *Ib.*

8. The use in an indictment, under section 5209, of the words "then and there" in alleging that the defendant was president or director of such bank and made alleged false entries, is not uncertain or repugnant merely because in one place they may refer to the whole of a day and in another to only one instant of the day. *Ib.*

9. The omission of the signs for dollars and cents in the recital of alleged false entries in reports and misnomer of reports are immaterial where reports are set out by their tenor in the indictment. *Ib.*

10. It is not necessary to allege specifically in such indictment that the reports were transmitted to the Comptroller of the Currency, or that they were published. *Ib.*

11. Allegations that the false entries were made with intent "to injure and defraud the said association and certain persons to the grand jurors unknown" are sufficient. *Ib.*

12. An indictment against the president of a national bank, under section 5209, for making false entries in the books of the bank, charging that it was done "with intent to defraud said association and certain persons to the grand jurors unknown" is sufficient so far as concerns the allegations of intent. *United States* v. *Potter, 56 Fed. Rep., 97.*

13. When indictment alleges that the false entries indicated that there was then in the paying teller's department of the bank certain amount in gold, legal tenders, and gold certificates, when in fact such amount was not there, it is not necessary that it should further allege that such amount was not then in other departments of the bank. *Ib.*

14. In addition to the entries themselves, the indictment need set out the context only when it so modifies the entries as to be in presumption of law a part of them. *Ib.*

15. The fact that the note teller's and paying teller's books, in which the president is charged with making the false entries are usually kept by those officers without interference by the president does not invalidate indictment thereon. *Ib.*

16. Counts charging false entries by the president in reports of condition of the bank, which allege that reports were made in conformity to the law and then set them out by their tenor are bad, for their failure to allege specifically that the reports were verified and attested by the cashier. *Ib.*

17. An indictment against the president of a national bank, alleging that he "unlawfully and willfully and with intent to injure and defraud the said association for the use, benefit, and advantage of himself, did misapply certain of the money and funds of the association which he * * * then and there with the intent aforesaid paid and caused to be paid" to certain persons named, was bad for failure to allege the fact that made such payment unlawful or criminal. *United States* v. *Eno, 56 Fed. Rep., 218.*

18. It is not essential that such indictment should allege that the acts charged were done without the knowledge and assent of the directors of the association. *Ib.*

19. Where the entry whose tenor is set forth contains the words "See schedule," it is not a valid objection to the indictment that these words are not explained. *Ib.*

20. It is sufficient if the indictment allege the substance of the reports in question without setting them out in full. *Ib.*

21. *United States* v. *Work, 57 Fed. Rep., 391, was decided in accordance with *United States* v. *French, 57 Fed. Rep., 382, and United States v. Potter, 56 Fed. Rep., 83 and 97.*

22. An allegation in an indictment under this section that defendant "did make a certain false entry in a certain report of the association" will not be

INDICTMENT—Continued.

construed to mean that the entry was made after the report was completed, and was, in fact, an alteration. *United States* v. *French et al., 57 Fed. Rep., 382.*

23.. The preparation and completion of the report, the making of the false entry therein, its verification, attestation, and delivery to the Comptroller, may be considered as simultaneous, and there is no repugnance in failing to allege that any or all of these things occurred in consecutive order. *Ib.*

24. Though the counts in an indictment under this section for aiding and abetting the cashier in making such false entries describe defendant as "being then and there a director" of the bank in question, it can not be held that they charge him in aiding and abetting in his official capacity. *Ib.*

25. Counts in such indictment, which charge defendant with procuring and counseling the false entry before the fact, are valid, for such acts are covered by the clause of the section extending the penalty to anyone who "abets" an officer or agent in the acts prohibited. *Ib.*

26. In indictment under Revised Statutes, Sec. 5209, for willfully misapplying the funds of a national bank, it is not necessary to charge that the funds had been previously intrusted to defendant; since such act may be done by an officer or agent of the association without his having previously received the funds into his manual possession. *United States* v. *Northway, 120 U. S., 327.*

27. Indictment charging president of a bank with aiding and abetting its cashier in the misapplication of its funds, it is not necessary to aver that he then and there knew that the person so aided and abetted was the cashier.— *Ib.*

28. A form of indictment which sufficiently describes and identifies the crime of abstracting the funds of a national bank created by Revised Statutes, Sec. 5209, and sufficiently states the character and capacity of the bank. *Ib.*

29 Indictment against president for false entry on books *held* sufficient in form and averments. *United States* v. *Britton, 107 U. S., 655.*

30. Indictment against president for fraudulent purchase of stock of the bank is bad if it fails to state for whose use purchase was made, or if it states that it was for use of the bank, or if it does not aver that it was not made to prevent loss on previous debt. *Ib.*

31. Indictment for perjury against officer for false statement under section 5211, Revised Statutes, is bad if, prior to act of 1881, chapter 82, his oath verifying report was taken before notary appointed by a State. *United States* v. *Curtis, 107 U. S., 671.*

INJUNCTION:

Sec. 5242 Revised Statutes, providing that no injunctions shall issue from a State court against a national bank before final judgment, does not deprive the Federal court of power to issue such injunction or to continue after removal of the case an injunction previously granted by a State court. *Hower* v. *Weiss Malting and Elevator Co. et. al., 55 Fed. Rep., 356.*

INSOLVENT BANKS: *See* Shareholders; Set-off; Receiver; Preferred claims.

1. National-banking associations were not subject to the bankrupt act while that act was in force. *In re Manufacturers' National Bank, 5 Biss., 499.*

2. The term "insolvency," as used in section 5242, Revised Statutes, forbidding transfer of the assets of national-banking associations after, or in contemplation of, such insolvency, has the same meaning as it had when applied to traders in the bankrupt act; that is, it does not mean an absolute inability of a debtor to pay his debt at some future time, upon a settlement and winding up of his affairs, but a present inability to pay in the ordinary course of business. *Case* v. *Citizens' Bank of Louisiana, 2 Woods, 23; Market Bank* v. *Pacific National Bank, 30 Hun., 50.*

3. It is not necessary that the facts upon which the Comptroller bases his action in appointing a receiver should be established by what is *competent legal evidence;* but he is left to be satisfied as best he can be, under the peculiar circumstances of each case, of the facts and the necessity for the exercise of his authority. *Platt* v. *Beebe, 57 N. Y., 330.*

4. A return of *nulla bona* upon an execution issued against the property of a national bank is proof of its insolvency. *Wheelock* v. *Kost, 77 Ill., 296.*

5. The creditors of an insolvent association must seek their remedy through the Comptroller, in the mode prescribed by the statute; they can not proceed

INSOLVENT BANKS—Continued.

directly in their own names against stockholders or the debtors of the bank. *Kennedy* v. *Gibson, 8 Wall., 498.*

6. The creditors of an insolvent national-banking association in the hands of a receiver are entitled to interest on their claims during the period of administration. *National Bank of Commonwealth* v. *Mechanics' National Bank. 94 U. S., 437; Chemical National Bank* v. *Bailey, 12 Blatch., 480; White* v. *Knox, 111 U. S., 784.*

7. Where a national bank has leased a banking house for a long term of years, and subsequently becomes insolvent, but during the time it continued business had not defaulted in paying the rent, the lessor has no claim against the receiver by reason of the insolvency or dissolution of the corporation or the forfeiture of its franchises, or by the refusal of the receiver to take under the contract and pay the rent. *Fidelity Safe Deposit and Trust Co.* v. *Armstrong, 35 Fed. Rep., 567.*

8. A subscriber who has made payments on his subscription to the proposed increase, believing that the statutory requirements would be complied with, is entitled to have the amount thereof allowed as a claim against the assets of the bank in the receiver's hands. *Armstrong* v. *Stanage, 37 Fed. Rep., 568.*

9. Revised Statutes, United States, sections 5234 and 5239, prescribing the method of enforcing the liability of the directors of national banks for violation of the banking law, are exclusive of other remedies, and a creditor of an insolvent bank for which a receiver has been appointed, can not sue its directors for the purpose of making them personally liable for the mismanagement of the bank. *National Exchange Bank* v. *Peters et al., 44 Fed. Rep., 13.*

10. Bank property attached by individual creditor after bank is insolvent can not be sold to pay his demand against the claim of a receiver subsequently appointed. *National Bank* v. *Colby, 21 Wall., 609.*

11. Depositor, when bank suspends payment and receiver is appointed, is entitled from date of his demand to interest on his deposit. *National Bank* v. *Mechanics' National Bank, 94 U. S., 437.*

12. It does not lose its corporate existence by mere default in paying its notes and the appointment of a receiver. *Ib.; Bank of Bethel* v. *Pahquioque Bank, 14 Wall., 383.*

13. Such associations may be sued, though a receiver has been appointed and is administering its concerns. *Ib.*

14. If failed bank was indebted to its subagent and the collections were entered in their books as a credit to such indebtedness, they were thereby reduced to possession and passed into the general funds of the failed bank. *Commercial National Bank* v. *Armstrong, 148 U. S., 50.*

15. By the terms of an arrangement for the failed bank to remit the 1st, 11th, and 21st of each month, the relations of debtor and creditor were created when the collections were fully made, the funds being on general deposit with the failed bank with the right in that bank to their use until the time of remittance should arrive. *Ib.*

16. Where a check of a depositor is accepted by a correspondent bank in payment of a draft for collection, which charges the same to the drawee and credits the drawer without separating the amount from its general funds, it holds the money as agent for the drawer, who, after insolvency, becomes a mere general creditor, notwithstanding the State constitution proves that "depositors who have not stipulated for interest shall for such deposits be entitled in case of insolvency to preference of claimant over all other creditors. *Anheuser-Busch Brewing Association* v. *Clayton, 56 Fed. Rep., 759.*

17. Sureties on indebtedness of insolvent bank are not entitled to prove any claim against it by reason of the enforcement of their liability as such. *Stewart* v. *Armstrong, 56 Fed. Rep., 167.*

18. A creditor of an insolvent national bank, who establishes his debt by suit and judgment after refusal of Comptroller to allow it, is entitled to share in dividends on debt and interest so established as of day of failure of bank, not for subsequent interest. *White* v. *Knox, 111 U. S., 784.*

19. The personal property of an insolvent bank in hands of a receiver is exempt from State taxation. *Rosenblatt* v. *Johnston, 104 U. S., 462.*

20. When a creditor of a national bank is entitled to interest on the amount of his dividend from the time it was declared by a receiver of the bank. *Armstrong* v. *American Exchange National Bank, 133 U. S., 433.*

21. Construction and application of Revised Statutes, Sec. 5212, as to transfers by insolvent national banks. *National Bank* v. *Butler, 129 U. S., 223,*

INSOLVENT BANKS—Continued.

22. What motive is sufficient under Revised Statutes, Sec. 5242, to invalidate a transfer by a national bank. *Ib.*

23. In estimating the dividends to be paid out of the assets of an insolvent association, the value of the claims at the time when the insolvency is declared is to be taken as the basis of distribution. *White v. Knox, 111 U. S., 784.*

INTEREST: *See* Usury; Insolvent banks.

1. The provision in section 30 of the act of 1864 "that where, by the law of any State, a different rate is limited for banks of issue organized under State laws, the rate so limited shall be allowed for associations organized in any such State under the act," is enabling, and not restrictive; and, therefore, a national-banking association in any State may stipulate for as high a rate of interest as by the laws of such State a natural person may, although State banks of issue are restricted to a less rate. *Tiffany v. National Bank of the State of Missouri, 18 Wall., 409.*

2. But it is not to be inferred from Tiffany v. National Bank of Missouri that whatever by the laws of the State is lawful for natural persons in acquiring title to negotiable paper by discount is lawful for national banks. *National Bank v. Johnson, 104 U. S., 271.*

3. The interest which a national-banking association may charge is limited to the rate allowed to the banks of the State generally; and the fact that a few of the State banks are specially authorized to take a higher rate is not a warrant for a national-banking association to do so. *Duncan v. First National Bank of Mount Pleasant, 11 Bank Mag., 787; Gruber v. First National Bank, 87 Penn. St., 468.*

4. Where the State law does not limit the rate of interest which may be charged on loans to corporations, a national-banking association located in that State can not charge more than 7 per cent interest on such loans. *In re Wild, 11 Blatch., 243.*

5. Where by the statutes of the State parties are authorized to contract for any rate of interest, national-banking associations in that State may likewise contract for any rate, and are not limited to 7 per cent. *Hinds v. Marmelejo, 60 Cal., 229; National Bank v. Bruhn, 64 Texas, 571.*

6. Bank may take the rate of interest allowed by the State to natural persons generally, and a higher rate where State banks of issue can take it. *Tiffany v. National Bank of Missouri, supra.*

7. May charge rate of interest allowed to natural persons in the State or Territory where bank is located, but can not take more, even on discount of paper for third party, without it being usury. *National Bank v. Johnson, supra.*

JURISDICTION: *See* Actions.

1. The tenth subdivision of section 629, Revised Statutes, which confers upon the circuit court of the United States jurisdiction of all suits by or against any national-banking association established in the district for which the court is held, has been repealed by the proviso to section 4 of the act of July 12, 1882. *National Bank of Jefferson v. Fare et al., 25 Fed. Rep., 209.*

2. The object of this proviso was to deprive the United States courts of jurisdiction of suits by or against national-banking associations in all cases where banks organized under State laws could not likewise sue or be sued in such courts. *Ib.*

3. But the proviso does not affect the right of the receiver of an insolvent association to sue in a Federal court. *Hendee v. Connecticut and P. R. R. Co., 26 Fed. Rep., 677.*

4. Nor would the act of July 12, 1882, take from the circuit court jurisdiction of a suit brought against a director for negligent performance of his duties; for, as such suits rest upon the requirements of the United States laws and by-laws made pursuant thereto, it is a case arising under the laws of the United States *Witters v. Foster, 28 Fed. Rep., 737.*

5. In an action against a national bank in a circuit court of the United States, if all the parties are citizens of the district in which the bank is situated, and the action does not come under section 5209 or section 5239 of the Revised Statutes, the circuit court has no jurisdiction. *Whittemore v. Amoskeag National Bank, 134 U. S., 527.*

6. The Federal courts have jurisdiction of an action between a national bank located in one State and a citizen of another State. *First National Bank v. Forest, 40 Fed. Rep., 705.*

7. An action between a receiver of an insolvent national bank and a depositor does not present a Federal question under Revised Statutes of the United

JURISDICTION—Continued.

States, section 5242, avoiding preferences to creditors of such an insolvent bank. *Tehan* v. *First National Bank et al., 39 Fed. Rep., 577.*

8. A receiver of an insolvent national bank is an officer of the United States within the meaning of section 563, Revised Statutes of the United States, which gives the district courts jurisdiction of "all suits at common law brought by the United States, or any officer thereof authorized by law to sue." *Stephens* v. *Bernays, 41 Fed. Rep., 401.*

9. State courts have jurisdiction of suits by and against national banking associations. *Bank of Bethel* v. *Pahqnioque Bank, 14 Wall., 383; Ordway* v. *Central National Bank, 47 Md., 217* and *Claflin* v. *Houseman 93 U. S., 130.*

10. Where a national banking association is sued in a State court, the suit must be brought in the city or county in which the bank is located. *Cadle* v. *Tracey, 11 Blatch., 101.*

11. The United States district court has jurisdiction of an action at law brought by the receiver of a national bank to recover an assessment made upon a stockholder, and the action may be maintained in such event against the executor of a deceased stockholder. *Stephens* v. *Bernays, supra.*

12. But in a State where the holder may sue without respect to the ownership an association may bring suit upon paper so acquired. *National Pemberton Bank* v. *Porter, 125 Mass., 333; Atlas National Bank* v. *Savery, 127 Mass., 75.*

13. But in *Talmage* v. *Third National Bank, 27 Hun., 61,* the supreme court of New York said: "The words of restriction to the place where said 'association is situated' apply to the county and municipal courts, and not to the State courts. In the State courts of general jurisdiction a national-banking association can be sued whenever an individual can be for the same cause."

14. A State court can entertain an action brought to recover of a national-banking association the penalty for taking usury. *Ordway* v. *The Central National Bank, 47 Md., 217; Hade* v. *McVay, 31 Ohio St., 231; Bletz* v. *Columbia National Bank, 87 Penn. St., 87.*

15. The State courts have jurisdiction of an action brought by a shareholder on behalf of himself and other shareholders to recover of the directors of an insolvent association damages for injuries resulting from their negligence and misconduct. *Brinckerhoff* v. *Bostwick, 88 N. Y., 52.*

16. A State court has no power to make an order directing the receiver of a national bank, who has been appointed by the Comptroller of the Currency, to pay a judgment obtained against the bank before the receiver was appointed. *Ocean National Bank* v. *Carll, 7 Hun, 237.*

17. State courts have no jurisdiction of the case of an embezzlement of the funds of the association by one of its officers. *Commonwealth* v. *Felton, 101 Mass., 204; Commonwealth ex rel. Torrey* v. *Ketner, 92 Penn. St., 372.*

18. The defense of usury may be set up in action brought in a State court. *National Bank of Winterset* v. *Eyre, 52 Iowa, 114.*

19. Neither the Comptroller nor the receiver by putting in an appearance to a suit can subject the United States to the jurisdiction of a court. *Case* v. *Terrell, 11 Wall., 199.*

20. A national-banking association is for jurisdictional purposes a citizen of the State in which it is located. *Davis* v. *Cook, 9 Nev., 134.*

21. The offense of making false entries in the books of a bank, for which an officer of the bank is liable to punishment, under section 5209, since it is not a crime of which the State courts have concurrent jurisdiction, under section 5328, is exclusively cognizable by the Federal courts. *In re Eno, 54 Fed. Rep., 69.*

22. Under the provisions of the act of August 13, 1888, national banks are deemed to be, for jurisdictional purposes, citizens of the State wherein they are located and they no longer possess the right of removal on the ground that they are Federal corporations. *Burnham et al.* v. *First National Bank of Leoti, 53 Fed. Rep., 163.*

23. When the citizenship is diverse and plaintiff is a resident of the district it is not necessary that he shall also reside in the particular division of the district in which the suit is brought, that a creditor's bill may be maintained in a Federal court upon a judgment procured in a different State court from the State in which the Federal court sits. *Merchants' National Bank et al.* v. *Chattanooga Construction Co., 53 Fed. Rep., 314.*

24. The Federal courts have jurisdiction of suits by receivers of national banks to collect the assets thereof without regard to the citizenship of the plaintiff. *Fisher* v. *Yoder, 53 Fed. Rep., 565.*

25. An action for money against a national bank whose corporate existence is admitted is not a suit arising under the laws of the United States. *Ulster County Savings Institution* v. *Fourth National Bank, 8 N. Y., 162.*

JURISDICTION—Continued.

26. The provision that the Federal courts shall not have jurisdiction of an action on a promissory note or other chose in action by an assignee thereof, unless the action might have been maintained in such courts if no assignment or transfer had been made (act August 13, 1888), does not apply to the indorsement and transfer of the payee of notes which were made to him merely that he might as agent of the maker raise money for it by negotiating them with third persons. *Hachusett National Bank* v. *Sioux City Stove Works, 56 Fed. Rep., 321.*

27. If the citizenship of original payee of promissory note is material to jurisdiction of an action by indorsee against maker, plaintiff must affirmatively plead it. *United States National Bank* v. *McNair, 56 Fed. Rep., 323.*

28. A suit on the official bond of the cashier of a national bank, conditioned for a faithful performance of the duties thereof, "according to law and the by-laws" of the bank, involves a Federal question and is maintainable in a Federal court irrespective of the citizenship of the parties. *Walker et al.* v. *Windsor National Bank, 56 Fed. Rep., 76.*

29. In a suit which is properly brought in a Federal court, because it involves a Federal question, the court has full jurisdiction of the defendant. who, though a resident of another district, waives his personal privilege of being sued in his district by voluntarily appearing. *Ib.*

30. A citizen of New York brought suit in the circuit court of North Carolina against a citizen of North Carolina on promissory note to cashier of national bank, which was also located there. Note had been indorsed to plaintiff. After indorsement a receiver had been appointed for the bank. *Held*, that the receiver would have been an assignee of the note although the assignment was brought about by operation of law, and that as bank could not have sued in circuit court neither could the receiver nor the plaintiff, as the court had no jurisdiction. *Ib.*

31. Under the above statute assignee can not maintain a suit on a promissory note unless the original payee could have prosecuted it. *Ib.*

32. The exemption of national banks from suits in State courts in other than their own county or city, by act of February 18, 1875 (18 Stat., 316, chap. 80), was a personal privilege which could be waived by appearing to such suit and not claiming the immunity. *First National Bank* v. *Morgan, 132 U. S., 141.*

33. The provision in act of July 12, 1882 (22 Stat., 163, chap. 290, sec. 4), respecting suits by or against national banks, refers only to suits brought after the passage of that act. *Ib.*

34. This court has jurisdiction to review a judgment in State courts involving the question whether a national bank is exempted from liability to account for bonds purchased by it on condition of selling back on demand. *Logan Bank* v. *Townsend, 139 U. S., 67.*

35. When transaction of transfer of national bank shares does not present a case arising under national-banking act, and so involving a Federal question. *Le Sassier* v. *Kennedy, 123 U. S., 521.*

LENDING CREDIT:

1. A national-banking association can not lend its credit. *Johnson* v. *Charlottesville National Bank, 3 Hughes, 657; Seligman* v. *Charlottesville National Bank, 3 Hughes, 647; National Bank of Commerce* v. *Atkinson, 55 Fed. Rep., 465.*

2. A national banking association can not take a pledge of its stock to secure a deposit made by it with another bank. Such a transaction amounts to a lending upon the security of its own shares. *Bank* v. *Lanier, 11 Wall., 369.*

3. Though a bank is prohibited from lending money upon the security of its own shares, yet, if the shares have been sold and the proceeds applied to the payment of the debt, the courts will not aid the shareholder to recover the value of the shares. He can dispute the validity of the transaction only while the contract is executory, and the security still subsists in the possession of the bank. *National Bank of Xenia* v. *Stewart, 107 U. S., 676.*

LIABILITY: *See* Officers; Shareholders.

1. And where an association receives United States bonds of one class for the purpose of having them converted into bonds of another class, it is not a mere mandatary, but is responsible for the failure to deliver the bonds on demand. *Leach* v. *Hale, 31 Iowa, 69.*

2. Where a national-banking association has taken collaterals to secure a loan, and, after the loan has been repaid, holds them to secure future advances,

LIABILITY—Continued.

it is not a gratuitous bailee; and it is responsible for the loss of such collaterals occasioned by its lack of ordinary care and diligence, though at the time the bailor was not indebted to it. *Third National Bank of Baltimore* v. *Boyd, 44 Md., 47.*

3. A bank receiving a certificate of deposit for collection, and mailing it to the drawer with a request for a remittance, is guilty of negligence. *First National Bank of Evansville* v. *Fourth National Bank of Louisville, 56 Fed. Rep., 967.*

4. A bank is charged with notice of letters duly mailed to it and received by the general bookkeeper, whose duty it is to open and distribute mail matter, although he conceals such letters to hide certain irregularities in his office, and thereby prevents their coming into the hands of the other bank officers. *Ib.*

5. The E. bank, on May 8, 1888, mailed to the L. bank for collection a certificate of deposit issued by P. & Co., which, the next day, negligently mailed it to P. & Co. with request to remit. On June 1 the L. bank credited the E. bank with the item in account current for May, and wrote that nothing had been heard from P. & Co. On June 22 the L. bank wrote that repeated letters about the item had remained unanswered. The L. bank now charged the E. bank with the item. No further correspondence ensued. P. & Co. continued in good credit until after January 1, 1889, when they failed. *Held,* That the L. bank was not responsible for more than nominal damages. *Ib.*

6. Where bank acquires title to real estate by conveyance from its president who held same under deed reciting full payment of purchase money, and bank has no actual knowledge that purchase money was not in fact paid, it is an innocent purchaser without notice, and is not chargeable with constructive notice because of the knowledge of its president. *First National Bank of Sheffield et al.* v. *Tompkins, 57 Fed. Rep., 20.*

7. Where grantor states to director of bank that he is willing to convey a half interest in certain land to the bank's president, with the understanding that such president was to deed the whole interest to the bank, and the president of the bank was to pay him by giving him credit upon notes then running against him in the bank. *Held,* Not to amount to notice to the director that the grantor intends to retain a vendor's lien, but rather imports a notice that no such lien is to be retained. *Ib.*

8. If a cashier, without authority to buy coin in behalf of his bank, does so buy it, and it goes into the funds of the bank, it is liable. *Merchants' Bank* v. *State Bank, 10 Wall., 604.*

9. National bank is liable for damages occasioned by the loss through gross negligence of a special deposit made in it with knowledge and acquiescence of its officers and directors. *National Bank* v. *Graham, 100 U. S., 699.*

LIEN: *See* Preferred claims.

1. An association has equitable lien upon dividends declared for any just debt due to it from the shareholders. *Hager* v. *Union National Bank, 63 Me., 509.*

2. But a creditor will not have a lien upon the funds of the association because checks given in settlement of balances were fraudulent, and were given at a time when the bank was hopelessly insolvent and its officers were contemplating flight. *Citizens' National Bank* v. *Dowd, 35 Fed. Rep., 340.*

3. Bank can not acquire a lien on its own stock held by its debtors, even if its by-laws are framed with that intention. *Bullard* v. *Bank, 18 Wall., 589.*

4. Loans by bank to stockholder do not give lien to bank on his stock. *Ib.; Bank* v. *Lanier, 11 Wall., 369.*

LIQUIDATION:

1. A national bank may go into voluntary liquidation and be closed by a vote of two-thirds of its shareholders, although contrary to the wishes and against the interest of the remainder. *Watkins* v. *National Bank of Lawrence, 32 Pac. Rep., 914.*

2. A national bank which has gone into voluntary liquidation will continue to exist as a body corporate for the purpose of suing and being sued until its affairs are completely settled. *National Bank* v. *Insurance Company, 104 U. S., 54; Ordway* v. *Central National Bank. 47 Md., 217.*

3. After an association goes into liquidation there is no authority on the part of its officers to transact any business in its name so as to bind its shareholders, except that which is implied in the duty of liquidation, unless such authority has been expressly conferred by the shareholders. *Richmond* v. *Irons, 121 U. S., 27.*

LIQUIDATION—Continued.

4. The Comptroller may appoint a receiver for a bank that has voted to go into voluntary liquidation. *Washington National Bank of Tacoma* v. *Eckels. Fed. Rep., 1893.*

5. Where a bank has gone into voluntary liquidation, and the Comptroller has no power to appoint a receiver, a proper court, in a case where such action is necessary to protect the interests of a creditor, will appoint a receiver for it. *Irons* v. *Manufacturers' National Bank, 6 Biss., 301.*

6. Where a national bank is insolvent and in process of voluntary liquidation, and its affairs are being greatly mismanaged by its managing agents, to the injury of its creditors and stockholders, and some of the creditors and stockholders are being favored to the injury of others, a receiver may be appointed in such a case, even where the bank only has been made a defendant. *Elwood* v. *First National Bank, 21 Kans., 673.*

7. Where after an association has gone into liquidation a receiver is appointed at the instance of the creditors, the expenses of such receivership must be paid by the creditors. The shareholders can not be made individually liable for such expenses. *Richmond* v. *Irons, supra.*

8. In case of book accounts in favor of depositors, interest begins to run against an association in liquidation from the date of the suspension of business. *Ib.*

9. Without express authority from the shareholders in a national bank its officers, after the bank goes into liquidation, can only bind them by acts implied by the duty of liquidation. *Ib.*

10. Creditors of national bank who, after it suspends payment and goes into voluntary liquidation, receive in settlement of their claims bills receivable, indorsed or guaranteed in the name of the bank by its president, can not claim as creditors against the shareholders, as the original debt is paid. *Ib.*

LOANS:

1. Sec. 5200, Revised Statutes, which provides that the total liabilities to any association of any person, etc., shall not exceed one-tenth part of the capital stock paid in, was intended only for the guidance of the association, and, though its franchises may be liable to forfeiture for violation of the law, the association may recover of the borrower the full amount of the loan. *Gold Mining Company* v. *Rocky Mountain National Bank, 96 U. S., 640;* *O'Hare* v. *Second National Bank of Titusville, 77 Penn. St., 96; Shoemaker* v. *The National Mechanics' Bank, 2 Abb., U. S., 416; Stewart* v. *National Union Bank of Maryland, 2 Abb., U. S., 424.*

2. A note is not illegal because at the time it was discounted by the association the maker was indebted to the association in a sum equal to more than one-tenth part of its capital. *O'Hare* v. *Second National Bank of Titusville, supra.*

3. And a court of equity will not enjoin an association, at the instance of the borrower, from transferring to innocent third persons notes and securities, on the ground that the notes represent part of a loan made in excess of 10 per cent of the capital of the association. *Elder* v. *First National Bank of Ottawa, 12 Kans., 238.*

4. Where a State bank makes a loan to one person of an amount in excess of one-tenth part of its capital, and is afterward converted into a national bank, it may, after conversion, extend the time for payment of such loan without violating section 5200, Revised Statutes. *Allen* v. *The First National Bank of Xenia, 24 Ohio St., 97.*

5. Defendant sued by national bank for moneys it loaned him can not set up as bar that they exceed one-tenth of capital paid in. *Gold Mining Co.* v. *National Bank, supra.*

6. Placing by one bank of its funds on permanent deposit with another is a loan within this enactment. *Bank* v. *Lanier, 11 Wall., 369.*

MANDAMUS:

The writ of mandamus can not issue in a case where its effect is to direct or control the head of an executive department in the discharge of an executive duty, involving the exercise of judgment or discretion. *United States ex rel. Boynton* v. *Blaine, 139 U. S., 306.*

MARRIED WOMEN:

A national-banking association may take as security for a loan the indorsement of a married woman, charging her separate estate. Such security is to be treated as personal security, within the meaning of the banking law, and not as a mortgage. *Third National Bank* v. *Blake, 73 N. Y., 260.*

MORTGAGE: *See* Real estate.

1. National-banking associations are by implication prohibited from taking mortgages on real estate as security for contemporaneous loans. *National Bank* v. *Matthews, 98 U. S., 621; Fowler* v. *Scully, 72 Penn. St., 456; Kansas Valley National Bank* v. *Rowell, 2 Dill., 371; Commonwealth Bank* v. *Clark, 4 Mo., 59; Crocker* v. *Whitney, 71 N. Y., 161; Fridley* v. *Bowen, 87 Ill., 151.*

2. But where such security has been taken, no one but the Government can be heard to complain that the association has exceeded its powers. *National Bank* v. *Matthews, supra; National Bank* v. *Whitney, 103 U. S., 99; Swope* v. *Leffingwell, 105 U. S., 3; Reynolds* v. *National Bank, 112 U. S., 405; Fortier* v. *National Bank, 112 U. S., 439.*

3. Where a national banking association sells real estate it may take a mortgage thereon to secure the payment of the purchase money. *New Orleans National Bank* v. *Raymond, 29 La. Ann., 355.*

4. An agreement by a national-banking association to the effect that, in case a note discounted by it shall not be paid, a mortgage given by the maker to his indorser shall inure to the benefit of the association, is not inhibited by the national-banking law. *First National Bank* v. *Haire, 36 Iowa, 443; National Bank* v. *Matthews, supra.*

5. A national bank may loan on security of a mortgage if not objected to by the United States. *National Bank* v. *Matthews, ib; National Bank* v. *Whitney, supra; Fortier, New Orleans National Bank, supra.*

NEGOTIABLE PAPER:

The president and secretary of a corporation are presumed to have authority to execute a promissory note in the name of the corporation, and the holder of such note will not be affected by the fact that such authority did not exist unless he is shown to have had notice thereof. *American Exchange National Bank* v. *Oregon Pottery Co., 55 Fed. Rep., 265.*

OATH OF DIRECTOR:

1. The directors of a bank at the time of its conversion into a national-banking association are not required to take the oath of directors. *Lockwood* v. *American National Bank, 9 R. 1., 308.*

2. Prior to the act of February 26, 1881, a notary public holding his commission under a State had no authority to administer the oath required by section 5211, Revised Statutes; and therefore a cashier who made oath before such notary to a false statement of the condition of his association was not guilty of perjury. *United States* v. *Curtis, 107 U. S., 671.*

OFFICERS :

1. Directors of national-banking associations may remove the president, both under the law of Congress and the articles of association, where the latter so provide. The power exists, though the association has adopted no by-laws. *Taylor* v. *Hutton, 43 Barb., 195.*

2. The officers of a national-banking association can hold their positions only by the tenure specified in section 5136, Revised Statutes, viz, the pleasure of the board of directors. *Harrington* v. *First National Bank of Chittenango, Thomp. N. B. Cas. 761; Taylor* v. *Hutton, supra.*

3. The executive officers of an association can not bind it as a gratuitous bailee, unless they have a special authority from the board of directors so to do, or there exists a general custom or usage to that effect. *First National Bank of Lyons* v. *Ocean National Bank, 60 N. Y., 278.*

4. The personal liability of directors of a national bank for violation of Revised Statutes, United States, section 5204, by declaring dividends in excess of net profits, and of section 5200, for loaning to separate persons, firms, or corporations amounts exceeding one-tenth of the capital stock can not be enforced in an action at law. *Welles* v. *Graves, 41 Fed. Rep., 459.*

5. The election of an individual as a director does not constitute him an agent of the corporation with authority to act separately and independently of his fellow members. It is the board duly convened and acting as a unit that is made the representative of the association. The assent or determination of the members of the board acting separately and individually is not the assent of the corporation. The law proceeds upon the theory that the directors shall meet and counsel with each other, and that any determination affecting the association shall be arrived at and expressed only after a consultation at a meeting of the board, attended by at least a majority of its members. *National Bank* v. *Drake 35 Kans., 564.*

6. An officer may, in the ordinary course of business, borrow money of the association. *Blair* v. *First National Bank of Mansfield, 10 Chicago Legal News, 84.*

7. All directors who participate in and assent to a loan in excess of one-tenth of the capital of the bank, in violation of section 5200, Revised Statutes, will be liable to the bank for all damages sustained by it in consequence of such loan. *Witters* v. *Sowles, 31 Fed. Rep., 1.*

8. If a cashier, without authority from the directors so to do, makes a loan in excess of one-tenth of the capital of the association, he will be liable, in case of loss, for the amount of the excess. *Second National Bank of Oswego* v. *Burt, 93 N. Y., 233.*

9. The directors of a national bank will not be held liable for loss occasioned to the bank through the frauds of a codirector in which they had no part, and which were perpetrated without their connivance or knowledge. It is not sufficient to charge them with liability that the frauds might have been prevented by the exercise on their part of a proper degree of supervision over the affairs of the bank. *Movius* v. *Lee, 30 Fed. Rep., 298.*

10. But directors of a national bank must exercise ordinary care and prudence in the administration of the affairs of the bank, and this includes something more than officiating as figureheads: they are entitled under the law to commit the banking business as defined to the duly authorized officers, but this does not absolve them from the duty of reasonable supervision nor ought they to be permitted to be shielded from liability because of want of knowledge of wrongdoing if that ignorance is the result of gross inattention. *Briggs* v. *Spaulding, 141 U. S., 131.*

11. Directors of a national bank are "officers" within the meaning of Revised Statutes, United States, section 5209, which makes it a misdemeanor for bank officers to make false entries in any book, report, or statement of the bank, with intent to deceive any of its officers. *United States* v. *Means et al., 42 Fed. Rep., 599.*

12. The president of a national bank has no power inherent in his office to bind the bank on the execution of a note in its name, but power to do so may be conferred on him by the board of directors, either expressly by resolution to that effect, or by subsequent ratification, or by acquiescence in transactions of a similar nature of which the directors have notice. *National Bank of Commerce* v. *Atkinson, 55 Fed. Rep., 465.*

13. If a president of a bank exercised the functions of a cashier, and was the sole managing officer of the bank, he had authority to borrow money for the use of the bank in the regular course of its business. *Simons et al.* v. *Fisher, 55 Fed. Rep., 905.*

14. Under section 5136 of the national-bank act, the cashier of a national bank has no power to bind it to pay the draft of a third person on one of its customers to be drawn at a future day, when it expects to have a deposit from him sufficient to cover it, and no action lies against the bank for its refusal to pay such a draft. *Flannagan et al.* v. *California National Bank et al., 56 Fed. Rep., 959.*

15. Persons elected directors of bank about which there is no suspicion of anything wrong, but which became bankrupt in ninety days, are not personally responsible, because they did not institute an investigation. *Briggs* v. *Spaulding. 141 U. S., 132.*

16. Duties of directors as to supervision over affairs of bank considered. *Ib.*

17. If director is seriously ill, the others may give him leave of absence for a year, and if frauds are committed while he is absent, and without his knowledge, he is not responsible. *Ib.*

18. Director is not precluded from resignation within the year by section 5145, Revised Statutes, providing that he shall hold office for one year, and until successor is elected. *Ib.*

19. It is within scope of general authority of cashier to receive offers for purchase of securities held by the bank, and to state whether or not bank owns securities in its possession. *Acuia Bank* v. *Stewart et al., 114 U. S., 224.*

PLACE OF BUSINESS:

1. The provisions requiring "the usual business" of the association to be transacted "at an office or banking house in the place specified in its organization certificate" must be construed reasonably; and a part of the legitimate business of the association which can not be transacted at the banking house may be done elsewhere. *Merchants' Bank* v. *State Bank, 10 Wall., 604.*

2. Although the general business of a national-banking association is to be transacted at its place of business, yet if the association is fully advised of the facts, and does not object, and there is no fraud, its officers, when acting within the general scope of their authority, may bind it by acts done at another place. *Burton* v. *Burley, 9 Biss., 253.*

POST-NOTES:

1. A certificate of deposit, endorsed by payee, is not in violation of section 5183 Revised Statutes which forbids national banks to issue any other notes to circulate as money than such as are authorized by the provisions of the statute. *In re Hunt, 141 Mass., 515.*

2. Certificates of deposit in the ordinary form, issued by a national bank to depositors and payable to order, are not post-notes within the prohibition of section 5183 Revised Statutes. *Riddle* v. *First National Bank of Butler, 2 Fed. Rep., 503.*

POWERS:

1. To the enumerated powers of national-banking associations are to be superadded all the powers incidental to the business of banking. *Pattison* v. *Syracuse National Bank, 80 N. Y., 82.*

2. A national bank may buy a check drawn upon another bank; and whether the check is payable to order or to bearer is immaterial. *First National Bank of Rochester* v. *Harris, 108 Mass., 514.*

3. A national-banking association, in the compromise of a claim growing out of its legitimate business, may take railroad stock. *First National Bank of Charlotte* v. *National Exchange Bank of Baltimore, 92 U. S., 122.*

4. And when necessary to do so, it may pay the difference between the value of the stock and the amount of the claim. *Ib.*

5. A national-banking association may take and hold the coupons of municipal bonds, and may maintain actions thereon. *First National Bank of North Bennington* v. *Town of Bennington, Browne's N. B. Cas., 437; Lyons* v. *Lyons National Bank, 19 Blatch., 279.*

6. A national-banking association may receive a deposit to be held by it as security for the faithful performance of a contract between the depositor and another. *Bushnell* v. *The Chautauqua County National Bank, 10 Hun, 378.*

7. Whatever the terms of an arrangement being made before the date of the drawee bank's certificate of authorization, it is invalid under Revised Statutes, section 5136, providing that no banking association "shall transact any business except such as is incidental and necessarily preliminary to its organization, until it has been authorized by the Comptroller of the Currency to commence the business of banking." *Armstrong* v. *National Bank of Springfield, 38 Fed. Rep., 883.*

8. Where an association has made or ratified a contract to give a person a certain number of the shares of its stock, upon condition that he will continue to do his business with it, and derives the benefit from this contract, the other party may recover of the association the value of the shares. *Rich* v. *State National Bank of Lincoln, 7 Nebr., 231.*

9. As the national-currency act of 1864 authorizes banks created under it to buy and sell coin, such bank, having coin in pledge, may sell and assign its special property therein. *Merchants' Bank* v. *State Bank, 10 Wall., 604.*

10. The clause requiring the usual business of the bank to be done at an office or banking house in the place selected does not prevent its purchase of coin at the banking house of another bank. *Ib.*

11. In adjusting and compromising claims growing out of a legitimate banking transaction, it may take stocks of other corporations with a view to selling them at a profit. *First National Bank* v. *National Exchange Bank, 92 U. S., 122.*

12. A national bank is not prohibited by law from guaranteeing payment of a note. *People's Bank* v. *National Bank, 101 U. S., 181.*

13. Under national-banking act one can exercise only the powers expressly granted and those necessarily incidental. *Logan Bank* v. *Townsend, 139 U. S., 67.*

PREFERRED CLAIMS. *See* Liens; Special deposits.

1. Section 3466 which gives the United States a priority for all claims it has against insolvent debtors, does not apply to the case of an insolvent national-banking association. *Cook County National Bank* v. *United States, 107 U. S., 445.*

2. A preference, to be within the meaning of section 5242, Revised Statutes, must be given to an existing creditor to secure a preëxisting debt. A transfer by an insolvent bank to secure a contemporaneous loan is not a violation of the law. *Casey* v. *La Société de Crédit Mobilier 2, Woods, 77.*

3. Revised Statutes, United States, section 5242, which prohibits all transfers by any national-banking association made after the commission of an act of insolvency, or in contemplation thereof, with the view to a preference

54 REPORT OF THE COMPTROLLER OF THE CURRENCY.

PREFERRED CLAIMS—Continued.

of one creditor over another, is directed to a preference, not to the giving of security when a debt is created; and if the transaction be free from fraud in fact, and is intended merely to adequately protect a loan made at the time, the creditor can retain property transferred to secure such a loan until the debt is paid, though the debtor is insolvent, and the creditor has reason at the time to believe that to be the fact. *Armstrong* v. *Chemical National Bank, 41 Fed. Rep., 234.*

4. A banker's lien for the amount of the balance of its general account does not exist when the securities have been deposited with the bank for a special purpose, or for the payment of a particular loan. *Ib.*

5. Section 5242, Revised Statutes, United States, does not prohibit a bank which has in good faith accepted the draft of a national bank the day before the latter's insolvency, and afterward paid the same, from applying the proceeds of collections made by it, on paper in its hands belonging to the insolvent bank, to the payment of the draft, since its lien on such collections runs from the date of the acceptance. *In re Armstrong, 41 Fed. Rep., 381.*

6. The insolvency need be in the contemplation of the bank only. It need not be known to the person to whom the transfer is made. *Case* v. *Citizens' Bank of Louisiana, 2 Woods 23.*

7. After the directors of an insolvent association have voted to close its doors, any transfer of assets whereby a creditor secures a preference must be presumed to be made with an intent to prefer. *National Security Bank* v. *Price, 22 Fed. Rep., 697.*

8. Where the officers of an association which is in danger of insolvency, *for the purpose and in the expectation of preventing a failure,* make a pledge of securities to a depositor to induce him not to withdraw his deposit, such a pledge is not a preference within the meaning of section 5242, Revised Statutes, and will not be set aside when the association afterward is declared insolvent. *Roberts* v. *Hill, 23 Fed. Rep., 311.*

9. Where an insolvent association receives a deposit a short time before closing its doors, its officers knowing of the insolvency at the time, the receipt of such deposit is a fraud upon the depositor, and no title passes to the association, and therefore the depositor may reclaim the whole amount of the deposit; and as he claims under his original title, and not under a transfer from the association, such reclamation does not amount to a preference. *Cragie et al.* v. *Hadley, 99 N. Y., 131.*

10. A trust was not impressed upon funds deposited on day the bank closed its doors in the absence of proof that the deposit had not gone into the general funds of the bank and lost its identity before reaching the receiver. *In re North River Bank, 14 N. Y., 261.*

11. Where the proceeds of an item indorsed "for collection and return" were mingled with other moneys of the bank, if it was a breach of trust it was a conversion, and plaintiff became a simple contract creditor, with no preference at law. *Philadelphia National Bank* v. *Dowd, 38 Fed. Rep. 172.*

12. Where by agreement and custom a national bank received drafts from its correspondent indorsed "for collection for the," and credited it to them as cash, with the understanding that any unpaid draft should be charged back, and where the collecting bank failed before collection, the proceeds of the draft coming into the hands of a receiver, the correspondent bank has the rights of a general creditor only. *First National Bank* v. *Armstrong, 39 Fed. Rep., 231.*

13. Where plaintiff and defendant banks for several years had acted as agents for each other in the collection of checks, notes, and drafts, and where plaintiff sent defendant a note "for collection and credit" which on maturity was paid by a check and credit was immediately given on the books, but defendant failed and the check passed into the hands of a receiver—*Held,* that in view of the course of dealing the two banks stood in the relation of debtor and creditor with respect to the amount of the check, and it became part of the assets of the bank. *Franklin County National Bank* v. *Beal, 49 Fed. Rep., 606.*

14. Whether the title to a check deposited with a bank passes to the bank before collection, so as to immediately create the relation of debtor and creditor between it and the depositor, is a question of fact, depending upon the circumstances and course of dealing in each particular case. *City of Somerville* v. *Beal, 49 Fed. Rep., 790.*

15. Where a bank in accordance with its custom credited checks deposited by a customer at the close of each day's business, retaining the right to subsequently charge off the same if returned unpaid from the clearing house, and the bank became insolvent on a succeeding day, title in the checks

PREFERRED CLAIMS—Continued.

passed to the bank so as to create the relation of debtor and creditor. *Ib.*

16. Where a national bank collected all papers sent to it by complainant under an arrangement which constituted the bank the agent of complainant, the latter can recover, on the ground of a trust, from a receiver of the bank such portion only of the proceeds of its paper sent to the bank as it shows has passed into the receiver's hands, either in its original or some substituted form. *Commercial National Bank* v. *Armstrong, 39 Fed. Rep., 684.*

17. Where checks and drafts sent from one bank to another indorsed "for collection" and credited "subject to payment" according to the dealings between the banks, and part of them were paid to the receiver of the latter bank after its failure and the balances were credited to it by the payors, the amount paid the receiver should be accounted for as a trust fund, but the balance as a general debt. *First National Bank* v. *Armstrong, 42 Fed. Rep., 193.*

18. Negotiable paper with restrictive indorsement credited by agent on date of receipt "subject to payment," although account is subject to be drawn upon, title is not transferred, and upon the insolvency of the agent before receiving notice of the collection of the item, the owner is entitled to the proceeds in the hands of the collecting agent. *Fifth National Bank* v. *Armstrong, 40 Fed. Rep., 46.*

19. The drawers of a draft deposited with a bank for collection, and by it forwarded to a correspondent bank, are entitled to the amount as against the receiver of the forwarding bank, which was insolvent, and known to be so by its officers when it received the draft, and suspended payment before the proceeds were withdrawn from the collecting bank. *Importers and Traders' National Bank* v. *Peters et al., 123 Court of Appeals, N. Y., 272.*

20. When a bank which has received a draft for collection sends it to another bank for that purpose, and on being advised that the latter bank has collected the draft credits the depositor and then becomes insolvent without having received the money from the collecting bank, the depositor remains the owner of the draft, and is entitled to its proceeds from the collecting bank against the receiver and the creditors of the insolvent bank. *Armstrong* v. *National Bank of Boyertown, 11 S. W. Rep., 411; Manufacturers' National Bank* v. *Continental Bank et al., 20 N. W. Rep., 193.*

21. A bank which collects a draft sent to it by another bank for that purpose with directions to remit the proceeds to a third bank for the owner's account does not thereby become a trustee, so that the fund can be followed into the hands of a receiver, although it had become mixed with the other cash of the bank before his appointment; especially when it appears that the business was carried on, and money paid out, for several days after the collection was probably made. *Merchants and Farmers' Bank* v. *Austin et al., 48 Fed. Rep., 25.*

22. A draft given to a bank in the ordinary course of business does not constitute an equitable assignment of the fund nor is it sufficient that draft be drawn by bank against its reserve fund in another city and given in exchange for clearing house certificates upon the president's representation that it owes a heavy debt at the clearing house which it is unable to meet and his statement, showing the amount of the reserve fund against which the draft was drawn. *Fourth Street National Bank* v. *Yardley, Receiver, 55 Fed. Rep., 850.*

23. Where bank sends paper to another bank for collection and credit on general account, the custom being to enter credit only when paper is collected, the relation being that of principal and agent until collection and receipt of money by the second bank, and if latter sends to another bank, which collects but does not remit until latter bank has failed, the former can recover the proceeds from the receiver thereof. *Beal* v. *National Exchange Bank of Dallas, 55 Fed. Rep., 894.*

24. In a package of miscellaneous bonds was the memorandum of the date, amount, and time when due, and also the words "$6,500 due Putnam." *Held*, that these facts did not show an equitable assignment by the bank to the plaintiff of $6,500 worth of bonds. To constitute an equitable assignment of property, there must be an appropriation or separation and the mere intent to appropriate is not sufficient. *Putnam Savings Bank* v. *Beal, 54 Fed. Rep. 577.*

25. Where the treasurer and tax collector of a county, without authority of law, deposit county money in a bank and receive certificates of deposit marked "special," the title to the moneys does not pass although there is no agreement that the identical bills shall be returned and they are mixed with

the bank's general funds, and the county is entitled to recover an equal amount from a receiver of the bank prior to the payment of the general depositors. *San Diego County v. California National Bank et al., 52 Fed. Rep., 59.*

26. The indorsement of a draft to a bank "for collection," accompanied by a credit of the amount to the endorser's account, does not transfer title to the bank, and correspondent of the bank who collects draft for it is responsible therefor to indorser. *Tyson v. Western National Bank of Baltimore, 26 Atl. Rep. 520.*

27. Paper for collection was indorsed, "Pay to (correspondent) bank or order for collection for (transmitting) bank." On insolvency of correspondent, *Held,* that the relation as to uncollected paper was that of principal and agent; that a subagent had collected some of such paper was not a commingling of these collections with the funds of the failed bank and did not relieve them from the trust obligation created by its agency nor create any difficulty in specially tracing it. *Commercial National Bank v. Armstrong, 148 U. S., 50.*

REAL ESTATE: *See* Mortgages.

1. Where a national-banking association acquires real estate which it is not authorized to take, the conveyance to it is not void, but only voidable. And the title of the association to such real estate is good until assailed in a direct proceeding by the Government. *National Bank v. Matthews, 98 U. S., 621; National Bank v. Whitney, 103 U. S., 99; Swope v. Leffingwell, 105 U. S., 3; Reynolds v. Crawfordsville Bank, 112 U. S., 405; Fortier v. New Orleans Bank, 112 U. S., 439.*

2. The amount of real estate which a national-banking association may purchase to secure a preëxisting debt is not limited to the exact amount of the debt, but as much may be purchased as is necessary to secure the debt due, so long as the security of such debt is the real object of the purchase. *Upton v. National Bank of South Reading, 120 Mass., 153.*

3. Where the purpose is to secure a debt, previously contracted, a national-banking association may take a conveyance of real estate, worth more than the debt, and pay the difference between the debt and the value of the property. *Libby v. Union National Bank, 99 Ill., 622.*

4. A national-banking association may take as security for a loan the stock of a corporation whose entire capital is vested in real estate. Such a loan does not amount to a lending upon mortgage. *Baldwin v. Canfield, 26 Minn., 43.*

5. A national-banking association, having taken a mortgage on real estate to secure a debt previously contracted, may, in order to protect itself, pay off a prior lien on the said real estate; and the lien which it thus acquires it may enforce. *Oran v. Merchants' National Bank, 16 Kans., 341; Holmes v. Boyd, 90 Ind., 332.*

6. Fact that bank at judgment sale of land mortgaged to it purchases the mortgaged property, and also other property which it was not authorized to acquire, does not invalidate its title as to the mortgaged property. *Reynolds v. Crawfordsville Bank, 112 U. S., 405.*

RECEIVER: *See* Insolvent banks; Preferred claims; Interest; Set-off.

1. Upon the appointment of a receiver all the assets of the association become, in his hands a trust fund which the statute of limitations does not touch or affect. *Riddle v. First National Bank, 27 Fed. Rep., 503.*

2. Claims arising out of the nonfeasance or malfeasance of the association should be paid ratably with the debts, technically so called. *Turner v. First National Bank of Keokuk et al., 26 Iowa, 562.*

3. A receiver, when appointed by the Comptroller, with the concurrence of the Secretary, is an officer of the United States. *Stanton v. Wilkeson, 8 Ben., 357.*

4. He represents the bank, its stockholders, and its creditors; but he does not in any sense represent the Government. *Case v. Terrell, 11 Wall., 199.*

5. The clause of section 50, act of 1864, which prescribes that the receiver shall be "under the direction of the Comptroller," means only that he shall be subject to the Comptroller's direction, not that he shall not act without orders. He may bring suit to collect assets without having been instructed to do so by the Comptroller. *Bank v. Kennedy, 17 Wall., 19.*

6. The receiver of a national bank is the instrument of the Comptroller, and may be removed by him. *Kennedy v. Gibson, 8 Wall., 505.*

RECEIVER—Continued.

7. The power of the Comptroller to appoint a receiver is not exclusive; it does not oust the courts of equity of their authority in the matter; and therefore a court of competent jurisdiction may place the bank in the hands of a receiver in cases where, according to the rules of equity, it may pursue such a course with regard to insolvent corporations generally. *Irons* v. *Manufacturers' National Bank, 6 Biss., 301; Wright* v. *Merchants' National Bank, 1 Flippin, 561.*

8. Suits brought by a receiver can not be settled or compounded upon an order of the Comptroller; this can be done only with the authority of the court. *Case* v. *Small, 2 Woods, 78.*

9. The decision of a receiver rejecting a claim is not final. The claimant still has the right to sue. *Bank of Bethel* v. *Pahquioque Bank, 14 Wall., 383.*

10. The receiver can not sell the real or personal property of the bank without an order from a court of competent jurisdiction. *Ellis* v. *Little, 27 Kans., 707.*

11. Nor can he sell upon the terms in conflict with the order. *Ib.*

12. And under an order permitting him to sell the property of the bank he can not exchange, trade, or barter it for other property. *Ib.*

13. A sale made by a receiver under order of a court is to all intents and purposes a judicial sale. *In re Third National Bank, 9 Biss., 535.*

14. As the power of a receiver of a national bank appointed by the Comptroller is limited, a person dealing with him in his official capacity is bound as a matter of law to have knowledge of his authority to act, and if contracts and agreements are entered into with the receiver in excess of his authority as conferred by law, the parties contract at their own peril and the estate of the bank can not be charged for the default or inability of a receiver acting outside of his functions as receiver and beyond the duties which it involves. *Ellis* v. *Little, 27 Kans., 707.*

15. The receiver can not charge the estate of the bank by any executory contract, unless authorized so to do by the provisions of the national-banking law and the order of a court of competent jurisdiction obtained upon the terms of said law. *Ib.*

16. The closing of a national bank by order of the examiner, the appointment of a receiver, and its dissolution by decree of a circuit court necessarily transfer the assets of the bank to the receiver. *Scott* v. *Armstrong. 146 U. S., 499.*

17. The receiver in such case takes the assets in trust for creditors, and in the absence of a statute to the contrary, subject to all claims and defences that might have been interposed against the insolvent corporation. *Ib.*

18. Receiver of national bank may sue for demands in his name as receiver, or in name of bank. *Bank* v. *Kennedy, 17 Wall., 19.*

19. Receiver of national bank appointed by Comptroller of the Currency is not accountable in equity to owner of real estate for rents thereof received by him and paid into United States Treasury, subject to disposition of Comptroller under Revised Statutes, Sec. 5234. *Hitz* v. *Jenks, 123 U. S. 297; Briggs* v. *Spaulding, 141 U. S., 132.*

20. The expenses of receivership of a national bank appointed in a creditor's suit, contesting a voluntary liquidation of the bank, can not be charged on stockholders as part of their statutory liability, but must come from the creditors at whose instance the receiver was appointed. *Ib.: Richmond* v. *Irons, 121 U. S., 27.*

21. On a bill filed by receiver against stockholders under section 50, where bank fails to pay its notes, action by Comptroller must precede institution of suit by receiver, and be set forth therein. *Kennedy* v. *Gibson, 8 Wall., 498.*

22. Creditors of the bank are not proper parties to such bill. *Ib.*

REDUCTION OF CAPITAL STOCK:

When a national banking association reduces its capital stock the amount of capital thus released belongs to the shareholders pro rata and must be returned to them; and it can not be retained by the association for a surplus. *Seeley* v. *New York National Exchange Bank, 8 Daly, 400; 4 Abb. N. C., 61; 78 N. Y., 608.*

REPORT: *See* False entry.

1. A national bank is not required to conform the headings of the various accounts on its books to any prescribed names, nor to the names stated in the form of report prescribed by the Comptroller, and therefore when a report is called for, if the person making it enters under the headings in the prescribed form a statement of the bank's condition, which is true with respect to the headings in said form, he has fulfilled the demands of the law. *United States* v. *Graves, 53 Fed. Rep., 634.*

2. The entry of "loans and discounts" in reports to the Comptroller does not guaranty the solvency of the makers of the paper, but is a statement that in truth and fact, at the date named in the report, the bank actually held and owned loans and discounts to the aggregate so reported. *Ib.*

3. Where the form of report, as prescribed by the Comptroller, contains heading of "Loans and Discounts," and also of "Overdrafts," it is the duty of the bank officer to make his entries in such report in such manner that each of these headings shall truthfully state the condition of his bank as to such heading. *Ib.*

4. A director of a bank is personally liable to the bank on paper made to it by a firm of which he is a member, and, in making a report of the condition of the bank to the Comptroller, the amount of such paper should be entered under the heading of "Liabilities of directors (individual and firm) as payers." *Ib.*

RESIGNATION:

1. The law providing no particular mode by which a director is to resign from the board, an oral resignation would be as good as any. *Morius v. Lee, 30 Fed. Rep., 298.*

2. The president being the head of the board, a resignation to him is a resignation to the board. *Ib.*

3. A director is not prohibited from resigning during the year. The apparent purpose of the provision in regard to the term of office is to make it conform to the time of the new election, and not to absolutely require every director to serve the full term. *Ib.*

RESTRAINING ACTS:

National-banking associations located outside of a State are subject to its restraining acts prohibiting all corporations, not authorized by the law of the State, from keeping therein offices for the purpose of discount and deposit. *National Bank of Fairhaven v. The Phœnix Warehousing Company, 6 Hun., 71.*

SET-OFF:

1. Against the proceeds of the bonds deposited to secure circulation the United States can set off no claim, except for money advanced to redeem notes. *Cook Co. National Bank v. United States, 107 U. S., 445.*

2. And upon the failure of any association its 5 per cent redemption fund can not be retained by the Treasurer to pay taxes due to the United States, but the fund passes to the Comptroller as an asset of the association. *Jackson v. United States, 20 Ct. Cls., 298.*

3. A person liable upon a note to an insolvent national bank may set off, against his indebtedness, the amount of his deposits with the bank. *Platt v. Bentley, Thomp. N. B., Cas., 758.*

4. But a debtor can not set off the amount of a deposit assigned to him after the act of insolvency committed. *Venango National Bank v. Taylor, 56 Penn. St., 14.*

5. The indorser of a note discounted by a national bank and which matures after the bank becomes insolvent and a receiver is appointed is entitled to set off against the note the amount of his deposit in the bank at the time of its failure. *Yardley v. Clothier, 51 Fed. Rep., 506.*

6. The commercial paper of a national bank becomes overdue and dishonored after the commission of an act of insolvency and appointment of a receiver, and is subject to all equities between the bank and the original party to whom it was payable. *U. S. D. C., N. D., Ill., May, 1890.*

7. A set-off under Illinois statute in favor of the maker of a note or bill is available if the paper is assigned after due, whether arising out of the same transaction or otherwise. *Ib.*

8. The ordinary equity rule of set-off in case of insolvency is that where the mutual obligations have grown out of the same transaction, insolvency on the one hand justifies the set-off of the debt due on the other, and there is nothing in the statutes relating to national banks which prevents the application of that rule to the receiver of an insolvent national bank under circumstances like those in this case. *Scott v. Armstrong, 146 U. S., 499.*

9. A customer of a national bank who, in good faith, borrows money of the bank, gives his note therefor due at a future day, and deposits the amount borrowed to be drawn against, any balance to be applied to the payment of the note when due, has an equitable (but not a legal) right, in case of

SET-OFF—Continued.

the insolvency and dissolution of the bank and the appointment of a receiver before the maturity of the note, to have the balance to his credit at the time of the insolvency applied to the payment of his indebtedness on the note. *Ib.*

10. Acts of Congress in relation to the administration of the assets of insolvent banks authorize no other rules of set-off than those recognized by courts in the settlement of the affairs of other insolvent corporations. *Yardley* v. *Clothier, 49 Fed. Rep., 337; Scott* v. *Armstrong, 146 U. S., 499.*

11. Set-off must be governed by the law of the place where, in case of controversy, suit must be brought to settle the rights of the parties. *Sarary* v. *Sarary, 3 Clark, 271; Gibbs* v. *Howard, 2d N. H., 296; Fose* v. *Philbrook, 3 Story, 335; Ruggles* v. *Kuler, 3 Johns., 263.*

12. A separate demand can not be set off against a joint one, or a joint debt against a separate one. *Gray* v. *Rollo, 18 Wall., 629; Scammon* v. *Kimball, 92 U. S., 362.*

13. Where, however, a note is signed by one as principal and others as sureties, the indebtedness of the bank to the principal may be set off. *Andrews* v. *Varnell, 46 N. H., 17; Himrod* v. *Baugh, 85 Ill. 435.*

14. Indorser of note held by the bank is entitled to set off, against his liability as such, any indebtedness from the bank to himself. *Yardley* v. *Clothier, 49 Fed. Rep., 337.*

15. An executor, administrator, or public officer is not entitled to set off against his liability as such any indebtedness from bank to himself individually, nor contra. *Scammon* v. *Kimball, 92 U. S., 362; Benton* v. *Hoomes, executor, 1 A. K. Marsh. 19; Stowe* v. *Yarwood, 14 Ill., 424.*

16. One indebted to bank can not set off a claim against bank acquired subsequent to its suspension. *Scott* v. *Armstrong, 146 U.S., 499; Venango National Bank* v. *Taylor, 56 Penn. St., 14; Colt* v. *Brown, 12 Gray, 233.*

17. Right of set-off is allowable where the indebtedness sought to be set off had or had not matured at time of bank's suspension. *Scott* v. *Armstrong, 146 U. S., 499; Skiles* v. *Huton, 110 Penn St., 254; Drake* v. *Rolio, 3 Biss., 273.*

SHAREHOLDERS:

1. One who appears on the books of the association as the owner of shares of its stock is individually liable, though he hold the stock merely as collateral security. *National Bank* v. *Case, 99 U. S., 628; Moore* v. *Jones, 3 Woods, 53; Bowdell* v. *Farmers and Merchants' National Bank of Baltimore, Browne's N. B. Cas., 147; Hale* v. *Walker, 31 Iowa, 344; Wheelock* v. *Kost, 77 Ill., 296.*

2. And a subscription to stock of a national bank, and payment in full on the subscription and entry of the subscriber's name on the books as a stockholder, constitutes the subscriber a shareholder without taking out a certificate. *Pacific National Bank* v. *Eaton, 141 U. S., 227.*

3. The individual liability of a shareholder adheres to his estate after his death until his place as a member of the association is taken by some new shareholder. *Davis* v. *Weed. 44 Conn., 569.*

4. The receiver has a valid claim against the estate generally of a deceased shareholder who died prior to the insolvency of the bank, but whose stock has not been transferred. *Richmond* v. *Irons, 121 U. S., 27; Davis* v. *Weed, supra.*

5. But a pledgee of shares of stock in a national bank who in good faith and with no fraudulent intent takes the security for his benefit in the name of an irresponsible trustee for the avowed purpose of avoiding individual liability as a shareholder, and who exercises none of the powers or rights of a stockholder, incurs no liability as such to creditors of the bank in case of its failure. *Anderson, Receiver,* v. *Warehouse Company, 111. U. S.,479.*

6. And where stock has been transferred as collateral security for a loan, *with the understanding that in case of default in the payment of the loan the shares shall be sold,* the transferee, upon default made, and before the bank closes its doors, may sell the stock for a nominal consideration. though his purpose be to avoid a personal liability; and such a transaction can not be set aside as a fraud upon the creditors of the association. *Magruder* v. *Colston, 44 Md., 349.*

7. If the trusteeship of one who holds stock in trust does not appear upon the books of the association he will be individually liable. *Davis Essex* v. *Baptist Society, 44 Conn., 582.*

8. The real owner of the stock is liable as a stockholder, though when he purchased the stock he had it transferred upon the books to another. *Davis* v. *Stevens, 17 Blatch., 259.*

SHAREHOLDERS—Continued.

9. The individual liability of the shareholders of an insolvent association may be enforced for the purpose of paying all of its liabilities, and not merely for the purpose of paying its "debts," technically so called. *Stanton* v. *Wilkeson, 8 Ben., 357.*

10. The individual liability of the stockholders must be restricted in its meaning to such contracts, debts, and engagements of the association as have been duly contracted in the ordinary course of its business. And, therefore, creditors of an association who make settlements *after the association is put into liquidation* and receive from the president payment of their claims in paper of the association, or of the individual notes of the president himself, indorsed or guaranteed in the name of the association, are not to be considered as creditors of the association entitled to subject the stockholders to individual liability; for these are new contracts. *Richmond* v. *Irons, 121, U. S., 27.*

11. The individual liability of the stockholders is enforcible only in behalf of all the creditors, and any security given by a stockholder for his liability in this respect should likewise be for the benefit of all the creditors. Accordingly, a mortgage of all the individual property of a stockholder, made after the bank has closed its doors, for the purpose of securing a single depositor, is void as against a judgment obtained against such stockholder in an action by the receiver to recover the amount of his individual liability. *Gatch* v. *Fitch, 34 Fed. Rep., 566.*

12. While it is undoubtedly the rule as regards stockholders that one put upon the books as a stockholder without his consent can not be held for any liability in respect to such stock, yet where the person to whom the stock is transferred is a director of the bank, and is concerned in the management of its affairs, he must be presumed to have knowledge of the fact that the stock stood in his name, and if he has not repudiated the transfer to himself, is liable as the holder of such stock. *Brown* v. *Finn, 34 Fed. Rep., 124.*

13. A national bank, having so received stock of another national bank, was sued as a stockholder. *Held*, that loan by national bank on such security is not prohibited, and if it were, defendant could not avoid liability by its own illegal act. *National Bank* v. *Case, 99 U. S., 628.*

14. Where stockholder, knowing that bank is to fail, collusively transfers his shares to an irresponsible person to avoid liability, his liability is not affected by such fraud. *Bowden* v. *Johnson, 107 U. S., 251.*

15. Bill filed by receiver against transferrer and transferee to enforce such liability will lie where it is for discovery as well as relief, as the transfer would be good between the parties. *Ib.*

16. A shareholder in national bank, who is liable for its debts, is liable for interest thereon to the extent of the bank's liability, and not in excess of the maximum liability fixed by statute. *Richmond* v. *Irons, 121 U. S., 27.*

17. A Federal court will not, even if it has the power, under section 5234, grant an order authorizing the receiver of a national bank to compound the statutory liability of certain stockholders by accepting payment of a gross sum less than is due in satisfaction and discharge thereof, although more money would thus be realized than by proceedings to collect the same in the usual way, when it appears probable that such stockholders have fraudulently conveyed their property to avoid their legal obligations as stockholders or to shield themselves from injury and exposure by litigation. *In re certain stockholders of the California National Bank of San Diego, 53 Fed. Rep., 38.*

18. A corporation which holds certain shares of stock in a national bank as collateral security for a loan and is carried on the registry of the bank as the holder of such stock "as pledgee," is not subject on the bank's insolvency to the statutory liability of a stockholder. *Pauley* v. *State Loan and Trust Co., 56 Fed. Rep., 430.*

19. A person who is entered on the books of a national bank as the owner of stock, but who is admitted to hold the stock in trust for the true owner, is not liable, as a stockholder, for the debts of the bank when the true owner has been adjudged so liable, although nothing is realized on the execution of such judgment. *Yardley* v. *Wilgus, 56 Fed. Rep., 965.*

20. Where stockholder of national bank sells to the bank, as agent for unknown principal, his stock and delivers to it his certificate and power of attorney for transfer, in blank, though no formal transfer is made, his responsibility for further assessments on the stock ceases. *Whitbeck* v. *Mercantile National Bank, 127 U. S., 193.*

SHAREHOLDERS—Continued.

21. Subscription to stock and payment in full and entry of name on books as a stockholder makes subscriber a shareholder without taking out a certificate. *Pacific National Bank* v. *Eaton, 111 U. S. 227; Thayer* v. *Butler, ib., 231; Butler* v. *Eaton, ib., 240.*

22. A pledgee of stock who in good faith takes the security for his benefit in name of an irresponsible trustee for the avowed purpose of avoiding individual liability as shareholder, incurs no liability as such. *Anderson* v. *Phil. Warehouse Co., 111 U. S. 479.*

23. The statutory liability of a shareholder in a national bank for the debts of the corporation survives against his personal representatives. *Richmond* v. *Irons, 121 U. S. 27.*

24. Shareholder in national bank continues liable for the company's debts until his stock is actually transferred or certificate surrendered for that purpose;
* a delivery to the president of the bank as vendee, and not as president, is insufficient to discharge the shareholder. *Ib.*

SPECIAL DEPOSITS: *See* Preferred claims; Set-off.

1. A national-banking association may receive special deposits. The provision in section 5228, Revised Statutes, authorizing an association "to deliver special deposits," implies that it may receive them as a part of its legitimate business; and this implication is as effectual as an express declaration to the same effect would have been. *National Bank* v. *Graham, 100 U. S., 699.*

2. Section 5228 of Revised Statutes, which provides that it shall be lawful for a national bank after its failure to "deliver special deposits," is an effectual recognition of its power to receive them. *Ib.*

3. National banking associations have power to receive special deposits either *gratuitously or otherwise. Pattison* v. *Syracuse National Bank, 80 N. Y., 82.*

STOCKS: *See* Broker; Collateral securities; Ultra vires.

TAXATION: *See* Circulation.

1. A State can not tax the capital stock of a national bank as such. The tax must be assessed upon the shares of the different stockholders. *Collins* v. *Chicago, 4 Biss., 472.*

2. Under Revised Statutes, United States, section 5219, which declares that nothing in the national-banking act shall prevent all the shares of stock of a national bank from being included in the assessment of the personal property of the owners of such shares, an assessment of the entire stock of a national bank *in solido* against the bank itself is invalid. *National Bank of Virginia* v. *City of Richmond et al., 42 Fed. Rep., 877.*

3. The assessment of the entire capital stock of a national bank *in solido* against the bank itself is invalid. The bank may pay the tax assessed upon the shares of its different stockholders, and it will have a lien thereon when it pays such tax until the same is satisfied; but if for any cause the tax levied upon the different stockholders is not paid by the bank, the property of the individual stockholders will be liable therefor. *First National Bank of Leoti* v. *Fisher, 45 Kans., 726.*

4. The individual stockholders of a national bank are allowed the same deductions from the assessment against them upon their shares of stock as other taxpayers in the State, owning moneyed capital, are allowed. *Ib.*

5. "Moneyed capital" in Revised Statutes, section 5219, embraces capital employed in national banks and that used by individuals in business for profit by use of it as money, but does not include that in the hands of a corporation, even if its business be such as to make its shares moneyed capital when in the hands of individuals, or if it invests its capital in securities payable in money. *Mercantile Bank* v. *New York, 121 U. S., 138; Newark Bank Co.* v. *Newark, ib., 163; Talbot* v. *Silver Bow County, Montana, 139 U. S., 438.*

6. Laws, New York, chapter 596, section 3, which provide that the stockholders in banks and trust companies organized under the authority of the State or of the United States, shall be assessed for the value of their shares of stock, but which omits to provide for the taxation of the shares of stock in other private corporations, does not contravene Revised Statutes, United States, section 5219, which forbids the taxation of shares of national banks at a greater rate than is assessed on other "moneyed capital" in the hands of the individual citizen of the State. *Palmer* v. *McMahon, 133 U. S., 660; Central National Bank* v. *United States, 137 U. S., 355.*

7. The shares of a national bank are taxable to the owners, and the bank is not liable primarily or as the agent of the shareholders, under the act of Con-

gress or the various laws of the State or Territory, for the payment of a tax levied upon such shares; but if such bank, through its proper officers, voluntarily lists such shares as the property of the bank for taxation, and the taxing officers of the State or Territory, in pursuance of such erroneous listing, tax the same in the name of the bank, equity will not relieve the bank from the payment of such tax by enjoining its collection in the absence of proper application to all the statutory tribunals authorized to hear such matter and determine and grant the proper relief. *Albuquerque National Bank* v. *Peoria et al.* (S. C. N. Mex.), *January 28, 1892.*

8. The entire interests of the shareholders may be taxed without any deduction for that portion of the capital which is invested in United States securities. *Van Allen* v. *The Assessors, 3 Wall., 573.*

9. New shares issued by a national-banking association can not be taxed until the increase of capital has been approved by the Comptroller of the Currency. *Charleston* v. *People's National Bank, 5 S. C., 123.*

10. The manifest intention of the law is to permit the State in which a national bank is located to tax, subject to the limitations prescribed, all the shares of its capital stock without regard to their ownership; and, therefore, a national bank may be taxed upon the shares which it holds in another national bank. *Bank of Redemption* v. *Boston, 125 U. S., 60.*

11. The undivided surplus of a national-banking association, unless invested in Federal securities, may be lawfully taxed by the State. *North Ward National Bank of Newark* v. *City of Newark, 10 Vroom, 380; First National Bank* v. *Peterborough, 56 N. H., 38.*

12. But, of course, if the surplus is taken into consideration in estimating the taxable value of the shares, it is not to be taxed separately. *North Ward National Bank* v. *City of Newark, supra.*

NOTE.—But it has been held in Maryland that the stock of an association represents its whole property, and where a tax is assessed upon the shares a separate tax upon the real or personal estate amounts to double taxation; and, therefore, where the organic laws of the State prohibit double taxation, such a tax upon the property of an association is void. *County Commissioners* v. *Farmers and Mechanics' National Bank, 48 Md., 117; National State Bank* v. *Young, 25 Iowa, 311,* wherein it was held that the State could tax only the shares *eo nomine* and the real estate.

13. The surplus fund of a national-banking association is not excluded in the valuation of its shares for taxation. *Strafford National Bank* v. *Dorer, 59 N. H., 316.*

14. Where shares of stock are assessed at their actual cash value, without any deduction for the real estate owned by the association, the real estate should not be taxed *eo nomine. Commissioners of Rice County* v. *Citizens' National Bank of Faribault, 23 Minn., 280.*

15. Real estate owned by a bank constitutes part of its assets, within the meaning of code of Mississippi providing that banks shall pay a privilege tax, whose amount varies with their "capital stock or assets," in lieu of all other taxes. *Vicksburg Bank* v. *Worrell, 7 So. Rep., 219.*

16. The State can not tax the circulating notes of national-banking associations. *Horne* v. *Greene, 25 Miss., 452;* contra, *Board of Commissioners* v. *Elston, 32 Ind., 27; Ruffin* v. *Board of Commissioners, 69 N. C., 198; Lily* v. *The Commissioners, 69 N. C., 300.*

17. Where the State banks are taxed upon the capital, no tax can be imposed upon the shares of national-banking associations; for, as the capital of the State banks may consist of the bonds of the United States, which are exempt from State taxation, a tax on capital is not equivalent to a tax on shares. *Van Allen* v. *The Assessors, 3 Wall., 573; Bradley* v. *The People, 4 Wall., 459.*

18. But though the tax upon the State banks is not *eo nomine* a tax on shares, yet if it is equivalent to such a tax the shares in the national-banking associations located in that State may be taxed. *Frazer* v. *Seibern, 16 Ohio St., 614; Van Slyke* v. *State, 23 Wis., 656; Boynoll* v. *State, 25 Wis., 112.*

19. Where by local legislation different rates are prescribed for different classes of moneyed capital, the rate imposed upon shares of national banks should approximate as closely as may be the rate imposed upon other moneyed capital of the same or similar class, viz, shares of State banks. *City National Bank* v. *Paducah, 5 Cent. L. J., 317.*

20. Congress meant no more than to require of the States, as a condition to the exercise of the power to tax the shares in national banks, that they should, as far as they had the capacity, tax in like manner the shares of banks of issue of their own creation. *Lionberger* v. *Rouse, 9 Wall., 468.*

TAXATION—Continued.

21. Therefore, where a State has previously contracted with the banks which it has chartered that they shall not be taxed above a certain rate, a tax upon national-bank shares at a greater rate is not invalid, if this rate is not greater than that assessed upon all the moneyed capital within the State, except that of the State banks. *Ib.*

22. Any system of assessment of taxes which exacts from the owner of the shares of a national-banking association a larger sum in proportion to the actual value of those shares than it does from other moneyed capital, valued in like manner, taxes the shares at a greater rate, notwithstanding that the percentage of tax on the valuation is the same as that applied to other moneyed capital. *Pelton* v. *Commercial National Bank, 101 U. S., 143.*

23. In estimating the value of the shares for the purpose of taxation reference may be had to all the property and values of the bank. *St. Louis National Bank* v. *Papin, 3 Cent., L. J., 669.*

24. If no excessive valuation is complained of, and a correct result is arrived at, equity will not restrain the collection of a tax because the method of computation was erroneous. *Ib.*

25. The shares may be valued for taxation at an amount exceeding their face value, if this amount is not at a greater rate than the valuation set upon other moneyed capital in the State. *Hepburn* v. *School Directors, 23 Wall., 480.*

26. Under the statute of New York, shares in national-banking associations should be taxed at their real or market value. *People* v. *The Commissioners of Taxes and Assessments, 94 U. S., 415.*

27. Where shares in national-banking associations are purposely valued proportionately higher than the other moneyed capital in the State, the assessment is void. *Pelton* v. *National Bank, 101 U. S., 143.*

28. And the collection of what is in excess of the rate imposed on the other moneyed capital may be enjoined. *Ib.*

29. A State statute creating a system of taxation of banks which does not discriminate against national banks is not unconstitutional. *Ib; Davenport Bank* v. *Davenport, 123 U. S., 83.*

30. Section 5219, Revised Statutes, does not require perfect equality between State and national banks, but only a system of taxation which shall work no discrimination between them. *Ib.*

31. The intention of Congress was that the rate of taxation of the shares should be the same as, or not greater than, the tax upon the moneyed capital of the individual citizen which is *subject and liable to taxation. People* v. *The Commissioners, 4 Wall., 244.*

32. The fact that by the statutes creating them, which statutes were passed prior to the national-banking law, State banks are entirely exempt from taxation will not render a tax upon the shares of national-banking associations void. *City of Richmond* v. *Scott, 48 Ind., 568.*

33. And a State tax upon shares in national-banking associations is not rendered invalid by an exemption of the shares of other corporations the capital of which consists of property required to be listed for taxation as such. *McIver* v. *Robinson, 53 Ala., 456.*

34. Merely a partial exemption of other moneyed capital will not invalidate a tax upon shares in national-banking associations. *Hepburn* v. *School Directors, 23 Wall., 480.*

35. But though Congress did not contemplate that there should be an absolute equality (which in the nature of things is impossible), yet it did intend that there should be a substantial equality; and therefore if the exemptions in favor of other moneyed capital are so palpable as to show that there is a serious discrimination against capital invested in the shares of national-banking associations the tax will be declared unlawful. *Boyer* v. *Boyer, 113 U. S., 690.*

36. A State law which does not permit a deduction to be made from the assessed value of bank shares for all debts due by the holder thereof, while authorizing such a deduction to be made from the assessed value of moneyed capital otherwise invested, is void. *People ex rel. Williams* v. *Wearer, 100 U. S., 539,* reversing *S. C., 67 N. Y., 516,* and overruling *People* v. *Dolan, 36 N. Y., 59.*

37. In the assessment and taxation of shares of national-bank stock the owners thereof, having no other credits or moneyed capital, are entitled to deduct their bona fide debts from the value of such shares of stock. *Wasson* v. *Bank, 8 N. E. Rep., 97.*

38. Revised Statutes, section 5219, providing that shares of national-bank stock may be taxed as part of the personality of the owner, and that each State

TAXATION—Continued.

may tax them in its own manner, except that the taxation shall not be at a greater rate than is imposed on other "moneyed capital" owned by citizens of the State, and that the shares of nonresidents shall only be taxed in the city wherein the bank is located, do not authorize the taxation of the stock of a bank *in solido* by the city in which it does business, but only the shares of individual owners residing in the city are taxable, and they must be taxed separately, in order that the owner may deduct from their value the amount of his personal indebtedness, where the State laws or municipal ordinances permit such deductions, and require equality of taxation. *First National Bank of Richmond* v. *City of Richmond et al., 39 Fed. Rep., 309; Whitbeck* v. *Mercantile Bank, 127 U. S., 193.*

39. The main purpose of Congress in fixing limits to State taxation on investments in the shares of national banks was to render it impossible for the State in levying such a tax *to create and foster an unequal and unfriendly competition by favoring institutions or individuals carrying on similar business and operations and investments of a like character;* and the language of the law is to be read in the light of this policy. And, therefore, the exemption of shares of stock in corporations *the business of which does not come into competition with that of the national bank (e. g.,* railroad companies, mining companies, manufacturing companies, and insurance companies) does not invalidate a tax upon national-bank shares. Capital thus employed is not "moneyed capital" within the meaning of the act of Congress. *Mercantile Bank* v. *New York, 121 U. S., 138; Newark Bank Co. v. Newark, ib., 163; Bank of Redemption* v. *Boston, ib., 60.*

40. The bonds of municipal corporations are not within the reason of the rule established by Congress for the taxation of national banks. *Central National Bank* v. *United States, 137 U. S., 355.*

41. Although deposits in savings banks constitute moneyed capital in the hands of individuals within the terms of any definition which can be given of that phrase, yet they are not within the meaning of the act of Congress in such a sense as to require that, if they are exempted from taxation, shares of stock in national banks must thereby also be exempted from taxation, for it can not be supposed that savings banks come into any possible competition with national banks. *Mercantile Bank* v. *New York, 121 U. S., 138; Newark Bank Co. v. Newark, ib., 63; Bank of Redemption* v. *Boston, 125, ib., 60.*

42. Under act Louisiana, 1888, section 27, relating to taxation of national-bank shares, making no deduction for that part of the bank's property entering into their value which consists of nontaxable State and national securities, which deduction may, under the act, be made by individuals, a tax on national-bank shares violates Revised Statutes of the United States, section 5219, prohibiting the assessment of such shares at a greater rate than moneyed capital in the hands of individual citizens, and it is immaterial that the same discrimination is made against other corporations. *Whitney National Bank* v. *Parker, 41 Fed. Rep., 402.*

43. The taxation of national-bank shares by the statute of Indiana without permitting the owner to deduct from their assessed value the amount of his bona fide indebtedness as he may in the case of other investments of moneyed capital, is a discrimination forbidden by the act of Congress. *Britton* v. *Evansville National Bank, 105 U. S., 322.*

44. Section 5219 prohibits an adverse discrimination by a local government in the valuation of national-bank stock for assessment as compared with an assessment by the same government for the same year of other moneyed capital invested so as to make a profit from the use thereof as money. *Puget Sound National Bank of Seattle* v. *King County et al., 57 Fed. Rep., 433.*

45. The State has a right to resort to the bank as a garnishee for the collection of its claims against stockholders for taxes, and legislation may require assessment of stock to be made to the bank *in solido. First National Bank of Aberdeen* v. *Chehalis Co. et al., Washington supreme court, March 18, 1893.*

46. The nontaxation of credits of individuals, such as accounts, promissory notes, and mortgages, is not unlawful discrimination against national banks whose capital is taxed. *Ib.*

47. A State tax upon shares is valid, though the tax is collected from the bank. *National Bank* v. *Commonwealth, 9 Wall., 353.*

48. And the State may require the banks to pay a tax rightfully laid upon the shares. *Ib.*

49. And where the tax on shares is payable by the association the collection of the tax may be enforced by distraint of its property. *First National Bank* v. *Douglas County, 3 Dill., 330.*

TAXATION—Continued.

50. But where the tax laws of the State make the bank the *mere agent* for paying the tax on shares, and direct it to retain so much of the dividends as will answer that purpose, other agents being required to pay taxes for their principals only when they have under their control the property, money, or credit of such principals, the bank can not be made liable unless it has the control of the property, etc., of its shareholders, or has dividends in its possession, or has failed to retain them. *Hershire v. First National Bank, 35 Iowa, 272.*

51. Act Louisiana, 1888, section 27, providing that shares in banks shall be assessed to shareholders, but requiring the bank to pay taxes so assessed, and authorizing it to collect the same from the shareholders, imposes a tax, not upon the bank, but upon its shares, as permitted by act of Congress, providing that a State may determine the manner of taxing the shares of national banks located in the State.' *Whitney National Bank v. Parker, 41 Fed. Rep., 402.*

52. No suit for the collection of a tax under State statutes imposed upon the shares of stock of a national bank can be maintained against the receiver of an insolvent national bank where the property represented by the shares has disappeared; for, there being nothing from which the receiver can be reimbursed, the tax will fall upon the assets of the bank, which belong to its creditors, and thereby violate the rule that a State can not tax the capital stock of a national bank. *City of Boston v. Beal, 51 Fed. Rep., 306.*

53. National-banking associations can not be subjected to a license or privilege tax. *Mayor v. First National Bank of Macon, 59 Ga., 648; City of Carthage v. First National Band of Carthage, 71 Mo., 508; National Bank of Chattanooga v. Mayor, 8 Heiskell, 814.*

54. Municipal officers can not assess a tax upon the shares of national-banking associations until authorized to do so by some law of the State. *Stetson v. City of Bangor, 56 Me., 274.*

55. The officers of a national-banking association can not be compelled to exhibit to the taxing officers of a State the books of the association showing the deposits of its customers. *First National Bank of Youngstown v. Hughes, Browne's N. B. Cas., 176.*

56. The tax imposed on State or national banks paying out the notes of individuals or State banks for circulation is constitutional. *Veazie Bank v. Fenno, 8 Wall., 533.*

57. So is the tax imposed on them for paying out the circulating notes of municipal corporations. *Merchants' National Bank of Little Rock v. United States, 101 U. S., 1.*

58. Such a tax is not a direct tax within the meaning of the clause of the Constitution which declares that "direct taxes shall be apportioned among the several States according to their respective numbers." *Veazie Bank v. Fenno and Mechanics' National Bank of Little Rock v. United States, supra.*

59. Where the tax on shares is collected from the association it may bring a suit to enjoin the collection of an illegal tax. *Cummings v. National Bank, 101 U. S., 153; Pelton v. Commercial National Bank, 101 U. S., 143; Boyer v. Boyer, 113, U. S., 148.*

60. No suit can be maintained against the receiver of an insolvent national bank where the property represented by the shares has disappeared, under a statute which provides that shares of stock in all banks, State and national, shall be taxed to the owners thereof, to be paid in the first instance by the bank itself, which for reimbursement shall have a lien upon the shares and all the rights of the shareholders in the bank property. *City of Boston v. Beal, 55 Fed. Rep., 26.*

61. The imposition of a tax upon the shares of the bank according to the Louisiana statute, which requires the bank to pay the tax and then look to the dividends upon the shares and to the stockholders for reimbursement, is a tax upon the bank itself. *Citizens' Bank of Louisiana v. Board of Assessors, 54 Fed. Rep., 73.*

62. In 1856 the State of Tennessee granted to the Bank of Commerce a charter which provides that the bank "shall have a lien on the stock for debts due it by the stockholders and shall pay to the State an annual tax of one-half of one per cent on each share of capital stock, which shall be in lieu of all other taxes." *Held,* that this charter exempts from taxation the property of the bank as well as the individual property of the shareholders in the corporate stock and its shares, and such construction is not affected by the fact that the United States Supreme Court decided that the charter tax was a tax on the shareholder only, and an exemption therefore of the shareholder, since such decision does not exclude from

TAXATION—Continued.

the exemption the corporation and its property. *State of Tennessee et al.* v. *Bank of Commerce et al.*, *53 Fed. Rep.*, *735*.

63. When the statute requires property to be assessed for taxation at its cash value, a bill to enjoin the collection of a tax solely on the ground that the property of other persons is assessed below its cash value, can not be maintained by a person whose property is also assessed below that value. *Albuquerque National Bank* v. *Perea*, *147 U. S.*, *87*.

64. Massachusetts laws for taxation of national banks do not deny them the equal protection of the laws guaranteed by the Constitution, nor impose an unequal tax in violation of the constitution of that State. *Bank of Redemption* v. *Boston*, *125 U. S.*, *60*.

65. If a bank by mistake declares a dividend or adds to its surplus when it is not in condition to do so, such dividend is subject to taxation and the mistake can not be corrected in action to recover the tax. *Central National Bank* v. *United States*, *137 U. S.*, *355*.

66. When an assessment on national-bank stock for taxation by a State is not made in contravention of the Federal Constitution or laws. *Palmer* v. *McMahon*, *133 U. S.*, *660*.

67. The same power of taxation in respect to national banks exists in the Territories that does in the States. *Talbott* v. *Silver Bow County*, *139 U. S.*, *158*.

68. When increase in valuation of national-bank shares over that of the moneyed capital of individuals is a discrimination forbidden by Revised Statutes, Sec. 5219. *Whitbeck* v. *Mercantile Bank*, *127 U. S.*, *193*.

69. Act of 1864, "to provide a national currency," etc., subjects shares of banks authorized by it to taxation by States, though part or whole of capital is invested in national securities exempt from State taxation, and is constitutional. *Van Allen* v. *Assessors*, *3 Wall.*, *573*.

70. New York act of 1865, subjecting shares of national banks to taxation, but not providing that the tax should not exceed rate imposed on State banks, is void, as there was no tax on shares of State banks—only on the capital. *Ib.*

71. Shares of stock in national banks are personal property, and the law creating them could give them a *citus* of their own, apart from owners, for purpose of taxation. This was done by act of 1864, section 41. *Tappan* v. *Merchants' National Bank*, *19 Wall.*, *490*.

72. State statutes taxing shares without permitting owner to deduct his indebtedness, as allowed to owners of other personal property, make a discrimination forbidden by acts of Congress. *Supervisors* v. *Stanley*, *105 U. S.*, *305; Evansville Bank* v. *Britton*, *ib.*, *322.* .

73. State statute is not void which requires. for purposes of taxation, that the cashier of each national bank within the state transmits to clerks of several towns in State a true list of its stockholders residing there. *Waite* v. *Dowley*, *94 U. S.*, *527*.

74. National-bank shares can not be subjected to State taxation where a large part relatively of other moneyed capital in hands of individual citizens in same taxing district is exempted. *Boyer* v. *Boyer*, *113 U. S.*, *689*.

75. Bank may, on behalf of stockholders, maintain suit to enjoin collection of State tax unlawfully assessed on shares. *Hills* v. *Exchange Bank*, *105 U. S.*, *319*.

76. Act of 1866, taxing every national bank or State bank on the amount of State-bank notes paid out is the proper restraint on the circulation of such notes. *Veazie Bank* v. *Fenno*, *8 Wall.*, *533*.

TRANSFER OF STOCK.   See Shareholders:

1. The transfer of shares in national-banking associations is not governed by different rules from those which are ordinarily applied to the transfer of shares in other corporate bodies. *Johnson* v. *Laflin*, *103 U. S.*, *800*.

2. The entry of the transaction in the books of the association is required, not for the translation of the title, but for the protection of the parties, and others dealing with the association, and to enable it to know who are its stockholders. *Ib.*

3. A shareholder in a national bank, while it is a going concern, has the absolute right, in the absence of fraud, to make a bona fide and actual sale and transfer of his shares at any time to any person capable in law of purchasing and holding the same, and of assuming the transferrer's liabilities in respect thereto; and this right is not in such cases subject to the control of the directors or other stockholders. *Johnson* v. *Laflin*, *5 Dill.*, *65*.

4. Under the pretense of prescribing the manner thereof, an association can not clog the transfer with useless restrictions. *Ib.*

TRANSFER OF STOCK—Continued.

5. When a shareholder, acting in good faith, delivers his certificates of stock, with a blank power of attorney for making the transfer, and receives the purchase money, the sale is complete and the title passes. *Ib.*

6. A shareholder who disposes of his stock will continue to be liable thereon until the transfer is noted on the books of the association. *Bowdell v. Farmers and Merchants' National Bank of Baltimore, Browne's N. B. Cas., 147.*

7. In such case the mere return of the dividends paid upon the stock to the person by whom the transfer was made will not be a sufficient repudiation thereof. *Ib.: Brown v. Finn, 34 Fed. Rep., 124.*

8. A national-banking association can not acquire a lien on the stock of a shareholder. And a by-law prohibiting a transfer until all liabilities of the shareholder to the association are discharged, or a provision to that effect in the certificates of stock, is void. *Bullard v. National Bank, 18 Wall., 589; Bank v. Lanier, 11 Wall., 369; Conklin v. The Second National Bank, 45 N. Y., 655.*

9. When bank's stock is sold by aid of fraudulent representations in regard to its solvency the purchaser is entitled to a complete recision of the fraudulent sale. *Florida Land and Improvement Co. v. Merrill, Receiver, 52 Fed. Rep., 77.*

10. When bank's stock is fraudulently sold, and the proceeds are turned over to the bank, and a receiver subsequently appointed, no creditor of the bank can be said to have any such interest in the proceeds as would prevent restitution and a recision of the sale, and such appointment of a receiver does not in itself show that there are creditors of the bank that had prior equities. *Ib.*

11. Where a cashier who is intrusted by the directors with the duty of transferring the stock of the association refuses, for insufficient reasons, to transfer shares, and the association subsequently becomes insolvent, the owner of the shares may maintain an action against the receiver for the injury sustained. *Case v. Citizens' Bank, 100 U. S., 446.*

12. Where a shareholder who has sold his stock has delivered to the bank the certificates of stock and a power of attorney, with the request that the transfer be made upon the books of the bank, and has had no reason to suppose that such transfer was not made, he will not, should the bank afterward become insolvent, be held liable as a shareholder, although he still appears as such on the books of the bank. *Whitney v. Butler, 118 U. S., 655.*

13. But where the president of the bank is himself the purchaser of the stock, then the delivery of the certificates and power of attorney to him with the request to make the transfer upon the books of the bank would not be sufficient to discharge the seller from liability as a stockholder. *Richmond v. Irons, 121 U. S., 27.*

14. Where a shareholder of a national bank makes a bona fide sale of his stock and goes with the purchaser to the bank, indorses the certificate, and delivers it to the cashier of the bank, with directions to make the transfer on the books, he has done all that is incumbent upon him to discharge his liability, and he is not liable, though the cashier failed to make the transfer, upon the subsequent suspension of the bank, for an assessment made by the Comptroller of the Currency, under Revised Statutes, section 5151, to pay the bank's debts. *Hayes v. Shoemaker, 39 Fed. Rep., 319.*

15. A transfer of shares for the purpose of avoiding liability, though made "out and out," is void. *National Bank v. Case, supra; Bowden v. Santos, 1 Hughes, 158.*

16. And where a shareholder, who has knowledge of the insolvent condition of the bank, transfers his shares, without consideration, to a person unable to respond to the assessment, the transfer may be set aside. *Bowden v. Johnson, 107 U. S., 125.*

17. Title to stock passes on delivery of certificates to purchaser with authority to have shares transferred on books of bank. *Johnston v. Laflin, 103 U. S., 800.*

18. Party who, as security for a loan, accepts stock which he causes to be transferred to him on books, incurs liability as a stockholder and is not relieved by colorable transfer with understanding that he may have it back on request. *National Bank v. Case, 99 U. S., 628.*

19. Bank cashier refusing to transfer on books of bank shares of capital stock pledged and sold for debt of one of its stockholders, receiver of bank is liable for value of stock at that time if bank had no lien thereon to justify such refusal. *Case v. Bank, 100 U. S., 446.*

ULTRA VIRES:

1. A national-banking association can not deal in stocks. The prohibition is to be implied from the failure to grant the power. *First National Bank* v. *National Exchange Bank, 93 U. S., 122.*

2. A national-banking association can not *purchase* negotiable paper. *Lazear* v. *National Union Bank of Baltimore, 52 Md., 78; First National Bank of Rochester* v. *Pierson, 24 Minn., 140; Farmers and Mechanics' Bank* v. *Baldwin, 23 Minn., 198.* But see *Smith* v. *The Exchange Bank of Pittsburg, 26 Ohio St., 111.*

3. Where the provisions of the national banking act prohibit certain acts by banks or their officers, without imposing any penalty or forfeiture applicable to particular transactions which had been executed, their validity can be questioned by the United States only and not by private parties. *Thompson* v. *St. Nicholas National Bank, 146 U. S., 240.*

4. Can make no valid loan or discount on security of their own stock unless necessary to prevent loss on debt previously contracted in good faith. *Bank* v. *Lanier, 11 Wall., 369.*

5. The national-banking act does not give a bank an absolute right to retain bonds coming into its possession by purchase under a contract which it was without legal authority to make. *Logan Bank* v. *Townsend, 139 U. S., 67.*

USURY: See Interest.

1. The usury laws of the States do not apply to national-banking associations. *Farmers and Mechanics' Bank* v. *Dearing, 91 U. S., 29; Central National Bank* v. *Pratt, 115 Mass., 539; First National Bank* v. *Garlinghouse, 22 Ohio St., 492; Davis* v. *Randall, 115 Mass., 547; Hintermister* v. *First National Bank, 64 N. Y., 212.*

2. And the remedies provided by the State for the taking of usury can not be resorted to. *Farmers and Mechanics' Bank* v. *Dearing, supra; Wiley* v. *Starbuck, 44 Ind., 208.*

3. The taking of illegal interest by a national-banking association does not render the contract void. *Farmers and Mechanics' Bank* v. *Dearing, supra.*

4. It does not invalidate an indorsement or a guaranty of the notes upon which the usurious interest was paid. *Oates* v. *First National Bank of Montgomery, 100 U. S., 239; Lazear* v. *National Union Bank of Baltimore, 52 Md., 78.*

5. But usury destroys the interest-bearing power of the obligation; and there will be no point of time from which it can bear interest. *Lucas* v. *Government National Bank, 78 Penn. St., 228.*

6. The usury works a forfeiture of the entire interest accruing after maturity and before judgment, as well as that which accrues before maturity. *Shunk* v. *The First National Bank of Gallion, 22 Ohio St., 508.*

7. The discounting of business paper by a national-banking association at a higher than the legal rate is usurious, though the law of the State fixes no limit to the rate which natural persons may take for the discount or purchase of such paper. *Johnson* v. *National Bank of Gloversville, 74 N. Y., 329; National Bank* v. *Johnson, 104 U. S., 271.*

8. By charging more than legal interest on overdrafts, a national-banking association loses the right to recovery any interest at all. *Third National Bank of Philadelphia* v. *Miller, 90 Penn. St., 241.*

9. The liabilities of antecedent parties to a note or bill will not be affected by the usurious character of the transaction between the payee and the association; and the association may recover the full amount of the note or bill from the maker or acceptor. *Smith* v. *The Exchange Bank of Pittsburg, 26 Ohio St., 111.*

10. Usurious interest which has been paid to a national-banking association can not be applied by way of payment, set-off, or counter claim in an action by the association to recover the amount of the loan, but a separate action must be brought therefor. *Barnet* v. *Muncie National Bank, 98 U. S., 555.*

11. Where a national-banking association has discounted notes for another bank at a usurious rate of interest, the fact that the other bank has charged illegal interest on those notes to its customers will not affect its right to set up the defense of usury in an action by the association. *Third National Bank of Philadelphia* v. *Miller, supra.*

12. The amount which may be recovered from the association as a penalty is twice the amount of interest paid, and not simply twice the amount in excess of the legal rate. *Crocker* v. *First National Bank of Chetopa, 3 Am. L. T. [N. S.], 350; Overholt* v. *National Bank of Mount Pleasant, 82 Penn. St., 490; Barnet* v. *Muncie National Bank, supra.*

USURY—Continued.

13. The purchase of accepted drafts by a national bank from the holder without his indorsement at a greater reduction than lawful interest on their face value is a discounting of those drafts within the meaning of Revised Statutes, United States, section 5197, which prohibits such bank from taking interest on any loan or discount made by it at a greater rate than is allowed by the laws of the State where it is situated. *Danforth et al. v. National State Bank of Elizabeth, 48 Fed. Rep., 271.*

14. Where a bankrupt has paid usurious interest, his assignee may bring an action against the association to recover the penalty. *Wright v. First National Bank of Greensburg, 8 Biss.. 243; Crocker v. First National Bank of Chetopa, 4 Dill., 358; 3 Am. L. T. N. S.. 350.*

15. The party who paid the usurious interest is the only party to the note who is entitled to sue for the penalty. *Lazear v. National Union Bank of Maryland, supra.*

16. Under Revised Statutes, United States, 5198, providing that a suit against a national bank for taking usurious interest must be commenced within two years from "the time the usurious transaction occurred," the limitation begins to run from the time when such interest is paid. *National Bank v. Carpenter, N. J.. 19 A., 181; Bobs v. People's National Bank. 21 Fed. Rep., 888.*

17. The penalty for all illegal interest paid to a national-banking association within two years prior to the commencement of proceedings may be recovered in a single action, whether the amount was in one payment or in several. *Hintermister v. First National Bank, 64 N. Y., 212.*

18. A note dated and signed by the makers in Tennessee and payable in Chicago, Ill., and forwarded by them to the payees in Chicago, to be used by the latter in raising money with which to pay off a prior note made by the same parties. must be held an Illinois contract and governed by the laws of Illinois relating to usury. *Buchanan et al. v. Drovers' National Bank of Chicago, 55 Fed. Rep.. 223.*

19. Bank loaned money upon note which it afterward discounted, the maker agreeing to open account with bank or to pay 2¼ per cent commission to the bank on the loan. As the money loaned belonged to the bank, commission held to be usury. *Union National Bank v. L. N. O. & C. Ry. Co., Ill., Supreme Court, May 9, 1893.*

20. An act of a legislature providing that no corporation shall set up defense of usury in any action does not render contracts by corporations for usurious interest enforcible and does not prevent corporations setting up a defense of illegality under section 5197, Revised Statutes. *Ib.*

21. When allegations of complaint are sufficient to sustain a judgment in an action against a national bank for exacting usurious interest. *First National Bank v. Morgan, 132 U. S., 141.*

22. Usurious interest paid a national bank on renewing a series of notes can not, in an action by the bank on the last of them, be applied in satisfaction of the debt. *Driesbach v. National Bank, 104 U. S., 52; Barnett v. National Bank, 98 U. S., 555.*

23. Remedy given by section 5198, Revised Statutes, for recovery of usurious interest paid to a national bank is exclusive. *Barnett v. National Bank, 98, U. S., 555; Stephens v. Monongahela Bank, 111 U. S., 187.*

24. The only forfeiture for usury declared by section 30 of act of 1864 is of entire interest. and no greater loss is incurred by such bank by reason of the usury laws of a State. *Farmers' National Bank v. Dearing, 91 U. S., 29.*

VOTING:

The provision of section 5144, Revised Statutes, which disqualifies shareholders "whose liability is past due and unpaid" from voting at meetings of shareholders, applies only to liability for unpaid subscriptions for stock. *United States ex rel. v Barry, 36 Fed. Rep., 246.*

NUMBER OF BANKS ORGANIZED, IN LIQUIDATION, AND IN OPERATION, WITH THEIR CAPITAL, BONDS ON DEPOSIT, AND CIRCULATION ISSUED, REDEEMED, AND OUTSTANDING ON OCTOBER 31, 1893.

States and Territories.	Banks. Organized.	In liquidation.	In operation.	Capital stock paid.	United States bonds on deposit.	Circulation. Issued.	Redeemed.	Outstanding.*
Maine	96	13	82	$11,220,600	$4,259,400	$40,516,200	$36,135,145	$4,381,055
New Hampshire	60	9	51	6,180,000	3,714,000	27,614,075	23,998,263	3,615,812
Vermont	67	19	48	7,035,000	3,480,500	35,695,900	32,550,327	3,145,573
Massachusetts	287	19	268	99,467,500	30,478,100	335,387,475	304,087,890	31,299,585
Rhode Island	64	5	59	20,277,050	7,621,250	72,396,235	64,707,253	7,688,982
Connecticut	98	14	84	22,999,370	7,880,500	93,268,490	85,503,433	7,765,057
Eastern States	672	79	593	167,179,520	57,433,750	604,878,375	546,982,311	57,896,064
New York	462	128	334	88,141,360	36,439,450	318,774,665	282,067,216	36,707,449
New Jersey	113	14	99	14,608,350	5,235,750	56,943,590	51,876,179	5,067,111
Pennsylvania	469	61	399	73,670,310	25,645,500	217,104,315	191,683,952	25,420,363
Delaware	18	......	18	2,133,985	926,000	7,903,005	7,132,970	860,035
Maryland	71	3	68	16,988,220	3,755,500	41,610,200	37,515,097	4,115,103
Dist. Columbia	18	5	13	2,827,000	1,155,400	6,437,980	5,413,617	1,024,303
Middle States	1,142	211	931	198,369,225	73,157,600	648,883,755	575,689,091	73,194,724
Virginia	52	16	36	4,796,300	1,594,250	13,800,360	12,246,979	1,553,381
West Virginia	38	8	30	2,961,000	962,500	8,454,830	7,469,105	985,727
North Carolina	31	7	24	2,926,000	917,600	7,418,250	6,565,867	882,383
South Carolina	18	4	14	1,748,000	474,750	6,015,215	5,573,984	441,231
Georgia	40	13	27	4,191,000	1,186,250	9,537,590	8,380,417	1,157,173
Florida	24	7	17	1,500,000	417,500	1,003,700	623,159	386,541
Alabama	38	9	29	3,844,000	1,133,500	6,672,980	5,492,939	1,180,041
Mississippi	15	3	12	1,115,000	353,750	943,050	648,595	294,455
Louisiana	25	5	20	3,935,000	1,152,500	11,697,820	10,318,514	1,379,306
Texas	254	32	222	25,926,175	5,624,100	13,625,980	8,433,799	5,192,181
Arkansas	13	4	9	1,100,000	200,000	1,724,010	1,447,800	276,210
Kentucky	107	27	80	14,512,900	4,050,500	38,268,675	33,937,549	4,331,126
Tennessee	77	26	51	9,590,000	1,369,000	12,792,510	11,422,533	1,369,977
Southern States	732	161	571	78,055,375	19,436,200	131,900,970	112,561,240	19,429,730
Missouri	199	40	70	23,865,000	2,345,300	19,898,055	17,401,856	2,466,199
Ohio	344	101	243	46,680,100	15,795,750	115,278,900	99,866,769	15,412,191
Indiana	181	67	114	13,987,000	5,122,050	56,778,745	51,255,945	5,522,800
Illinois	291	78	213	39,408,500	6,916,000	57,900,305	51,177,027	6,732,278
Michigan	167	67	100	14,834,000	5,215,500	33,588,800	28,467,494	5,121,366
Wisconsin	119	37	82	9,480,200	2,400,250	15,353,210	13,131,780	2,221,460
Iowa	230	61	169	14,915,000	3,722,500	26,254,350	22,605,074	3,648,376
Minnesota	104	27	77	16,335,000	2,005,800	14,357,240	12,341,105	2,016,135
North Dakota	42	10	32	2,615,000	644,000	1,817,370	1,219,407	597,963
South Dakota	52	13	39	2,610,000	742,250	2,154,000	1,464,065	689,935
Kansas	213	76	137	12,174,100	3,045,750	11,916,130	8,889,121	3,027,009
Nebraska	165	30	135	13,598,100	3,122,500	10,261,670	7,348,880	2,912,790
Western States	2,027	607	1,420	210,502,000	51,077,650	365,567,865	315,259,423	50,308,442
Nevada	3	1	2	282,000	70,500	317,390	266,989	50,401
Oregon	42	3	39	3,795,000	757,300	2,704,690	1,924,588	780,102
Colorado	65	13	52	9,125,000	1,717,750	6,974,530	5,364,473	1,610,057
Idaho	14	1	13	825,000	200,250	689,320	511,072	178,248
Montana	41	16	25	4,675,000	902,100	2,997,230	2,120,037	877,193
Wyoming	14	2	12	1,360,000	312,500	934,720	680,362	254,358
Washington	77	16	61	7,480,000	1,720,500	3,734,250	2,071,473	1,662,777
California	48	12	36	8,975,000	1,543,750	5,558,280	4,118,640	1,439,640
Utah	17	3	14	2,800,000	475,000	2,155,690	1,086,767	468,923
New Mexico	15	5	10	1,075,000	340,000	1,866,640	1,550,211	316,429
Arizona	8	3	5	400,000	100,500	212,110	115,650	96,460
Oklahoma	7	1	6	300,000	75,000	109,070	25,480	83,590
Indian Ter	6	......	6	360,000	90,000	111,470	29,740	81,730
Pacific States and Territories	357	76	281	41,452,000	8,313,150	28,365,390	20,465,482	7,899,968
Add for mutilated notes								
Total currency banks						1,779,686,355	1,570,959,487	208,728,868
Add gold banks						3,465,210	3,367,413	97,827
United States	4,930	1,134	3,796	695,558,120	209,416,350	1,783,151,595	1,574,324,900	208,826,695

* Including $21,197,938 for which lawful money has been deposited with the Treasurer of the United States to retire an equal amount of circulation which has not been presented for redemption.

† Four banks restored to solvency and resumed business, making total going banks now 3,796.

THE NUMBER AND CAPITAL, BY STATES, OF NATIONAL BANKS ORGANIZED DURING THE YEAR ENDED OCTOBER 31, 1893.

States and Territories.	No. of banks.	Capital.	States and Territories.	No. of banks.	Capital.
Pennsylvania	25	$2,375,000	Arizona	1	$100,000
New York	11	2,050,000	Colorado	1	50,000
Texas	10	610,000	Idaho	1	50,000
Iowa	10	500,000	Kansas	1	50,000
Illinois	7	500,000	Kentucky	1	50,000
Indiana	7	500,000	Michigan	1	100,000
Ohio	7	495,000	Montana	1	50,000
Minnesota	6	330,000	Missouri	1	100,000
Wisconsin	5	1,750,000	New Jersey	1	50,000
Nebraska	3	150,000	North Carolina	1	50,000
California	2	150,000	North Dakota	1	50,000
Florida	2	150,000	South Dakota	1	50,000
Maine	2	160,000	Tennessee	1	60,000
Maryland	2	150,000	Vermont	1	50,000
Massachusetts	2	300,000	West Virginia	1	50,000
Oklahoma	2	100,000			
Alabama	1	50,000	Total	119	11,230,000

STATEMENT SHOWING BY STATES THE NUMBER OF NATIONAL BANKS IN ACTIVE OPERATION OCTOBER 31, 1893.

Alabama	29	Nebraska	135
Arizona	5	Nevada	2
Arkansas	9	New Hampshire	51
California	36	New Jersey	99
Colorado	52	New Mexico	10
Connecticut	84	New York	334
Delaware	18	North Carolina	24
District of Columbia	13	North Dakota	32
Florida	17	Ohio	243
Georgia	27	Oklahoma	6
Idaho	13	Oregon	39
Illinois	213	Pennsylvania	399
Indiana	114	Rhode Island	59
Indian Territory	6	South Carolina	14
Iowa	169	South Dakota	39
Kansas	137	Tennessee	51
Kentucky	80	Texas	222
Louisiana	20	Utah	14
Maine	83	Vermont	48
Maryland	68	Virginia	36
Massachusetts	268	Washington	61
Michigan	100	West Virginia	30
Minnesota	77	Wisconsin	82
Mississippi	12	Wyoming	12
Missouri	79		
Montana	25	Total	3,796

STATEMENT SHOWING TOTAL NUMBER OF NATIONAL BANKS NOW IN OPERATION AND THE NUMBER PASSED OUT OF THE SYSTEM SINCE FEBRUARY 25, 1863.

Passed into voluntary liquidation to wind up affairs	713
Less number placed in the hands of a receiver	10
	703
Passed into liquidation for purpose of reorganization	84
Passed into liquidation upon expiration of corporate existence *	103
Placed in the hands of a receiver	248
	1,138
Less number restored to solvency and resumed business	4
Total passed out of system	1,134

* Total number of banks organized since February 25, 1863, 4,930; number now in operation, 3,796. Sixty-four of these have been reorganized.

NUMBER AND AUTHORIZED CAPITAL OF BANKS ORGANIZED AND THE NUMBER AND CAPITAL OF BANKS CLOSED IN EACH YEAR ENDED OCTOBER 31 SINCE THE ESTABLISHMENT OF THE NATIONAL BANKING SYSTEM, WITH THE YEARLY INCREASE OR DECREASE.

Year.	Organized.		Closed.				Net yearly increase.		Net yearly decrease.	
			In voluntary liquidation.		Insolvent.					
	No.	Capital.	No.	Capital.	No.	Capital.	No.	Capital.	No.	Capital.
1863	134	$16,378,700					134	$16,378,700		
1864	453	79,366,950	3				450	79,366,950		
1865	1,014	242,542,982	6	$330,000	1	$50,000	1,007	242,162,982		
1866	62	8,515,150	4	659,000	2	500,000	56	7,365,150		
1867	10	4,260,300	12	2,160,000	6	1,170,000		930,300	8	
1868	12	1,210,000	18	2,445,500	4	410,000			10	1,645,500
1869	9	1,500,000	17	3,372,710	1	50,000			9	1,922,710
1870	22	2,736,000	14	2,550,000	1	250,000	7			64,000
1871	170	19,510,000	11	1,450,000			159	18,060,000		
1872	175	18,988,000	11	2,180,500	6	1,806,100	158	15,001,400		
1873	68	7,602,700	21	3,524,700	11	3,825,000	36	253,000		
1874	71	6,745,500	20	2,795,000	3	250,000	48	3,700,500		
1875	107	12,104,000	38	3,820,000	5	1,000,000	64	7,283,800		
1876	36	3,189,800	32	2,565,000	9	965,000			5	340,200
1877	29	2,580,000	26	2,539,500	10	3,344,000			7	3,294,500
1878	28	2,775,000	41	4,237,500	14	2,612,500			27	4,075,000
1879	38	3,595,000	33	3,750,000	8	1,230,000			3	1,385,000
1880	57	6,374,170	9	570,000	3	700,000	45	5,104,170		
1881	86	9,651,050	26	1,920,000			60	7,731,050		
1882	227	30,038,300	78	16,120,000	3	1,561,300	146	12,357,000		
1883	262	28,654,350	40	7,736,000	2	250,000	220	20,668,350		
1884	191	10,042,230	30	3,647,250	11	1,285,000	150	11,109,980		
1885	145	16,938,000	85	17,856,590	4	600,000	56			1,518,590
1886	174	21,358,000	25	1,651,100	8	650,000	141	19,056,900		
1887	225	30,546,000	25	2,537,450	8	1,550,100	192	26,458,550		
1888	132	12,053,000	34	4,171,000	8	1,900,000	90	5,982,000		
1889	211	21,240,000	41	4,316,000	2	250,000	168	16,674,000		
1890	307	36,250,000	50	5,050,000	9	750,000	248	30,450,000		
1891	193	20,700,000	41	4,485,000	25	3,622,000	127	12,593,000		
1892	163	15,285,000	53	6,157,500	17	2,450,000	93	6,677,500		
1893	119	11,230,000	46	6,035,000	67	11,035,000	6		113	5,840,000
Total	4,930	709,978,182	890	120,623,500	248	44,065,900	3,974	565,374,282	182	20,085,500
Deduct decrease							182	20,085,500		
Total							*3,792	545,288,782		

* Four banks restored to solvency making 3,796 going banks.

† The total authorized capital stock on October 31 was $695,953,165, the paid-in capital $695,558,120, including the capital stock of liquidating and insolvent banks which have not deposited lawful money for the retirement of their circulating notes.

STATEMENT SHOWING, BY STATES, THE NUMBER AND CAPITAL OF ALL BANKS EXTENDED UNDER ACT OF JULY 12, 1882.

States and Territories.	No. of banks.	Capital.	States and Territories.	No. of banks.	Capital.
Alabama	6	$885,000	Montana	2	$650,000
Arkansas	2	350,000	Nebraska	8	1,400,000
California	3	2,100,000	New Hampshire	38	4,905,000
Colorado	6	1,010,000	New Jersey	53	10,783,350
Connecticut	73	22,450,820	New York	225	72,872,460
Delaware	11	1,503,185	North Carolina	4	850,000
District of Columbia	5	1,277,000	South Carolina	9	1,535,000
Georgia	9	1,806,000	Ohio	103	17,329,000
Illinois	83	10,018,000	Oregon	1	250,000
Indiana	46	5,629,000	Pennsylvania	174	45,951,000
Iowa	47	4,170,000	Rhode Island	59	19,959,800
Idaho	1	100,000	Tennessee	13	2,570,000
Kansas	9	825,000	Texas	7	985,000
Kentucky	23	6,611,500	Utah	1	500,000
Louisiana	6	2,600,000	Vermont	32	5,956,000
Maine	56	9,835,000	Virginia	14	2,391,000
Maryland	29	12,060,000	West Virginia	13	1,491,000
Massachusetts	209	88,612,500	Wisconsin	22	2,085,000
Michigan	29	2,440,000	Wyoming	1	100,000
Minnesota	18	5,315,000			
Missouri	16	3,775,000	Total	1,460	375,949,005

STATEMENT SHOWING THE NUMBER, CAPITAL AND CIRCULATION OF NATIONAL BANKS WHICH WILL REACH THE EXPIRATION OF THEIR CORPORATE EXISTENCE DURING THE PERIOD OF TEN YEARS FROM 1894 TO 1903 INCLUSIVE.

Year.	No. of banks.	Capital.	Circulation.
1894	51	$7,008,000	$2,114,950
1895	78	12,257,000	3,596,225
1896	22	2,453,800	830,215
1897	25	3,714,000	1,026,675
1898	24	2,579,000	943,200
1899	32	4,330,000	1,930,500
1900	47	8,157,100	3,011,885
1901	101	13,863,150	4,766,650
1902	203	37,892,300	8,512,537
1903	194	25,021,500	5,735,125
Total	777	117,275,850	32,407,992

STATEMENT SHOWING THE TITLE, LOCATION, CAPITAL, AND CIRCULATION OF BANKS, THE CORPORATE EXISTENCE OF WHICH EXPIRED DURING THE YEAR ENDED OCTOBER 31, 1893, AND OF ASSOCIATIONS WHICH SUCCEEDED THEM.

Title and location.	Capital.	Circulation.
The Lumberman's National Bank of Muskegon, Mich	$100,000	$22,500
The Phœnix National Bank of Medina, Ohio	75,000	17,000
The First National Bank of Chelsea, Vt	50,000	11,250
The Farmers' National Bank of Owatonna, Minn	75,000	17,100
	300,000	67,850
The National Lumberman's Bank of Muskegon, Mich	100,000	22,500
The Old Phœnix National Bank of Medina, Ohio	75,000	35,100
The National Bank of Orange County, Chelsea, Vt	50,000	22,500
The National Farmers' Bank of Owatonna, Minn	80,000	18,000
	305,000	98,100

STATEMENT SHOWING THE NUMBER, CAPITAL, AND CIRCULATION BY STATES, OF NATIONAL BANKS, THE CORPORATE EXISTENCE OF WHICH WAS EXTENDED DURING THE YEAR ENDED OCTOBER 31, 1893.

State.	No. of banks.	Capital.	Circulation.	State.	No. of banks.	Capital.	Circulation.
California	1	$100,000	$22,500	New Jersey	1	$100,000	$22,500
Colorado	1	50,000	11,250	New York	2	200,000	67,500
Georgia	1	56,000	12,600	Ohio	2	160,000	137,700
Illinois	4	325,000	118,125	Pennsylvania	1	150,000	36,000
Indiana	1	50,000	11,250	South Carolina	1	75,000	17,100
Iowa	1	50,000	18,000	South Dakota	1	50,000	11,250
Kansas	1	50,000	45,000	Tennessee	2	310,000	58,500
Kentucky	2	430,000	225,000	Texas	2	310,000	90,000
Louisiana	1	300,000	125,000	Vermont	1	100,000	5,400
Maine	2	205,000	58,500	Wisconsin	1	100,000	22,500
Massachusetts	6	1,450,000	373,500	Wyoming	1	100,000	22,500
Michigan	1	50,000	11,250				
Minnesota	2	125,000	29,250	Total	40	5,046,000	1,585,925
Montana	1	150,000	33,750				

STATEMENT SHOWING THE NATIONAL BANKS, THE CORPORATE EXISTENCE OF WHICH WILL EXPIRE DURING THE YEAR ENDING OCTOBER 31, 1894, WITH THE DATE OF EXPIRATION, CAPITAL, AND AMOUNT OF UNITED STATES BONDS AND CIRCULATING NOTES.

Charter number.	Title and location.	State.	Date of expiration.	Capital.	Bonds.	Circulation.
			1893.			
2132	The Kellogg National Bank, Green Bay	Wis ..	Dec. 23	$100,000	$25,000	$22,500
			1894.			
2138	The Rochester National Bank, Rochester...	N. H..	Feb. 16	50,000	12,500	11,250
2135	The Commercial National Bank of Charlotte.	N.C ..	Feb. 16	175,000	50,000	45,000
2137	The National Bank of Boyertown	Pa	Feb. 19	100,000	100,000	90,000
2172	The Athol National Bank, Athol	Mass .	Mar. 6	100,000	100,000	90,000
2141	The National Bank of Pontiac.............	Ill	Mar. 25	50,100	12,500	11,250
2143	The First National Bank of Hancock	Mich .	Apr. 6	200,000	50,000	45,000
2152	The Home National Bank of Brockton	Mass .	Apr. 8	200,000	150,000	135,000
2142	The National Bank of Schwenksville.......	Pa....	Apr. 14	100,000	25,000	22,500
2153	The Safety Fund National Bank of Fitchburg.	Mass .	Apr. 17	200,000	200,000	180,000
2144	The People's National Bank of Martinsburg.	W.Va.	Apr. 30	75,000	18,750	16,875
2146	The First National Bank of East Liverpool.	Ohio ..	...do	50,000	50,000	45,000
2145	The Second National Bank of Bay City	Mich .	May 5	250,000	200,000	180,000
2151	The Wilber National Bank of Oneonta.....	N. Y ..	May 12	100,000	100,000	90,000
2147	The Mattoon National Bank, Mattoon......	Ill	May 14	60,000	15,000	13,500
2148	The Citizens' National Bank of Winchester.	Ky ...	May 16	175,000	50,000	45,000
2150	The Marion National Bank of Lebanon	Ky ...	May 25	150,000	40,000	36,000
2174	The First National Bank of Florida, at Jacksonville.	Fla ...	May 26	50,000	50,000	45,000
2156	The First National Bank of Farmer City...	Ill	May 30	50,000	12,500	11,250
2154	The First National Bank of Belleville......	Ill	June 10	100,000	50,000	45,000
2155	The People's National Bank of Rock Island.	Ill	June 17	100,000	50,000	45,000
2179	The First National Bank of Colorado Springs.	Colo ..	June 24	100,000	25,000	22,500
2158	The First National Bank of San Jose	Cal ...	July 11	500,000	50,000	45,000
2160	The National Exchange Bank of Steubenville.	Ohio ..	July 17	100,000	100,000	90,000
2159	The First National Bank of Kasson	Minn .	July 22	50,000	13,000	11,700
2161	The Merchants' National Bank of Louisville	Ky	...do	500,000	50,000	44,950
2165	The Farmers' National Bank of Princeton..	Ill	July 24	110,000	27,500	24,750
2184	The First National Bank of La Grange	Ind ...	July 30	65,000	25,000	22,500
2187	The People's National Bank of Independence.	Iowa..	...do	75,000	20,000	18,000
2168	The First National Bank of Jackson........	Tenn .	July 31	100,000	25,000	22,500
2164	The Citizens' National Bank of Louisville..	Ky ...	Aug. 1	500,000	50,000	45,000
2175	The First National Bank of Fairfield	Me ...	...do	50,000	15,000	13,500
2183	The First National Bank of Crown Point...	Ind ...	Aug. 4	50,000	20,000	18,000
2166	The Second National Bank of New Albany.	Ind ...	Aug. 6	100,000	25,000	22,500
2171	The Third National Bank of Louisville	Ky	...do	400,000	50,000	45,000
2180	The People's National Bank of Princeton...	Ind ...	Aug. 11	75,000	25,000	22,500
2181	The Centerville National Bank of Thurman	Ohio .	Aug. 13	50,000	45,000	40,500
2186	The Citizens' National Bank of Romeo	Mich .	Aug. 19	100,000	25,000	22,500
2176	The Union National Bank of Streator.......	Ill	Aug. 24	100,000	25,000	22,500
2189	The First National Bank of Waco	Tex ...	Sept. 7	500,000	50,000	45,000
2185	The Mount Sterling National Bank, Mount Sterling.	Ky ...	Sept. 8	100,000	25,000	22,500
2188	The Citizens' National Bank of Evansville .	Ind ...	Sept. 12	200,000	* 50,000	45,000
2207	The Boonville National Bank, Boonville....	Ind ...	Sept. 17	50,000	50,000	45,000
2193	The First National Bank of Petaluma	Cal ...	Sept. 25	200,000	50,000	45,000
2203	The First National Bank of New Lisbon....	Ohio .	Sept. 26	50,000	12,500	11,250
2204	The First National Bank of Arcola..........	Ill	Sept. 28	50,000	12,500	11,250
2212	The Oakland National Bank, Oakland......	Ill	Oct. 15	53,000	13,250	11,925
2205	The Second National Bank of Monmouth ...	Ill	Oct. 20	75,000	20,000	18,000
2221	The National Bank of McMinnville	Tenn .	Oct. 30	70,000	20,000	18,000
	Total		....	6,708,000	2,280,000	2,006,950

STATEMENT GIVING TITLES, CAPITAL, AND CIRCULATION ISSUED, REDEEMED, AND OUTSTANDING, OF NATIONAL BANKS WHICH SUSPENDED BUSINESS AND WERE PLACED IN THE HANDS OF A RECEIVER DURING THE YEAR ENDED OCTOBER 31, 1893; ALSO SIMILAR INFORMATION WITH RESPECT TO SEVEN BANKS IN THE HANDS OF EXAMINERS.

Name and location of bank.	Date of authority to commence business.	Date of suspension.	Capital stock.	Issued.	Redeemed.	Outstanding.
Newton National Bank. Newton, Kans.	Jan. 28, 1890	Dec. 15, 1892	$100,000	$48,740	$17,630	$31,110
First National Bank, Del Norte, Colo..	Mar. 18, 1890	Dec. 19, 1892	50,000	11,250	....	11,250
Bankers' and Merchants' National Bank, Dallas, Texas	Jan. 21, 1890	Jan. 17, 1893	500,000	44,600	10,560	33,440
Capital National Bank, Lincoln, Nebr.	June 29, 1883	Jan. 21, 1893	300,000	43,700	....	43,700
First National Bank, Little Rock, Ark.	Apr. 12, 1866	Feb. 1, 1893	500,000	63,495	14,631	48,864
Alabama National Bank, Mobile, Ala.	May 13, 1871	Mar. 14, 1893	150,000	42,800	800	42,000
Commercial National Bank, Nashville, Tenn	July 22, 1884	Mar. 25, 1893	500,000	45,000	11,700	33,300
First National Bank, Ponca, Nebr....	Jan. 28, 1887	Apr. 27, 1893	50,000	11,250	....	11,250
Second National Bank, Columbia, Tenn.	Oct. 3, 1881	Apr. 28, 1893	100,000	22,500	....	22,500
Chemical National Bank, Chicago, Ill.	Dec. 15, 1891	May 9, 1893	1,000,000	45,000	....	45,000
Columbia National Bank, Chicago, Ill.	Apr. 23, 1887	May 11, 1893	1,000,000	45,000	....	45,000
First National Bank, Cedar Falls, Iowa.	Sept. 1, 1874	May 16, 1893	50,000	11,250	....	11,250
First National Bank, Brunswick, Ga..	Feb. 2, 1884	May 18, 1893	200,000	44,000	....	44,000
Oglethorpe National Bank, Brunswick, Ga	July 16, 1887	....do	150,000	32,900	....	32,900
Evanston National Bank, Evanston, Ill.	June 29, 1892	....do	100,000	22,500	....	22,500
National Bank of Deposit. New York, N. Y.	Aug. 5, 1887	May 22, 1893	300,000	45,000	....	45,000
Elmira National Bank, Elmira, N. Y..	Aug. 30, 1889	May 23, 1893	200,000	43,000	4,460	38,510
First National Bank, Brady, Texas....	Jan. 7, 1890	May 26, 1893	50,000	10,800	....	10,800
National Bank of North Dakota, Fargo, N. Dak	Mar. 12, 1890	May 29, 1893	250,000	44,250	....	44,250
First National Bank, Lakota, N. Dak.	Oct. 23, 1889	....do	50,000	11,250	....	11,250
Gulf National Bank, Tampa, Fla......	Dec. 2, 1890	....do	50,000	11,250	....	11,250
Merchants' National Bank, Tacoma, Wash	May 2, 1884	June 1,1893	250,000	45,000	7,980	37,020
Citizens' National Bank. Spokane Falls, Wash	Apr. 8, 1890	June 6, 1893	150,000	33,000	....	33,000
Citizens' National Bank, Hillsboro, Ohio	Sept. 4, 1872	June 8, 1893	100,000	24,550	....	24,550
First National Bank, Arkansas City, Kans	June 30, 1885	June 15, 1893	125,000	27,520	....	27,520
City National Bank, Brownwood, Texas	June 17, 1890	June 16, 1893	150,000	33,750	....	33,750
Linn County National Bank, Albany, Oregon	May 31, 1890	June 19, 1893	100,000	21,700	....	21,700
Consolidated National Bank, San Diego, Cal	Sept. 22, 1883	June 21, 1893	250,000	55,300	....	55,300
City National Bank, Greenville, Mich.	Aug. 28, 1884	June 22, 1893	50,000	11,250	....	11,250
First National Bank. Whatcom, Wash.	Aug. 26, 1889	....do	50,000	11,250	....	11,250
Columbia National Bank, New Whatcom, Wash	June 28, 1890	June 23, 1893	100,000	22,500	....	22,500
First National Bank, Port Angeles, Wash	May 10, 1890	June 26, 1893	50,000	10,750	....	10,750
Nebraska National Bank, Beatrice, Nebr	Dec. 21, 1889	June 30, 1893	100,000	21,780	....	21,780
First National Bank, Philipsburg, Mont	Dec. 5, 1891	July 1, 1893	50,000	11,250	....	11,250
First National Bank, Ouray, Colo. a ..	Sept. 2, 1889	....do	50,000	11,250	....	11,250
Albuquerque National Bank, Albuquerque, N. Mex	July 14, 1884	July 3, 1893	175,000	45,000	850	44,150
Puget Sound National Bank, Everett, Wash. a	Sept. 23, 1892	July 5, 1893	50,000	11,250	....	11,250
First National Bank, Hot Springs, S. Dak	July 15, 1890	July 7, 1893	50,000	11,250	....	11,250
Livingston National Bank, Livingston, Mont	Sept. 11, 1889	....do	50,000	10,750	....	10,750
Northern National Bank, Big Rapids, Mich	June 5, 1871	July 8, 1893	100,000	33,250	....	33,250
Lloyds National Bank, Jamestown, N. Dak	May 4, 1891	July 10, 1893	100,000	22,500	....	22,500
First National Bank. Starkville, Miss.	Apr. 30, 1887	July 14, 1893	60,000	13,500	....	13,500
First National Bank, Cedartown, Ga...	July 16, 1889	July 17, 1893	75,000	16,370	....	16,370
Commercial National Bank, Denver, Colo	Sept. 6, 1889	July 18, 1893	250,000	45,000	....	45,000
Bozeman National Bank, Bozeman, Mont. b	Oct. 23, 1882	July 19, 1893	50,000	11,250	....	11,250
First National Bank, Vernon, Tex	May 13, 1889	July 22, 1893	100,000	22,500	1,170	21,330
State National Bank, Knoxville, Tenn	Aug. 28, 1889	....do	100,000	21,800	....	21,800
First National Bank, Orlando, Fla	Mar. 16, 1886	July 24, 1893	150,000	33,750	....	33,750

a Was in hands of receiver, but resumed prior to October 31.
b Was in hands of receiver, but resumed subsequent to October 31.

STATEMENT GIVING TITLES OF NATIONAL BANKS WHICH SUSPENDED BUSINESS AND WERE PLACED IN THE HANDS OF A RECEIVER, ETC.—Continued.

Name and location of bank.	Date of authority to commence business.	Date of suspension.	Capital stock.	Circulation.		
				Issued.	Redeemed.	Outstanding.
Merchants' National Bank, Great Falls, Mont	Oct. 7, 1890	July 24, 1893	$100,000	$22,500	....	$22,500
Tacoma National Bank, Tacoma, Wash. a	Apr. 13, 1883	....do	200,000	45,000	....	45,000
National Bank of the Commonwealth, Manchester, N. H	Feb. 9, 1892	July 25, 1893	200,000	67,500	....	67,500
Indianapolis National Bank, Indianapolis, Ind	Nov. 21, 1864	....do	300,000	57,212	....	57,210
First National Bank, Spokane, Wash. b.	Oct. 24, 1882	July 26, 1893	250,000	45,000	....	45,000
First National Bank, Middlesboro, Ky .	Jan. 8, 1890	July 27, 1893	50,000	11,250	....	11,252
First National Bank, Helena, Mont. c ..	Apr. 5, 1866	....do	500,000	45,000	....	45,000
Montana National Bank, Helena, Mont.	Nov. 11, 1882	....do	500,000	45,000	....	45,000
National Granite State Bank, Exeter, N. H	May 15, 1865	....do	50,000	41,137	$760	40,377
Chamberlain National Bank, Chamberlain, S. Dak	Apr. 8, 1890	July 28. 1893	50,000	11,250	....	11,250
First National Bank, Great Falls, Mont	July 1, 1886	....do	250,000	45,000	....	45,000
First National Bank, Kankakee, Ill. d.	Feb. 20, 1871	July 29, 1893	50,000	11,250	....	11,250
Stock Growers' National Bank, Miles City, Mont	Dec. 20, 1884	....do	75,000	17,100	....	17,100
Bellingham Bay National Bank, New Whatcom, Wash. c	Feb. 7, 1889	July 31, 1893	60,000	13,500	....	13,500
El Paso National Bank, of Texas, El Paso, Tex	Dec. 22. 1886	Aug. 1, 1893	150,000	33,750	....	33,750
Texas National Bank, San Antonio, Tex	Jan. 31, 1885	Aug. 4, 1893	100,000	22,500	....	22,500
Citizens' National Bank, Muncie, Ind. d.	Mar. 15, 1875	....do	200,000	45,000	....	45,000
First National Bank, Marion, Kans ...	July 28, 1883	Aug. 16, 1893	75,000	21,900	....	21,900
National Bank of South Pennsylvania, Hyndman, Pa. a	June 2, 1889	Aug. 17, 1893	50,000	11,250	....	11,250
Washington National Bank, Tacoma, Wash	Apr. 23, 1889	Aug. 24, 1893	100,000	43,500	....	43,500
Port Townsend National Bank, Port Townsend, Wash	Apr. 18, 1890	Sept. 18, 1893	100,000	22,500	....	22,500
First National Bank, North Manchester, Ind	Mar. 17, 1883	Oct. 4. 1893	50,000	27,000	....	27,000
First National Bank, Sundance, Wyo.	June 16, 1890	....do	50,000	11,250	....	11,250
Hutchinson National Bank, Hutchinson, Kans. b	May 29, 1884	Oct. 18, 1893	100,000	22,500	....	22,500
Socorro National Bank, Socorro, N. Mex. a	May 26, 1891	Oct. 19, 1893	50,000	11,250	....	11,250
First National Bank, Dayton, Tenn ...	July 10, 1890	Oct. 21, 1893	50,000	11,250	....	11,250

a Was in hands of examiner, but resumed subsequent to October 31.
b Placed in hands of receiver, subsequent to October 31.
c In hands of examiner.
d Was in hands of receiver, but resumed subsequent to October 31.

STATEMENT GIVING TITLES OF NATIONAL BANKS WHICH WENT INTO VOLUNTARY LIQUIDATION DURING THE YEAR ENDED OCTOBER 31, 1893, WITH DATE OF AUTHORITY TO COMMENCE BUSINESS, DATE OF LIQUIDATION, CAPITAL, AND CIRCULATION ISSUED, REDEEMED, AND OUTSTANDING.

Name and location of bank.	Date of authority to commence business.	Date of closing.	Capital stock.	Circulation.		
				Issued.	Redeemed.	Outstanding.
First National Bank, South Sioux City, Nebr.	Apr. 22, 1891	Oct. 27, 1892	$50,000	$10,250	$2,150	$8,100
Continental National Bank, Kansas City, Mo	Aug. 2, 1892	Nov. 11, 1892	200,000	44,500	7,550	36,956
First National Bank, Clyde, Kans..	Jan. 31, 1884	Nov. 15, 1892	50,000	10,750	3,270	7,480
Eugene National Bank, Eugene City, Oregon	Mar. 8, 1889	Nov. 26, 1892	50,000	11,250	3,530	7,720
First National Bank, Batesville, Ohio	Jan. 18, 1875	Dec. 1, 1892	60,000	13,500	3,310	10,190
Commercial National Bank, Sioux City, Iowa	Sept. 16, 1891	...do	150,000	33,750	13,650	20,100
State National Bank, Lincoln, Nebr.	Nov. 16, 1871	Dec. 3, 1892	200,000	45,000	17,225	27,775
Woodson National Bank, Yates Center, Kans	Jan. 14, 1884	Dec. 5, 1892	50,000	10,750	2,010	8,740
First National Bank, Pontiac, Mich	Jan. 3, 1882	Dec. 31, 1892	100,000	21,750	18,213	3,537
First National Bank, Castle, Mont.	May 22, 1891	Jan. 4, 1893	65,000	14,020	2,960	11,060
National Pemberton Bank, Lawrence, Mass.	Apr. 24, 1865	Jan. 10, 1893	150,000	143,010	38,920	104,000
First National Bank, Lorain, Ohio.	Feb. 6, 1882	...do	75,000	16,095	2,210	13,885
Finney County National Bank, Garden City, Kans.	June 20, 1888	Jan. 12, 1893	50,000	10,750	1,120	9,630
Lumberman's National Bank, Muskegon, Mich	Feb. 3, 1873	Jan. 16, 1893	100,000	22,500	5,320	17,180
Covington City National Bank, Covington, Ky.	Aug. 10, 1871	Feb. 1, 1893	500,000	225,000	41,970	183,030
Phoenix National Bank, Medina, Ohio	Mar. 10, 1873	Feb. 10, 1893	75,000	17,100	3,237	13,863
Merchants' National Bank, Macon, Ga	June 29, 1887	Feb. 14, 1893	100,000	21,800	6,170	15,630
Ætna National Bank, Kansas City, Mo	Mar. 10, 1890	Mar. 9, 1893	250,000	44,550	6,350	38,200
Citizens' National Bank, Orlando, Fla	Oct. 12, 1887	Mar. 22, 1893	100,000	21,880	3,420	18,460
First National Bank, Lexington, Ill	Nov. 23, 1882	Apr. 1, 1893	50,000	16,410	2,660	13,750
First National Bank, Ida Grove, Iowa	Oct. 10, 1888	May 1, 1893	150,000	32,650	2,680	29,970
First National Bank, Burnet, Tex.	July 18, 1883	May 22, 1893	75,000	16,150	1,150	15,000
First National Bank, Springfield, Mo	Aug. 18, 1870	...do	50,000	11,250	1,385	9,865
Southern National Bank, New Orleans, La.	June 6, 1890	May 25, 1893	500,000	45,000	6,700	38,300
Decatur National Bank, Decatur, Ill	Aug. 12, 1873	May 31, 1893	100,000	22,500	2,350	20,150
First National Bank, Chelsea, Vt..	July 19, 1873	June 10, 1893	50,000	11,250		11,250
First National Bank, Santa Monica, Cal	Feb. 16, 1888	...do	50,000	10,250	890	9,360
Lake National Bank, Wolfboro N. H.	July 26, 1865	June 29, 1893	50,000	29,360	1,978	27,382
Farmers' National Bank, Owatonna, Minn	July 24, 1873	June 30, 1893	75,000	17,100	1,420	15,680
First National Bank, Wa Keeney, Kans.	Aug. 18, 1887	...do	50,000	10,290	110	10,180
Fourth National Bank, Chattanooga, Tenn	June 28, 1889	July 6, 1893	150,000	44,200	1,540	42,660
Farmers and Merchants' National Bank, Rockwall, Tex.	Mar. 30, 1892	July 11, 1893	50,000	11,250	1,620	9,030
North Texas National Bank, Dallas, Tex.	Jan. 6, 1888	July 13, 1893	1,000,000	45,000	2,100	42,900
Hoquiam National Bank, Hoquiam, Wash.	Aug. 8, 1890	July 18, 1893	50,000	11,250	500	10,750
Gallatin Valley National Bank, Bozeman, Mont	Nov. 14, 1883	July 24, 1893	100,000	22,000	1,170	20,830
Gate City National Bank, Atlanta, Ga	May 3, 1879	July 25, 1893	250,000	44,000	10,570	33,430
First National Bank, Big Timber, Mont	June 29, 1891	July 27, 1893	50,000	10,750	510	10,240
Orono National Bank, Orono, Me	May 13, 1865	July 29, 1893	50,000	13,720	1,230	12,490
Central National Bank, Dallas, Tex.	Sept. 25, 1889	Aug. 3, 1893	150,000	33,750	1,650	32,100
Merchants' National Bank, Fort Worth, Tex	Feb. 1, 1887	Aug. 15, 1893	250,000	45,000		45,000
Dillon National Bank, Dillon, Mont	May 2, 1884	Aug. 24, 1893	50,000	10,750		10,750

STATEMENT GIVING TITLES OF NATIONAL BANKS WHICH WENT INTO VOLUNTARY
LIQUIDATION DURING THE YEAR ENDED OCTOBER 31, 1893, ETC.—Continued.

Name and location of bank.	Date of authority to commence business.	Date of closing.	Capital stock.	Circulation.		
				Issued.	Re. deemed.	Outstanding.
Farmers' National Bank, Constantine, Mich	Dec. 4, 1874	Aug. 28, 1893	$50,000	$11,250	$1,050	$10,200
First National Bank, Mankato, Kans	July 6, 1887	Sept. 12, 1893	60,000	13,500	1,190	12,310
Gray National Bank, Middletown Springs, Vt	Apr. 9, 1884	Sept. 15, 1893	50,000	11,250	900	10,350
Frankfort National Bank, Frankfort, Ky	Aug. 13, 1889	Sept. 21, 1893	100,000	22,500	....	22,500
First National Bank, Slaughter, Wash	Nov. 3, 1890	Oct. 25, 1893	50,000	11,250	....	11,250
Total			6,085,000			

STATEMENT GIVING TITLES OF NATIONAL BANKS WHICH SUSPENDED DURING THE
YEAR ENDED OCTOBER 31, 1893, AND RESUMED BUSINESS PRIOR TO OCTOBER
31, WITH CAPITAL, DATE OF SUSPENSION, AND DATE OF RESUMPTION.

Name and location.	Capital.	Date of suspension.	Authorized to resume.
		1892.	1893.
The Black Hills National Bank, Rapid City, S. Dak	$125,000	Dec. 13	Feb. 17
		1893.	
The Gate City National Bank, Atlanta, Ga	250,000	Feb. 21	July 3
The Capital National Bank, Indianapolis, Ind	300,000	May 11	June 19
The Washington National Bank, Spokane Falls, Wash	250,000	June 6	July 6
The First National Bank, Palouse City, Wash	75,000	June 6	June 9
The American National Bank, Omaha, Nebr	200,000	June 13	Sept. 7
The First National Bank, Grundy Center, Iowa	50,000	June 16	Sept. 1
The Southern California National Bank, Los Angeles, Cal	200,000	June 21	July 10
The First National Bank, Los Angeles, Cal	200,000	June 21	July 14
The First National Bank, San Diego, Cal	300,000	June 21	July 5
The First National Bank, Santa Ana, Cal	150,000	June 22	July 21
The First National Bank, Kendallville, Ind	50,000	June 22	Aug. 1
The First National Bank, San Bernardino, Cal	100,000	June 23	July 21
The Second National Bank, Ashland, Ky	50,000	June 27	July 14
The First National Bank, Rico, Colo	50,000	June 30	Aug. 16
The First National Bank, Provo, Utah	50,000	June 30	Sept. 11
The National Bank of Commerce, Provo City, Utah	50,000	July 1	July 11
The First National Bank, Ouray, Colo	50,000	July 1	Oct. 17
The First National Bank, Cisco, Tex	50,000	July 3	July 25
The American National Bank, Leadville, Colo	100,000	July 3	Aug. 17
The Central National Bank, Pueblo, Colo	50,000	July 5	Aug. 23
The American National Bank, Pueblo, Colo	250,000	July 5	Sept. 4
The Puget Sound National Bank, Everett, Wash	50,000	July 5	Oct. 23
The National Bank of Ashland, Nebr	100,000	July 5	Aug. 31
The First National Bank, Winston, N. C	200,000	July 5	Sept. 18
The Western National Bank, Pueblo, Colo	50,000	July 5	Sept. 11
The Commercial National Bank, Ogden, Utah	150,000	July 8	Sept. 7
The First National Bank, Cherryvale, Kans	50,000	July 14	Sept. 1
The National Bank of Kansas City, Kansas City, Mo	1,000,000	July 14	Oct. 4
The Missouri National Bank, Kansas City, Mo	250,000	July 17	July 29
The Union National Bank, Denver, Colo	1,000,000	July 17	Aug. 21
The First National Bank, Fort Scott, Kans	300,000	July 18	Aug. 16
The National Bank of Commerce, Denver, Colo	500,000	July 18	Aug. 17
The State National Bank, Denver, Colo	300,000	July 19	Aug. 29
The German National Bank, Denver, Colo	200,000	July 19	Aug. 29
The People's National Bank, Denver, Colo	600,000	July 19	Aug. 21
The Oklahoma National Bank, Oklahoma City, Okla	50,000	July 19	Sept. 22
The First National Bank, Harrisonville, Mo	50,000	July 20	Sept. 1
The First National Bank, Cañon City, Colo	50,000	July 20	Aug. 29
The First National Bank, Anthony, Kans	50,000	July 20	Aug. 18
The Greeley National Bank, Greeley, Colo	50,000	July 20	Aug. 14
The First National Bank, Grand Junction, Colo	50,000	July 20	Aug. 30
The First National Bank, Cheyenne, Wyo	200,000	July 20	Sept. 9
The Farmers' National Bank, Henrietta, Texas	50,000	July 21	Aug. 5
The State National Bank, Vernon, Tex	100,000	July 21	Aug. 28
The First National Bank, Russell, Kans	80,000	July 22	Sept. 14
The Milwaukee National Bank of Wisconsin, Milwaukee, Wis	250,000	July 22	Sept. 25
The Kentucky National Bank, Louisville, Ky	1,000,000	July 22	Oct. 2
The Louisville City National Bank, Louisville, Ky	400,000	July 24	Aug. 29
The Merchants' National Bank, Louisville, Ky	500,000	July 25	Aug. 29
The Fourth National Bank, Louisville, Ky	300,000	July 25	Aug. 23
The Farmers' National Bank, Findlay, Ohio	80,000	July 25	Oct. 2
The Oregon National Bank, Portland, Oregon	200,000	July 27	Sept. 9

STATEMENT GIVING TITLES OF NATIONAL BANKS WHICH SUSPENDED DURING THE YEAR ENDED OCTOBER 31, 1893, ETC.—Continued.

Name and location.	Capital.	Date of suspension.	Authorized to resume.
		1893.	1893.
The Ellensburg National Bank, Ellensburg, Wash	$50,000	July 27	Oct. 21
The Commercial National Bank, Portland, Oregon	250,000	July 29	Sept. 26
The Ainsworth National Bank, Portland, Oregon	100,000	July 29	Sept. 15
The First National Bank, Ashland, Wis	125,000	July 31	Aug. 29
The National Park Bank, Livingston, Mont	100,000	July 31	Sept. 25
The First National Bank, East Portland, Oregon	100,000	July 31	Sept. 16
The First National Bank, The Dalles, Oregon	50,000	July 31	Aug. 25
The First National Bank, Birmingham, Ala	250,000	Aug. 2	Oct. 9
The Waupaca County National Bank, Waupaca, Wis	50,000	Aug. 2	Aug. 28
The First National Bank, Hammond, Ind	50,000	Aug. 4	Sept. 25
The National German-American Bank, St. Paul, Minn	2,000,000	Aug. 4	Oct. 30
The First National Bank, Platteville, Wis	50,000	Aug. 4	Aug. 29
The First National Bank, Mankato, Minn	150,000	Aug. 4	Sept. 7
The National Citizens' Bank, Mankato, Minn	100,000	Aug. 4	Sept. 7
The Mankato National Bank, Mankato, Minn	100,000	Aug. 5	Sept. 7
The National Bank of Sturgis, Mich	65,000	Aug. 7	Sept. 7
The First National Bank, White Sulphur Springs, Mont	200,000	Aug. 5	Oct. 11
The First National Bank, Nashville, Tenn	1,000,000	Aug. 9	Sept. 11
The Union National Bank, Rochester, Minn	50,000	Aug. 9	Oct. 2
The American National Bank, Nashville, Tenn	1,000,000	Aug. 10	Sept. 1
The First National Bank, Decatur, Ala	100,000	Aug. 10	Sept. 18
The Waxahachie National Bank, Waxahachie, Tex	100,000	Aug. 11	Aug. 19
The Citizens' National Bank, Attica, Ind	50,000	Aug. 12	Aug. 21
The First National Bank, Gadsden, Ala	50,000	Aug. 12	Sept. 12
The Union National Bank, Racine, Wis	150,000	Aug. 16	Oct. 23
The First National Bank, Dubuque, Iowa	200,000	Aug. 17	Aug. 30
The People's National Bank, Winston, N. C.	100,000	Aug. 18	Sept. 21
The First National Bank, Le Mars, Iowa	100,000	Aug. 18	Sept. 11
The Le Mars National Bank, Le Mars, Iowa	100,000	Aug. 18	Sept. 16
The First National Bank, San Marcos, Tex	80,000	Aug. 21	Aug. 28
The First National Bank, Lockhart, Tex	50,000	Aug. 22	Aug. 28
The First National Bank, Hawarden, Iowa	75,000	Aug. 24	Sept. 25
The First National Bank, York, Nebr	50,000	Aug. 28	Oct. 21
The Hutchinson National Bank, Hutchinson, Kans	100,000	July 18	Aug. 7
Total	18,205,000		

STATEMENT GIVING TITLES, CAPITAL, AND DATE OF SUSPENSION, OF NATIONAL BANKS WHICH SUSPENDED DURING THE YEAR ENDED OCTOBER 31, 1893, AND WERE PLACED IN THE HANDS OF NATIONAL BANK EXAMINERS, PENDING RESUMPTION OF BUSINESS OR THE APPOINTMENT OF A RECEIVER.

Name and Location.	Capital.	Date of suspension.
The Tacoma National Bank, Tacoma, Wash	$200,000	July 24, 1893
The First National Bank, Spokane, Wash	250,000	July 26, 1893
The First National Bank, Helena, Mont	500,000	July 27, 1893
The Bellingham Bay National Bank, New Whatcom, Wash	60,000	July 31, 1893
The National Bank of South Pennsylvania, Hyndman, Pa	50,000	Aug. 27, 1893
The Hutchinson National Bank, Hutchinson, Kans	100,000	Oct. 18, 1893
The Socorro National Bank, Socorro, New Mex	50,000	Oct. 19, 1893

STATEMENT SHOWING BY STATES AND GEOGRAPHICAL DIVISIONS THE NUMBER AND CAPITAL STOCK OF NATIONAL BANKS WHICH SUSPENDED DURING THE YEAR ENDED OCTOBER 31, 1893, TOGETHER WITH THE NUMBER AND CAPITAL OF THOSE WHICH RESUMED, FAILED, AND WERE PLACED IN CHARGE OF EXAMINERS.

States and Territories.	Suspensions.		Resumptions.		Failures.		In charge of examiners.	
	No.	Capital.	No.	Capital.	No.	Capital.	No.	Capital.
New Hampshire — Total Eastern States	2	$250,000	....	....	2	$250,000	....	....
New York	2	500,000	....	....	2	500,000	....	....
Pennsylvania	1	50,000	....	....	..	....	1	$50,000
Total Middle States	3	550,000	....	....	2	500,000	1	50,000
North Carolina	2	300,000	2	$300,000	..	....	....	....
Georgia	4	675,000	1	250,000	3	425,000	....	....
Florida	2	200,000	....	....	2	200,000	....	....
Alabama	4	550,000	3	400,000	1	150,000	....	....
Mississippi	1	60,000	....	....	1	60,000	....	....
Texas	12	1,480,000	6	430,000	6	1,050,000	....	....
Arkansas	1	500,000	....	....	1	500,000	....	....
Kentucky	6	2,300,000	5	2,250,000	1	50,000	....	....
Tennessee	6	2,750,000	2	2,000,000	4	750,000	....	....
Total Southern States	38	8,815,000	19	5,630,000	19	3,185,000	....	....
Missouri	3	1,300,000	3	1,300,000	..	....	....	....
Ohio	2	180,000	1	80,000	1	100,000	....	....
Indiana	7	1,000,000	4	450,000	3	530,000	....	....
Illinois	4	2,150,000	....	....	4	2,150,000	....	....
Michigan	3	215,000	1	65,000	2	150,000	....	....
Wisconsin	5	625,000	5	625,000	..	....	....	....
Iowa	6	575,000	5	525,000	1	50,000	....	....
Minnesota	5	2,400,000	5	2,400,000	..	....	....	....
Kansas	8	880,000	4	480,000	3	300,000	1	100,000
Nebraska	6	800,000	3	350,000	3	450,000	....	....
Total Western States	49	10,125,000	31	6,275,000	17	3,750,000	1	100,000
Oregon	6	800,000	5	700,000	1	100,000	....	....
Colorado	16	3,600,000	14	3,300,000	2	300,000	....	....
Utah	3	250,000	3	230,000	..	....	....	....
Montana	10	1,875,000	2	300,000	7	1,075,000	1	500,000
Wyoming	2	250,000	1	200,000	1	50,000	....	....
New Mexico	2	225,000	....	....	1	175,000	1	50,000
North Dakota	3	400,000	....	....	3	400,000	....	....
South Dakota	3	225,000	1	125,000	2	100,000	....	....
Washington	14	1,735,000	4	425,000	7	800,000	3	510,000
California	6	1,200,000	5	950,000	1	250,000	....	....
Oklahoma Territory	1	50,000	1	50,000	..	....	....	....
Total Pacific States and Territories	66	10,610,000	36	6,300,000	25	3,250,000	5	1,060,000
Total United States	158	30,350,000	86	18,205,000	65	10,935,000	7	1,210,000

STATEMENT SHOWING THE AMOUNT OF AUTHORIZED CAPITAL STOCK OF THE NATIONAL BANKS ON THE FIRST DAY OF EACH MONTH FROM JANUARY 1, 1872, TO NOVEMBER 1, 1895, THE AMOUNT OF UNITED STATES BONDS ON DEPOSIT TO SECURE CIRCULATION, THE AMOUNT OF CIRCULATION SECURED BY THE BONDS ON DEPOSIT, THE AMOUNT OF LAWFUL MONEY TO REDEEM CIRCULATION, AND THE TOTAL AMOUNT OF NATIONAL-BANK NOTES OUTSTANDING, INCLUDING NOTES OF NATIONAL GOLD BANKS.

Date.	Authorized capital stock.	U. S. bonds on deposit to secure circulation.	Circulation secured by U. S. bonds.	Lawful money on deposit to redeem circulation.	Total national-bank notes outstanding.
1872.					
January	$409,408,976	$370,240,500	$328,465,431	$2,976,154	$331,441,585
February	470,457,651	371,558,900	330,253,550	3,034,020	334,187,579
March	471,822,651	373,764,450	332,094,399	4,205,720	336,300,119
April	472,656,351	374,637,450	333,556,529	4,190,113	337,755,642
May	475,458,651	376,732,850	334,521,855	3,566,059	338,087,914
June	477,012,051	378,341,200	335,644,365	3,288,259	338,932,624
July	479,852,051	380,440,700	337,664,795	3,230,159	340,903,954
August	482,906,851	382,552,200	339,094,675	3,174,359	342,269,034
September	484,223,351	381,918,200	340,649,060	2,970,604	343,620,654
October	486,106,851	383,977,200	342,227,690	3,105,564	345,328,254
November	487,136,851	384,968,900	343,112,772	2,508,986	345,621,758
December	487,699,551	385,951,400	344,097,112	2,404,876	346,501,988
1873.					
January	487,781,551	386,355,300	344,582,812	2,484,086	347,066,898
February	489,380,851	386,640,800	345,358,892	2,802,141	348,251,033
March	490,480,151	387,415,100	345,507,312	2,651,951	348,159,263
April	492,898,951	388,218,350	346,164,392	2,579,189	348,743,581
May	494,428,951	388,983,800	346,834,666	2,641,964	349,476,630
June	496,480,951	389,775,000	347,185,711	2,300,703	349,486,414
July	496,496,501	390,410,550	347,267,001	1,917,603	349,184,664
August	497,921,501	390,855,250	347,802,361	2,104,498	349,966,859
September	498,801,501	391,618,450	348,715,421	2,104,498	350,819,919
October	499,111,501	392,616,000	350,173,226	2,350,896	352,524,122
November	499,232,701	392,852,100	350,412,046	2,009,096	352,421,142
December	499,533,401	393,215,900	350,692,966	1,928,796	352,621,762
1874.					
January	499,003,401	393,000,900	348,624,953	2,223,283	350,848,236
February	498,632,201	392,644,300	348,255,299	2,776,278	351,031,577
March	498,150,901	392,506,050	348,203,489	3,081,323	351,284,812
April	497,505,901	392,809,200	348,505,184	3,120,623	351,625,807
May	497,020,901	392,937,100	348,323,390	3,360,932	351,684,322
June	497,657,401	392,803,000	348,290,340	3,560,162	351,850,520
July	498,777,401	391,171,200	347,182,820	4,798,212	351,981,032
August	500,347,401	388,506,100	344,851,526	7,867,254	352,718,780
September	500,706,401	385,889,100	342,310,386	11,057,679	353,368,065
October	502,181,401	385,649,150	342,270,676	11,707,870	353,978,546
November	502,931,401	385,421,750	342,367,844	11,709,402	354,077,246
December	503,301,401	385,378,250	342,685,175	12,021,071	354,706,246
1875.					
January	503,347,901	385,128,250	342,333,837	11,794,413	354,128,250
February	503,467,901	384,174,950	341,121,249	13,152,121	351,273,370
March	503,858,521	382,076,650	338,048,494	15,300,850	354,249,344
April	505,763,300	380,661,600	337,855,479	17,593,099	355,448,578
May	506,103,801	379,506,900	336,697,831	18,349,762	355,047,593
June	508,531,283	379,126,400	336,110,532	18,344,941	354,455,473
July	509,386,283	376,314,500	334,698,341	19,709,667	354,408,008
August	510,706,283	374,891,362	333,468,611	19,440,077	353,118,688
September	510,903,171	373,056,762	323,324,225	18,535,727	351,859,952
October	511,084,471	371,489,262	331,249,470	19,300,112	350,539,582
November	511,613,765	367,549,412	327,578,260	20,638,642	348,246,902
December	510,686,765	365,836,912	326,725,728	21,095,102	347,820,830
1876.					
January	511,155,865	363,601,662	324,484,539	21,995,217	346,479,756
February	510,619,905	361,430,462	321,319,645	22,648,884	343,968,529
March	510,189,171	356,732,150	318,413,293	24,405,780	342,819,073
April	509,701,671	350,216,350	312,850,786	27,627,308	340,478,094
May	507,881,671	346,715,350	310,084,721	28,755,191	338,839,912
June	506,013,371	344,463,850	307,912,468	28,753,462	336,665,930
July	506,608,371	341,394,750	305,417,013	27,581,323	332,998,336
August	505,226,171	340,071,850	303,756,276	25,982,339	329,738,615
September	504,071,171	338,673,850	302,847,886	23,087,016	325,934,902
October	504,027,171	337,955,800	301,819,811	22,532,933	324,352,744
November	502,752,171	337,727,800	301,658,372	21,582,936	323,241,308
December	502,652,171	338,261,800	301,844,917	20,114,674	321,959,591

STATEMENT SHOWING THE AMOUNT OF AUTHORIZED CAPITAL STOCK OF THE
NATIONAL BANKS ON THE FIRST DAY OF EACH MONTH, ETC.—Continued.

Date.	Authorized capital stock.	U. S. bonds on deposit to secure circulation.	Circulation secured by U. S. bonds.	Lawful money on deposit to redeem circulation.	Total national-bank notes outstanding.
1877.					
January	501,392,171	338,191,300	302,020,242	19,575,364	321,505,606
February	497,335,071	338,885,450	302,201,132	18,160,486	320,361,618
March	496,770,571	338,866,550	302,416,700	16,728,336	319,145,036
April	494,783,571	340,537,600	303,523,225	16,146,363	319,669,588
May	493,821,771	340,732,100	304,407,450	15,386,137	319,793,587
June	493,126,271	340,415,100	304,766,940	14,329,272	319,096,212
July	487,868,771	338,713,600	303,108,350	13,940,522	317,048,872
August	487,221,771	337,761,600	302,239,212	14,426,746	316,665,958
September	486,605,271	337,684,650	302,440,152	14,246,546	316,686,698
October	486,449,271	338,002,450	302,885,797	14,438,272	317,324,069
November	486,677,771	343,048,900	305,094,140	13,113,091	318,207,231
December	486,742,771	345,130,550	308,642,795	11,988,924	320,631,719
1878.					
January	485,557,771	346,187,550	309,890,415	11,782,090	321,672,505
February	484,836,371	346,302,050	310,240,005	11,839,305	322,079,310
March	482,052,071	346,522,550	310,301,472	11,688,519	321,989,901
April	482,144,671	346,336,250	310,008,832	12,184,082	322,193,514
May	481,019,671	347,711,850	310,826,422	12,315,257	323,141,679
June	480,660,571	349,166,450	312,435,402	11,552,623	323,988,085
July	479,627,996	349,546,400	313,020,832	11,493,452	324,514,284
August	477,675,996	348,880,900	312,905,592	10,910,967	323,906,559
September	477,698,296	349,049,450	313,154,792	10,294,370	323,449,162
October	476,335,396	349,560,650	313,159,592	9,988,127	323,147,719
November	473,865,396	349,408,900	312,830,797	9,629,918	322,460,715
December	473,859,396	349,795,000	313,355,839	9,935,217	323,291,056
1879.					
January	471,609,396	349,068,000	313,218,189	10,573,485	323,791,674
February	469,995,856	348,039,200	312,725,809	11,673,060	324,399,769
March	467,778,606	350,600,400	313,091,639	12,354,531	326,046,170
April	465,890,006	351,196,400	314,244,779	12,882,417	327,127,196
May	464,608,206	352,250,550	315,628,352	13,516,558	329,144,910
June	463,223,515	353,422,300	316,335,949	13,203,462	329,539,411
July	462,813,515	354,254,600	317,315,679	12,376,018	329,691,697
August	462,822,515	353,201,800	316,412,560	13,545,677	329,958,237
September	462,507,515	355,638,950	317,534,289	13,258,698	330,792,987
October	463,117,515	359,030,500	320,868,979	13,403,261	334,272,240
November	462,392,515	363,802,400	324,051,279	13,127,139	337,181,418
December	461,842,515	365,194,900	326,684,059	13,381,719	340,065,778
1880.					
January	461,557,515	367,021,000	328,773,639	13,613,697	342,387,336
February	461,715,515	364,765,900	326,785,599	16,945,310	343,730,907
March	462,407,585	362,728,050	325,032,790	18,604,197	343,636,089
April	464,177,585	363,656,050	325,425,390	18,959,687	344,385,077
May	464,507,585	363,061,650	325,519,740	19,410,910	344,930,650
June	464,915,185	362,715,050	325,301,700	19,882,033	345,183,733
July	465,205,185	361,652,050	324,242,730	20,262,697	344,505,427
August	465,915,185	361,152,050	323,886,720	20,266,967	344,153,687
September	466,267,285	361,113,450	323,903,330	20,153,448	344,056,778
October	466,245,085	359,935,450	323,056,550	20,848,363	343,904,893
November	466,500,085	359,748,050	322,798,130	21,035,977	343,834,107
December	467,639,085	359,808,550	322,206,550	21,500,091	343,706,641
1881.					
January	467,039,084	350,823,550	322,832,101	21,523,102	344,355,203
February	466,981,785	359,811,050	322,654,721	21,895,077	344,550,698
March	466,640,185	345,739,050	305,587,202	38,447,716	344,034,918
April	466,890,185	351,480,000	300,034,317	38,538,105	347,572,422
May	467,542,685	354,683,000	316,226,247	36,374,320	352,600,567
June	468,557,685	358,829,900	318,497,814	35,653,904	354,151,718
July	469,382,685	360,488,400	321,148,399	33,894,276	355,042,675
August	470,322,685	362,684,000	323,478,586	33,846,027	357,324,613
September	471,282,935	364,285,500	325,824,740	32,675,940	358,000,680
October	472,565,935	365,751,500	326,513,546	32,237,394	358,750,940
November	466,307,335	369,608,500	329,180,122	31,164,128	360,344,250
December	467,907,335	371,336,100	331,729,592	30,438,878	362,168,410
1882.					
January	470,018,135	371,692,100	332,398,922	30,023,066	362,421,988
February	472,303,135	371,270,200	331,682,622	30,913,792	362,596,414
March	473,866,240	370,602,700	331,230,311	30,713,969	361,944,280
April	475,411,240	369,900,700	331,242,702	30,383,935	361,626,637
May	478,013,940	366,350,050	327,729,622	33,340,677	361,070,290
June	482,954,940	364,079,350	323,910,522	35,955,612	359,875,334

STATEMENT SHOWING THE AMOUNT OF AUTHORIZED CAPITAL STOCK OF THR NATIONAL BANKS ON THE FIRST DAY OF EACH MONTH, ETC.—Continued.

Date.	Authorized capital stock.	U. S. bonds on deposit to secure circulation.	Circulation secured by U. S. bonds.	Lawful money on deposit to redeem circulation.	Total national-bank notes outstanding.
1882.					
July	$486,511,335	$361,212,700	$320,312,832	$38,429,202	$358,742,034
August	487,803,635	362,736,500	319,805,161	39,017,621	358,822,782
September	487,538,635	361,452,350	320,760,739	39,745,163	360,514,902
October	489,741,635	362,043,250	323,487,353	39,401,781	362,889,134
November	491,591,635	362,505,650	324,301,343	38,423,404	362,727,747
December	493,176,635	362,174,250	323,820,480	38,723,848	362,544,328
1883.					
January	492,076,635	360,531,650	322,386,120	40,265,049	362,651,169
February	491,199,635	359,567,450	321,626,353	40,540,877	362,167,230
March	498,262,135	358,163,800	320,235,601	41,084,788	361,320,389
April	498,017,135	357,201,400	319,849,816	39,945,249	359,795,065
May	500,260,135	357,339,750	319,899,521	39,368,605	359,268,126
June	505,379,135	356,588,600	319,013,856	39,150,326	358,164,182
July	507,208,135	356,596,500	319,219,806	37,565,704	356,815,510
August	510,283,135	357,298,500	319,461,846	36,310,284	355,772,130
September	513,543,135	355,674,150	318,367,216	36,222,005	354,589,221
October	515,528,135	353,308,650	316,278,066	37,064,605	353,342,671
November	516,608,135	352,877,300	316,020,326	35,993,461	352,013,787
December	516,348,135	351,174,600	314,573,106	36,385,055	350,958,161
1884.					
January	518,081,135	347,538,200	310,953,321	39,529,507	350,482,828
February	517,380,635	343,475,550	307,828,001	41,071,892	349,490,893
March	519,104,635	341,533,050	306,100,465	40,532,837	346,633,302
April	521,573,635	339,116,150	303,699,075	41,015,561	344,714,636
May	524,348,635	337,618,650	302,533,855	40,571,613	343,105,468
June	525,992,165	336,257,150	301,238,845	39,768,855	341,007,700
July	528,784,165	334,147,850	299,369,370	40,130,513	339,499,833
August	530,784,165	332,588,600	297,982,165	39,913,971	337,897,136
September	532,274,165	331,371,100	297,136,455	39,495,690	336,632,145
October	532,749,165	329,186,000	295,375,999	40,453,209	335,829,228
November	532,554,165	325,316,300	291,849,059	41,710,163	333,559,813
December	531,875,165	320,244,700	287,277,980	44,235,274	331,513,254
1885.					
January	529,910,165	318,655,050	285,496,055	43,662,568	329,158,623
February	530,380,165	317,282,600	284,127,895	42,784,663	326,912,558
March	530,590,165	315,854,500	282,772,315	41,888,596	324,660,911
April	531,151,165	315,386,850	282,336,725	39,881,941	322,218,666
May	531,241,165	315,127,450	282,434,075	38,468,630	320,902,705
June	530,830,865	313,428,700	280,831,610	38,032,217	318,863,827
July	531,540,465	312,145,200	279,528,175	39,541,757	319,069,932
August	532,328,465	310,225,150	277,826,775	39,503,567	317,330,342
September	532,749,965	309,768,050	277,371,525	39,613,802	316,985,327
October	532,034,965	309,074,550	277,149,661	40,274,772	317,424,433
November	532,877,965	308,364,550	276,304,189	39,542,979	315,847,168
December	533,447,965	307,544,250	275,821,779	41,704,029	317,525,808
1886.					
January	534,378,265	306,008,750	274,466,748	42,976,706	317,443,454
February	535,398,265	302,257,000	271,065,593	46,951,839	318,017,432
March	537,896,965	296,780,400	266,047,488	52,049,017	318,096,505
April	538,652,065	289,729,650	259,405,300	56,826,227	316,231,527
May	540,414,565	285,447,950	255,322,541	58,555,047	313,877,588
June	543,069,565	279,537,400	250,257,632	61,580,662	311,838,294
July	545,206,565	275,974,800	247,087,961	61,922,499	309,010,460
August	549,542,565	273,540,800	244,675,012	62,151,745	306,826,757
September	550,252,565	270,524,150	242,168,247	62,505,757	304,674,004
October	553,002,565	261,848,900	234,682,736	68,828,505	303,511,241
November	552,775,165	245,444,050	219,710,656	81,819,233	301,529,889
December	553,855,165	234,991,800	210,525,601	88,781,909	299,307,510
1887.					
January	555,805,165	229,438,350	205,316,106	91,455,875	296,771,981
February	557,684,165	223,926,650	200,268,346	92,806,395	293,074,741
March	559,986,665	213,619,150	191,004,726	98,039,485	289,044,211
April	561,321,665	206,938,000	185,009,551	102,114,704	287,124,255
May	564,346,665	202,446,550	181,026,016	103,979,299	285,005,315
June	571,581,665	200,939,100	179,309,020	103,051,817	282,360,891
July	574,703,665	191,906,700	171,629,341	107,588,447	279,217,788
August	578,826,215	189,445,800	169,302,430	107,150,817	276,454,277
September	581,046,215	190,096,950	169,951,385	104,313,124	274,264,509
October	582,683,715	189,017,100	169,931,680	102,962,170	272,893,850
November	583,188,715	188,828,000	169,215,067	102,826,136	272,041,203
December	584,203,715	187,147,000	167,863,819	102,019,176	269,882,995

STATEMENT SHOWING THE AMOUNT OF AUTHORIZED CAPITAL STOCK OF THE NATIONAL BANKS ON THE FIRST DAY OF EACH MONTH, ETC.—Continued.

Date.	Authorized capital stock.	U. S. bonds on deposit to secure circulation.	Circulation secured by U. S. bonds.	Lawful money on deposit to redeem circulation.	Total national-bank notes outstanding.
1888.					
January	$584,726,915	$184,444,950	$165,205,724	$103,193,154	$268,398,878
February	586,505,915	182,764,950	163,833,205	102,024,952	265,858,157
March	588,785,915	182,161,700	163,235,505	99,492,361	262,727,866
April	589,637,915	181,863,700	162,743,135	97,427,882	260,171,017
May	591,437,915	182,033,450	162,891,912	95,692,133	258,584,045
June	592,467,915	180,005,150	161,134,338	94,675,310	255,809,648
July	592,852,915	178,312,650	159,642,657	92,719,664	252,362,321
August	594,631,915	177,438,800	158,874,203	90,758,447	249,632,650
September	595,313,915	176,508,850	158,133,712	88,294,850	246,428,562
October	596,041,015	173,280,250	155,365,068	88,236,639	243,601,707
November	596,796,015	170,003,350	152,366,328	87,018,909	239,385,237
December	597,457,315	166,796,550	149,487,373	86,955,794	236,443,167
1889.					
January	598,239,065	163,480,900	146,372,588	87,287,439	233,660,027
February	599,709,365	160,463,950	143,580,313	85,688,716	229,269,029
March	600,684,365	157,485,700	140,874,515	83,520,212	224,394,727
April	602,404,365	154,590,150	138,193,798	83,032,333	221,226,131
May	603,264,365	151,522,350	135,375,463	83,320,725	218,696,188
June	607,390,365	149,829,850	133,769,313	81,753,704	215,523,017
July	609,670,365	148,121,450	132,244,437	79,134,526	211,378,963
August	612,535,365	147,758,450	131,890,777	76,273,662	208,164,439
September	614,925,365	148,150,700	132,101,128	73,701,013	205,802,141
October	617,844,365	147,037,200	131,225,172	72,437,560	203,662,732
November	620,174,365	145,668,150	130,207,285	71,816,130	202,023,415
December	621,959,365	144,709,250	129,388,116	70,258,081	199,646,197
1890.					
January	623,791,365	142,849,900	127,742,440	69,487,965	197,230,405
February	630,003,865	142,266,750	126,747,030	67,895,259	194,642,289
March	632,757,865	143,197,000	127,410,251	64,857,292	192,267,543
April	637,372,865	143,600,750	128,046,801	62,480,331	190,527,132
May	638,932,865	144,216,150	128,920,916	60,665,663	189,586,579
June	644,587,865	144,658,650	128,976,526	58,573,322	187,549,848
July	646,937,865	145,228,300	129,767,150	56,203,625	185,970,775
August	651,367,865	145,434,750	129,854,561	54,537,072	184,391,633
September	652,352,865	143,102,350	127,625,431	55,455,037	183,280,468
October	655,002,865	140,428,600	125,430,316	56,440,709	181,871,025
November	659,782,865	140,190,900	124,958,736	54,796,907	179,755,643
December	662,947,865	140,427,400	125,253,195	53,315,181	178,568,376
1891.					
January	665,267,865	140,510,650	125,660,361	51,627,485	177,287,846
February	666,977,865	140,720,700	125,859,360	49,762,379	175,721,739
March	669,007,865	140,790,200	125,957,235	47,706,139	173,663,374
April	671,477,865	141,036,150	126,054,415	45,750,649	171,805,064
May	672,197,865	140,949,900	125,970,955	44,448,421	170,419,376
June	673,422,865	141,310,150	126,267,575	42,969,884	169,237,459
July	676,247,865	142,508,300	127,221,391	40,706,183	167,927,574
August	681,742,865	146,089,650	129,708,040	38,845,019	168,543,059
September	683,125,865	149,830,200	133,790,690	37,543,649	171,334,339
October	684,660,865	151,220,100	135,093,378	36,842,328	171,935,706
November	684,755,865	152,050,350	136,753,837	35,430,721	172,184,558
December	685,515,865	155,283,700	138,605,343	34,388,264	172,993,607
1892.					
January	685,762,265	157,205,050	140,081,203	32,991,382	173,078,585
February	687,332,265	158,515,050	141,435,288	31,770,208	173,205,496
March	688,332,265	159,513,800	142,319,978	30,301,897	172,621,875
April	688,923,665	160,447,800	143,355,178	29,174,273	172,529,451
May	689,298,665	161,352,550	143,954,506	28,522,069	172,476,575
June	690,908,665	162,540,050	144,680,363	27,818,986	172,499,349
July	692,123,665	163,190,050	145,683,023	27,000,827	172,683,850
August	694,428,665	163,500,550	146,132,463	26,395,250	172,527,713
September	695,263,665	164,012,050	146,460,033	26,196,390	172,656,429
October	695,563,665	164,498,550	147,191,593	25,595,167	172,786,760
November	693,868,665	164,883,000	147,241,063	25,191,083	172,432,146
December	695,308,665	166,511,500	148,010,239	25,604,632	173,614,371
1893.					
January	695,148,665	168,247,000	150,526,651	23,877,773	174,404,424
February	696,089,665	169,282,350	151,197,221	23,194,032	174,391,253
March	696,119,665	171,094,550	152,887,461	22,534,927	175,422,388
April	695,949,665	172,220,050	153,860,410	22,234,128	176,094,544
May	695,554,665	173,258,800	155,142,318	21,723,296	176,865,614
June	698,451,665	174,530,050	156,028,010	21,136,245	177,164,255
July	698,824,665	176,588,250	151,900,959	20,812,773	178,713,692
August	699,034,665	182,617,850	163,221,294	20,533,854	183,755,148
September	697,963,165	201,096,350	178,616,718	20,303,650	198,980,368
October	698,128,165	209,407,100	187,864,985	20,825,595	208,690,580
November	695,953,165	209,410,350	188,016,228	21,295,765	209,311,993

CHANGES IN CAPITAL, BONDS, AND CIRCULATION, BY GEOGRAPHICAL DIVISIONS.

States and Territories.	Banks existing October 31, 1892.				Banks organized during year ended October 31, 1893.			
	No.	Capital.	Bonds.	Circulation.	No.	Capital.	Bonds.	Circulation.
Maine	82	$11,135,000	$3,861,400	$3,475,260	2	$100,000	$40,000	$36,000
New Hampshire	54	6,230,000	2,938,000	2,614,200				
Vermont	49	7,160,000	3,050,000	2,745,000	1	50,000	12,500	11,250
Massachusetts	267	99,633,150	22,217,450	19,995,705	2	300,000	125,000	112,500
Rhode Island	59	20,277,050	6,142,250	5,528,025				
Connecticut	84	22,999,370	6,273,000	5,645,700				
Division No. 1	595	167,494,570	44,482,100	40,033,890	5	510,000	177,500	150,750
New York	325	85,896,060	22,396,700	20,157,030	11	2,050,000	870,000	783,000
New Jersey	96	14,558,350	4,318,250	3,886,425	1	50,000	12,500	11,250
Pennsylvania	374	71,227,390	18,448,050	16,603,245	25	2,375,000	933,750	840,375
Division No. 2	797	171,681,800	45,163,000	40,646,700	37	4,475,000	1,816,250	1,634,625
Delaware	18	2,133,985	740,000	666,000				
Maryland	66	16,829,960	2,861,000	2,574,900	2	150,000	62,500	56,250
District Columbia	13	2,827,000	900,000	810,000				
Virginia	36	4,696,300	1,418,750	1,276,875				
West Virginia	29	2,856,560	816,250	734,625	1	50,000	12,500	11,250
Division No. 3	162	29,343,805	6,736,000	6,062,400	3	200,000	75,000	67,500
North Carolina	23	2,876,000	819,000	737,100	1	50,000	12,500	11,250
South Carolina	14	1,623,000	468,750	421,875				
Georgia	32	4,541,000	1,086,250	977,625				
Florida	18	1,350,000	380,000	342,000	2	150,000	37,500	33,750
Alabama	29	3,919,000	1,152,000	1,036,800	1	50,000	24,500	22,050
Mississippi	13	1,165,000	353,750	318,375				
Louisiana	21	4,435,000	1,202,500	1,082,250				
Texas	223	27,058,455	5,390,350	4,851,315	10	610,000	152,500	137,250
Arkansas	10	1,600,000	260,000	234,000				
Kentucky	82	15,389,400	3,982,500	3,584,250	1	50,000	50,000	45,000
Tennessee	55	10,181,380	1,479,000	1,331,100	1	60,000	15,000	13,500
Division No. 4	520	74,138,235	16,574,100	14,916,690	16	970,000	292,000	262,800
Ohio	240	45,864,670	12,070,500	10,863,450	7	495,000	154,400	138,600
Indiana	110	13,706,850	4,376,050	3,938,445	7	500,000	137,500	123,750
Illinois	212	39,996,000	6,444,500	5,800,050	7	500,000	130,000	117,000
Michigan	104	15,034,000	3,293,000	2,963,700	1	100,000	25,000	22,500
Wisconsin	77	7,517,050	2,034,250	1,830,825	5	1,750,000	250,000	225,000
Division No. 5	743	122,118,570	28,218,300	25,396,470	27	3,345,000	696,500	626,850
Iowa	162	14,550,000	3,527,000	3,174,300	10	500,000	125,000	112,500
Minnesota	72	15,958,850	1,920,800	1,736,820	6	330,000	82,500	74,250
Missouri	81	24,240,000	2,495,300	2,245,770	1	100,000	25,000	22,500
Kansas	144	12,844,100	2,997,250	2,697,525	1	50,000	12,500	11,250
Nebraska	137	13,668,100	3,087,500	2,778,750	3	150,000	37,500	33,750
Division No. 6	596	81,261,050	14,036,850	12,633,165	21	1,130,000	282,500	254,250
Colorado	53	9,075,000	1,699,250	1,529,325	1	50,000	25,000	22,500
Nevada	2	282,000	70,500	63,450				
California	36	8,675,000	1,518,750	1,366,875	2	150,000	37,500	33,750
Oregon	41	3,945,000	794,800	715,320				
Arizona	4	300,000	75,500	67,950	1	100,000	25,000	22,500
Division No. 7	136	22,277,000	4,158,800	3,742,920	4	300,000	87,500	78,750
Indian Territory	6	357,300	90,000	81,000				
Oklahoma	4	190,000	50,000	45,000	2	100,000	25,000	22,500
North Dakota	34	2,515,000	619,000	557,100	1	50,000	12,500	11,250
South Dakota	40	2,735,000	704,750	634,275	1	50,000	12,500	11,250
Idaho	12	750,000	193,750	174,375	1	50,000	12,500	11,250
Montana	35	4,810,000	943,350	849,015	1	50,000	12,500	11,250
New Mexico	11	1,070,000	340,000	306,000				
Utah	14	2,800,000	475,000	427,500				
Washington	70	7,680,000	1,758,000	1,582,200				
Wyoming	13	1,360,000	340,000	306,000				
Division No. 8	239	24,497,300	5,513,850	4,962,465	6	300,000	75,000	67,500
United States	3,788	692,812,330	164,883,000	148,394,700	119	11,230,000	3,502,250	3,152,025

CHANGES IN CAPITAL, BONDS, AND CIRCULATION, BY GEOGRAPHICAL DIVISIONS—Continued.

States and Territories.	Increase in capital, bonds, and circulation of banks existing October 31, 1892, and number of banks concerned in such increase.				Total increase in capital, bonds, and circulation and number of banks concerned in such increase.			
	No.	Capital.	Bonds.	Circulation.	No.	Capital.	Bonds.	Circulation.
Maine	17		$403,000	$362,700	19	$160,000	$443,000	$398,700
New Hampshire	14		869,500	782,550	14		869,500	782,550
Vermont	10		436,500	392,850	11	50,000	449,000	404,100
Massachusetts	100	$250,000	8,332,150	7,498,935	102	550,000	8,457,150	7,611,435
Rhode Island	19		1,479,000	1,331,100	19		1,479,000	1,331,100
Connecticut	23		1,599,500	1,439,550	23		1,599,500	1,439,550
Division No. 1	183	250,000	13,119,650	11,807,685	188	760,000	13,297,150	11,967,435
New York	106	500,000	14,656,750	13,191,075	117	2,550,000	15,526,750	13,974,075
New Jersey	16		955,000	859,500	17	50,000	967,500	870,750
Pennsylvania	95	411,000	6,718,700	6,046,850	120	2,786,000	7,652,450	6,887,205
Division No. 2	217	911,000	22,330,450	20,097,405	254	5,386,000	24,146,700	21,732,030
Delaware	4		179,000	161,100	4		179,000	161,100
Maryland	9		1,044,000	939,600	11	150,000	1,106,500	995,850
Dist. Columbia	3		225,400	202,860	3		225,400	202,860
Virginia	6	100,000	169,500	152,550	6	100,000	169,500	152,550
West Virginia	5		133,750	120,375	6	50,000	146,250	131,625
Division No. 3	27	100,000	1,751,650	1,576,485	30	300,000	1,826,650	1,643,985
North Carolina	4		86,000	77,400	5	50,000	98,500	88,650
South Carolina	2	125,000	6,000	5,400	2	125,000	6,000	5,400
Georgia	4		137,500	123,750	4		137,500	123,750
Florida	1	100,000	25,000	22,500	3	250,000	62,500	56,250
Alabama	2	25,000	19,500	17,550	3	75,000	44,000	39,600
Mississippi								
Louisiana								
Texas	5	100,000	112,550	101,295	15	710,000	265,050	238,545
Arkansas								
Kentucky	12	300,000	268,000	241,200	13	350,000	318,000	286,200
Tennessee	1		20,000	18,000	2	60,000	35,000	31,500
Division No. 4	31	650,000	674,550	607,095	47	1,620,000	966,550	869,895
Ohio	64	365,000	3,672,100	3,304,890	71	860,000	3,826,100	3,443,490
Indiana	8		718,500	646,650	15	500,000	856,000	770,400
Illinois	22	80,000	464,000	417,500	29	580,000	594,000	534,600
Michigan	16	50,000	1,957,500	1,761,750	17	150,000	1,982,500	1,784,250
Wisconsin	7	290,000	78,500	70,650	12	2,040,000	328,500	295,650
Division No. 5	117	785,000	6,890,600	6,201,540	144	4,130,000	7,587,100	6,828,390
Iowa	10	240,000	195,500	175,950	20	740,000	320,500	288,450
Minnesota	1	50,000	12,500	11,250	7	380,000	95,000	85,500
Missouri					1	100,000	25,000	22,500
Kansas	6		117,500	105,750	7	50,000	130,000	117,000
Nebraska	3	50,000	50,000	45,000	6	200,000	87,500	78,750
Division No. 6	20	340,000	375,500	337,950	41	1,470,000	658,000	592,200
Colorado	1		6,000	5,400	2	50,000	31,000	27,900
Nevada								
California	1	200,000			3	350,000	37,500	33,750
Oregon								
Arizona					1	100,000	25,000	22,500
Division No. 7	2	200,000	6,000	5,400	6	500,000	93,500	84,150
Indian Territory								
Oklahoma					2	100,000	25,000	22,500
North Dakota	1	50,000	12,500	11,250	2	100,000	25,000	22,500
South Dakota	3	25,000	50,000	45,000	4	75,000	62,500	56,250
Idaho					1	50,000	12,500	11,250
Montana					1	50,000	12,500	11,250
New Mexico								
Utah								
Washington								
Wyoming								
Division No. 8	4	75,000	62,500	56,250	10	375,000	137,500	123,750
United States	601	3,311,000	45,210,900	40,689,810	720	14,541,000	48,713,150	43,841,835

CHANGES IN CAPITAL, BONDS, AND CIRCULATION, BY GEOGRAPHICAL DIVISIONS—
Continued.

Decrease in capital, bonds, and circulation, with number of banks concerned in such decrease.

States and Territories.	Failed and liquidating banks.				By banks existing October 31, 1892.			
	No.	Capital.	Bonds.	Circulation.	No.	Capital.	Bonds.	Circulation.
Maine	1	$50,000	$12,500	$11,250				
New Hampshire	3	300,000	112,500	101,250				
Vermont	2	100,000	25,000	22,500	2	$100,000	$6,000	$5,400
Massachusetts	1	150,000	150,000	135,000	2	200,000		
Rhode Island					1		50,000	45,000
Connecticut								
Division No. 1	7	600,000	300,000	270,000	5	300,000	56,000	50,400
New York	2	500,000	100,000	90,000	7	100,000	1,305,000	1,174,500
New Jersey					1	10,000		
Pennsylvania					3	150,000	50,000	45,000
Division No. 2	2	500,000	100,000	90,000	11	260,000	1,355,000	1,219,500
Delaware								
Maryland					1		100,000	90,000
Dist. Columbia								
Virginia								
West Virginia								
Division No. 3					1		100,000	90,000
North Carolina								
South Carolina								
Georgia	5	775,000	168,750	151,875				
Florida	3	300,000	75,000	67,500				
Alabama	1	150,000	50,000	45,000				
Mississippi	1	60,000	15,000	13,500	1	50,000		
Louisiana	1	500,000	50,000	45,000				
Texas	11	2,575,000	356,300	320,670	6	1,110,000	62,500	56,250
Arkansas	1	150,000	50,000	45,000	1		10,000	9,000
Kentucky	3	650,000	287,500	258,750	3	746,500		
Tennessee	5	900,000	162,500	146,250	1		20,000	18,000
Division No. 4	31	6,060,000	1,215,050	1,093,545	12	1,906,500	92,500	83,250
Ohio	4	310,000	77,750	69,975				
Indiana	3	550,000	112,500	101,250	3		197,500	177,750
Illinois	6	2,300,000	175,000	157,500				
Michigan	5	400,000	112,500	101,250	2	150,000		
Wisconsin					1	65,000		
Division No. 5	18	3,560,000	4,777,750	429,975	6	215,000	197,500	177,750
Iowa	3	350,000	87,500	78,750	2	150,000	12,500	11,250
Minnesota	1	75,000	19,000	17,100				
Missouri	3	500,000	112,500	101,250	1	25,000		
Kansas	8	560,000	146,250	131,625	5	255,000	25,000	22,500
Nebraska	5	700,000	150,000	135,000	1	10,000	2,500	2,250
Division No. 6	20	2,185,000	515,250	463,725	9	440,000	40,000	36,000
Colorado	2	300,000	62,500	56,250				
Nevada								
California	2	300,000	75,000	67,500				
Oregon	2	150,000	37,500	33,750				
Arizona								
Division No. 7	6	750,000	175,000	157,500				
Indian Territory								
Oklahoma								
North Dakota	3	400,000	87,500	78,750				
South Dakota	2	100,000	25,000	22,500	1	75,000		
Idaho								
Montana	11	1,340,000	247,740	222,975				
New Mexico	1	175,000	50,000	45,000				
Utah								
Washington	9	900,000	237,500	213,750	1	50,000	12,500	11,250
Wyoming	1	50,000	12,500	11,250				
Division No. 8	27	2,965,000	660,250	594,225	2	125,000	12,500	11,250
United States	111	16,620,000	3,443,300	3,098,970	46	3,246,500	1,853,500	1,668,150

CHANGES IN CAPITAL, BONDS, AND CIRCULATION, BY GEOGRAPHICAL DIVISIONS—Continued.

States and Territories	Increase and decrease during year ended October 31, 1892.					
	Total increase.			Total decrease.		
	Capital.	Bonds.	Circulation.	Capital.	Bonds.	Circulation.
Maine	$160,000	$443,000	$398,700	$50,000	$12,500	$11,250
New Hampshire		869,500	782,550	300,000	112,500	101,250
Vermont	50,000	449,000	404,100	200,000	31,000	27,900
Massachusetts	550,000	8,457,150	7,611,435	350,000	150,000	135,000
Rhode Island		1,479,000	1,331,100		50,000	75,000
Connecticut		1,599,500	1,439,550			
Division No. 1	760,000	13,297,150*	11,967,435	900,000	350,000	320,400
New York	2,550,000	15,526,750	13,974,075	600,000	1,405,000	1,264,500
New Jersey	50,000	967,500	870,750	10,000		
Pennsylvania	2,786,000	7,652,450	6,887,205	150,000	50,000	45,000
Division No. 2	5,386,000	24,146,700	21,732,030	760,000	1,455,000	1,309,500
Delaware		179,000	161,100			
Maryland	150,000	1,700,500	995,850		100,000	90,000
District of Columbia		225,400	202,860			
Virginia	100,000	169,500	152,550			
West Virginia	50,000	146,250	131,625			
Division No. 3	300,000	1,826,650	1,643,985		100,000	90,000
North Carolina	50,000	98,500	88,650			
South Carolina	125,000	6,000	5,400			
Georgia		137,500	123,750	775,000	168,750	151,875
Florida	250,000	62,500	56,250	300,000	75,000	67,500
Alabama	75,000	44,000	39,600	150,000	50,000	45,000
Mississippi				110,000	15,000	13,500
Louisiana				500,000	50,000	45,000
Texas	710,000	265,050	238,545	3,685,000	418,800	376,920
Arkansas				150,000	60,000	54,000
Kentucky	350,000	318,000	266,200	1,396,500	287,500	258,750
Tennessee	60,000	35,000	31,500	900,000	182,500	164,250
Division No. 4	1,620,000	966,550	869,895	7,966,500	1,307,550	1,176,795
Ohio	860,000	3,826,100	3,443,490	310,000	77,750	69,975
Indiana	500,000	856,000	770,400	550,000	310,000	279,000
Illinois	580,000	594,000	534,600	2,300,000	175,000	157,500
Michigan	150,000	1,982,500	1,784,250	550,000	112,500	101,250
Wisconsin	2,040,000	328,500	295,650	65,000		
Division No. 5	4,130,000	7,587,100	6,828,390	3,775,000	675,250	607,725
Iowa	740,000	320,500	288,450	500,000	100,000	90,000
Minnesota	380,000	95,000	85,500	75,000	19,000	17,100
Missouri	100,000	25,000	22,500	525,000	112,500	101,250
Kansas	50,000	130,000	117,000	815,000	171,250	154,125
Nebraska	200,000	87,500	78,750	710,000	152,300	137,250
Division No. 6	1,470,000	658,000	592,200	2,625,000	555,250	4,997,725
Colorado	50,000	31,000	27,900	300,000	62,500	56,250
Nevada						
California	350,000	37,500	33,750	300,000	75,000	67,500
Oregon				150,000	37,500	33,750
Arizona	100,000	25,000	22,500			
Division No. 7	500,000	93,500	84,150	750,000	175,000	157,500
Indian Territory						
Oklahoma	100,000	25,000	22,500			
North Dakota	100,000	25,000	22,500	400,000	87,500	78,750
South Dakota	75,000	62,500	56,250	175,000	25,000	22,500
Idaho	50,000	12,500	11,250			
Montana	50,000	12,500	11,250	1,310,000	247,750	222,975
New Mexico				175,000	50,000	45,000
Utah						
Washington				950,000	250,000	225,000
Wyoming				50,000	12,500	11,250
Division No. 8	375,000	137,500	123,750	3,000,000	672,750	605,475
United States	14,541,000	48,713,150	43,841,835	19,866,500	5,296,800	4,767,120

CHANGES IN CAPITAL, BONDS, AND CIRCULATION, BY GEOGRAPHICAL DIVISIONS—Continued.

States and Territories.	Net increase and decrease—capital, bonds, and circulation.					
	Net increase.			Net decrease.		
	Capital.	Bonds.	Circulation.	Capital.	Bonds.	Circulation.
Maine	$110,000	$430,500	$387,450			
New Hampshire		757,000	681,300	$300,000		
Vermont		418,000	376,200	150,000		
Massachusetts	200,000	8,307,150	7,476,435			
Rhode Island		1,429,000	1,286,100			
Connecticut		1,599,500	1,439,550			
Division No. 1	310,000	12,941,150	11,647,035	450,000		
New York	1,950,000	14,121,750	12,709,575			
New Jersey	40,000	907,500	870,750			
Pennsylvania	2,636,000	7,602,450	6,842,205			
Division No. 2	4,626,000	22,691,700	20,422,530			
Delaware		179,000	161,100			
Maryland	150,000	1,006,500	905,850			
District of Columbia		225,400	202,860			
Virginia	100,000	169,500	152,550			
West Virginia	50,000	146,250	131,625			
Division No. 3	300,000	1,726,650	1,553,985			
North Carolina	50,000	98,650	88,650			
South Carolina	125,000	6,000	5,400			
Georgia				775,000	$31,250	$28,125
Florida				50,000	12,500	11,250
Alabama				75,000	6,000	5,400
Mississippi				110,000	15,000	13,500
Louisiana				500,000	50,000	45,000
Texas				2,975,000	153,750	138,375
Arkansas				150,000	60,000	54,000
Kentucky		30,500	27,450	1,046,500		
Tennessee				840,000	147,500	132,750
Division No. 4	175,000	135,000	121,500	6,521,500	476,000	428,400
Ohio	550,000	3,748,350	3,373,515			
Indiana		546,000	491,400	50,000		
Illinois		419,000	377,100	1,720,000		
Michigan		1,870,000	1,683,000	400,000		
Wisconsin	1,975,000	328,500	295,650			
Division No. 5	2,525,000	6,911,850	6,220,665	2,170,000		
Iowa	240,000	220,500	198,450			
Minnesota	305,000	76,000	68,400			
Missouri				425,000	87,500	78,750
Kansas				765,000	41,250	37,125
Nebraska				510,000	65,000	58,500
Division No. 6	545,000	296,500	266,850	1,700,000	193,750	174,375
Colorado				250,000	31,500	28,350
Nevada						
California	50,000				37,500	33,750
Oregon				150,000	37,500	33,750
Arizona	100,000	25,000	22,500			
Division No. 7	150,000	25,000	22,500	400,000	106,500	95,850
Indian Territory						
Oklahoma	100,000	25,000	22,500			
North Dakota				300,000	62,500	56,250
South Dakota		37,500	33,750	100,000		
Idaho	50,000	12,500	11,250			
Montana				1,290,000	235,250	211,725
New Mexico				175,000	50,000	45,000
Utah						
Washington				950,000	250,000	225,000
Wyoming				50,000	12,500	11,250
Division No. 8	150,000	75,000	67,500	2,865,000	610,250	549,225
United States*	8,781,000	44,802,850	40,322,565	14,106,500	1,366,500	1,247,850

* In explanation of apparent differences in figures representing capital, bonds, and circulation, the decrease under each of these heads includes a number of failed and liquidating banks which have not yet withdrawn their bonds and provided for their outstanding circulation.

DECREASE OR INCREASE OF NATIONAL BANK CIRCULATION DURING EACH OF THE YEARS ENDED OCTOBER 31, 1886 TO 1893, INCLUSIVE, AND THE AMOUNT OF LAWFUL MONEY ON DEPOSIT AT THE END OF EACH YEAR.

National-bank notes outstanding October 31, 1886, including notes of national gold banks...................... $301,529,889
Less lawful money on deposit at same date, including deposits of national gold banks......................... 81,819,233
                                                                      $219,710,656

Net decrease of circulation....................................... 56,593,533
Net outstanding as above, October 31, 1886........................... 219,710,656
National-bank notes outstanding October 31, 1887, includ-
ing notes of national gold banks...................... 272,041,203
Less lawful money on deposit at same date, including de-
posits of national gold banks......................... 102,826,136
                                                                      169,215,067

Net decrease of circulation....................................... 50,495,589
Net outstanding as above, October 31, 1887........................... 169,215,067
National-bank notes outstanding October 31, 1888, includ-
ing notes of national gold banks...................... 239,385,237
Less lawful money on deposit at same date, including
deposits of national gold banks........................ 87,018,909
                                                                      152,366,328

Net decrease of circulation....................................... 16,848,739
Net outstanding as above, October 31, 1888........................... 152,366,328
National-bank notes outstanding October 31, 1889, includ-
ing notes of national gold banks...................... 202,023,415
Less lawful money on deposit at same date, including
deposits of national gold banks........................ 71,816,130
                                                                      130,207,285

Net decrease of circulation....................................... 22,159,043
Net outstanding as above, October 31, 1889........................... 130,207,285
National-bank notes outstanding October 31, 1890, includ-
ing notes of national gold banks...................... 179,755,643
Less lawful money on deposit at same date, including
deposits of national gold banks........................ 54,796,907
                                                                      124,958,736

Net decrease of circulation....................................... 5,248,549
Net outstanding as above, October 31, 1890........................... 124,958,736
National-bank notes outstanding October 31, 1891, includ-
ing notes of national gold banks...................... 172,184,558
Less lawful money on deposit at same date, including
deposits of national gold banks........................ 35,430,721
                                                                      136,753,837

Net increase of circulation....................................... 11,795,101
Net outstanding as above October 31, 1891........................... 136,753,837
National-bank notes outstanding October 31, 1892, includ-
ing notes of national gold banks...................... 172,432,146
Less lawful money on deposit at same date, including
deposits of national gold banks........................ 25,191,083
                                                                      147,241,063

Net increase of circulation....................................... 10,487,226
Net outstanding as above October 31, 1892........................... 147,241,063
National-bank notes outstanding October 31, 1893, includ-
ing notes of national gold banks...................... 209,311,993
Less lawful money on deposit at same date, including
deposits of national gold banks........................ 21,295,765
                                                                      188,016,228

Net increase of circulation....................................... 40,775,165

The gross increase of circulation, including the notes of gold banks and those of failed and liquidated associations, was $36,886,972.

STATEMENT SHOWING BY STATES THE AMOUNT OF NATIONAL-BANK CIRCULATION ISSUED, THE AMOUNT OF LAWFUL MONEY DEPOSITED IN THE UNITED STATES TREASURY TO RETIRE NATIONAL-BANK CIRCULATION FROM JUNE 20, 1874, TO OCTOBER 31, 1893, AND AMOUNT REMAINING ON DEPOSIT AT LATTER DATE.

States and Territories.	Additional circulation issued since June 20, 1874.	Lawful money deposited to retire national-bank circulation since June 20, 1874.				Lawful money on deposit with the United States Treasurer at date.
		For redemption of notes of liquidating banks.	To retire circulation under act of June 20, 1874.	To retire circulation under act of July 12, 1882.	Total deposits.	
Maine	$3,880,059	$900,037.00	$4,465,235.00	$2,568,018.00	$7,933,290.00	$469,872
New Hampshire	3,180,735	658,045.00	2,391,060.00	1,466,008.00	4,495,113.00	341,214
Vermont	4,512,515	1,107,657.00	5,015,003.00	1,957,682.00	8,080,342.00	348,011
Massachusetts	50,952,915	2,146,100.00	53,952,314.00	24,809,896.50	80,768,310.50	3,461,942
Rhode Island	8,959,955	317,017.00	8,858,456.00	5,977,042.00	15,152,575.00	736,945
Connecticut	10,943,800	1,070,361.00	13,777,507.00	6,422,927.00	21,270,795.00	977,449
New York	63,015,230	9,666,225.00	58,697,361.50	15,563,431.50	83,927,018.00	4,046,284
New Jersey	7,255,170	1,431,988.00	9,022,902.00	3,095,420.00	13,550,400.00	578,598
Pennsylvania	39,272,910	5,011,351.00	36,145,273.50	15,837,882.00	56,994,507.00	2,597,492
Delaware	1,082,210		997,000.00	458,645.00	1,455,645.00	105,135
Maryland	5,122,195	184,800.00	6,348,665.00	3,665,625.00	10,199,090.00	548,036
District of Columbia	1,020,000	455,664.00	899,740.00	76,310.00	1,431,714.00	20,578
Virginia	2,392,470	1,208,860.00	2,377,275.00	723,430.00	4,309,574.00	175,892
West Virginia	998,609	950,310.00	922,740.00	551,015.00	2,424,065.00	92,177
North Carolina	1,735,880	389,660.00	2,153,210.00	76,920.00	2,619,790.00	51,618
South Carolina	410,580	81,050.00	1,896,675.00	129,830.00	2,107,555.00	53,648
Georgia	1,488,840	430,925.00	1,678,855.00	547,910.00	2,657,690.00	144,212
Florida	470,250	85,590.00	7,790.00		93,380.00	30,515
Alabama	1,249,020	360,398.00	1,076,320.00	143,972.00	1,580,690.00	157,214
Mississippi	356,600		38,450.00		38,450.00	137
Louisiana	2,908,560	711,413.00	3,088,180.00	830,970.00	5,230,563.00	222,971
Texas	6,038,510	434,867.00	1,157,358.00	90,805.00	1,683,030.00	173,903
Arkansas	646,450	130,625.00	412,120.00	63,205.00	605,950.00	55,620
Kentucky	8,451,239	1,027,506.00	8,680,066.00	1,302,992.00	12,010,564.00	596,614
Tennessee	2,376,920	1,162,401.00	2,190,756.00	445,818.00	3,798,975.00	334,781
Missouri	4,730,010	1,596,705.00	6,204,341.00	611,649.00	8,412,695.00	360,288
Ohio	24,763,636	8,242,179.00	19,948,956.00	5,014,379.00	33,205,514.00	1,320,749
Indiana	9,183,990	5,523,215.00	12,036,725.50	1,233,092.00	18,793,032.50	713,526
Illinois	9,172,295	4,021,058.00	11,907,966.00	1,619,663.00	17,548,687.00	587,583
Michigan	7,347,420	3,391,706.00	5,585,005.00	401,384.00	9,378,095.00	390,851
Wisconsin	3,774,350	1,359,293.00	2,702,388.00	638,828.00	4,700,509.00	160,728
Iowa	5,639,090	2,014,207.50	4,838,043.50	646,965.00	7,499,216.00	272,376
Minnesota	2,819,015	1,103,304.50	2,614,826.50	430,914.00	4,149,045.00	126,344
Kansas	3,950,165	1,663,935.00	1,016,065.00	71,301.00	2,751,301.00	324,477
Nebraska	3,747,920	423,437.50	1,153,915.00	221,080.00	1,799,332.00	125,923
Nevada	76,950		13,500.00		13,500.00	904
Oregon	781,750	43,670.00	180,860.00	82,450.00	306,980.00	47,084
Colorado	2,323,505	369,975.00	712,720.00	263,810.00	1,346,505.00	81,627
Idaho	225,405	11,250.00	90,268.00	14,762.00	116,280.00	4,655
Montana	1,157,470	236,710.00	334,610.00	29,470.00	600,790.00	53,602
Wyoming	206,345	24,750.00	20,250.00		45,000.00	7,653
North Dakota	898,200	107,640.00	195,570.00		303,210.00	4,613
South Dakota	859,715	155,870.00	100,330.00		256,200.00	42,045
Washington	2,088,445	151,700.00	385,850.00		537,550.00	60,278
California	3,041,370	279,890.00	1,340,500.00		1,620,390.00	115,170
Utah	756,050	161,191.00	527,547.00	42,903.00	731,641.00	30,928
New Mexico	382,500	59,750.00	285,200.00		344,950.00	23,526
Arizona	143,540	50,590.00	2,500.00		53,090.00	970
Oklahoma	90,000	21,800.00			21,800.00	15,090
Indian Territory	81,000					
Lawful money deposited prior to June 20, 1874, and remaining at that date					3,813,675.00	
Total	*317,021,767	61,916,685.50	299,048,338.50	97,989,304.00	†462,768,008.00	†21,197,938

* This includes circulation issued under act of July 12, 1882.
† Exclusive of $97,827 on deposit to retire circulation of national gold banks.

STATEMENT SHOWING THE AMOUNT OF NATIONAL-BANK NOTES OUTSTANDING, THE AMOUNT OF LAWFUL MONEY ON DEPOSIT WITH THE TREASURER OF THE UNITED STATES TO REDEEM NATIONAL-BANK NOTES, AND THE KINDS AND AMOUNTS OF UNITED STATES BONDS ON DEPOSIT TO SECURE CIRCULATION AND PUBLIC DEPOSITS ON OCTOBER 31, 1893, WITH THE CHANGES DURING THE PRECEDING YEAR AND THE PRECEDING MONTH.

National-bank notes.	October 31, 1892.	September 30, 1893.
Total circulation.		
Total amount outstanding at the dates named	$172,327,194	$208,592,172
Additional circulation issued during the intervals:		
To new banks	2,268,250	47,200
To banks increasing circulation	42,097,130	1,150,725
Aggregate	216,692,574	209,790,157
Surrendered and destroyed during the intervals	7,478,408	575,991
Total amount outstanding Oct. 31, 1893*	209,214,166	209,214,166
Increase in total circulation since Oct. 31, 1892	36,886,972	
Increase in total circulation since Sept. 30, 1893		621,994
Circulation based on United States bonds.		
Amount outstanding at the dates named	147,241,063	187,864,984
Additional issued during the intervals as above	44,365,380	1,197,985
Aggregate	191,606,443	189,062,969
Retired during the intervals:		
By insolvent banks	637,160	267,600
By liquidating banks	1,003,792	11,250
By reducing banks	1,959,263	7,891
Total retired during the intervals	3,590,215	1,046,741
Outstanding against bonds Oct. 31, 1893	188,016,228	188,016,228
Increase in circulation since Oct. 31, 1892	40,775,165	
Increase in circulation since Sept. 30, 1893		151,244

Circulation secured by lawful money.	October 31, 1892.	October 31, 1893.
Amount of outstanding circulation represented by lawful money on deposit with the Treasurer United States to redeem notes:		
Of insolvent national banks	$1,108,559	$1,335,614
Of liquidating national banks	5,056,407	4,732,400
Of national banks reducing circulation under section 4 of the act of June 20, 1874	3,287,019	1,886,834
Of national banks retiring circulation under section 6 of the act of July 12, 1882	15,633,246	13,243,090
Total lawful money on deposit	25,086,131	21,197,938
Lawful money deposited in October, 1893		1,064,820
National-bank notes redeemed in October, 1893		594,070
Decrease in aggregate deposit since Oct. 31, 1892	3,888,193	
Increase in aggregate deposit since Sept. 30, 1893		470,750

United States registered bonds on deposit.	To secure circulating notes.	To secure public deposits.
Pacific Railroad bonds, 6 per cents	$16,576,000	$1,170,000
Funded loan of 1891, 4½ per cents continued at 2 per cent	22,320,850	1,538,000
Funded loan of 1907, 4 per cents	170,519,500	12,203,000
Total on deposit October 31, 1893	209,416,350	14,911,000

*Circulation of national gold banks, not included in the above, $97,827.

STATEMENT SHOWING PROFITS UPON CIRCULATING NOTES BASED UPON A DEPOSIT OF $100,000 BONDS, OCTOBER 31, 1893.

October 31, 1893—2 per cents.

$100,000 twos at 96, interest		$2,000.00
Circulation, 90 per cent on par value	$90,000.00	
Loanable circulation at 6 per cent		5,400.00
Gross receipts		7,400.00
Deduct—		
1 per cent tax on circulation	900.00	
Annual cost of redemption	45.00	
Express charges	3.00	
Cost of plates for circulation	7.50	
Agents' fees	7.00	
		962.50
Net receipts		6,437.50
$96,000 loaned at 6 per cent		5,760.00
Profit on circulation		677.50

Total profit on $22,020,550 bonds, $149,189.23.
Percentage on maximum circulation obtainable, 0.677½ per cent.

October 31, 1893—4 per cents.

$100,000 fours at 111.1712 premium, interest		$4,000.00
Circulation, 90 per cent on par value	$90,000.00	
Loanable circulation at 6 per cent		5,400.00
Gross receipts		9,400.00
Deduct—		
1 per cent tax on circulation	900.00	
Annual cost of redemption	45.00	
Express charges	3.00	
Cost of plates for circulation	7.50	
Agents' fees	7.00	
Sinking fund reinvested quarterly to liquidate premium	533.25	
		1,495.75
Net receipts		7,904.25
$111,171.20 loaned at 6 per cent		6,670.27
Profit on circulation		1,233.98

Total profit on $112,141,700 bonds, $1,754,000.16.
Percentage on maximum circulation obtainable, 1.234 per cent.

October 31, 1893—6 per cents.

100,000 sixes at 103.5943 premium, interest		$6,000.00
Circulation, 90 per cent on par value	$90,000.00	
Loanable circulation at 6 per cent		5,400.00
Gross receipts		11,400.00
Deduct—		
1 per cent tax on circulation	$900.00	
Annual cost of redemption	45.00	
Express charges	3.00	
Cost of plates for circulation	7.50	
Agents' fees	7.00	
Sinking fund reinvested semiannually to liquidate premium	1,307.78	
		2,270.28
Net receipts		9,129.72
$105,594.50 loaned at 6 per cent		6,335.67
Profit on circulation		2,794.05

Total profit on $12,426,000 bonds, $347,488.65.
Percentage on maximum circulation obtainable, 2.794 per cent.

STATEMENT SHOWING QUARTERLY INCREASE OR DECREASE OF NATIONAL-BANK CIRCULATION, FROM JANUARY 14, 1875, TO OCTOBER 31, 1893.

	National bank.		Increase.	Decrease.
	Issued.	Retired.		
From Jan. 14 to Jan. 31, 1875	$537,580	$255,600	$281,980	
For quarter ended—				
Apr. 30, 1875	4,409,220	3,336,804	1,072,416	
July 31, 1875	4,124,165	5,423,970		$1,299,761
Oct. 31, 1875	1,915,710	5,553,971		3,638,261
Jan. 31, 1876	2,504,600	3,852,731		1,348,131
Apr. 30, 1876	877,580	5,425,539		4,547,959
July 31, 1876	1,107,110	9,663,984		8,556,874
Oct. 31, 1876	2,604,390	8,564,727		5,960,333
Jan. 31, 1877	3,188,630	4,759,015		1,570,386
Apr. 30, 1877	4,363,010	5,005,596		642,586
July 31, 1877	3,000,230	4,984,399		1,984,169
Oct. 31, 1877	5,754,160	3,516,321	2,237,839	
Jan. 31, 1878	6,725,585	2,701,885	4,023,700	
Apr. 30, 1878	3,036,760	1,906,720	1,130,039	
July 31, 1878	4,252,980	3,453,080	797,900	
Oct. 31, 1878	2,276,360	2,924,430		648,070
Jan. 31, 1879	3,097,060	747,327	2,349,733	
Apr. 30, 1879	7,039,300	1,822,988	5,216,312	
July 31, 1879	3,674,830	2,715,524	959,306	
Oct. 31, 1879	9,122,300	1,754,558	7,367,742	
Jan. 31, 1880	7,289,805	674,129	6,615,676	
Apr. 30, 1880	3,163,820	1,555,766	1,608,054	
July 31, 1880	1,748,660	2,427,398		678,738
Oct. 31, 1880	1,199,930	1,535,760		335,830
Jan. 31, 1881	2,234,780	1,361,534	873,246	
Apr. 30, 1881	12,690,890	4,426,596	8,264,294	
July 31, 1881	9,569,410	4,734,578	4,834,832	
Oct. 31, 1881	6,484,550	3,182,551	3,301,999	
Jan. 31, 1882	5,625,200	3,354,153	2,271,047	
Apr. 30, 1882	2,991,400	4,414,865		1,423,465
July 31, 1882	4,054,740	5,741,456		1,086,710
Oct. 31, 1882	9,792,910	5,611,497	4,181,413	
Jan. 31, 1883	4,588,850	4,927,020		338,170
Apr. 30, 1883	3,638,650	6,510,245		2,871,595
July 31, 1883	3,527,100	6,868,245		3,341,145
Oct. 31, 1883	2,755,600	6,369,273		3,613,673
Jan. 31, 1884	2,748,270	5,172,714		2,424,444
Apr. 30, 1884	2,052,294	8,430,804		6,378,510
July 31, 1884	2,778,960	7,883,997		5,105,037
Oct. 31, 1884	2,792,170	6,833,874		4,041,704
Jan. 31, 1885	1,265,520	7,812,055		6,576,535
Apr. 30, 1885	2,125,260	8,135,112		6,009,852
July 31, 1885	2,160,110	5,731,673		3,571,563
Oct. 31, 1885	5,591,760	6,758,154		1,166,394
Jan. 31, 1886	7,751,794	5,581,261	2,170,533	
Apr. 30, 1886	4,700,384	8,397,163		3,696,779
July 31, 1886	1,469,325	8,425,486		6,956,161
Oct. 31, 1886	1,566,700	6,468,227		4,901,527
Jan. 31, 1887	1,243,550	9,580,973		8,337,423
Apr. 30, 1887	2,961,775	11,014,057		8,052,282
July 31, 1887	2,936,670	11,307,718		8,371,048
Oct. 31, 1887	4,021,350	8,421,529		4,400,179
Jan. 31, 1888	6,144,629	12,190,159		6,045,530
Apr. 30, 1888	7,755,416	15,005,579		7,250,163
July 31, 1888	6,188,531	15,115,185		8,926,654
Oct. 31, 1888	1,049,765	11,277,768		10,228,003
Jan. 31, 1889	930,445	11,031,498		10,101,053
Apr. 30, 1889	1,179,165	11,789,161		10,609,996
July 31, 1889	1,376,200	11,791,639		10,415,438
Oct. 31, 1889	1,783,020	7,894,453		6,110,533
Jan. 31, 1890	1,428,895	8,865,001		7,436,106
Apr. 30, 1890	3,469,345	8,496,305		5,026,960
July 31, 1890	2,481,990	7,515,116		5,063,126
Oct. 31, 1890	1,817,525	6,444,175		4,626,650
Jan. 31, 1891	1,765,540	5,896,594		4,131,054
Apr. 30, 1891	1,397,135	6,578,579		5,181,444
July 31, 1891	4,065,775	5,973,521		1,907,716
Oct. 31, 1891	8,230,000	4,462,850	3,767,150	
Jan. 31, 1892	5,241,445	4,220,507	1,020,938	
Apr. 30, 1892	3,217,945	3,934,429		716,484
July 31, 1892	2,992,805	2,824,744	168,061	
Oct. 31, 1892	2,271,669	2,439,286		167,617
Jan. 31, 1893	4,384,625	2,426,418	1,958,207	
Apr. 30, 1893	4,735,660	2,267,346	2,468,314	
July 31, 1893	8,523,700	1,612,297	6,911,403	
Oct. 31, 1893	26,724,395	1,186,029	25,538,366	
Total	312,287,267	439,314,632	101,392,500	228,419,865
Surrendered to this office and retired from Jan. 14, 1875, to Oct. 31, 1893		16,489,240		16,489,240
Grand total	312,287,267	455,803,872	101,392,500	244,909,105

STATEMENT SHOWING NATIONAL-BANK NOTES ISSUED, REDEEMED, AND OUTSTANDING, BY DENOMINATIONS AND AMOUNTS, ON OCTOBER 31, IN EACH YEAR FROM 1864 TO 1893, INCLUSIVE.

Year		Ones.	Twos.	Fives.	Tens.	Twenties.	Fifties.	One hundreds.	Five hundreds.	One thousands.	Total.	Issued during current year.
1864	Issued	$2,020,167	$1,340,778	$20,924,100	$19,708,260	$6,530,920	$2,491,300	$2,903,400	$250,000		$56,813,080	$58,813,980
	Redeemed											
	Outstanding	2,020,167	1,346,778	20,024,100	19,708,260	6,536,920	2,491,300	2,003,400	250,000		56,813,080	
1865	Issued			84,790,000	53,493,210	28,209,500	10,349,700	15,033,600	5,446,500	4,401,000	205,099,455	146,285,475
	Redeemed			104,829	195,800	26,580	46,550	89,500		1,010	464,250	
	Outstanding			84,691,160	53,297,410	28,182,920	10,303,160	14,941,100	5,446,500	4,403,000	204,635,205	
1866	Issued	7,099,182	5,156,012	111,115,620	75,807,000	42,278,700	16,473,700	24,057,300	6,669,500	4,726,000	294,585,214	89,485,759
	Redeemed	7,640	11,700	153,175	225,390	42,040	76,650	172,700	302,500	507,000	1,403,255	
	Outstanding	7,091,502	5,144,302	110,962,445	75,581,610	42,236,640	16,397,050	24,484,800	6,367,000	4,221,000	293,080,959	
1867	Issued	8,390,179	5,622,722	113,535,300	77,899,270	43,615,720	17,469,850	26,243,600	6,691,500	4,724,000	304,202,141	9,616,927
	Redeemed	58,606	42,350	753,855	510,620	198,080	432,300	877,000	71,500	1,563,000	5,107,317	
	Outstanding	8,337,573	5,580,350	112,781,445	77,388,650	43,417,640	17,037,550	25,366,600	6,620,000	3,165,000	299,094,824	
1868	Issued	8,947,798	5,990,468	115,738,140	79,257,620	44,430,700	17,775,450	26,766,600	6,744,500	4,746,000	310,307,276	6,165,135
	Redeemed	272,997	156,016	2,515,093	1,300,500	759,760	880,950	1,598,000	909,000	1,858,000	10,250,318	
	Outstanding	8,674,801	5,834,452	113,223,045	77,957,120	43,670,940	16,894,500	25,168,600	5,835,500	2,888,000	300,116,958	
1869	Issued	9,663,584	6,468,392	118,074,740	81,107,820	45,490,040	18,205,350	27,526,300	6,836,500	4,769,000	318,743,726	8,376,450
	Redeemed	973,427	1,437,318	5,146,030	2,817,390	1,496,400	1,502,050	2,708,100	1,347,000	2,501,000	19,018,935	
	Outstanding	8,690,157	5,819,240	113,528,710	78,260,430	43,993,640	16,703,300	24,818,200	5,491,500	2,268,000	299,724,791	
1870	Issued	10,843,093	7,256,558	124,376,620	85,118,050	48,208,890	19,180,600	28,667,200	6,980,000	4,779,000	335,411,001	16,667,875
	Redeemed	2,752,088	3,114,890	9,035,250	5,060,560	2,701,960	2,501,050	4,587,500	2,096,000	3,380,000	33,552,320	
	Outstanding	8,091,005	5,367,544	115,341,370	80,058,300	45,507,020	16,679,550	24,079,700	4,884,000	1,399,000	301,859,275	
1871	Issued	12,673,807	8,482,434	142,195,820	96,246,360	56,132,040	21,896,850	32,365,500	7,326,500	4,843,000	384,072,311	48,060,710
	Redeemed	5,471,799	3,114,890	17,014,975	9,689,570	5,076,520	4,277,250	7,816,100	3,078,000	4,028,000	59,597,104	
	Outstanding	7,202,068	5,367,544	125,180,845	88,556,730	51,055,520	17,529,600	24,519,400	4,248,500	815,000	324,475,207	
1872	Issued	14,297,360	9,365,256	159,666,740	112,513,760	64,513,760	24,850,950	36,779,700	7,810,500	4,933,000	434,900,786	50,888,475
	Redeemed	7,019,386	4,616,778	29,803,335	16,997,020	8,777,040	6,300,000	11,098,900	3,933,500	4,315,000	93,969,961	
	Outstanding	6,377,972	4,748,478	129,863,405	95,537,500	55,736,720	18,550,950	25,680,800	3,877,000	618,000	340,990,625	
1873	Issued	15,536,189	10,390,222	174,472,280	125,603,990	62,164,360	27,097,100	41,061,000	8,233,000	5,158,000	481,196,101	49,235,375
	Redeemed	9,891,606	6,241,446	45,700,815	25,730,700	13,061,424	8,448,800	11,495,700	4,829,000	4,530,000	132,848,487	
	Outstanding	5,634,583	4,148,776	128,762,465	99,873,290	59,102,960	19,538,300	27,255,300	3,404,000	628,000	348,347,671	
1874	Issued	16,550,250	11,078,256	196,215,080	133,370,780	79,242,180	33,348,500	49,250,200	8,057,000	5,250,000	532,902,605	51,766,044
	Redeemed	11,143,606	7,110,036	65,208,025	39,127,070	19,832,160	11,577,800	19,657,200	5,836,000	4,683,000	184,176,899	
	Outstanding	5,406,653	3,968,188	131,007,655	94,243,690	59,410,020	21,770,700	29,593,000	2,819,000	567,000	348,735,906	

STATEMENT SHOWING NATIONAL-BANK NOTES ISSUED, REDEEMED, AND OUTSTANDING, BY DENOMINATIONS AND AMOUNTS, ETC.—Continued.

Year		Ones.	Twos.	Fives.	Tens.	Twenties.	Fifties.	One hundreds.	Five hundreds.	One thousands.	Total.	Issued during current year.
1875	Issued	$18,048,176	$12,079,504	$235,275,920	$174,105,076	$105,921,280	$44,209,250	$64,585,800	$9,223,000	$5,540,000	$668,988,000	$136,025,195
	Redeemed	14,092,126	9,233,246	124,633,860	76,085,320	40,489,280	19,051,850	29,942,800	7,236,500	5,047,000	325,811,982	
	Outstanding	3,956,050	2,846,253	110,642,060	98,019,750	65,432,000	25,157,400	34,643,000	1,986,500	493,000	343,176,018	
1876	Issued	18,851,264	12,614,896	258,917,640	200,086,520	121,729,810	49,281,750	71,092,000	9,345,500	5,549,000	747,468,410	78,480,410
	Redeemed	15,556,708	10,219,092	161,910,280	103,692,140	57,444,920	25,789,200	39,578,500	8,108,500	5,272,000	427,601,340	
	Outstanding	3,294,556	2,365,804	97,007,360	96,394,380	64,284,920	23,492,550	31,513,500	1,237,000	277,000	319,867,070	
1877	Issued	20,618,024	13,793,936	284,064,240	222,660,640	135,525,000	53,990,050	76,733,700	9,906,000	5,878,000	823,079,650	75,611,240
	Redeemed	16,815,568	11,111,052	190,579,340	124,347,790	70,470,560	31,733,950	47,931,700	8,807,500	5,411,000	507,208,460	
	Outstanding	3,802,456	2,682,884	93,504,900	98,312,850	65,054,500	22,256,100	28,802,000	1,188,500	467,000	315,871,190	
1878	Issued	22,480,415	15,035,530	305,956,440	241,572,930	140,883,340	57,379,900	81,292,300	10,090,000	6,214,000	886,904,855	63,825,205
	Redeemed	18,194,196	12,653,384	213,417,165	135,591,490	79,063,560	36,411,100	54,185,900	9,417,500	5,900,000	567,261,295	
	Outstanding	4,286,219	2,982,146	92,539,275	102,081,440	61,819,780	20,968,800	27,106,400	642,500	314,000	319,640,560	
1879	Issued	23,169,677	15,495,038	327,892,200	259,043,230	157,399,020	60,589,050	85,074,000	10,270,000	6,350,000	945,281,215	58,376,360
	Redeemed	19,600,477	13,002,540	229,980,380	149,305,990	85,146,860	39,203,150	58,160,400	9,643,500	6,057,000	610,160,297	
	Outstanding	3,569,200	2,492,498	97,911,820	109,736,240	72,252,160	21,325,900	26,913,000	620,500	293,000	335,120,918	
1880	Issued	23,169,677	15,495,038	345,659,880	272,031,680	165,327,960	62,694,250	87,951,000	10,366,500	6,373,000	989,068,983	43,787,770
	Redeemed	20,875,215	13,887,778	245,749,120	155,211,100	90,096,400	41,274,950	61,060,100	8,742,000	6,124,000	647,020,663	
	Outstanding	2,294,462	1,607,260	99,910,760	113,820,580	75,231,560	21,419,300	26,890,900	624,500	249,000	342,046,322	
1881	Issued	23,169,677	15,495,038	368,062,520	291,775,190	178,810,340	67,879,700	95,973,200	10,964,500	7,154,000	1,062,290,165	73,221,180
	Redeemed	21,838,565	14,572,868	267,552,863	173,466,350	98,099,840	44,594,500	66,020,200	10,247,500	6,943,000	703,365,263	
	Outstanding	1,331,112	922,170	100,430,080	121,308,840	80,716,500	23,285,200	29,953,000	717,000	211,000	358,924,902	
1882	Issued	23,169,677	15,495,038	393,487,120	310,422,600	195,035,680	72,667,200	103,513,800	11,378,500	7,197,000	1,142,368,615	80,076,450
	Redeemed	22,353,877	14,968,280	296,566,165	107,709,340	111,434,140	49,000,340	71,913,000	10,440,000	6,990,000	781,383,902	
	Outstanding	815,800	526,758	96,920,955	122,713,260	83,601,540	23,658,100	31,600,800	938,500	207,000	360,982,713	
1883	Issued	23,169,677	15,495,038	417,236,040	345,440,860	211,576,920	77,801,450	111,474,200	11,566,500	7,287,000	1,221,047,685	78,681,070
	Redeemed	23,598,909	15,141,896	325,712,835	227,123,550	128,492,760	54,535,150	78,912,500	10,683,500	7,092,000	870,288,010	
	Outstanding	575,788	353,232	91,523,205	118,317,310	83,084,160	23,266,300	32,561,700	883,000	195,000	350,759,675	
1884	Issued	23,169,677	15,495,038	440,505,940	371,821,020	228,841,820	83,051,500	110,977,000	11,853,000	7,379,000	1,302,093,995	81,046,310
	Redeemed	22,671,936	15,206,570	355,196,755	260,501,070	149,635,240	60,828,650	87,454,300	11,990,500	7,156,000	969,641,051	
	Outstanding	497,741	288,468	85,309,155	111,319,050	79,206,580	22,222,850	32,522,700	862,500	223,000	332,452,944	
1885	Issued	23,169,677	15,495,038	466,042,000	398,040,010	246,363,460	87,927,650	128,770,600	11,947,000	7,379,000	1,385,134,435	83,040,440
	Redeemed	22,731,963	15,257,734	384,085,330	293,828,720	171,975,940	67,288,100	97,192,200	11,363,500	7,238,000	1,070,261,507	
	Outstanding	437,714	237,284	81,956,670	104,211,290	75,087,520	20,639,550	31,578,400	583,500	141,000	314,672,928	

		Issued	Redeemed	Outstanding
1886	Issued			
	Redeemed			
	Outstanding			
1887	Issued			
	Redeemed			
	Outstanding			
1888	Issued			
	Redeemed			
	Outstanding			
1889	Issued			
	Redeemed			
	Outstanding			
1890	Issued			
	Redeemed			
	Outstanding			
1891	Issued			
	Redeemed			
	Outstanding			
1892	Issued			
	Redeemed			
	Outstanding			
1893	Issued			
	Redeemed			
	Outstanding			

[Note.—First issue Dec. 21, 1862; first redemption Apr. 5, 1865.]

10665 CUR——7

STATEMENT OF NATIONAL GOLD BANK NOTES ISSUED, REDEEMED, AND OUTSTANDING OCTOBER 31, 1893.

Denominations.	Issued.	Redeemed.	Outstanding.
Fives	$364,140	$343,775	$20,365
Tens	746,470	717,740	28,730
Twenties	722,580	698,500	24,080
Fifties	404,850	396,800	8,050
One hundreds	809,700	795,200	14,500
Five hundreds	342,500	340,500	2,000
One thousands	75,000	75,000	....
Total	3,465,240	3,367,515	97,725
Fractions unredeemed	....	—102	+102
		3,367,413	97,827

STATEMENT OF NATIONAL-BANK NOTES ISSUED DURING THE YEAR ENDED OCTOBER 31, 1893, WITH THE TOTAL AMOUNT ISSUED, REDEEMED, AND OUTSTANDING.

Denominations.	Issued during the year.	Issued previous years.	Total issued to Oct. 31, 1893.	Total redemptions Oct. 31, 1893.	Circulation outstanding Oct. 31, 1893.
Ones	....	$23,169,677	$23,169,677	$22,810,808.00	$358,869.00
Twos	....	15,495,038	15,495,038	15,319,508.00	175,530.00
Fives	$28,285,240	577,190,300	605,475,540	543,392,670.00	62,082,870.00
Tens	27,868,370	491,530,600	519,398,970	452,019,540.00	66,479,430.00
Twenties	18,511,460	308,389,420	326,900,880	278,070,440.00	48,830,440.00
Fifties	3,885,200	102,085,550	105,970,750	95,400,300.00	10,570,450.00
One hundreds	7,634,400	156,315,100	163,949,500	143,918,400.00	20,031,100.00
Five hundreds	....	11,947,000	11,947,000	11,807,500.00	139,500.00
One thousands	....	7,379,000	7,379,000	7,346,000.00	33,000.00
Total	86,184,670	1,693,501,685	1,779,686,355	1,570,985,166.00	208,701,189.00
Unpresented fractions of notes to be deducted from notes redeemed and added to amount of currency outstanding				—27,677.25	+27,677.25
Total				1,570,957,488.75	208,728,866.25

MONTHLY STATEMENT OF ADDITIONAL CIRCULATION ISSUED ON BONDS FOR YEARS ENDED OCTOBER 31, FROM 1883 TO 1893.

Month.	1883–'84.	1884–'85.	1885–'86.	1886–'87.	1887–'88.
November	$445,240	$208,580	$2,363,300	$444,905	$1,687,807
December	1,177,010	379,930	2,600,545	366,765	2,039,803
January	1,126,020	677,010	2,727,889	431,880	2,416,929
February	509,004	512,310	2,054,053	447,560	1,889,790
March	579,850	548,330	1,340,990	1,640,800	2,835,660
April	963,440	1,053,370	404,441	864,325	3,009,065
May	733,960	403,790	478,035	674,500	2,910,246
June	1,101,050	701,490	500,780	1,657,890	2,122,695
July	943,950	1,072,330	490,510	604,280	1,155,590
August	1,279,030	1,154,460	527,970	999,510	492,355
September	943,390	1,914,710	571,230	1,435,040	251,020
October	569,750	2,516,340	467,500	1,586,800	396,390
Total	10,371,694	11,142,650	15,488,203	11,163,345	21,138,341

MONTHLY STATEMENT OF ADDITIONAL CIRCULATION ISSUED ON BONDS FOR YEARS ENDED OCTOBER 31, FROM 1883 TO 1893—Continued.

Month.	1888–'89.	1889–'90.	1890–'91.	1891–'92.	1892–'93.
November	$244,765	$507,435	$603,580	$1,065,780	$1,823,925
December	285,320	379,255	672,180	1,765,320	1,661,460
January	400,360	542,205	485,780	1,510,335	899,240
February	435,070	951,840	391,020	984,090	1,980,340
March	345,100	1,164,000	542,375	1,217,400	1,294,990
April	308,095	1,353,505	463,740	1,016,455	1,460,330
May	505,890	794,120	424,740	1,022,180	938,330
June	447,390	921,115	1,044,715	1,264,160	2,149,600
July	422,020	766,755	2,596,320	766,465	5,435,770
August	466,750	660,160	4,223,350	891,370	15,600,975
September	673,055	625,885	2,138,390	775,210	9,913,435
October	644,115	531,480	1,868,260	605,089	1,197,985
Total	5,209,730	9,197,755	15,458,450	13,723,864	44,365,380

STATEMENT SHOWING BY DENOMINATIONS, THE AMOUNT OF NATIONAL-BANK NOTES ISSUED AND REDEEMED SINCE THE ORGANIZATION OF THE SYSTEM, AND THE AMOUNT OUTSTANDING OCTOBER 31, 1893.

Denominations.	Number of notes—			Amounts—		
	Issued.	Redeemed.	Outstanding.	Issued.	Redeemed.	Outstanding.
Ones	$23,169,677	$22,810,808	$358,869	$23,169,677	$22,810,808.00	$358,869.00
Twos	7,747,519	7,659,754	87,765	15,495,038	15,319,508.00	175,530.00
Fives	121,095,108	108,678,534	12,416,574	605,475,510	543,392,670.00	62,082,870.00
Tens	51,939,897	45,291,954	6,647,943	519,398,970	452,919,540.00	66,479,430.00
Twenties	16,345,044	13,903,522	2,441,522	326,900,880	278,070,440.00	48,830,440.00
Fifties	2,119,415	1,008,006	211,409	105,970,750	95,400,300.00	10,570,450.00
One Hundreds	1,639,493	1,439,184	200,311	163,949,500	143,918,400.00	20,031,100.00
Five Hundreds	23,894	23,615	279	11,947,000	11,807,500.00	139,500.00
One Thousands	7,379	7,346	33	7,379,000	7,346,000.00	33,000.00
	224,087,428	201,722,723	22,364,705	1,779,686,355	1,570,985,166.00	208,701,189.00

Unpresented fractions of notes to be deducted from notes redeemed and added to the amount of notes outstanding 27,677.25   27,677.25

Total 1,570,957,488.75   208,728,866.25

STATEMENT SHOWING THE AMOUNT OF INCOMPLETE CURRENCY ISSUED BY THE BUREAU DURING THE YEAR ENDED OCTOBER 31, 1893.

National-bank currency in the vault October 31, 1892 .... $45,293,400
Amount received from the Bureau of Engraving and Printing during the year ended October 31, 1893 101,598,800

Total 146,892,200
Amount issued to banks during the year $86,184,670
Amount withdrawn from vault for cancellation 1,598,630
                                                                         87,783,300

Balance in vault at close of business October 31, 1893 59,108,900

STATEMENT SHOWING, BY STATES, THE AMOUNT OF "ADDITIONAL CIRCULATION" ISSUED AND RETIRED DURING THE YEAR ENDED OCTOBER 31, 1893, AND TOTAL AMOUNT ISSUED AND RETIRED SINCE JUNE 20, 1874.

States and Territories.	Circulation issued.			Circulation retired.		
	Under act of July 12, 1882.	Additional.	Total.	Under act of June 20, 1874.	Insolvent and liquidating banks.	Total.
Maine		$380,700	$380,700	$96,812	$127,144	$223,956
New Hampshire		778,040	778,040	61,156	101,839	162,995
Vermont	$44,420	390,590	435,010	70,490	7,153	77,643
Massachusetts		7,645,820	7,645,820	673,899	389,627	1,063,526
Rhode Island		1,331,100	1,331,100	170,406	8,040	178,446
Connecticut		1,460,250	1,460,250	193,752	128,899	322,651
New York	69,360	14,045,410	14,084,770	578,827	674,864	1,253,691
New Jersey	10,880	837,020	847,900	117,231	118,453	235,684
Pennsylvania		6,413,565	6,413,565	656,343	276,585	932,928
Delaware		107,400	107,400	17,405	25,010	42,415
Maryland		888,300	888,300	107,054	41,205	148,259
District of Columbia		229,850	229,850	3,964		3,964
Virginia	23,700	157,950	181,650	41,489	6,315	47,804
West Virginia		154,110	154,110	26,430	9,581	36,011
North Carolina		88,720	88,720	12,213		12,213
South Carolina		5,400	5,400	15,075		15,075
Georgia		112,500	112,500	41,303	11,910	53,213
Florida		56,250	56,250	30,030		30,030
Alabama	30,000	28,350	58,350	41,597		41,597
Mississippi				10		10
Louisiana	45,000		45,000	48,137	77,825	125,902
Texas		351,060	351,960	64,041	16,370	80,411
Arkansas				18,011	9,000	27,011
Kentucky		286,200	286,200	174,819	51,857	226,676
Tennessee		31,500	31,500	73,514		73,514
Missouri	7,380	22,500	29,880	73,117	38,790	111,907
Ohio	4,000	3,469,530	3,473,530	319,918	258,035	577,953
Indiana		903,800	903,800	117,012	151,076	268,088
Illinois	67,645	530,085	597,730	93,846	9,815	103,661
Michigan	2,100	2,074,400	2,076,500	126,313	9,482	135,796
Wisconsin		295,760	295,760	42,997	60,186	103,183
Iowa		299,720	299,720	76,326	24,939	101,265
Minnesota		96,740	96,740	36,074	5,460	41,534
Kansas	8,100	141,760	149,860	157,459	19,230	176,689
Nebraska		90,095	90,095	73,139	1,500	74,639
Nevada				35		35
Oregon				8,250		8,250
Colorado		16,650	16,650	12,247	72,686	84,933
Idaho		22,510	22,510	2,616	270	2,886
Montana		56,250	56,250	7,020	1,040	8,060
Wyoming				17,097		17,097
North Dakota		33,750	33,750	3,880		3,880
South Dakota		56,240	56,240	30,705		30,705
Washington		11,260	11,260	30,150	7,100	37,250
California		33,750	33,750	29,080	76,570	105,650
Utah	42,900		42,900	15,797	39,841	55,638
New Mexico				11,962		11,962
Arizona		22,500	22,500	420		420
Oklahoma		22,500	22,500	4,800		4,800
Indian Territory		10	10			
Alaska						
Total	355,485	44,009,895	44,365,380	4,624,268	2,857,697	7,481,965
Surrendered to this office and retired						205,362
From June 20, 1874, to October 31, 1892				272,665,387	294,273,046	139,815,052	434,088,008
Surrendered and retired same dates						16,343,878
Grand total October 31, 1893.				317,030,767	298,897,314	142,672,749	458,119,303

Notes of gold banks are not included in the above table.

STATEMENT EXHIBITING THE AMOUNT OF NATIONAL-BANK NOTES RECEIVED MONTHLY FOR REDEMPTION BY THE COMPTROLLER OF THE CURRENCY DURING THE YEAR ENDED OCTOBER 31, 1893, AND THE AMOUNT RECEIVED DURING THE SAME PERIOD AT THE REDEMPTION AGENCY OF THE TREASURY, TOGETHER WITH THE TOTAL AMOUNT RECEIVED SINCE THE APPROVAL OF THE ACT OF JUNE 20, 1874.

Months.	Received by the Comptroller of the Currency.					Received at the United States Treasury redemption agency.
	From national banks in connection with reduction of circulation and replacement with now notes.	From the redemption agency.			Total.	
		For replacement with new notes.	For reduction of circulation under act of June 20, 1874.	Insolvent and liquidating national banks.		
November, 1892	$30	$3,786,199	$467,860	$639,334	$4,893,423	$5,471,649
December, 1892	20	3,918,450	344,452	472,093	4,735,015	6,969,662
January, 1893	1,870	4,401,750	396,231	504,288	5,304,139	9,731,987
February, 1893	540	4,627,035	323,202	487,430	5,438,207	5,864,411
March, 1893	670	4,380,268	297,141	441,584	5,119,663	5,524,568
April, 1893	13,386	3,328,593	185,933	345,971	3,873,877	6,991,570
May, 1893	1,380	4,369,915	212,196	449,040	5,032,531	8,150,482
June, 1893	15,400	3,760,096	155,331	335,331	4,206,218	5,082,039
July, 1893	5,050	2,572,730	117,091	299,784	2,995,555	3,877,423
August, 1893	2,940	1,953,845	86,121	204,677	2,247,583	2,609,855
September, 1893	90,880	1,375,588	60,107	154,246	1,686,821	7,275,730
October, 1893		3,609,090	205,132	290,491	4,104,713	12,505,692
Total	132,220	42,023,559	2,857,697	4,624,269	49,637,745	80,145,068
Received from June 20, 1874, to Oct. 31, 1892	16,853,295	910,795,682	294,214,745	139,690,061	1,361,553,783	2,190,112,040
Grand total	16,985,515	952,819,241	297,072,442	144,314,330	1,411,191,528	2,270,257,108

Notes of gold banks are not included in the above table.

STATEMENT SHOWING THE NATIONAL-BANK NOTES RECEIVED AT THE BUREAU AND DESTROYED YEARLY SINCE THE ESTABLISHMENT OF THE SYSTEM.

Prior to November 1, 1865	$175,490	During year ended October 31—	
During year ended October 31—		1882	$74,917,611
1866	1,050,382	1883	82,913,766
1867	3,401,423	1884	93,178,418
1868	4,602,825	1885	91,048,723
1869	8,603,729	1886	59,989,810
1870	14,305,689	1887	47,726,083
1871	24,344,047	1888	59,568,525
1872	30,211,720	1889	52,207,027
1873	36,433,171	1890	44,447,467
1874	49,939,741	1891	45,981,463
1875	137,897,696	1892	43,885,319
1876	98,672,716	1893	44,895,466
1877	76,918,963	Additional amount of insolvent and	
1878	57,381,249	liquidating national-bank notes	
1879	41,101,830	destroyed	154,870,457
1880	35,539,660		
1881	54,941,130	Total	1,570,953,196

Notes of gold banks are not included in above table.

There was in the vault of the redemption division of this office, awaiting destruction, at the close of business October 31, 1892 ... $127,582.50
Received during the year ended October 31, 1893 ... 49,644,870.00

Total ... 49,772,452.50
Withdrawn and destroyed during the year ... 49,526,860.00

Balance in vault October 31, 1893 ... 245,592.50

STATEMENT SHOWING AMOUNT OF TAX ON CIRCULATION, COST OF REDEMPTION, ASSESSMENT FOR PLATES, AND EXAMINERS' FEES FOR THE YEAR ENDED JUNE 30, 1893.

Semiannual duty on circulation	$1,443,489.69
Cost of redemption of notes by the United States Treasurer	103,032.96
Assessment for cost of plates, new banks	14,225.00
Assessment for cost of plates, extended banks	5,200.00
Assessment for examiners' fees (sec. 5240, Revised Statutes)	162,444.59
Total	1,728,392.24

STATEMENT SHOWING BY COMPARISON THE AMOUNT OF TAXES ASSESSED AS SEMI-ANNUAL DUTY ON CIRCULATING NOTES, COST OF REDEMPTION, COST OF PLATES, AND EXAMINERS' FEES FOR THE PAST ELEVEN YEARS.

Years.	Semiannual duty on circulation.	Cost of redemption of notes by the United States Treasurer.	Assessment for cost of plates, new banks.	Assessment for cost of plates, extended banks.	Assessment for examiners' fees (sec. 5240, R. S.).	Total.
1883	$3,132,006.73	$147,592.27	$25,980.00	$34,120.00	$94,606.16	$3,434,305.16
1884	3,024,668.24	160,896.65	18,845.00	1,950.00	99,642.05	3,306,001.94
1885	2,794,584.01	181,857.16	13,150.00	97,800.00	107,781.73	3,195,172.90
1886	2,592,021.33	168,243.35	14,810.00	24,825.00	107,272.83	2,907,172.51
1887	2,044,922.75	138,967.00	18,850.00	1,750.00	110,219.88	2,314,709.63
1888	1,616,127.53	141,141.48	14,100.00	3,900.00	121,777.86	1,897,046.87
1889	1,410,331.84	131,190.67	12,200.00	575.00	130,725.79	1,685,023.30
1890	1,254,839.65	107,843.39	24,175.00	725.00	136,772.71	1,524,355.75
1891	1,216,104.72	99,366.52	18,575.00	7,200.00	138,969.39	1,480,215.63
1892	1,331,287.26	100,593.70	15,700.00	8,100.00	161,983.68	1,617,664.64
1893	1,443,489.69	103,032.96	14,225.00	5,200.00	162,444.59	1,728,392.24
Total	21,860,383.75	1,480,725.15	190,610.00	186,145.00	1,372,196.67	25,090,060.57

STATEMENT SHOWING THE TOTAL CAPITAL AND BONDS OF NATIONAL BANKS WHICH DO NOT ISSUE CIRCULATING NOTES.

	Capital.	Bonds.
Chemical National Bank, New York, N. Y	$300,000	$50,000
Mechanics' National Bank, New York, N. Y	2,000,000	50,000
National Bank of Washington, D. C.	200,000	50,000
National Bank of Cockeysville, Md	50,000	12,500
Total	2,550,000	162,500

STATEMENT SHOWING THE AMOUNT AND KINDS OF UNITED STATES BONDS HELD
TO SECURE CIRCULATING NOTES OF NATIONAL BANKS ON JUNE 30 OF EACH
YEAR FROM 1865 TO 1893, AND THE AMOUNT OWNED AND HELD BY THE BANKS
FOR OTHER PURPOSES, INCLUDING THOSE DEPOSITED WITH THE TREASURER TO
SECURE PUBLIC DEPOSITS.

Years.	United States bonds held as security for circulation.					United States bonds held for other purposes at nearest date.	Grand total.
	6 per cent bonds.	5 per cent bonds.	4½ per cent bonds.	4 per cent bonds.	Total.		
1865 ..	$170,382,500	$65,576,600	....	....	$235,959,100	$155,785,750	$391,744,850
1866 ..	241,083,500	86,226,850	....	....	327,310,350	121,152,950	448,463,300
1867 ..	251,430,400	89,177,100	....	....	340,607,500	84,002,650	424,610,150
1868 ..	250,726,950	90,768,950	....	....	341,495,900	80,922,500	422,118,400
1869 ..	255,190,350	87,661,250	....	....	342,851,600	55,102,000	397,953,600
1870 ..	247,335,350	94,923,200	....	....	342,278,550	43,980,600	386,259,150
1871 ..	220,497,750	139,387,800	....	....	359,885,550	30,450,800	393,336,350
1872 ..	173,251,450	207,189,250	....	....	380,440,700	31,868,200	412,308,900
1873 ..	160,923,500	229,487,050	....	....	390,410,550	25,724,400	416,134,150
1874 ..	154,370,700	236,800,500	....	....	391,171,200	25,347,100	416,518,300
1875 ..	136,955,100	239,359,400	....	....	376,314,500	26,960,200	403,214,700
1876 ..	100,313,450	232,081,300	....	....	341,394,750	45,170,300	386,565,050
1877 ..	87,690,300	206,651,050	$14,372,250	....	338,713,600	47,315,050	386,028,650
1878 ..	82,421,200	109,514,550	48,418,650	$19,162,000	340,546,400	68,859,900	418,397,300
1879 ..	56,642,800	144,616,300	35,056,550	118,538,950	354,254,600	76,603,520	430,858,120
1880 ..	58,056,150	139,758,650	37,760,950	126,076,300	361,652,050	42,831,300	404,483,350
1881 ..	61,901,800	172,348,350	32,600,500	93,637,700	360,488,400	63,849,950	424,338,350
	Continued at 3½ per cent.	Continued at 3½ per cent.					
1882 ..	25,142,600	202,487,650 { 7,402,800}	32,752,650	97,429,800	357,812,700	43,122,550	400,935,250
1883 ..	385,700	{ 3 per cents: } { 200,877,850} 172,412,550	39,408,500	104,954,650	353,029,500	34,094,150	387,123,650
1884 ..	....	172,412,550	46,546,400	111,690,900	330,649,850	31,203,000	161,852,850
	Pacifics:						
1885 ..	3,520,000	142,240,850	48,483,050	117,901,300	312,145,200	32,195,800	344,341,000
1886 ..	3,565,000	107,782,100	50,484,200	114,143,500	275,974,800	31,345,550	307,320,350
1887 ..	3,175,000	5,205,930	67,743,100	115,842,650	191,966,700	33,147,750	224,814,450
1888 ..	3,181,000	37,500	69,670,300	105,423,850	178,312,650	63,618,150	211,930,800
1889 ..	4,324,000	....	42,409,900	101,387,550	148,121,450	51,642,100	199,763,550
1890 ..	4,913,000	....	39,486,750	100,828,550	145,224,300	35,287,350	180,515,650
1891 ..	7,957,000	....	22,565,950	111,985,950	142,508,900	30,114,150	172,623,050
			Continued at 2 per cent.				
1892 ..	11,600,000	....	21,825,350	129,764,700	163,190,050	20,301,600	183,491,650
1893 ..	12,426,000	....	22,020,550	142,141,700	176,588,250	18,334,050	194,922,300

STATEMENT SHOWING THE AMOUNT OF UNITED STATES BONDS HELD TO SECURE
CIRCULATING NOTES OF NATIONAL BANKS FOR THE YEARS ENDED OCTOBER 31,
FROM 1882 TO 1893, INCLUSIVE, AND EXHIBITING THE CHANGES WHICH OCCURRED
IN THE SEVERAL CLASSES OF BONDS.

Year.	Number of banks.	United States bonds held as security for circulation.					United States bonds held for other purposes at nearest date.	Grand total.
		4½ per cent bonds.	4 per cent bonds.	3 per cent. bonds.	Pacific 6 per cent bonds.	Total.		
1882.......	2,301	$33,754,650	$104,927,500	{$10,621,950} {179,675,550}	$3,526,000	$362,505,650	$37,563,750	$400,069,400
1883.......	2,522	41,319,700	106,164,850	{ * 602,000} {201,327,700}	3,463,000	352,877,300	30,674,050	383,551,350
1884.......	2,671	49,537,450	116,705,450	155,604,400	3,460,000	325,316,300	30,419,600	355,735,900
1885.......	2,727	49,547,250	116,391,650	138,920,650	3,505,000	308,361,550	31,780,100	340,144,650
1886.......	2,868	57,436,850	115,383,150	60,038,050	3,586,000	245,444,050	32,431,400	277,875,450
1887.......	3,061	69,696,100	115,731,400	144,500	3,256,000	188,828,000	34,671,350	223,499,350
1888.......	3,151	66,121,750	100,413,600	....	3,468,000	170,003,350	60,715,050	230,718,400
1889.......	3,319	41,066,150	100,040,000	....	4,553,000	145,608,150	48,501,200	194,169,350
1890.......	3,567	28,116,700	105,402,200	....	6,072,000	140,190,900	30,684,000	170,874,900
1891.......	3,694	{199,400} {Continued at 2 p. ct.} {21,648,100}	120,858,850	....	10,244,000	152,950,350	24,871,950	177,822,500
1892.......	3,788	21,897,850	131,133,150	....	11,852,000	164,883,000	20,104,250	185,047,250
1893.......	3,796	22,020,550	142,141,700	....	12,426,000	176,588,250	17,576,950	194,165,200

* Three and one-half per cent.

STATEMENT SHOWING THE AMOUNT OF INTEREST-BEARING BONDED DEBT OF THE UNITED STATES FROM 1865 to 1893, INCLUSIVE.

Date.	6 per cent.	5 per cent.	4½ per cent.*	4 per cent.†	6 per cent.‡	Total.
Aug. 31, 1865 ...	$908, 518, 091	$199, 792, 100			$1, 258, 000	$1, 109, 568, 191
June 30, 1866 ...	1, 008, 388, 469	198, 528, 435			6, 642, 000	1, 212, 958, 904
June 30, 1867 ...	1, 421, 110, 719	198, 533, 435			14, 762, 000	1, 634, 406, 154
June 30, 1868 ..	1, 841, 521, 800	221, 588, 400			20, 089, 000	2, 002, 199, 200
June 30, 1869 ...	1, 886, 341, 300	221, 589, 300			58, 638, 320	2, 166. 568, 920
June 30, 1870 ...	1, 764, 932, 300	221, 589, 300			64, 457, 320	2, 050. 978, 920
June 30, 1871 ...	1, 613, 897, 300	274, 236, 450			64, 618, 832	1, 952, 752, 582
June 30, 1872 ...	1, 374, 883, 800	414, 567, 300			64, 623, 512	1, 845, 074, 612
June 30, 1873 ...	1, 281, 238, 650	414, 567, 300			64, 623, 512	1, 760, 429, 462
June 30, 1874 ...	1, 213, 624, 700	510. 628, 050			64, 623, 512	1, 788, 876, 262
June 30, 1875 ...	1, 100, 865, 550	607, 132, 750			64, 623, 512	1, 772, 621, 812
June 30, 1876 . .	984, 999, 650	711, 685, 800			64, 623, 512	1, 761, 308, 962
June 30, 1877 ...	854, 621, 850	703, 266, 650	$140, 000, 000		64, 623, 512	1, 761, 512, 012
June 30, 1878 ...	738, 619, 000	703, 266, 650	240, 000, 000	$98, 850, 000	64, 623, 512	1, 845, 359, 162
June 30, 1879 ...	310, 932, 500	646, 905, 500	250, 000, 000	679, 878, 110	64, 623, 512	1, 952, 339, 622
June 30, 1880 ...	235, 780, 400	484, 864, 900	250, 000, 000	739, 347, 800	64, 623, 512	1, 774, 616, 612
June 30, 1881 ...	196, 378, 600	439, 841, 350	250, 000, 000	739, 347, 800	64, 623, 512	1, 690, 191, 262
	Continued at 3½ per cent.	Continued at 3½ per cent.				
June 30, 1882 ..	58, 957, 150	401, 503, 000	250, 000, 000	739, 349, 350	64, 623, 512	1, 514, 433, 912
		32, 082, 600				
		Funded into 3 per cents,				
June 30, 1883 ...		act July 12,	250, 000, 000	737, 942, 200	64, 623, 512	1, 388, 852, 662
		1882.				
		304, 204, 350				
June 30, 1884 ...		224. 612, 150	250, 000, 000	737, 661, 700	64, 623, 512	1, 276, 987, 362
June 30, 1885 ...		194, 190, 500	250, 000, 000	737, 719, 850	64, 623, 512	1, 246, 533, 862
June 30, 1886 ...		144, 046, 600	250, 000, 000	737, 759, 700	64, 623, 512	1, 196, 429, 812
June 30, 1887 ...		19, 716, 500	250, 000, 000	737, 800, 600	64, 623, 512	1, 072, 140, 612
June 30, 1888 ...			222, 207, 050	714, 177, 400	64. 623, 512	1, 001, 007, 962
June 30, 1889 ...			139, 639, 000	676, 095, 350	64, 623, 512	880, 357, 862
June 30, 1890 ...			109, 015, 750	602, 193, 500	64, 623, 512	775, 832, 762
June 30, 1891 ...			50. 869, 200	559, 566, 000	64, 623, 512	675, 058, 712
			Continued at 2 per cent.			
June 30, 1892 ...			25, 364, 500	559, 581, 250	64, 623, 512	649, 569, 262
June 30, 1893 ...			25, 364, 500	559, 604, 150	64, 623, 512	649, 592, 162
Oct. 31, 1893 ...			25, 364, 500	559, 609, 850	64, 623, 512	649, 597, 862

* Funded loan 1891; authorizing act July 14, 1870, and January 20, 1871; date of maturity, 1891.
† Funded loan 1907; authorizing act July 14, 1870, and January 20, 1871; date of maturity, 1907.
‡ Pacific railroad bonds; authorizing act July 1, 1862, and July 2, 1864, date of maturity, 1895 to 1899. The refunding certificates amounting to $64,600 are not included in the table.
The public debt reached the maximum August 31, 1865, and amounted to $2,844,649,626. The non-interest-bearing obligations amounted to $461,616,311, the interest-bearing debt being $2,383,033,315. On October 31, 1893, the interest-bearing debt amounted to $559,609,850.

STATEMENT SHOWING THE MARKET PRICES OF UNITED STATES BONDS BY WEEKS DURING THE YEAR ENDED OCTOBER 31, PREPARED BY THE ACTUARY OF THE TREASURY.

Week ended –	2 per cent.			4 per cent.		
	Opening.	Highest.	Lowest.	Opening.	Highest.	Lowest.
November 4, 1892	100½	100½	100	114¾-115	114¾-115	114½-114¾
November 11, 1892	100	100¼	100	114¼-115	114¾-115½	114¼-115
November 18, 1892	100¼	100¼	100¼	114½-115	114½-115¼	114½-114⅞
November 25, 1892	100¼	100¼	100¼	114½-115¼	114½-115¼	114½-114⅞
December 2, 1892	100¼	100¼	100	114½-115	114¾-115¼	113-113¾
December 9, 1892	100	100	100	113-113¾	113-113¾	113-113½
December 16, 1892	100	100	100	113-113½	113½-113¾	113-113½
December 23, 1892	100	100	100	113-113½	113-113½	112½-113¼
December 30, 1892	100	100	100	112½-113¼	113¼-114	112½-113¼
January 6, 1893	100	100	100	113-114	113½-114½	113-114
January 13, 1893	100	100	100	113¾-114½	113¾-114½	113¼-113⅜
January 20, 1893	100	100	100	113¼-114	113½-114¼	113½-114
January 27, 1893	100	100	100	113½-114¼	113¾-114½	113½-114¼
February 3, 1893	100	100	100	113¾-114½	113¾-114½	113-114½
February 10, 1893	100	100	99½	113¾-114½	113¾-114½	112¾-113¼
February 17, 1893	99½	99½	99½	112¼-113	112½-113¼	112¼-113
February 24, 1893	99½	99½	99½	112¼-113	112¼-113¼	112-113
March 3, 1893	99½	99½	99½	112½-113¼	112½-113¼	111½-112¼
March 10, 1893	99½	99½	99½	111½-112¼	111½-112¼	111½-112¼
March 17, 1893	99½	99½	99⅜	111½-112	111½-112½	111½-112
March 24, 1893	99½	99½	99½	111½-112½	112-112¾	111½-112½
March 31, 1893	99½	99½	99⅛	112-112¾	113-113¾	112-112⅝
April 7, 1893	99½	99½	99½	113-113¾	113-113¾	113-113¾
April 14, 1893	99	99½	99	113-113¾	113-113¾	113-113¾
April 21, 1893	99½	99⅛	99	113-113⅜	113-113¾	112½-113¼
April 28, 1893	99	99	99	112¾-113¼	113-113½	112¾-113¼
May 5, 1893	99	99	99	112¾-113½	112¾-113½	112½-113¼
May 12, 1893	99	99	99	112½-113¼	112½-113¼	112¼-113
May 19, 1893	99	99	99	112½-113¼	112¾-113½	112½-113¼
May 26, 1893	99	99	99	112¾-113½	113-113¾	112¾-113½
June 2, 1893	99	99	99	112¾-113½	112¾-113½	111½-112½
June 9, 1893	99	99	98½	111¼-112¼	111½-112¼	110½-111½
June 16, 1893	98	98	98	110½-111½	110½-111½	109-110
June 23, 1893	98	98	97	109-110	109¼-110	109-109¾
June 30, 1893	96	96	96	109-110	109-110	109-110
July 7, 1893	96	98	96	108¾-109¾	110-111	108¾-109¾
July 14, 1893	96	97½	96	110-111	111-112	110-111
July 21, 1893	97	97	97	111-112	111-112	110½-111½
July 28, 1893	97	97	96	110½-111½	110½-111½	108½-109½
August 4, 1893	96	96	95	108½-109½	109-110	108-109
August 11, 1893	95	95	95	109-110	110-111½	109-110
August 18, 1893	95	95½	95	110-111½	111½-112½	110-111½
August 25, 1893	95	97	95	111½-112½	112-113	111-112
September 1, 1893	97	98	97	111-112½	111-112½	110-111½
September 8, 1893	98	98	98	110½-111½	110½-111½	110-111½
September 15, 1893	99½	99½	98	110½-111½	110½-111½	110-111
September 22, 1893	98	98	98	110-111	110-111	110-111
September 29, 1893	98	98	98	110-111	110-111	110-111
October 6, 1893	98	98	98	110-111	110-111½	110-111
October 13, 1893	98	98	98	110½-111½	111-112	110½-111½
October 20, 1893	98	98	97	110¾-111½	111¼-112	110¾-111½
October 27, 1893	98	98	97	111-111¾	111-111¾	111-111¾

STATEMENT SHOWING THE INVESTMENT VALUE OF UNITED STATES 4½ AND 4 PER CENT BONDS FROM 1885 TO 1893, INCLUSIVE, FOR EACH QUARTERLY PERIOD.

Date.	4½ per cent bonds.		4 per cent bonds.	
	Average price flat.	Rate of interest realized by investors.	Average price flat.	Rate of interest realized by investors.
1885:	Per cent.	Per cent.	Per cent.	Per cent.
January	112.7788	2.655	121.9086	2.726
April	112.4350	2.488	121.8028	2.721
July	112.7525	2.365	122.6462	2.668
October	112.9421	2.250	123.4004	2.619
1886:				
January	112.7000	2.208	123,4325	2.607
April	112.4759	2.150	126.2980	2.444
July	111.8156	2.149	126.4975	2.420
October	111.9855	2.003	128.6650	2.289
1887:				
January	110.2775	2.290	127.8325	2.320
April	110.1947	2.019	129.2451	2.227
July	109.1475	2.340	127.8425	2.284
October	108.5553	2.339	125.7885	2.390
1888:				
January	108.2375	2.280	126.1275	2.341
April	107.1025	2.478	124.6400	2.449
July	107.5175	2.195	127.4825	2.230
October	108.4213	1.693	128.1204	2.178
1889:				
January	108.9255	1.254	127.2837	2.208
April	108.1848	1.240	129.1902	2.080
July	107.0048	1.421	128.3894	2.109
October	105.8241	1.645	127.1944	2.160
1890:				
January	104.7885	1.856	125.6178	2.236
April	103.7500	2.151	122.1175	2.435
July	103.3825	1.966	122.3200	2.407
October	104.1296	0.409	123.5602	2.309
1891:				
January	103.1106	0.424	120.9279	2.463
April	101.7590	1.363	122.0264	2.372
July	100.3846	5.971	117.3317	2.676
October			116.7546	2.701
1892:				
January	2 cents at par		116.6719	2.693
April			116.1575	2.715
July			116.4557	2.677
October			115.0978	2.766
1893:				
January			113.8250	2.849
April			113.3646	2.877
July			110.5450	3.079
October			111.2356	3.011

TABLE BY STATES, TERRITORIES, AND RESERVE CITIES, EXHIBITING THE NUMBER OF BANKS IN EACH, CAPITAL, BONDS ACTUALLY HELD ON OCTOBER 3, 1893, MINIMUM AMOUNT OF BONDS REQUIRED BY LAW, AND THE EXCESS OF BONDS ON OCTOBER 3, 1893, AND SEPTEMBER 30, 1892.

States, Territories, and reserve cities.	No. of banks.	Capital.	United States bonds.		Excess of bonds.	
			Held October 3, 1893.	Minimum required.	October 3, 1893.	September 30, 1892.
Maine	83	$11,220,600	$4,246,900	$2,130,000	$2,116,900	$1,751,400
New Hampshire	51	6,130,000	3,689,000	1,507,500	2,181,500	1,369,875
Vermont	48	6,985,000	3,445,000	1,458,750	1,986,250	1,572,500
Massachusetts	214	46,117,500	19,977,100	8,381,875	11,595,225	8,045,275
Boston	55	53,350,000	10,565,000	2,750,000	7,815,000	2,860,000
Rhode Island	59	20,277,050	7,721,250	2,437,500	5,283,750	3,804,750
Connecticut	84	22,999,370	7,845,500	3,412,000	4,433,500	2,770,925
Division No. 1	594	167,079,520	57,489,750	22,077,625	35,412,125	22,174,725
New York	274	33,674,360	17,180,700	7,841,240	9,699,460	6,965,035
New York City	49	51,250,000	18,148,500	2,450,000	15,698,500	4,309,000
Albany	6	1,550,000	600,000	300,000	300,000	....
Brooklyn	5	1,352,000	642,000	250,000	392,000	292,000
New Jersey	99	14,608,350	5,237,250	2,962,087	2,275,163	1,377,163
Pennsylvania	326	39,103,900	15,258,500	8,658,490	6,600,010	4,138,708
Philadelphia	41	22,765,000	6,707,500	2,037,500	4,670,000	2,150,000
Pittsburg	29	11,640,000	3,226,500	1,425,000	1,801,500	505,000
Division No. 2	829	175,943,670	67,000,950	25,564,317	41,436,633	19,737,406
Delaware	18	2,133,985	926,000	455,000	471,000	284,800
Maryland	46	3,724,320	1,710,500	918,155	792,345	671,000
Baltimore	22	13,243,260	2,020,000	1,100,000	920,000	200,000
District of Columbia	1	252,600	250,000	50,000	200,000	200,000
Washington	12	2,575,000	905,400	600,000	305,400	75,000
Virginia	36	4,796,300	1,594,250	985,250	609,000	433,750
West Virginia	30	2,961,000	962,500	738,750	223,750	92,588
Division No. 3	165	29,685,865	8,368,650	4,847,155	3,521,495	1,957,138
North Carolina	24	2,676,000	867,600	644,000	223,600	137,705
South Carolina	14	1,748,000	474,750	399,500	75,250	75,500
Georgia	27	3,766,000	1,005,000	754,000	251,000	151,000
Florida	17	1,300,000	367,500	325,000	42,500	42,500
Alabama	28	3,504,000	1,083,500	717,250	366,250	366,000
Mississippi	12	1,055,000	338,750	263,750	75,000	62,500
Louisiana	11	810,000	252,500	202,500	50,000	50,000
New Orleans	9	3,125,000	900,000	450,000	450,000	430,000
Texas	222	23,596,175	5,180,600	5,011,544	169,056	70,476
Arkansas	9	1,100,000	250,000	250,000	....	10,000
Kentucky	71	10,061,400	3,405,500	2,259,100	1,146,400	1,164,275
Louisville	10	4,401,500	555,000	500,000	55,000	....
Tennessee	52	9,400,000	1,364,000	1,331,250	32,750	27,880
Division No. 4	506	66,633,075	16,044,700	13,107,894	2,936,806	2,607,842
Ohio	218	27,495,100	10,078,750	5,982,775	4,095,975	2,602,707
Cincinnati	13	9,100,000	4,175,000	650,000	3,525,000	2,117,000
Cleveland	11	9,050,000	1,465,000	550,000	915,000	175,000
Indiana	115	13,777,000	5,072,050	3,081,750	1,990,300	1,246,800
Illinois	191	17,295,450	5,646,000	4,230,113	1,415,887	964,250
Chicago	21	20,900,000	1,200,000	1,050,000	150,000	150,000
Michigan	92	10,234,000	3,693,000	2,171,000	1,522,000	163,250
Detroit	8	4,400,000	1,450,000	400,000	1,050,000	100,000
Wisconsin	76	7,019,319	1,875,250	1,667,330	207,920	• 73,587
Milwaukee	5	2,300,000	450,000	250,000	200,000	200,000
Division No. 5	750	121,570,869	35,105,050	20,032,968	15,072,082	7,792,594
Iowa	165	14,000,000	3,522,500	3,137,500	385,000	284,500
Des Moines	4	700,000	175,000	150,000	25,000	....
Minnesota	65	6,080,070	1,355,800	1,276,267	79,533	93,838
St. Paul	4	2,800,000	250,000	200,000	50,000	50,000
Minneapolis	7	5,450,000	350,000	350,000	....	....
Missouri	57	4,615,000	1,195,300	1,141,250	54,050	47,800
St. Louis	9	10,700,000	450,000	450,000	....	....
Kansas City	8	5,550,000	400,000	400,000	....	25,000
St. Joseph	4	2,000,000	250,000	200,000	50,000	125,000
Kansas	136	11,647,100	2,881,500	2,599,275	282,225	169,725
Nebraska	121	7,793,170	2,042,500	1,948,292	94,208	71,725
Omaha	9	4,150,000	780,000	450,000	330,000	280,000
Lincoln	4	1,000,000	175,000	175,000	....	....
Division No. 6	593	76,485,340	13,827,600	12,477,584	1,350,016	1,147,588

TABLE, BY STATES, TERRITORIES, AND RESERVE CITIES EXHIBITING THE NUMBER
OF BANKS IN EACH, CAPITAL, ETC.—Continued.

States, Territories, and reserve cities.	No. of banks.	Capital.	United States bonds.		Excess of bonds.	
			Held October 3, 1893.	Minimum required.	October 3, 1893.	September 30, 1892.
Colorado	51	$8, 775, 000	$1, 642, 750	$1, 318, 750	$324, 000	$320, 500
Nevada	2	282, 000	70, 500	70, 500		
California	33	6, 625, 000	1, 306, 250	1, 068, 750	237, 500	300, 000
San Francisco	2	2, 500, 000	100, 000	100, 000		
Oregon	39	3, 795, 000	776, 050	773, 750	2, 300	2, 300
Arizona	5	400, 000	100, 500	100, 000	500	500
Division No. 7	132	21, 377, 000	3, 996, 050	3, 431, 750	564, 300	623, 300
North Dakota	32	2, 215, 000	569, 000	553, 750	15, 250	15, 250
South Dakota	39	2, 510, 000	692, 250	627, 500	64, 750	2, 250
Idaho	13	825, 000	206, 250	206, 250		6, 550
Montana	22	2, 775, 000	575, 600	568, 750	6, 850	8, 350
New Mexico	10	750, 000	265, 000	187, 500	77, 500	80, 000
Utah	14	2, 800, 000	475, 000	462, 500	12, 500	12, 500
Washington	57	6, 020, 000	1, 380, 500	1, 380, 000	500	39, 150
Wyoming	13	1, 210, 000	302, 500	302, 500		
Oklahoma	6	300, 000	75, 000	75, 000		3, 750
Indian Territory	6	360, 000	90, 000	90, 000		2, 700
Division No. 8	212	19, 765, 000	4, 631, 100	4, 453, 750	177, 350	170, 500
United States	3, 781	678, 540, 339	206, 463, 850	105, 993, 043	100, 470, 807	56, 211, 093

TABLE, BY STATES, TERRITORIES, AND RESERVE CITIES, EXHIBITING THE NUMBER OF BANKS IN EACH, WITH CAPITAL OF $150,000 AND UNDER, FOR THE YEARS 1892 AND 1893, AND THE INCREASE OR DECREASE IN BANKS AND CAPITAL DURING THE INTERVAL.

States, Territories, and reserve cities.	September 30, 1892.		October 3, 1893.		Increase.		Decrease.	
	No.	Capital.	No.	Capital.	No.	Capital.	No.	Capital.
Maine	66	$5,390,000	68	$5,520,600	2	$130,600		
New Hampshire	46	4,572,500	43	4,430,000			3	$142,500
Vermont	38	3,710,000	37	3,635,000			1	75,000
Massachusetts	103	12,260,700	103	11,327,500				933,200
Boston								
Rhode Island	23	2,550,000	23	2,550,000				
Connecticut	34	3,648,300	34	3,648,000				300
Division No. 1	310	32,131,500	308	31,111,100	2	130,600	4	1,150,800
New York	213	18,994,660	222	19,524,960	9	530,300		
New York City								
Albany								
Brooklyn								
New Jersey	63	5,768,350	66	5,848,350	1	80,000		
Pennsylvania	240	20,627,370	263	22,033,960	23	1,406,590		
Philadelphia	1	150,000	1	150,000				
Pittsburg	1	100,000	1	100,000				
Division No. 2	527	45,640,380	556	47,657,270	33	2,016,890		
Delaware	14	1,020,800	14	1,020,800				
Maryland	40	2,910,000	43	3,072,620	3	162,620		
Baltimore								
District of Columbia								
Washington	1	100,000	1	100,000				
Virginia	27	2,141,000	27	2,141,000				
West Virginia	24	1,994,650	26	2,155,000	2	160,350		
Division No. 3	106	8,166,450	111	8,489,420	5	322,970		
North Carolina	18	1,525,180	19	1,576,000	1	50,820		
South Carolina	11	973,000	11	998,000				25,000
Georgia	23	1,941,000	20	1,616,000			3	325,000
Florida	18	1,350,000	17	1,300,000			1	50,000
Alabama	22	1,744,000	22	1,669,000				75,000
Mississippi	13	1,165,000	12	1,055,000			1	110,000
Louisiana	10	610,000	10	610,000				
New Orleans								
Texas	194	15,105,495	197	15,046,175	3	59,320		
Arkansas	7	600,000	7	600,000				
Kentucky	49	4,652,900	49	4,636,400				16,500
Louisville								
Tennessee	42	3,204,455	40	2,925,000			2	279,455
Division No. 4	407	32,871,030	404	32,031,575	4	135,140	7	855,955
Ohio	171	14,563,170	171	14,531,100				32,070
Cincinnati								
Cleveland								
Indiana	83	7,297,000	94	8,127,000	11	830,000		
Illinois	168	12,671,000	171	12,920,450	3	249,000		
Chicago								
Michigan	85	6,919,000	83	6,884,000			2	35,000
Detroit								
Wisconsin	67	5,042,650	69	5,269,319	2	226,669		
Milwaukee								
Division No. 5	574	46,492,820	588	47,731,869	16	1,305,669	2	67,070
Iowa	147	10,120,000	153	10,150,000	6	30,000		
Des Moines	2	200,000	2	200,000				
Minnesota	52	3,293,850	58	3,705,070	6	411,220		
St. Paul								
Minneapolis								
Missouri	53	3,740,000	53	3,765,000				25,000
St. Louis								
Kansas City	1	100,000					1	100,000
St. Joseph	1	100,000	1	100,000				
Kansas	134	9,492,100	129	8,997,100			5	495,000
Nebraska	121	7,718,100	120	7,593,170			1	124,930
Omaha								
Lincoln	1	100,000	1	100,000				
Division No. 6	512	34,864,050	517	34,610,340	12	466,220	7	719,930

TABLE, BY STATES, TERRITORIES, AND RESERVE CITIES, EXHIBITING THE NUMBER OF BANKS IN EACH, WITH CAPITAL OF $150,000 AND UNDER, ETC.—Continued.

States, Territories, and reserve cities.	September 30, 1892.		October 3, 1893.		Increase.		Decrease.	
	No.	Capital.	No.	Capital.	No.	Capital.	No.	Capital.
Colorado	38	$2,515,000	37	$2,475,000			1	$40,000
Nevada	1	82,000	1	82,000				
California	22	2,075,000	22	2,075,000				
San Francisco								
Oregon	36	2,245,000	34	2,095,000			2	150,000
Arizona	4	300,000	5	400,000	1	$100,000		
Division No. 7	101	7,217,000	99	7,127,000	1	100,000	3	190,000
North Dakota	31	2,015,000	31	2,015,000				
South Dakota	39	2,410,000	38	2,310,000			1	100,000
Idaho	11	700,000	13	825,000	2	125,000		
Montana	26	1,990,000	18	1,475,000	.c		8	515,000
New Mexico	10	740,000	10	750,000		10,000		
Utah	8	650,000	8	650,000				
Washington	54	3,825,400	45	3,120,000			0	705,400
Wyoming	11	810,000	11	810,000				
Oklahoma	4	185,000	6	300,000	2	115,000		
Indian Territory	6	349,200	6	360,000		10,800		
Division No. 8	200	13,674,600	186	12,615,000	4	260,800	18	1,320,400
United States	2,737	221,057,830	2,769	221,373,574	77	4,738,289	41	4.304.155

TABLE, BY STATES, TERRITORIES, AND RESERVE CITIES, EXHIBITING THE NUMBER OF BANKS IN EACH, WITH CAPITAL EXCEEDING $150,000, FOR THE YEARS 1892 AND 1893, AND THE INCREASE OR DECREASE IN BANKS AND CAPITAL DURING THE INTERVAL.

States, Territories, and reserve cities.	September 30, 1892.		October 3, 1893.		Increase.		Decrease.	
	No.	Capital.	No.	Capital.	No.	Capital.	No.	Capital.
Maine	15	$5,700,000	15	$5,700,000				
New Hampshire	8	1,700,000	8	1,700,000				
Vermont	11	3,450,000	11	3,350,000				$100,000
Massachusetts	110	33,870,000	111	34,790,000	1	$920,000		
Boston	55	53,100,000	55	53,350,000				250,000
Rhode Island	36	17,727,050	36	17,727,050				
Connecticut	50	19,351,070	50	19,351,370				300
Division No.1	285	134,898,120	286	135,968,420	1	1,170,300		100,000
New York	53	14,340,400	52	14,149,400			1	100,000
New York City	48	49,650,000	49	51,250,000	1	1,600,000		
Albany	6	1,550,000	6	1,550,000				
Brooklyn	5	1,352,000	5	1,352,000				
New Jersey	30	8,760,000	30	8,760,000				
Pennsylvania	63	17,115,020	63	17,070,000				45,020
Philadelphia	40	22,315,000	40	22,615,000		300,000		
Pittsburg	25	10,800,000	28	11,540,000	3	740,000		
Division No.2	270	125,891,420	273	128,286,400	4	2,640,000	1	145,020
Delaware	4	1,113,185	4	1,113,185				
Maryland	3	651,700	3	651,700				
Baltimore	22	13,243,260	22	13,243,260				
District of Columbia	1	252,000	1	252,000				
Washington	11	2,475,000	11	2,475,000				
Virginia	9	2,515,300	9	2,655,300				140,000
West Virginia	4	806,000	4	806,000				
Division No.3	54	21,056,445	54	21,196,445				140,000
North Carolina	5	1,100,000	5	1,100,000				
South Carolina	3	650,000	3	750,000				100,000
Georgia	9	2,600,000	7	2,150,000			2	450,000
Florida								
Alabama	7	2,175,000	6	1,925,000			1	250,000
Mississippi								
Louisiana	1	200,000	1	200,000				
New Orleans	10	3,625,000	9	3,125,000			1	500,000
Texas	20	11,210,000	25	8,550,000			4	2,660,000
Arkansas	3	1,000,000	2	500,000			1	500,000
Kentucky	23	5,825,000	22	5,425,000			1	400,000
Louisville	10	4,501,500	10	4,401,500				500,000
Tennessee	13	6,975,000	12	6,475,000				500,000
Division No. 4	113	40,261,500	102	34,601,500		100,000	11	5,760,000
Ohio	45	12,326,700	47	12,964,000	2	637,300		
Cincinnati	13	9,100,000	13	9,100,000				
Cleveland	10	8,050,000	11	9,050,000	1	1,000,000		
Indiana	23	6,150,000	21	5,650,000			2	500,000
Illinois	20	4,375,000	20	4,375,000				
Chicago	23	22,900,000	21	20,900,000			2	12,000,000
Michigan	11	3,715,000	9	3,350,000			2	365,000
Detroit	8	4,400,000	8	4,400,000				
Wisconsin	7	1,610,000	7	1,750,000		140,000		
Milwaukee	5	850,000	5	2,300,000	2	1,450,000		
Division No. 5	163	73,476,700	162	73,839,000	5	3,227,300	6	2,865,000
Iowa	10	3,700,000	12	3,850,000	2	150,000		
Des Moines	2	500,000	2	500,000				
Minnesota	7	2,375,000	7	2,375,000				
St. Paul	5	4,800,000	4	2,800,000			1	2,000,000
Minneapolis	7	4,931,000	7	5,450,000		519,000		
Missouri	4	850,000	4	850,000				
St. Louis	9	10,700,000	9	10,700,000				
Kansas City	10	6,800,000	8	5,550,000			2	
St. Joseph	3	1,900,000	3	1,900,000				
Kansas	8	2,950,000	7	2,650,000			1	300,000
Nebraska	1	200,000	1	200,000				
Omaha	9	4,150,000	9	4,150,000				
Lincoln	5	1,350,000	3	900,000			2	450,000
Division No. 6	80	45,206,000	76	41,875,000	2	669,000	6	2,750,000

TABLE, BY STATES, TERRITORIES, AND RESERVE CITIES, EXHIBITING THE NUMBER OF BANKS IN EACH, WITH CAPITAL EXCEEDING $150,000, ETC.—Continued.

States, Territories, and reserve cities.	September 30, 1892.		October 3, 1893.		Increase.		Decrease.	
	No.	Capital.	No.	Capital.	No.	Capital.	No.	Capital.
Colorado	15	$6,550,000	14	$6,300,000			1	$250,000
Nevada	1	200,000	1	200,000				
California	12	3,600,000	11	3,550,000			1	50,000
San Francisco	2	2,500,000	2	2,500,000				
Oregon	5	1,700,000	5	1,700,000				
Arizona								
Division No. 7	35	14,550,000	33	14,250,000			2	300,000
North Dakota	2	450,000	1	200,000			1	250,000
South Dakota	1	200,000	1	200,000				
Idaho								
Montana	8	2,750,000	4	1,300,000			4	1,450,000
New Mexico	1	175,000					1	175,000
Utah	6	2,150,000	6	2,150,000				
Washington	16	4,050,000	12	2,900,000			4	1,150,000
Wyoming	2	400,000	2	400,000				
Oklahoma								
Indian Territory								
Division No. 8	36	10,175,000	26	7,150,000			10	3,025,000
United States	1,036	465,515,185	1,012	457,166,765	12	$7,946,600	36	14,915,020

COMPARATIVE STATEMENT OF THE RESOURCES AND LIABILITIES OF THE NATIONAL BANKS FROM 1864 TO 1893, INCLUSIVE.

	Oct. 3, 1864.	Oct. 2, 1865.	Oct. 1, 1866.	Oct. 7, 1867.	Oct. 5, 1868.	Oct. 9, 1869.	Oct. 8, 1870.	Oct. 2, 1871.
	508 banks.	1,513 banks.	1,644 banks.	1,642 banks.	1,643 banks.	1,617 banks.	1,648 banks.	1,767 banks.
RESOURCES.	Millions.	Millions.	Millions.	Millions.	Millions.	Millions.	Millions.	Millions.
Loans	$93.2	$487.2	$603.3	$609.7	$657.7	$682.9	$715.9	$831.6
Bonds for circulation			331.8	338.6	340.5	339.5	340.9	364.5
Other United States bonds	108.1	427.7	95.0	80.3	74.1	44.6	37.7	45.8
Stocks, bonds, etc			15.9	21.5	20.7	22.2	23.6	24.5
Due from banks	34.0	107.3	122.9	103.6	110.1	100.8	109.4	143.2
Real estate	2.2	14.7	17.1	20.6	22.7	23.2	27.5	30.1
Specie			18.1	9.2	12.8	13.1	23.0	18.5	13.2
Legal-tender notes	44.8	190.0	202.8	157.4	156.1	129.6	122.7	107.0
National-bank notes	4.7	16.2	17.4	11.8	11.8	10.8	12.5	14.3
Clearing-house exchanges		72.3	103.7	134.6	143.2	108.8	79.1	115.2
U. S. certificates of deposit								
Due from U. S. Treasurer								
Other resources	10.1	26.3	7.9	8.6	9.6	9.8	22.9	41.2
Total	297.1	1,359.8	1,527.0	1,499.5	1,559.6	1,497.2	1,510.7	1,730.6
LIABILITIES.								
Capital stock	86.8	393.2	415.5	420.1	420.6	426.4	430.4	458.3
Surplus fund	2.0	38.7	53.3	66.7	78.0	86.2	94.1	101.1
Undivided profits	6.0	32.4	32.6	33.8	36.1	40.7	38.6	42.0
Circulation outstanding	45.2	171.3	290.0	297.9	298.7	296.0	293.9	317.4
Due to depositors	122.2	549.1	598.0	568.2	603.1	523.0	512.8	631.4
Due to banks	34.9	174.2	137.5	112.8	123.1	118.9	130.0	171.9
Other liabilities		.9	.1				6.0	10.9	8.5
Total	297.1	1,359.8	1,527.0	1,499.5	1,559.6	1,497.2	1,510.7	1,730.6

	Oct. 3, 1872.	Sept. 12, 1873.	Oct. 2, 1874.	Oct. 1, 1875.	Oct. 2, 1876.	Oct. 1, 1877.	Oct. 1, 1878.	Oct. 2, 1879.
	1,919 banks.	1,976 banks.	2,004 banks.	2,087 banks.	2,089 banks.	2,080 banks.	2,053 banks.	2,048 banks.
RESOURCES.	Millions.	Millions.	Millions.	Millions.	Millions.	Millions.	Millions.	Millions.
Loans	$877.2	$944.2	$954.4	$984.7	$931.3	$891.9	$834.0	$878.5
Bonds for circulation	382.0	288.3	383.3	370.3	337.2	336.8	347.6	357.3
Other United States bonds	27.6	23.6	28.0	28.1	47.8	45.0	94.7	71.2
Stocks, bonds, etc	23.5	23.7	27.8	33.5	34.4	34.5	36.9	39.7
Due from banks	128.2	149.5	134.8	144.7	146.9	129.9	138.9	167.3
Real estate	32.3	34.7	38.1	42.4	43.1	45.2	46.7	47.8
Specie	10.2	19.9	21.2	8.1	21.4	22.7	30.7	42.2
Legal-tender notes	102.1	92.4	80.0	76.5	84.2	66.9	64.4	69.2
National-bank notes	15.8	16.1	18.5	18.5	15.9	15.6	16.9	16.7
Clearing-house exchanges	125.0	100.3	109.7	87.9	100.0	74.5	82.4	113.0
United States certificates of deposit	6.7	20.6	42.8	48.8	29.2	33.4	32.7	20.8
Due from United States Treasurer			20.3	19.6	16.7	16.0	16.5	17.0
Other resources	25.2	17.3	18.3	19.1	19.1	28.7	24.9	22.1
Total	1,755.8	1,830.6	1,877.2	1,882.2	1,827.2	1,741.1	1,767.3	1,868.8
LIABILITIES.								
Capital stock	479.6	491.0	493.8	504.8	499.8	479.5	466.2	454.1
Surplus fund	110.3	120.3	129.0	134.4	132.2	122.8	116.9	114.8
Undivided profits	46.0	54.5	51.5	53.0	46.4	44.5	40.9	40.3
Circulation outstanding	335.1	340.3	334.2	319.1	292.2	291.0	301.9	313.8
Due to depositors	628.0	640.0	683.8	679.4	666.2	630.4	668.4	736.0
Due to banks	143.8	173.0	175.8	170.7	179.8	161.6	165.1	201.2
Other liabilities	11.5	11.5	9.1	11.8	10.6	10.4	7.9	6.7
Total	1,755.8	1,830.6	1,877.2	1,882.2	1,827.2	1,741.1	1,767.3	1,868.8

COMPARATIVE STATEMENT OF THE RESOURCES AND LIABILITIES OF THE NATIONAL
BANKS FROM 1864 TO 1893, INCLUSIVE—Continued.

	Oct. 1, 1880.	Oct. 1, 1881.	Oct. 3, 1882.	Oct. 2, 1883.	Sept. 30, 1884.	Oct. 1, 1885.	Oct. 7, 1886.
	2,090 banks.	2,132 banks.	2,269 banks.	2,501 banks.	2,664 banks.	2,714 banks.	2,852 banks.
RESOURCES.	Millions.	Millions.	Millions.	Millions.	Millions.	Millions.	Millions.
Loans	$1,041.0	$1,173.8	$1,243.2	$1,309.2	$1,245.3	$1,306.1	$1,451.0
Bonds for circulation	357.8	363.3	357.6	351.4	327.4	307.7	258.5
Other United States bonds	43.6	56.5	37.4	30.7	30.4	31.8	32.4
Stocks, bonds, etc	48.9	61.9	66.2	71.1	71.4	77.5	81.8
Due from banks	213.5	230.8	198.9	208.9	194.2	235.3	241.4
Real estate	48.0	47.3	46.5	48.3	49.9	51.3	54.1
Specie	109.3	114.3	102.9	107.8	128.6	174.9	156.4
Legal-tender notes	56.6	53.2	63.2	70.7	77.0	69.7	62.8
National-bank notes	18.2	17.7	20.7	22.7	23.3	23.1	22.7
Clearing-house exchanges	121.1	189.2	208.4	96.4	66.3	84.9	95.5
United States certificates of deposit	7.7	6.7	8.7	10.0	14.2	18.8	5.9
Due from United States Treasurer	17.1	17.5	17.2	16.6	17.7	14.9	14.0
Other resources	23.0	26.2	28.0	28.9	33.8	36.9	37.4
Total	2,105.8	2,368.4	2,399.8	2,372.7	2,279.5	2,432.9	2,513.0
LIABILITIES.							
Capital stock	457.6	463.8	483.1	509.7	524.3	527.5	548.5
Surplus fund	120.5	128.1	132.0	142.0	147.0	146.6	157.3
Undivided profits	46.1	56.4	61.2	61.6	63.2	59.3	66.5
Circulation outstanding	317.3	320.2	315.0	310.5	289.8	269.0	228.8
Due to depositors	887.9	1,083.1	1,134.9	1,063.6	993.0	1,116.7	1,189.5
Due to banks	267.9	294.9	259.9	270.4	246.4	299.7	308.6
Other liabilities	8.5	11.9	13.7	14.9	15.8	14.1	14.9
Total	2,105.8	2,358.4	2,399.8	2,372.7	2,279.5	2,432.9	2,513.9

	Oct. 5, 1887.	Oct. 4, 1888.	Sept. 30, 1889.	Oct. 2, 1890.	Sept. 25, 1891.	Sept. 30, 1892.	Oct. 3, 1893.
	3,049 banks.	3,120 banks.	3,290 banks.	3,540 banks.	3,677 banks.	3,773 banks.	3,781 banks.
RESOURCES.	Millions.	Millions.	Millions.	Millions.	Millions.	Millions.	Millions.
Loans	$1,587.5	$1,628.1	$1,817.3	$1,986.1	$2,005.5	$2,171.0	$1,843.6
Bonds for circulation	189.1	177.6	146.5	140.0	150.0	163.3	209.4
Other United States bonds	34.7	63.6	48.5	30.7	24.9	20.2	17.6
Stocks, bonds, etc	88.8	96.3	109.3	115.5	125.2	154.5	148.6
Due from banks	256.3	282.5	335.4	336.2	338.7	409.6	277.5
Real estate	58.0	61.1	69.4	76.8	83.3	87.9	89.2
Specie	165.1	181.3	161.3	195.9	183.5	209.1	224.7
Legal-tender notes	73.7	82.0	86.8	80.6	97.6	104.3	114.7
National-bank notes	21.0	21.3	20.9	18.5	20.0	19.6	22.4
Clearing-house exchanges	88.8	74.2	136.8	106.8	122.0	105.5	106.2
United States certificates of deposit	6.2	12.3	12.0	6.2	15.7	14.0	7.0
Due from United States Treasurer	9.3	9.0	7.4	6.9	8.0	8.2	10.2
Other resources	40.8	42.1	42.8	41.3	38.7	43.0	41.4
Total	2,620.2	2,731.4	2,998.3	3,141.5	3,213.1	3,510.1	3,109.5
LIABILITIES.							
Capital stock	578.5	588.4	612.6	650.4	677.4	686.6	678.5
Surplus fund	173.9	183.1	197.4	213.0	227.6	238.9	246.8
Undivided profits	71.5	70.3	84.0	97.0	103.3	101.6	103.5
Circulation	167.3	155.4	128.5	123.0	131.3	143.4	183.0
Due to depositors	1,274.7	1,350.7	1,522.0	1,594.2	1,608.6	1,779.3	1,465.4
Due to banks	329.6	358.1	425.3	426.4	430.6	530.7	340.3
Other liabilities	24.7	25.4	27.6	36.9	34.3	29.6	83.0
Total	2,620.2	2,731.4	2,998.3	3,141.5	3,213.1	3,510.1	3,109.5

STATEMENT PRESENTING AN ABSTRACT OF THE RESOURCES AND LIABILITIES OF THE NATIONAL BANKS AT CLOSE OF BUSINESS OCTOBER 3, 1893; THE CONDITION OF BANKS IN NEW YORK CITY, IN THE THREE CENTRAL RESERVE CITIES, IN OTHER RESERVE CITIES, AND OF THE COUNTRY BANKS BEING SHOWN SEPARATELY.

	Central reserve cities.		Other reserve cities.*	Country banks.	Aggregate.
	New York City.	New York, Chicago, and St. Louis.			
	49 banks.	79 banks.			
RESOURCES.					
Loans and discounts	$281,040,663	$376,920,353	$402,908,027	$990,838,969	$1,830,607,349
Overdrafts	279,802	912,531	1,132,949	10,921,338	12,966,818
Bonds for circulation	18,148,500	19,798,500	36,141,400	150,523,950	206,463,850
Bonds for deposits	960,000	1,510,000	4,715,000	8,591,000	14,816,000
United States bonds on hand	79,450	341,150	680,150	1,739,650	2,760,950
Stocks, securities, claims, etc	28,349,305	35,327,576	27,006,845	86,235,529	148,569,950
Due from reserve agents			51,570,537	106,929,107	158,499,644
Due from other national banks	23,845,425	38,317,080	30,734,823	25,688,112	94,740,015
Due from State banks and bankers	3,695,143	8,317,338	5,738,370	10,173,399	24,229,107
Banking-house, furniture, and fixtures	11,444,322	13,214,254	16,751,372	42,357,201	72,322,827
Other real estate and mortgages owned	756,548	1,442,822	3,628,518	11,757,609	16,828,949
Current expenses	1,360,021	1,627,117	2,277,386	7,167,494	11,071,997
Premiums	1,144,421	1,237,501	3,360,755	9,383,611	13,981,867
Checks and cash items	2,742,847	2,903,048	3,322,522	9,134,195	15,359,765
Exchanges for clearing house	57,499,566	64,386,261	37,895,497	3,899,637	106,181,395
Bills of other national banks	1,468,723	4,739,305	3,310,362	14,352,944	22,402,611
Fractional currency, nickels, and cents	41,034	80,739	214,802	731,273	1,026,814
Specie	75,703,063	102,114,662	46,617,813	75,971,385	224,703,860
Legal-tender notes	31,082,821	48,776,286	24,954,842	40,978,224	114,799,352
United States certificates of deposit	1,420,000	1,950,000	4,855,000	215,000	7,020,000
Redemption fund	811,112	885,362	1,590,577	6,501,475	8,977,414
Due from United States Treasurer	654,882	852,933	224,470	185,338	1,262,750
Total	542,531,655	725,654,817	769,632,025	1,614,276,442	3,109,563,284
LIABILITIES.					
Capital stock	51,250,000	82,850,000	163,001,760	432,688,579	678,540,339
Surplus fund	41,533,247	55,111,747	58,690,211	132,948,823	246,750,781
Undivided profits	18,784,747	22,306,821	19,454,548	61,713,294	103,474,663
National-bank notes outstanding	15,818,057	17,079,068	32,208,182	133,672,476	182,959,726
State-bank notes outstanding	24,325	24,325	6,640	44,104	75,069
Dividends unpaid	210,591	293,055	793,903	1,787,740	2,874,698
Individual deposits	249,606,107	330,903,431	353,790,743	766,520,157	1,451,124,331
United States deposits	690,687	1,154,363	3,514,369	5,877,403	10,546,135
Deposits of United States disbursing officers	100,216	145,830	1,259,552	2,371,056	3,776,438
Due to National banks	100,751,310	129,716,256	71,558,391	25,149,332	226,423,979
Due to banks and bankers	45,105,498	67,183,055	39,457,486	16,250,557	122,891,098
Notes and bills rediscounted			3,137,972	17,928,765	21,066,737
Bills payable		250,000	10,556,104	16,628,834	27,426,938
Liabilities other than those above stated	18,636,865	18,636,866	12,292,163	703,323	31,632,352
Total	542,531,655	725,654,817	769,632,025	1,614,276,442	3,109,563,284

*Other reserve cities are Boston, Philadelphia, Baltimore, Albany, Brooklyn, Pittsburg, Washington, New Orleans, Louisville, Cincinnati, Cleveland, Detroit, Milwaukee, Des Moines, Minneapolis, St. Paul, Kansas City, St. Joseph, Lincoln, Omaha, and San Francisco.

STATEMENT SHOWING THE HIGHEST AND LOWEST POINTS REACHED IN THE PRINCI-
PAL ITEMS OF RESOURCES AND LIABILITIES DURING THE EXISTENCE OF THE SYSTEM.

	January 1, 1866.	October 3, 1893.	Highest point reached.		Lowest point reached.	
			Amount.	Date.	Amount.	Date.
Capital	$403, 357, 346	$678, 540, 338	$686, 573, 015	Sept. 30, 1892	$403, 357, 346	Jan. 1, 1866
Capital, surplus, and undivided profits ...	475, 330, 204	1, 028, 765, 781	1, 028, 765, 781	Oct. 3, 1893	475, 330, 204	Do.
Circulation	213, 239, 530	182, 959, 725	341, 320, 256	Dec. 26, 1873	122, 928, 084	Oct. 2, 1890
Total investments in United States bonds.	440, 380, 350	224, 040, 800	712, 437, 900	Apr. 4, 1879	170, 653, 059	Do.
Individual deposits ...	520, 212, 174	1, 451, 124, 330	1, 765, 422, 983	Sept. 30, 1892	591, 407, 586	Oct. 8, 1870
Loans and discounts..	500, 650, 109	1, 830, 667, 349	2, 153, 498, 829	....do	500, 650, 109	Jan. 1, 1866
Cash:						
National-bank notes	20, 406, 442	22, 402, 611	28, 809, 699	Dec. 31, 1883	11, 841, 104	Oct. 7, 1867
Legal-tender notes .	187, 846, 548	114, 709, 352	205, 793, 578	Oct. 1, 1866	52, 156, 439	Mar. 11, 1881
Specie...............	16, 909, 363	224, 703, 860	224, 703, 860	Oct. 3, 1893	8, 050, 330	Oct. 1, 1875

STATEMENT SHOWING THE PERCENTAGES OF LOANS, UNITED STATES BONDS, AND
SPECIE TO THE AGGREGATE FUNDS OF NATIONAL BANKS, 1886 TO 1893.

	1886.	1887.	1888.	1889.	1890.	1891.	1892.	1893.
	Per cent.	Per cent.	Per cent.	Per cent.	Per cent.	Per cent.	Per cent.	Per cent.
Loans and discounts	41. 32	70. 52	71. 04	72. 26	74. 37	72. 92	73. 35	68. 75
United States bonds	36. 36	9. 98	9. 87	7. 80	6. 44	6. 41	6. 25	8. 41
Specie	1. 57	7. 37	11. 90	6. 58	7. 40	6. 73	7. 12	4. 31
Total	79. 25	87. 87	92. 81	86. 64	88. 21	86. 06	86. 72	81. 47

STATEMENT EXHIBITING A CLASSIFICATION OF LOANS MADE BY THE NATIONAL BANKS IN THE CENTRAL RESERVE CITIES, NEW YORK, CHICAGO, AND ST. LOUIS, AND OTHER RESERVE CITIES, IN GROUPS, TOGETHER WITH COUNTRY BANKS ON APPROXIMATE DATES FOR THE PAST FIVE YEARS.

SEPTEMBER 30, 1889.

	No. of banks.	On paper with single name, unsecured.	On paper with indorsers, otherwise unsecured.	Ou demand, with U. S. bonds, other bonds, stocks, or collaterals as security.	On time, bonds, other bonds, stocks, or collaterals as security.	Total.
New York	45	$31,866,578	$119,366,417	$109,579,495	$43,085,676	$303,898,166
Chicago	20	15,947,708	31,275,073	12,702,779	12,455,515	72,381,075
St. Louis	5	866,900	7,863,955	1,816,621	2,897,770	13,475,246
Group No. 1, 4 cities	129	43,237,334	145,457,842	54,280,694	43,847,643	286,823,504
Group No. 2, 4 cities	43	8,308,283	29,328,014	9,770,705	12,056,470	59,463,472
Group No. 3, 4 cities	33	8,618,618	30,473,645	8,337,056	6,419,197	62,848,510
Group No. 4, 4 cities	23	9,051,215	16,140,667	3,432,808	7,661,230	36,285,921
Country	2,992	154,475,783	636,484,510	54,314,240	125,279,276	970,553,839
Total	3,290	272,372,410	1,025,390,153	254,264,398	253,702,777	1,805,729,739

OCTOBER 2, 1890.

New York	47	$29,044,063	$122,226,701	$102,372,932	$43,466,652	$297,110,551
Chicago	19	16,714,673	27,897,562	17,125,219	16,506,704	78,244,158
St. Louis	8	2,172,008	16,274,789	4,346,312	6,681,993	29,475,102
Group No. 1, 5 cities *†	138	45,604,039	146,363,799	56,582,852	48,664,875	297,216,165
Group No. 2, 4 cities*	50	8,683,687	33,311,338	11,002,538	13,140,182	66,137,745
Group No. 3, 6 cities *†	46	21,118,680	55,649,978	10,540,565	10,752,917	98,062,140
Group No. 4, 4 cities	25	10,116,981	18,602,080	6,225,020	10,313,144	45,257,225
Country	3,207	164,605,256	685,600,401	63,538,244	144,715,700	1,058,519,601
Total	3,540	298,119,987	1,105,926,851	271,733,682	294,242,167	1,970,022,687

SEPTEMBER 25, 1891.

	No. of banks.	On paper with single name, unsecured.	On paper with one or more indorsers, otherwise unsecured.	On demand with indorsers, otherwise unsecured.	On demand with U. S. bonds, other bonds, stocks, or collaterals as security.	On time, with U. S. bonds, other bonds, stocks, or collaterals as security.	Total.
New York	49	$25,125,313	$116,957,046	$2,925,418	$113,787,196	$42,783,829	$301,578,802
Chicago	21	17,937,791	34,889,300	3,704,939	13,525,638	17,508,229	87,565,897
St. Louis	9	2,093,451	14,617,141	558,571	3,999,711	6,505,233	27,864,107
Group—							
No. 1, 5 cities *†	136	42,118,748	141,021,853	9,015,155	54,233,863	48,397,495	294,787,114
No. 2, 4 cities*	54	8,457,434	29,991,803	1,084,034	11,149,928	14,393,999	65,077,198
No. 3, 7 cities*†	49	18,809,101	54,500,479	3,361,241	9,923,642	11,684,959	98,279,422
No. 4, 4 cities*	26	7,498,961	14,130,558	2,106,638	5,596,114	9,954,626	39,286,897
Country	3,333	150,412,548	662,814,133	35,679,262	54,065,103	162,943,757	1,074,014,803
Total	7,677	281,453,347	1,068,922,313	58,435,285	266,281,195	314,262,127	1,989,354,240

* Group No. 1, Boston, Albany, Brooklyn, Philadelphia, and Pittsburg. Group No. 2, Baltimore, Washington, New Orleans, and Louisville. Group No. 3. Cincinnati, Cleveland, Detroit, Milwaukee, Des Moines, and Minneapolis. Group No. 4, Kansas City, St. Joseph, Lincoln, Omaha, and San Francisco.
† Lincoln, not a reserve city prior to 1893.

STATEMENT EXHIBITING A CLASSIFICATION OF LOANS MADE BY THE NATIONAL
BANKS IN THE CENTRAL RESERVE CITIES, ETC.—Continued.

SEPTEMBER 30, 1892.

	No. of banks.	On demand, paper with one or more individual or firm names.	On demand, secured by stocks, bonds, and other personal securities.	On time, paper with two or more individual or firm names.	On time, single-name paper (one person or firm) without other security.	On time, secured by stocks, bonds, and other personal securities, or on mortgages or other real-estate security.	Total.
New York	48	$4,931,784	$117,751,227	$117,796,025	$38,147,905	$65,573,000	$344,199,941
Chicago	23	7,853,323	16,617,397	40,307,355	18,128,149	21,006,801	103,913,025
St. Louis	9	1,079,406	4,722,783	16,137,981	2,744,362	8,192,840	32,877,372
Group—							
No. 1, 5 cities*†	133	11,998,687	52,893,245	144,730,329	53,328,579	54,982,554	317,983,394
No. 2, 4 cities*	54	2,072,198	10,740,223	30,656,759	8,910,933	14,945,457	67,325,570
No. 3, 7 cities*†	50	8,028,468	12,133,686	55,564,357	20,377,874	13,879,881	109,984,266
No. 4, 4 cities*	26	5,751,077	2,698,736	14,320,995	7,380,208	11,288,439	41,445,455
Country	3,430	54,205,372	55,770,992	677,626,891	171,265,156	176,901,395	1,135,769,806
Total	3,773	95,920,315	273,328,289	1,097,196,692	320,283,166	366,770,367	2,153,498,829

OCTOBER 3, 1893.

New York	49	$6,216,350	$93,897,446	$110,225,762	$26,864,953	$43,836,150	$281,040,663
Chicago	21	5,509,670	13,815,614	24,522,359	13,515,691	15,558,954	72,922,290
St. Louis	9	1,626,168	3,350,523	9,424,921	1,863,841	6,691,944	22,957,399
Group—							
No. 1, 5 cities*†	136	10,442,401	47,358,410	131,164,892	39,637,045	51,575,820	280,178,570
No. 2, 4 cities*	53	1,565,493	9,456,808	27,400,578	6,985,533	13,418,670	58,827,084
No. 3, 7 cities*†	52	7,767,904	10,060,849	43,579,125	14,580,606	14,390,163	90,378,650
No. 4, 5 cities†	27	5,382,436	3,058,636	11,880,155	5,114,318	8,088,175	33,523,722
Country	3,434	52,576,784	75,118,992	562,082,320	136,125,133	164,935,738	990,838,968
Total	3,781	91,087,210	256,117,281	920,280,115	244,687,123	318,495,617	1,830,667,349

* Group No. 1, Boston, Albany, Brooklyn, Philadelphia, and Pittsburg. Group No. 2, Baltimore, Washington, New Orleans, and Louisville. Group No. 3, Cincinnati, Cleveland, Detroit, Milwaukee, Des Moines, St. Paul, and Minneapolis. Group No. 4, Kansas City, St. Joseph, Lincoln, Omaha, and San Francisco.

† Lincoln not a reserve city prior to 1893.

STATEMENT SHOWING THE CLASSIFICATION OF THE LOANS BY NATIONAL BANKS IN NEW YORK CITY FOR THE LAST EIGHT YEARS.

Loans and discounts.	Oct. 7, 1886.	Oct. 5, 1887.	Oct. 4, 1888.	Sept. 30, 1889.	Oct. 2, 1890.
	45 banks.	47 banks.	46 banks.	45 banks.	47 banks.
On indorsed paper	$121,381.380	$115,316,625	$117,707,044	$119,369,404	$122,220,904
On single-name paper	24,646,008	17,585,496	28,626,205	31,866,578	29,044,063
On U. S. bonds on demand	2,002,550	1,445,900	2,132,159	1,124,109	583,820
On other stocks, etc., on demand	91,636,791	95,075,844	108,466,001	108,258.112	101,789,112
On real-estate security	211,432	146,885	113,494	201,878	228,778
All other loans	13,854,215	28,443,431	35,450,488	43,078.085	43,237,874
Total	253,732,376	258,014,181	292,495,481	303,898,166	297,110,551

Loans and discounts.	Sept. 25, 1891.
	49 banks.
On paper, with single name, unsecured	$25,125.313
On paper, with one or more indorsers, otherwise unsecured	116,957,046
On demand, with one or more indorsers, otherwise unsecured	2,925,418
On demand, with U. S. bonds, other bonds, stocks, or collaterals, as security	113,787,196
On time, with U. S. bonds, other bonds, stocks, or collaterals, as security	42,783,829
Total	301,578,802

Loans and discounts.	Sept. 30, 1892.	Oct. 3, 1893.
	48 banks.	49 banks.
On demand, paper with one or more individual or firm names	$4,931,784	$6,216,350.57
On demand, secured by stocks, bonds, and other personal securities	117,751.227	93,897,446.82
On time, paper with two or more individual or firm names	117,796,025	110,225,762.11
On time, single-name paper (one person or firm) without other security	38,147,905	26,864,953.38
On time, secured by stocks, bonds, and other personal securities, or on mortgages or other real-estate security	65,573,000	43,836,150.94
Total	344,199,941	281,040,663.82

CLASSIFICATION OF THE LOANS AND DISCOUNTS OF THE NATIONAL BANKS IN THE RESERVE CITIES AND IN THE STATES AND TERRITORIES ON OCTOBER 3, 1893.

Cities, States, and Territories.	No. of banks.	On demand, paper with one or more individual or firm names.	On demand, secured by stocks, bonds, and other personal securities.	On time, paper with two or more individual or firm names.	On time, single-name paper (one person or firm) without other security.	On time, secured by stocks, bonds, and other personal securities, or on mortgages or other real estate security.	Total.
New York City	49	$6,216,350	$93,897,446	$110,225,762	$26,864,953	$43,836,150	$281,040,663
Chicago	21	5,509,670	13,815,614	24,522,359	13,515,691	15,558,954	72,922,290
St. Louis	9	1,626,168	3,350,523	9.424.021	1,863,841	6,691,944	22,957,399
Boston	55	7,473,487	20,444,592	65,931,982	20,526,027	22,328,975	136,705,006
Albany	6	544,822	3,115,209	3,329,892	376,820	368,633	7,735,378
Brooklyn	5	37,100	3,543,380	4,088,394	329,000	1.148,902	9,146,777
Philadelphia	41	1,430,377	15,003,780	37,317,161	16,467,703	20,466,852	90,985,874
Pittsburg	29	956,614	5,251,448	20.497,460	1,937,493	7,262,455	35,905,472
Baltimore	22	903,842	4,278,666	14,383,850	5,899,995	4,731,462	30,197,818
Washington City	12	175,045	1,409,245	3,634,161	33,487	764,737	6,016,677
New Orleans	9	370,339	3,126,328	5,252,834	814,811	4,275,234	13,839,548

CLASSIFICATION OF THE LOANS AND DISCOUNTS OF THE NATIONAL BANKS IN THE RESERVE CITIES, ETC.—Continued.

Cities, States, and Territories.	No. of banks.	On demand, paper with one or more individual or firm names.	On demand, secured by stocks, bonds, and other personal securities.	On time, paper with two or more individual or firm names.	On time, single name paper (one person or firm) without other security.	On time, secured by stocks, bonds, and other personal securities, or on mortgages or other real estate securities.	Total.
Louisville	10	$116,206	$642,567	$4,129,731	$237,238	$3,647,235	$8,773,639
Cincinnati	13	1,704,731	2,483,965	9,422,523	4,888,908	3,571,107	22,071,236
Cleveland	11	1,207,206	3,962,536	13,487,134	2,015,703	3,507,270	24,179,851
Detroit	8	1,299,103	1,264,575	7,963,458	1,147,924	1,782,453	13,457,516
Milwaukee	5	790,748	1,001,172	3,084,008	829,740	1,070,984	6,776,653
Des Moines	4	34,145	89,760	875,164	412,497	543,471	1,955,040
St. Paul	4	1,191,014	653,599	3,119,244	2,596,231	2,078,612	9,638,702
Minneapolis	7	1,540,954	605,238	5,627,591	2,689,601	1,836,263	12,299,649
Kansas City	8	672,515	1,383,923	3,733,560	2,122,817	3,372,958	11,285,776
St. Joseph	4	499,238	81,294	2,050,999	741,994	1,082,704	4,456,211
Lincoln	4	185,040	109,899	1,492,088	228,344	606,416	2,621,790
Omaha	9	364,220	325,678	4,147,552	1,767,793	2,665,604	9,270,849
San Francisco	2	3,661,440	1,157,839	455,955	253,369	360,490	5,889,094
Total of cities	347	38,510,420	180,998,289	358,197,794	108,561,990	153,559,878	839,828,360
Maine	83	797,978	900,420	15,654,029	1,153,419	2,777,810	21,283,653
New Hampshire	51	1,772,497	1,675,833	5,189,069	528,502	1,676,464	10,842,367
Vermont	48	1,173,429	739,862	4,472,787	1,039,966	1,753,231	13,179,277
Massachusetts	214	4,200,573	8,301,571	57,256,281	16,975,429	15,478,048	102,211,905
Rhode Island	59	548,220	1,482,107	17,896,470	7,005,168	7,090,582	34,022,550
Connecticut	84	1,745,398	3,835,592	25,317,781	6,059,113	6,775,261	43,733,147
New York	274	5,225,165	4,600,032	71,718,085	9,016,484	8,177,141	98,736,909
New Jersey	99	1,518,940	7,696,006	30,643,040	2,950,006	4,484,366	47,293,261
Pennsylvania	326	2,542,326	23,664,989	59,665,711	10,930,622	9,558,664	106,362,313
Delaware	18	168,488	345,916	4,053,383	108,560	756,844	5,433,192
Maryland	46	177,750	330,354	8,040,534	516,811	1,079,393	10,144,844
District of Columbia	1	500	70,191	265,226		187,285	523,204
Virginia	36	927,185	1,259,914	9,201,772	1,043,009	2,017,180	15,049,062
West Virginia	30	115,708	38,832	5,803,603	240,201	594,179	6,792,525
North Carolina	24	219,432	119,209	3,539,753	638,012	1,156,964	5,673,372
South Carolina	14	54,800	352,769	2,727,387	166,244	2,664,954	5,966,156
Georgia	27	138,882	810,034	4,124,056	729,981	1,973,071	7,782,025
Florida	17	110,167	122,144	1,577,472	926,660	691,223	3,427,668
Alabama	28	509,937	453,024	2,331,283	931,804	1,701,647	5,927,607
Mississippi	12	56,189	180,645	814,530	258,536	900,034	2,209,937
Louisiana	11	107,948	78,468	1,067,379	457,916	392,497	2,104,210
Texas	222	1,784,924	907,455	17,219,871	10,671,117	11,551,703	42,135,072
Arkansas	9	72,147	145,215	1,066,040	221,802	593,135	2,101,342
Kentucky	71	842,650	398,536	13,061,163	1,272,609	3,229,458	18,804,418
Tennessee	52	1,157,011	1,510,908	8,935,311	2,320,403	4,201,502	18,134,197
Ohio	218	1,767,944	1,806,383	43,742,819	7,437,069	9,509,503	64,323,721
Indiana	115	2,197,304	879,093	20,351,075	3,444,594	3,970,170	30,843,138
Illinois	191	4,763,706	1,949,180	22,050,536	6,987,487	6,566,527	42,317,438
Michigan	92	1,291,276	799,952	17,688,932	4,874,085	3,656,072	28,310,300
Wisconsin	76	988,452	926,432	12,872,584	2,484,641	2,742,497	20,014,607
Iowa	165	2,177,433	876,143	14,485,546	7,234,609	6,712,299	31,486,032
Minnesota	65	741,646	572,511	7,216,611	2,960,406	3,747,170	15,247,345
Missouri	57	345,543	128,578	5,450,724	1,042,689	1,423,296	8,390,834
Kansas	136	432,815	280,805	7,132,738	3,388,113	8,438,242	19,672,715
Nebraska	121	798,143	415,113	7,941,831	2,762,377	4,228,115	16,145,581
Colorado	51	1,846,115	1,461,441	7,691,255	5,604,343	5,274,871	21,878,028
Nevada	2	288,243	54,368	48,913	96,948	47,512	535,086
California	33	2,793,379	1,843,779	2,910,787	1,136,862	1,890,104	10,574,913
Oregon	39	1,914,126	1,019,477	2,718,227	2,375,345	1,372,176	9,399,353
Arizona	5	57,161	43,967	194,667	46,299	133,238	475,334
North Dakota	32	168,306	219,970	952,504	614,154	3,830,937	5,815,874
South Dakota	39	161,106	146,071	1,044,351	786,436	2,321,888	4,459,854
Idaho	13	323,003	100,717	688,963	207,916	274,046	1,594,617
Montana	22	1,280,205	121,444	2,907,362	2,509,732	1,022,311	7,931,056
New Mexico	10	114,120	68,875	693,944	465,803	280,954	1,623,698
Utah	14	418,147	207,314	1,478,270	860,899	1,446,352	4,410,989
Washington	57	1,652,076	1,135,615	4,794,420	1,025,941	3,010,307	12,219,021
Wyoming	13	56,504	35,734	814,942	812,527	740,776	2,460,786
Oklahoma	6	29,947		105,430	49,963	86,267	331,608
Indian Territory	6	922		308,041	105,494	87,329	501,788
Total of country banks	3,434	52,576,784	75,118,992	562,082,320	136,125,133	164,935,738	990,838,968
United States *	3,781	91,087,210	256,117,281	920,280,115	244,687,123	318,495,617	1,830,667,349

* Cents not included.

TABLE, BY STATES, TERRITORIES, AND RESERVE CITIES, EXHIBITING THE AMOUNT OF EACH KIND OF COIN AND COIN CERTIFICATE HELD BY THE NATIONAL BANKS ON OCTOBER 4, 1888, SEPTEMBER 30, 1889, OCTOBER 2, 1890, SEPTEMBER 25, 1891, SEPTEMBER 30, 1892, AND OCTOBER 3, 1893.

OCTOBER 4, 1888.

States, etc.	Gold coin.	Gold Treasury certificates.	Gold clearing-house certificates.	Silver coin.		Silver Treasury certificates.	Total.
				Dollars.	Fractional.		
Maine	$608,811.76	$8,400		$36,088	$28,894.91	$35,303	$717,497.67
New Hampshire	272,931.70	7,780		71,483	28,661.80	16,432	397,288.50
Vermont	324,242.49	7,600		40,823	28,023.36	5,045	405,733.85
Massachusetts	2,075,139.18	239,520		315,188	200,543.74	140,182	2,970,552.92
Boston	3,995,172.09	6,619,800		108,687	81,047.76	693,321	11,498,027.85
Rhode Island	399,863.35	67,670		59,372	44,740.69	87,102	658,748.04
Connecticut	1,288,182.11	182,770		134,863	103,636.67	86,480	1,795,931.73
Division No. 1	8,964,342.68	7,133,540		766,504	515,548.93	1,003,845	18,443,780.61
New York	3,489,057.48	1,216,790		385,126	266,313.30	255,317	5,612,603.78
New York City	7,138,669.50	64,305,120		362,213	219,845.64	1,771,348	73,797,196.14
Albany	402,900.50	535,700		18,500	8,171.00	14,000	979,331.50
New Jersey	1,091,490.59	309,470		194,805	107,949.01	171,323	1,875,037.60
Pennsylvania	3,748,764.42	284,160		641,141	251,439.41	191,152	5,016,656.83
Philadelphia	2,264,915.00	172,450	$8,890,000	346,946	169,237.19	548,152	12,391,700.19
Pittsburg	2,130,858.70	823,100		154,299	38,003.53	94,708	3,240,969.23
Division No. 2	20,266,716.19	67,646,790	8,890,000	2,003,030	1,060,959.08	3,046,000	102,913,495.27
Delaware	131,453.50	22,610		46,450	29,751.09	37,894	268,188.59
Maryland	322,302.12	44,180		69,251	35,612.29	65,154	536,499.41
Baltimore	1,385,293.50	468,680		101,658	39,337.36	240,872	2,244,840.86
District of Columbia	96,471.00	116,500		4,060	5,260.50	6,980	229,271.50
Washington	201,783.00	531,046		13,165	14,974.50	192,624	953,586.50
Virginia	394,598.00	9,480		87,750	42,127.05	84,470	618,431.05
West Virginia	225,096.13	10,400		19,157	9,963.02	8,309	272,925.15
Division No. 3	2,756,997.25	1,202,920		341,497	177,025.81	645,303	5,123,743.06
North Carolina	160,598.00			50,873	17,418.10	10	228,899.10
South Carolina	108,983.00	420		63,841	19,142.05	8,562	200,948.05
Georgia	144,273.63	55,500		191,526	24,005.03	116,619	531,923.66
Florida	39,363.00	3,580		46,468	16,552.39	1,385	107,338.39
Alabama	306,792.00	19,520		52,607	13,180.30	45,293	437,302.36
Mississippi	64,869.50	4,000		32,122	8,503.65	40,185	149,680.15
Louisiana	12,480.00	4,500		26,565	16,668.05	76,736	136,949.05
New Orleans	123,442.00	127,920		114,592	61,523.85	505,643	933,120.85
Texas	481,531.20	139,590		416,152	49,749.95	218,363	1,305,386.15
Arkansas	33,175.00	14,270		25,523	7,572.10	40,210	120,750.10
Kentucky	389,062.36	41,390		67,570	15,984.33	36,895	550,001.69
Louisville	290,748.00	1,500		43,630	5,022.75	1,400	342,300.75
Tennessee	392,423.00	117,100		215,062	39,858.85	72,270	836,713.85
Division No. 4	2,547,730.69	529,290		1,346,531	295,181.46	1,163,571	5,882,304.15
Ohio	2,422,423.80	146,640		292,133	116,657.86	45,973	3,023,827.66
Cincinnati	360,997.50	271,000		60,582	11,671.75	156,500	860,721.25
Cleveland	729,789.50	180,000		39,132	14,904.91	25,000	988,826.41
Indiana	1,729,041.62	113,250		205,120	62,733.89	40,370	2,150,521.51
Illinois	1,972,502.50	198,920		247,130	104,820.92	98,558	2,621,031.42
Chicago	9,757,108.50	2,426,750		215,851	254,807.10	416,725	13,071,241.60
Michigan	1,154,512.93	29,310		135,933	45,064.67	20,575	1,385,425.60
Detroit	972,174.50	5,960		45,385	53,500.36	12,535	1,089,554.86
Wisconsin	785,011.87	12,390		93,807	46,524.54	11,371	949,014.41
Milwaukee	455,377.00	100,000		20,233	9,040.00	8,534	593,184.00
Division No. 5	20,347,930.72	3,484,160		1,355,276	719,726.00	836,147	26,743,248.72
Iowa	1,240,734.58	75,680		176,286	74,774.07	58,790	1,626,264.65
Minnesota	1,794,471.24	5,880		265,136	91,569.40	12,160	2,169,216.64
Missouri	220,667.00	9,000		34,539	8,621.51	8,587	281,414.51
St. Louis	487,219.00	355,000		20,000	7,878.00	92,400	962,497.00
Kansas City	1,054,752.50	251,200		72,817	38,738.97	87,120	1,504,628.47
St. Joseph	89,740.00	50,260		4,378	3,668.70	26,327	174,373.70
Kansas	967,519.80	24,290		134,328	48,451.10	03,047	1,218,505.90
Nebraska	505,725.45	15,960		69,250	22,980.85	32,582	736,498.30
Omaha	881,497.10	32,950		67,536	28,085.12	11,540	1,022,208.22
Division No. 6	7,332,326.67	820,190		844,270	325,367.72	393,453	9,715,607.39

AMOUNT OF EACH KIND OF COIN AND COIN CERTIFICATE HELD BY THE NATIONAL BANKS, ETC.—Continued.

OCTOBER 4, 1888—Continued.

States, etc.	Gold coin.	Gold Treasury certificates.	Gold clearing-house certificates.	Silver coin.		Silver Treasury certificates.	Total.
				Dollars.	Fractional.		
Colorado	$1,334,134.65	$6,490	....	$74,457	$28,756.56	$11,698	$1,455,536.21
Nevada	40,727.50	60	....	5,629	2,845.09	285	55,546.59
California	2,280,137.90	122,180	....	113,289	42,964.08	52,220	2,616,790.98
San Francisco	928,622.50	3,650	$180,000	14,643	15,255.32	....	1,142,170.82
Oregon	875,572.50	12,190	....	18,034	13,979.80	20,843	940,619.30
Arizona	14,010.00	....	....	500	1,437.10	....	15,947.10
Division No. 7	5,485,205.05	144,570	180,000	226,552	105,237.95	85,046	6,226,601.00
Dakota	371,845.10	17,240	....	50,879	21,154.90	9,496	470,615.00
Idaho	101,784.50	1,630	....	6,762	1,217.35	6,117	117,510.85
Montana	736,950.00	40,600	....	48,589	11,744.00	32,224	870,407.00
New Mexico	108,269.50	1,000	....	8,557	4,522.35	2,100	124,448.85
Utah	323,806.30	55,500	....	6,213	5,597.45	5,009	396,127.75
Washington	670,097.70	10,700	....	42,344	7,804.29	8,895	749,740.99
Wyoming	198,992.60	660	....	4,927	4,804.40	792	210,176.00
Division No. 8	2,521,647.70	127,330	....	168,271	56,844.74	64,933	2,939,026.44
United States	70,222,905.95	81,088,790	9,070,000	7,051,931	3,255,891.69	7,298,298	177,987,816.64

SEPTEMBER 30, 1889.

States, etc.	Gold coin.	Gold Treasury certificates.	Gold clearing-house certificates.	Silver coin.		Silver Treasury certificates.	Total.
				Dollars.	Fractional.		
Maine	$611,151.51	$4,830	....	$39,928	$36,167.51	$40,036	$732,113.02
New Hampshire	276,224.05	5,300	....	56,872	37,729.89	25,014	401,139.94
Vermont	317,710.80	10,210	....	25,589	39,073.69	12,650	405,233.49
Massachusetts	2,201,966.47	294,200	....	252,370	247,212.02	250,783	3,246,531.49
Boston	4,457,576.00	5,369,820	....	87,897	86,117.54	703,018	10,704,428.54
Rhode Island	421,327.35	89,560	....	41,795	71,292.71	76,139	700,113.96
Connecticut	1,305,898.51	262,820	....	91,519	112,373.23	158,487	1,931,097.74
Division No. 1	9,591,854.59	6,036,740	....	595,970	629,966.59	1,265,127	18,120,658.18
New York	3,232,797.64	1,036,370	....	253,903	267,762.70	362,524	5,153,357.34
New York City	7,096,549.50	48,025,260	....	220,609	255,586.02	2,589,708	59,087,892.62
Albany	329,347.70	450,000	....	17,160	6,047.00	21,482	824,036.70
New Jersey	1,071,054.42	189,270	....	104,237	172,035.35	296,980	1,834,176.77
Pennsylvania	3,670,770.53	350,740	....	464,605	267,083.43	389,397	5,142,595.96
Philadelphia	1,573,016.00	467,430	$7,000,000	217,425	182,861.02	757,031	10,197,793.02
Pittsburg	1,743,812.00	974,000	....	119,502	52,607.95	179,576	3,069,497.95
Division No. 2	18,717,977.79	52,393,070	7,000,000	1,397,531	1,203,983.47	4,596,788	85,309,350.26
Delaware	138,871.00	11,800	....	42,155	22,915.64	71,120	286,951.64
Maryland	301,597.97	50,670	....	41,350	41,876.02	77,104	512,597.99
Baltimore	1,024,545.50	1,343,040	225,000	34,394	42,230.88	287,840	2,977,050.38
District of Columbia	98,840.50	90,000	....	3,783	1,481.25	9,891	203,995.75
Washington	108,076.00	601,020	....	11,247	19,582.00	201,611	941,536.00
Virginia	311,021.50	8,730	....	70,684	35,029.83	84,927	519,992.33
West Virginia	216,166.66	13,800	....	13,778	11,744.25	15,856	271,344.93
Division No. 3	2,109,119.15	2,119,150	225,000	216,391	175,459.87	748,340	5,713,469.02
North Carolina	155,029.76	570	....	62,844	40,393.09	4,441	263,277.85
South Carolina	95,171.00	....	....	57,593	24,570.90	38,096	215,430.90
Georgia	215,454.38	21,920	....	93,578	40,800.81	117,964	489,717.19
Florida	46,536.90	1,800	....	48,190	10,762.70	1,463	108,812.60
Alabama	163,601.50	13,170	....	108,060	28,635.55	88,315	401,782.05
Mississippi	33,641.50	1,800	....	33,651	14,649.15	40,763	124,504.65
Louisiana	15,267.50	8,040	....	14,092	8,988.35	52,074	98,461.85
New Orleans	68,241.00	58,900	....	46,232	38,379.15	415,410	627,162.15
Texas	472,210.55	71,290	....	234,301	59,236.95	281,188	1,118,226.50
Arkansas	34,144.50	12,200	....	38,880	6,745.65	43,681	135,660.15
Kentucky	444,211.50	41,370	....	51,507	27,370.71	36,814	601,271.21
Louisville	330,711.50	63,500	....	23,766	8,654.90	45,285	471,917.40
Tennessee	454,167.50	118,000	....	122,823	38,110.87	88,574	821,735.37
Division No. 4	2,528,389.00	412,080	....	935,526	347,298.78	1,254,008	5,477,961.87

AMOUNT OF EACH KIND OF COIN AND COIN CERTIFICATE HELD BY THE NATIONAL BANKS, ETC.—Continued.

SEPTEMBER 30, 1889—Continued.

States, etc.	Gold coin.	Gold Treasury certificates.	Gold clearinghouse certificates.	Silver coin.		Silver Treasury certificates.	Total.
				Dollars.	Fractional.		
Ohio	$2,425,974.67	$109,300		$254,526	$151,936.95	$76,972	$3,018,709.62
Cincinnati	317,739.00	312,000		50,708	17,977.40	292,400	990,824.40
Cleveland	631,680.00	240,000		31,729	6,834.97	25,000	935,243.97
Indiana	1,680,614.69	256,750		151,382	99,572.80	84,079	2,272,998.49
Illinois	1,837,607.81	190,390		211,287	144,057.64	98,129	2,481,471.45
Chicago	11,594,795.00	2,622,000		221,473	135,375.19	769,150	15,342,793.19
Michigan	1,082,062.69	39,240		118,554	73,262.97	34,005	1,347,124.66
Detroit	995,425.50	57,370		50,497	54,499.05	61,423	1,219,714.55
Wisconsin	806,332.15	11,885		60,886	49,836.25	22,825	951,759.40
Milwaukee	602,185.00	120,000		12,169	7,820.00	6,700	748,874.00
Division No. 5	21,974,416.51	3,958,930		1,163,211	741,673.22	1,471,283	29,309,513.73
Iowa	902,414.10	56,120		145,479	82,074.65	58,976	1,245,663.75
Minnesota	1,752,021.30	7,310		199,613	113,786.93	25,662	2,099,023.23
Missouri	251,010.20	10,290		40,955	22,257.64	31,090	355,608.84
St. Louis	1,061,101.00	395,000		25,200	15,032.60	81,000	1,577,333.60
Kansas City	1,284,739.50	130,540		80,227	40,736.45	162,110	1,698,352.95
St. Joseph	148,987.50	80,400		14,458	5,989.55	66,907	316,802.05
Kansas	849,880.59	26,150		134,444	63,584.90	85,027	1,159,086.49
Nebraska	546,096.15	13,730		57,780	33,492.32	57,859	708,957.47
Omaha	950,567.32	15,000		86,172	32,387.98	22,946	1,107,673.30
Division No. 6	7,747,417.66	735,200		784,355	409,943.02	591,643	10,268,561.68
Colorado	1,738,927.52	28,790		76,934	43,207.80	27,495	1,915,354.32
Nevada	38,590.00	500		804	3,713.05	140	43,297.65
California	2,118,974.50	24,550	$110,000	141,314	52,423.33	21,291	2,468,552.83
San Francisco	824,265.00	140,410	40,000	7,500	4,800.00	2,500	1,019,475.00
Oregon	984,984.50	1,390		19,868	24,138.23	18,080	1,048,460.73
Arizona	16,005.00			142	1,076.70		17,223.70
Division No. 7	5,721,746.52	195,190	150,000	246,562	129,359.71	69,506	6,512,364.23
Dakota	348,812.10	16,560		26,778	20,238.46	22,808	435,196.56
Idaho	109,630.00	7,000		9,220	3,663.48	6,689	136,202.48
Montana	614,095.00	42,050		47,385	24,084.20	14,905	743,019.20
New Mexico	147,122.50			13,062	5,790.55	725	166,700.05
Utah	457,235.53	76,990		19,003	8,217.65	8,353	569,799.18
Washington	1,248,730.00	17,190		51,079	22,159.50	12,903	1,352,061.50
Wyoming	194,983.50	200		7,030	6,462.40	2,915	211,590.90
Division No. 8	3,120,608.63	159,990		173,457	91,216.24	69,298	3,614,509.87
United States	71,601,529.94	66,010,950	7,375,000	5,543,006	3,728,900.90	10,067,062	164,326,448.84

OCTOBER 2, 1890.

States, etc.	Gold coin.	Gold Treasury certificates.	Gold clearinghouse certificates.	Silver coin.		Silver Treasury certificates.	Total.
				Dollars.	Fractional.		
Maine	$602,874.89	$41,820		$48,059	$39,218.33	$67,884	$799,856.22
New Hampshire	268,771.25	4,150		56,098	49,127.21	55,647	433,793.46
Vermont	316,702.85	12,120		30,081	37,316.78	28,414	424,634.63
Massachusetts	2,306,246.38	330,130		293,386	252,934.59	369,949	3,552,645.97
Boston	3,651,524.50	6,538,790		80,266	92,004.01	996,026	11,358,610.51
Rhode Island	408,039.36	156,540		36,931	80,276.60	140,846	817,632.96
Connecticut	1,384,923.24	288,270		104,210	117,233.67	283,495	2,178,131.91
Division No. 1	8,934,082.47	7,371,820		649,031	668,111.19	1,942,261	19,565,305.66
New York	3,060,378.34	630,170		287,419	276,835.54	255,673	4,510,675.88
New York City	8,631,003.00	65,551,590		267,232	328,370.08	3,681,745	78,459,940.03
Albany	415,144.50	511,000		15,435	8,554.75	16,792	966,921.25
Brooklyn	132,848.00	584,200		13,333	32,783.20	180,871	944,035.20
New Jersey	1,167,601.91	256,520		155,844	183,705.67	444,643	2,208,314.58
Pennsylvania	3,929,012.10	402,830		491,700	314,143.18	480,232	5,617,917.28
Philadelphia	1,731,829.50	3,150,210	$3,150,000	310,751	281,162.31	923,777	9,553,729.81
Pittsburg	1,738,876.50	906,380		187,768	70,891.15	314,846	3,218,761.65
Division No. 2	20,806,693.85	71,992,900	3,150,000	1,735,477	5,496,445.83	6,298,779	105,480,295.68

AMOUNT OF EACH KIND OF COIN AND COIN CERTIFICATE HELD BY THE NATIONAL
BANKS, ETC.—Continued.

OCTOBER 2, 1890—Continued.

States, etc.	Gold coin.	Gold Treasury certificates.	Gold-clearing-house certificates.	Silver coin. Dollars.	Silver coin. Fractional.	Silver Treasury certificates.	Total.
Delaware	$156,931.14	$7,000		$30,291	$25,558.11	$85,829	$305,600.25
Maryland	294,910.81	67,450		51,340	48,257.85	110,370	572,328.66
Baltimore	457,112.50	2,260,200		75,102	50,451.38	381,720	3,224,585.88
District of Columbia	103,923.50	110,000		7,287	5,485.75	13,792	240,488.25
Washington	108,436.50	1,131,890		7,863	42,164.55	297,724	1,588,078.05
Virginia	369,895.00	47,680		74,555	35,531.80	129,120	656,781.80
West Virginia	257,912.28	14,850		24,910	20,057.17	21,340	339,060.45
Division No. 3	1,749,121.73	3,639,070		271,348	227,506.61	1,039,895	6,926,941.34
North Carolina	184,338.30	50		27,627	23,101.20	8,172	243,798.50
South Carolina	223,350.35	2,080		57,233	24,123.73	13,486	320,273.08
Georgia	422,448.69	73,60		123,053	32,397.10	123,989	776,147.79
Florida	29,654.65			71,554	18,243.98	4,635	124,087.63
Alabama	289,812.00	20,820		95,971	28,156.55	65,369	495,128.55
Mississippi	39,719.00	2,70		34,836	19,943.15	30,054	127,252.15
Louisiana	7,530.00	15,740		25,520	13,295.45	53,915	116,000.45
New Orleans	154,462.50	301,500		56,915	34,445.98	424,191	971,514.48
Texas	737,805.15	194,410		352,724	84,456.12	355,980	1,725,375.27
Arkansas	30,010.00	15,850		31,451	17,905.99	36,519	131,786.99
Kentucky	548,288.80	44,400		76,660	33,482.20	41,829	744,660.00
Louisville	218,568.00	34,600		26,548	10,348.05	32,296	322,360.05
Tennessee	422,654.50	100,880		201,882	55,865.52	90,422	889,704.02
Division No. 4	3,308,641.94	816,180		1,182,574	390,836.02	1,289,857	6,988,088.96
Ohio	2,420,812.37	103,810		304,608	150,806.22	125,131	3,105,257.59
Cincinnati	275,719.66	475,000		69,236	27,373.89	172,950	1,020,279.49
Cleveland	786,965.50	177.00		25,466	15,010.25	22,032	1,026,473.75
Indiana	1,932,387.58	145,496		214,933	111,890.35	175,912	2,580,612.93
Illinois	1,807,274.55	237,256		222,857	143,473.63	148,488	2,559,343.18
Chicago	10,849,786.50	5,215,400		197,478	216,478.72	527,516	17,006,659.22
Michigan	1,158,699.04	59,253		117,510	85,285.85	66,559	1,487,303.89
Detroit	822,327.50	116,580		40,353	46,008.05	49,720	1,075,888.55
Wisconsin	896,186.70	39,840		71,724	60,309.08	52,137	1,120,286.78
Milwaukee	617,000.00	225,000		21,948	7,820.00	7,891	879,659.00
Division No. 5	21,567,159.34	6,794,620		1,286,203	865,446.04	1,348,336	31,861,764.38
Iowa	1,192,871.10	67,350		103,018	90,547.24	117,644	1,661,430.34
Minnesota	651,600.70	4,840		47,698	34,221.15	27,443	765,802.85
St. Paul	1,017,869.45			104,950	65,461.05	118,105	1,306,385.50
Minneapolis	739,050.25	30,00		46,002	25,192.00	11,200	851,444.25
Missouri	257,902.50	11,120		57,679	23,049.05	40,072	300,812.55
St. Louis	497,523.50	1,848,790		27,221	14,413.14	672,484	3,060,431.64
Kansas City	886,925.00	152,450		124,995	31,585.12	170,276	1,367,211.12
St. Joseph	162,267.50	71,260		12,168	7,222.05	44,430	297,356.55
Kansas	856,101.30	97,500		150,003	67,525.70	107,770	1,279,839.00
Nebraska	636,827.75	24,170		72,475	44,779 37	73,640	851,892.12
Omaha	1,811,377.50	36,390		88,490	24,400.70	37,500	1,908,224.20
Division No. 6	8,710,406.55	2,343,850		924,689	430,456.57	1,421,428	13,830,830.12
Colorado	1,920,630.90	31,550		92,634	42,211.00	40,113	2,127,138.91
Nevada	40,932.50	22.0		3,787	4,450.20	218	49,616.70
California	1,800,211.50	57,140	*29,000	100,966	50,488.30	28,831	2,066,636.80
San Francisco	843,042.50	2,000	290,000	11,000	5,570.00	8,000	1,159,612.50
Oregon	1,301,926.50	2,270		17,729	20,640.20	16,999	1,359,564.70
Arizona	49,770.00	340		1,800	1,113.70	520	53,543.70
Division No. 7	5,956,513.91	93,520	319,000	227,916	124,482.40	94,681	6,816,113.31
North Dakota	162,277.90	26,070		13,263	12,779.40	42,774	257,164.30
South Dakota	186,939.90	17,100		14,870	11,517.30	23,047	253,474.20
Idaho	98,263.40	2,070		2,098	1,341.25	3,801	107,573.65
Montana	668,008.05	60,320		56,132	34,918.99	30,487	850,766.04
New Mexico	214,217.50			12,265	6,022.60		232,505.10
Utah	444,215.50	110,000		20,288	13,392.31	48,730	645,654.81
Washington	1,826,303.80	56,790		80,906	30,841.54	31,682	1,826,521.34
Wyoming	218,145.00	2,140		9,010	5,327.95	5,251	230,879.95
Oklahoma	11,485.00	150		840	821.08	4,545	17,847.08
Indian Territory	1,457.50			2,612	360.42	3,721	8,150.92
Division No. 8	3,632,213.55	283,640		212,296	117,322.84	194,047	4,439,519.39
United States	74,664,833.34	93,335,600	3,469,000	6,489,534	4,320,007.56	3,629,284	195,908,858.84

AMOUNT OF EACH KIND OF COIN AND COIN CERTIFICATE HELD BY THE NATIONAL BANKS, ETC.—Continued.

SEPTEMBER 25, 1891.

States, etc.	Gold coin.	Gold Treasury certificates.	Gold clearing-house certificates.	Silver coin. Dollars.	Silver coin. Fractional.	Silver Treasury certificates.	Total.
Maine	$686,071.30	$48,770		$37,428	$40,981.04	$90,391	$903,641.34
New Hampshire	274,384.50	25,790		57,414	43,181.41	71,550	472,319.91
Vermont	334,232.20	18,110		30,175	48,748.68	45,545	476,810.88
Massachusetts	2,451,009.49	268,250		230,782	273,482.61	400,108	3,713,632.10
Boston	3,414,499.35	3,835,130		63,776	131,608.95	1,481,750	8,920,773.30
Rhode Island	419,431.90	210,670		41,332	83,205.28	187,918	942,557.18
Connecticut	1,520,844.90	351,440		77,653	123,855.48	313,274	2,393,067.38
Division No. 1..	9,106,473.64	4,758,160		538,560	745,063.45	2,680,545	17,828,802.09
New York	3,236,137.64	605,770		261,779	305,934.46	328,675	4,788,296.10
New York City ..	9,845,117.00	37,523,360		155,216	401,567.49	5,871,631	53,796,801.49
Albany	348,577.00	454,000		19,700	10,103.50	19,911	852,291.50
Brooklyn	126,711.50	392,000		2,455	43,268.53	271,502	835,907.03
New Jersey	1,253,476.56	302,290		152,978	193,413.20	528,855	2,431,017.82
Pennsylvania	4,307,482.36	487,960		506,752	328,088.40	686,739	6,317,921.82
Philadelphia	1,872,449.00	1,740,720	$6,675,000	264,836	268,583.55	1,651,178	12,472,766.55
Pittsburg	2,203,511.50	515,580		119,402	69,718.85	237,345	3,145,557.35
Division No. 2..	23,183,162.56	42,081,680	6,675,000	1,483,118	1,621,583.10	9,595,896	84,640,739.66
Delaware	128,212.00	14,080		36,235	31,758.45	99,319	310,504.45
Maryland	368,635.46	66,550		45,342	50,316.09	113,452	644,295.55
Baltimore	596,612.50	1,271,650		84,218	50,786.80	667,738	2,680,005.39
District of Columbia .	117,550.50	120,000		2,735	2,151.75	22,892	265,338.25
Washington	136,071.40	1,234,180		17,946	22,667.30	385,291	1,796,155.70
Virginia	535,150.34	59,730		91,024	67,721.30	120,797	874,422.64
West Virginia	273,611.68	15,340		24,683	24,359.81	32,132	370,126.49
Division No. 3..	2,155,852.88	2,782,430		302,183	258,761.59	1,441,621	6,940,848.47
North Carolina	266,716.86	4,420		42,276	36,255.48	15,090	364,758.34
South Carolina	66,441.85	500		45,165	33,700.25	7,461	153,268.10
Georgia	237,152.80	18,880		89,823	44,567.30	126,984	517,407.10
Florida	62,301.40	2,550		49,843	22,598.95	13,571	150,864.35
Alabama	221,738.50	23,400		79,710	24,780.75	78,974	428,612.25
Mississippi	53,490.50	3,540		21,465	9,580.95	32,373	120,449.45
Louisiana	28,490.50	4,040		38,781	18,327.50	45,526	135,174.00
New Orleans	187,836.50	258,320		74,992	38,571.95	626,495	1,186,215.45
Texas	949,942.20	80,460		395,071	102,383.91	491,866	2,019,723.11
Arkansas	70,445.00	17,950		22,383	4,942.30	25,341	141,061.30
Kentucky	536,133.67	48,990		70,747	37,181.86	63,370	756,422.53
Louisville	319,407.00	24,800		40,197	10,319.35	14,200	408,923.35
Tennessee	538,586.50	92,840		204,343	62,196.31	83,551	981,516.81
Division No. 4..	3,538,692.28	580,690		1,174,786	445,415.86	1,624,802	7,364,386.14
Ohio	2,801,760.86	165,840		283,858	176,114.08	168,081	3,595,653.94
Cincinnati	353,328.50	747,450		67,766	29,437.74	470,212	1,668,194.24
Cleveland	743,412.50	266,000		34,045	23,507.00	28,621	1,095,585.50
Indiana	2,261,623.30	395,930		220,358	124,001.38	219,825	3,221,737.68
Illinois	2,423,284.75	407,290		280,268	187,171.87	249,155	3,547,109.62
Chicago	13,018,145.50	5,449,500		222,513	201,803.25	1,250,501	20,142,612.75
Michigan	1,384,806.09	69,700		127,808	92,223.39	93,171	1,767,768.48
Detroit	725,296.00	38,000		33,017	37,310.00	94,797	928,420.00
Wisconsin	1,284,673.74	45,300		87,007	74,814.01	61,831	1,553,625.75
Milwaukee	674,550.00	170,000		16,230	12,722.02	40,754	914,236.02
Division No. 5..	25,670,921.24	7,755,010		1,372,870	959,164.74	2,677,038	38,435,003.98
Iowa	1,308,988.24	67,260		177,600	99,872.29	111,520	1,785,339.44
Des Moines	112,710.00			18,404	9,522.35	50,000	190,636.35
Minnesota	735,091.94	20,300		54,611	37,661.04	53,304	900,967.98
St. Paul	1,714,857.97	14,000		30,906	18,063.95	227,210	2,005,037.92
Minneapolis	616,167.50			53,091	23,045.65	181,750	874,054.15
Missouri	304,751.00	13,030		62,396	35,253.18	42,105	457,535.18
St. Louis	1,437,512.00	1,412,350		37,117	16,771.70	832,430	3,736,180.70
Kansas City	1,038,627.50	178,640		141,931	34,802.35	264,032	1,658,092.85
St. Joseph	195,733.50	27,080		21,533	10,657.20	72,751	327,754.70
Kansas	1,115,800.05	45,210		133,377	63,423.52	134,639	1,492,449.57
Nebraska	771,823.90	26,660		78,552	45,625.84	71,496	994,157.74
Omaha	1,672,940.40	43,500		91,303	42,766.26	52,193	1,902,702.66
Division No. 6..	11,025,004.00	1,868,030		900,911	437,525.24	2,093,430	16,324,909.24

AMOUNT OF EACH KIND OF COIN AND COIN CERTIFICATE HELD BY THE NATIONAL
BANKS, ETC.—Continued.

SEPTEMBER 25, 1891—Continued.

States, etc.	Gold coin.	Gold Treasury certificates.	Gold clearing-house certificates.	Silver coin. Dollars.	Silver coin. Fractional.	Silver Treasury certificates.	Total.
Colorado	$1,886,841.60	$52,720		$208,684	$52,031.04	$52,510	$2,252,792.64
Nevada	37,210.00			1,770	2,015.45	280	41,275.45
California	1,701,832.50	21,890	$35,000	98,455	74,232.40	19,025	1,951,334.90
San Francisco	1,020,225.00		590,000	13,090	23,200.00	3,000	1,655,425.00
Oregon	1,409,640.07	4,230		18,037	34,093.08	13,675	1,480,276.95
Arizona	36,130.00			2,927	1,766.85		40,823.85
Division No. 7	6,097,880.07	78,840	625,000	342,873	187,939.72	80,396	7,421,928.79
North Dakota	185,076.72	25,800		11,882	13,713.20	41,002	277,473.92
South Dakota	175,387.50	19,400		20,557	10,172.39	39,712	265,228.89
Idaho	128,640.90	260		9,150	5,211.75	13,885	157,137.65
Montana	738,850.00	64,200		48,915	45,281.69	42,690	939,936.69
New Mexico	145,850.00			13,492	6,343.15	2,041	167,726.15
Utah	526,641.35	101,400		40,558	21,825.36	18,716	709,140.71
Washington	1,556,435.60	57,580		71,538	53,877.93	35,985	1,775,416.53
Wyoming	217,156.00	190		11,355	5,883.65	6,467	241,051.65
Oklahoma	6,385.00			709	101.25	720	7,915.25
Indian Territory	5,647.50			5,116	886.60	5,780	17,430.10
Division No. 8	3,686,060.57	268,830		233,272	163,296.97	206,998	4,558,457.54
United States	84,464,347.24	60,173,670	7,300,000	6,348,573	4,818,750.67	20,409,735	183,515,075.91

SEPTEMBER 30, 1892.

Maine	$743,629.30	$77,870		$43,077	$47,450.76	$101,324	$1,013,351.15
New Hampshire	318,934.18	34,330		65,434	48,332.48	81,675	548,705.66
Vermont	367,132.50	18,490		32,705	48,565.19	38,643	505,625.69
Massachusetts	2,705,756.35	228,090		236,327	296,995.63	589,326	4,056,494.98
Boston	3,713,014.00	4,990,210		63,391	128,725.55	1,864,358	10,760,298.55
Rhode Island	482,412.30	197,120		29,248	95,906.80	105,167	999,854.10
Connecticut	1,622,266.05	230,410		82,265	148,681.97	334,144	2,417,767.02
Division No. 1	9,953,744.77	5,776,520		552,537	814,658.38	3,204,637	20,302,097.15
New York	3,475,672.03	774,700		231,719	304,826.98	413,385	5,200,303.01
New York City	12,146,883.00	44,618,480		151,290	467,497.07	5,183,921	62,568,071.07
Albany	312,807.50	438,000		11,083	10,161.45	29,422	802,073.95
Brooklyn	130,174.50	462,250		17,740	46,330.09	250,547	907,051.49
New Jersey	1,318,017.17	332,690		156,190	186,759.75	549,640	2,543,296.02
Pennsylvania	4,407,338.18	501,920		405,726	369,144.33	832,631	6,606,759.51
Philadelphia	2,102,139.50	2,109,380	$7,730,000	313,277	287,504.54	2,079,813	14,622,204.04
Pittsburg	2,682,329.50	661,600		135,889	121,539.35	488,635	4,089,992.85
Division No. 2	26,575,361.38	49,899,020	7,730,000	1,513,514	1,793,863.46	9,827,004	97,339,752.84
Delaware	137,330.90	11,580		26,690	41,537.95	118,133	335,271.85
Maryland	385,510.60	71,320		34,845	45,902.60	161,455	699,042.26
Baltimore	983,166.00	1,130,400		67,828	71,094.10	941,804	3,194,382.10
District of Columbia	83,847.00	142,000		3,995	3,144.25	48,512	281,498.25
Washington	243,560.40	1,098,780		17,076	33,284.20	372,710	1,766,310.60
Virginia	420,718.40	62,000		82,215	75,014.08	135,313	775,260.48
West Virginia	292,404.53	26,260		37,112	28,806.55	90,406	474,989.08
Division No. 3	2,546,546.80	2,542,340		270,661	298,783.73	1,868,423	7,526,754.62
North Carolina	241,342.00	2,640		53,132	38,128.68	10,364	345,606.68
South Carolina	91,060.35			86,845	38,200.90	35,852	252,858.25
Georgia	258,390.94	27,300		128,375	79,903.93	80,786	577,755.87
Florida	58,459.28	1,540		105,042	26,018.15	5,856	197,515.43
Alabama	238,697.00	44,800		107,093	39,305.00	88,008	519,403.00
Mississippi	102,270.80	2,970		10,744	10,573.65	21,510	148,068.45
Louisiana	42,275.50	6,040		36,205	14,020.05	41,580	140,210.55
New Orleans	133,561.00	373,090		76,557	52,243.18	1,601,183	2,236,634.18
Texas	1,224,397.90	146,540		485,916	110,597.23	558,565	2,535,016.13
Arkansas	71,275.00	21,480		39,672	10,972.55	41,506	184,805.55
Kentucky	483,863.25	54,030		81,881	39,961.54	85,353	745,088.79
Louisville	462,426.00	39,780		29,652	10,544.63	27,320	569,722.61
Tennessee	566,592.50	115,120		184,994	73,738.11	130,260	1,070,710.01
Division No. 4	3,975,511.52	836,230		1,426,698	553,807.60	2,729,049	9,521,296.12

AMOUNT OF EACH KIND OF COIN AND COIN CERTIFICATE HELD BY THE NATIONAL BANKS, ETC.—Continued.

SEPTEMBER 30, 1892—Continued.

States, etc.	Gold coin.	Gold Treasury certificates.	Gold clearing-house certificates.	Silver coin. Dollars.	Silver coin. Fractional.	Silver Treasury certificates.	Total.
Ohio	$2,922,193.04	$108,830		$329,524	$189,223.72	$208,833	$3,848,603.76
Cincinnati	539,215.00	815,770		94,767	21,092.15	557,460	2,028,304.15
Cleveland	1,035,070.50	302,000		32,171	22,970.00	41,000	1,433,211.50
Indiana	2,458,641.26	591,150		236,457	136,619.34	218,749	3,641,616.60
Illinois	2,841,613.78	436,160		284,849	189,027.43	239,032	3,991,582.21
Chicago	14,644,030.00	5,969,880		223,114	188,982.90	1,289,847	22,315,853.90
Michigan	1,400,258.38	60,780		118,760	89,904.61	99,811	1,769,522.99
Detroit	933,042.50	50,150		25,767	48,841.05	113,304	1,170,104.55
Wisconsin	1,507,862.29	55,420		05,142	73,420.66	105,291	1,837,144.05
Milwaukee	819,550.00	125,000		0,323	10,050.00	9,533	974,365.00
Division No. 5	29,106,476.75	8,605,140		1,449,883	971,046.86	2,883,703	43,010,309.61
Iowa	1,471,192.70	118,780		168,038	127,160.25	156,434	2,041,613.95
Des Moines	123,268.00	7,000		13,336	20,272.15	9,800	173,676.15
Minnesota	854,245.45	9,830		62,676	42,302.76	49,718	1,018,862.21
St. Paul	1,691,711.80	2,170		82,300	17,786.67	17,250	1,811,218.17
Minneapolis	671,912.50	5,000		53,664	42,627.78	74,200	847,404.28
Missouri	314,155.70	15,390		59,235	26,089.05	52,567	467,436.75
St. Louis	1,319,193.00	2,082.480		34,223	22,701.85	1,132,924	4,591,524.85
Kansas City	841,267.50	252,920		141,923	45,403.75	240,561	1,522,074.25
St. Joseph	173,012.00	58,580		15,577	7,726.30	79,322	334,217.30
Kansas	1,123,074.05	55,750		142,572	77,017.91	169,483	1,567,896.96
Nebraska	992,968.81	26,730		86,085	59,647.88	92,805	1,258,236.69
Omaha	2,025,212.00	10,000		86,217	54,602.05	50,724	2,226,755.05
Division No. 6	11,601,213.51	2,644,630		945,846	543,439.40	2,125,788	17,860,916.91
Colorado	2,546,291.85	83,630		109,925	83,157.24	98,779	3,011,783.09
Nevada	44,765.00			1,682	2,247.30		48,694.30
California	1,552,025.00	19,940	$80,000	77,040	71,898.79	31,602	1,832,505.79
San Francisco	1,086,610.00	402,100	50,000	30,000	13,460.60	7,000	1,580,170.00
Oregon	1,313,437.50	3,020		25,772	37,877.11	13,908	1,394,014.61
Arizona	68,310.00			3,245	5,036.85		77,091.85
Division No. 7	6,611,939.35	508,690	130,000	337,664	213,677.29	151,289	7,953,259.64
North Dakota	296,862.00	22,950		19,852	23,244.85	21,757	384,665.85
South Dakota	271,733.50	10,620		28,457	17,031.04	28,550	356,400.54
Idaho	164,863.40	1,230		9,006	9,816.13	6,920	192,735.53
Montana	030,457.50	71,810		61,270	57,349.65	46,194	1,167,081.15
New Mexico	160,492.50	4,860		20,884	8,788.33	1,032	196,056.83
Utah	746,022.75	73,910		41,159	27,066.03	17,874	906,031.78
Washington	1,744,552.10	49,570		78,160	60,455.45	58,323	1,991,060.55
Wyoming	303,330.35	360		17,513	8,502.67	3,412	333,208.02
Oklahoma	20,307.00	460		6,469	1,478.70	8,804	37,518.70
Indian Territory	12,537.50	1,840		4,611	2,611.35	9,633	31,232.85
Division No. 8	4,651,158.60	237,610		288,281	216,431.20	202,508	5,505,091.80
United States	95,021,952.77	71,050,180	7,860,000	6,785,084	5,405,710.92	22,993,451	209,116,378.69

OCTOBER 3, 1893.

Maine	842,423.72	39,040		55,197	57,070.41	120,658	1,114,389.13
New Hampshire	320,892.77	20,610		78,704	56,768.07	99,076	585,050.84
Vermont	447,051.50	25,250		70,613	55,837.60	44,600	643,991.41
Massachusetts	2,905,423.46	192,640		464,610	398,723.97	559,546	4,520,952.43
Boston	5,389,926.00	2,000,540		112,772	165,428.60	2,275,122	9,952,788.60
Rhode Island	666,006.50	124,740		84,123	131,248.30	188,449	1,195,466.80
Connecticut	1,879,951.13	390,220		115,100	158,702.10	343,726	2,896,699.23
Division No. 1	12,453,205.33	2,820,040		981,128	1,023,779.11	3,631,186	20,909,338.44
New York	4,265,473.42	651,960		390,172	390,822.75	453,725	6,152,153.17
New York City	36,739,700.00	32,403,940		248,996	431,664.90	5,878,703	75,703,663.90
Albany	341,297.50	305,500		28,965	18,779.85	20,701	715,243.35
Brooklyn	230,202.50	202,200		29,400	45,632.52	291,948	799,383.02
New Jersey	1,896,615.60	321,550		179,012	225,137.05	607,339	3,229,653.66
Pennsylvania	5,987,729.21	504,930		736,307	452,204.05	962,407	8,733,577.88
Philadelphia	2,632,646.50	545,920	5,075,000	331,899	302,585.84	2,239,360	11,127,420.34
Pittsburg	2,757,432.99	321,860		171,173	135,898.35	626,470	4,012,840.34
Division No. 2	54,851,097.74	35,347,860	5,075,000	2,115,924	2,002,725.91	11,080,728	110,473,335.65

AMOUNTS OF EACH KIND OF COIN AND COIN CERTIFICATE HELD BY THE NATIONAL BANKS, ETC.—Continued.

OCTOBER 3, 1893—Continued.

States, etc.	Gold coin.	Gold treasury certificates.	Gold clearing-house certificates.	Silver coin.		Silver treasury certificates.	Total.
				Dollars.	Fractional.		
Delaware	$211,816.20	$13,000		$36,436	$38,287.57	$115,631	$415,170.77
Maryland	355,314.06	73,480		31,562	49,117.71	206,402	715,875.77
Baltimore	993,039.00	911,850		67,800	95,295.70	872,817	2,940,801.70
District of Columbia	100,091.50	92,000		2,965	7,035.00	26,026	237,027.50
Washington City	249,777.40	631,510		14,705	23,939.00	478,887	1,398,848.40
Virginia	515,262.50	28,380		104,431	80,296.06	217,004	945,373.56
West Virginia	397,572.43	35,870		42,105	33,751.17	83,685	592,983.60
Division No. 3.	2,831,783.09	1,786,120		300,004	327,722.21	2,001,052	7,246,681.30
North Carolina	238,353.00	1,150		69,888	44,680.00	18,883	373,454.06
South Carolina	167,993.50			45,576	31,425.40	18,099	263,093.90
Georgia	255,415.50	3,460		78,628	46,837.65	83,556	467,897.15
Florida	96,466.85	11,150		99,800	19,796.40	26,084	253,297.25
Alabama	239,398.00	42,290		101,310	27,363.95	64,894	495,255.95
Mississippi	92,495.00	2,500		20,935	14,938.13	8,005	138,903.13
Louisiana	54,619.50	1,300		26,714	12,765.35	38,399	133,797.85
New Orleans	104,789.00	200,050		61,669	72,071.21	741,024	1,179,603.21
Texas	2,270,293.00	212,750		518,887	116,656.26	380,421	3,498,977.26
Arkansas	104,866.10	11,500		16,383	13,902.50	63,852	210,503.60
Kentucky	527,131.75	48,200		89,868	36,469.95	82,686	781,355.70
Louisville	481,052.00	25,600		26,456	15,354.86	27,000	576,062.86
Tennessee	829,375.00	54,120		237,407	79,123.70	274,930	1,474,964.70
Division No. 4.	5,483,348.20	614,070		1,393,491	531,385.42	1,827,932	9,850,226.62
Ohio	3,832,540.61	213,270		337,866	204,305.66	228,775	4,816,757.27
Cincinnati	755,040.00	311,500		56,869	20,182.90	496,815	1,640,406.90
Cleveland	1,250,002.50	255,000		100,964	44,002.00	42,000	1,692,028.50
Indiana	3,508,701.82	176,720		225,689	110,972.19	223,801	4,335,884.01
Illinois	3,122,530.83	361,550		220,830	171,949.22	299,755	4,176,615.05
Chicago	12,013,600.00	3,987,650		476,195	549,920.25	5,744,558	22,771,923.25
Michigan	1,741,785.07	69,340		183,910	113,902.17	132,235	2,241,172.24
Detroit	828,852.50	13,000		37,041	36,943.88	55,234	971,071.38
Wisconsin	1,978,276.10	34,770		125,880	73,163.22	117,542	2,329,617.32
Milwaukee	1,299,677.50	125,000		33,898	22,456.60	108,825	1,589,857.10
Division No. 5.	30,421,006.93	5,547,800		1,799,148	1,347,858.09	7,449,540	46,565,353.02
Iowa	1,956,792.50	121,980		155,898	93,284.17	161,229	2,489,183.67
Des Moines	83,307.50	3,500		9,728	9,796.25	8,696	115,527.75
Minnesota	1,257,439.70	9,000		58,085	46,771.81	57,068	1,428,364.51
St. Paul	1,908,636.50	18,500		102,400	29,745.00	117,508	2,176,790.10
Minneapolis	887,000.00	10,000		18,617	12,160.65	47,750	975,527.65
Missouri	356,081.50	13,320		56,347	26,740.60	69,711	522,200.10
St. Louis	1,756,230.50	772,820		32,269	23,634.25	1,054,721	3,639,674.75
Kansas City	959,705.00	59,220		96,210	35,873.60	103,709	1,254,807.60
St. Joseph	280,218.50	13,200		27,382	12,603.50	111,658	445,062.00
Kansas	1,373,733.54	61,840		141,071	79,839.27	149,762	1,806,245.81
Nebraska	936,728.36	11,200		57,730	35,682.30	70,848	1,112,188.66
Lincoln	232,505.00			23,598	9,735.41	5,547	271,385.41
Omaha	1,436,160.00	28,500		80,537	36,849.92	118,030	1,700,096.92
Division No. 6.	13,425,038.60	1,123,080		859,892	452,726.33	2,076,327	17,937,063.93
Colorado	2,278,765.15	83,250		173,794	75,183.53	45,426	2,656,418.68
Nevada	47,980.00			2,010	3,281.00	205	53,476.00
California	1,751,707.50	4,260		53,802	41,473.66	21,822	1,873,065.16
San Francisco	1,025,350.00	25,000	$5,000	7,520	17,890.00	1,500	1,082,260.00
Oregon	1,456,827.25	90		14,676	30,766.18	21,290	1,523,649.43
Arizona	106,437.50	500		5,732	5,381.90	1,700	119,751.40
Division No. 7.	6,667,067.40	113,100	5,000	257,534	173,979.27	91,943	7,308,623.67
North Dakota	212,625.20	10,800		7,916	12,408.20	25,459	260,208.40
South Dakota	275,480.50	9,350		18,264	12,511.80	53,998	364,604.30
Idaho	207,265.00	450		6,446	4,615.69	9,153	227,930.59
Montana	776,789.70	11,410		86,579	33,459.20	41,370	949,607.90
New Mexico	148,491.00	5,450		24,387	11,551.85	1,989	191,868.85
Utah	623,959.50	75,180		21,616	20,232.95	34,927	775,915.45
Washington	1,093,607.60	55,780		65,977	41,145.95	20,766	1,277,366.55
Wyoming	196,491.50	620		10,161	8,383.55	3,217	218,873.05
Oklahoma	42,615.00			7,378	1,601.00	22,727	74,321.00
Indian Territory	35,475.00	1,400		9,999	3,092.35	13,575	63,541.35
Division No. 8.	3,607,890.90	170,440		258,723	149,002.54	227,181	4,413,237.44
United States	139,740,438.19	47,522,510	5,080,000	7,965,844	6,009,178.88	28,385,889	224,703,860.07

STATEMENT EXHIBITING, BY STATES, TERRITORIES, AND RESERVE CITIES, THE AMOUNT OF COIN AND COIN CERTIFICATES HELD BY THE NATIONAL BANKS ON SEPTEMBER 30, 1889, OCTOBER 2, 1890, SEPTEMBER 25, 1891, SEPTEMBER 30, 1892, AND OCTOBER 3, 1893.

States, etc.	September 30, 1889.	October 2, 1890.	September 25, 1891.	September 30, 1892.	October 3, 1893.
Maine	$732,113.02	$799,856.22	$903,641.34	$1,013,351.15	$1,114,389.13
New Hampshire	401,139.94	433,793.46	472,319.91	543,795.66	585,050.84
Vermont	405,243.49	424,634.63	476,810.88	505,625.69	643,991.41
Massachusetts	3,246,531.49	3,552,615.97	3,713,632.10	4,056,494.98	4,529,952.43
Boston	10,704,428.54	11,358,610.51	8,926,773.30	10,760,298.55	9,952,788.60
Rhode Island	700,113.96	817,632.96	942,557.18	939,854.10	1,195,466.80
Connecticut	1,931,657.74	2,178,131.91	2,303,067.38	2,417,767.02	2,896,699.27
Division No. 1	18,120,658.18	19,565,305.00	17,828,802.09	20,302,097.15	20,909,338.44
New York	5,153,357.31	4,510,675.88	4,788,296.10	5,200,308.01	6,152,153.17
New York City	59,087,892.52	78,459,940.03	53,796,891.49	62,508,071.07	75,704,963.90
Albany	824,036.70	966,921.25	852,291.50	802,073.95	715,243.35
Brooklyn		944,035.20	835,997.03	907,051.49	799,383.02
New Jersey	1,834,176.77	2,298,311.58	2,431,017.82	2,543,296.92	3,229,651.45
Pennsylvania	5,142,595.96	5,617,917.28	6,317,921.82	6,606,759.51	8,733,577.88
Philadelphia	10,497,793.02	9,553,729.81	12,472,766.55	14,622,204.04	11,127,420.34
Pittsburg	3,069,497.95	3,218,761.65	3,145,557.35	4,089,092.85	4,012,840.34
Division No. 2	85,309,359.20	105,480,295.08	84,640,739,66	97,339,752.84	110,473,335.65
Delaware	286,951.64	305,609.25	310,504.45	335,271.85	415,170.77
Maryland	512,597.99	572,328.66	644,295.55	699,042.26	715,875.77
Baltimore	2,977,050.38	3,224,585.88	2,689,005.39	3,194,382.10	2,940,801.70
District of Columbia	203,905.75	240,488.25	265,394.25	281,498.25	237,627.50
Washington	941,536.09	1,588,078.05	1,796,155.70	1,786,310.60	1,398,848.40
Virginia	519,992.33	656,781.80	874,422.64	775,260.48	945,373.56
West Virginia	271,344.93	309,669.45	370,126.49	474,989.08	592,983.60
Division No. 3	5,713,469.02	6,926,941.34	6,940,848.47	7,526,754.62	7,246,081.30
North Carolina	263,277.85	243,798.50	364,758.34	345,606.68	373,454.06
South Carolina	215,430.90	320,273.08	153,258.10	252,858.25	263,093.90
Georgia	489,717.19	770,147.79	517,407.10	574,755.87	467,897.15
Florida	108,812.60	124,087.63	150,804.35	197,515.43	253,297.25
Alabama	401,782.05	495,128.55	428,612.25	519,463.00	495,255.95
Mississippi	124,504.65	127,252.15	120,449.45	148,068.45	138,963.13
Louisiana	98,461.85	116,090.45	135,174.00	140,210.55	133,797.85
New Orleans	627,162.15	971,514.48	1,186,215.45	2,236,634.18	1,179,603.21
Texas	1,118,226.50	1,725,375.27	2,019,723.11	2,535,016.13	3,498,977.26
Arkansas	135,600.15	131,786.99	141,061.30	181,805.55	210,503.60
Kentucky	601,273.21	744,660.00	756,422.53	745,988.79	784,355.70
Louisville	471,917.40	322,360.05	408,923.35	509,722.63	576,062.86
Tennessee	821,735.37	889,704.02	981,510.81	1,070,710.61	1,474,964.70
Division No. 4	5,477,901.87	6,988,088.96	7,364,380.14	9,521,296.12	9,850,226.62
Ohio	3,018,709.62	3,105,257.59	3,595,653.94	3,848,603.76	4,810,757.27
Cincinnati	994,821.40	1,020,279.49	1,668,194.24	2,028,304.15	1,640,466.90
Cleveland	9.5,243.97	1,026,473.75	1,095,585.50	1,433,211.50	1,692,023.50
Indiana	2,272,998.49	2,580,612.93	3,221,737.68	3,641,616.60	4,353,884.01
Illinois	2,481,471.45	2,559,343.18	3,547,169.62	3,991,582.21	4,176,615.05
Chicago	15,342,793.19	17,006,659.22	20,142,612.75	22,315,853.90	22,771,923.25
Michigan	1,317,124.66	1,487,303.89	1,767,768.48	1,769,522.99	2,241,172.24
Detroit	1,219,714.55	1,075,888.55	928,420.00	1,176,104.55	971,071.38
Wisconsin	951,750.40	1,120,286.78	1,553,625.75	1,837,144.95	2,329,637.22
Milwaukee	748,874.00	879,659.00	914,236.02	974,305.00	1,589,857.10
Division No. 5	29,309,513.73	31,801,764.38	38,435,003.98	43,016,309.61	46,565,351.02
Iowa	1,215,663.75	1,601,430.34	1,785,339.44	2,041,613.95	2,483,183.67
Des Moines			190,636.35	173,076.15	115,527.75
Minnesota	2,099,623.23	765,802.85	990,967.98	1,018,862.21	1,428,364.51
St. Paul		1,306,385.50	2,005,637.92	1,811,218.47	2,176,790.10
Minneapolis		851,444.25	874,054.15	817,404.28	975,527.65
Missouri	353,608.84	390,812.55	457,535.18	467,436.75	522,200.10
St. Louis	1,577,333.60	3,060,431.64	3,736,180.70	4,591,524.85	3,639,674.75
Kansas City	1,606,352.95	1,367,211.12	1,658,692.85	1,522,071.25	1,254,807.60
St. Joseph	316,862.05	297,356.55	327,754.70	334,217.30	445,062.60
Kansas	1,159,086.49	1,279,839.60	1,492,449.57	1,567,896.96	1,806,215.81
Nebraska	708,957.47	851,802.12	994,157.71	1,258,236.69	1,112,188.66
Omaha	1,107,673.30	1,008,224.20	1,002,702.66	2,226,755.05	1,700,096.92
Lincoln					271,385.41
Division No. 6	10,268,561.68	13,830,830.12	16,324,909.24	17,860,916.91	17,937,063.93

STATEMENT EXHIBITING, BY STATES, TERRITORIES, AND RESERVE CITIES, THE
AMOUNT OF COIN AND COIN CERTIFICATES, ETC.—Continued.

States, etc.	September 30, 1889.	October 2, 1890.	September 25, 1891.	September 30, 1892.	October 3, 1893.
Colorado	$1,915,354.32	$2,127,138.91	$2,252,792.64	$3,011,783.09	$2,656,418.68
Nevada	43,297.65	49,616.70	41,275.45	48,694.30	53,476.00
California	2,468,552.83	2,066,636.80	1,951,334.90	1,832,505.79	1,673,065.16
San Francisco	1,019,175.00	1,150,612.50	1,655,425.00	1,589,170.00	1,082,260.00
Oregon	1,048,460.73	1,359,561.70	1,480,276.95	1,394,014.61	1,523,649.43
Arizona	17,223.70	53,543.70	40,823.85	77,091.85	119,754.40
Division No. 7	6,512,364.23	6,816,113.31	7,421,928.79	7,953,259.64	7,308,623.67
Dakota	435,196.56				
North Dakota		257,164.30	277,473.92	384,665.85	269,208.40
South Dakota		253,474.20	265,228.89	356,400.54	364,604.30
Idaho	136,202.48	107,573.65	157,147.65	192,735.53	227,930.59
Montana	743,019.20	850,766.04	939,936.69	1,167,081.15	949,607.00
New Mexico	106,700.05	232,505.10	167,726.15	196,650.83	191,868.85
Utah	569,799.18	645,634.81	709,140.71	906,031.78	775,915.45
Washington	1,352,061.50	1,826,523.34	1,775,416.53	1,991,060.55	1,277,366.55
Wyoming	211,590.90	239,879.95	241,051.65	333,208.02	218,873.05
Oklahoma		17,847.08	7,915.25	37,518.70	74,321.00
Indian Territory		8,150.92	17,430.10	31,232.85	63,541.35
Division No. 8	3,614,569.87	4,558,519.39	4,558,457.54	5,595,091.80	4,413,237.44
United States	161,326,448.84	195,908,858.84	183,515,075.91	209,116,378.69	224,703,860.07

STATEMENT EXHIBITING THE CHANGES IN DEPOSITS AND RESERVE SINCE JUNE
20, 1874; ALSO, ON OR ABOUT OCTOBER 1 OF EACH YEAR IN EACH CENTRAL
RESERVE CITY, IN ALL THE RESERVE CITIES, AND IN STATES AND TERRITO-
RIES, WITH A GENERAL SUMMARY EMBRACING ALL ACTIVE NATIONAL BANKS.

NEW YORK CITY.

Date.	No. of banks.	Net deposits.	Reserve required (25 per cent).*	Reserve held.		Classification of reserve.			
				Amount	Ratio to deposits.	Specie.	Other lawful money.	Due from agents.	Redemption fund.
		Millions.	Millions.	Millions.	Per cent.	Millions.	Millions.	Millions.	Millions.
Oct. 2, 1874	48	204.6	51.2	68.3	33.4	14.4	52.4	....	1.5
Oct. 1, 1875	48	202.3	50.7	60.5	29.9	5.0	54.4	....	1.1
Oct. 2, 1876	47	197.9	49.5	60.7	30.7	14.6	45.3	....	0.8
Oct. 1, 1877	47	174.9	43.7	48.1	27.5	13.0	34.3	....	0.8
Oct. 1, 1878	47	189.8	47.4	50.9	26.8	13.3	36.5	....	1.1
Oct. 2, 1879	47	210.2	52.6	53.1	25.3	19.4	32.6	....	1.1
Oct. 1, 1880	47	268.1	67.0	70.6	26.4	58.7	11.0	....	0.9
Oct. 1, 1881	48	268.8	67.2	62.5	23.3	50.6	10.9	....	1.0
Oct. 3, 1882	50	254.0	63.5	64.4	25.4	44.5	18.9	....	1.0
Oct. 2, 1883	48	266.9	66.7	70.8	26.5	50.3	19.7	....	0.9
Sept. 30, 1884	44	255.0	63.7	90.8	35.6	63.1	27.0	....	0.7
Oct. 1, 1885	44	312.9	78.2	115.7	37.0	91.5	23.7	....	0.5
Oct. 7, 1886	45	282.8	70.7	77.0	27.2	64.1	12.5	....	0.4
Oct. 5, 1887	47	284.3	71.1	80.1	28.2	63.6	16.1	....	0.4
Oct. 4, 1888	46	342.2	85.5	96.4	28.2	73.9	22.1	....	0.3
Sept. 30, 1889	45	338.2	84.5	84.9	25.1	59.1	25.6	....	0.2
Oct. 2, 1890	47	332.6	83.2	92.5	27.8	78.4	13.9	....	0.2
Sept. 25, 1891	49	327.8	81.9	86.1	26.3	53.8	32.0	....	0.3
Sept. 30, 1892	48	391.9	97.9	103.4	26.4	62.6	40.5	....	0.3
Oct. 3, 1893	49	309.9	77.5	100.0	35.1	75.7	32.5	....	0.8
Average for 20 years	47	275.7	67.6	77.2	28.6	48.4	28.1	....	0.7

* All lawful money.

STATEMENT EXHIBITING THE CHANGES IN DEPOSITS AND RESERVE SINCE JUNE 20, 1874, ETC.—Continued.

RESERVE CITIES.*

[Reserved 25 per cent, one-half in lawful money.]

Date.	No. of banks.	Net deposits.	Reserve required (15 per cent).*	Reserve held.		Classification of reserve.			
				Amount.	Ratio to deposits.	Specie.	Other lawful money.	Due from agents.	Redemption fund.
		Millions.	Millions.	Millions.	Per cent.	Millions.	Millions.	Millions.	Millions.
Oct. 2, 1874	182	221.4	55.3	76.0	34.3	4.5	36.7	31.1	3.7
Oct. 1, 1875	188	223.9	56.0	74.5	33.3	1.5	37.1	32.3	3.6
Oct. 2, 1876	189	217.0	54.2	76.1	35.1	4.0	37.1	82.0	3.0
Oct. 1, 1877	188	201.1	51.0	67.3	33.0	5.6	34.3	24.4	3.0
Oct. 1, 1878	184	199.9	50.0	71.1	35.6	9.4	29.4	29.1	3.2
Oct. 2, 1879	181	288.8	57.2	83.5	36.5	11.3	33.0	35.7	3.5
Oct. 1, 1880	181	280.4	72.4	105.2	36.2	28.3	25.0	48.2	3.7
Oct. 1, 1881	189	335.4	83.9	100.8	30.0	34.6	21.9	40.6	3.7
Oct. 3, 1882	193	318.8	79.7	89.1	28.0	28.3	24.1	33.2	3.5
Oct. 2, 1883	200	323.9	81.0	100.6	31.1	26.3	30.1	40.8	3.4
Sept. 30, 1884	203	307.9	77.0	99.0	32.2	30.3	33.3	32.3	3.1
Oct. 1, 1885	203	364.5	91.1	122.2	33.5	42.0	34.9	42.4	2.9
Oct. 7, 1886	217	381.5	95.4	114.0	29.9	44.5	26.0	41.3	2.2
Oct. 5, 1887	223	336.5	84.6	100.7	29.7	36.3	23.2	40.0	1.2
Oct. 4, 1888	224	384.9	96.2	116.9	30.4	40.0	24.5	51.5	0.9
Sept. 30, 1889	228	419.0	104.8	121.0	29.1	37.8	26.7	56.7	0.6
Oct. 2, 1890	250	457.8	114.4	129.8	28.3	43.1	24.9	61.0	0.7
Sept. 25, 1891	265	451.9	113.0	138.8	30.7	45.5	31.5	61.0	0.8
Sept. 30, 1892	263	519.3	129.8	156.1	30.1	53.1	29.0	73.0	1.0
Oct. 3, 1893	268	392.6	98.1	129.6	35.1	46.6	29.8	51.6	1.6

* Includes Chicago and St. Louis up to October 5, 1887.

STATES AND TERRITORIES.

Oct. 2, 1874	1,774	293.4	44.0	100.6	34.3	2.4	33.7	52.7	11.9
Oct. 1, 1875	1,851	307.9	46.3	108.1	32.5	1.6	33.7	53.3	11.6
Oct. 2, 1876	1,853	291.7	43.8	99.9	34.3	2.7	31.0	55.4	10.8
Oct. 1, 1877	1,845	290.1	43.6	95.4	32.9	4.2	31.6	48.9	10.7
Oct. 1, 1878	1,822	289.1	43.4	106.1	36.7	8.0	31.1	56.0	11.0
Oct. 2, 1879	1,820	329.9	49.5	124.3	37.7	11.5	30.3	71.3	11.2
Oct. 1, 1880	1,859	410.5	61.6	147.2	35.8	21.2	28.3	86.4	11.3
Oct. 1, 1881	1,895	507.2	76.1	158.3	31.2	27.5	27.1	92.4	11.4
Oct. 3, 1882	2,026	545.8	81.9	150.4	27.5	30.0	30.0	80.1	11.3
Oct. 2, 1883	2,253	577.9	86.7	157.5	27.2	31.2	30.8	84.1	11.3
Sept. 30, 1884	2,417	535.8	80.4	156.3	29.2	35.2	30.9	79.7	10.5
Oct. 1, 1885	2,467	570.8	85.6	177.5	31.1	41.5	29.9	95.9	10.2
Oct. 7, 1886	2,590	637.6	95.6	186.2	29.2	47.8	30.1	99.5	8.7
Oct. 5, 1887	2,756	690.6	103.6	190.9	27.6	50.8	32.6	100.9	6.6
Oct. 4, 1888	2,847	739.2	110.9	209.8	28.4	50.2	34.5	119.0	6.2
Sept. 30, 1889	2,992	807.6	121.1	224.6	27.8	50.5	36.2	132.4	5.5
Oct. 2, 1890	3,207	859.2	128.9	225.5	26.2	54.3	37.7	128.5	5.2
Sept. 25, 1891	3,333	861.8	129.3	235.5	27.3	60.3	36.8	133.0	5.4
Sept. 30, 1892	3,430	975.5	146.3	274.8	28.2	66.6	38.9	163.5	5.8
Oct. 3, 1893	3,434	767.5	115.1	239.6	30.0	75.9	41.2	106.9	6.6

* Reserve 15 per cent, two-fifths in lawful money.

SUMMARY.

Oct. 2, 1874	2,004	719.5	150.1	244.9	34.0	21.3	122.8	83.8	17.1
Oct. 1, 1875	2,987	734.1	152.2	235.1	32.0	8.1	125.2	85.6	16.3
Oct. 2, 1876	2,089	706.6	147.5	236.7	33.5	21.3	113.4	87.4	14.6
Oct. 1, 1877	2,080	669.1	138.3	219.8	31.5	22.8	100.2	73.3	14.5
Oct. 1, 1878	2,053	678.8	140.8	228.1	33.6	30.7	97.0	85.1	15.3
Oct. 2, 1879	2,048	768.9	150.3	260.9	33.9	42.2	95.9	107.0	15.8
Oct. 1, 1880	2,090	968.0	201.0	321.0	33.4	108.2	64.3	134.6	15.9
Oct. 1, 1881	2,132	1,111.6	227.2	321.6	28.9	112.7	59.9	133.0	16.1
Oct. 3, 1882	2,269	1,118.6	225.1	303.9	27.2	102.8	72.0	113.3	15.8
Oct. 2, 1883	2,501	1,168.7	234.4	328.9	28.1	107.8	80.6	124.9	15.6
Sept. 30, 1884	2,664	1,098.7	221.1	346.1	31.6	128.6	91.2	112.0	14.3
Oct. 1, 1885	2,714	1,218.2	254.9	415.4	33.3	175.0	88.5	138.3	13.6
Oct. 7, 1886	2,852	1,301.8	261.7	377.2	29.0	156.4	68.7	140.8	11.4
Oct. 5, 1887	3,019	1,388.4	278.0	394.2	28.4	165.1	79.9	140.9	8.3
Oct. 4, 1888	3,140	1,513.6	311.9	446.2	28.9	178.1	90.1	170.5	7.6
Sept. 30, 1889	3,290	1,655.5	333.1	459.6	27.6	164.3	99.7	189.1	6.4
Oct. 2, 1890	3,540	1,758.7	351.7	478.2	27.2	195.9	86.8	189.5	6.1
Sept. 25, 1891	3,677	1,758.6	353.5	497.4	28.3	183.5	113.3	191.0	6.6
Sept. 30, 1892	3,773	2,022.5	408.1	570.9	28.2	200.1	118.3	236.4	7.1
Oct. 3, 1893	3,781	1,573.7	316.6	513.9	32.6	224.7	121.7	158.5	9.0

LAWFUL MONEY RESERVE OF THE NATIONAL BANKS, AS SHOWN BY THEIR

	Cities, States, and Territories.	No. of banks.	Deposits.	Reserve required, 25 per cent.	Reserve held.	Ratio of reserve.
						Per cent.
1	New York City	49	$309,971,554	$77,492,888	$109,010,997	35.17
2	Chicago	21	85,756,781	21,439,195	38,987,815	45.46
3	St. Louis	9	17,907,671	4,476,918	5,721,498	31.95
	Total of central reserve cities	79	413,636,006	103,409,001	153,726,310	37.16
1	Boston	55	103,648,459	25,912,115	35,029,946	33.80
2	Albany	6	8,786,023	2,196,506	3,185,179	36.25
3	Brooklyn	5	11,095,830	2,773,958	3,581,757	32.28
4	Philadelphia	41	85,736,506	21,434,126	28,154,044	32.84
5	Pittsburg	29	29,400,063	7,350,016	8,615,282	29.30
6	Baltimore	22	20,757,620	5,189,405	6,490,129	31.27
7	Washington	12	7,437,372	1,859,343	3,115,446	41.89
8	New Orleans	9	12,751,208	3,187,802	2,574,644	20.19
9	Louisville	10	6,732,465	1,683,116	2,107,012	31.31
10	Cincinnati	13	21,505,545	5,301,386	7,756,198	35.97
11	Cleveland	11	16,035,405	4,008,851	4,964,221	30.96
12	Detroit	8	10,977,753	2,744,438	3,074,743	28.01
13	Milwaukee	5	8,820,278	2,205,069	4,017,000	45.54
14	Des Moines	4	1,732,135	433,034	580,582	34.04
15	St. Paul	4	9,280,8:0	2,320,207	3,449,771	37.17
16	Minneapolis	7	7,879,637	1,969,909	2,290,504	29.07
17	Kansas City	8	9,886,007	2,471,502	3,768,839	38.12
18	St. Joseph	4	4,186,919	1,046,730	1,583,158	37.81
19	Lincoln	4	1,874,554	468,639	470,716	25.11
20	Omaha	9	10,277,743	2,569,436	3,583,038	34.86
21	San Francisco	2	3,743,044	935,761	1,186,960	31.71
	Total of other reserve cities	208	392,605,396	98,151,349	129,588,769	33.01
	Total of all reserve cities	347	806,241,402	201,560,350	283,315,079	35.14
					(15 per cent.)	
1	Maine	83	12,042,451	1,896,368	4,154,999	32.87
2	New Hampshire	51	8,541,464	1,281,220	2,737,773	32.05
3	Vermont	48	8,165,195	1,224,779	2,570,751	31.48
4	Massachusetts	214	66,692,945	10,003,942	18,999,917	28.49
5	Rhode Island	59	17,932,473	2,689,871	5,535,899	30.87
6	Connecticut	84	28,301,464	4,245,219	9,625,540	34.01
7	New York	274	85,916,966	12,887,545	22,179,983	25.82
8	New Jersey	99	48,159,208	7,223,881	14,212,487	29.51
9	Pennsylvania	326	98,175,070	14,726,260	27,822,085	28.14
10	Delaware	18	4,549,454	682,373	1,397,751	30.73
11	Maryland	46	9,673,229	1,450,986	2,542,317	26.28
12	District of Columbia	1	744,974	111,746	381,436	51.20
13	Virginia	36	12,151,919	1,822,788	2,828,670	23.28
14	West Virginia	30	5,587,142	838,071	1,717,169	30.74
15	North Carolina	24	3,327,184	499,078	980,747	29.75
16	South Carolina	14	3,344,581	501,687	678,839	20.30
17	Georgia	27	4,076,162	611,424	1,256,759	30.83
18	Florida	17	3,158,906	473,836	935,391	29.61
19	Alabama	28	3,284,731	492,710	1,119,622	34.09
20	Mississippi	12	1,216,019	182,403	487,199	40.07
21	Louisiana	11	1,236,669	185,500	360,407	20.15
22	Texas	222	25,249,035	3,787,355	8,553,246	33.88
23	Arkansas	9	1,241,291	186,194	487,366	39.24
24	Kentucky	71	10,424,122	1,563,618	2,762,746	26.50
25	Tennessee	52	10,739,343	1,610,902	3,827,598	35.64
26	Ohio	218	51,070,779	7,660,617	14,782,260	28.94
27	Indiana	115	25,484,213	3,822,632	9,530,171	37.40
28	Illinois	191	37,654,221	5,648,138	12,446,825	33.06
29	Michigan	92	23,121,492	3,468,224	6,617,274	28.75
30	Wisconsin	76	18,666,027	2,799,904	6,051,753	32.43
31	Iowa	165	24,556,709	3,683,506	7,834,296	31.90
32	Minnesota	65	12,376,966	1,856,545	3,782,356	30.16
33	Missouri	57	6,029,822	904,473	1,835,901	30.45
34	Kansas	136	15,904,721	2,385,708	6,200,177	38.98
35	Nebraska	121	12,103,798	1,815,570	3,811,911	31.49
36	Colorado	51	18,646,221	2,796,933	6,497,811	34.85
37	Nevada	2	363,989	54,598	83,343	22.90
38	California	33	8,692,178	1,303,872	2,441,411	28.09
39	Oregon	39	7,470,836	1,120,626	1,902,140	25.46
40	Arizona	5	449,636	67,445	202,792	45.10
41	North Dakota	32	4,619,680	692,953	1,029,002	22.27
42	South Dakota	39	3,657,411	548,612	982,468	20.86
43	Idaho	13	1,336,283	200,443	315,151	25.83
44	Montana	22	6,914,192	1,037,129	2,188,802	31.66
45	New Mexico	10	1,383,763	207,565	361,292	26.11
46	Utah	14	2,739,375	410,900	1,109,205	40.49
47	Washington	57	6,975,001	1,046,250	1,744,008	25.02
48	Wyoming	13	1,755,349	263,302	403,246	22.97
49	Oklahoma	6	562,133	84,320	264,125	46.99
50	Indian Territory	6	410,702	61,605	200,724	48.87
	Total of country banks	3,434	767,477,513	115,121,627	230,595,191	30.05
	Total of United States	3,781	1,573,718,915	316,681,977	513,910,270	32.66

Reports of Condition at the Close of Business October 3, 1893.

Cash reserve. Required.	Held.	Specie.	Legal tenders.	United States certificates of deposit.	Due from reserve agents.	Redemption fund with Treasurer.	
$76,681,776	$108,205,885	$75,703,064	$31,082,821	$1,420,000	....	$811,112	1
21,385,195	38,935,815	22,771,923	15,611,892	520,000	....	54,000	2
4,456,668	5,701,248	3,639,075	2,051,573	10,000	....	20,250	3
102,523,639	152,840,948	102,114,662	48,776,286	1,950,000	....	885,362	
12,718,755	16,360,548	9,952,789	5,527,759	880,000	$18,194,793	474,605	1
1,084,755	1,119,354	715,243	404,111	....	2,038,830	26,995	2
1,373,750	1,512,878	799,383	713,495	....	2,012,439	26,440	3
10,567,113	17,600,250	11,127,420	4,242,830	2,230,000	10,253,894	299,900	4
3,607,837	6,006,046	4,012,840	1,993,206	....	2,474,891	131,302	5
2,551,862	4,867,655	2,910,802	1,246,853	680,000	1,536,794	85,680	6
910,427	2,623,877	1,398,848	965,029	200,000	453,079	38,490	7
1,573,651	1,986,157	1,179,603	816,554	....	537,987	40,500	8
829,183	1,523,732	576,063	917,689	....	559,110	24,750	9
2,601,756	5,273,635	1,640,407	2,828,228	805,000	2,294,688	187,875	10
1,976,119	2,922,029	1,692,029	1,230,000	....	1,985,580	56,612	11
1,339,594	1,552,701	971,071	581,633	....	1,456,789	65,250	12
1,002,410	2,376,428	1,589,857	786,571	....	1,020,322	20,250	13
212,010	257,612	115,528	142,084	....	321,757	7,213	14
1,154,479	2,388,626	2,176,790	211,836	....	1,019,895	11,250	15
978,105	1,410,528	975,528	435,000	....	860,276	13,700	16
1,226,751	2,258,527	1,254,808	1,003,719	....	1,492,312	18,000	17
517,740	730,612	445,062	285,550	....	841,296	11,250	18
230,382	314,205	271,385	42,880	....	148,576	7,875	19
1,267,168	2,227,802	1,700,097	527,705	....	1,320,136	35,100	20
465,630	1,104,370	1,082,260	22,110	....	78,090	4,500	21
48,280,386	76,427,655	46,617,813	24,954,842	4,855,000	51,570,537	1,590,577	
150,804,025	229,268,603	148,732,475	73,731,128	6,805,000	51,570,537	2,475,939	
683,485	1,483,719	1,114,389	369,330	....	2,483,625	187,655	1
446,086	868,800	585,051	283,749	....	1,702,968	166,005	2
437,347	1,089,756	643,991	436,767	....	1,358,580	131,413	3
3,649,031	6,864,671	4,520,952	2,157,719	125,000	11,314,881	881,365	4
938,044	1,761,257	1,195,467	565,790	....	3,429,881	344,761	5
1,559,961	3,990,247	2,896,699	1,093,548	....	5,289,977	315,316	6
4,853,689	8,780,917	6,152,153	3,548,794	80,000	11,645,713	753,323	7
2,797,840	5,730,324	3,229,654	2,490,670	10,000	8,252,963	229,260	8
5,027,951	13,791,432	8,733,578	5,057,854	....	13,174,270	656,383	9
256,301	617,786	415,171	202,615	....	738,345	41,620	10
551,556	1,255,217	715,876	539,341	....	1,215,004	72,090	11
40,198	290,880	237,627	53,253	....	79,306	11,250	12
703,446	1,900,201	945,374	954,827	....	864,290	64,173	13
318,926	1,104,368	592,984	511,384	....	572,045	40,756	14
185,986	658,274	373,454	284,820	....	297,359	34,114	15
192,950	503,468	263,094	240,374	....	156,058	19,313	16
228,698	829,301	467,897	361,404	....	387,778	30,680	17
182,919	564,763	253,297	311,466	....	354,091	16,537	18
180,899	778,277	495,256	283,021	....	300,885	40,460	19
67,496	304,683	138,963	165,720	....	168,854	13,662	20
69,655	192,333	133,798	58,535	....	156,771	11,363	21
1,425,075	6,063,711	3,498,977	2,564,734	....	2,264,868	224,667	22
70,757	353,599	210,504	143,095	....	124,467	9,300	23
567,727	1,432,062	784,356	647,706	....	1,186,382	141,302	24
620,428	2,673,787	1,474,905	1,198,882	....	1,093,999	50,832	25
2,895,419	8,592,489	4,816,757	3,775,732	....	5,767,700	422,071	26
1,443,946	6,725,562	4,335,884	2,389,678	....	2,591,843	212,766	27
2,160,141	6,153,024	4,176,615	1,976,409	....	6,046,019	247,782	28
1,325,174	3,255,158	2,241,172	1,013,986	....	3,236,827	155,289	29
1,087,281	3,161,772	2,329,637	832,135	....	2,808,280	81,701	30
1,411,434	3,752,209	2,489,184	1,263,025	....	3,927,167	154,920	31
718,976	1,853,008	1,428,365	424,643	....	1,820,243	59,105	32
340,794	885,375	522,209	363,166	....	898,037	52,489	33
965,174	2,786,612	1,806,246	980,396	....	3,290,762	122,773	34
691,279	1,494,010	1,112,189	381,821	....	2,230,530	87,371	35
1,090,112	4,252,171	2,656,419	1,595,752	....	2,173,987	71,653	36
20,570	53,563	53,476	87	....	26,607	3,173	37
498,816	1,944,671	1,873,065	71,606	....	439,909	56,831	38
435,042	1,571,812	1,523,649	48,163	....	297,306	33,022	39
25,309	140,141	119,754	20,387	....	58,478	4,173	40
267,594	487,192	269,208	217,984	....	517,841	23,909	41
208,189	568,660	364,604	204,056	....	885,668	28,140	42
76,665	279,399	227,930	51,469	....	56,971	8,781	43
404,691	1,419,979	949,608	461,371	....	752,422	25,401	44
78,456	237,103	191,869	45,234	....	112,764	11,425	45
156,052	903,978	775,916	128,062	....	181,452	20,775	46
395,011	1,307,385	1,277,367	90,018	....	318,891	58,722	47
100,076	252,087	218,873	33,214	....	138,047	13,112	48
32,378	131,618	74,321	60,297	....	126,132	3,375	49
23,022	87,756	63,541	24,215	....	108,918	4,050	50
43,448,061	117,164,609	75,971,585	40,978,224	215,000	106,929,107	6,501,475	
194,202,056	346,433,212	224,703,860	114,709,356	7,020,000	158,499,644	8,977,414	

STATEMENT SHOWING AMOUNT OF DEPOSITS HELD BY NATIONAL BANKS, AMOUNT OF LAWFUL MONEY RESERVE REQUIRED, AND RATIO OF SAME; ALSO AMOUNT, RATIO AND CLASSIFICATION OF RESERVE ACTUALLY HELD ON DECEMBER 9, 1892, MARCH 6, MAY 4, JULY 12, AND OCTOBER 3, 1893.

	No. of banks	Deposits	Reserve required.		Reserve held.		Classification of reserve held.		
			Ratio.	Amount	Ratio.	Amount	Lawful money in bank.	Due from reserve agents.	Redemption with treasurer.
December 9, 1892.		*Millions.*	*P. ct.*	*Millions.*	*Per ct.*	*Millions.*	*Millions.*	*Millions.*	*Millions.*
Central reserve cities	80	488.4	25	122.1	27.26	133.1	132.8	....	0.4
Other reserve cities	265	495.2	25	123.8	28.68	142.0	77.8	63.1	1.0
Outside of reserve cities	3,439	975.6	15	146.3	26.21	255.7	108.0	141.8	5.8
Total	3,784	1,959.2	....	392.2	27.10	530.8	318.6	204.9	7.2
March 6, 1893.									
Central reserve cities	80	489.0	25	122.5	26.51	129.9	129.5	....	0.4
Other reserve cities	265	473.3	25	118.3	29.47	139.5	75.2	63.2	1.1
Outside of reserve cities	3,461	981.8	15	147.2	25.93	254.5	109.2	139.4	5.9
Total	3,806	1,945.0	....	388.0	26.94	523.9	313.9	202.6	7.4
May 4, 1893.									
Central reserve cities	79	472.4	25	118.1	28.30	133.7	133.3	....	0.4
Other reserve cities	260	467.6	25	116.9	28.56	133.5	78.8	53.5	1.1
Outside of reserve cities	3,482	970.4	15	145.5	24.47	237.3	110.7	120.8	5.9
Total	3,830	1,910.4	....	380.5	26.42	504.6	322.8	174.3	7.4
July 12, 1893.									
Central reserve cities	79	405.7	25	101.4	26.24	106.4	106.0	....	0.4
Other reserve cities	209	404.5	25	101.1	29.20	118.1	68.4	48.5	1.2
Outside of reserve cities	3,459	864.4	15	129.7	26.80	231.6	114.8	110.8	6.0
Total	3,807	1,674.6	....	332.2	27.24	456.1	289.2	159.3	7.6
October 3, 1893.									
Central reserve cities	79	413.6	25	103.4	37.16	153.7	152.9	....	0.9
Other reserve cities	268	392.0	25	98.1	35.14	129.6	76.4	51.5	1.5
Outside of reserve cities	3,434	767.5	15	115.1	30.05	230.6	117.1	106.9	6.5
Total	3,781	1,573.7	....	316.6	32.66	513.9	346.4	158.4	8.9

LIABILITIES OF THE NATIONAL BANKS, AND THE RESERVE REQUIRED AND HELD ON THREE DATES IN THE YEARS 1888, 1889, 1890, 1891, 1892, AND 1893.

STATES AND TERRITORIES EXCLUSIVE OF RESERVE CITIES.

Date.	No. of banks.	Net deposits.	Reserve required.	Reserve held.		Classification of reserve.			
				Amount.	Ratio to deposits.	Specie.	Other lawful money.	Due from agents.	Redemption fund.
		Millions.	*Millions.*	*Millions.*	*Per cent.*	*Millions.*	*Millions.*	*Millions.*	*Millions.*
Apr. 30, 1888	2,849	707.5	106.1	193.9	27.4	51.0	33.8	102.8	6.4
June 30, 1888	2,829	711.8	106.8	199.2	28.0	49.1	31.5	112.2	6.3
Oct. 4, 1888	2,847	739.3	110.9	209.8	28.4	50.2	34.5	118.9	6.2
May 13, 1889	2,914	769.8	115.5	223.9	29.1	53.5	36.9	127.8	5.6
July 12, 1889	2,944	789.1	118.4	229.3	29.1	53.3	37.2	133.3	5.6
Sept. 30, 1889	2,992	807.6	121.1	224.6	27.8	50.5	36.2	132.4	5.5
May 17, 1890	3,125	845.3	126.8	223.2	26.4	52.9	37.3	127.6	5.4
July 18, 1890	3,151	835.4	124.3	222.2	26.6	52.7	37.1	127.0	5.3
Oct. 2, 1890	3,207	859.2	128.9	225.5	26.2	54.3	37.7	128.5	5.2
May 4, 1891	3,296	847.4	127.1	225.1	26.6	61.3	36.5	122.1	5.2
July 9, 1891	3,309	846.8	127.0	224.7	26.5	62.8	36.4	120.3	5.1
Sept. 25, 1891	3,383	861.8	129.3	235.5	27.3	60.3	36.8	133.0	5.4
May 17, 1892	3,393	929.2	139.4	274.2	29.5	65.3	38.7	164.5	5.7
July 12, 1892	3,418	950.3	142.5	282.2	29.7	66.4	38.8	171.2	5.8
Sept. 30, 1892	3,430	975.6	146.3	274.8	28.2	66.6	38.9	163.5	5.8
May 4, 1893	3,482	970.5	145.6	237.4	24.4	72.8	37.9	120.8	5.9
July 12, 1893	3,459	864.5	129.7	231.6	26.8	73.2	41.6	110.8	6.0
Oct. 3, 1893	3,434	767.5	115.1	239.6	30.0	75.9	41.2	106.9	6.6

NEW YORK CITY.

Date.	No. of banks.	Net deposits.	Reserve required.	Reserve held.		Classification of reserve.			
				Amount.	Ratio to deposits.	Specie.	Other lawful money.	Due from agents.	Redemption fund.
Apr. 30, 1888	46	316.7	79.2	94.8	29.9	69.4	25.0	....	0.4
June 30, 1888	46	338.4	84.6	102.7	30.3	73.4	28.8	....	0.4
Oct. 4, 1888	46	342.2	85.5	96.4	28.2	73.9	22.1	....	0.3
May 13, 1889	45	361.0	90.2	103.7	28.7	71.5	32.0	....	0.2
July 12, 1889	45	359.2	89.8	97.3	27.1	61.8	35.3	....	0.2
Sept. 30, 1889	45	338.2	84.5	84.9	25.1	59.1	25.6	....	0.2
May 17, 1890	46	322.3	80.6	85.0	26.4	65.2	19.6	....	0.2
July 18, 1890	47	326.8	81.7	88.4	27.0	64.2	24.0	....	0.2
Oct. 2, 1890	47	332.6	83.2	92.5	27.8	78.4	13.9	....	0.2
May 4, 1891	47	327.1	81.8	68.3	26.9	58.6	29.5	....	0.2
July 9, 1891	49	330.3	82.6	98.9	29.9	55.6	43.1	....	0.2
Sept. 25, 1891	49	327.8	81.9	86.1	26.3	53.8	32.0	....	0.3
May 17, 1892	48	437.3	109.3	127.8	29.2	85.2	42.3	....	0.3
July 12, 1892	48	424.5	106.1	124.7	29.4	75.8	48.5	....	0.4
Sept. 30, 1892	48	391.9	98.0	103.4	26.4	62.6	40.6	....	0.2
May 4, 1893	49	345.0	86.2	98.4	28.5	63.5	34.5	....	0.4
July 12, 1893	49	304.4	76.1	77.0	25.3	55.0	21.6	....	0.4
Oct. 3, 1893	49	309.9	77.5	109.0	35.1	75.7	32.5	....	0.8

LIABILITIES OF THE NATIONAL BANKS AND THE RESERVE REQUIRED AND HELD ON THREE DATES, ETC.—Continued.

CHICAGO.

Date.	No. of banks.	Net deposits.	Reserve required.	Reserve held.		Classification of reserve.			
				Amount.	Ratio to deposits.	Specie.	Other lawful money.	Due from agents.	Redemption fund.
		Millions.	Millions.	Millions.	Per cent.	Millions.	Millions.	Millions.	Millions.
Apr. 30, 1888	18	71.3	17.8	21.2	29.7	13.4	7.8	....	0.05
June 30, 1888	19	71.8	18.0	22.5	31.4	14.1	8.4	....	0.05
Oct. 4, 1888	19	69.3	17.3	21.0	30.2	13.1	7.8	....	0.05
May 13, 1889	19	74.3	18.6	26.4	35.5	14.6	11.7	....	0.05
July 12, 1889	19	77.6	19.4	24.7	31.8	15.1	9.6	....	0.05
Sept. 30, 1889	20	78.7	19.7	25.0	31.7	15.3	9.6	....	0.05
May 17, 1890	20	85.0	21.3	26.4	31.0	15.3	11.0	....	0.05
July 18, 1890	19	84.1	21.0	24.5	29.1	14.7	9.8	....	0.05
Oct. 2, 1890	19	82.9	20.7	24.8	30.0	17.0	7.8	....	0.05
May 4, 1891	20	96.0	24.0	32.5	33.9	19.7	12.7	....	0.05
July 9, 1891	20	91.8	22.9	28.5	31.0	19.3	9.1	....	0.05
Sept. 25, 1891	21	92.9	23.2	31.2	33.6	20.1	11.0	....	0.05
May 17, 1892	22	111.4	27.9	36.8	33.0	23.3	13.4	....	0.05
July 12, 1892	22	114.4	28.6	34.0	29.8	23.1	10.9	....	0.05
Sept. 30, 1892	23	106.5	26.7	30.5	28.6	22.3	8.2	....	0.05
May 4, 1893	21	99.6	24.9	29.3	29.4	21.6	7.7	....	0.05
July 12, 1893	21	81.3	20.4	24.9	30.6	15.4	9.5	....	0.05
Oct. 3, 1893	21	85.8	21.4	39.0	45.4	22.8	16.2	....	0.05

ST. LOUIS.

Date.	No. of banks.	Net deposits.	Reserve required.	Reserve held.		Classification of reserve.			
				Amount.	Ratio to deposits.	Specie.	Other lawful money.	Due from agents.	Redemption fund.
Apr. 30, 1888	4	8.7	2.2	3.5	40.1	1.6	1.8	....	0.03
June 30, 1888	4	8.9	2.2	3.7	42.0	1.8	1.9	....	0.03
Oct. 4, 1888	4	7.9	2.0	2.1	27.1	1.0	1.1	....	0.02
May 13, 1889	4	7.5	1.9	3.5	46.8	1.9	1.7	....	0.01
July 12, 1889	5	11.3	2.8	4.6	40.1	2.2	2.3	....	0.01
Sept. 30, 1889	5	12.0	3.0	3.2	26.7	1.6	1.6	....	0.01
May 17, 1890	8	26.0	6.5	6.5	25.0	3.3	3.1	....	0.02
July 18, 1890	8	27.2	6.8	6.6	24.4	3.3	3.3	....	0.02
Oct. 2, 1890	8	26.2	6.5	5.6	21.3	3.1	2.5	....	0.02
May 4, 1891	8	25.0	6.2	6.1	24.4	3.7	2.4	....	0.02
July 9, 1891	9	23.6	5.9	5.6	23.8	4.0	1.6	....	0.02
Sept. 25, 1891	9	24.2	6.1	5.8	23.8	3.8	2.0	....	0.02
May 17, 1892	9	27.8	7.0	7.9	28.4	5.9	2.0	....	0.02
July 12, 1892	9	27.5	6.9	6.5	23.6	5.0	1.4	....	0.02
Sept. 30, 1892	9	29.2	7.3	6.2	21.1	4.6	1.5	....	0.02
May 4, 1893	9	27.7	6.9	5.9	21.4	3.7	2.2	....	0.02
July 12, 1893	9	19.9	4.9	4.5	22.6	2.5	2.0	....	0.02
Oct. 3, 1893	9	17.9	4.4	5.7	31.9	3.7	2.0	....	0.02

LIABILITIES OF THE NATIONAL BANKS AND THE RESERVE REQUIRED AND HELD ON THREE DATES, ETC.—Continued.

OTHER RESERVE CITIES.

Date.	No. of banks.	Net deposits.	Reserve required.	Reserve held.		Classification of reserve.			
				Amount.	Ratio to deposits.	Specie.	Other lawful money.	Due from agents.	Redemption fund.
		Millions.	*Millions.*	*Millions.*	*Per cent.*	*Millions.*	*Millions.*	*Millions.*	*Millions.*
Apr. 30, 1888	221	355.4	88.8	105.9	29.8	36.7	24.5	43.7	1.0
June 30, 1888	224	372.5	93.1	113.4	30.4	42.9	23.6	45.9	1.0
Oct. 4, 1888	224	384.9	96.2	116.9	30.4	40.0	24.4	51.5	0.9
May 13, 1889	224	415.3	103.8	132.8	32.0	43.7	28.9	59.6	0.7
July 12, 1889	226	427.8	106.9	131.4	31.0	43.5	27.9	59.3	0.6
Sept. 30, 1889	228	419.0	104.8	121.9	29.1	37.8	26.7	56.7	0.6
May 17, 1890	239	425.0	106.2	122.8	28.9	41.4	25.2	55.6	0.6
July 18, 1890	259	461.9	115.5	131.3	28.4	43.7	28.1	58.8	0.7
Oct. 2, 1890	259	457.8	114.4	129.8	28.3	43.1	24.9	61.0	0.7
May 4, 1891	262	448.9	112.2	136.9	30.5	51.6	26.7	57.9	0.7
July 9, 1891	263	442.0	110.5	134.1	30.3	49.1	29.0	55.3	0.7
Sept. 25, 1891	265	451.9	113.0	138.8	30.7	45.5	31.5	61.0	0.8
May 17, 1892	262	520.6	130.1	184.0	35.4	59.3	38.0	85.8	0.9
July 12, 1892	262	534.3	133.6	178.6	33.4	59.0	37.4	81.3	0.9
Sept. 30, 1892	263	519.3	129.8	156.1	30.1	53.0	29.1	72.9	1.0
May 4, 1893	269	467.6	116.9	133.6	28.5	45.6	33.3	53.5	1.2
July 12, 1893	269	404.5	101.1	118.1	29.2	40.6	27.8	48.5	1.2
Oct. 3, 1893	268	392.6	98.2	129.6	35.1	46.6	29.8	51.6	1.6

SUMMARY.

Apr. 30, 1888	3,096	1,459.6	294.1	419.3	28.7	172.1	92.9	146.5	7.9
June 30, 1888	3,120	1,503.5	304.7	441.5	29.4	181.3	94.3	158.1	7.8
Oct. 4, 1888	3,140	1,543.6	312.0	446.2	28.9	178.1	90.0	170.5	7.6
May 13, 1889	3,206	1,627.9	330.0	490.3	30.1	185.2	111.2	187.4	6.6
July 12, 1889	3,239	1,665.0	337.3	487.3	29.3	175.9	112.3	192.5	6.5
Sept. 30, 1889	3,290	1,665.5	333.1	460.6	27.8	164.3	99.7	189.1	6.4
May 17, 1890	3,438	1,709.6	311.4	463.9	27.2	178.1	96.2	183.2	6.3
July 18, 1890	3,484	1,735.4	349.3	473.0	27.3	178.6	102.3	185.8	6.3
Oct. 2, 1890	3,540	1,758.7	353.7	478.2	27.2	195.9	86.8	189.5	6.1
May 4, 1891	3,633	1,744.6	351.3	488.9	28.0	104.9	107.8	180.0	6.2
July 9, 1891	3,652	1,734.5	348.9	491.8	28.3	190.8	119.3	175.6	6.1
Sept. 25, 1891	3,677	1,758.6	353.5	497.4	28.3	183.5	113.5	194.0	6.6
May 17, 1892	3,734	2,026.3	413.7	630.7	31.1	239.0	134.4	250.3	7.0
July 12, 1892	3,759	2,051.0	417.7	626.0	30.5	229.3	137.1	252.5	7.1
Sept. 30, 1892	3,773	2,022.5	408.1	571.0	28.2	209.1	118.3	236.4	7.2
May 4, 1893	3,830	1,910.4	380.5	504.6	26.4	207.2	115.6	174.3	7.5
July 12, 1893	3,807	1,674.6	332.2	456.1	27.2	186.7	102.5	159.3	7.6
Oct. 3, 1893	3,781	1,573.7	316.6	513.9	32.6	224.7	121.7	158.5	9.0

STATE OF THE LAWFUL MONEY RESERVE OF THE NATIONAL BANKS AS

STATES AND

	Dates.	No. of banks.	Net deposits.	Reserve required.
1	Oct. 5, 1887	2,756	$699,622,007	$103,503,301
2	Dec. 7, 1887	2,778	684,059,721	102,608,958
3	Feb. 14, 1888	2,787	707,423,152	106,113,472
4	Apr. 30, 1888	2,809	707,530,013	106,129,502
5	June 20, 1888	2,827	711,849,213	106,777,382
6	Oct. 4, 1888	2,847	739,325,350	110,898,802
7	Dec. 12, 1888	2,858	730,883,243	109,632,486
8	Feb. 26, 1889	2,878	757,591,413	113,638,712
9	May 13, 1889	2,914	769,817,794	115,472,669
10	July 12, 1889	2,944	789,081,203	118,362,180
11	Sept. 30, 1889	2,992	807,628,795	121,144,318
12	Dec. 11, 1889	3,026	807,532,815	121,129,922
13	Feb. 28, 1890	3,076	823,504,222	125,025,633
14	May 17, 1890	3,125	845,329,596	126,799,439
15	July 18, 1890	3,151	835,341,554	124,301,233
16	Oct. 2, 1890	3,207	859,249,215	128,887,382
17	Dec. 19, 1890	3,241	819,407,422	122,911,113
18	Feb. 26, 1891	3,205	828,643,459	124,296,519
19	May 4, 1891	3,296	847,402,314	127,110,347
20	July 9, 1891	3,309	846,759,676	127,013,951
21	Sept. 25, 1891	3,333	861,837,570	129,275,635
22	Dec. 2, 1891	3,349	867,016,129	130,052,419
23	Mar. 1, 1892	3,370	909,876,403	136,481,460
24	May 17, 1892	3,393	929,173,506	139,376,025
25	July 12, 1892	3,418	950,252,797	142,537,920
26	Sept. 30, 1892	3,430	975,542,131	146,331,320
27	Dec. 9, 1892	3,439	975,622,088	146,343,313
28	Mar. 6, 1893	3,461	981,760,606	147,264,090
29	May 4, 1893	3,482	970,413,360	145,562,004
30	July 12, 1893	3,459	864,468,926	120,670,338
31	Oct. 3, 1893	3,434	767,477,513	115,121,627

RESERVE

1	Oct. 5, 1887	293	$697,767,889	$174,441,972
2	Dec. 7, 1887	292	695,790,194	173,947,548
3	Feb. 14, 1888	290	747,718,913	186,929,728
4	Apr. 30, 1888	289	752,040,152	188,010,038
5	June 30, 1888	293	791,629,383	197,907,346
6	Oct. 4, 1888	293	804,241,438	201,060,359
7	Dec. 12, 1888	292	774,053,284	193,513,321
8	Feb. 26, 1889	291	840,117,539	210,029,385
9	May 13, 1889	292	858,084,652	214,521,163
10	July 12, 1889	295	875,916,968	218,979,242
11	Sept. 30, 1889	298	847,868,586	211,967,147
12	Dec. 11, 1889	300	801,625,021	200,406,255
13	Feb. 28, 1890	307	844,646,301	211,161,575
14	May 17, 1890	313	858,292,596	214,573,149
15	July 18, 1890	333	900,058,542	225,014,635
16	Oct. 2, 1890	333	899,412,106	224,853,027
17	Dec. 19, 1890	332	814,046,939	203,511,735
18	Feb. 26, 1891	335	877,301,354	219,347,838
19	May 4, 1891	337	897,207,393	224,301,848
20	July 9, 1891	343	887,727,112	221,937,778
21	Sept. 25, 1891	344	896,799,090	224,199,774
22	Dec. 2, 1891	343	916,744,509	229,186,127
23	Mar. 1, 1892	341	1,061,786,647	265,446,662
24	May 17, 1892	341	1,097,165,067	274,291,266
25	July 12, 1892	341	1,100,686,179	275,171,544
26	Sept. 30, 1892	343	1,046,937,693	261,734,423
27	Dec. 9, 1892	345	983,607,295	245,901,824
28	Mar. 6, 1893	345	963,289,771	240,822,443
29	May 4, 1893	348	939,906,774	234,999,194
30	July 12, 1893	348	810,184,800	202,546,200
31	Oct. 3, 1893	347	806,241,402	201,560,350

SHOWN BY THE REPORTS FROM OCTOBER 5, 1887, TO OCTOBER 3, 1893.

TERRITORIES.

Amount.	Ratio to liabilities.	Specie.	Legal tenders.	United States certificates of deposit.	Due from reserve agents.	Redemption fund with Treasurer.	
	Per cent.						
$19.3,919,164	27.6	$50,821,078	$32,129,956	$475,000	$100,879,879	$6,613,271	1
185,893,160	27.2	51,606,357	31,997,316	520,000	95,002,125	6,587,062	2
201,787,492	28.5	51,835,866	32,264,781	510,000	110,663,685	6,483,157	3
193,936,932	27.4	50,968,350	33,260,051	515,000	102,759,410	6,414,118	4
199,150,391	28.0	49,123,608	31,021,956	505,000	112,183,937	6,324,800	5
209,844,956	28.4	50,188,336	33,789,747	689,000	118,950,556	6,236,317	6
200,111,504	27.4	50,661,056	33,326,867	530,000	109,573,502	6,020,079	7
224,480,351	29.6	52,214,875	34,734,244	855,000	130,841,596	5,834,636	8
224,875,655	29.1	53,540,166	36,235,912	705,000	127,753,288	5,642,269	9
229,353,725	29.1	53,312,874	36,758,352	485,000	133,246,766	5,550,733	10
224,634,194	27.8	50,467,067	35,712,394	510,000	132,423,322	5,520,401	11
212,516,298	26.3	52,496,023	37,389,775	510,000	116,716,620	5,403,880	12
233,749,310	28.0	55,084,885	38,450,332	505,000	134,379,587	5,329,506	13
223,205,878	26.4	52,806,449	36,823,184	475,000	127,639,363	5,371,882	14
222,203,056	26.6	52,752,311	36,074,235	440,000	127,015,635	5,320,875	15
225,523,671	26.2	54,250,695	37,218,060	440,000	128,452,576	5,162,340	16
210,262,300	25.7	57,551,701	37,502,841	445,000	109,582,313	5,120,445	17
220,938,230	27.7	61,575,870	36,682,708	425,000	126,076,254	5,178,398	18
225,163,434	26.6	61,304,104	36,524,884	425,000	122,115,434	5,194,976	19
224,652,075	26.5	62,776,089	36,038,178	415,000	120,273,937	5,148,871	20
235,508,045	27.3	60,314,566	36,394,039	440,000	132,984,453	5,374,967	21
235,620,574	27.2	61,590,899	36,532,677	415,000	131,609,289	5,472,700	22
270,973,086	29.8	62,867,013	37,017,682	440,000	165,633,135	5,615,256	23
274,120,725	29.5	65,324,747	38,308,295	405,000	164,423,561	5,668,122	24
282,158,477	29.7	66,394,006	38,605,004	405,000	171,219,102	5,733,365	25
274,769,504	23.2	66,575,758	38,525,290	395,000	163,509,922	5,763,534	26
255,727,465	26.2	68,405,704	39,247,152	360,000	141,848,825	5,866,094	27
254,568,781	25.9	71,346,320	37,527,765	355,000	130,429,002	5,910,694	28
237,431,814	24.4	72,812,241	37,573,847	345,000	120,758,208	5,942,518	29
231,651,807	26.8	73,103,849	41,353,526	315,000	110,834,812	6,044,680	30
230,595,191	30.0	75,971,385	40,978,224	215,000	106,929,107	6,501,475	31

CITIES.

$203,201,575	29.1	$114,264,376	$41,621,319	$5,715,000	$39,993,700	$1,607,171	1
196,092,726	28.2	107,544,286	43,304,650	5,645,000	37,957,340	1,581,441	2
227,815,221	30.5	121,994,748	50,052,886	9,610,000	44,647,555	1,510,052	3
225,407,142	30.0	121,085,661	50,314,156	8,815,000	43,718,493	1,473,832	4
242,342,065	30.6	132,168,579	50,975,687	11,810,000	45,949,662	1,441,037	5
236,321,317	29.4	127,799,480	47,309,714	8,385,000	51,508,038	1,319,085	6
228,126,466	29.5	122,073,222	49,228,103	8,600,000	47,013,606	1,121,355	7
259,776,653	30.9	130,060,926	53,890,616	12,950,000	61,800,509	1,025,512	8
266,431,684	31.1	131,627,286	61,602,473	12,650,000	59,619,008	932,917	9
257,944,870	29.5	122,500,005	60,250,305	14,405,000	59,343,308	907,047	10
234,930,688	27.7	113,858,462	51,039,699	12,435,000	56,712,959	884,568	11
223,275,478	27.8	118,593,435	47,101,119	8,535,000	48,173,145	872,779	12
237,434,449	28.1	126,461,252	48,101,270	8,325,000	53,684,545	862,592	13
240,691,424	28.0	125,269,045	51,205,808	7,060,000	55,566,043	939,628	14
250,833,366	27.9	125,851,752	55,806,133	9,385,000	58,806,133	984,247	15
252,720,301	28.1	141,668,163	44,614,285	5,715,000	60,999,210	961,257	16
234,027,627	28.7	132,511,305	44,614,285	5,315,000	59,638,370	948,667	17
261,136,678	29.8	139,664,492	52,890,612	11,230,000	56,569,349	955,146	18
263,820,903	29.4	134,636,268	60,250,305	11,090,000	57,889,288	963,982	19
267,083,198	30.1	127,993,448	64,961,633	18,430,000	55,317,148	980,969	20
261,860,394	29.2	129,200,599	61,221,549	15,280,000	61,005,875	1,161,461	21
277,898,632	30.3	146,307,135	57,321,677	8,350,000	64,719,249	1,209,571	22
346,349,747	32.6	167,280,955	62,428,053	23,610,000	91,717,863	1,282,876	23
356,540,373	32.5	178,719,360	69,673,107	26,000,000	85,825,510	1,322,396	24
343,758,250	31.2	162,924,474	65,218,052	22,710,000	81,254,538	1,359,226	25
296,183,715	28.3	142,540,621	65,742,655	13,600,000	72,924,409	1,376,639	26
275,144,704	27.9	141,489,866	60,108,183	6,110,009	63,699,335	1,416,320	27
269,397,689	27.9	136,995,496	53,408,009	14,320,000	63,183,047	1,491,137	28
267,211,601	28.4	134,409,931	65,937,316	11,785,000	53,553,912	1,525,472	29
224,546,270	27.7	113,647,324	54,480,151	6,345,000	48,517,867	1,555,928	30
283,315,079	35.1	148,732,475	73,731,128	6,805,000	51,570,537	2,475,939	31

TABLE SHOWING, BY GEOGRAPHICAL DIVISIONS, THE RESERVE CITIES AND CENTRAL RESERVE CITIES, THE NUMBER OF BANKS IN OPERATION AT EVERY DATE ON WHICH REPORTS OF CONDITION HAVE BEEN MADE, FROM MARCH 7, 1884, TO OCTOBER 3, 1893, INCLUSIVE, TOGETHER WITH THE AMOUNT OF RESERVE REQUIRED AND THE AMOUNT HELD AT EACH OF THOSE DATES, AND THE CLASSIFICATION OF THE RESERVE HELD, SHOWING AMOUNTS AND PERCENTAGES IN EACH CASE.

[Division No. 1.—Maine, New Hampshire, Vermont, Massachusetts, Rhode Island, and Connecticut, excluding reserve cities.]

Dates.	No. of banks	Amount of reserve required, 15 per cent of net deposits.	Reserve held.		Classification of reserve held.				
			Amount.	Ratio.	Lawful money (6 per cent).		With reserve agents (9 per cent).		Five per cent redemption fund.
					Amount.	Ratio.	Amount.	Ratio.	
1884.				*Per ct.*		*Per ct*		*Per ct.*	
Mar. 7....	514	$15,959,007	$32,510,001	30.56	$7,875,750	7.40	$20,374,517	19.15	$4,260,634
Apr. 24...	514	16,081,733	31,256,427	27.15	8,138,314	7.59	18,787,103	17.52	4,331,010
June 20...	514	15,103,686	27,470,663	27.28	8,231,410	8.17	14,972,792	14.87	4,266,461
Sept. 30...	514	15,614,046	32,199,345	30.93	8,199,770	7.88	19,833,278	19.05	4,166,297
Dec. 20 ...	515	15,216,181	31,576,643	31.13	8,273,291	8.16	19,211,124	18.94	4,092,228
1885.									
Mar. 10...	514	15,553,913	33,563,396	32.37	8,416,689	9.12	21,146,721	20.30	3,999,986
May 6....	511	16,093,617	34,886,766	32.52	8,641,121	8.05	22,184,176	20.68	4,061,469
July 1....	512	16,580,066	34,597,448	31.31	8,951,595	8.10	21,637,813	19.58	4,008,040
Oct. 1	506	17,218,577	34,416,314	29.98	9,549,345	8.32	20,832,605	18.15	4,034,364
Dec. 24 ...	506	17,150,864	32,831,670	28.71	9,562,800	8.36	19,311,376	16.89	3,957,494
1886.									
Mar. 1....	507	17,185,207	32,588,870	28.44	9,772,588	8.53	18,960,980	16.56	3,846,302
June 3....	510	16,473,718	32,509,786	27.91	10,304,208	8.85	18,555,748	15.93	3,649,830
Aug. 27...	509	17,388,516	31,345,786	27.04	10,316,259	8.90	17,449,280	15.05	3,580,249
Oct. 7....	510	18,295,909	35,762,441	20.32	10,335,491	8.47	21,995,854	18.03	3,431,096
Dec. 28 ...	511	17,815,957	33,229,398	27.98	10,888,902	9.17	19,338,260	16.28	3,002,236
1887.									
Mar. 4....	511	17,464,118	34,081,099	29.27	10,261,663	8.81	21,137,117	18.15	2,682,319
May 13...	513	17,918,113	33,354,311	27.92	10,470,249	8.77	20,384,444	17.06	2,499,618
Aug. 1...	512	17,228,499	28,645,014	24.91	10,202,657	8.88	16,106,385	14.02	2,335,972
Oct. 5....	512	17,758,954	32,079,549	27.10	10,081,047	8.51	19,698,402	16.64	2,300,100
Dec. 7	514	17,341,009	29,625,990	25.04	10,316,792	8.92	17,045,118	14.74	2,264,080
1888.									
Feb. 14...	514	18,229,526	33,096,440	27.23	9,937,633	8.18	20,928,685	17.22	2,230,122
Apr. 30...	514	18,287,862	32,928,907	27.01	10,402,526	8.53	20,330,966	16.68	2,195,415
June 30...	515	18,929,571	35,172,829	27.87	10,017,520	7.96	22,986,251	18.21	2,139,058
Oct. 4.....	515	19,889,503	36,517,994	27.56	10,745,705	8.11	23,704,062	17.88	2,098,167
Dec. 12 ...	516	19,338,797	33,598,583	26.06	10,781,645	8.37	20,835,576	16.16	1,978,362
1889.									
Feb. 26...	517	19,631,288	36,075,905	27.57	10,535,537	8.05	23,657,943	18.08	1,882,425
May 13...	518	20,634,607	40,204,495	29.29	11,125,880	8.09	27,409,248	19.92	1,759,357
July 12...	521	21,622,302	40,580,347	28.15	11,779,205	8.17	27,066,971	18.77	1,734,171
Sept. 30...	522	21,643,953	38,925,305	26.97	11,534,535	7.99	25,693,206	17.81	1,697,564
Dec. 11 ...	523	20,841,025	33,618,578	21.22	11,673,180	8.40	20,382,427	14.67	1,592,971
1890.									
Feb. 28 ...	521	20,878,978	36,300,363	26.08	11,504,237	8.26	23,270,173	16.72	1,525,053
May 17...	527	21,229,739	36,242,622	25.61	11,090,798	7.84	23,622,164	16.61	1,529,660
July 18...	527	22,127,475	37,817,047	25.64	12,361,578	8.38	23,909,780	16.21	1,542,688
Oct. 2....	527	22,292,444	37,840,955	25.34	12,182,922	8.20	23,896,058	16.08	1,431,320
Dec. 19 ...	527	20,763,952	34,649,318	25.03	12,134,781	8.77	21,119,223	15.26	1,395,314
1891.									
Feb. 26 ...	528	20,499,180	33,004,361	24.15	12,034,234	8.81	19,554,271	14.31	1,415,856
May 4....	528	21,301,304	35,962,153	25.32	12,111,658	8.53	22,443,506	15.80	1,406,989
July 9....	530	22,232,922	41,064,136	27.70	13,388,475	9.03	26,267,239	17.72	1,408,424
Sept. 25...	530	21,827,710	38,281,908	26.31	12,769,927	8.79	23,904,951	16.47	1,527,032
Dec. 2....	530	22,188,502	38,708,647	26.17	13,003,798	8.85	24,050,937	16.26	1,563,912
1892.									
Mar. 1....	533	22,847,267	42,870,874	28.15	12,813,421	8.41	28,400,953	18.65	1,646,500
May 17...	532	23,690,464	41,816,761	28.40	13,366,465	8.46	29,823,145	18.88	1,657,151
July 12...	537	24,761,277	47,840,955	28.08	14,094,485	8.51	32,658,140	19.42	1,688,330
Sept. 30...	540	24,777,370	42,937,529	25.99	13,876,306	8.40	27,359,249	16.56	1,701,974
Dec. 9	540	24,549,292	40,133,652	24.52	14,164,898	8.65	24,244,231	14.75	1,724,523
1893.									
Mar. 6....	542	24,021,757	37,092,878	23.16	13,883,932	8.67	21,498,375	13.41	1,710,571
May 4	542	23,874,620	36,540,695	22.96	14,102,910	9.05	20,363,464	12.79	1,774,291
July 12...	541	23,046,083	42,980,406	27.97	15,128,587	10.01	25,694,349	16.72	1,857,200
Oct. 3....	539	21,341,390	43,624,879	30.66	15,988,452	11.24	25,579,912	17.85	2,056,515

TABLE SHOWING, BY GEOGRAPHICAL DIVISIONS, THE RESERVE CITIES AND CENTRAL RESERVE CITIES, THE NUMBER OF BANKS IN OPERATION, ETC.—Continued.

[Division No. 2.—New York, New Jersey, and Pennsylvania, excluding reserve cities.]

Dates.	No. of banks	Amount of reserve required, 15 per cent of net deposits.	Reserve held.		Classification of reserve held.						
			Amount.	Ratio.	Lawful money (6 per cent).		With reserve agents (9 per cent).		Five per cent redemption fund.		
					Amount.	Ratio.	Amount.	Ratio.			
1884.				*Per ct.*		*Per ct.*		*Per ct.*			
Mar. 7....	550	$27,003,470	$53,829,445	29.90	$10,983,453	9.43	$33,924,115	18.84	$2,921,877		
Apr. 24...	554	27,240,954	53,358,232	29.38	18,854,082	10.38	31,556,160	17.38	2,947,990		
June 20...	561	25,502,602	45,241,608	26.61	18,801,649	11.06	23,558,015	13.86	2,881,974		
Sept.30...	563	25,245,939	49,189,650	20.23	18,694,389	11.11	27,634,801	16.42	2,860,460		
Dec. 20 ...	560	24,531,549	50,799,729	31.06	18,036,445	11.03	29,977,889	18.33	2,785,386		
1885.											
Mar. 10...	559	25,258,857	55,463,538	32.94	18,925,754	11.24	33,766,999	20.05	2,770,785		
May 6....	553	25,204,559	53,071,049	31.58	20,044,604	11.93	30,262,857	18.01	2,763,578		
July 1....	561	25,615,082	51,945,847	30.42	19,178,305	11.23	30,093,212	17.59	2,734,330		
Oct. 1....	557	26,291,732	56,170,958	32.05	20,055,448	11.44	33,297,308	19.00	2,818,202		
Dec. 24 ...	567	26,843,401	58,345,580	32.60	18,913,441	10.57	36,653,591	20.48	2,778,548		
1886.											
Mar. 1....	570	27,453,354	56,026,945	30.61	18,060,011	10.36	34,334,359	18.76	2,732,575		
June 3...	571	27,533,873	54,618,301	29.75	20,795,357	11.33	31,241,898	17.02	2,581,136		
Aug.27...	572	28,253,322	56,916,208	30.21	20,185,336	10.71	34,176,300	18.14	2,554,572		
Oct. 7....	572	28,830,549	54,836,089	28.53	20,102,341	10.51	32,249,120	16.78	2,394,628		
Dec. 28 ...	575	28,792,675	53,341,795	27.79	20,260,434	10.61	30,849,802	10.07	2,131,650		
1887.											
Mar. 4....	576	29,020,465	54,867,767	28.36	19,405,628	10.03	33,449,631	17.29	2,012,508		
May 13...	580	29,685,015	56,208,209	28.48	20,193,151	10.20	34,160,474	17.26	1,914,584		
Aug. 1 ...	586	29,837,428	51,361,676	25.82	19,291,157	9.70	30,226,408	15.20	2,844,111		
Oct. 5 ...	587	30,064,960	52,990,784	26.44	19,775,576	9.87	31,370,441,	15.65	1,844,767		
Dec. 7	591	30,090,137	52,172,378	26.01	20,038,795	9.99	30,215,646	15.01	1,817,937		
1888.											
Feb. 14 ...	593	31,181,582	57,520,460	27.67	20,111,377	9.67	35,617,574	17.13	1,791,509		
Apr. 30 ...	596	31,422,827	55,782,017	26.63	20,936,380	9.99	33,066,277	15.78	1,779,360		
June 30...	598	31,184,285	56,274,855	27.07	19,371,217	9.31	35,146,229	16.91	1,757,400		
Oct. 4	601	32,650,370	62,056,372	28.50	21,624,590	9.93	38,705,110	17.78	1,726,762		
Dec. 12 ...	603	32,101,080	57,440,943	26.77	20,803,560	9.69	34,986,054	16.30	1,651,329		
1889.											
Feb. 26...	603	32,774,651	63,083,678	28.96	21,144,626	9.68	40,351,399	18.47	1,587,653		
May 13...	607	33,020,608	62,586,794	28.43	21,670,363	9.84	39,393,656	17.89	1,522,775		
July 12...	608	33,539,199	64,388,650	28.78	21,675,391	9.09	41,229,456	18.43	1,483,803		
Sept.30...	615	34,329,752	61,470,079	26.86	20,674,866	0.17	39,007,835	17.04	1,474,586		
Dec. 11 ...	617	34,059,110	56,484,694	24.88	21,179,732	9.23	33,807,848	14.91	1,437,114		
1890.											
Feb. 28 ...	625	34,511,854	61,087,952	26.55	21,451,064	9.72	38,212,806	16.61	1,423,992		
May 17...	629	34,518,143	56,082,396	24.76	20,335,343	8.84	35,226,537	15.31	1,420,516		
July 18*..	626	33,516,164	57,433,692	25.70	20,674,866	9.25	35,410,567	15.85	1,348,319		
Oct. 2....	633	34,306,011	56,273,548	24.65	20,867,126	0.12	34,120,446	14.92	1,285,976		
Dec. 19 ...	640	32,687,250	52,770,142	24.22	21,676,126	0.95	29,824,190	13.64	1,260,826		
1891.											
Feb. 26 ...	647	33,316,855	60,131,790	27.07	22,108,571	10.00	36,659,926	16.51	1,273,293		
May 4....	655	33,826,152	57,350,851	25.44	21,838,631	9.68	34,242,908	15.18	1,278,112		
July 9 ...	657	33,855,163	58,352,440	25.85	23,393,089	10.36	33,605,293	11.92	1,264,067		
Sept.25...	658	34,601,023	60,307,438	26.14	22,805,895	9.89	36,214,263	15.70	1,287,340		
Dec. 2 ...	658	34,616,832	59,361,535	25.72	22,237,717	9.20	35,820,101	15.52	1,303,717		
1892.											
Mar. 1 ...	659	36,154,961	69,465,248	28.82	21,790,282	9.04	46,353,240	19.23	1,321,726		
May 17...	666	37,433,634	70,853,519	28.30	23,085,521	9.25	46,432,159	18.61	1,335,839		
July 12...	671	38,002,339	75,068,925	29.56	24,013,764	9.46	49,612,882	19.54	1,342,279		
Sept.30...	671	39,635,609	72,090,357	27.28	24,252,012	9.18	46,485,078	17.59	1,353,177		
Dec. 9 ...	672	39,300,157	65,465,561	24.99	24,192,628	9.23	39,904,523	15.23	1,368,410		
1893.											
Mar. 6....	677	39,498,038	65,213,004	24.77	24,292,569	9.23	39,537,518	15.01	1,382,917		
May 4....	688	40,041,889	64,213,611	24.05	26,108,649	9.78	36,722,845	13.76	1,382,117		
July 12 ..	697	37,420,310	62,907,053	25.24	27,705,403	11.11	33,829,395	13.56	1,432,255		
Oct. 3	699	34,837,686	64,014,555	27.56	29,302,703	12.62	33,072,889	11.24	1,638,966		

*Brooklyn transferred to division No. 9 from July 18, 1890.

TABLE SHOWING, BY GEOGRAPHICAL DIVISIONS, THE RESERVE CITIES AND CENTRAL RESERVE CITIES, THE NUMBER OF BANKS IN OPERATION, ETC.—Continued.

[Division No. 3.—Delaware, Maryland, Virginia, West Virginia, and the District of Columbia, excluding reserve cities.]

Dates.	No. of banks	Amount of reserve required, 15 per cent of net deposits.	Reserve held.		Classification of reserve held.				
			Amount.	Ratio.	Lawful money (6 per cent).		With reserve agents (9 per cent).		Five per cent redemption fund.
					Amount.	Ratio.	Amount.	Ratio.	
1884.				*Per ct.*		*Per ct.*		*Per ct.*	
Mar. 7....	83	$3,877,353	$6,822,590	26.36	$2,873,867	11.12	$3,582,088	13.86	$366,035
Apr. 21...	83	3,812,038	6,446,814	25.37	3,045,651	11.98	3,027,832	11.91	373,331
June 20 ..	83	3,513,153	5,375,113	22.95	2,975,931	12.71	2,025,960	8.65	373,222
Sept.30...	88	3,702,825	6,837,101	27.70	3,220,417	13.05	3,246,528	13.15	370,156
Dec. 20 ...	88	3,365,854	6,467,992	28.82	2,942,926	13.12	3,164,161	14.10	360,905
1885.									
Mar. 10...	88	3,361,044	6,282,532	28.04	3,043,637	13.58	2,895,186	12.92	343,709
May 6	87	2,854,130	6,624,698	29.56	2,985,242	15.69	2,289,321	12.03	350,135
July 1.....	87	2,919,436	5,311,397	27.29	2,758,277	14.17	2,199,065	11.30	353,155
Oct. 1	88	3,286,346	7,338,927	33.50	3,134,687	14.31	3,850,486	17.57	353,754
Dec. 24 ...	89	3,162,147	7,070,981	33.54	2,887,760	13.70	3,825,340	18.15	357,881
1886.									
Mar. 1....	89	3,163,328	6,579,113	31.20	3,079,948	14.60	3,153,202	14.95	345,963
June 3 ...	90	3,259,103	6,761,884	31.12	3,414,420	15.71	3,034,136	13.97	313,325
Aug.27...	91	3,490,359	3,337,721	31.53	3,313,468	14.24	3,714,380	15.96	309,873
Oct. 7.....	89	3,525,434	7,125,856	30.32	3,405,443	14.49	3,414,134	14.53	306,279
Dec. 28 ...	91	3,459,845	6,826,991	29.60	3,124,102	13.54	3,414,702	14.80	288,187
1887.									
Mar. 4....	91	3,541,988	6,685,225	28.31	3,061,122	12.96	3,370,508	14.27	253,535
May 13 ...	92	3,434,211	6,233,763	27.16	3,351,755	14.64	2,640,664	11.53	241,344
Aug. 1 ...	93	3,681,532	6,591,665	26.86	8,397,925	13.84	2,952,617	12.03	241,123
Oct. 5.....	94	3,789,907	6,641,421	26.29	3,402,471	13.47	3,004,141	11.89	234,809
Dec. 7	94	3,748,997	6,728,437	26.92	3,329,980	13.32	3,157,971	12.64	240,476
1888.									
Feb. 14...	94	3,827,470	6,737,364	26.40	3,272,849	12.83	3,236,123	12.68	228,392
Apr. 30...	94	3,789,898	6,554,763	25.94	3,340,776	13.22	2,988,503	11.83	225,484
June30...	95	3,902,911	6,688,570	25.71	3,320,174	12.76	3,156,750	12.11	217,646
Oct.4....	96	4,364,275	8,474,938	29.13	3,672,305	12.62	4,582,280	15.75	220,353
Dec. 12 ...	96	4,159,106	7,612,357	27.45	3,502,069	12.63	3,898,858	14.06	211,430
1889.									
Feb. 26 ...	96	4,210,619	7,830,630	27.90	3,583,377	12.77	4,043,241	14.40	204,012
May 13 ...	98	4,129,743	7,338,116	26.65	3,852,193	13.99	3,283,681	11.93	201,939
July 12...	102	4,262,053	7,356,738	25.89	3,644,247	12.77	3,528,845	12.42	193,646
Sept.30 ..	104	4,431,299	7,396,267	25.00	3,387,152	11.46	3,808,964	12.89	194,151
Dec. 11 ...	105	4,285,277	7,058,474	24.71	3,483,691	12.19	3,399,343	11.90	175,440
1890.									
Feb. 28 ...	107	4,364,478	7,384,234	25.38	3,252,139	11.18	3,956,771	13.60	175,324
May 17 ...	108	4,549,745	7,767,257	25.55	3,652,805	12.02	3,942,458	12.97	171,994
July 18...	110	3,888,424	8,567,845	26.28	3,689,922	11.32	4,701,987	14.43	175,935
Oct.2.....	112	5,127,124	8,665,176	25.35	3,925,154	11.48	4,575,269	13.39	164,753
Dec. 10 ...	113	4,821,664	8,137,749	25.32	4,178,148	13.00	3,793,410	11.80	166,191
1891.									
Feb. 26 ...	115	4,870,435	8,552,098	26.34	4,157,438	12.84	4,225,817	13.01	168,843
May 4	116	4,867,413	8,078,827	24.90	4,553,151	14.03	3,355,717	10.34	169,959
July 9.....	117	4,915,034	8,368,584	25.38	4,424,507	13.42	3,774,134	11.42	169,043
Sept.25 ..	121	5,211,836	9,103,332	26.20	4,351,771	12.52	4,562,235	13.13	189,326
Dec.2	122	5,050,142	8,947,957	26.58	4,273,584	12.69	4,482,701	13.32	191,672
1892.									
Mar. 1....	123	5,197,888	9,553,079	27.57	4,043,320	11.67	5,312,345	15.33	197,414
May 17...	123	5,339,549	10,024,832	28.16	4,579,861	12.87	5,254,667	14.76	190,304
July 12...	125	5,525,165	10,051,025	27.39	4,539,597	12.32	5,306,624	14.41	204,804
Sept.30 ..	126	5,866,785	10,466,007	27.21	4,555,393	11.65	5,880,531	15.04	206,140
Dec.9	128	5,734,312	9,573,896	25.04	4,297,482	11.21	5,070,908	13.26	205,506
1893.									
Mar. 6	129	5,620,043	8,825,413	23.53	4,141,262	11.05	4,473,944	11.91	210,237
May 4 .	129	5,168,525	8,182,254	22.44	4,474,082	12.27	3,497,972	9.59	210,197
July 12 .	131	5,216,620	8,791,799	25.16	5,007,147	14.33	3,578,550	10.24	206,102
Oct.3....	131	4,905,961	8,867,343	27.11	5,168,452	15.80	3,468,996	10.61	220,895

TABLE SHOWING, BY GEOGRAPHICAL DIVISIONS, THE RESERVE CITIES AND CENTRAL RESERVE CITIES, THE NUMBER OF BANKS IN OPERATION, ETC.—Continued.

[Division No. 4.—North Carolina, South Carolina, Georgia, Florida, Alabama, Mississippi, Louisiana. Texas, Arkansas, Kentucky, and Tennessee, excluding reserve cities.]

Dates.	No. of banks	Amount of reserve required, 15 per cent of net deposits.	Reserve held.		Classification of reserve held.					
			Amount.	Ratio.	Lawful money (6 per cent).		With reserve agents (9 per cent).		Five per cent redemption fund.
					Amount.	Ratio.	Amount.	Ratio.	
1884.				*Per ct.*		*Per ct.*		*Per ct.*	
Mar. 7....	201	$6,816,062	$13,644.672	30.03	$6,883,358	15.15	$5,979,687	13.16	$781.627
Apr. 24...	204	6.874,431	12,348,517	26.95	6,803,162	14.84	4,762,025	10.39	781,330
June 20 ..	208	6,449,163	11,304,136	26.43	6,826,409	15.88	3,782,006	8.80	755,721
Sept. 30 ..	216	6,012,864	11,168,505	27.72	6,334,635	15.72	4,087,148	10.15	746,482
Dec. 20 ...	220	6,491,216	14,560,732	33.67	7,007,016	16.19	6,806,367	15.73	747,349
1885.									
Mar. 10...	226	0,069,784	15,098,820	33.96	7,064,807	17.91	6,385,184	14.36	748,829
May 6....	229	6,483,495	13,065,477	30.23	7,563,398	17.50	4,765,739	11.03	736,340
July 1....	232	6,442,590	12,404,357	28.88	7,159,393	16.67	4,592,187	10.55	712,777
Oct. 1	232	6,388,330	11,374,404	27.88	6,826,279	16.03	4,322,628	10.15	725,487
Dec. 24 ...	235	7,112,914	15,834,011	33.25	8,001,784	16.80	7,141,940	15.00	690,287
1886.									
Mar. 1....	240	7,583,952	16,308,788	32.26	8,523,863	16.86	7,114,169	14.07	670,756
June 3 ...	245	7,493,063	15,598,452	31.23	8,108,413	16.23	6,863,196	13.74	626,843
Aug. 27...	251	7,301,499	13,956,929	28.67	7,650,399	15.72	5,690,062	11.71	607,468
Oct. 7....	251	7,520,093	13,507,692	27.12	7,565,181	15.09	5,474,973	10.92	557,538
Dec. 28 ...	253	8,863,744	21,696,851	35.70	9,659,357	16.35	10,914,071	18.47	523,423
1887.									
Mar. 4....	265	9,951,682	22,483,366	33.89	10,365,005	15.02	11,607,039	17.50	511,262
May 13...	279	9,493,413	18,693,369	28.86	9,623,458	15.35	7,965,043	12.71	501,868
Aug. 1....	290	9,227,123	15,981,046	25.98	8,924,863	14.51	6,555,611	10.66	500,602
Oct. 5....	296	9,183,326	16,341,034	26.69	9,728,521	15.80	6,100,154	9.96	512,359
Dec. 7 ...	301	9,671,142	18,063,708	29.41	10,375,365	16.10	8,072,837	12.52	515,506
1888.									
Feb. 14 ...	305	10,241,743	21,109,205	30.92	11,248,310	16.47	9,353,121	13.70	507,774
Apr. 30...	307	9,775,180	17,945,763	27.51	9,916,320	15.22	7,522,773	11.54	506,670
June 30 ..	313	9,683,437	17,925,943	27.77	9,397,854	14.56	8,027,614	12.44	500,475
Oct. 4 ...	318	9,543,970	16,380,467	25.74	9,557,311	15.02	6,338,284	9.96	484,872
Dec. 12 ...	321	10,201,944	19,622,145	28.85	9,752,368	14.34	9,382,165	13.79	487,612
1889.									
Feb. 26 ...	324	11,495,298	26,797,309	34.97	12,195,333	15.91	14,122,446	18.42	479,590
May 13...	339	11,100,507	22,345,576	30.20	11,482,281	15.52	10,385,059	14.03	478,236
July 12...	346	11,035,036	20,836,091	28.32	11,054,098	15.03	9,301,242	12.64	480,751
Sept. 30...	364	11,566,487	20,011,741	25.96	10,771,020	13.97	8,756,707	11.36	487,014
Dec. 11 ...	374	12,872,658	24,737,345	28.83	11,495,248	13.39	12,731,317	14.84	510,780
1890.									
Feb. 28 ...	393	14,175,895	30,120,238	31.87	14,846,750	15.71	14,753,742	15.61	519,746
May 17...	406	13,714,957	23,414,837	25.61	12,862,873	14.07	10,017,319	10.96	534,645
July 18...	424	13,739,515	21,907,965	23.02	12,007,302	13.21	9,268,102	10.12	542,560
Oct. 2	448	13,710,442	22,101,525	24.18	12,400,753	13.57	9,139,407	10.00	561,368
Dec. 19 ...	459	13,510,003	23,155,918	25.71	13,418,057	14.90	9,173,073	10.18	564,788
1891.									
Feb. 26 ...	467	13,804,224	26,336,774	28.62	14,779,704	16.06	10,970,713	11.92	586,267
May 4....	477	13,436,294	22,473,091	25.09	12,991,105	14.50	8,691,629	9.93	590,357
July 9 ...	479	12,738,158	21,907,300	25.12	12,403,539	14.61	8,344,295	9.83	584,526
Sept.25...	478	12,036,628	20,885,765	26.03	11,898,504	14.83	8,394,262	10.46	592,909
Dec.2 ...	481	12,811,339	26,036,093	30.48	13,545,523	15.86	11,877,366	13.91	613,204
1892.									
Mar. 1....	489	13,763,268	30,781,096	33.55	15,204,417	16.57	14,949,816	16.29	626,863
May 17...	496	13,622,353	28,184,556	31.03	15,403,496	16.04	12,974,795	14.29	616,265
July 12...	500	13,467,057	27,206,231	30.30	13,781,480	15.35	12,765,316	14.22	656,405
Sept.30...	500	13,626,945	24,577,400	27.05	12,747,780	14.03	11,175,373	12.30	654,247
Dec.9 ...	501	14,813,578	29,429,783	29.80	14,677,877	14.86	14,089,551	14.27	662,355
1893.									
Mar. 1....	501	15,395,493	30,895,770	30.10	15,764,518	15.36	14,497,952	14.13	633,320
May 4....	502	14,806,327	26,856,363	27.21	14,982,806	15.18	11,241,220	14.39	672,337
July 12...	493	12,813,068	24,628,630	28.83	15,166,526	17.76	8,847,103	10.35	625,001
Oct. 3....	487	10,694,707	21,458,980	31.89	14,354,238	21.33	6,491,512	9.65	613,230

TABLE SHOWING, BY GEOGRAPHICAL DIVISIONS, THE RESERVE CITIES AND CENTRAL
RESERVE CITIES, THE NUMBER OF BANKS IN OPERATION, ETC.—Continued.

[Division No. 5.—Ohio, Indiana, Illinois, Michigan, and Wisconsin, excluding reserve cities.]

Dates.	No. of banks	Amount of reserve required, 15 per cent of net deposits.	Reserve held.		Classification of reserve held.					
			Amount.	Ratio.	Lawful money (6 per cent).		With reserve agents (9 per cent).		Five per cent redemption fund.
					Amount.	Ratio.	Amount.	Ratio.	
1884.				*Per ct.*		*Per ct.*		*Per ct.*	
Mar. 7....	558	$17,808,933	$34,832,320	29.34	$16,461,984	13.87	$16,636,811	14.01	$1,733,525
Apr. 24...	560	17,392,601	32,294,594	27.81	16,913,978	14.59	13,623,182	11.75	1,757,434
June 20...	569	16,640,340	30,968,073	29.15	16,186,847	14.59	13,081,876	11.79	1,699,350
Sept. 30...	574	15,784,489	31,545,494	29.98	16,127,236	15.33	13,764,179	13.08	1,651,079
Dec. 20 ...	572	15,040,275	33,478,235	33.39	15,563,364	15.52	16,332,719	16.29	1,582,152
1885.									
Mar. 10...	567	15,800,092	36,876,186	35.07	16,882,609	16.03	18,475,898	17.54	1,517,079
May 6	568	15,954,519	35,963,108	33.81	17,117,106	16.09	17,336,757	16.30	1,509,305
July 1	567	16,118,869	36,162,987	33.65	15,936,885	11.83	18,738,134	17.45	1,487,958
Oct. 1	570	16,501,187	37,477,345	34.07	17,019,462	15.47	18,934,890	17.21	1,522,093
Dec. 24 ...	570	16,497,191	36,226,910	32.93	16,050,698	14.59	18,653,616	16.96	1,522,596
1886.									
Mar. 1	571	17,184,663	38,467,958	33.57	16,692,494	14.57	20,284,810	17.78	1,490,654
June 3 ...	575	17,452,850	36,682,622	31.53	17,840,509	15.34	17,426,446	14.98	1,406,667
Aug. 27...	582	18,315,951	41,364,412	33.88	17,118.272	14.02	22,867,315	18.73	1,378,825
Oct. 7.....	580	18,438,101	39,891,410	32.45	17,974,624	14.62	20,591,220	16.75	1,322,566
Dec. 28 ...	576	18,828.474	40,251,058	32.07	18,082,937	14.41	20,974,170	16.71	1,193,951
1887.									
Mar. 4	582	19,446,236	42,186,629	32.54	18,037,638	13.91	23,012,354	17.75	1,136,637
May 13 ...	584	20,082,778	41,806,938	31.27	19,111,576	14.27	21,673,401	16.19	1,081,958
Aug. 1....	594	20,814,218	44,475,533	32.05	18,401,230	13.26	25,021,687	18.03	1,052,616
Oct. 5.....	598	20,570,959	40,983,916	29.88	19,171,016	13.98	20,771,852	15.14	1,011,048
Dec. 7	600	20,237,953	39,116,212	28.99	18,425,529	13.66	19,629,800	14.55	1,060,883
1888.									
Feb. 14 ...	603	20,788,469	40,918,158	29.52	18.290,041	13.20	21,600,663	15.59	1,027,454
Apr. 30...	606	20,795,516	39,175,386	28.26	18,869,677	13.61	19,298,656	13.92	1,007,053
June 30 ...	609	20,756,627	39,806,200	28.77	17,754,453	12.83	21,045,051	15.21	1,006,696
Oct. 4.....	611	21,297,373	42,224,352	29.74	18,466,510	13.01	22,763,433	16.03	991,409
Dec. 12 ...	615	21,150,669	42,006,506	20.85	18,089,328	12.83	23,025,148	16.33	982,030
1889.									
Feb. 26 ...	620	22,108,190	46,152,837	31.31	18,299,545	12.42	26,888,639	18.24	964,653
May 13 ...	622	22,532,982	45,216,707	30.10	19,984,145	13.30	24,287,408	16.17	945,154
July 12 ...	624	22,197,384	48,488,996	31.35	20,064,249	12.97	27,489,591	17.78	935,153
Sept. 30...	626	23,355,251	47,310,106	30.39	19,052,153	12.24	27,327,970	17.55	929,983
Dec. 11 ...	630	23,037,979	43,421,760	28.27	19,053,439	12.41	23,439,190	15.26	929,131
1890.									
Feb. 28	635	23,999,083	47,348,221	29.59	19,385,160	12.12	27,013,130	16.90	910,925
May 17 ...	644	24,458,347	45,815,953	28.10	19,214,280	11.78	25,672,588	15.74	929,085
July 18 ...	650	25,234,240	47,608,327	28.30	19,719,230	11.72	26,955,389	16.02	933,708
Oct. 2.....	650	25,804,618	48,563,276	28.23	20,110,638	11.72	27,493,759	15.98	919,879
Dec. 19 ...	655	25,120,570	46,041,313	27.49	20,682,244	12.35	24,440,070	14.60	910,029
1891.									
Feb. 26 ...	654	26,052,632	52,440,599	30.20	21,751,135	12.52	29,785,731	17.15	912,733
May 4 ...	657	26,750,845	50,936,356	28.56	22,312,308	12.51	27,709,586	15.54	914,402
July 9....	660	27,027,984	49,364,907	27.40	22,496,181	12.49	25,973,487	14.41	893,939
Sept. 25...	663	28,583,963	56,609,151	29.74	23,177,047	12.16	32,572,518	17.06	919,589
Dec. 2	666	28,159,822	52,506,985	27.97	22,416,277	11.95	29,173,153	15.54	917,555
1892.									
Mar. 1....	672	29,753,103	60,508,503	30.50	22,473,202	11.33	37,105,510	18.71	929,785
May 17 ...	674	30,056,393	60,761,493	30.32	23,505,074	11.73	36,314,168	18.12	942,251
July 12...	678	30,026,267	62,196,543	30.46	23,899,691	11.71	37,353,557	18.29	913,292
Sept. 30...	680	31,553,491	62,336,327	29.61	21,987,436	11.87	36,395,159	17.29	953,692
Dec. 9	683	31,321,325	56,657,506	27.13	24,707,288	13.36	30,917,479	9.79	1,002,739
1893.									
Mar. 6	690	31,702,621	56,060,568	26.53	21,647,925	11.66	30,368,515	14.37	1,044,128
May 4	695	31,387,409	50,916,834	24.33	21,605,190	12.21	24,258,308	11.59	1,051,336
July 12 ...	696	27,270,886	50,291,654	27.66	27,220,984	14.97	21,992,775	12.10	1,077,895
Oct. 3	692	23,399,510	49,458,283	31.70	27,888,005	17.88	20,450,669	13.11	1,119,609

TABLE SHOWING, BY GEOGRAPHICAL DIVISIONS, THE RESERVE CITIES AND CENTRAL RESERVE CITIES, THE NUMBER OF BANKS IN OPERATION, ETC.—Continued.

[Division No. 6.—Iowa, Minnesota, Missouri, Kansas, and Nebraska (Omaha transferred to division No. 0, October 5, 1887; Kansas City and St. Joseph transferred to division No. 9, May 13, 1887), excluding reserve cities.]

Dates.	No. of banks	Amount of reserve required, 15 per cent of net deposits.	Reserve held.		Classification of reserve held.					
			Amount.	Ratio.	Lawful money (6 per cent).		With reserve agents (9 per cent).		Five per cent redemption fund.
					Amount.	Ratio.	Amount.	Ratio.	
1884.				*Per ct.*		*Per ct.*		*Per ct.*	
Mar. 7 ...	287	$9,365,609	$16,334,768	26.16	$7,297,414	11.69	$8,526,486	13.66	$510,868
Apr. 24 ...	298	9,712,110	17,385,106	26.85	8,463,026	13.07	8,406,680	12.98	515,330
June 20 ..	309	9,546,762	16,682,585	26.21	9,366,030	14.72	6,806,044	10.69	510,451
Sept. 30 ..	329	9,158,231	16,305,178	26.70	8,130,878	13.32	7,677,976	12.58	494,324
Dec. 20 ..	329	8,643,147	15,874,452	27.55	7,734,917	13.42	7,642,884	13.26	496,651
1885.									
Mar. 10 ...	336	9,202,146	18,064,151	29.45	8,442,274	13.76	9,131,647	14.89	490,230
May 6	340	9,643,675	19,112,096	29.73	8,803,813	13.69	9,806,853	15.25	502,330
July 1	346	10,105,532	20,186,373	29.96	8,868,049	13.16	10,827,681	16.07	490,613
Oct. 1	359	10,526,279	19,159,727	27.30	8,896,805	12.68	9,768,829	13.92	494,093
Dec. 24 ...	363	10,511,542	19,128,184	27.30	9,300,286	13.28	9,315,121	13.29	503,777
1886.									
Mar. 1....	377	10,872,988	19,373,302	26.73	8,838,140	12.19	10,043,854	13.86	491,308
June 3 ...	391	12,203,046	23,020,432	28.70	11,204,906	13.77	11,339,220	13.94	476,396
Aug. 27...	404	12,349,300	24,464,927	29.72	10,229,545	12.43	13,747,424	16.70	487,951
Oct. 7.....	406	12,377,733	21,931,867	26.58	11,010,342	13.35	10,422,066	12.63	490,459
Dec. 28 ..	418	12,811,418	23,073,002	26.99	11,752,951	13.76	10,848,107	12.70	451,044
1887.									
Mar. 4....	427	14,184,873	27,752,343	29.35	11,860,366	12.54	15,441,590	16.33	450,387
May 13...	428	13,368,183	26,721,847	29.99	12,010,369	13.48	14,290,849	16.04	422,619
Aug. 1....	438	12,435,313	25,056,695	30.22	10,458,690	12.62	14,175,709	17.10	422,236
Oct. 5.....	455	12,258,402	22,367,310	27.37	10,275,484	12.57	11,690,633	14.27	431,193
Dec. 7	462	11,440,774	20,023,408	26.25	9,831,122	12.89	9,753,960	12.79	438,326
1888.									
Feb. 14 ...	460	11,915,472	24,167,651	30.42	10,418,840	13.12	13,308,839	16.75	439,981
Apr. 30...	468	12,191,175	24,217,974	29.80	10,851,912	13.35	12,924,379	15.90	441,683
June 30 ..	471	12,423,419	25,981,996	30.62	10,547,101	12.73	14,367,358	17.35	449,537
Oct. 4.....	476	12,646,574	23,898,707	28.35	10,011,697	11.87	13,496,321	15.94	450,689
Dec. 12 ...	480	12,102,286	20,169,802	25.00	10,197,298	12.64	9,520,418	11.80	452,086
1889.									
Feb. 26 ...	487	12,420,637	22,812,398	27.55	10,019,197	12.10	12,336,471	14.90	456,730
May 13 ...	490	12,585,262	23,606,074	28.13	10,460,419	12.47	12,687,257	15.12	458,394
July 12 ...	497	12,925,286	24,386,707	28.30	10,374,952	12.04	13,553,976	15.73	457,497
Sept. 30 ..	503	13,015,631	23,831,360	27.46	9,352,807	10.78	14,013,997	16.15	461,556
Dec. 11 ...	516	13,209,115	23,663,534	26.87	10,728,448	12.18	12,464,371	14.15	470,715
1890.									
Feb. 28 ...	522	14,037,495	26,557,782	28.38	10,142,221	10.84	15,945,079	17.04	470,481
May 17...	531	14,672,093	28,417,458	29.05	10,120,380	10.36	17,803,225	18.20	481,844
July 18*..	522	11,820,328	23,587,972	29.93	8,660,227	10.99	14,559,610	18.48	462,910
Oct. 2.....	529	12,650,537	25,045,606	29.70	9,057,219	10.72	15,542,676	18.43	465,711
Dec. 19 ...	526	12,020,920	21,800,313	27.32	9,113,606	11.37	12,303,422	15.36	473,285
1891.									
Feb. 26 ...	525	12,152,020	24,124,918	29.78	9,109,692	11.24	14,518,746	17.96	466,480
May 4	526	12,807,895	24,484,809	28.68	9,883,476	10.99	14,634,337	17.14	467,086
July 9†..	525	12,271,889	21,873,399	26.74	9,271,189	11.33	12,140,446	14.84	461,764
Sept. 25 ..	534	12,709,609	24,150,965	28.53	8,975,041	10.59	14,702,960	17.35	472,355
Dec. 2	540	12,764,884	23,452,871	27.56	9,081,102	10.67	13,887,498	16.32	484,271
1892.									
Mar. 1....	540	14,021,847	28,524,563	30.51	9,292,759	9.94	18,745,334	20.05	486,470
May 17...	539	14,113,353	28,830,733	30.65	9,659,618	10.27	18,696,824	19.87	485,291
July 12 ...	541	14,379,925	29,371,591	30.64	9,901,201	10.33	18,986,849	19.81	483,538
Sept. 30...	543	14,520,103	29,190,867	30.16	9,940,427	10.27	18,768,907	19.20	481,533
Dec. 9	544	14,516,112	24,440,147	25.23	9,899,800	10.23	14,052,376	14.52	487,971
1893.									
Mar. 6....	547	15,316,641	28,052,373	27.47	10,538,687	10.32	17,025,851	16.67	487,865
May 4§ ..	547	14,435,303	25,361,913	26.35	10,331,862	10.74	14,558,770	15.13	471,281
July 12...	544	12,300,120	23,245,212	28.35	9,868,175	13.30	11,799,613	14.39	465,534
Oct. 3....	544	10,645,802	23,414,641	32.90	10,771,244	15.18	12,166,739	17.14	476,658

* St. Paul and Minneapolis transferred to division No. 9 from July 18, 1890.
† Des Moines transferred to division No. 9 from July 9, 1891.
§ Lincoln transferred to division No. 9 from May 4, 1893.

TABLE SHOWING, BY GEOGRAPHICAL DIVISIONS, THE RESERVE CITIES AND CENTRAL RESERVE CITIES, THE NUMBER OF BANKS IN OPERATION, ETC.—Continued.

[Division No. 7.—Colorado, Nevada, California, and Oregon, excluding reserve cities.]

Dates.	No. of banks	Amount of reserve required, 15 per cent of net deposits.	Reserve held.		Classification of reserve held.				Five per cent redemption fund.
			Amount.	Ratio.	Lawful money (6 per cent).		With reserve agents (9 per cent).		
					Amount.	Ratio.	Amount.	Ratio.	
1884.				*Per ct.*		*Per ct.*		*Per ct.*	
Mar. 7....	43	$3,005,761	$5,626,902	28.08	$3,217,300	16.05	$2,287,585	11.46	$122,603
Apr. 24...	43	3,028,531	5,791,614	28.68	3,207,082	15.88	2,462,838	12.20	121,624
June 20 ..	45	2,748,621	5,492,659	29.97	3,664,908	20.00	1,717,837	9.37	109,914
Sept. 30 ..	46	2,660,548	5,798,350	32.69	3,346,017	18.86	2,341,155	13.20	111,187
Dec. 20 ...	47	2,560,777	5,524,939	32.36	3,180,260	18.63	2,239,427	13.12	105,252
1885.									
Mar. 10...	47	2,663,353	5,978,551	33.67	3,450,529	19.43	2,419,586	13.63	108,436
May 6....	49	2,683,438	5,699,692	31.86	3,336,534	18.65	2,256,198	12.64	106,960
July 1....	50	2,721,004	5,697,478	31.41	2,966,876	16.36	2,626,141	14.48	104,461
Oct. 1	51	2,920,866	6,635,005	34.07	3,260,554	16.71	3,264,417	16.70	110,034
Dec. 24 ...	54	3,189,900	7,038,522	33.10	3,732,709	17.55	3,192,688	15.01	113,125
1886.									
Mar. 1....	57	3,320,624	7,529,082	33.92	3,947,515	17.78	3,465,653	15.61	116,814
June 2 ...	61	3,598,749	7,672,897	31.98	4,034,927	16.82	3,527,877	14.70	110,093
Aug. 27 ..	67	3,863,286	8,288,012	32.18	4,096,387	15.91	4,075,587	15.82	116,038
Oct. 7	68	3,971,589	7,896,910	29.83	4,104,213	15.50	3,672,731	13.87	119,966
Dec. 28 ...	71	4,329,961	9,221,771	31.95	5,276,940	18.28	3,828,979	13.26	115,853
1887.									
Mar. 4....	71	4,674,444	10,289,333	33.02	5,672,302	18.20	4,501,028	14.45	115,003
May 13...	75	5,276,435	11,540,554	32.81	5,990,889	17.03	5,438,612	15.46	611,053
Aug. 1 ...	83	5,719,220	11,799,916	30.95	6,134,729	16.09	5,548,590	14.55	116,507
Oct. 5	86	6,330,097	13,784,605	32.66	7,270,703	17.24	6,385,396	15.13	122,506
Dec. 7	80	6,291,325	12,852,230	30.71	7,510,479	17.98	5,218,778	12.44	122,973
1888.									
Feb. 14 ...	87	6,149,731	12,446,002	30.36	7,457,014	18.19	4,861,593	11.86	128,205
Apr. 30...	94	6,042,609	11,396,749	28.29	6,557,882	16.28	4,708,066	11.69	130,801
June 30 ..	96	5,924,963	11,614,948	29.46	6,338,182	16.05	5,171,147	13.09	125,619
Oct. 4	98	6,036,317	12,503,944	31.07	6,338,048	16.05	6,034,814	15.03	131,685
Dec. 12...	96	5,935,642	11,717,220	29.61	6,780,265	17.16	4,800,478	12.13	127,486
1889.									
Feb. 26 ...	98	6,215,145	13,833,283	33.39	7,408,611	17.88	6,297,797	15.20	126,875
May 13...	102	6,418,018	13,674,031	31.96	7,084,911	16.56	6,459,741	15.10	129,379
July 12 ..	102	6,409,509	14,125,458	32.75	7,124,899	16.52	6,870,159	15.93	130,400
Sept. 30 ..	107	6,871,682	15,136,846	33.04	6,826,811	14.90	8,181,249	17.86	128,786
Dec. 11 ...	109	6,822,808	13,759,793	30.25	7,133,414	15.16	6,489,222	14.27	137,160
1890.									
Feb. 28 ...	111	6,985,597	14,398,961	30.92	7,499,805	16.10	6,756,913	14.51	142,243
May 17...	114	7,280,605	14,457,219	29.79	7,148,956	14.73	7,166,979	14.77	141,284
July 18...	118	7,407,945	14,436,316	29.23	6,844,003	13.85	7,450,124	15.08	142,099
Oct. 2	120	7,973,078	15,402,798	28.98	7,188,163	13.52	8,070,144	15.18	144,491
Dec. 19 ...	123	7,220,289	12,965,412	26.94	7,689,352	15.97	5,126,361	10.65	149,699
1891.									
Feb. 26 ...	126	7,002,973	13,974,031	29.93	7,904,310	16.93	5,916,675	12.67	153,046
May 4....	127	7,411,637	14,707,475	29.65	8,210,360	16.55	6,335,458	12.77	161,657
July 9....	125	7,251,722	13,418,378	29.75	7,670,382	15.86	5,590,972	11.56	157,024
Sept. 25 ..	125	7,410,697	14,096,112	28.47	7,112,951	14.40	6,782,556	13.73	170,605
Dec. 2	126	7,230,867	13,262,170	27.51	7,049,001	14.62	6,038,406	12.53	174,763
1892.									
Mar. 1....	127	7,512,533	16,105,600	32.16	7,878,251	15.73	8,045,713	16.06	181,633
May 17...	129	7,708,768	16,803,460	32.70	7,998,033	15.56	8,621,376	16.78	184,051
July 12...	129	7,811,979	16,013,909	30.75	7,837,323	15.05	7,992,300	15.35	184,286
Sept. 30 ..	130	8,061,098	17,134,307	31.88	7,956,810	14.81	8,998,901	16.75	178,596
Dec. 9....	129	7,864,815	15,736,998	30.01	8,226,157	15.69	7,335,308	13.99	175,533
1893.									
Mar. 6 ...	129	7,832,953	15,397,197	29.48	8,326,499	15.95	6,896,302	13.21	174,696
May 4 ...	131	7,784,155	13,821,022	26.64	8,054,327	15.52	5,589,749	10.78	177,946
July 12 ..	118	5,369,641	9,017,696	25.23	6,735,237	18.85	2,123,215	5.94	159,244
Oct. 3	125	5,276,029	10,924,705	31.06	7,822,217	22.24	2,937,809	8.35	164,679

TABLE SHOWING, BY GEOGRAPHICAL DIVISIONS, THE RESERVE CITIES AND CENTRAL RESERVE CITIES, THE NUMBER OF BANKS IN OPERATION, ETC.—Continued.

[Division No. 8.—Arizona, North Dakota, South Dakota, Idaho, Montana, New Mexico, Utah, Washington, Wyoming, Oklahoma, and Indian Territory.]

Dates.	No. of banks	Amount of reserve required, 15 per cent of net deposits.	Reserve held.		Classification of reserve held.				
			Amount.	Ratio.	Lawful money (6 per cent).		With reserve agents (9 per cent).		Five per cent redemption fund.
					Amount.	Ratio.	Amount.	Ratio.	
1884.				*Per ct.*		*Per ct.*		*Per ct.*	
Mar. 7....	78	$2,206,520	$3,406,474	24.16	$2,332,136	15.85	$935,815	6.50	$118,523
Apr. 24...	84	2,236,816	3,584,760	24.83	2,421,783	16.10	1,038,881	6.90	124,096
June 20...	87	2,194,632	3,402,605	23.26	2,377,061	16.25	899,284	6.15	126,350
Sept.30...	87	2,162,177	3,263,041	22.64	2,077,673	14.41	1,066,754	7.40	118,614
Dec. 20 ...	86	2,195,537	3,581,574	24.49	2,357,403	16.12	1,111,624	7.62	109,547
1885.									
Mar. 10...	88	2,132,223	3,703,384	26.05	2,525,590	17.77	1,068,609	7.52	109,185
May 6....	89	2,124,749	3,587,907	25.33	2,387,887	16.86	1,089,153	7.69	110,957
July 1....	92	2,317,930	3,939,596	25.48	2,354,579	15.24	1,473,460	9.53	111,557
Oct. 1....	94	2,492,432	4,420,239	26.60	2,600,691	15.65	1,701,733	10.26	114,815
Dec. 24 ...	107	2,653,914	4,881,391	27.80	3,166,234	18.03	1,594,293	9.08	120,864
1886.									
Mar. 1....	107	2,643,604	4,716,817	26.86	3,057,426	17.41	1,535,412	8.74	123.077
June3....	109	2,745,657	4,688,187	25.61	3,091,659	16.89	1,471,191	8.04	125,339
Aug.27...	113	2,615,777	5,173,789	29.07	3,135,269	17.98	1,913,185	10.97	125,335
Oct. 7....	114	2,675,213	5,149,624	28.87	3,360,600	18.79	1,669,970	9.36	119,045
Dec. 28 ...	111	2,852,550	5,258,108	27.65	3,560,333	18.70	1,577,946	8.25	119,829
1887.									
Mar. 4....	121	3,019,568	4,961,765	24.65	3,418,756	16.98	1,421,601	7.06	121,408
May 13...	125	3,258,730	4,782,756	22.02	3,357,718	15.46	1,303,545	6.00	121,493
Aug. 1....	128	3,501,233	5,626,017	24.13	3,402,525	14.96	2,010,740	8.57	122,752
Oct. 5....	128	3,630,096	5,730,545	23.68	3,715,196	15.35	1,888,860	7.80	126,489
Dec. 7....	130	3,787,621	6,290,797	24.91	4,255,601	16.85	1,908,315	7.56	126,881
1888.									
Feb. 14...	131	3,779,467	5,791,312	22.98	3,874,586	15.38	1,787,096	7.09	129,630
Apr. 30...	130	3,824,435	5,935,373	23.28	3,887,931	15.25	1,919,790	7.53	127,652
June30...	130	3,972,189	6,292,050	23.76	3,871,153	14.63	2,289,557	8.65	129,360
Oct. 4....	132	4,461,321	7,758,182	26.08	4,241,947	14.26	3,386,255	11.39	129,940
Dec. 12 ...	131	4,552,960	7,853,939	25.88	4,599,390	15.15	3,124,805	10.29	129,744
1889.									
Feb. 26 ...	133	4,782,884	7,894,311	24.76	4,617,893	14.48	3,143,660	9.86	132,758
May 13...	138	5,050,912	8,813,862	26.18	4,829,576	14.34	3,847,235	11.43	137,051
July 12...	144	5,311,411	9,191,020	25.96	4,849,185	13.69	4,206,523	11.88	135,312
Sept.30...	151	5,928,263	10,555,490	26.71	4,778,295	12.09	5,633,344	14.25	143,851
Dec. 11 ...	152	6,001,950	9,742,120	24.35	5,648,649	24.12	3,942,902	9.85	150,569
1890.									
Feb. 28 ...	159	6,072,253	10,551,560	26.07	5,958,811	14.72	4,440,876	10.77	151,842
May 17...	166	6,366,800	10,108,136	23.81	5,760,189	13.57	4,188,093	9.87	159,854
July 18*..	174	6,567,112	10,813,892	24.77	5,911,199	13.50	4,760,076	10.87	172,617
Oct. 2†...	188	7,023,128	11,958,489	25.54	6,157,780	13.15	5,614,817	11.99	185,842
Dec. 19 ...	198	6,766,459	10,652,105	23.61	6,667,228	14.78	3,793,564	8.41	191,313
1891.									
Feb. 26 ...	203	6,598,191	11,364,659	25.84	6,748,401	15.34	4,414,375	10.04	201,880
May 4....	210	6,678,807	11,160,782	25.07	6,452,075	14.49	4,502,293	10.11	206,414
July 9....	216	6,689,079	10,878,920	24.40	6,181,605	13.86	4,488,131	10.06	209,184
Sept.25...	224	6,891,169	12,033,371	26.20	6,036,951	13.13	5,790,699	12.60	215,721
Dec. 2 ...	226	7,229,641	13,344,276	27.69	6,841,534	14.19	6,279,127	13.03	223,615
1892.									
Mar. 1....	227	7,230,593	13,161,123	27.31	6,819,040	14.15	6,120,218	12.70	224,865
May 17...	234	7,411,511	13,815,371	27.96	7,279,974	11.73	6,306,427	12.76	228,970
July 12...	237	7,873,909	14,409,298	27.45	7,035,463	13.40	7,143,404	13.61	230,431
Sept.30...	240	8,209,517	15,860,840	28.80	7,179,884	13.04	8,446,721	15.34	234,235
Dec. 9....	242	8,243,692	14,289,922	26.00	7,846,416	14.28	6,204,449	11.29	239,057
1893.									
Mar. 6 ...	246	7,876,561	13,031,248	24.82	7,633,693	14.54	5,160,596	9.83	236,959
May 4 ...	248	7,763,764	11,539,126	22.29	6,773,232	13.09	4,525,880	8.74	240,014
July 12 ...	233	6,217,700	9,729,507	23.47	6,525,046	15.74	2,983,012	7.20	221,444
Oct. 3....	217	4,620,530	8,831,805	28.67	5,869,298	19.05	2,760,584	8.96	201,023

*Oklahoma included from July 18, 1890.   † Indian Territory included from Oct. 2, 1890.

TABLE SHOWING, BY GEOGRAPHICAL DIVISIONS, THE RESERVE CITIES, THE NUMBER OF BANKS IN OPERATION, ETC.—Continued.

[Division No. 9.—Reserve cities—Chicago, St. Louis, Boston, Albany, Brooklyn, Philadelphia, Pittsburg, Baltimore, Washington, New Orleans, Louisville, Cincinnati, Cleveland, Detroit, Milwaukee, Des Moines, St. Paul, Minneapolis, Kansas City, St. Joseph, Lincoln, Omaha, and San Francisco.]

Dates.	No. of banks	Amount of reserve required, 25 per cent of net deposits.	Reserve held.		Classification of reserve held.					
			Amount.	Ratio.	Lawful money (12½ per cent).		With reserve agents (12½ per cent).		Five per cent redemption fund.
					Amount.	Ratio.	Amount.	Ratio.	
1884.				*Per ct.*		*Per ct.*		*Per ct.*	
Mar. 7....	202	$85,297,501	$111,255,631	32.61	$61,563,512	18.04	$46,437,308	13.61	$3,254,811
Apr. 24...	202	84,514,593	104,165,958	30.81	62,160,250	18.39	38,827,197	11.49	3,178,511
June 20 ..	204	75,708,561	91,103,676	30.08	59,623,045	19.69	28,403,338	9.38	3,077,293
Sept. 30...	203	76,984,342	99,022,475	32.16	63,578,992	20.65	32,340,900	10.50	3,102,583
Dec. 20 ...	203	78,739,375	103,685,153	32.92	66,011.790	20.96	34,672,781	11.01	3,000,582
1885.									
Mar. 10...	202	83,462,537	118,522,306	35.50	74,383,404	22.28	41,172,443	12.33	2,966,459
May 6....	202	86,628,766	123,962,577	35.77	80,109,098	23.12	40,912,049	11.81	2,941,430
July 1....	202	80,118,594	123,423,045	34.62	79,828,139	22.30	40,661,809	11.41	2,933,097
Oct. 1.....	203	91,118,639	122,186,751	33.52	76,907,632	21.10	42,402,600	11.63	2,876,510
Dec. 24 ...	202	91,151,185	117,043,608	32.11	74,674,927	20.48	39,551,479	10.88	2,817,202
1886.									
Mar. 1....	205	94,506,304	124,034,337	32.81	77,446,730	20.49	43,904,247	11.61	2,683,357
June 3 ...	212	96,810,237	122,784,157	31.71	80,738,933	20.85	39,507,423	10.22	2,477,801
Aug. 27...	215	93,802,959	110,584,456	29.42	68,232,506	18.19	40,072,689	10.68	2,279,261
Oct. 7.....	217	95,363,719	113,951,757	29.88	70,489,135	18.48	41,271,509	10.82	2,191,113
Dec. 28 ...	218	94,305,102	112,821,235	29.91	70,683,785	18.72	40,371,942	10.70	1,815,508
1887.									
Mar. 4....	220	99,518,660	124,447,510	31.26	73,631,556	18.50	49,217,253	12.36	1,598,701
May 13*...	210	86,270,869	106,121,301	30.75	64,496,954	18.69	40,210,839	11.65	1,413,508
Aug. 11...	221	83,889,166	98,389,074	29.32	59,504,534	17.73	37,672,349	11.23	1,213,010
Oct. 5.....	223	81,621,164	100,714,683	29.75	59,521,848	17.59	39,993,709	11.82	1,196,076
Dec. 7	223	84,031,602	97,132,024	28.90	58,086,213	17.28	37,957,340	11.29	1,088,471
1888.									
Feb. 14...	222	88,281,012	107,015,750	30.31	61,380,008	17.38	44,647,555	12.63	1,018,187
Apr. 30...	221	88,841,975	105,914,479	29.80	61,211,749	17.22	43,718,493	12.30	984,257
June 30..	224	93,119,904	113,366,426	30.44	66,493,977	17.85	45,940,662	12.34	955,472
Oct. 4.....	224	96,217,307	116,864,734	30.36	64,447,941	16.75	51,508,038	13.38	908,755
Dec. 12 ...	223	92,796,351	110,791,225	29.85	62,071,624	16.96	47,013,696	12.67	805,905
1889.									
Feb. 26 ...	223	100,132,732	129,178,251	32.25	66,585,765	16.62	61,860,599	15.44	731,887
May 13 ...	224	103,814,057	132,810,931	31.98	72,531,581	17.47	59,619,008	14.36	660,342
July 12...	226	106,953,841	131,366,446	30.71	71,388,356	16.69	59,343,308	13.87	634,702
Sept. 30...	228	101,752,379	121,912,119	29.10	64,592,017	15.42	50,712,959	13.51	607,143
Dec. 11 ...	229	99,449,783	112,113,813	28.18	63,330,689	15.92	48,173,145	12.09	609,079
1890.									
Feb. 28 ...	234	102,211,212	119,560,033	29.24	65,270,448	15.96	53,684,545	13.13	605,000
May 17...	239	106,243,919	122,780,265	28.80	66,575,944	15.67	55,566,943	13.08	647,378
July 18½..	250	115,477,384	131,308,097	28.43	71,778,457	15.54	58,806,133	12.73	723,507
Oct. 2.....	259	114,438,382	129,777,284	28.35	68,071,517	14.87	60,999,210	13.33	706,557
Dec. 19 ...	258	104,320,461	120,929,702	28.98	69,599,015	16.68	50,658,370	12.14	602,317
1891.									
Feb. 26 ...	260	109,081,974	133,621,929	30.17	74,395,392	17.05	56,569,349	12.96	695,246
May 4 ...	262	112,226,005	136,955,966	30.50	78,363,336	17.46	57,889,288	12.90	703,342
July 9§...	265	110,503,938	134,147,404	30.35	78,122,409	17.67	55,317,148	12.51	707,844
Sept. 25...	265	112,977,749	138,786,632	30.71	76,990,726	17.04	61,003,875	13.50	790,031
Dec. 2	264	112,935,945	142,314,957	31.50	76,766,567	16.99	64,710,249	14.32	838,141
1892.									
Mar. 1....	261	124,370,037	177,149,110	35.61	84,522,051	16.99	91,717,863	18.44	909,196
May 17...	262	130,145,842	184,027,948	35.35	97,255,972	18.68	85,825,510	16.49	946,466
July 12...	262	133,586,733	178,591,949	33.42	96,347,405	18.01	81,254,528	15.21	990,016
Sept. 30...	263	129,825,359	156,098,942	30.06	82,164,838	15.82	72,924,409	14.04	1,009,695
Dec. 9.....	265	123,799,238	142,005,438	28.68	77,869,593	15.72	63,099,335	12.74	1,036,510
1893.									
Mar. 6....	265	118,326,127	139,488,339	29.47	75,206,055	15.89	63,183,047	13.35	1,099,237
May 4 ¶..	269	116,908,521	133,535,121	28.56	78,843,637	16.86	53,553,912	11.45	1,137,572
July 12...	269	101,124,664	118,104,158	29.20	68,417,483	16.91	48,517,867	11.99	1,168,808
Oct. 3.....	268	98,151,349	129,588,769	33.01	70,427,655	19.47	51,570,537	13.14	1,590,577

* Kansas City and St. Joseph included from May 13, 1887, and Chicago and St. Louis transferred to division No. 10.

† Omaha included from August 1, 1887.

‡ Minneapolis, St. Paul, and Brooklyn included from July 18, 1890.

§ Des Moines included from July 9, 1891.

¶ Lincoln included from May 4, 1893.

TABLE SHOWING, BY GEOGRAPHICAL DIVISIONS, THE CENTRAL RESERVE CITIES, THE
NUMBER OF BANKS IN OPERATION, ETC.—Continued.

[Division No. 10.—Central reserve cities—New York, Chicago, and St. Louis.]

Dates.	New York City.			Chicago.			St. Louis.		
	No. of banks.	Amount of reserve required, 25 per cent of net deposits.	Ratio of reserve held.	No. of banks.	Amount of reserve required, 25 per cent of net deposits.	Ratio of reserve held.	No. of banks.	Amount of reserve required, 25 per cent of net deposits.	Ratio of reserve held.
1884.		Per ct.			Per ct.				Per ct.
Mar. 7	47	$75,373,069	28.94						
Apr. 24	47	70,540,863	26.65						
June 20	45	57,948,702	20.82						
Sept. 30	44	64,737,684	35.63						
Dec. 20	44	68,335,552	38.29						
1885.									
Mar. 10	44	73,191,705	40.12						
May 6	44	74,436,136	41.48						
July 1	45	78,181,211	42.47						
Oct. 1	44	78,214,626	36.98						
Dec. 24	45	75,516,839	32.76						
1886.									
Mar. 1	45	80,887,727	31.28						
June 3	45	71,187,977	30.28						
Aug. 27	45	70,386,879	27.46						
Oct. 7	45	70,607,561	27.24						
Dec. 28	45	73,607,025	29.89						
1887.									
Mar. 4	45	78,607,422	28.70						
May 13	46	74,921,637	27.64	18	$16,903,940	30.41	5	$2,280.864	36.40
Aug. 1	46	73,497,514	28.11	18	16,579,934	33.14	5	2,710,600	31.89
Oct. 5	47	71,084,776	28.18	18	16,161,735	30.53	5	2,574,207	26.44
Dec. 7	47	72,379,059	27.18	18	15,537,512	28.80	4	1,999,375	29.79
1888.									
Feb. 14	46	80,277,202	30.29	18	16,167,806	31.68	4	2,202.808	34.05
Apr. 30	46	79,168,388	29.93	18	17,822,500	29.75	4	2,177,175	40.11
June 30	46	81,608,091	30.34	19	17,961,506	31.37	4	2,217,845	42.10
Oct. 4	46	85,529,988	28.16	19	17,332,756	30.24	4	1,970,308	27.07
Dec. 12	46	82,630,532	29.12	19	16,056,945	30.88	4	2,020,493	28.90
1889.									
Feb. 26	45	91,060,618	28.72	19	16,813,643	33.60	4	2,013,392	42.12
May 13	45	90,257,718	28.73	19	18,564,211	35.50	4	1,885,147	46.75
July 12	45	80,801,522	27.08	19	19,411,765	31.79	5	2,812,114	40.95
Sept. 30	45	81,536,699	25.10	20	19,682,820	31.69	5	2,995,249	26.71
Dec. 11	46	79,476,706	26.99	20	18,500,455	30.29	5	2,979,311	24.80
1890.									
Feb. 28	46	84,259,377	26.17	20	19,020,602	30.17	7	5,670,384	28.57
May 17	46	89,585,344	26.39	20	21,248,980	31.01	8	6,494,906	25.03
July 18	47	81,702,359	27.05	19	21,034.078	29.09	8	6,800.814	24.42
Oct. 2	47	85,147,968	27.81	19	20,721,496	29.98	8	6,545,181	21.35
Dec. 19	47	75,113,249	28.11	19	18,398,815	31.42	8	5,679,210	24.28
1891.									
Feb. 26	47	84,503,622	28.91	20	19,713.708	32.77	8	6,048,537	24.49
May 4	47	81,835,203	26.96	20	23,491.723	33.88	8	6,248,857	24.40
July 9	49	82,571,595	29.93	20	22,913,151	31.02	9	5,913.094	23.78
Sept. 25	49	81,940,346	26.26	21	23,216,492	33.62	9	6,065,187	23.83
Dec. 2	49	88,258,830	28.69	21	22,112.475	31.53	9	5,878,877	27.32
1892.									
Mar. 1	49	109,948,706	29.31	22	24,426.854	33.45	9	6,701,065	28.34
May 17	48	109,335,717	29.23	22	27,847,903	33.01	9	6,961,804	28.36
July 12	48	106,122,173	29.36	22	28,594,133	29.77	9	6,868.505	23.61
Sept. 30	48	97,967,550	26.39	23	26,634,476	28.64	9	7,307,038	21.07
Dec. 9	48	90,338,433	26.89	23	25,124,297	30.07	9	6,639,856	21.60
1893.									
Mar. 6	48	90,009,093	26.34	23	25,249,086	28.03	9	7,238,137	23.39
May 4	49	86,253,700	28.52	21	24,896,048	29.45	9	6,940,925	21.43
July 12	49	76,107,584	25.30	21	20,343,433	30.61	9	4,970,519	22.60
Oct. 3	49	77,492,888	35.17	21	21,439,195	45.46	9	4,476,918	31.95

AVERAGE WEEKLY DEPOSITS, CIRCULATION, AND RESERVE OF THE NATIONAL
BANKS OF NEW YORK CITY, AS REPORTED TO THE NEW YORK CLEARING HOUSE,
FOR THE MONTHS GIVEN, IN THE YEARS 1887, 1888, 1889, 1890, 1891, 1892, AND
1893.

Week ended—	Liabilities.			Reserve.			
	Circulation.	Net deposits.	Total.	Specie.	Legal tenders.	Total.	Ratio to liabilities.
							Per cent.
Sept. 3, 1887	$8,112,000	$281,345,100	$289,457,100	$59,175,700	$18,786,100	$77,961,800	26.93
Sept. 10, 1887	8,115,000	279,915,600	288,031,200	58,851,300	17,769,000	76,620,300	26.40
Sept. 17, 1887	8,126,000	279,288,500	287,414,500	59,052,900	16,389,600	75,442,500	26.25
Sept. 24, 1887	8,235,300	278,573,000	286,808,300	60,635,900	16,259,600	76,895,500	26.81
Oct. 1, 1887	8,202,500	281,647,300	289,819,800	64,619,200	15,767,500	80,386,700	27.73
Oct. 8, 1887	8,186,800	285,703,700	293,890,500	64,317,500	16,269,700	80,587,200	27.42
Oct. 15, 1887	8,199,100	280,861,500	238,060,600	64,663,100	16,885,100	81,548,500	27.36
Oct. 22, 1887	8,216,200	289,542,800	297,759,000	64,918,700	16,735,800	81,651,500	27.42
Oct. 29, 1887	8,115,100	289,601,900	297,717,000	66,005,800	17,542,400	83,548,200	28.06
Nov. 5, 1887	8,046,100	289,951,700	298,030,800	64,639,800	17,810,700	82,450,500	27.07
Nov. 12 1887	8,033,700	288,289,700	296,323,400	63,791,600	18,070,800	81,862,400	27.63
Sept. 1, 1888	7,770,400	311,477,200	319,247,600	73,344,200	30,867,300	104,031,500	29.79
Sept. 8, 1888	7,850,400	336,495,600	344,346,000	69,844,500	28,797,600	98,642,100	28.65
Sept. 15, 1888	7,892,900	312,995,600	320,888,500	69,723,700	28,238,900	97,962,600	30.53
Sept. 22, 1888	7,927,700	333,959,700	341,887,400	70,051,900	26,320,600	96,375,500	28.02
Sept. 29, 1888	6,896,400	336,016,200	342,852,600	74,146,500	24,994,100	89,140,600	28.92
Oct. 6, 1888	6,515,300	349,506,800	356,022,100	74,411,300	23,204,300	97,615,600	27.42
Oct. 13, 1888	6,516,700	337,755,000	344,271,700	73,901,500	22,017,800	95,919,300	27.86
Oct. 20, 1888	6,488,700	343,953,000	350,441,700	81,457,700	21,386,600	102,844,500	29.35
Oct. 27, 1888	6,484,500	343,813,200	350,297,700	81,212,600	21,329,800	102,542,400	29.27
Nov. 3, 1888	6,363,200	343,587,300	349,950,500	80,140,200	21,703,800	101,841,000	29.10
Sept. 7, 1889	3,961,900	345,344,200	349,306,100	65,635,100	31,687,500	97,322,600	27.86
Sept. 14, 1889	3,978,100	346,601,000	350,574,100	63,824,300	30,527,100	94,351,400	26.91
Sept. 21, 1889	3,931,300	342,298,800	346,230,100	60,894,900	29,468,400	90,363,300	26.10
Sept. 28, 1889	3,945,500	340,542,700	344,488,200	60,375,900	28,933,700	89,309,600	25.93
Oct. 5, 1889	3,957,100	334,991,500	338,948,600	58,407,200	27,257,900	85,665,100	25.27
Oct. 12, 1889	3,943,900	323,923,400	333,867,300	59,565,900	24,873,400	84,439,300	25.29
Oct. 19, 1889	3,893,200	328,225,600	332,118,800	62,537,900	23,570,300	86,108,200	25.93
Oct. 26, 1889	4,037,400	325,328,100	329,365,500	62,403,200	22,715,200	85,118,400	25.84
Nov. 2, 1889	4,053,600	325,635,600	329,689,200	62,450,000	22,748,700	85,198,700	25.84
Nov. 9, 1889	3,991,200	320,166,700	324,157,900	61,240,500	20,416,800	81,657,300	25.19
Sept. 6, 1890	3,690,700	309,128,200	312,818,900	68,678,800	19,062,800	87,741,600	28.05
Sept. 13, 1890	3,700,100	304,626,200	308,326,300	56,963,600	19,146,500	76,110,100	24.68
Sept. 20, 1890	3,585,700	309,181,200	312,766,900	63,598,600	17,403,400	80,992,000	25.90
Sept. 27, 1890	3,479,300	324,335,300	327,814,600	79,205,500	16,692,300	95,897,800	29.25
Oct. 4, 1890	3,505,000	331,436,600	334,941,600	80,839,400	15,353,900	96,193,300	28.72
Oct. 11, 1890	3,521,300	325,794,800	329,316,100	73,148,900	14,436,700	87,585,600	26.60
Oct. 18, 1890	3,518,800	320,667,900	324,186,700	66,552,400	14,642,500	81,194,900	25.05
Oct. 25, 1890	3,497,200	317,395,500	320,892,700	65,680,500	15,611,800	81,292,300	25.33
Nov. 1, 1890	3,500,800	314,709,700	318,210,500	66,088,800	16,334,300	82,423,100	25.90
Nov. 8, 1890	3,493,500	309,975,100	313,468,600	62,360,900	15,517,400	77,878,300	24.84
Sept. 5, 1891	5,459,400	332,378,600	337,838,000	49,293,200	44,509,800	93,803,000	27.77
Sept. 12, 1891	5,527,000	332,578,000	338,105,000	51,750,700	41,488,500	93,239,200	27.58
Sept. 19, 1891	5,501,200	335,317,300	340,818,500	53,005,900	39,540,900	92,611,800	27.17
Sept. 26, 1891	5,567,700	333,004,000	338,571,700	52,824,200	35,676,300	88,500,500	26.14
Oct. 3, 1891	5,619,000	331,492,100	337,111,100	54,783,100	32,879,900	87,663,300	26.06
Oct. 10, 1891	5,629,100	332,294,100	337,923,200	59,731,800	30,905,700	90,637,500	26.82
Oct. 17, 1891	5,576,500	339,667,000	345,243,500	65,532,000	29,610,500	95,142,500	27.56
Oct. 24, 1891	5,573,400	341,023,400	346,596,400	69,327,700	27,347,300	96,675,000	27.89
Oct. 31, 1891	5,592,000	343,572,700	349,165,300	71,771,500	26,779,400	98,550,900	28.22
Nov. 7, 1891	5,587,400	345,411,300	350,998,700	71,728,600	23,665,800	95,394,400	27.18
Sept. 3, 1892	5,424,200	419,587,400	425,011,600	67,609,700	45,381,700	113,081,400	26.61
Sept. 10, 1892	5,530,800	414,929,500	420,460,300	66,210,100	44,185,600	110,395,700	26.26
Sept. 17, 1892	5,601,000	408,312,700	413,913,700	65,742,400	43,884,100	109,626,500	26.49
Sept. 24, 1892	5,612,600	399,038,400	404,651,000	63,667,200	43,760,700	107,427,900	26.55
Oct. 1, 1892	5,672,000	395,234,300	400,906,300	62,208,200	43,225,300	105,433,500	26.30
Oct. 8, 1892	5,573,900	390,012,300	395,586,200	62,137,500	39,862,800	102,000,300	25.78
Oct. 15, 1892	5,569,100	384,724,200	390,293,300	62,030,800	37,053,900	99,084,700	25.39
Oct. 22, 1892	5,608,800	378,739,600	384,348,400	61,205,200	39,529,900	90,735,100	25.89
Oct. 29, 1892	5,633,700	374,072,300	379,706,000	62,313,900	36,526,000	98,839,900	26.03
Nov. 5, 1892	5,650,800	371,530,500	377,181,300	62,274,600	34,685,500	96,960,100	25.71
Sept. 2, 1893	9,911,600	301,665,200	311,576,800	57,584,800	18,727,900	76,312,700	24.49
Sept. 9, 1893	11,200,400	299,816,400	311,025,800	59,174,600	20,345,900	79,520,500	25.56
Sept. 16, 1893	12,723,600	304,808,300	317,531,900	65,946,100	21,650,100	87,596,100	27.58
Sept. 23, 1893	13,610,300	310,368,900	323,979,200	67,942,900	27,048,100	91,991,000	28.32
Sept. 30, 1893	11,385,600	317,329,300	331,724,900	69,703,000	32,358,300	102,061,300	29.52
Oct. 7, 1893	14,940,000	325,891,300	340,831,300	72,369,000	35,435,000	107,804,000	30.76
Oct. 14, 1893	14,956,800	335,951,400	350,911,200	75,563,400	37,728,600	113,292,000	31.62
Oct. 21, 1893	11,699,500	344,672,800	356,363,300	79,564,100	37,728,600	122,462,000	32.28
Oct. 28, 1893	11,610,800	351,660,600	363,271,400	80,472,200	49,418,600	129,890,800	34.07
Nov. 4, 1893	14,409,900	365,638,100	380,048,000	81,118,200	54,757,600	135,875,800	35.75

TABLE SHOWING THE MOVEMENT OF THE RESERVE OF THE NATIONAL BANKS IN NEW YORK CITY DURING OCTOBER FOR THE LAST SIXTEEN YEARS.

Week ended—	Specie.	Legal tenders.	Total.	Ratio of reserve to— Circulation and deposits.	Deposits.
				Per cent.	Per cent.
October 5, 1878	$14,995,800	$38,304,900	$53,300,700	25.7	28.4
October 12, 1878	12,184,600	37,685,100	49,869,700	24.4	27.0
October 10, 1878	13,531,400	36,576,000	50,107,400	24.7	27.3
October 26, 1878	17,384,200	35,690,500	53,074,700	25.8	28.5
October 4, 1879	18,979,600	34,368,000	53,347,600	23.3	25.8
October 11, 1879	20,901,800	32,820,300	53,722,100	23.4	25.9
October 18, 1879	24,686,500	29,305,200	53,991,700	23.5	26.1
October 25, 1879	25,636,000	26,713,900	52,349,000	23.0	25.5
October 2, 1880	59,823,700	11,129,100	70,952,800	25.4	26.4
October 9, 1880	62,521,300	10,785,000	73,306,300	25.4	27.2
October 16, 1880	62,760,600	10,939,200	73,699,800	25.5	27.1
October 23, 1880	60,888,200	10,988,200	71,876,400	24.8	26.6
October 30, 1880	61,471,600	10,925,000	72,396,600	25.0	26.7
October 1, 1881	54,954,600	12,150,400	67,105,000	23.1	24.6
October 8, 1881	53,287,900	12,153,800	65,441,700	23.1	24.8
October 15, 1881	51,008,300	12,452,700	63,461,000	23.2	25.9
October 22, 1881	54,016,200	12,496,500	66,512,700	24.6	26.6
October 29, 1881	55,961,300	12,047,900	68,909,100	25.6	27.0
October 7, 1882	47,016,000	18,381,500	65,400,500	24.0	26.4
October 14, 1882	48,281,000	18,002,700	66,283,700	24.7	26.3
October 21, 1882	49,518,200	17,023,900	66,542,100	25.0	26.8
October 28, 1882	48,374,300	17,204,700	65,578,900	24.8	26.5
October 6, 1883	51,586,700	20,122,500	71,709,200	25.5	27.0
October 13, 1883	50,894,000	21,145,800	72,039,800	25.4	26.8
October 20, 1883	47,262,900	20,719,700	67,982,600	24.5	25.9
October 27, 1883	46,372,800	20,617,600	66,990,400	24.5	25.9
October 4, 1884	67,470,600	25,817,300	93,287,900	34.5	36.3
October 11, 1884	68,922,500	27,654,100	96,576,600	35.2	36.9
October 18, 1884	67,579,400	27,875,500	95,454,900	34.8	36.5
October 25, 1884	67,638,000	27,354,200	94,992,200	34.6	36.3
October 3, 1885	92,351,600	24,516,600	116,868,200	36.0	37.1
October 10, 1885	93,612,500	23,002,000	116,614,500	35.8	37.0
October 17, 1885	91,945,300	22,221,100	114,166,400	34.9	36.0
October 24, 1885	87,309,100	21,059,800	108,368,900	33.5	34.5
October 30, 1885	84,954,600	21,874,900	106,829,500	33.0	34.1
October 2, 1886	64,111,700	14,607,700	78,719,400	27.1	27.9
October 9, 1886	65,723,800	13,209,100	78,932,900	27.0	27.7
October 16, 1886	65,228,600	13,133,100	78,361,700	26.7	27.4
October 23, 1886	65,668,400	12,803,800	78,472,200	26.9	27.7
October 30, 1886	66,195,100	13,177,200	79,372,300	27.1	27.9
October 1, 1887	64,619,200	15,767,500	80,386,700	27.7	28.5
October 8, 1887	64,317,500	16,229,700	80,587,200	27.4	28.2
October 15, 1887	64,663,100	16,885,400	81,548,500	27.3	28.1
October 22, 1887	64,918,700	16,735,500	81,654,500	27.4	28.2
October 29, 1887	66,005,800	17,542,600	82,848,400	27.8	28.6
October 6, 1888	74,411,300	23,204,300	97,615,600	27.4	27.9
October 13, 1888	73,901,500	23,017,800	95,919,300	27.8	28.4
October 20, 1888	81,457,700	21,386,800	102,844,500	29.3	29.9
October 27, 1888	81,212,600	21,329,800	102,542,400	29.3	29.8
October 5, 1889	58,407,200	27,247,900	85,655,100	25.3	25.6
October 12, 1889	59,565,900	24,873,400	84,439,300	25.3	25.6
October 19, 1889	62,537,000	23,570,900	86,198,200	25.9	26.2
October 26, 1889	62,403,200	22,715,200	85,118,400	25.8	26.2
October 4, 1890	80,839,400	15,353,900	96,193,300	28.7	29.0
October 11, 1890	73,148,900	14,436,700	87,585,600	26.6	26.9
October 18, 1890	66,552,400	14,642,500	81,194,900	25.0	25.3
October 25, 1890	65,680,500	15,611,800	81,292,300	25.3	25.6
October 3, 1891	54,783,400	32,879,900	87,663,300	26.0	26.4
October 10, 1891	59,731,800	30,905,700	90,637,500	26.8	27.3
October 17, 1891	65,532,000	29,610,500	95,142,500	27.6	28.0
October 24, 1891	69,327,700	27,347,300	90,675,000	27.9	28.3
October 31, 1891	71,771,500	26,779,400	98,550,900	28.2	28.7
October 1, 1892	62,208,200	43,225,300	105,433,500	26.3	26.7
October 8, 1892	62,137,500	39,862,800	102,000,300	25.8	26.1
October 15, 1892	62,030,900	37,053,900	99,084,700	25.4	25.5
October 22, 1892	61,205,200	38,529,900	99,735,100	25.9	26.3
October 29, 1892	62,311,900	36,526,600	98,839,000	26.0	26.4
October 7, 1893	72,369,000	35,435,000	107,804,000	31.6	33.1
October 14, 1893	75,563,400	37,728,600	113,292,060	32.3	33.7
October 21, 1893	79,504,100	42,957,900	122,462,000	34.1	35.5
October 28, 1893	80,472,200	49,418,600	129,890,800	35.2	36.6

ABSTRACT OF REPORTS OF EARNINGS AND DIVIDENDS

FROM SEPTEMBER 1, 1892,

	States, reserve cities, and Territories.	No. of banks.	Capital stock.	Surplus.	Capital and surplus.	Gross earnings.
1	Maine....................	81	$11,060,000.00	$2,704.920.00	$13,764,920.00	$808,033.29
2	New Hampshire..........	54	6,320,000.00	1,600,180.20	7,920.180.20	531,062.40
3	Vermont	49	7,160,000.00	1,861,900.00	9,021,900.00	546,157.15
4	Massachusetts	211	45,967,500.00	15,613,577.71	61,581,077.71	3,730,763.76
5	Boston..................	55	53,100,000.00	14,336,557.74	67,436,557.74	3,564,256.30
6	Rhode Island...........	59	20,277,050.00	5,430,728.07	25,707,778.07	1,124,191.86
7	Connecticut............	84	22,009,370.00	7,678,539.74	30,077,909.74	1,768,860.72
	Division No. 1......	593	166,883,920.00	49,226,403.46	216,110,323.46	12,073,277.48
8	New York	267	33,346,460.00	11,193,385.63	44,539,845.63	3,879,706.48
9	New York City	48	49,650,000.00	40,756,964.14	90,406,964.14	9,258,023.07
10	Albany	6	1,550,000.00	1,285,000.00	2,835,000.00	400,471.22
11	Brooklyn............	5	1,352,000.00	2,082,000.00	3,434,000.00	330,386.58
12	New Jersey	98	14,568,350.00	7,251.418.68	21,819,768.68	1,993,360.80
13	Pennsylvania	308	37,772,390.00	17,132,131.81	54,904,521.81	4,129,563.34
14	Philadelphia	41	22,465.000.00	14,106,303.08	36,571,303.08	2,729,449.82
15	Pittsburg	26	10,900,000.00	7,045,612.19	17,945,612.19	1,368,842.31
	Division No. 2......	799	171,604,200.00	100,852,815.53	272,457,015.53	23,999,803.62
16	Delaware...............	18	2,133,985.00	1,007,926.12	3,141,911.12	207,105.60
17	Maryland	44	3,611,700.00	1,345,771.98	4,957,471.98	417,566.88
18	Baltimore	22	13,243,260.00	4,526,900.00	17,770,160.00	1,023,185.66
19	District of Columbia	1	252,000.00	100,000.00	352,000.00	31,092.15
20	Washington............	12	2,575,000.00	1,235,000.00	3,810,000.00	316,209.76
21	Virginia	36	4,696,300.00	2,557,600.00	7,253,900.00	649,480.03
22	West Virginia	28	2,811,000.00	727,003.18	3,538,033.18	323,899.16
	Division No. 3......	161	29,323,245.00	11,500,231.28	40,823,476.28	2,962,548.24
23	North Carolina...........	23	2,626,000.00	766,127.31	3,392,127.31	253,807.38
24	South Carolina	14	1,623,000.00	829,100.00	2,452,100.00	220,959.39
25	Georgia	32	4,541,000.00	1,223,580.42	5,764,580.42	443,741.40
26	Florida.................	19	1,450,000.00	293,000.00	1,743,000.00	250,078.82
27	Alabama	29	3,919,000.00	983,180.09	4,902,180.09	348,604.32
28	Mississippi.............	13	1,115,000.00	456,859.36	1,571,859.36	134,355.10
29	Louisiana	11	810,000.00	254,252.42	1,064,252.42	109,508.20
30	New Orleans	10	3,625,000.00	2,088,085.81	5,713,985.81	644,001.42
31	Texas	222	25,880,000.00	4,900,697.60	30,780,697.60	2,968,045.45
32	Arkansas	10	1,600,000.00	496,250.00	2,096,250.00	162,458.00
33	Kentucky...............	72	10,597,900.00	2,832,561.12	13,430,461.12	919,553.11
34	Louisville.............	10	4,901,500.00	1,023,800.00	5,925,300.00	350,049.83
35	Tennessee..............	55	10,639,240.00	2,222,359.19	12,861,599.19	935,982.03
	Division No. 4......	520	73,327,640.00	18,379,753.32	91,707,393.32	7,750,145.35

OF NATIONAL BANKS IN THE UNITED STATES.

TO MARCH 1, 1893.

Charged off.		Net earnings.	Dividends.	Ratios.			
Losses and premiums.	Expenses and taxes.			Net earnings to capital and surplus.	Dividends to capital and surplus.	Dividends to capital.	
				Per cent.	Per cent.	Per cent.	
$173,665.61	$208,645.77	$425,721.91	$418,975.00	3.09	3.04	3.79	1
90,472.44	173,013.35	267,576.64	231,700.00	3.38	2.93	3.67	2
129,082.29	173,271.83	243,803.03	250,500.00	2.70	2.78	3.50	3
550,600.20	1,424,356.63	1,755,746.93	1,557,206.68	2.85	2.53	3.39	4
376,779.32	1,454,391.42	1,733,085.56	1,415,250.00	2.57	2.10	2.67	5
130,024.10	264,227.14	729,943.62	518,197.25	2.84	2.02	2.56	6
218,311.90	469,272.32	1,081,285.50	873,375.00	3.52	2.85	3.80	7
1,668,935.86	4,167,178.46	6,237,163.16	5,265,293.93	2.89	2.44	3.75	
515,236.80	1,486,775.26	1,877,694.42	1,261,823.98	4.22	2.83	3.78	8
857,003.24	4,509,537.57	3,891,482.26	2,423,132.76	4.30	2.68	4.88	9
89,616.16	161,823.54	149,031.52	199,851.20	5.26	7.05	12.89	10
17,411.16	142,141.00	170,834.42	92,112.00	4.07	2.68	6.83	11
231,700.75	656,553.86	1,015,106.19	723,347.00	4.65	3.32	4.97	12
723,868.74	1,237,865.74	2,167,828.86	1,311,851.10	3.95	2.39	3.47	13
327,035.14	1,020,686.63	1,381,428.05	805,950.00	3.78	2.20	3.59	14
171,790.71	458,067.26	738,984.34	420,000.00	4.12	2.34	3.85	15
2,933,662.70	9,673,750.86	11,392,390.06	7,258,048.04	4.18	2.66	4.92	
14,882.03	64,334.51	127,889.06	103,202.82	4.07	3.28	4.84	16
44,902.26	181,079.42	191,585.20	139,194.71	3.86	2.81	3.86	17
62,320.06	329,958.46	630,937.14	456,558.30	3.55	2.57	3.45	18
5,000.00	9,866.61	16,225.54	10,080.00	4.61	2.86	4.00	19
25,887.89	141,736.56	142,583.31	72,500.00	3.74	1.90	2.82	20
55,265.70	261,495.44	332,727.80	183,505.00	4.59	2.53	3.91	21
40,549.52	121,503.22	161,846.42	98,290.00	4.57	2.78	3.50	22
248,807.55	1,100,974.22	1,603,766.47	1,063,390.83	3.93	2.61	3.63	
16,623.84	99,725.26	137,458.28	105,330.00	4.05	3.11	4.01	23
88,208.70	123,631.07	9,719.62	185,120.00	0.40	7.55	11.41	24
102,056.92	230,376.37	111,508.11	146,300.00	1.93	2.54	3.22	25
13,924.25	119,423.89	116,730.68	45,500.00	6.09	2.61	3.14	26
89,065.76	173,053.35	86,485.21	136,235.00	1.76	2.78	3.48	27
10,914.25	71,972.31	51,468.54	47,650.00	3.27	3.03	4.03	28
6,738.08	47,364.49	55,405.63	35,400.00	5.21	3.33	4.37	29
122,231.29	286,221.12	235,518.71	158,000.00	4.12	2.77	4.36	30
596,485.22	1,093,137.79	1,278,422.44	1,201,148.67	4.15	3.91	4.65	31
36,158.31	60,438.91	65,861.68	68,000.00	3.14	3.24	4.25	32
158,041.42	298,907.05	462,604.64	405,315.00	3.44	3.02	3.82	33
34,232.78	134,960.40	189,856.65	158,500.00	3.20	2.67	3.23	34
129,864.98	401,407.47	410,709.58	386,462.00	3.19	3.00	3.63	35
1,395,545.80	3,143,019.78	3,211,579.77	3,081,960.67	3.50	3.36	4.20	

ABSTRACT OF REPORTS OF EARNINGS AND DIVIDENDS OF

FROM SEPTEMBER 1, 1892,

	States, reserve cities, and Territories.	No. of banks.	Capital stock.	Surplus.	Capital and surplus.	Gross earnings.
36	Ohio	213	$26,883,100.00	$7,491,626.89	$34,324,726.89	$2,890,376.84
37	Cincinnati	13	9,100,000.00	2,700,000.00	11,800,000.00	1,011,208.82
38	Cleveland	11	8,050,000.00	1,777,500.00	9,827,500.00	663,286.25
39	Indiana	108	13,567,660.00	4,755,662.20	18,323,322.20	1,652,107.24
40	Illinois	188	17,556,000.00	6,353,166.69	23,906,166.69	2,131,163.51
41	Chicago	22	22,900,000.00	11,316,300.00	34,216,300.00	3,202,027.72
42	Michigan	95	10,469,000.00	3,169,907.39	13,638,907.39	1,224,287.02
43	Detroit	8	4,400,000.00	666,000.00	5,066,000.00	557,514.02
44	Wisconsin	73	6,670,000.00	2,031,414.02	8,701,414.02	1,026,461.37
45	Milwaukee	3	625,000.00	475,000.00	1,100,000.00	197,689.79
	Division No. 5	734	120,170,760.00	40,733,577.19	160,904,337.19	14,556,122.58
46	Iowa	153	13,940,000.00	3,069,208.27	17,009,208.27	1,485,432.56
47	Des Moines	4	700,000.00	313,000.00	1,013,000.00	105,883.36
48	Minnesota	60	5,740,310.00	1,114,590.58	6,854,900.58	743,800.94
49	St. Paul	5	4,800,000.00	1,326,000.00	6,126,000.00	518,401.29
50	Minneapolis	7	5,450,000.00	650,000.00	6,100,000.00	693,929.31
51	Missouri	57	4,590,000.00	793,503.35	5,383,503.35	472,959.09
52	St. Louis	9	10,700,000.00	1,796,707.96	12,496,707.96	1,069,907.86
53	Kansas City	10	6,800,000.00	725,600.00	7,525,600.00	704,782.06
54	St. Joseph	4	2,000,000.00	220,000.00	2,220,000.00	182,138.62
55	Kansas	139	12,342,100.00	1,806,081.17	14,148,181.17	1,413,751.52
56	Nebraska	125	8,820,200.00	1,702,911.44	10,523,141.44	1,146,800.00
57	Omaha	9	4,000,000.00	477,400.00	4,477,400.00	588,206.89
58	Lincoln *					
	Division No. 6	582	70,882,610.00	13,995,122.77	93,877,732.77	9,035,993.50
59	Colorado	53	9,100,000.00	2,366,306.81	11,466,306.81	1,559,358.51
60	Nevada	2	282,000.00	128,000.00	410,000.00	44,409.29
61	California	34	5,675,000.00	1,175,043.00	6,850,043.00	632,418.09
62	San Francisco	2	2,500,000.00	1,075,000.03	3,575,000.00	269,025.87
63	Oregon	41	3,995,000.00	917,000.00	4,912,000.00	568,843.51
64	Arizona	4	300,000.00	36,360.89	336,360.89	57,041.65
	Division No. 7	136	21,852,000.00	5,697,710.70	27,549,710.70	3,131,096.92
65	North Dakota	33	2,465,000.00	535,018.65	3,000,018.65	417,741.73
66	South Dakota	40	2,610,000.00	644,825.00	3,254,825.00	349,635.62
67	Idaho	9	625,000.00	213,000.00	838,000.00	141,136.58
68	Montana	34	4,740,000.00	774,083.90	5,514,083.90	816,906.02
69	New Mexico	11	925,000.00	199,556.74	1,121,556.74	135,792.11
70	Oklahoma	4	200,000.00	15,000.00	215,000.00	41,573.88
71	Indian Territory	6	360,000.00	27,100.00	387,100.00	42,984.96
72	Utah	14	2,800,000.00	968,800.00	3,768,800.00	280,596.62
73	Wyoming	13	1,210,000.00	206,550.00	1,416,550.00	135,424.96
74	Washington	70	7,895,000.00	1,744,889.66	9,639,889.66	906,862.79
	Division No. 8	234	23,830,000.00	5,328,823.95	29,158,823.95	3,358,645.27
	United States	3,759	686,874,375.00	245,714,438.20	932,588,813.20	76,867,632.96

* Included in State of Nebraska.

NATIONAL BANKS IN THE UNITED STATES—Continued.

TO MARCH 1, 1893.

Charged off.		Net earnings.	Dividends.	Ratios.			
Losses and premiums.	Expenses and taxes.			Net earnings to capital and surplus.	Dividends to capital and surplus.	Dividends to capital.	
				Per cent.	*Per cent.*	*Per cent.*	
$252,409.82	$1,054,496.72	$1,583,470.30	$984,060.02	4.61	2.86	3.67	36
65,640.83	388,436.97	557,119.02	345,500.00	4.72	2.93	3.80	37
51,990.88	205,989.27	345,306.10	261,500.00	3.51	2.66	3.25	38
187,205.64	634,927.92	829,884.68	575,435.00	4.53	3.14	4.24	39
162,826.88	735,256.37	1,233,080.26	784,589.96	5.16	3.28	4.47	40
432,654.99	1,396,646.02	1,372,726.71	857,000.00	4.01	2.50	3.74	41
160,756.99	511,254.97	543,275.06	516,812.28	3.98	3.81	4.97	42
40,492.16	342,660.04	174,361.82	126,000.00	3.44	2.49	2.86	43
75,378.65	384,209.83	566,872.89	418,356.75	6.51	4.80	6.27	44
22,210.22	119,021.33	56,458.24	48,000.00	5.13	4.36	7.08	45
1,460,666.06	5,832,902.14	7,262,554.08	4,917,254.01	4.51	3.06	4.09	
141,637.84	607,011.54	736,783.18	589,750.00	4.33	3.47	4.23	46
14,934.62	36,057.75	54,800.99	34,000.00	5.42	3.36	4.86	47
119,100.27	272,821.26	351,870.41	316,925.00	5.13	4.62	5.52	48
64,438.65	125,716.30	328,246.34	225,000.00	5.36	3.67	4.60	49
173,048.62	147,306.73	282,673.96	162,500.00	4.63	2.66	2.98	50
40,911.00	208,589.89	223,458.20	184,068.28	4.15	3.42	4.01	51
68,119.11	518,078.29	454,710.46	261,000.00	3.63	2.09	2.44	52
256,887.83	377,678.68	70,215.55	118,375.00	0.93	1.57	1.74	53
49,932.76	63,393.94	62,811.92	66,000.00	2.83	2.97	3.30	54
355,217.03	601,653.46	456,881.03	374,073.50	2.23	2.64	3.03	55
160,963.47	498,087.96	487,748.37	385,978.59	4.64	3.67	4.38	56
129,406.34	359,226.74	99,573.84	85,000.00	2.22	1.90	2.13	57
							58
1,575,506.54	3,851,592.51	3,608,834.45	2,842,670.37	3.84	2.99	3.51	
260,368.27	668,084.62	630,905.62	429,750.00	5.50	3.75	4.72	59
1,148.93	17,743.35	25,517.01	17,460.00	6.22	4.26	6.19	60
249,055.94	253,364.22	129,937.93	281,500.00	1.90	4.11	4.96	61
9,224.74	69,744.85	191,056.28	115,000.00	5.32	3.22	4.60	62
67,156.21	190,953.63	310,733.67	207,133.10	6.33	4.22	5.18	63
2,332.21	17,987.80	36,721.64	19,000.00	10.92	5.65	6.83	64
589,286.30	1,217,878.47	1,323,932.15	1,069,843.10	4.81	3.81	4.90	
75,295.23	140,582.46	201,854.04	134,700.00	6.73	4.49	5.46	65
60,325.20	151,808.78	137,501.64	98,050.00	4.22	3.01	3.76	66
4,897.23	55,232.67	81,006.08	49,000.00	9.07	5.85	7.84	67
172,906.92	383,858.22	260,140.88	180,250.00	4.72	3.27	3.80	68
15,102.49	69,187.02	51,502.60	21,750.00	4.58	1.93	2.35	69
7,295.09	13,202.67	21,076.12	7,500.00	9.80	3.49	3.75	70
392.84	14,482.46	28,109.66	9,000.00	7.26	2.56	2.75	71
9,824.34	123,410.93	147,361.35	123,500.00	3.91	3.28	4.41	72
37,138.14	69,860.75	28,426.07	34,350.00	2.01	2.42	2.84	73
75,367.44	427,045.81	494,449.54	376,750.00	5.13	3.91	4.77	74
458,544.92	1,448,671.77	1,451,428.58	1,035,750.00	4.98	3.55	4.35	
10,330,955.73	30,444,968.51	36,091,708.72	26,474,210.95	3.87	2.84	3.85	

ABSTRACT OF REPORTS OF EARNINGS AND DIVIDENDS

FROM MARCH 1, 1893,

	States, reserve cities, and Territories.	No. of banks.	Capital stock.	Surplus.	Capital and surplus.	Gross earnings.
1	Maine	82	$11,160,000.00	$2,717,441.87	$13,877,441.87	$812,815.52
2	New Hampshire	53	6,370,000.00	1,570,409.83	7,940,409.83	545,745.72
3	Vermont	48	7,010,000.00	1,825,250.00	8,835,250.00	510,525.65
4	Massachusetts	213	45,967,500.00	15,598,607.66	61,566,107.66	3,709,285.93
5	Boston	55	53,100,000.00	14,762,100.00	67,862,100.00	3,785,201.02
6	Rhode Island	59	20,277,050.00	5,086,019.62	25,363,069.62	1,213,748.97
7	Connecticut	84	22,500,370.00	7,770,977.35	30,370,347.35	1,751,894.58
	Division No. 1	504	166,483,920.00	49,330,806.33	215,814,726.33	12,349,217.39
8	New York	268	33,244,060.00	11,413,780.21	44,657,840.21	3,890,759.51
9	New York City	47	49,350,000.00	41,272,289.09	90,622,289.00	9,291,462.23
10	Albany	6	1,550,000.00	1.290,000.00	2,840,000.00	261,222.85
11	Brooklyn	5	1,352,000.00	2,000,000.00	3,442,000.00	510,050.16
12	New Jersey	99	14,603,350.00	7,416,766.61	22,020,116.61	1,934,717.98
13	Pennsylvania	318	38,564,868.00	17,672,306.00	56,237,174.00	4,357,663.29
14	Philadelphia	41	22,765,000.00	14,306,503.08	37,071,503.08	2,624,118.16
15	Pittsburg	27	11,100,000.00	7,218,528.09	18,318,528.09	1,280,360,97
	Division No. 2	811	172,529,278.00	102,680,173.00	275,209,451.08	23,977,375.15
16	Delaware	18	2,808,985.00	953,996.47	3,762,981.47	200,790.15
17	Maryland	44	3,611,700.00	1,377,350.00	4,989,050.00	389,439.04
18	Baltimore	22	13,243,260.00	4,505,312.60	17,748,572.60	1,039,721.61
19	District of Columbia	1	252,000.00	100,000.00	352,000.00	32,133.98
20	Washington	12	2,575,000.00	1,305,000.00	3,880,000.00	304,324.96
21	Virginia	36	4.796,300.00	2,624,200.00	7,420,500.00	613,232.04
22	West Virginia	30	2,951,000.00	764,672.00	3,715,672.00	293,671.67
	Division No. 3	163	30,238,245.00	11,630,531.07	41,868,776.07	2,873,313.45
23	North Carolina	23	2,626,000.00	729,559.38	3,355,559.38	249,835.52
24	South Carolina	14	1,748,000.00	840,000.00	2,588,000.00	304,755.59
25	Georgia	28	4,016,000.00	1,090,653.12	5,106,653.12	416,843.72
26	Florida	18	1,450,000.00	286,411.00	1,736,411.00	281,177.56
27	Alabama	28	3,769,000.00	972,457.50	4,741,457.50	368,456.65
28	Mississippi	12	1,055,000.00	456,750.00	1,511,750.00	162,979.12
29	Louisiana	11	810,000.00	289,943.72	1,099,943.72	148,231.28
30	New Orleans	9	3,125,000.00	2,206,000.00	5,331,000.00	723,878.83
31	Texas	220	24,870,500.00	5,016,689.50	29,887,189.50	2,758,882.03
32	Arkansas	9	1,100,000.00	380,250.00	1,480,250.00	136,616.13
33	Kentucky	72	10,157,900.00	2,831,018.64	12,988,918.64	939,788.81
34	Louisville	10	4,901,500.00	1,030,300.00	5,931,800.00	356,174.33
35	Tennessee	54	9,647,300.00	2,119,362.95	11,766,662.95	890,550.23
	Division No. 4	508	69,276,200.00	18,249,995.81	87,526,195.81	7,747,278.80
36	Ohio	207	27,185,100.00	7,681,158.69	34,866,258.69	2,815,143.16
37	Cincinnati	13	9,100,000.00	2,745,000.00	11,845,000.00	913,146.51
38	Cleveland	11	9,050,000.00	1,800,000.00	10,850,000.00	731,813.53
39	Indiana	113	13,997,000.00	4,813,822.97	18,810,822.97	1,669,355.48
40	Illinois	187	16,946,000.00	6,301,805.58	23,247,805.58	2,111,906.93
41	Chicago	21	20,900,000.00	11,522,700.00	32,422,700.00	2,963,141.32
42	Michigan	94	10,379,000.00	3,166,849.31	13,545,849.31	1,179,751.96
43	Detroit	8	4,400,000.00	677,000.00	5,077,000.00	572,370.28
44	Wisconsin	74	6,895,000.00	2,070,849.02	8,965,849.02	922,707.65
45	Milwaukee	5	1,250,000.00	475,000.00	1,725,000.00	284,735.39
	Division No. 5	733	120.102,100.00	41,254,185.57	161,356,285.57	14,139,102.21

OF NATIONAL BANKS IN THE UNITED STATES—Continued.

TO SEPTEMBER 1, 1893.

Charged off.		Net earnings.	Dividends.	Ratios.			
Losses and premiums.	Expenses and taxes.			Net earnings to capital and surplus.	Dividends to capital and surplus.	Dividends to capital.	
				Per cent.	*Per cent.*	*Per cent.*	
$182,171.49	$211,425.30	$439,218.73	$409,600.00	3.16	2.95	3.67	1
139,415.43	180,439.04	225,801.25	215,300.00	2.84	2.71	3.38	2
133,441.64	170,899.07	206,184.94	216,625.00	2.33	2.45	3.09	3
682,524.00	1,228,392.29	1,708,369.64	1,483,013.23	2.92	2.41	3.23	4
414,656.85	1,595,844.89	1,774,699.28	1,471,000.00	2.62	2.17	2.77	5
311,897.98	271,272.70	630,638.29	609,722.25	2.49	2.37	2.96	6
255,369.92	477,760.87	1,018,763.79	828,982.00				7
2,119,417.31	4,136,034.16	6,093,765.92	5,225,242.48	2.82	2.42	3.14	
759,144.36	1,536,470.85	1,595,144.36	1,202,310.13	3.57	2.69	3.62	8
1,241,603.01	4,008,807.36	4,041,051.86	2,438,220.00	4.46	2.69	4.94	9
16,848.44	128,243.59	116,130.82	60,346.00	4.09	2.12	3.89	10
31,908.49	153,895.70	142,267.97	91,860.00	4.13	2.67	6.79	11
298,760.41	628,718.55	1,007,239.02	670,647.00	4.57	3.05	4.59	12
682,656.60	1,490,998.53	2,184,008.16	1,234,376.00	4.46	2.19	3.20	13
301,500.71	1,063,785.65	1,168,825.80	810,650.00	3.15	2.19	3.56	14
67,768.35	517,745.29	703,847.33	423,500.00	3.84	2.31	3.82	15
3,490,194.31	9,528,665.52	10,958,515.32	6,931,009.13	3.98	2.52	4.02	
75,473.41	67,050.58	58,266.16	94,486.82	1.55	2.51	3.36	16
47,917.51	163,324.90	178,196.63	131,644.00	3.57	2.64	3.64	17
95,370.22	377,809.60	566,541.79	500,123.30	3.19	2.82	3.78	18
4,000.00	10,714.23	17,419.75	10,080.00	4.95	2.86	4.00	19
14,434.83	142,893.77	146,996.26	72,500.00	3.79	1.86	2.82	20
57,296.67	281,032.88	274,962.49	202,065.00	3.70	2.72	4.21	21
22,407.90	103,955.06	167,308.71	100,740.00	4.50	2.71	3.41	22
316,900.54	1,146,781.02	1,409,631.89	1,111,638.12	3.37	2.66	3.68	
13,910.06	94,826.90	141,098.56	85,750.00	4.20	2.56	3.27	23
29,509.70	122,272.51	152,973.38	177,620.00	5.91	6.86	10.16	24
168,533.54	161,840.56	86,569.82	107,240.00	1.70	2.10	2.67	25
55,999.11	138,591.62	86,586.83	38,500.00	4.99	2.22	2.66	26
40,537.42	169,319.52	158,599.71	123,735.00	3.34	2.61	3.28	27
53,129.47	65,305.33	44,544.32	41,050.00	2.95	2.72	3.89	28
4,060.30	50,557.91	93,613.07	29,000.00	8.51	2.64	3.80	29
107,593.12	316,487.75	299,797.96	139,000.00	5.62	2.61	4.45	30
442,415.21	1,123,228.63	1,188,238.19	619,650.00	3.98	2.07	2.49	31
33,841.95	64,733.85	38,040.33	26,000.00	2.57	1.76	2.36	32
167,668.88	300,130.73	471,980.20	389,386.00	3.63	3.00	3.83	33
54,369.31	156,844.41	144,960.61	149,500.00	2.44	2.52	3.05	34
134,245.63	439,588.82	305,724.78	214,392.00	2.60	1.87	2.22	35
1,325,813.70	3,208,728.34	3,212,736.76	2,140,823.00	3.67	2.45	3.09	
536,723.85	1,093,861.73	1,184,554.58	852,863.33	3.40	2.44	3.14	36
177,209.28	436,132.94	299,804.29	316,250.00	2.53	2.67	3.47	37
60,709.38	325,281.68	335,822.47	261,500.00	3.10	2.41	2.89	38
238,724.38	667,372.59	763,258.51	513,205.00	4.06	2.73	3.67	39
244,058.24	903,741.68	958,197.01	707,150.00	4.12	3.04	4.17	40
455,439.50	1,219,350.63	1,293,351.19	897,000.00	3.99	2.49	3.86	41
226,600.76	473,111.88	480,039.32	381,550.00	3.54	2.82	3.68	42
84,026.10	357,047.79	130,696.39	131,000.00	2.57	2.38	2.98	43
87,896.70	377,128.52	457,682.43	261,125.00	5.10	2.91	3.78	44
20,323.35	137,644.16	127,367.88	80,000.00	7.38	4.64	6.40	45
2,132,311.54	5,976,076.60	6,030,774.07	4,311,643.33	3.74	2.67	3.06	

ABSTRACT OF REPORTS OF EARNINGS AND DIVIDENDS

FROM MARCH 1, 1893, TO

States, reserve cities, and Territories.	No. of banks.	Capital stock.	Surplus.	Capital and surplus.	Gross earnings.
46 Iowa	157	$13,612,500.00	$3,057,744.19	$16,670,244.19	$1,475,280.10
47 Des Moines	4	700,000.00	234,000.00	934,000.00	101,142.46
48 Minnesota	65	5,880,230.00	1,103,734.85	6,983,964.85	611,542.29
49 St. Paul	5	4,800,000.00	1,328,000.00	6,128,000.00	447,269.05
50 Minneapolis	7	5,450,000.00	664,000.00	6,114,000.00	406,070.21
51 Missouri	57	4,640,000.00	802,760.35	5,442,760.35	448,737.91
52 St. Louis	9	10,700,000.00	2,033,000.00	12,733,000.00	1,002,984.50
53 Kansas City	9	6,550,000.00	730,700.00	7,280,700.00	590,792.50
54 St. Joseph	4	2,000,000.00	223,500.00	2,223,500.00	180,913.63
55 Kansas	138	12,192,100.00	1,754,195.93	13,946,295.93	1,338,791.99
56 Nebraska	120	7,758,100.00	1,595,325.49	9,353,425.49	926,272.48
57 Omaha	9	4,150,000.00	487,600.00	4,637,600.00	480,849.01
58 Lincoln	4	1,000,000.00	148,000.00	1,148,000.00	139,610.42
Division No. 6	588	79,432,930.00	14,162,560.81	93,595,490.81	8,156,156.55
59 Colorado	52	9,020,000.00	2,359,883.84	11,379,883.84	1,430,110.09
60 Nevada	2	282,000.00	128,000.00	410,000.00	38,517.54
61 California	35	5,575,000.00	1,135,743.00	6,710,743.00	591,378.60
62 San Francisco	2	2,500,000.00	1,100,000.00	3,600,000.00	265,707.13
63 Oregon	39	3,795,000.00	910,251.28	4,705,251.28	461,914.28
64 Arizona	4	300,000.00	36,150.00	336,150.00	46,914.51
Division No. 7	134	21,472,000.00	5,670,028.12	27,142,028.12	2,836,642.15
65 North Dakota	33	2,315,000.00	513,221.47	2,828,221.47	253,570.16
66 South Dakota	38	2,560,000.00	596,375.00	3,156,375.00	276,840.46
67 Idaho	11	725,000.00	252,000.00	977,000.00	124,998.87
68 Montana	32	4,375,000.00	676,483.90	5,051,483.90	704,840.29
69 New Mexico	10	750,000.00	188,107.20	938,107.20	112,932.54
70 Oklahoma	5	250,000.00	16,000.00	266,000.00	53,372.14
71 Indian Territory	6	360,000.00	42,200.00	402,200.00	41,598.14
72 Utah	14	2,800,000.00	965,700.00	3,765,700.00	266,062.94
73 Wyoming	13	1,210,000.00	180,600.00	1,390,600.00	130,485.50
74 Washington	65	6,930,000.00	1,713,939.66	8,643,939.66	783,189.97
Division No. 8	227	22,275,000.00	5,144,627.23	27,419,627.23	2,747,894.01
United States	3,758	381,809,673.00	248,122,908.02	929,932,581.02	74,827,039.71

OF NATIONAL BANKS IN THE UNITED STATES—Continued.

SEPTEMBER 1, 1893—Continued.

Charged off.		Net earnings.	Dividends.	Ratios.			
Losses and premiums.	Expenses and taxes.			Net earnings to capital and surplus.	Dividends to capital and surplus.	Dividends to capital.	
				Per cent.	Per cent.	Per cent.	
$182,234.53	$620,565.49	$663,480.08	$433,800.00	3.98	2.60	3.12	46
15,461.43	45,476.08	40,204.95	127,000.00	4.30	1.36	1.81	47
146,868.63	322,655.86	142,037.80	199,200.00	2.03	2.85	3.39	48
192,795.19	181,617.71	72,826.15	215,000.00	1.19	3.51	4.48	49
26,280.79	189,454.53	190,337.89	187,581.06	3.11	3.07	3.44	50
50,406.66	202,364.14	195,967.11	127,003.42	3.60	2.33	2.74	51
70,915.11	479,351.29	432,718.10	231,000.00	3.56	1.03	2.16	52
133,638.14	358,749.81	98,404.55	101,500.00	1.35	1.39	1.55	53
47,271.62	73,301.99	60,240.62	28,000.00	2.71	1.26	1.40	54
451,900.99	531,402.83	355,488.17	303,805.00	2.55	2.18	2.49	55
57,732.42	516,208.86	352,331.20	256,462.85	3.77	2.74	3.31	56
92,337.22	319,781.79	74,730.00	83,000.00	1.61	1.75	1.85	57
8,667.64	78,096.39	52,846.39	13,000.00	4.60	1.13	1.30	58
1,476,510.37	3,928,033.77	2,751,612.41	2,304,352.33	2.94	2.46	2.90	
233,325.38	644,805.86	551,978.85	154,000.00	4.85	1.35	1.70	59
4,472.73	13,305.96	20,678.85	17,460.00	5.04	4.26	6.19	60
71,613.24	235,258.52	284,526.81	174,750.00	4.24	2.60	3.13	61
16,948.47	67,803.79	180,654.96	115,040.00	5.03	3.19	4.60	62
41,320.40	198,395.99	225,197.89	166,900.00	4.79	3.55	4.40	63
2,426.75	27,792.53	15,795.23	6,000.00	4.70	1.78	2.00	64
370,106.97	1,187,402.56	1,279,132.62	634,110.00	4.72	2.34	2.95	
22,790.44	161,552.64	69,317.08	58,116.65	2.45	2.05	2.51	65
79,387.30	187,787.47	9,665.63	30,250.00	3.06	9.58	1.10	66
6,742.66	39,746.66	78,509.52	8,000.00	8.04	8.19	1.10	67
127,726.44	288,064.34	280,049.51	156,000.00	5.72	3.09	3.57	68
12,406.11	52,321.61	48,204.82	4,500.00	5.14	4.80	0.60	69
3,325.54	22,219.09	27,827.51	7,000.00	10.46	2.63	2.80	70
3,225.06	16,988.38	21,384.76	9,400.00	5.32	2.34	2.61	71
23,643.11	117,980.15	124,439.68	83,000.00	3.30	2.20	2.96	72
75,777.48	60,329.50	**5,618.48**	15,750.00	**0.40**	1.13	1.30	73
117,793.00	405,102.68	260,294.29	127,250.00	3.01	1.47	1.84	74
472,727.11	1,352,092.52	923,074.38	499,266.65	3.37	1.82	2.24	
11,703,981.85	30,463,814.49	32,659,243.37	23,158,985.04	3.51	2.49	3.40	

NOTE.—Figures printed in boldface type signify loss.

TABLE, BY STATES AND RESERVE CITIES, SHOWING RATIOS TO CAPITAL, AND TO
FROM MARCH 1, 1889,

States, Territories, and reserve cities	Ratio of dividends to capital for six months ended—										Ratio of dividends to capital and surplus for six months ended—			
	Mar. 1, 1889	Sept. 1, 1889	Mar. 1, 1890	Sept. 1, 1890	Mar. 1, 1891	Sept. 1, 1891	Mar. 1, 1892	Sept. 1, 1892	Mar. 1, 1893	Sept. 1, 1893	Mar. 1, 1889	Sept. 1, 1889	Mar. 1, 1890	Sept. 1, 1890
	P. ct.	P. ct.	P. ct.	P. ct.	P. ct.	P. ct.	P. ct.	P. ct.	P. ct.	P. ct.	P. ct.	P. ct.	P. ct.	P. ct.
1 Maine	3.9	3.9	3.9	4.1	3.8	3.5	3.6	3.8	3.7	3.1	3.1	3.1	3.1	3.1
2 New Hampshire	3.9	3.9	3.9	4.3	5.5	3.9	3.9	3.7	3.4	3.1	3.1	3.1	3.1	3.4
3 Vermont	3.7	3.5	3.6	3.6	3.6	3.5	3.5	3.5	3.1	3.1	2.8	2.9	2.9	
4 Massachusetts	3.5	3.3	4.0	3.1	3.5	3.0	3.4	1.1	3.4	3.2	2.7	2.5	3.0	2.3
5 Boston	2.9	2.8	2.6	2.8	2.8	2.8	2.6	2.7	2.7	2.8	2.3	2.2	2.1	2.2
6 Rhode Island	3.2	3.2	3.0	2.6	2.9	3.1	3.1	3.0	2.6	2.9	2.6	2.6	2.4	2.1
7 Connecticut	3.5	3.5	3.5	3.5	3.7	3.7	3.7	3.7	3.8	3.7	2.7	2.7	2.7	2.7
8 New York	3.9	3.9	4.1	4.7	3.7	3.9	4.0	4.2	3.8	3.6	3.0	3.0	3.0	3.5
9 New York City	4.3	4.2	4.7	4.7	4.9	4.7	4.9	4.0	4.9	4.0	2.6	2.8	2.7	2.7
10 Albany	5.0	5.7	4.4	4.0	4.4	4.8	5.5	3.4	12.9	3.9	2.9	3.1	2.4	2.1
11 Brooklyn					6.7	6.8	6.8	6.8	6.8	6.8				
12 New Jersey	4.4	4.6	4.4	4.9	4.5	4.6	1.5	4.5	5.0	4.6	3.2	3.2	3.1	3.4
13 Pennsylvania	3.9	4.0	3.8	3.7	3.8	3.8	3.6	4.0	3.5	3.2	2.8	2.9	2.7	2.6
14 Philadelphia	3.6	3.6	3.6	3.5	3.6	3.7	3.5	3.6	3.6	3.6	2.4	2.4	2.4	2.3
15 Pittsburg	3.6	3.7	3.7	3.7	3.7	3.7	3.7	3.7	3.8	3.8	2.4	2.4	2.4	2.4
16 Delaware	4.7	5.1	5.0	4.9	4.9	4.8	4.7	4.8	4.8	3.4	3.4	3.6	3.5	3.4
17 Maryland	4.0	4.2	3.9	3.8	3.8	3.8	5.2	3.8	3.9	3.6	3.0	3.0	2.9	2.8
18 Baltimore	3.7	3.9	3.6	3.8	3.4	3.5	3.1	3.7	3.4	3.8	2.8	2.9	2.7	2.8
19 District of Columbia	4.0	4.0	4.0	4.0	4.0	4.0	4.0	4.0	4.0	4.0	3.2	3.2	3.2	2.9
20 Washington	3.3	4.6	3.0	2.4	2.5	2.5	2.8	2.8	2.8	2.8	2.4	3.2	2.1	1.7
21 Virginia	4.4	3.8	3.8	3.8	4.3	3.9	4.1	4.0	3.9	4.2	3.1	2.7	2.7	2.7
22 West Virginia	4.0	3.9	4.0	5.0	3.5	3.9	5.3	3.2	3.5	3.4	3.2	3.1	3.1	4.9
23 North Carolina	3.8	3.4	3.7	3.7	4.0	4.3	4.2	4.0	4.0	3.3	3.0	2.7	2.9	3.0
24 South Carolina	4.5	4.5	4.5	4.5	4.6	4.8	14.8	4.9	11.4	10.2	3.1	3.1	3.1	3.0
25 Georgia	3.1	4.3	4.9	3.5	5.0	3.6	3.3	3.2	3.2	2.7	2.4	3.3	3.8	2.7
26 Florida	3.2	4.5	3.8	3.1	4.6	4.3	3.3	3.3	3.1	2.7	2.8	3.9	3.3	2.7
27 Alabama	4.0	3.8	3.9	4.0	3.8	3.3	3.6	3.4	3.5	3.3	3.3	3.0	3.2	3.2
28 Mississippi	4.4	6.5	6.2	4.2	5.3	4.0	4.6	3.7	4.0	3.5	3.5	5.1	4.6	3.2
29 Louisiana	2.0	2.0	3.0	4.2	3.7	3.3	3.9	3.3	4.4	3.6	1.7	1.6	3.2	3.3
30 New Orleans	4.6	3.8	4.7	4.1	4.3	4.1	3.7	3.4	4.4	4.4	3.1	2.6	3.0	2.7
31 Texas	5.0	4.3	5.9	3.9	4.2	3.4	4.6	4.3	4.6	2.5	4.0	3.5	4.8	3.2
32 Arkansas	5.9	7.1	6.2	13.9	6.0	4.1	4.0	2.9	4.2	2.4	4.8	5.9	5.0	11.1
33 Kentucky	3.7	3.8	3.9	3.5	3.6	3.6	3.8	4.3	3.8	3.8	3.0	3.1	3.1	2.8
34 Louisville	3.7	3.7	3.5	3.2	3.2	2.8	3.2	2.4	3.2	3.0	2.9	2.9	2.8	2.6
35 Tennessee	3.7	3.4	3.9	3.1	3.5	3.2	3.7	3.1	3.6	2.2	3.1	2.8	3.2	2.5
36 Ohio	3.7	3.9	4.1	3.8	4.7	3.7	3.6	3.8	3.7	3.1	3.0	3.1	3.2	3.0
37 Cincinnati	3.6	3.4	3.6	3.7	3.8	3.8	3.2	3.6	3.8	3.5	3.0	2.8	2.9	3.0
38 Cleveland	2.9	2.9	3.2	5.7	3.2	2.8	3.3	3.2	3.2	2.9	2.5	2.5	2.7	4.8
39 Indiana	5.7	4.2	4.2	4.5	5.1	4.8	4.9	5.0	4.2	3.7	4.4	3.2	3.2	3.4
40 Illinois	5.0	4.9	5.1	5.3	5.2	5.1	4.6	4.5	4.5	4.2	3.8	3.7	3.9	3.9
41 Chicago	4.4	3.9	10.9	4.0	4.0	4.5	4.0	3.7	3.7	3.9	3.3	2.8	7.7	2.9
42 Michigan	4.3	4.4	4.9	4.1	4.4	4.7	4.5	4.5	5.0	3.7	3.5	3.5	4.0	3.2
43 Detroit	4.0	3.9	3.9	3.7	3.4	3.3	3.3	3.3	2.9	3.0	3.6	3.4	3.4	3.2
44 Wisconsin	5.3	4.8	6.1	8.5	4.1	4.8	4.7	4.5	6.3	3.8	4.1	3.7	4.7	6.7
45 Milwaukee	4.9	4.9	4.9	4.9	4.9	4.5	5.6	5.5	7.7	6.4	3.4	3.4	3.2	3.2
46 Iowa	5.1	4.9	5.5	5.7	5.7	5.6	4.9	4.6	4.2	3.2	4.0	3.9	4.3	4.4
47 Des Moines					4.8	5.0	5.0	4.9	18.1					
48 Minnesota	3.6	3.2	3.6	3.4	3.8	3.5	4.7	4.4	5.5	3.4	3.1	2.7	3.1	2.9
49 St. Paul					4.2	4.5	4.1	4.0	4.7	4.5				
50 Minneapolis					2.9	3.1	2.5	2.5	3.0	3.4				
51 Missouri	4.7	5.2	4.5	4.1	5.0	3.4	4.0	3.9	4.0	2.7	3.8	4.3	3.7	3.5
52 St. Louis	2.5	3.5	3.2	3.1	3.3	3.3	2.8	2.7	2.4	2.2	2.0	2.7	2.7	2.8
53 Kansas City	4.0	4.2	3.8	4.0	3.5	2.2	3.1	1.6	1.7	1.5	3.0	3.7	3.4	3.6
54 St. Joseph	3.3	8.5	3.6	2.8	3.3	3.3	3.3	3.3	1.4	2.4	15.3	3.3	3.4	3.6
55 Kansas	4.2	4.4	3.6	3.2	3.2	2.6	3.0	2.8	3.0	2.5	3.6	3.8	3.1	2.7
56 Nebraska	5.2	5.2	4.8	4.3	3.5	3.4	4.0	3.6	4.4	3.3	4.4	4.4	4.0	3.6
57 Omaha	3.2	3.9	3.7	3.3	3.3	3.2	2.8	2.3	2.1	1.9	2.5	3.4	3.3	3.0
58 Lincoln										1.3				
59 Colorado	5.8	5.9	12.0	11.7	5.1	4.0	4.5	4.5	4.7	1.7	4.2	4.3	9.5	8.0
60 Nevada	4.4	6.0	6.0	6.0	6.0	6.0	6.0	7.1	6.2	6.2	3.5	4.4	4.4	4.4
61 California	4.7	4.4	4.4	4.6	4.9	4.6	4.2	4.0	5.0	3.1	3.9	3.1	3.6	3.7
62 San Francisco	3.8	4.0	5.6	4.0	4.0	1.6	4.0	4.0	4.6	4.6	3.3	3.4	4.3	3.1
63 Oregon	3.7	3.9	3.5	4.7	4.5	4.2	4.2	8.8	5.2	4.4	3.1	3.3	2.9	3.4
64 Arizona	6.0	6.0	6.0	6.0	4.5	5.0	6.0	4.5	6.3	2.0	5.2	5.0	4.8	4.0
65 Dakota	5.6	3.2									4.5	2.6		
66 North Dakota			6.2	3.4	5.0	4.1	4.5	3.2	5.5	2.5			5.0	2.8
67 South Dakota			5.0	2.8	3.7	2.9	3.3	2.9	2.6	3.6	1.2		4.3	2.2
68 Idaho	4.9	1.1	1.3	1.0	11.2	6.2	14.8	1.5	7.8	1.1	4.1	1.0	1.0	0.8
69 Montana	2.1	0.9	7.7	4.0	4.0	3.6	2.4	3.9	2.7	3.8	1.7	0.7	6.4	3.3
70 New Mexico	3.8	6.7	6.0	6.3	6.3	7.0	5.7	1.6	2.3	0.6	3.1	5.5	4.9	5.0
71 Utah	7.3	4.3	5.8	4.2	2.6	5.3	4.5	4.7	4.4	3.0	4.7	3.1	4.1	3.0
72 Washington	4.5	7.9	5.0	3.3	6.0	3.6	3.5	5.2	4.8	1.8	3.2	5.7	3.8	2.6
73 Wyoming	1.7	2.3	2.3	2.4	2.7	2.5	2.5	3.6	2.8	1.3	1.4	1.9	1.0	2.0
74 Oklahoma					2.2	2.5	4.0	7.7	3.7	2.8				
75 Indian Territory					1.4	5.3	3.6	3.0	2.7	2.6				
Average	3.0	3.9	4.3	3.9	3.9	3.8	3.8	3.7	3.8	3.4	3.0	2.9	3.2	2.9

NOTE.- Figures printed in bold-face type in

CAPITAL AND SURPLUS, OF THE EARNINGS AND DIVIDENDS OF NATIONAL BANKS TO SEPTEMBER 1, 1893.

Ratio of dividends to capital and surplus for six months ended—						Ratio of earnings to capital and surplus for six months ended—										
Mar. 1, 1891	Sept. 1, 1891	Mar. 1, 1892	Sept. 1, 1892	Mar. 1, 1893	Sept. 1, 1893	Mar. 1, 1889	Sept. 1, 1889	Mar. 1, 1890	Sept. 1, 1890	Mar. 1, 1891	Sept. 1, 1891	Mar. 1, 1892	Sept. 1, 1892	Mar. 1, 1893	Sept. 1, 1893	
P. ct.	P. ct.	P. ct.	P. ct.	P. ct.	P. ct.	P. ct.	P. ct.	P. ct.	P. ct.	P. ct.	P. ct.	P. ct.	P. ct.	P. ct.	P. ct.	
3.2	3.0	2.8	2.9	3.0	2.9	4.4	3.9	4.0	3.7	4.5	2.8	2.0	3.0	3.0	3.2	1
4.4	3.1	3.1	3.0	2.9	2.7	4.0	3.2	3.6	3.9	4.2	3.4	3.1	2.7	3.4	2.8	2
2.9	2.8	2.8	2.7	2.8	2.4	4.0	3.7	3.4	3.6	3.9	2.9	3.4	3.1	2.7	2.8	3
2.6	2.3	2.5	0.8	2.5	2.4	3.4	3.4	2.6	3.2	3.1	3.0	2.5	2.5	2.8	2.9	4
2.2	2.2	2.1	2.2	2.1	2.2	3.9	3.4	1.7	2.7	3.3	3.2	1.9	2.4	2.6	2.6	5
2.4	2.5	2.5	2.5	2.0	2.4	3.5	2.5	3.0	0.9	3.1	2.5	2.8	2.2	2.8	2.5	6
2.8	2.8	2.6	2.8	2.8	2.7	3.3	3.2	3.6	3.8	3.7	3.3	3.5	3.1	3.5	3.4	7
2.9	3.0	3.0	3.1	2.8	2.7	4.7	4.3	4.4	4.5	4.4	3.5	3.8	4.0	4.2	3.6	8
2.8	2.7	2.7	2.7	2.7	2.7	4.0	4.9	4.5	5.3	5.2	4.7	4.4	3.8	4.3	4.5	9
2.4	2.6	3.0	2.3	7.0	2.1	3.4	5.4	2.3	0.6	1.6	4.0	3.9	4.0	5.3	4.1	10
2.8	2.8	2.7	2.7	2.7	2.7					5.5	4.9	3.6	4.2	5.0	4.1	11
3.1	3.2	1.0	3.1	3.3	3.0	5.0	5.6	6.1	5.5	5.3	4.7	4.6	4.3	4.6	4.6	12
2.6	2.7	2.5	2.8	2.4	2.2	4.6	4.1	4.5	3.9	4.5	3.3	4.0	3.4	3.9	4.1	13
2.3	2.3	2.2	2.2	2.2	2.2	3.5	3.8	3.5	3.5	3.0	3.7	3.3	2.8	3.8	3.1	14
2.3	2.4	2.3	2.3	2.3	2.3	3.8	3.9	4.2	4.1	4.5	3.2	3.7	3.9	4.1	3.8	15
3.4	3.3	3.3	3.3	3.3	2.5	4.9	4.7	4.2	4.9	4.5	1.9	3.6	3.8	4.1	1.6	16
2.8	2.8	3.8	2.8	2.8	2.6	4.3	4.8	4.3	3.9	4.2	3.9	4.1	3.8	3.9	3.6	17
2.6	2.6	2.4	2.8	2.6	2.8	4.1	3.0	3.6	3.2	3.3	3.0	3.2	2.8	3.5	3.2	18
2.9	2.9	2.9	2.9	2.9	2.9	4.2	4.1	4.5	4.3	7.8	3.2	3.5	4.9	4.6	4.9	19
1.8	1.7	1.9	1.9	1.9	1.9	4.8	5.8	6.2	5.5	4.5	3.8	3.5	3.8	3.7	3.8	20
2.9	2.6	2.7	2.6	2.5	2.7	4.8	4.7	4.0	5.8	5.5	4.4	4.6	4.7	4.6	3.7	21
2.7	3.1	4.3	2.6	2.8	2.7	4.3	4.5	4.4	5.0	5.7	5.0	5.7	4.2	4.6	4.5	22
3.2	3.4	3.3	3.1	3.1	2.6	4.2	5.1	4.0	3.4	4.1	5.4	3.9	4.5	4.0	4.2	23
3.1	3.0	9.6	3.1	7.5	6.9	4.8	7.1	4.4	7.2	5.6	6.8	3.2	6.8	0.4	5.9	24
3.8	2.8	2.6	2.5	2.5	2.1	3.7	3.7	4.6	4.5	4.7	5.2	2.4	3.2	1.9	1.7	25
3.9	3.6	2.8	2.8	2.6	2.2	4.6	5.7	6.2	5.5	7.6	8.4	5.7	6.1	6.7	5.0	26
3.1	2.7	2.9	2.6	2.8	2.6	4.3	6.1	6.3	5.4	4.1	3.4	2.7	2.4	1.8	3.3	27
3.0	3.0	3.3	2.7	3.0	2.7	5.0	8.8	6.0	6.9	4.4	7.0	3.0	4.6	3.3	3.0	28
3.0	2.7	3.1	2.5	3.3	2.6	4.6	5.1	6.8	9.4	6.6	8.4	4.3	5.8	5.2	8.5	29
3.0	2.7	2.5	2.2	2.8	2.6	5.3	6.2	5.6	4.1	4.0	4.1	1.3	4.3	4.1	5.6	30
3.8	2.9	3.9	3.6	3.9	2.1	5.7	6.1	6.3	5.8	5.9	5.4	3.5	4.3	4.1	4.0	31
4.8	3.2	3.1	2.2	3.2	1.8	7.4	7.9	6.4	10.5	6.8	5.0	5.1	3.5	3.1	2.6	32
2.8	2.8	2.4	3.4	3.0	3.0	4.1	4.0	4.4	4.7	4.8	2.9	3.5	3.4	3.4	3.6	33
2.6	2.3	2.6	2.0	2.7	2.5	4.1	3.7	5.4	2.9	4.0	0.9	2.9	1.1	3.2	2.4	34
2.9	2.7	3.0	2.5	3.0	1.9	5.1	3.7	4.8	5.1	4.6	3.1	3.5	2.6	3.2	2.6	35
3.7	2.9	2.8	3.0	2.9	2.4	4.3	4.1	4.0	3.9	4.5	3.6	4.1	3.8	4.6	3.4	36
3.0	3.0	2.9	2.8	2.9	2.7	4.2	4.0	4.7	5.5	5.3	3.8	4.0	2.6	4.7	2.5	37
2.7	2.4	2.6	2.6	2.7	2.4	3.8	3.8	3.7	4.1	4.2	3.7	6.0	3.1	3.5	3.1	38
3.8	3.7	3.6	3.6	3.1	2.7	4.6	4.4	5.0	4.4	5.4	4.3	4.6	4.4	4.5	4.1	39
3.9	3.8	3.4	3.3	3.3	3.0	5.8	5.3	5.4	4.9	6.1	5.9	5.3	4.7	5.2	4.1	40
2.7	3.0	2.8	2.6	2.5	2.5	5.5	5.3	6.1	6.3	6.2	7.8	6.1	5.3	4.0	4.0	41
3.5	3.7	3.5	3.4	3.8	2.8	4.5	4.7	4.0	4.9	5.7	4.6	4.4	4.2	4.0	3.5	42
3.0	2.9	2.9	2.9	2.5	2.6	5.0	4.7	4.3	3.5	3.6	3.3	2.5	3.5	3.4	2.6	43
3.2	3.7	3.6	3.4	4.8	2.9	5.5	6.0	5.8	6.5	6.1	5.8	5.2	5.1	6.5	5.1	44
4.5	4.6	3.9	3.7	3.5	2.6	10.0	4.7	6.2	5.2	4.4	3.1	6.7	5.4	5.1	7.4	45
			3.5	3.4	1.4	4.8	5.1	5.1	4.8	5.4	4.7	4.2	4.5	4.3	4.0	46
	3.2	3.5	3.5	3.4	1.4						8.7	4.5	2.6	5.4	4.3	47
3.1	3.0	3.7	3.6	4.6	2.8	4.6	3.3	5.4	3.5	5.2	3.6	6.8	4.2	5.1	2.0	48
3.3	3.5	3.2	3.2	3.7	3.5					4.8	4.1	4.9	5.0	5.4	1.2	49
2.6	2.7	2.2	2.2	2.7	3.1					4.5	5.0	4.7	1.2	4.6	3.1	50
4.3	3.0	3.4	3.4	3.4	2.3	4.9	4.2	4.6	4.1	5.3	4.3	3.7	4.0	4.1	3.6	51
2.9	2.9	2.4	2.4	2.1	1.0	4.9	4.8	2.8	7.6	4.6	4.8	2.7	3.9	3.6	3.6	52
3.1	1.9	2.7	1.4	1.6	1.4	5.6	4.9	4.8	4.4	3.7	1.0	2.0	0.4	0.9	1.3	53
3.0	3.0	3.0	3.0	3.0	1.3	7.7	8.5	5.8	5.5	5.1	3.4	3.3	3.8	2.8	2.7	54
2.8	2.3	2.6	2.5	2.5	2.2	5.1	3.7	3.8	3.2	3.5	2.4	2.6	2.6	2.2	2.5	55
3.0	2.9	3.4	3.0	3.7	2.7	7.0	6.1	5.9	4.9	4.6	3.5	4.5	3.6	4.6	3.8	56
2.9	2.8	2.5	2.0	1.9	1.7	5.4	4.9	4.8	3.8	4.8	3.0	1.5	0.5	2.2	1.6	57
					1.1										4.6	58
4.1	3.3	3.6	3.6	3.7	1.3	9.8	10.0	9.1	9.0	9.3	6.1	6.0	4.9	5.5	4.8	59
4.4	4.4	4.1	4.9	4.3	4.3	6.1	6.1	5.3	6.3	4.8	5.6	5.0	6.0	6.2	5.0	60
4.0	3.6	3.3	3.2	4.1	2.6	6.0	6.2	5.3	4.9	5.5	5.1	4.6	4.3	1.9	4.2	61
3.0	1.2	3.0	2.9	3.2	3.2	5.6	6.8	4.4	5.2	5.4	5.1	5.7	5.4	5.3	5.0	62
3.6	3.6	3.6	7.3	4.2	3.5	8.5	7.9	7.5	8.4	8.6	6.5	5.2	6.0	6.3	4.8	63
3.9	4.3	5.6	3.8	5.6	1.8	12.5	8.6	10.2	7.2	6.3	7.6	8.4	7.0	10.9	4.7	64
						6.7	4.1									65
4.1	3.4	3.8	2.6	4.5	2.1			7.1	2.7	5.0	4.2	6.8	3.3	6.7	2.4	66
2.3	2.6	2.3	2.0	3.0	9.6			5.0	3.5	4.5	1.4	3.2	2.3	4.2	3.1	67
7.9	4.4	11.0	1.1	5.8	0.8	8.0	6.5	6.0	4.8	11.1	7.4	9.3	7.8	9.7	8.0	68
3.1	2.1	3.4	2.3	3.3	3.1	8.3	4.7	11.9	9.5	6.6	5.6	6.6	5.9	4.7	5.7	69
5.1	5.8	4.7	3.8	1.9	0.5	5.8	5.9	6.0	6.3	6.3	4.0	5.3	4.8	4.6	5.1	70
2.0	3.8	3.4	3.5	3.3	2.2	12.3	8.5	8.7	6.3	6.5	7.3	2.2	4.5	3.9	3.3	71
4.8	2.9	2.8	4.3	3.9	1.5	10.9	10.3	9.5	8.1	7.8	5.5	5.3	4.7	3.0	3.0	72
2.3	2.2	2.1	3.1	2.4	1.1	1.8	1.4	2.5	3.4	1.3	4.5	3.0	0.5	2.0	0.4	73
2.2	2.4	3.8	7.1	3.5	2.6					4.0	4.7	6.3	11.9	9.8	10.5	74
1.4	5.1	3.5	2.9	2.6	2.3					4.6	5.8	6.1	4.9	7.3	5.3	75
3.0	2.8	2.8	2.7	2.8	2.5	4.5	4.3	4.3	4.3	4.6	4.0	3.8	3.5	3.9	3.5	

column for 1890, 1892, and 1893 signify percentage of loss

EARNINGS AND DIVIDENDS OF THE NATIONAL BANKS, ARRANGED BY GEOGRAPHICAL DIVISIONS, FOR SEMIANNUAL PERIODS FROM SEPTEMBER 1884, TO SEPTEMBER, 1893.

Geographical divisions.	No. of banks	Capital.	Surplus.	Dividends.	Net earnings.	Ratios.		
						Dividends to capital.	Dividends to capital and surplus.	Earnings to capital and surplus.
						Pr. ct.	Pr. ct.	Pr. ct.
Sept., 1884, to Mar., 1885:								
New England States...	567	$167,400,370	$41,413,826	$5,661,537	$4,388,812	3.4	2.7	2.1
Middle States..........	732	173,212,145	64,741,009	7,156,680	7,474,752	4.1	3.0	3.1
Southern States........	278	42,648,400	11,527,942	1,760,726	2,426,858	4.2	3.3	4.5
Western States	1,073	139,638,800	31,088,344	5,828,707	7,310,780	4.2	3.4	4.3
Total	2,650	522,899,715	148,771,121	20,437,650	21,601,202	3.9	3.0	3.2
Mar., 1885, to Sept., 1885:								
New England States...	562	165,668,370	40,786,007	5,391,401	4,725,395	3.3	2.6	2.3
Middle States..........	731	172,907,352	64,247,888	6,953,332	7,297,150	4.0	2.9	3.1
Southern States........	287	43,500,300	11,505,477	1,655,261	2,282,782	3.8	3.0	4.2
Western States	1,085	142,523,580	30,364,123	6,218,477	7,718,959	4.5	3.6	4.5
Total	2,665	524,599,602	146,903,495	20,218,471	22,024,295	3.9	3.0	3.3
Sept., 1885, to Mar., 1886:								
New England States...	559	165,203,920	41,128,387	5,375,226	5,925,381	3.2	2.6	2.8
Middle States..........	738	172,435,295	67,583,309	7,044,535	9,484,324	4.0	2.9	3.9
Southern States........	294	44,437,400	12,053,524	1,969,190	2,705,274	4.4	3.4	4.7
Western States	1,117	148,879,580	32,767,699	6,946,485	9,412,687	4.6	3.8	5.2
Total	2,708	530,956,195	153,532,919	21,335,436	27,527,666	4.0	3.1	4.0
Mar., 1886, to Sept., 1886:								
New England States...	563	165,352,320	41,581,845	5,338,635	6,736,479	3.2	2.5	3.2
Middle States..........	744	173,628,875	70,044,187	7,328,798	9,789,135	4.2	3.0	4.0
Southern States........	303	45,444,000	11,967,321	1,994,537	2,553,055	4.3	3.4	4.0
Western States	1,174	153,138,453	33,470,425	6,485,172	8,834,050	4.2	3.5	4.7
Total	2,784	537,563,648	157,064,778	21,147,142	27,912,719	3.9	3.0	4.0
Sept., 1886, to Mar., 1887:								
New England States...	563	165,252,370	41,897,072	5,318,480	6,176,707	3.2	2.6	3.0
Middle States..........	754	175,873,735	73,445,033	7,574,627	12,072,419	4.3	3.0	4.8
Southern States........	313	46,213,240	12,483,050	2,143,870	2,646,893	4.6	3.6	4.5
Western States	1,225	161,016,425	35,926,745	7,111,610	10,883,275	4.4	3.6	5.5
Total	2,855	548,355,770	163,731,900	22,148,587	31,698,794	4.0	3.1	4.5
Mar., 1887, to Sept., 1887:								
New England States...	566	164,837,370	43,118,790	5,355,787	7,224,781	3.2	2.6	3.5
Middle States..........	764	176,635,656	76,574,179	7,357,400	11,360,893	4.2	2.9	4.5
Southern States........	349	51,515,315	13,247,285	2,137,328	3,298,973	4.1	3.3	5.0
Western States	1,269	165,556,200	38,314,290	7,153,305	10,953,427	4.3	3.5	5.4
Total	2,942	558,544,541	171,254,553	22,003,820	32,808,074	3.9	3.0	4.5
Sept., 1887, to Mar., 1888:								
New England States...	567	164,405,020	43,459,769	5,426,178	6,187,595	3.3	2.6	3.0
Middle States..........	780	181,382,395	80,679,527	7,346,515	11,201,708	4.0	2.8	4.2
Southern States........	358	53,124,400	14,258,403	2,298,039	3,257,542	4.3	3.4	4.8
Western States	1,339	176,224,933	40,999,447	8,017,876	11,954,449	4.5	3.7	5.5
Total	3,044	577,136,748	179,397,147	23,088,607	32,601,294	4.0	3.0	4.3
Mar., 1888, to Sept., 1888:								
New England States...	568	164,640,820	44,197,418	5,349,582	6,730,240	3.2	2.6	3.2
Middle States..........	793	184,220,575	82,908,779	7,564,822	11,544,258	4.1	2.8	4.3
Southern States........	369	54,802,800	14,844,534	2,189,837	3,105,202	4.0	3.1	4.4
Western States	1,363	179,865,950	42,376,280	8,338,710	11,379,032	4.6	3.8	5.1
Total	3,093	583,529,145	184,416,991	23,443,051	32,759,192	4.0	3.0	4.3
Sept., 1888, to Mar., 1889:								
New England States...	568	164,506,720	44,904,040	5,508,163	6,932,212	3.3	2.6	3.3
Middle States..........	795	184,628,445	86,496,967	7,370,692	12,241,390	4.0	2.7	4.5
Southern States........	382	56,074,485	15,715,136	2,357,718	3,497,410	4.1	3.2	4.8
Western States	1,401	187,144,200	45,391,957	8,045,400	12,478,868	4.3	3.5	5.3
Total	3,147	593,253,850	192,507,500	23,290,973	35,109,889	3.9	3.0	4.5

EARNINGS AND DIVIDENDS OF THE NATIONAL BANKS, ETC.—Continued.

Geographical divisions.	No. of banks	Capital.	Surplus.	Dividends.	Net earnings.	Dividends to capital.	Dividends to capital and surplus.	Earnings to capital and surplus.
						Pr. ct.	*Pr. ct.*	*Pr. ct.*
Mar., 1889, to Sept., 1889:								
New England States...	571	$165,101,920	$45,476,953	$5,307,086	$6,920,889	3.2	2.5	3.3
Middle States.........	796	184,195,745	87,936,236	7,646,874	12,060,433	4.1	2.8	4.5
Southern States.......	483	58,905,530	16,387,359	2,365,368	3,816,370	4.0	3.1	5.1
Western States........	1,425	191,247,990	47,328,336	8,016,259	11,708,674	4.2	3.4	4.9
Total...............	3,194	599,451,185	197,128,884	23,325,587	34,508,375	3.9	2.9	4.3
Sept., 1889, to Mar., 1890:								
New England States...	576	165,631,980	46,157,181	5,520,977	5,606,830	3.3	2.6	2.6
Middle States.........	831	186,198,725	91,010,405	7,629,170	12,208,788	4.1	2.8	4.4
Southern States.......	436	62,949,360	17,141,070	2,861,628	4,220,776	4.5	3.6	5.3
Western States........	1,471	200,625,480	50,237,778	10,237,091	12,203,145	5.1	4.1	5.2
Total...............	3,294	615,405,545	204,546,434	26,249,766	35,248,539	4.3	3.2	4.3
Mar., 1890, to Sept., 1890:								
New England States...	582	165,500,920	46,488,598	5,144,588	6,239,358	3.1	2.4	2.9
Middle States.........	834	188,261,155	94,608,921	7,046,301	12,534,630	4.2	2.8	4.4
Southern States.......	475	68,491,105	18,081,496	2,695,210	4,730,666	3.9	3.1	5.5
Western States........	1,521	212,520,506	52,690,124	9,123,018	13,302,370	4.3	3.4	5.0
Total...............	3,412	634,773,746	211,869,139	24,009,117	36,807,024	3.9	2.9	4.3
Sept., 1890, to Mar., 1891:								
New England States...	583	165,525,420	47,263,871	5,530,473	7,275,215	3.3	2.6	3.4
Middle States.........	851	189,215,745	98,365,397	7,720,433	13,189,635	4.1	2.7	4.6
Southern States.......	522	75,175,100	19,232,961	3,026,402	4,842,139	4.0	3.2	5.1
Western States........	1,586	222,670,320	54,368,512	9,491,377	14,838,085	4.3	3.4	5.4
Total...............	3,542	652,586,585	219,430,741	25,768,775	40,145,074	3.9	3.0	4.6
Mar., 1891, to Sept., 1891:								
New England States...	589	165,392,090	48,053,953	5,231,854	6,512,910	3.2	2.4	3.0
Middle States.........	874	192,973,876	99,692,776	7,911,627	11,475,715	4.1	2.7	3.9
Southern States.......	544	78,244,000	20,344,334	2,778,024	4,290,226	3.6	2.8	4.4
Western States........	1,605	231,019,971	58,011,532	9,104,730	13,329,789	3.9	3.2	4.6
Total...............	3,612	667,629,937	226,102,595	25,026,235	35,617,640	3.7	2.8	4.0
Sept., 1891, to Mar., 1892:								
New England States...	585	165,668,920	48,438,842	5,292,014	5,422,799	3.2	2.5	2.5
Middle States.........	880	192,304,940	103,561,327	7,463,453	11,764,329	3.9	2.5	3.9
Southern States.......	558	78,227,550	21,026,567	3,350,369	3,412,941	4.3	3.4	3.4
Western States........	1,648	239,155,900	61,650,165	9,441,017	13,763,021	3.9	3.1	4.6
Total...............	3,671	675,356,310	234,676,901	25,546,853	34,363,090	3.8	2.8	3.8
Mar., 1892, to Sept., 1892:								
New England States...	587	165,018,920	48,072,364	4,300,264	5,542,203	2.6	2.0	2.6
Middle States.........	882	182,464,745	105,487,995	8,147,702	10,855,644	4.2	2.7	3.6
Southern States.......	570	79,620,155	21,456,227	3,007,204	3,780,308	3.8	2.9	3.7
Western States........	1,662	241,072,830	62,745,27.	9,394,600	12,116,679	3.9	3.1	4.0
Total...............	3,701	679,076,650	237,761,865	24,853,860	32,294,924	3.7	2.7	3.5
Sept., 1892, to Mar., 1893:								
New England States...	593	166,883,920	49,226,463	5,265,294	6,237,163	3.7	2.4	2.9
Middle States.........	896	193,420,145	109,068,414	8,019,584	12,501,582	4.2	2.6	4.1
Southern States.......	584	80,834,940	21,064,386	3,363,815	3,706,154	4.2	3.3	3.6
Western States........	1,686	245,735,370	65,755,255	9,825,517	13,646,809	4.0	3.2	4.4
Total...............	3,759	686,874,375	245,714,438	26,474,210	36,091,708	3.8	2.8	3.9
Mar., 1893, to Sept., 1893:								
New England States...	594	166,483,920	49,330,806	5,225,243	6,093,766	3.1	2.4	2.8
Middle States.........	908	195,020,223	110,921,832	7,740,742	11,925,936	4.0	2.5	3.9
Southern States.......	574	77,023,500	21,638,808	3,442,628	3,654,948	3.2	2.5	3.7
Western States........	1,682	243,282,030	66,231,402	7,749,372	10,984,593	3.1	2.5	3.5
Total...............	3,758	681,809,673	248,122,908	24,158,085	32,659,243	3.4	2.5	3.5
General average.....	3,213	603,877,957	195,718,573	23,468,174	32,321,091	3.9	2.9	4.0

NATIONAL BANKS WHICH HAVE GONE INTO VOLUNTARY LIQUIDATION UNDER THE PROVISIONS OF SECTIONS 5220 AND 5221 OF THE REVISED STATUTES OF THE UNITED STATES, WITH THE DATES OF LIQUIDATION, THE AMOUNT OF CAPITAL, CIRCULATION ISSUED AND RETIRED, AND CIRCULATION OUTSTANDING OCTOBER 31, 1893.

Name and location of bank.	Date of liquidation.	Capital.	Circulation.		
			Issued.	Retired.	Outstanding.
First National Bank, Penn Yan, N.Y.* ..	Apr. 6, 1864				
First National Bank, Norwich, Conn.* ..	May 2, 1864				
Second National Bank, Ottumwa, Iowa†..	....do				
Second National Bank, Canton, Ohio†...	Oct. 3, 1864				
First National Bank, Lansing, Mich.† ..	Dec. 5, 1864				
First National Bank, Columbia, Mo.....	Sept. 19, 1864	$100,000	$90,000	$89,875	$125
First National Bank, Carondelet, Mo....	Mar. 15, 1865	30,000	25,500	25,399	101
First National Bank, Utica, N. Y.*	June 9, 1865				
Pittston National Bank, Pittston, Pa....	Sept. 16, 1865	200,000			
Fourth National Bank, Indianapolis, Ind.	Nov. 30, 1865	100,000	100,000	99,373	627
Berkshire National Bank, Adams, Mass.‡	Dec. 8, 1865	100,000			
National Union Bank, Rochester, N. Y..	Apr. 26, 1866	400,000	192,500	191,358	942
First National Bank, Leonardsville, N.Y.	July 11, 1866	50,000	45,000	44,420	580
Farmers' National Bank, Richmond, Va.	Oct. 22, 1866	100,000	85,000	83,293	1,707
Farmers' National Bank, Waukesha, Wis....................................	Nov. 25, 1866	100,000	90,000	89,545	455
National Bank of Metropolis, Washington, D. C..............................	Nov. 28, 1866	200,000	180,000	177,128	2,872
First National Bank, Providence, Pa...	Mar. 1, 1867	100,000	50,000	88,805	1,195
National State Bank, Dubuque, Iowa...	Mar. 9, 1867	150,000	127,000	125,765	1,235
First National Bank of Newton, Newtonville, Mass...................	Mar. 11, 1867	150,000	130,000	128,832	1,168
First National Bank, New Ulm, Minn..	Apr. 18, 1867	60,000	54,000	53,250	750
National Bank of Crawford County, Meadville, Pa....................	Apr. 19, 1867	300,000			
Kittanning National Bank, Kittanning, Pa.‡..................................	Apr. 29, 1867	200,000			
City National Bank, Savannah, Ga.†....	May 28, 1867	100,000			
Ohio National Bank, Cincinnati, Ohio...	July 3, 1867	500,000	450,000	444,260	5,740
First National Bank, Kingston, N. Y...	Sept. 26, 1867	200,000	180,000	177,825	2,175
First National Bank, Bluffton, Ind......	Dec. 5, 1867	50,000	45,000	44,586	414
National Exchange Bank, Richmond, Va.	....do	200,000	180,000	179,380	620
First National Bank, Skaneateles, N. Y.	Dec. 21, 1867	150,000	135,000	133,808	1,112
First National Bank, Jackson, Miss.....	Dec. 26, 1867	100,000	45,500	43,715	1,785
First National Bank, Downingtown, Pa.	Jan. 14, 1868	100,000	90,000	89,026	974
First National Bank, Titusville, Pa.....	Jan. 15, 1868	100,000	86,750	85,790	960
Appleton National Bank, Appleton, Wis.	Jan. 21, 1868	50,000	45,050	44,380	620
National Bank of Whitestown, N. Y....	Feb. 14, 1868	120,000	45,500	45,258	242
First National Bank, New Brunswick, N. J......................................	Feb. 26, 1868	100,000	90,000	88,734	1,266
First National Bank, Cuyahoga Falls, Ohio	Mar. 4, 1868	50,000	45,000	44,472	528
First National Bank, Cedarburg, Wis...	Mar. 23, 1868	100,000	90,000	89,527	473
Commercial National Bank, Cincinnati, Ohio	Apr. 28, 1868	500,000	345,950	343,945	2,005
Second National Bank, Watertown, N. Y.	July 21, 1868	100,000	90,000	88,980	1,020
First National Bank, South Worcester, N. Y...................................	Aug. 4, 1868	175,500	157,400	155,826	1,574
National Mechanics and Farmers' Bank, Albany, N. Y........................	....do	350,000	314,950	313,015	1,935
Second National Bank, Des Moines, Iowa.	Aug. 5, 1868	50,000	42,500	42,162	338
First National Bank, Steubenville, Ohio.	Aug. 8, 1868	150,000	135,000	133,337	1,663
First National Bank, Plumer, Pa........	Aug. 25, 1868	100,000	87,500	86,202	1,298
First National Bank, Danville, Va.......	Sept. 30, 1868	50,000	45,000	44,710	290
First National Bank, Dorchester, Mass.	Nov. 24, 1868	150,000	132,500	130,627	1,873
First National Bank, Oskaloosa, Iowa ..	Dec. 17, 1868	75,000	67,500	66,992	508
Merchants and Mechanics' National Bank, Troy, N. Y.....................	Dec. 31, 1868	300,000	184,750	183,198	1,552
National Savings Bank, Wheeling, W. Va.	Jan. 7, 1869	100,000	90,000	89,455	545
First National Bank, Marion, Ohio	Jan. 12, 1869	125,000	109,850	109,019	831
National Insurance Bank, Detroit, Mich	Feb. 26, 1869	200,000	85,000	84,473	527
National Bank of Lansingburg, N. Y....	Mar. 6, 1869	150,000	135,000	133,802	1,198
National Bank of North America, New York, N. Y.............................	Apr. 15, 1869	1,000,000	333,000	330,865	2,135
First National Bank, Hallowell, Mo	Apr. 19, 1869	60,000	53,350	52,946	404
First National Bank, Clyde, N. Y	Apr. 23, 1869	50,000	44,000	43,280	720
Pacific National Bank, New York, N. Y	May 10, 1869	422,700	134,990	134,082	908
Grocers' National Bank, New York, N. Y	June 7, 1869	390,000	85,250	84,921	329
Savannah National Bank, Savannah, Ga.	June 22, 1869	100,000	85,000	84,500	500
First National Bank, Frostburg, Md......	July 10, 1869	50,000	45,000	44,757	243
First National Bank, La Salle, Ill	Aug. 30, 1869	50,000	45,000	44,535	465
National Bank of Commerce, Georgetown, D. C...............................	Oct. 28, 1869	100,000	90,000	89,100	900

* New bank with same title. † Never completed organization. ‡ Consolidated with another bank.

NATIONAL BANKS WHICH HAVE GONE INTO VOLUNTARY LIQUIDATION UNDER THE PRO-
VISIONS OF SECTIONS 5220 AND 5221 OF THE REVISED STATUTES, ETC.--Cont'd.

Name and location of bank.	Date of liquidation.	Capital.	Circulation.		
			Issued.	Retired.	Outstanding.
Miners' National Bank, Salt Lake City, Utah	Dec. 2, 1869	$150, 000	$135, 000	$134, 116	$884
First National Bank, Vinton, Iowa	Dec. 13, 1869	50, 000	42, 500	42, 303	197
National Exchange Bank, Philadelphia, Pa	Jan. 8, 1870	300, 000	175, 750	173, 910	1, 840
First National Bank, Decatur, Ill	Jan. 10, 1870	100, 000	85, 250	84, 226	1, 024
National Union Bank, Owego, N. Y	Jan. 11, 1870	100, 000	88, 250	87, 338	912
First National Bank, Berlin, Wis	Jan. 25. 1870	500, 000	44, 000	43, 627	373
Central National Bank. Cincinnati, Ohio.	Mar. 31, 1870	500, 000	425, 000	421, 305	3, 695
First National Bank, Dayton, Ohio.	Apr. 9, 1870	150, 000	135, 000	133, 851	1, 149
National Bank of Chemung, Elmira, N.Y.	June 10, 1870	100, 000	90, 000	89, 498	502
Merchants' National Bank, Milwaukee, Wis.	June 14, 1870	100, 000	90, 000	89, 345	655
First National Bank, St. Louis, Mo	July 16, 1870	200, 000	179, 990	178, 597	1, 393
Chemung Canal National Bank, Elmira, N. Y	Aug. 3, 1870	100, 000	90, 000	89, 174	826
Central National Bank, Omaha Nebr. *	Sept. 23, 1870	100, 000			
First National Bank, Clarksville. Va	Oct. 13, 1870	50, 000	27, 000	26, 895	105
First National Bank, Burlington, Vt	Oct. 15, 1870	300, 000	270, 000	267, 018	2, 082
First National Bank, Lebanon, Ohio	Oct. 24, 1870	100, 000	85, 000	84, 348	652
National Exchange Bank, Lansingburg, N. Y	Dec. 27, 1870	100, 000	90, 000	89, 428	572
Muskingum National Bank, Zanesville, Ohio	Jan. 7, 1871	100, 000	90, 000	89, 300	700
United National Bank, Winona, Minn	Feb. 15, 1871	50, 000	45, 000	44, 615	385
First National Bank, Des Moines, Iowa.	Mar. 25, 1871	100, 000	90, 000	89, 213	787
Saratoga County National Bank, Waterford, N. Y	Mar. 28, 1871	150, 000	135, 000	134, 048	952
State National Bank, St. Joseph. Mo	Mar. 31, 1871	100, 000	90, 000	89, 461	539
First National Bank, Fenton, Mich	May 2, 1871	100, 000	49, 500	49, 033	467
First National Bank, Wellsburg, W. Va	June 24, 1871	100, 000	90, 000	89, 278	722
Clarke National Bank, Rochester, N. Y.	Aug. 11, 1871	200, 000	180, 000	178, 278	1, 722
Commercial National Bank, Oshkosh, Wis	Nov. 22, 1871	100, 000	90, 000	89, 323	677
Fort Madison National Bank, Fort Madison, Iowa	Dec. 26, 1871	75, 000	67, 500	66, 990	510
National Bank of Maysville, Ky	Jan. 6, 1872	300, 000	270, 000	268, 754	1, 246
Fourth National Bank, Syracuse, N. Y.	Jan. 9, 1872	105. 500	91, 700	90, 879	821
American National Bank, New York, N. Y.	May 10, 1872	500, 000	450, 000	444, 150	5, 850
Carroll County National Bank, Sandwich, N. H	May 24, 1872	50, 000	45, 000	44, 468	532
Second National Bank, Portland, Me	June 24, 1872	100, 000	81, 000	80, 029	971
Atlantic National Bank, Brooklyn, N. Y.	July 15, 1872	200, 000	165, 000	163, 720	1. 280
Merchants and Farmers' National Bank, Quincy, Ill	Aug. 8, 1872	150, 000	135, 000	133, 725	1. 275
First National Bank, Rochester, N. Y.	Aug. 9, 1872	400, 000	206, 100	203, 875	2, 225
Lawrenceburg National Bank, Lawrenceburg, Ind	Sept. 10, 1872	200, 000	180, 000	178, 052	1, 918
Jewett City National Bank, Jewett City, Conn	Oct. 4, 1872	60, 000	48, 750	48, 277	473
First National Bank, Knoxville, Tenn	Oct. 22, 1872	100, 000	80, 910	80, 112	798
First National Bank, Goshen. Ind	Nov. 7, 1872	115, 000	103, 500	102, 283	1, 217
Kidder National Gold Bank, Boston, Mass	Nov. 8, 1872	300, 000	120, 000	120, 000	
Second National Bank, Zanesville, Ohio.	Nov. 16, 1872	154, 700	138, 140	136, 513	1, 627
Orange County National Bank, Chelsea, Vt	Jan. 14, 1873	200, 000	180, 000	177, 871	2, 129
Second National Bank, Syracuse, N. Y.	Feb. 18, 1873	100, 000	90, 000	88, 880	1, 120
Richmond National Bank, Richmond, Ind. *	Feb. 28, 1873	230. 000	207, 000	207, 000	
First National Bank, Adams, N. Y	Mar. 7, 1873	75, 000	66, 900	66, 015	885
Mechanics' National Bank, Syracuse, N. Y	Mar. 11, 1873	140, 000	93, 800	92, 880	920
Farmers and Mechanics' National Bank, Rochester, N. Y.	Apr. 15, 1873	100, 000	83, 250	82, 377	873
Montana National Bank, Helena, Mont	do	100, 000	31, 500	31, 385	115
First National Bank, Havana, N. Y.	June 3, 1873	50, 000	45, 000	44, 415	585
Merchants and Farmers' National Bank, Ithaca, N. Y	June 30, 1873	50, 000	45, 000	44, 321	679
National Bank of Cazenovia, N. Y	July 18, 1873	150, 000	116, 770	115, 341	1, 429
Merchants' National Bank, Memphis. Tenn	Aug. 30, 1873	250, 000	225, 000	222, 413	2, 587
Manufacturers' National Bank, Chicago, Ill	Sept. 25, 1873	500, 000	438, 750	433, 392	5, 358
Second National Bank, Chicago, Ill	do	100, 000	97, 500	96, 176	1, 324

* New bank with same title.

NATIONAL BANKS WHICH HAVE GONE INTO VOLUNTARY LIQUIDATION UNDER THE PRO-
VISIONS OF SECTIONS 5220 AND 5221 OF THE REVISED STATUTES, ETC.—Cont'd.

Name and location of bank.	Date of liquidation.	Capital.	Circulation.		
			Issued.	Retired.	Outstanding.
Merchants' National Bank, Dubuque, Iowa	Sept. 30, 1873	$200,000	$180,000	$176,472	$3,528
Beloit National Bank, Beloit, Wis	Oct. 2, 1873	50,000	45,000	44,319	6·1
Union National Bank, St. Louis, Mo	Oct. 22, 1873	500,000	150,300	148,473	1,827
City National Bank, Green Bay, Wis	Nov. 29, 1873	50,000	45,000	44,325	675
First National Bank, Shelbina, Mo	Jan. 1, 1874	100,000	90,000	89,300	700
Second National Bank, Nashville, Tenn	Jan. 8, 1874	125,000	92,920	91,715	1,205
First National Bank, Oneida, N. Y	Jan. 13, 1874	125,000	110,500	108,956	1,544
Merchants' National Bank, Hastings, Minn	Feb. 7, 1874	100,000	90,000	88,541	1,459
National Bank of Tecumseh, Mich	Mar. 3, 1874	50,000	15,000	44,315	685
Gallatin National Bank, Shawneetown, Ill	Mar. 7, 1874	250,000	225,000	223,057	1,943
First National Bank, Brookville, Pa	Mar. 26, 1874	100,000	90,000	88,845	1,155
Citizens' National Bank, Sioux City, Iowa	Apr. 14, 1874	50,000	45,000	44,850	150
Citizens' National Bank, Charlottesville, Va	Apr. 27, 1874	100,000	90,000	89,279	721
Farmers' National Bank, Warren, Ill	Apr. 28, 1874	50,000	45,000	44,463	537
First National Bank, Medina, Ohio	May 6, 1874	75,000	45,000	44,735	265
Croton River National Bank, South East, N. Y	May 25, 1874	200,000	166,550	163,638	2,912
Merchants' National Bank of West Virginia, Wheeling, W. Va	July 7, 1874	500,000	450,000	444,880	5,120
Central National Bank, Baltimore, Md	July 15, 1874	200,000	180,000	178,878	1,122
Second National Bank, Leavenworth, Kans	July 22, 1874	100,000	90,000	87,942	2,058
Teutonia National Bank, New Orleans, La	Sept. 2, 1874	300,000	270,000	268,060	1,940
City National Bank, Chattanooga, Tenn	Sept. 10, 1874	170,000	148,001	147,069	932
First National Bank, Cairo, Ill	Oct. 10, 1874	100,000	90,000	88,672	1,328
First National Bank, Olatho, Kans	Nov. 9, 1874	50,000	45,000	44,660	340
First National Bank, Beverly, Ohio	Nov. 10, 1874	102,000	90,000	88,581	1,419
Union National Bank, Lafayette, Ind	Dec. 4, 1874	250,000	224,095	220,380	3,715
Ambler National Bank, Jacksonville, Fla.*	Dec. 7, 1874	42,500			
Mechanics' National Bank, Chicago, Ill	Dec. 30, 1874	250,000	125,000	123,960	1,940
First National Bank, Evansville, Wis	Jan. 9, 1875	55,000	45,000	44,563	437
First National Bank, Baxter Springs, Kans	Jan. 12, 1875	50,000	36,000	35,655	345
People's National Bank, Pueblo, Colo	do	50,000	27,000	26,834	166
National Bank of Commerce, Green Bay, Wis	do	100,000	90,000	89,235	765
First National Bank, Millersburg, Ohio	do	100,000	60,400	60,045	355
First National Bank, Staunton, Va	Jan. 23, 1875	100,000	90,000	89,107	893
National City Bank, Milwaukee, Wis	Feb. 24, 1875	100,000	60,000	59,170	820
Irasburg National Bank of Orleans, Irasburg, Vt	Mar. 17, 1875	75,000	67,500	66,569	931
First National Bank, Pekin, Ill	Mar. 25, 1875	100,000	90,000	88,725	1,275
Merchants and Planters' National Bank, Augusta, Ga	Mar. 30, 1875	200,000	169,000	167,345	1,655
Monticello National Bank, Monticello, Iowa	do	100,000	45,000	44,735	265
Iowa City National Bank, Iowa City, Iowa	Apr. 14, 1875	125,000	104,800	103,176	1,624
First National Bank, Wheeling, W. Va	Apr. 22, 1875	250,000	225,000	221,884	3,116
First National Bank, Mount Clemens, Mich	May 20, 1875	50,000	27,000	20,910	90
First National Bank, Knob Noster, Mo	May 29, 1875	50,000	43,800	43,440	360
First National Bank, Brodhead, Wis	June 21, 1875	50,000	45,000	44,507	493
Auburn City National Bank, Auburn, N. Y	June 26, 1875	200,000	141,300	138,987	2,313
First National Bank, Eldorado, Kans	June 30, 1875	50,000	45,000	44,530	470
First National Bank, Junction City, Kans	July 1, 1875	50,000	45,000	44,705	295
First National Bank, Chetopa, Kans	July 19, 1875	50,000	36,000	35,701	299
First National Bank, Golden, Colo	Aug. 25, 1875	50,000	27,000	26,818	182
National Bank of Jefferson, Wis	Aug. 26, 1875	60,000	54,000	53,022	978
Green Lane National Bank, Green Lane, Pa	Sept. 9, 1875	100,000	90,000	89,688	312
State National Bank, Topeka, Kans	Sept. 15, 1875	60,000	30,000	30,477	123
Farmers' National Bank, Marshalltown, Iowa	Sept. 18, 1875	50,000	27,000	26,810	160
Richland National Bank, Mansfield, Ohio	Sept. 25, 1875	150,000	131,300	128,027	2,273
Planters' National Bank, Louisville, Ky	Sept. 30, 1875	350,000	315,000	310,479	4,521
First National Bank, Gallatin, Tenn	Oct. 1, 1875	75,000	45,000	44,630	370
First National Bank, Charlestown, W. Va	Oct. 2, 1875	100,000	90,000	89,156	844

* No circulation.

NATIONAL BANKS WHICH HAVE GONE INTO VOLUNTARY LIQUIDATION UNDER THE PRO-
VISIONS OF SECTIONS 5220 AND 5221 OF THE REVISED STATUTES, ETC.—Cont'd.

Name and location of bank.	Date of liquidation.	Capital.	Circulation.		
			Issued.	Retired.	Outstanding.
People's National Bank, Winchester, Ill.	Oct. 4, 1875	$75,000	$67,500	$66,869	$631
First National Bank, New Lexington, Ohio	Oct. 12, 1875	50,000	45,000	44,658	342
First National Bank, Ishpeming, Mich..	Oct. 20, 1875	50,000	45,000	44,594	406
Fayette County National Bank, Washington, Ohio	Oct. 26, 1875	100,000	81,280	80,617	663
Merchants' National Bank, Fort Wayne, Ind	Nov. 8, 1875	100,000	46,820	46,265	555
Kansas City National Bank, Kansas City, Mo	Nov. 13, 1875	100,000	65,991	65,140	851
First National Bank, Schoolcraft, Mich.	Nov. 17, 1875	50,000	45,000	44,512	488
First National Bank, Curwensville, Pa ..	Dec. 17, 1875	100,000	90,000	88,583	1,417
National Marine Bank. St. Paul, Minn ..	Dec. 28, 1875	100,000	59,710	58,345	1,365
First National Bank, Rochester, Ind.....	Jan. 11, 1876	50,000	45,000	43,049	1,951
First National Bank, Lodi, Ohio..........	...do	100,000	90,000	88,562	1,438
Iron National Bank, Portsmouth, Ohio ..	Jan. 19, 1876	100,000	90,000	89,197	803
First National Bank, Ashland, Nebr.....	Jan. 26, 1876	50,000	45,000	44,626	374
First National Bank, Paxton, Ill.........	Jan. 28, 1876	50,000	45,000	44,408	592
First National Bank, Bloomfield, Iowa...	Feb. 5, 1876	55,000	49,500	48,505	995
Marietta National Bank, Marietta, Ohio .	Feb. 16, 1876	150,000	90,000	88,133	1,867
Salt Lake City National Bank, Salt Lake City, Utah	Feb. 21, 1876	100,000	45,000	44,162	838
First National Bank, La Grange, Mo	Feb. 24, 1876	50,000	45,000	44,483	517
First National Bank, Atlantic, Iowa.....	Mar. 7, 1876	50,000	45,000	44,506	494
First National Bank, Spencer, Ind.......	Mar. 11, 1876	70,000	63,000	62,564	436
National Currency Bank, New York, N. Y	Mar. 23, 1876	100,000	45,000	44,000	1,000
Caverna National Bank, Caverna, Ky....	May 13, 1876	50,000	45,000	44,675	325
City National Bank, Pittsburg, Pa	May 25, 1876	200,000	68,929	68,325	604
National State Bank, Des Moines, Iowa..	June 21, 1876	100,000	50,795	49,530	1,265
First National Bank, Trenton, Mo.......	June 22, 1876	50,000	45,000	44,546	454
First National Bank, Bristol, Tenn	July 10, 1876	50,000	45,000	44,692	308
First National Bank, Leon, Iowa.........	July 11, 1876	60,000	45,000	44,113	887
Anderson County National Bank, Lawrenceburg, Ky	July 20, 1876	100,000	45,000	44,740	260
First National Bank, Newport, Ind.......	Aug. 7, 1876	60,000	45,000	44,488	512
First National Bank, DePere, Wis........	Aug. 17, 1876	50,000	31,500	31,259	241
Second National Bank, Lawrence, Kans .	Aug. 23, 1876	100,000	67,500	66,830	670
Commercial National Bank, Versailles, Ky	Aug. 26, 1876	170,000	153,000	151,229	1,771
State National Bank. Atlanta, Ga........	Aug. 31, 1876	200,000	73,725	72,645	1,080
Syracuse National Bank, Syracuse, N. Y.	Sept. 25, 1876	200,000	117,961	114,518	3,443
First National Bank, Northumberland, Pa	Oct. 6, 1876	100,000	62,106	60,341	1,765
First National Bank, Lancaster, Mo	Nov. 14, 1876	50,000	27,000	26,857	143
First National Bank, Council Grove, Kans	Nov. 28, 1876	50,000	26,500	26,163	337
National Bank Commerce, Chicago, Ill...	Dec. 2, 1876	250,000	71,465	70,261	1,204
First National Bank, Palmyra, Mo	Dec. 12, 1876	100,000	46,140	44,963	1,177
First National Bank, Newton, Iowa	Dec. 16, 1876	50,000	45,000	43,876	1,124
National Southern Kentucky Bank, Bowling Green, Ky	Dec. 23, 1876	50,000	27,000	26,772	228
First National Bank, Monroe, Iowa	Jan. 1, 1877	60,000	35,700	35,391	309
First National Bank, New London, Conn.	Jan. 9, 1877	100,000	38,300	36,591	1,709
Winona Deposit National Bank, Winona, Minn	Jan. 28, 1877	100,000	63,285	61,947	1,338
First National Bank, South Charleston, Ohio	Feb. 24, 1877	100,000	90,000	88,154	1,846
Lake Ontario National Bank, Oswego, N. Y	...do	275,000	66,405	62,371	4,034
First National Bank, Sidney, Ohio	Feb. 26, 1877	52,000	46,200	45,272	928
Chillicothe National Bank, Ohio..........	Apr. 9, 1877	100,000	53,825	52,270	1,555
First National Bank, Manhattan, Kans..	Apr. 13, 1877	52,000	44,200	43,638	562
National Bank, Monticello, Ky...........	Apr. 23, 1877	60,000	49,500	48,560	940
First National Bank, Rockville, Ind	Apr. 25, 1877	200,000	173,090	170,135	2,955
Georgia National Bank, Atlanta, Ga	May 31, 1877	100,000	45,000	43,705	1,295
First National Bank, Adrian, Mich	June 11, 1877	100,000	43,500	42,936	564
First National Bank, Napoleon, Ohio	June 30, 1877	50,000	45,000	44,157	843
First National Bank, Lancaster, Ohio	Aug. 1, 1877	60,000	54,000	52,361	1,639
First National Bank, Minerva, Ohio.....	Aug. 24, 1877	50,000	45,000	44,373	627
Kinney National Bank, Portsmouth, Ohio.	Aug. 28, 1877	100,000	90,000	89,000	1,000
First National Bank, Green Bay, Wis....	Oct. 19, 1877	50,000	45,000	43,941	1,059
National Exchange Bank, Wakefield, R.I.	Oct. 27, 1877	70,000	34,650	33,801	849
First National Bank, Union City, Ind	Nov. 10, 1877	50,000	45,000	44,065	935
First National Bank, Negaunee, Mich ...	Nov. 13, 1877	50,000	45,000	44,270	730
Tenth National Bank, New York, N. Y ..	Nov. 24, 1877	500,000	441,000	422,788	18,212
First National Bank, Paola, Kans.......	Dec. 1, 1877	50,000	44,350	43,577	773
National Exchange Bank, Troy, N. Y	Dec. 6, 1877	100,000	90,000	87,945	2,055
Second National Bank, Lafayette, Ind....	Dec. 20, 1877	200,000	52,167	48,819	3,348
State National Bank, Minneapolis, Minn.	Dec. 31, 1877	100,000	82,500	80,300	2,200
Second National Bank, St. Louis, Mo....	Jan. 8, 1878	200,000	53,055	48,920	4,135

NATIONAL BANKS WHICH HAVE GONE INTO VOLUNTARY LIQUIDATION UNDER THE PROVISIONS OF SECTIONS 5220 AND 5221 OF THE REVISED STATUTES, ETC.—Cont'd.

Name and location of bank.	Date of liquidation.	Capital.	Circulation. Issued.	Retired.	Outstanding.
First National Bank, Sullivan, Ind	Jan. 8, 1878	$50,000	$45,000	$44,495	$505
Rockland County National Bank, Nyack, N. Y	Jan. 10, 1878	100,000	89,000	87.286	1,714
First National Bank, Wyandotte, Kans	Jan. 19, 1878	50,000	45,000	44.261	739
First National Bank, Boone, Iowa	Jan. 22, 1878	50,000	32,400	31.835	545
First National Bank, Pleasant Hill, Mo	Feb. 7, 1878	50,000	45,000	41,198	802
National Bank of Gloversville, N. Y	Feb. 28, 1878	100,000	64,750	63,867	883
First National Bank, Independence, Mo	Mar. 1, 1878	50,000	27,000	25,671	1,329
National State Bank, Lima, Ind	Mar. 2, 1878	100,000	33,471	32,257	1,214
First National Bank, Tell City, Ind	Mar. 4, 1878	50,000	44,500	44,030	470
First National Bank, Pomeroy, Ohio	Mar. 5, 1878	200,000	75,713	71,987	3,726
Eleventh Ward National Bank, Boston, Mass	Mar. 14, 1878	200,000	89,400	88,365	1,035
First National Bank, Prophetstown, Ill	Mar. 19, 1878	50,000	45,000	44,585	415
First National Bank, Jackson, Mich	Mar. 26, 1878	100,000	88,400	86,615	1,785
First National Bank, Eau Claire, Wis	Mar. 30, 1878	60,000	38,461	37,765	696
First National Bank, Washington, Ohio	Apr. 5, 1878	200,000	69,750	67,141	2.609
First National Bank, Middleport, Ohio	Apr. 20, 1878	80,000	31,500	31,125	375
First National Bank, Streator, Ill	Apr. 24. 1878	50,000	40,500	40,075	425
First National Bank, Muir, Mich	Apr. 25, 1878	50,000	44,200	43,669	531
Kane County National Bank, St. Charles, Ill	May 31. 1878	50,000	26,300	25,878	422
First National Bank, Carthage, Mo	June 1, 1878	50,000	44,500	43,870	630
Security National Bank, Worcester, Mass.	June 5, 1878	100,000	49,000	48,400	600
First National Bank, Lake City, Colo	June 15, 1878	50,000	29,300	29,119	181
People's National Bank, Norfolk, Va	July 31, 1878	100,000	85,705	84.290	1,415
Topeka National Bank, Topeka, Kans	Aug. 7, 1878	100,000	89,300	87,511	1,789
First National Bank, St. Joseph, Mo	Aug. 13, 1878	100,000	67,110	65.000	2,110
First National Bank, Winchester, Ind	Aug. 24, 1878	60,000	52.700	51,154	1,546
Muscatine National Bank, Muscatine, Iowa	Sept. 2, 1878	100,000	44,200	42.381	1,819
Traders' National Bank, Chicago, Ill	Sept. 4. 1878	200,000	43.700	40,700	2,991
Union National Bank, Rahway, N. J	Sept. 10, 1878	100.000	89,200	86.948	2.252
First National Bank, Sparta, Wis	Sept. 14, 1878	50,000	45,000	43,964	1,036
Herkimer County National Bank, Little Falls, N. Y	Oct. 11, 1878	200,000	178.300	173,769	4,531
Farmers' National Bank, Bangor, Mo	Nov. 22, 1878	100,000	89,100	87,522	1,578
Pacific National Bank, Council Bluffs, Iowa	Nov. 30, 1878	100,000	45,000	43,780	1,220
First National Bank, Anamosa, Iowa	Dec. 14, 1878	50,000	44,500	43,477	1,023
Smithfield National Bank, Pittsburg, Pa.	Dec. 16, 1878	200,000	78.750	77,050	1,700
First National Bank, Buchanan, Mich	Dec. 21, 1878	50,000	27,000	26,638	362
First National Bank, Prairie City, Ill	Dec. 24, 1878	50,000	27,000	25,960	1,040
Corn Exchange National Bank, Chicago, Ill	Jan. 4, 1879	500.000	59,160	53,670	5.490
Franklin National Bank, Columbus, Ohio	do	100,000	93,070	90,013	3,057
Traders' National Bank, Bangor, Me	Jan. 14, 1879	100,000	76,400	73,911	2,489
First National Bank, Genie, N. H	do	60,000	45,597	44,031	1,566
First National Bank, Salem, N. C	do	150,000	128,200	125,075	3,125
First National Bank, Granville, Ohio	do	50,000	34,365	32,929	1,436
Commercial National Bank, Petersburg, Va	do	120,000	99,800	96.758	3,042
First National Gold Bank, Stockton, Cal	do	300,000	238,600	225,811	12,789
First National Bank, Sheboygan, Wis	do	50,000	45,000	44.282	718
First National Bank, Boscobel, Wis	Jan. 21, 1879	50,000	43,900	42,956	944
National Marine Bank, Oswego, N. Y	Jan. 25, 1879	120,000	44,300	42,028	2,272
Central National Bank, Hightstown, N. J	Feb. 15, 1879	100,000	32,400	31,918	482
Brookville National Bank, Brookville, Ind	Feb. 18, 1879	100,000	89,000	86,340	2,660
Farmers' National Bank, Centreville, Iowa	Feb. 27, 1879	50,000	41.500	40,928	572
First National Bank, Clarinda, Iowa	Mar. 1, 1879	50,000	45,000	44,277	723
Waterville National Bank, Waterville, Me	Mar. 3, 1879	125,000	110,300	107,293	3,007
First National Bank, Tremont, Pa	Mar. 4, 1879	75,000	64,600	62.053	2,547
First National Bank, Atlanta, Ill	Apr. 15, 1879	50,000	26,500	26,010	490
Union National Bank, Aurora, Ill	Apr. 22, 1879	125,000	82,000	79,446	2,554
National Bank of Menasha, Wis	Apr. 26, 1879	50,000	44,500	43,596	904
National Exchange Bank, Jefferson City, Mo	May 8, 1879	50,000	45,000	43,975	1,025
First National Bank, Hannibal, Mo	May 15, 1879	100,000	88,200	84,690	3,510
Merchants' National Bank, Winona, Minn	June 16, 1879	100,000	35,000	34,377	623
Farmers' National Bank, Keithsburg, Ill	July 3, 1879	50,000	27,000	26,365	635
First National Bank, Franklin, Ky	July 5, 1879	100,000	51,000	52,625	1,375
National Bank of Salem, Salem, Ind	July 8, 1879	50,000	44,400	43,839	561
Fourth National Bank, Memphis, Tenn	July 19, 1879	125,000	45,000	43,455	1,545
Bedford National Bank, Bedford, Ind	July 21, 1879	100,000	87,200	85,694	1,506
First National Bank, Alton, Iowa	Aug. 15, 1879	50,000	26,500	25,594	906

NATIONAL BANKS WHICH HAVE GONE INTO VOLUNTARY LIQUIDATION UNDER THE PRO-
VISIONS OF SECTIONS 5220 AND 5221 OF THE REVISED STATUTES, ETC.—Cont'd.

Name and location of bank.	Date of liquidation.	Capital.	Circulation.		
			Issued.	Retired.	Outstanding.
First National Bank, Deer Lodge, Mont.	Aug. 16, 1879	$50,000	$45,000	$44,020	$980
First National Bank, Batavia, Ill.	Aug. 30, 1879	50,000	44,300	42,482	1,818
National Gold Bank and Trust Company, San Francisco, Cal	Sept. 1, 1879	750,000	40,000	29,645	10,355
Gainesville National Bank, Gainesville, Ala	Nov. 25, 1879	100,000	90,000	87,492	2,508
First National Bank, Hackensack, N. J..	Dec. 6, 1879	100,000	90,000	88,070	1,930
National Bank of Delevan, Delevan, Wis.	Jan. 7, 1880	50,000	27,000	25,995	1,005
Mechanics' National Bank, Nashville, Tenn	Jan. 13, 1880	100,000	90,000	86,050	3,950
Manchester National Bank, Manchester, Ohio	...do	50,000	48,303	46,857	1,446
First National Bank, Meyersdale, Pa	Mar. 5, 1880	50,000	30,600	30,210	390
First National Bank, Mifflinburg, Pa.	Mar. 8, 1880	100,000	90,000	86,835	3,165
National Bank of Michigan, Marshall, Mich	May 14, 1880	120,000	100,800	97,465	3,335
National Exchange Bank, Houston, Tex.	Sept. 10, 1880	100,000	31,500	30,324	1,176
Ascutney National Bank, Windsor, Vt.	Oct. 19, 1880	100,000	90,000	87,297	2,703
First National Bank, Seneca Falls, N. Y.	Nov. 23, 1880	60,000	54,000	52,828	1,172
First National Bank, Baraboo, Wis	Nov. 27, 1880	50,000	27,000	26,437	563
Bundy National Bank, Newcastle, Ind	Dec. 6, 1880	50,000	45,000	44,574	426
Vineland National Bank, Vineland, N. J	Jan. 11, 1881	50,000	45,000	44,465	535
Ocean County National Bank, Toms River, N. J	...do	100,000	119,405	114,920	4,485
Hungerford National Bank, Adams, N. Y.	Jan. 27, 1881	50,000	45,000	42,440	2,560
Merchants' National Bank, Minneapolis, Minn	Jan. 31, 1881	150,000	98,268	96,460	1,808
Farmers' National Bank, Mechanicsburg, Ohio	Feb. 18, 1881	100,000	30,140	29,175	965
First National Bank, Green Spring, Ohio.	...do	50,000	45,000	44,129	871
First National Bank, Cannon Falls, Minn	Feb. 21, 1881	50,000	45,000	44,483	517
First National Bank, Coshocton, Ohio ..	...do	50,000	53,058	51,882	1,176
Manufacturers' National Bank, Three Rivers, Mich	Feb. 25, 1881	50,000	45,000	44,045	955
First National Bank, Lansing, Iowa....	...do	50,000	45,000	43,625	1,375
First National Bank, Watertown, N. Y.	May 26, 1881	100,000	75,510	71,945	3,565
First National Bank, Americus, Ga.	June 17, 1881	60,000	45,000	44,049	951
First National Bank, St. Joseph, Mich..	June 30, 1881	50,000	26,500	25,706	794
First National Bank, Logan, Ohio	July 8, 1881	50,000	45,000	43,660	1,340
First National Bank, Rochelle, Ill	Aug. 9, 1881	50,000	45,000	44,115	885
First Natioul Bank, Shakopee, Minn....	Aug. 10, 1881	50,000	45,000	43,755	1,245
National State Bank, Oskaloosa, Iowa..	Aug. 13, 1881	50,000	81,665	81,157	508
First National Bank, Hobart, N. Y	Aug. 27, 1881	100,000	90,000	87,271	2,729
Attica National Bank, Attica, N. Y	Aug. 30, 1881	50,000	45,000	44,380	620
National Bank of Brighton, Boston, Mass.	Oct. 4, 1881	300,000	270,000	261,907	8,013
Clement National Bank, Rutland, Vt..	Aug. 1, 1881	100,000			
First National Bank, Lisbon, Iowa.......	Nov. 1, 1881	50,000	45,000	44,170	830
First National Bank, Warsaw, Ind	Dec. 1, 1881	50,000	48,500	47,010	1,490
Brighton National Bank, Brighton, Iowa.	Dec. 15, 1881	50,000	45,000	43,967	1,033
Merchants' National Bank, Denver, Colo.	Dec. 24, 1881	120,000	72,000	70,790	1,210
Merchants' National Bank, Holly, Mich.	Dec. 31, 1881	50,000	45,000	43,963	1,037
First National Bank, Alliance, Ohio	Jan. 3, 1882	50,000	45,000	43,849	1,151
National Union Bank, New Loudon, Conn	Jan. 10, 1882	300,000	112,818	108,536	4,282
National Bank of Royalton, Vt............	...do	100,000	90,000	87,337	2,663
First National Bank, Whitehall, N. Y..	Jan. 18, 1882	50,000	45,000	42,631	2,369
National Bank of Pulaski, Tenn	Jan. 23, 1882	70,000	43,700	42,000	1,700
First National Bank, Alton, Ill	Mar. 30, 1882	100,000	90,000	86,480	3,520
Havana National Bank, Havana, N. Y..	Apr. 15, 1882	50,000	45,000	43,419	1,581
First National Bank, Brownsville, Pa ..	May 2, 1882	75,000	67,500	64,480	3,020
Second National Bank, Franklin, Ind ...	June 20, 1882	100,000	81,060	76,280	4,780
Merchants' National Bank, Georgetown, Colo	June 22, 1882	50,000	45,000	44,263	737
Commercial National Bank, Toledo, Ohio.	July 6, 1882	100,000	90,000	88,100	1,900
Harmony National Bank, Harmony, Pa.	July 7, 1882	50,000	45,000	43,840	1,160
First National Bank, Liberty, Ind	July 22, 1882	60,000	54,000	52,468	1,532
Manufacturers' National Bank, Amsterdam, N. Y.	Aug. 1, 1882	80,000	72,000	70,410	1,590
First National Bank, Bay City, Mich....	Nov. 8, 1882	400,000	156,100	151,403	4,697
First National Bank, Ripley, Ohio......	Nov. 10, 1882	100,000	69,201	64,394	4,394
National Bank of State of New York, New York, N. Y	Dec. 6, 1882	800,000	379,004	384,112	12,892
First National Bank, Wellington, Ohio.	Dec. 12, 1882	100,000	90,000	87,377	2,623
Second National Bank, Jefferson, Ohio..	Dec. 26, 1882	100,000	90,000	87,159	2,841
First National Bank, Painesville, Ohio ..	Dec. 30, 1882	200,000	162,800	155,521	7,279
Saint Nicholas National Bank, New York, N. Y	...do	500,000	450,000	426,851	23,149

* New bank with same title; no circulation.

NATIONAL BANKS WHICH HAVE GONE INTO VOLUNTARY LIQUIDATION UNDER THE PRO
VISIONS OF SECTIONS 5220 AND 5221 OF THE REVISED STATUTES, ETC.—Cont'd.

Name and location of bank.	Date of liquidation.	Capital.	Circulation.		
			Issued.	Retired.	Outstanding.
Fifth National Bank, Chicago, Ill	Dec. 30, 1882	$500, 000	$29, 700	$22, 878	$6, 822
First National Bank, Dowagiac, Mich	Jan. 3, 1883	50, 000	45, 000	43, 493	1, 507
First National Bank, Greenville, Ill	Jan. 9, 1883	150, 000	50, 400	56, 654	2, 746
Merchants' National Bank, East Saginaw, Mich	...do	200, 000	101, 100	95, 982	5, 118
Logan County National Bank, Russellville, Ky	...do	50, 000	40, 050	39. 070	980
National Bank of Vandalia, Ill	Jan. 11, 1883	100, 000	90, 000	86, 650	3, 350
Traders' National Bank, Charlotte, N. C.	Jan. 16, 1883	50, 000	38, 800	37, 634	1, 166
First National Bank, Norfolk, Nebr	Feb. 3, 1883	45, 000	11, 240	11, 060	180
First National Bank, Midland City, Mich. *	Feb. 5, 1883	30, 000			
Citizens' National Bank, New Ulm, Minn	Mar. 1. 1883	50, 000	27. 000	26, 280	720
National Bank of Owen, Owenton, Ky	Mar. 5, 1883	56, 000	48, 900	47, 295	1, 605
Merchants' National Bank, Nashville, Tenn	June 30, 1883	300, 000	141, 200	136, 450	4, 750
Indiana National Bank, Bedford, Ind	Aug. 25, 1883	35, 000	11, 250	11, 250	
Stockton National Bank. Stockton, Cal	Oct. 1, 1883	100, 000	90, 000	88, 250	1, 750
Wall Street National Bank, New York, N. Y.	Oct. 15, 1883	500, 000	102. 800	93, 549	9. 251
Commercial National Bank, Reading, Pa.	Oct. 23, 1883	150, 000	135, 000	131, 190	3, 810
Corn Exchange National Bank, Chicago, Ill. *	Nov. 10, 1883	700, 000			
Farmers' National Bank, Sullivan, Ind	Dec. 24, 1883	50, 000	45. 000	43, 380	1, 620
City National Bank, La Salle, Ill	Jan. 8, 1884	100, 000	22, 500	21, 590	910
Hunt County National Bank, Greenville, Tex	Jan. 22, 1884	68, 250	17, 300	16. 550	750
Waldoboro National Bank, Waldoboro, Me	Jan. 31, 1884	50, 000	44, 000	41, 760	2, 240
Third National Bank, Nashville, Tenn	Feb. 20, 1884	300, 000	167, 600	161. 435	6, 165
Madison County National Bank, Anderson, Ind	Mar. 25, 1884	50, 000	45, 000	43. 910	1, 090
First National Bank, Phœnix. Ariz	Apr. 7, 1884	50. 000	11. 240	11, 070	170
Cobbossee National Bank, Gardiner, Me.	Apr. 18, 1884	150, 000	90, 000	85, 541	4, 459
Mechanics and Traders' National Bank, New York, N. Y.	Apr. 24, 1884	200, 000	85, 400	78, 675	6, 725
Princeton National Bank, Princeton, N. J.	May 17. 1884	100, 000	72. 500	70, 090	2, 410
Kearsarge National Bank, Warner, N. H.	June 30, 1884	50, 000	23, 586	22, 537	1, 049
Second National Bank, Lansing, Mich	July 31, 1884	50, 000	40, 000	37, 096	2, 904
First National Bank, Ellensburg, Wash	Aug. 9, 1884	50, 000	13, 500	13, 230	270
German National Bank, Millerstown, Pa.	Aug. 12, 1884	50, 000	45. 000	42, 095	2 905
Exchange National Bank, Cincinnati, Ohio	Aug. 27, 1884	500, 000	78, 000	74, 690	3. 310
First National Bank, Rushville, Ill	Sept. 30, 1884	75, 000	66. 500	62, 438	4, 062
Mechanics' National Bank, Peoria, Ill	Oct. 4, 1884	100, 000	72, 000	67, 593	4. 407
First National Bank, Freeport, Pa	Oct. 10, 1884	50, 000	44. 200	41, 750	2, 450
Genesee County National Bank, Batavia, N. Y.	Oct. 11, 1884	50, 000	45, 000	43, 745	1, 255
Valley National Bank, Red Oak. Iowa	Oct. 20, 1884	50, 000	22, 150	20, 830	1, 320
Merchants' National Bank, Bismarck, N. Dak	Oct. 28, 1884	73, 000	22, 500	22, 140	360
Manufacturers' National Bank, Minneapolis, Minn	Nov. 1, 1884	300, 000	45, 000	43. 360	1, 640
Farmers and Merchants' National Bank, Uhrichsville, Ohio	Nov. 10, 1884	50, 000	34, 600	33. 260	1, 340
Metropolitan National Bank, New York, N. Y.	Nov. 18, 1884	3, 000, 000	1, 447, 000	1, 336, 222	110, 778
First National Bank, Grand Forks, N. Dak	Dec. 2, 1884	50, 000	19, 250	18, 910	340
Iron National Bank, Gunnison, Colo	Dec. 8, 1884	50, 000	11, 250	10, 950	300
Freehold National Banking Company, Freehold, N. J	Dec. 10, 1884	50, 000	93, 000	87, 387	5, 613
Albia National Bank, Albia, Iowa	Dec. 16, 1884	50. 000	11, 240	11, 020	220
First National Bank, Carlinville, Ill	...do	50, 000	22, 450	20, 977	1, 473
Freeman's National Bank, Augusta, Me	Dec. 26, 1884	100, 000	90, 000	81, 671	5, 329
First National Bank, Kokomo, Ind	Jan. 1, 1885	250, 000	45, 000	42, 785	2, 215
First National Bank, Sabetha, Kans	Jan. 2, 1885	50, 000	10, 740	10, 585	155
First National Bank, Wyoming, Ill	Jan. 13, 1885	50, 000	11, 2 0	10, 670	530
First National Bank, Tarentum, Pa	...do	50, 000	42, 500	40. 130	2 370
First National Bank, Walnut, Ill	Jan. 21, 1885	60, 000	36, 000	34, 710	1, 290
Farmers' National Bank, Franklin, Tenn	Jan. 24, 1885	50, 000	10, 740	9, 565	1, 175
Citizens' National Bank, Sabetha, Kans.	Jan. 27. 1885	50, 000	11, 240	10, 990	250
First National Bank, Tucson, Ariz	Jan. 31, 1885	100, 000	28, 100	27, 550	550
Ripon National Bank, Ripon, Wis	Feb. 7, 1885	50, 000	16, 200	15, 885	315
Farmers' National Bank, Franklin, Ohio	Apr. 1, 1885	50, 000	27, 350	26, 175	1, 175

* No circulation issued.

NATIONAL BANKS WHICH HAVE GONE INTO VOLUNTARY LIQUIDATION UNDER THE PRO-
VISIONS OF SECTIONS 5220 AND 5221 OF THE REVISED STATUTES, ETC.—Cont'd.

Name and location of bank.	Date of liquidation.	Capital.	Circulation. Issued.	Retired.	Outstanding.
First National Bank, Prescott, Ariz.....	Apr. 9, 1885	$50,000	$11,250	$10,860	$390
National Union Bank, Swanton, Vt.......	Apr. 28, 1885	50,000	43,800	40,840	2,960
German National Bank, Memphis, Tenn.	May 6, 1885	175,300	120,100	107,028	13,072
Merchants and Farmers' National Bank, Shakopee, Minn......................	May 12, 1885	50,000	10,240	10,000	240
First National Bank, Superior, Wis.....	May 16, 1885	60,000	18,900	18,510	390
Shetucket National Bank, Norwich, Conn	May 18, 1885	100,000	72,000	67,698	4,302
Cumberland National Bank, Cumberland, R. I....................................	June 5, 1885	125,000	106,200	100,190	6,010
First National Bank, Columbia, Tenn...	July 14, 1885	100,000	66,800	62,340	4,460
Union National Bank, New York, N. Y..	July 21, 1885	1,200,000	25,100	15,819	9,281
First National Bank, Centerville, Ind...	Oct. 3, 1885	50,000	27,350	25,200	2,150
Manufacturers' National Bank, Appleton, Wis	Oct. 10, 1885	50,000	45,000	42,856	2,144
First National Bank, Plankinton, S. Dak.	Oct. 21, 1885	50,000	11,250	10,700	650
Valley National Bank, St. Louis, Mo.....	Dec. 4, 1885	250,000	44,960	41,165	3,795
First National Bank, Belton, Tex........	Jan. 6, 1886	50,000	23,490	22,260	1,230
First National Bank, Granville, Ohio....	Feb. 15, 1886	50,000	26,500	25,210	1,290
Concordia National Bank, Concordia, Kans......................................	Mar. 12, 1886	50,000	11,240	10,920	320
Citizens' National Bank, Beloit, Wis	Mar. 22, 1886	50,000	11,240	10,540	700
First National Bank, Dayton, Wash......	Mar. 24, 1886	50,000	13,490	12,940	550
First National Bank, Macomb, Ill	Apr. 14, 1886	100,000	89,520	82,404	7,116
First National Bank, Jesup, Iowa........	Apr. 20, 1886	50,000	25,760	24,980	780
Dallas National Bank, Dallas, Tex.......	May 8, 1886	150,000	33,750	31,770	1,980
First National Bank, Lewistown, Ill.....	May 12, 1886	50,000	45,000	41,110	3,890
First National Bank, Cedar Rapids, Iowa	May 28, 1886	100,000	35,490	32,422	3,068
First National Bank, Socorro, N. Mex ...	July 31, 1886	50,000	15,500	14,430	1,070
Custer County National Bank, Broken Bow, Nebr	Aug. 9, 1886	50,000	11,240	11,240	....
Roanoke National Bank, Roanoke, Va ..	Sept. 16, 1886	50,000	11,250	10,390	860
First National Bank, Brownville, Nebr...	....do	50,000	39,680	36,115	3,565
First National Bank, Leslie, Mich.......	Sept. 25, 1886	50,000	13,410	12,110	1,300
Mount Vernon National Bank, Mount Vernon, Ill	Oct. 11, 1886	51,100	45,000	42,177	2,823
National Bank, Piedmont, W. Va........	Oct. 14, 1886	50,000	45,000	40,940	4,060
First National Bank, St. Clair, Mich......	Oct. 20, 1886	50,000	39,310	37,050	2,260
First National Bank, Milford, Mich	Oct. 21, 1886	50,000	45,000	41,350	3,650
National Bank of Kingwood, W. Va......	....do	125,000	96,140	85,850	10,290
Merchants' National Bank, Lima, Ohio ..	Oct. 22, 1886	50,000	45,000	41,320	3,680
Hubbard National Bank, Hubbard, Ohio.	Oct. 23, 1886	50,000	45,000	42,882	2,118
Commercial National Bank, Marshalltown, Ohio	Oct. 25, 1886	100,000	22,500	20,980	1,520
First National Bank, Indianapolis, Ind .	Nov. 11, 1886	500,000	162,325	149,585	12,740
First National Bank, Concord, Mich	Nov. 27, 1886	50,000	11,250	10,970	280
Jamestown National Bank, Jamestown, N. Dak	Nov. 29, 1886	50,000	11,250	10,590	660
First National Bank, Berea, Ohio	Dec. 1, 1886	50,000	45,000	42,631	2,369
First National Bank, Allerton, Iowa	Dec. 6, 1886	50,000	11,250	10,240	1,010
Second National Bank, Hillsdale, Mich..	Dec. 18, 1886	50,000	13,892	11,043	2,849
Topton National Bank, Topton, Pa......	Dec. 28, 1886	50,000	18,000	16,510	1,490
First National Bank, Warsaw, Ill	Dec. 31, 1886	50,000	38,250	33,605	4,645
First National Bank, Hamburg, Iowa ...	....do	50,000	13,500	12,235	1,265
Darlington National Bank, Darlington, S. C	Feb. 10, 1887	100,000	22,500	21,470	1,030
Union National Bank, Cincinnati, Ohio..	Feb. 14, 1887	500,000	237,230	215,947	21,283
Roberts' National Bank, Titusville, Pa..	Feb. 28, 1887	100,000	75,610	70,030	5,580
National Bank of Rahway, N. J	Mar. 9, 1887	100,000	42,500	36,977	5,523
Olney National Bank, Olney, Ill.........	Mar. 11, 1887	60,000	27,000	25,820	1,180
Metropolitan National Bank, Leavenworth, Kans	Mar. 15, 1887	100,000	22,500	21,000	1,500
Ontario County National Bank, Canandaigua, N. Y	Mar. 23, 1887	50,000	11,250	10,620	630
Winsted National Bank, Winsted, Conn.	Apr. 12, 1887	50,000	11,250	10,115	1,135
Council Bluffs National Bank, Council Bluffs, Iowa.............................	May 5, 1887	100,000	22,500	21,230	1,270
First National Bank, Homer, Ill	June 22, 1887	50,000	11,250	10,925	325
First National Bank, Beloit, Wis........	June 30, 1887	50,000	11,250	10,290	960
Mystic National Bank, Mystic, Conn ...	July 7, 1887	52,450	47,205	44,365	2,840
Exchange National Bank, Louisiana, Mo.	July 12, 1887	50,000	11,250	10,823	415
Exchange National Bank, Downs, Kans.	Aug. 1, 1887	50,000	11,250	10,845	385
First National Bank, Tecumseh, Nebr ..	Nov. 3, 1887	50,000	11,700	11,180	520
Third National Bank, St. Paul, Minn ...	Nov. 4, 1887	500,000	45,000	41,820	3,180
First National Bank, Marshall, Mo......	Dec. 6, 1887	100,000	22,500	21,550	950
First National Bank, Greene, Iowa	Dec. 13, 1887	50,000	10,750	9,740	1,010
Fulton National Bank, New York, N.Y.*	Dec. 20, 1887	300,000	....	....	....
Fayetteville National Bank, Fayetteville, N. C	Dec. 31, 1887	200,000	39,580	35,731	3,849

* No circulation.

NATIONAL BANKS WHICH HAVE GONE INTO VOLUNTARY LIQUIDATION UNDER THE PROVISIONS OF SECTIONS 5220 AND 5221 OF THE REVISED STATUTES, ETC.—Cont'd.

Name and location of bank.	Date of liquidation.	Capital.	Circulation.		
			Issued.	Retired.	Outstanding.
National Bank, Somerset, Ky	Dec. 31, 1887	$50,000	$45,000	$38,105	$6,895
First National Bank, Richburg, N. Y	Jan. 10, 1888	50,000	25,905	24,450	1,455
Scituate National Bank, Scituate, R. I	Jan. 11, 1888	50,000	35,018	31,826	3,192
National Bank, Franklin, Ind	Jan. 31, 1888	50,000	11,250	10,445	805
First National Bank, Hampton, Iowa	Feb. 1, 1888	50,000	11,250	10,280	970
First National Bank, Greensburg, Kans.	Feb. 10, 1888	50,000	11,240	10,775	465
First National Bank, Central City, Nebr.	Feb. 11, 1888	50,000	10,710	10,190	520
Duluth National Bank, Duluth, Minn	Feb. 20, 1888	300,000	45,000	40,670	4,330
Bismarck National Bank, Bismarck, N. Dak	Mar. 1, 1888	50,000	11,250	10,570	680
First National Bank, Ashton, S. Dak	Mar. 6, 1888	50,000	11,250	10,430	820
Citizens' National Bank, Sioux Falls, S. Dak	Apr. 24, 1888	50,000	11,250	10,815	435
First National Bank, Stanton, Mich	Apr. 30, 1888	50,000	11,250	10,350	900
First National Bank, Fairmont, Nebr	May 1, 1888	50,000	11,250	10,800	450
First National Bank, Greenleaf, Kans	May 9, 1888	50,000	11,250	10,870	880
National Bank Genesee, Batavia, N. Y	May 21, 1888	75,000	44,434	37,9000	6,534
Strong City National Bank, Strong City, Kans	May 26, 1888	50,000	11,250	10,640	610
Citizens' National Bank, Saginaw, Mich.	June 1, 1888	100,000	45,000	40,400	4,600
Saugerties National Bank, Saugerties, N. Y	June 16, 1888	125,000	93,316	81,973	11,343
Hyde National Bank, Titusville, Pa	June 21, 1888	300,000	74,730	60,400	14,330
State National Bank, Omaha, Nebr	July 18, 1888	100,000	22,500	19,850	2,650
Cincinnati National Bank, Cincinnati, Ohio	Aug. 1, 1888	280,000	52,510	44,680	7,830
First National Bank, Worthington, Minn	Sept. 5, 1888	75,000	16,875	16,130	745
South Framingham National Bank, South Framingham, Mass	Sept. 8, 1888	100,000	21,720	18,380	3,340
First National Bank, Alameda, Cal	Sept. 4, 1888	100,000	27,000	22,800	4,140
First National Bank, Grass Valley, Cal.	Sept. 18, 1888	50,000	11,250	9,790	1,460
Merchants' National Bank of West Virginia, Morgantown, W. Va	Oct. 4, 1888	110,000	80,830	69,170	11,660
First National Bank, Cawker City, Kans.	Oct. 9, 1888	50,000	11,250	9,750	1,500
San Diego National Bank, San Diego, Cal	Nov. 7, 1888	100,000	22,500	19,350	3,150
National Exchange Bank, Auburn, N. Y.	Nov. 16, 1888	200,000	97,520	82,930	14,590
National Bank of Dayton, Wash	Nov. 21, 1888	50,000	11,250	9,590	1,660
First National Bank, Colby, Kans	...do	50,000	11,250	10,700	550
First National Bank, Russell Springs, Kans	...do	50,000	10,690	9,900	790
First National Bank, Columbia, S. Dak	Nov. 26, 1888	50,000	11,250	10,545	705
Citizens' National Bank, Kingman, Kans	Dec. 24, 1888	50,000	11,250	9,510	1,740
Bowery National Bank, New York, N. Y.	Jan. 2, 1889	250,000	217,710	186,080	31,630
Second National Bank, Ionia, Mich	Jan. 8, 1889	50,000	21,870	17,424	4,446
First National Bank, Johnstown, N. Y.	Jan. 16, 1889	100,000	86,590	77,858	8,732
First National Bank, Canandaigua, N. Y.	Jan. 26, 1889	75,000	17,100	12,215	4,785
Pendleton National Bank, Pendleton, Oregon	Feb. 4, 1889	50,000	11,250	9,910	1,340
Iowa City National Bank, Iowa City, Iowa	Feb. 7, 1889	200,000	45,000	38,320	6,780
Fleming County National Bank, Flemingsburg, Ky	Feb. 9, 1889	50,000	26,622	21,392	5,230
Merchants' National Bank, El Dorado, Kans	Feb. 26, 1889	100,000	22,500	20,910	1,560
Merchants' National Bank, Des Moines, Iowa	Mar. 1, 1889	100,000	22,500	18,925	3,575
Norwich National Bank, Norwich, Conn.	Mar. 15, 1889	220,000	77,150	60,165	16,985
First National Bank, Franklin, Nebr	Mar. 27, 1889	60,000	13,000	12,279	721
Farmers and Mechanics' National Bank, Buffalo, N. Y	Apr. 3, 1889	200,000	26,100	20,782	5,318
First National Bank, Du Bois City, Pa	Apr. 8, 1889	50,000	11,250	9,850	1,400
First National Bank, Cimarron, Kans.	Apr. 27, 1889	50,000	10,170	9,615	555
Traders' National Bank, San Antonio, Tex	Apr. 29, 1889	100,000	22,500	18,380	4,120
Merchants' National Bank, Duluth, Minn	May 20, 1889	200,000	45,000	41,520	3,480
Wright County National Bank, Clarion, Iowa	June 19, 1889	50,000	11,250	9,210	2,040
National Bank, Lawrence, Kans	June 29, 1889	100,000	49,809	39,044	10,765
National Bank, Le Roy, N. Y	...do	100,000	22,500	19,270	3,230
Halstead National Bank, Halstead, Kans	...do	50,000	11,250	10,300	950
Farmers' National Bank, Mt. Sterling, Ky	July 1, 1889	250,000	195,690	152,300	43,380
First National Bank, Keyport, N. J	...do	50,000	11,250	10,310	940
National Bank, Huntsville, Ala	...do	50,000	44,900	32,312	12,588
German National Bank, Newton, Kans	July 19, 1889	60,000	13,500	11,240	2,260
First National Bank, Clay Center, Nebr.	Aug. 8, 1889	50,000	11,250	10,320	930

NATIONAL BANKS WHICH HAVE GONE INTO VOLUNTARY LIQUIDATION UNDER THE PRO-
VISIONS OF SECTIONS 5220 AND 5221 OF THE REVISED STATUTES, ETC.—Cont'd.

Name and location of bank.	Date of liquidation.	Capital.	Circulation.		
			Issued.	Retired.	Outstanding.
Vernon National Bank, Vernon, Tex.*	Aug. 17, 1889	$60,000			
Butler National Bank, Butler, Mo	Aug. 23, 1889	66,000	$14,850	$12,280	$2,570
Second National Bank, Lebanon, Tenn	Sept. 18, 1889	50,000	11,250	8,030	3,220
National Bank, Kinderhook, N. Y	Oct. 1, 1889	125,000	78,220	65,163	13,057
First National Bank, Woodstock, Ill	Oct. 31, 1889	50,000	27,000	22,140	4,860
Farmers and Merchants' National Bank, Valley City, N. Dak	Dec. 1, 1889	65,000	14,630	12,000	2,630
Union National Bank, La Crosse, Wis	Dec. 9, 1889	100,000	22,500	19,440	3,060
Harper County National Bank, Anthony, Kans	Dec. 20, 1889	50,000	11,250	8,760	2,490
Lumberman's National Bank, Williamsport, Pa	Dec. 31, 1889	100,000	32,580	24,525	8,055
First National Bank. South Haven, Mich	....do	50,000	11,250	8,861	2,389
Durango National Bank, Durango, Colo	Jan. 6, 1890	50,000	11,250	11,250	
First National Bank, Fox Lake. Wis	Jan. 11, 1890	50,000	48,605	38,857	9,748
First National Bank, Ogallala, Nebr	....do	50,000	11,250	9,300	1,950
First National Bank, Stockton, Kans	Jan. 15, 1890	50,000	11,250	9,750	1,500
First National Bank, Rulo, Nebr	Jan. 20, 1890	50,000	30,300	23,450	6,910
First National Bank. Eagle Grove, Iowa	....do	50,000	11,250	10,060	1,190
Toledo National Bank, Toledo, Ohio	Jan. 21, 1890	100,000	35,920	24,455	11,465
National Exchange Bank, Kansas City, Mo	Jan. 28, 1890	200,000	45,000	33,280	11,720
National Bank, New Castle, Ky	Feb. 4, 1890	60,000	17,670	13,160	4,510
Plymouth National Bank, Plymouth, Mich	Feb. 25, 1890	50,000	11,250	9,785	1,465
First National Bank, Lockport, N. Y	Feb. 28, 1890	100,000	28,573	19,788	8,785
Merchants' National Bank, Amsterdam, N. Y	Mar. 15, 1890	100,000	32,680	29,000	3,680
National Bank of Texas, Galveston, Tex	Mar. 19, 1890	100,000	37,487	28,058	9,429
Bowie National Bank, Bowie, Tex.*	Mar. 27, 1890	50,000			
First National Bank, Union Springs, N. Y	Mar. 31, 1890	50,000	15,805	11,179	4,626
Ferris National Bank, Swanton, Vt	Apr. 18, 1890	50,000	11,240	*11,240	
First National Bank, Rock Island, Ill	Apr. 19, 1890	100,000	24,654	18,398	6,256
First National Bank. Ketchum. Idaho	Apr. 28, 1890	50,000	11,250	9,620	1,630
Winchester National Bank, Winchester, Ky	Apr. 29, 1890	200,000	45,000	32,650	12,350
First National Bank, Harper, Kans	Apr. 30, 1890	50,000	11,250	8,550	2,700
First National Bank. Loup City, Nebr	June 21, 1890	50,000	11,250	9,450	1,800
American National Bank, Waco, Tex	June 24, 1890	250,000	45,000	34,650	10,350
Hamilton County National Bank, Webster City, Iowa	June 30, 1890	50,000	11,250	8,970	2,280
Planters' National Bank, Henderson, Ky	....do	150,000	33,750	23,970	9,780
Wakefield National Bank, Wakefield, R. I	July 1, 1890	100,000	59,249	45,793	13,456
Jewell County National Bank, Mankato, Kans	July 2, 1890	50,000	11,250	9,560	1,690
Citizens' National Bank. Flint, Mich	Aug. 5, 1890	125,000	32,641	21,735	10,906
N. Village Bank, Bowdoinham, Me	Aug. 28, 1890	50,000	35,748	26,401	9,347
La Fayette National Bank, La Fayette, Ind	Aug. 29, 1890	300,000	64,033	41,168	22,865
Lincoln National Bank, Stanford, Ky	Sept. 8, 1890	200,000	45,000	34,910	10,090
Canastota National Bank, Canastota, N. Y	Sept. 25, 1890	55,000	55,927	41,561	14,366
First National Bank, Whitehall, Mich	Sept. 30, 1890	50,000	11,250	7,020	4,230
Meade County National Bank, Meade Center, Kans	Oct. 6, 1890	50,000	11,250	8,020	3,230
Farmers' National Bank. South Charleston. Ohio	Oct. 15, 1890	50,000	11,710	9,330	2,380
First National Bank, Columbus, Ohio	....do	300,000	220,465	156,745	63,720
Commercial National Bank, St. Paul, Minn	Oct. 27, 1890	500,000	45,000	33,000	12,000
German American National Bank, Kansas City, Mo	Dec. 5, 1890	250,000	45,000	31,350	13,650
First National Bank, Hill City, Kans	Dec. 20, 1890	50,000	10,750	8,440	2,310
First National Bank. Frankfort, Kans	Jan. 8, 1891	100,000	22,500	16,400	6,100
Second National Bank, Owosso, Mich	Jan. 13, 1891	60,000	13,500	10,480	3,020
West Side National Bank, Wichita, Kans	....do	100,000	22,500	15,430	7,070
Anthony National Bank, Anthony, Kans	....do	50,000	10,750	6,840	3,910
Commercial National Bank, Rochester, N. Y	Jan. 27, 1891	200,000	41,820	28,890	12,030
Mercantile National Bank, Louisiana, Mo	....do	50,000	11,250	7,270	3,980
National Bank, El Dorado, Kans	Feb. 9, 1891	50,000	10,745	7,385	3,360
First National Bank, Suffolk, Va	Feb. 12, 1891	50,000	11,250	7,960	3,290
Citizens' National Bank, Medicine Lodge, Kans	Feb. 19, 1891	50,000	11,250	8,138	3,112
Rome National Bank, Rome, Ga	Feb. 23, 1891	100,000	22,500	16,110	6,390

* No circulation.

NATIONAL BANKS WHICH HAVE GONE INTO VOLUNTARY LIQUIDATION UNDER THE PRO-
VISIONS OF SECTIONS 5220 AND 5221 OF THE REVISED STATUTES, ETC.—Cont'd.

Name and location of bank.	Date of liquidation.	Capital.	Circulation.		
			Issued.	Retired.	Outstanding.
Windsor National Bank, Windsor, Vt...	Feb. 24, 1891	$50,000	$22,500	$15,705	$6,795
Beadle County National Bank, Huron, S. Dak	Feb. 26, 1891	50,000	22,500	14,260	8,240
American National Bank, Sioux City, Iowa	Mar. 12, 1891	150,000	33,750	25,695	8,055
United States National Bank, Atchison, Kans	Mar. 24, 1891	250,000	45,000	29,390	15,610
First National Bank, Ashland, Kans....	Apr. 15, 1891	50,000	11,250	8,030	3,220
Washington National Bank, New York, N. Y	Apr. 13, 1891	300,000	45,000	32,410	12,590
First National Bank, Burr Oak, Kans...	May 15, 1891	50,000	11,250	7,660	3,590
Glenwood National Bank, Glenwood Springs, Colo	May 23, 1891	100,000	'22,500	15,280	7,220
First National Bank, Cardiff, Tenn	May 25, 1891	50,000	11,250	6,520	4,730
East Saginaw National Bank, East Saginaw, Mich	June 23, 1891	150,000	33,750	19,650	14,100
Twin City National Bank, New Brighton, Minn	...do	50,000	11,250	5,510	5,740
Merchants' National Bank, Binghamton, N. Y	June 25, 1891	100,000	61,638	46,833	14,805
First National Bank, Merced, Cal	June 30, 1891	200,000	43,400	28,630	14,770
National Bank of Union County, Morganfield, Ky	...do	100,000	88,090	52,100	35,990
Citizens' National Bank, Belton, Tex....	July 1, 1891	50,000	10,750	5,270	5,480
Citizens' National Bank, Gatesville, Tex	...do	50,000	11,250	5,960	5,290
Ord National Bank, Ord, Nebr	Aug. 22, 1891	50,000	11,250	6,490	4,760
First National Bank, Indianola, Nebr...	Aug. 31, 1891	50,000	11,250	7,185	4,065
National Bank, Anderson, S. C	Sept. 1, 1891	50,000	14,050	7,680	6,370
First National Bank, Flushing, Mich	Sept. 21, 1891	50,000	11,250	6,220	5,030
First National Bank, Francestown, N. H.	Oct. 10, 1891	100,000	61,135	35,470	25,665
Columbus National Bank, New York, N. Y.	Oct. 15, 1891	200,000	45,000	34,450	10,550
Citizens' National Bank, Colorado, Tex.	Nov. 3, 1891	60,000	13,500	5,970	7,530
First National Bank, La Grange, Ga	Dec. 1, 1891	50,000	11,700	8,260	3,440
Produce National Bank, Philadelphia, Pa.	Dec. 8, 1891	300,000	45,000	27,983	17,017
Merchants' National Bank, Kansas City, Mo	Dec. 22, 1891	1,000,000	45,000	19,990	25,010
First National Bank, Manitowoc, Wis...	Dec. 26, 1891	50,000	14,816	6,646	8,170
First National Bank, Fairfield, Tex	Dec. 28, 1891	50,000	11,250	6,200	5,050
Commonwealth National Bank, Philadelphia, Pa	Dec. 31, 1891	208,000	65,480	32,990	32,490
Merchants' National Bank, Fort Dodge, Iowa	...do	100,000	22,500	10,493	12,007
Giles National Bank, Pulaski, Tenn	Jan. 12, 1892	100,000	22,500	9,684	12,816
First National Bank, Quanah, Tex	...do	50,000	11,250	4,980	6,270
Northwestern National Bank, Aberdeen, S. Dak	Jan. 15, 1892	100,000	22,500	12,440	10,060
Castleton National Bank, Castleton, Vt.	Jan. 22, 1892	50,000	14,630	6,670	7,960
First National Bank, Chamberlain, S. Dak	Feb. 6, 1892	50,000	11,250	5,420	5,830
Sedan National Bank, Sedan, Kans	Feb. 9, 1892	50,000	11,250	5,620	5,630
Bronson National Bank, Painted Post, N. Y	Feb. 29, 1892	50,000	22,500	12,270	10,230
First National Bank, Ainsworth, Nebr..	Mar. 3, 1892	50,000	11,250	4,630	6,620
First National Bank, Leoti, Kans	Mar. 4, 1892	50,000	10,250	6,480	3,770
First National Bank, Blaine, Wash......	Mar. 9, 1892	50,000	11,250	6,650	4,600
Erath County National Bank, Stephenville, Tex	Mar. 15, 1892	50,000	11,250	5,750	5,500
American National Bank, Birmingham, Ala	Mar. 22, 1892	250,000	45,000	24,050	20,950
First National Bank, Wilber, Nebr	...do	50,000	13,000	5,940	7,060
First National Bank, Greenville, Mich..	Mar. 28, 1892	50,000	11,250	6,057	5,193
National Exchange Bank, Columbus, Ohio	Apr. 1, 1892	100,000	50,670	21,085	29,585
Citizens' National Bank, Roanoke, Va...	Apr. 4, 1892	100,000	21,700	10,983	10,717
Inter-State National Bank, New York, N. Y	Apr. 15, 1892	200,000	45,000	24,080	20,920
First National Bank, Platte City, Mo....	Apr. 25, 1892	50,000	11,250	4,470	6,780
First National Bank, Jetmore, Kans......	Apr. 30, 1892	50,000	11,250	5,250	6,000
Tampa National Bank, Tampa, Fla	May 2, 1892	50,000	11,250	4,760	6,490
Birmingham National Bank, Birmingham, Ala	...do	250,000	45,000	24,050	20,950
First National Bank, Stafford, Kans.....	June 15, 1892	50,000	11,250	5,050	6,200
National Bank Commerce, Hutchinson, Kans	...do	100,000	22,500	9,750	12,750
First National Bank, Grafton, Mass.....	June 21, 1892	100,000	25,102	10,894	14,208
First National Bank, Dorchester, Nebr..	July 5, 1892	50,000	11,250	4,350	6,900

NATIONAL BANKS WHICH HAVE GONE INTO VOLUNTARY LIQUIDATION UNDER THE PRO-
VISIONS OF SECTIONS 5220 AND 5221 OF THE REVISED STATUTES, ETC.—Cont'd.

Name and location of bank.	Date of liquidation.	Capital.	Circulation.		
			Issued.	Retired.	Outstand-ing.
First National Bank, Salina, Kans	July 5, 1892	$150,000	$33,750	$11,670	$22,080
Lincoln National Bank, Lincoln, Nebr	July 12, 1892	100,000	22,500	11,165	11,335
First National Bank, Aurora, Mo	July 22, 1892	50,000	11,250	3,750	7,500
Farmers' and Traders' National Bank, Oskaloosa, Iowa	July 30, 1892	100,000	22,500	8,200	14,300
First National Bank, San Luis Obispo, Cal	Aug. 27, 1892	150,000	33,750	13,140	20,610
First National Bank, De Smet, S. Dak	Sept. 14, 1892	50,000	11,250	4,950	6,300
Merchants' National Bank, Chatta-nooga, Tenn	Sept. 24, 1892	250,000	45,000	11,620	33,380
National Bank of the Republic, Tacoma, Wash	Oct. 1, 1892	200,000	45,000	15,190	29,810
First National Bank, South Sioux City, Nebr	Oct. 27, 1892	50,000	10,250	2,150	8,100
Continental National Bank, Kansas City, Mo	Nov. 11, 1892	200,000	44,500	7,550	36,950
First National Bank, Clyde, Kans	Nov. 15, 1892	50,000	10,750	3,270	7,480
Eugene National Bank, Eugene City, Oregon	Nov. 26, 1892	50,000	11,250	3,530	7,720
Commercial National Bank, Sioux City, Iowa	Dec. 1, 1892	150,000	33,750	13,650	20,100
First National Bank, Batesville, Ohio	...do	60,000	13,500	3,310	10,190
State National Bank, Lincoln, Nebr	Dec. 3, 1892	200,000	45,000	17,225	27,775
Woodson National Bank, Yates Center, Kans	Dec. 5, 1892	50,000	10,750	2,010	8,740
First National Bank, Pontiac, Mich	Dec. 31, 1892	100,000	21,750	18,213	3,537
First National Bank, Castle, Mont	Jan. 4, 1893	65,000	14,020	2,960	11,060
National Pemberton Bank, Lawrence, Mass	Jan. 10, 1893	150,000	143,010	38,920	104,090
First National Bank, Lorain, Ohio	...do	75,000	16,095	2,210	13,885
Covington City National Bank, Coving-ton, Ky	Feb. 1, 1893	500,000	225,000	41,970	183,030
Merchants' National Bank, Macon, Ga	Feb. 14, 1893	100,000	21,800	6,170	15,630
Ætna National Bank, Kansas City, Mo	Mar. 9, 1893	250,000	44,550	6,350	38,200
Citizens' National Bank, Orlando, Fla	Mar. 22, 1893	100,000	21,880	3,420	18,460
First National Bank, Lexington, Ill	Apr. 1, 1893	50,000	16,410	2,660	13,750
First National Bank, Ida Grove, Iowa	May 1, 1893	150,000	32,650	2,680	29,970
First National Bank, Burnet, Tex	May 22, 1893	75,000	16,150	1,150	15,000
Southern National Bank, New Orleans, La	June 5, 1893	500,000	45,000	6,700	38,300
First National Bank, Santa Monica, Cal	June 17, 1893	50,000	10,250	890	9,360
Finney County National Bank, Garden City, Kans	June 20, 1893	50,000	10,750	1,120	9,630
Lake National Bank, Wolfborough, N.H.	June 29, 1893	50,000	29,360	1,978	27,382
First National Bank, Wa Keeney, Kans	June 30, 1893	50,000	10,290	110	10,180
First National Bank, Springfield, Mo	July 6, 1893	50,000	11,250	1,385	9,805
Farmers and Merchants' National Bank, Rockwall, Tex	July 11, 1893	50,000	11,250	1,620	9,630
North Texas National Bank, Dallas, Tex.	July 13, 1893	1,000,000	45,000	2,100	42,900
Hoquiam National Bank, Hoquiam, Wash	July 18, 1893	50,000	11,250	500	10,750
Gate City National Bank, Atlanta, Ga	July 25, 1893	250,000	44,000	10,570	33,430
First National Bank, Big Timber, Mont.	July 27, 1893	50,000	10,750	510	10,240
Orono National Bank, Orono, Me	July 29, 1893	50,000	13,720	1,250	12,490
Central National Bank, Dallas, Tex	Aug. 3, 1893	150,000	33,750	1,650	32,100
Fourth National Bank, Chattanooga, Tenn	Aug. 10, 1893	150,000	44,200	1,540	42,660
Merchants' National Bank, Fort Worth, Tex	Aug. 15, 1893	250,000	45,000		45,000
Gallatin Valley National Bank, Boze-man, Mont	Aug. 18, 1893	100,000	22,000	1,170	20,830
Farmers' National Bank, Constantine, Mich	Sept. 4, 1893	50,000	11,250	1,050	10,200
First National Bank, Mankato, Kans	Sept. 15, 1893	60,000	13,500	1,190	12,310
Dillon National Bank, Dillon, Mont	Sept. 20, 1893	50,000	10,750		10,750
Gray National Bank, Middletown Springs, Vt	...do	50,000	11,250	900	10,350
Frankfort National Bank, Frankfort, Ky.	Sept. 21, 1893	100,000	22,500		22,500
First National Bank, Slaughter, Wash	Oct. 25, 1893	50,000	11,250		11,250
Total		86,613,010	44,140,984	40,720,119	3,420,865

NATIONAL BANKS IN LIQUIDATION UNDER SECTION 7, ACT JULY 12, 1882, WITH DATE OF EXPIRATION OF CHARTER, CIRCULATION ISSUED, RETIRED, AND OUT-STANDING, SUCCEEDED BY ASSOCIATIONS WITH THE SAME OR DIFFERENT TITLE, OCTOBER 31, 1893.

Name and location of bank.	Date of liquidation.	Capital.	Circulation.		
			Issued.	Retired.	Outstanding.
First National Bank, Kittanning, Pa	July 2, 1882	$200,000	$199,500	$191,725	$7,775
National Bank of Beaver County, New Brighton, Pa	Nov. 12, 1884	200,000	97,300	90,626	6,674
National Bank, Beaver Dam, Wis	Dec. 24, 1884	50,000	41,100	39,020	2,080
Merchants' National Bank, Cleveland, Ohio	Dec. 27, 1884	800,000	228,100	205,670	22,430
Union National Bank, Chicago, Ill	Dec. 29, 1884	1,000,000	62,800	49,435	13,365
First National Bank, Le Roy, N. Y	Jan. 2, 1885	150,000	135,000	127,088	7,912
Evansville National Bank, Evansville, Ind	Jan. 3, 1885	800,000	543,050	492,982	50,068
National Albany Exchange Bank, Albany, N. Y	Jan. 10, 1885	300,000	243,900	229,840	14,060
National Bank, Galena, Ill...............	Jan. 11, 1885	100,000	55,900	51,274	4,626
National State Bank, Lafayette, Ind.....	Jan. 16, 1885	300,000	117,000	102,774	14,226
First National Bank, Knoxville, Ill......	....do	60,000	43,600	41,037	2,563
Farmers' National Bank, Ripley, Ohio....	Jan. 17, 1885	100,000	87,400	80,771	6,629
City National Bank, Grand Rapids, Mich.	Jan. 21, 1885	300,000	45,000	40,858	4,142
Lee County National Bank, Dixon, Ill ...	....do	100,000	41,500	38,232	3,268
Fort Wayne National Bank, Fort Wayne, Ind	Jan. 25, 1885	350,000	257,300	240,144	17,156
National Exchange Bank, Tiffin, Ohio ...	Mar. 1, 1885	125,000	50,500	44,210	6,290
National Bank, Malone, N. Y	Mar. 9, 1885	200,000	65,900	59,206	6,694
Jefferson National Bank, Steubenville, Ohio	Mar. 21, 1885	150,000	132,600	124,042	8,558
First National Bank, Battle Creek, Mich	Mar. 28, 1885	100,000	89,200	82,875	6,325
Central National Bank, Danville, Ky....	....do	200,000	180,000	167,114	12,886
Knox County National Bank, Mount Vernon, Ohio..........................	Apr. 1, 1885	75,000	53,200	48,500	4,700
First National Bank, Houghton, Mich...	Apr. 18, 1885	100,000	45,000	39,804	5,196
National Bank, Fort Edward, N. Y	Apr. 22, 1885	100,000	88,960	82,381	6,519
National Bank, Salem, N. Y.............	May 4, 1885	100,000	86,100	80,911	5,189
National Exchange Bank, Seneca Falls, N. Y	May 6, 1885	100,000	88,400	83,889	4,511
Trumbull National Bank, Warren, Ohio.	July 5, 1885	150,000	132,400	122,995	9,405
Attleboro National Bank, North Attleboro, Mass	July 17, 1885	100,000	84,300	79,194	5,106
American National Bank, Detroit, Mich.	July 24, 1885	400,000	251,500	235,635	15,865
First National Bank, Paris, Ill	Aug. 12, 1885	125,000	111,500	102,637	8,863
First National Bank, St. Johns, Mich....	Aug. 14, 1885	50,000	21,000	18,915	2,085
Second National Bank, Pontiac, Mich...	Sept. 1, 18-5	100,000	43,000	39,748	3,252
Raleigh National Bank, Raleigh, N. C ...	Sept. 5, 1885	400,000	123,900	109,169	14,731
First National Bank, Danville, Ky	Sept. 22, 1885	150,000	130,500	119,158	11,342
Ohio National Bank, Cleveland, Ohio....	Jan. 1, 1889	400,000	57,763	45,265	12,498
National Bank, Lebanon, Ky	Apr. 7, 1889	100,000	45,000	38,511	6,489
Monmouth National Bank, Monmouth, Ill	Aug. 18, 1890	100,000	21,800	13,811	7,989
Muskegon National Bank, Muskegon, Mich	Aug. 27, 1890	100,000	21,720	16,085	5,635
First National Bank, Richmond, Ky.....	Oct. 3, 1890	250,000	66,979	44,494	22,485
First National Bank, Port Huron, Mich .	Oct. 15, 1890	135,000	57,480	40,443	17,037
Union National Bank, Oshkosh, Wis	Jan. 23, 1891	200,000	45,000	29,350	15,650
First National Bank, Grand Haven, Mich.	June 5, 1891	200,000	45,000	28,043	16,957
First National Bank, Plymouth, Mich....	Nov. 14, 1891	50,000	45,000	24,195	20,805
National Bank, Wooster, Ohio	Nov. 29, 1891	53,900	48,510	21,627	26,883
Defiance National Bank, Defiance, Ohio .	Dec. 7, 1891	100,000	22,500	10,666	11,834
First National Bank, New London, Ohio.	Mar. 23, 1892	50,000	11,250	6,138	5,112
Citizens' National Bank, Mankato, Minn.	Apr. 27, 1892	70,000	15,750	6,824	8,926
Third National Bank, Sandusky, Ohio...	Sept. 19, 1892	200,000	45,000	14,063	30,937
Third National Bank, Urbana, Ohio......	Oct. 15, 1892	100,000	22,500	7,132	15,368
Lumberman's National Bank, Muskegon, Mich	Jan. 16, 1893	100,000	22,500	5,320	17,180
Phoenix National Bank, Medina, Ohio....	Feb. 10, 1893	75,000	17,100	3,237	13,863
First National Bank, Chelsea, Vt	June 10, 1893	50,000	11,250	....	11,250
Farmers' National Bank, Owatonna, Minn.....................................	June 30, 1893	75,000	17,100	1,420	15,680
Total................................	....	9,943,900	4,615,552	4,018,483	597,069

NATIONAL BANKS WHICH HAVE GONE INTO VOLUNTARY LIQUIDATION UNDER THE PROVISIONS OF SECTIONS 5220 AND 5221 OF THE REVISED STATUTES OF THE UNITED STATES, FOR THE PURPOSE OF ORGANIZING NEW ASSOCIATIONS WITH THE SAME OR DIFFERENT TITLE, WITH DATE OF LIQUIDATION, AMOUNT OF CAPITAL, CIRCULATION ISSUED, RETIRED, AND OUTSTANDING ON OCTOBER 31, 1883.

Name and location of bank.	Date of liquidation.	Capital.	Circulation. Issued.	Retired.	Outstanding.
First National Bank, Roudont, N. Y.	Oct. 30, 1880	$300,000	$270,000	$259,817	$10,183
First National Bank, Huntington, Ind.	Jan. 31, 1881	100,000	90,000	87,115	2,885
First National Bank, Indianapolis, Ind.	July 5, 1881	300,000	279,248	263,177	16,071
First National Bank, Valparaiso, Ind.	Apr. 24, 1882	50,000	45,000	43,313	1,687
First National Bank, Stillwater, Minn.	Apr. 29, 1882	130,000	83,456	81,025	2,431
First National Bank, Chicago, Ill	do	1,000,000	90,000	82,483	7,517
First National Bank, Woodstock, Ill	Apr. 30, 1882	50,000	45,000	43,405	1,595
Second National Bank, Cincinnati, Ohio.	Apr. 28, 1882	200,000	180,000	172,580	7,420
Second National Bank, New York, N. Y.	do	300,000	376,890	365,045	11,845
First National Bank, Portsmouth, N. H.	Apr. 29, 1882	300,000	286,000	275,755	10,245
First National Bank, Richmond, Ind.	May 5, 1882	200,000	87,400	81,739	5,661
Second National Bank, Cleveland, Ohio.	May 6, 1882	1,000,000	510,800	489,905	20,895
First National Bank, New Haven, Conn.	do	500,000	355,310	345,230	10,080
First National Bank, Akron, Ohio	May 2, 1882	100,000	114,822	108,647	6,175
First National Bank, Worcester, Mass	May 4, 1882	300,000	252,000	244,555	7,445
First National Bank, Barre, Mass	May 9, 1882	150,000	135,000	130,246	4,754
First National Bank, Davenport, Iowa	do	100,000	45,000	42,077	2,923
First National Bank, Kendallville, Ind.	May 12, 1882	150,000	90,000	86,732	3,268
First National Bank, Cleveland, Ohio	May 13, 1882	300,000	266,462	254,337	12,125
First National Bank, Youngstown, Ohio	May 15, 1882	500,000	441,529	429,943	11,586
First National Bank, Evansville, Ind.	do	500,000	442,870	425,325	17,545
First National Bank, Salem, Ohio	do	50,000	110,540	106,550	3,990
First National Bank, Scranton, Pa	May 18, 1882	200,000	45,000	40,935	4,065
First National Bank, Centerville, Ind	do	50,000	64,525	61,404	3,121
First National Bank, Fort Wayne, Ind.	May 22, 1882	300,000	45,000	39,938	5,062
First National Bank, Strasburg, Pa	do	100,000	79,200	76,362	2,838
First National Bank, Marietta, Pa	May 27, 1882	100,000	99,000	95,410	3,590
First National Bank, Lafayette, Ind	May 31, 1882	150,000	175,000	165,653	9,407
First National Bank, McConnelsville, Ohio	do	50,000	84,640	80,979	3,661
First National Bank, Milwaukee, Wis	do	200,000	229,170	221,232	7,938
Second National Bank, Akron, Ohio	May 31, 1882	100,000	102,706	98,917	3,789
First National Bank, Ann Arbor, Mich.	June 1, 1882	100,000	85,078	81,219	3,859
First National Bank, Geneva, Ohio	do	100,000	90,000	85,830	4,170
First National Bank, Oberlin, Ohio	do	50,000	58,382	55,165	3,217
First National Bank, Philadelphia, Pa	June 10, 1882	1,000,000	799,800	760,555	39,245
First National Bank, Troy, Ohio	do	200,000	180,000	173,614	6,380
Third National Bank, Cincinnati, Ohio	June 14, 1882	800,000	609,500	585,530	23,970
First National Bank, Cambridge City, Ind	June 15, 1882	50,000	45,000	42,444	2,556
First National Bank, Lyons, Iowa	do	100,000	90,000	86,043	3,957
First National Bank, Detroit, Mich	June 17, 1882	500,000	336,345	327,458	8,887
First National Bank, Wilkesbarre, Pa	June 20, 1882	375,000	337,500	323,990	13,510
First National Bank, Iowa City, Iowa	June 24, 1882	100,000	88,400	85,810	2,590
First National Bank, Nashua, N. H.	do	100,000	90,000	85,622	4,378
First National Bank, Johnstown, Pa	do	60,000	54,000	51,930	2,070
First National Bank, Pittsburg, Pa	June 29, 1882	750,000	594,000	576,215	17,785
First National Bank, Terre Haute, Ind	do	200,000	141,575	133,963	7,612
First National Bank, Hollidaysburg, Pa.	June 30, 1882	50,000	45,000	43,565	1,435
First National Bank, Bath, Me	do	200,000	180,000	172,624	7,376
First National Bank, Janesville, Wis	do	125,000	121,050	116,900	4,150
First National Bank, Michigan City, Ind.	do	100,000	45,000	43,992	1,008
First National Bank, Monmouth, Ill	July 3, 1882	75,000	45,000	43,459	1,541
First National Bank, Marion, Iowa	July 11, 1882	50,000	45,000	43,096	1,904
First National Bank, Marlboro, Mass	Aug. 3, 1882	200,000	180,000	173,946	6,054
National Bank of Stanford, Ky	Oct. 3, 1882	150,000	135,000	130,739	4,261
First National Bank, Sandusky, Ohio	Oct. 6, 1882	150,000	90,000	85,752	4,248
First National Bank, Sandy Hill, N. Y.	Dec. 31, 1882	50,000	45,000	42,864	2,136
First National Bank, Lawrenceburg, Ind	Feb. 24, 1883	100,000	90,000	86,405	3,595
First National Bank, Cambridge, Ohio	do	100,000	80,800	77,783	3,017
First National Bank, Oshkosh, Wis	do	100,000	47,800	45,885	1,915
First National Bank, Grand Rapids, Mich	do	400,000	155,900	150,540	5,360
First National Bank, Delphos, Ohio	do	50,000	45,000	42,105	2,895
First National Bank, Freeport, Ill	do	100,000	53,500	51,208	2,292
First National Bank, Elyria, Ohio	do	100,000	90,000	86,368	3,632
First National Bank, Troy, N. Y.	do	300,000	229,550	220,335	9,215
Second National Bank, Detroit, Mich	do	1,000,000	363,700	344,563	19,137
Second National Bank, Peoria, Ill	do	100,000	90,000	84,003	5,997
National Fort Plain Bank, Fort Plain, N. Y.	do	200,000	174,300	167,686	6,614
Logansport National Bank, Logansport, Ind	Dec. 1, 1883	100,000	16,850	15,190	1,660
National Bank of Birmingham, Ala	May 14, 1884	50,000	45,000	43,479	1,521
First National Bank, Westfield, N. Y.	June 1, 1884	50,000	42,800	40,043	2,757
First National Bank, Independence, Iowa	Oct. 31, 1884	100,000	90,000	85,805	4,195

NATIONAL BANKS WHICH HAVE GONE INTO VOLUNTARY LIQUIDATION UNDER THE PRO-
VISIONS OF SECTIONS 5220 AND 5221 OF THE REVISED STATUTES OF THE UNITED
STATES, FOR THE PURPOSE OF ORGANIZING NEW ASSOCIATIONS WITH THE SAME OR
DIFFERENT TITLE, WITH DATE OF LIQUIDATION, AMOUNT OF CAPITAL, CIRCULA-
TION ISSUED, RETIRED, AND OUTSTANDING ON OCTOBER 31, 1893—Continued.

Name and location of bank.	Date of liquidation.	Capital.	Circulation.		
			Issued.	Retired.	Outstanding.
First National Bank. Sturgis, Mich	Dec. 31, 1884	$50,000	$43,850	$41,539	$2,311
National Bank, Rutland, Vt.............	Jan. 13, 1885	500,000	238,700	222,182	16,518
Kent National Bank, Chestertown, Md..	Feb. 12, 1885	50,000	18,200	16,800	1,400
National Fulton County Bank, Glovers- ville, N.Y..........................	Feb. 20, 1885	150,000	135,000	127,598	7,402
First National Bank, Centralia, Ill.......	Feb. 25, 1885	80,000	70,600	65,920	4,680
National Exchange Bank, Albion, Mich.	Feb. 28, 1885	75,000	30,600	28,408	2,192
First National Bank, Paris, Mo.........	Mar. 31, 1885	100,000	89,155	80,292	8,863
First National Bank, Yakima, Wash....	June 20, 1885	50,000	14,650	14,090	560
First National Bank, Flint, Mich	June 30, 1885	200,000	122,500	113,353	9,147
Farmers' National Bank, Stanford, Ky..	Dec. 31, 1888	200,000	45,000	34,552	10,448
Adams National Bank, Adams, N.Y	July 10, 1889	50,000	12,240	10,210	2,030
Poland National Bank, Poland, N.Y.....	Jan. 14, 1890	50,000	13,500	11,050	2,450
Sandy River National Bank, Farming- ton, Me...............................	Nov. 1, 1890	75,000	58,260	39,187	19,073
Second National Bank, Aurora, Ill......	July 13, 1891	100,000	22,500	11,682	10,818
Indiana National Bank, Lafayette, Ind..	Nov. 30, 1891	100,000	90,000	40,571	49,429
Decatur National Bank, Decatur, Ill...	May 31, 1893	100,000	22,500	2,350	20,150
Total.................................		18,245,000	12,694,713	12,053,338	641,375

NATIONAL BANKS IN LIQUIDATION UNDER SECTION 7, ACT JULY 12, 1882, WITH DATE OF EXPIRATION OF CHARTER, CIRCULATION ISSUED, RETIRED, AND OUTSTANDING OCTOBER 31, 1893.

Name and location of bank.	Date of liquidation.	Capital.	Circulation.		
			Issued.	Retired.	Outstanding.
First National Bank, Pontiac, Mich	Dec. 31, 1881	$50,000	$88,890	$85,353	$3,537
First National Bank, Washington, Iowa.	Apr. 11, 1882	100,000	88,565	85,664	2,901
First National Bank, Fremont, Ohio	May 22, 1882	100,000	90,000	86,125	3,875
Second National Bank, Dayton, Ohio	May 26, 1882	300,000	262,941	252,167	10,774
First National Bank, Girard, Pa	June 1, 1882	100,000	90,000	86,915	3,085
First National Bank, Xenia, Ohio	Feb. 24, 1883	120,000	108,000	103,605	4,395
First National Bank, Peru, Ill	...do	100,000	45,000	42,069	2,931
First National Bank, Elmira, N. Y	...do	100,000	90,000	86,300	3,700
First National Bank, Chittenango, N. Y.	...do	150,000	135,000	130,725	4,275
First National Bank, Eaton, Ohio	July 4, 1884	50,000	44,300	41,295	3,005
First National Bank, Leominster, Mass.	July 5, 1884	300,000	244,400	235,045	9,355
First National Bank, Winona, Minn	July 21, 1884	50,000	44,200	42,201	1,990
American National Bank, Hallowell, Me.	Sept. 10, 1884	75,000	67,500	64,290	3,210
First National Bank, Attica, Ind	Oct. 28, 1884	50,000	50,400	47,794	2,600
Citizens' National Bank, Indianapolis, Ind	Nov. 11, 1884	300,000	87,800	76,395	11,405
First National Bank, North East, Pa	Dec. 23, 1884	50,000	24,550	22,599	1,951
First National Bank, Galva, Ill	Jan. 2, 1885	50,000	36,000	33,386	2,614
First National Bank, Thorntown, Ind	Jan. 13, 1885	50,000	43,740	40,320	3,420
Muncie National Bank, Muncie, Ind	Jan. 28, 1885	200,000	161,000	151,063	9,937
Merchants' National Bank, Evansville, Ind	Feb. 6, 1885	250,000	90,800	80,477	10,323
Saybrook National Bank, Essex, Conn	Feb. 20, 1885	100,000	61,200	57,985	3,215
Union National Bank, Albany, N. Y	Mar. 7, 1885	250,000	144,400	135,990	8,410
Battenkill National Bank, Manchester, Vt	Mar. 21, 1885	75,000	57,700	54,077	3,623
First National Bank, Owosso, Mich	Apr. 14, 1885	60,000	47,700	44,704	2,996
Coventry National Bank, Anthony, R. I.	Apr. 17, 1885	100,000	89,000	83,942	5,058
State National Bank, Keokuk, Iowa	May 23, 1885	150,000	45,000	40,385	4,615
Tolland County National Bank, Tolland, Conn	June 6, 1885	100,000	44,100	40,691	3,409
City National Bank, Hartford, Conn	June 9, 1885	550,000	90,000	79,568	10,432
West River National Bank, Jamaica, Vt.	Aug. 17, 1885	60,000	54,000	50,993	3,007
National Bank of Lebanon, Tenn	Aug. 30, 1886	50,000	24,550	22,125	2,425
Greene County National Bank, Springfield, Mo	Feb. 8, 1888	100,000	22,500	18,362	4,138
Union Stock Yards National Bank, Chicago, Ill	Feb. 29, 1888	500,000	45,000	38,674	6,326
First National Bank, Decatur, Mich	Sept. 20, 1890	50,000	11,250	7,536	3,714
First National Bank, Mason, Mich	Oct. 28, 1890	50,000	13,500	9,345	4,155
First National Bank, Holly, Mich	Oct. 31, 1890	60,000	24,950	17,643	7,307
German National Bank, Evansville, Ind.	Dec. 24, 1890	250,000	98,030	75,157	22,873
Farmers and Merchants' National Bank, Vandalia, Ill	Jan. 10, 1891	100,000	22,500	13,670	8,830
National Bank of Chester, S. C	Mar. 2, 1891	100,000	33,250	21,945	11,305
First National Bank, Burlington, Wis	Dec. 19, 1891	50,000	10,750	4,952	5,798
Lansing National Bank, Lansing, Mich	Mar. 5, 1892	185,600	36,700	15,820	20,880
Ashtabula National Bank, Ashtabula, Ohio	July 11, 1892	80,000	67,850	24,770	43,080
Second National Bank of New Mexico, Santa Fe, N. Mex	July 17, 1892	150,000	33,750	10,754	22,996
Total		5,721,600	2,970,766	2,662,876	307,890

180   REPORT OF THE COMPTROLLER OF THE CURRENCY.

NATIONAL BANKS WHICH HAVE BEEN PLACED IN THE HANDS OF RECEIVERS,
DATE OF FAILURE, CAUSE OF FAILURE, DIVIDENDS PAID WHILE SOLVENT,
REDEEM CIRCULATION, THE AMOUNT REDEEMED, AND THE AMOUNT OUTSTANDING

	Name and location of bank.	Charter number.	Organization. Date.	Capital.	Surplus.	Total dividends paid during existence as a national banking association. Amount.	Per cent.
1	First National Bank, Attica, N. Y	199	Jan. 14, 1864	$50,000			
2	Venango National Bank, Franklin, Pa.	1176	May 20, 1865	300,000			
3	Merchants' National Bank, Washington, D. C.	627	Dec. 14, 1864	200,000			
4	First National Bank, Medina, N. Y	229	Feb. 3, 1864	50,000			
5	Tennessee National Bank, Memphis, Tenn.	1225	June 5, 1865	100,000			
6	First National Bank, Selma, Ala	1537	Aug. 24, 1865	100,000	$1,780		
7	First National Bank, New Orleans, La.	162	Dec. 18, 1863	500,000			
8	National Unadilla Bank, Unadilla, N. Y.	1463	July 17, 1865	150,000			
9	Farmers and Citizens' National Bank, Brooklyn, N. Y.	1223	June 5, 1865	300,000			
10	Croton National Bank, New York, N. Y.	1556	Sept. 9, 1865	200,000			
11	First National Bank, Bethel, Conn.	1141	May 15, 1865	60,000	2,236		
12	First National Bank, Keokuk, Iowa	80	Sept. 9, 1863	50,000			
13	National Bank of Vicksburg, Miss.	803	Feb. 14, 1865	50,000			
14	First National Bank, Rockford, Ill.	429	May 20, 1864	50,000			
15	First National Bank of Nevada, Austin, Nev.	1331	June 23, 1865	155,000	465	$7,500	4.9
16	Ocean National Bank, New York, N. Y.	1232	June 6, 1865	1,000,000		421,052	42.1
17	Union Square National Bank, New York, N. Y.	1691	Mar. 13, 1869	250,000			
18	Eighth National Bank, New York, N. Y.	384	Apr. 16, 1864	250,000		140,000	56
19	Fourth National Bank, Philadelphia, Pa.	286	Feb. 26, 1864	100,000			
20	Waverly National Bank, Waverly, N. Y.	1192	May 29, 1865	106,100	9,424	24,403	23
21	First National Bank, Fort Smith, Ark.	1631	Feb. 6, 1866	50,000		18,000	36
22	Scandinavian National Bank, Chicago, Ill.	1978	May 7, 1872	250,000			
23	Wallkill National Bank, Middletown, N. Y.	1473	July 21, 1865	175,000		103,250	59
24	Crescent City National Bank, New Orleans, La.	1937	Feb. 15, 1872	500,000		25,000	5
25	Atlantic National Bank, New York, N. Y.	1388	July 1, 1865	300,000	59,472	183,000	61
26	First National Bank, Washington, D. C.	26	July 16, 1863	500,000		805,000	161
27	National Bank of the Commonwealth, New York, N. Y.	1372	July 1, 1865	750,000		429,250	57.2
28	Merchants' National Bank, Petersburg, Va.	1548	Sept. 1, 1865	140,000		134,200	95.9
29	First National Bank, Petersburg, Va.	1378	July 1, 1865	120,000		97,770	81.5
30	First National Bank, Mansfield, Ohio.	436	May 24, 1864	100,000		102,066	102.6
31	New Orleans National Banking Association, New Orleans, La.	1825	May 27, 1871	600,000		108,000	18
32	First National Bank, Carlisle, Pa.	21	June 29, 1863	50,000		42,000	84
33	First National Bank, Anderson, Ind.	44	July 31, 1863	50,000		31,150	62.3
34	First National Bank, Topeka, Kans.	1666	Aug. 23, 1866	50,000		46,000	92
35	First National Bank, Norfolk, Va.	271	Feb. 23, 1864	100,000		90,500	90.5
36	Gibson County National Bank, Princeton, Ind.	2066	Nov. 30, 1872	50,000		6,000	12
37	First National Bank of Utah, Salt Lake City, Utah.	1695	Nov. 15, 1869	100,000		125,000	125
38	Cook County National Bank, Chicago, Ill.	1845	July 8, 1871	300,000		53,333	17.8
39	First National Bank, Tiffin, Ohio.	900	Mar. 16, 1865	100,000		108,279	108.2
40	Charlottesville National Bank, Charlottesville, Va.	1468	July 19, 1865	100,000		149,245	149.2
41	Miners' National Bank, Georgetown, Colo.	2199	Oct. 30, 1874	150,000		4,500	3
42	Fourth National Bank, Chicago, Ill.*	276	Feb. 24, 1864	100,000		184,008	184
43	First National Bank, Bedford, Iowa	2298	Sept. 18, 1875	50,000			

* Formerly in voluntary liquidation.

TOGETHER WITH CAPITAL AND SURPLUS AT DATE OF ORGANIZATION AND AT CIRCULATION ISSUED, LAWFUL MONEY DEPOSITED WITH THE TREASURER TO OCTOBER 31, 1893.

	Failures.			Lawful money deposited.	Circulation.			
Capital.	Surplus.	Receiver appointed.	Cause of failure.		Issued.	Redeemed.	Outstanding.	
$50,000	....	Apr. 14, 1865	W	$44,000	$44,000	$43,757	$243	1
300,000	....	May 1, 1866	U	85,000	85,000	84,789	211	2
200,000	....	May 8, 1866	U	180,000	180,000	179,364	636	3
50,000	$2,288	Mar. 13, 1867	T	40,000	40,000	39,761	239	4
100,000	20,435	Mar. 21, 1867	V	90,000	90,000	89,738	262	5
100,000	4,788	Apr. 30, 1867	B	85,000	85,000	84,591	409	6
500,000	37,903	May 20, 1867	Q	180,000	180,000	178,866	1,134	7
120,000	....	Aug. 20, 1867	W	100,000	100,000	99,800	200	8
300,000	32,000	Sept. 6, 1867	U	253,900	253,900	252,842	1,058	9
200,000	....	Oct. 1, 1867	G	180,000	180,000	179,676	324	10
60,000	4,610	Feb. 28, 1868	N	26,300	26,300	26,145	155	11
100,000	20,000	Mar. 3, 1868	Q	90,000	90,000	89,664	336	12
50,000	5,000	Apr. 24.1868	N	25,500	25,500	25,443	57	13
50,000	1,400	Mar. 15.1869	B	45,000	45,000	44,723	277	14
250,000	5,580	Oct. 14,1869	U	129,700	129,700	128,737	963	15
1,000,000	150,000	Dec. 13,1871	V	800,000	800,000	793,057	6,943	16
200,000	....	Dec. 15,1871	U	50,000	50,000	49,742	258	17
250,000	40,000	....do	F	243,393	243,393	241,092	2,301	18
200,000	33,905	Dec. 20,1871	U	179,000	179,000	177,840	1,160	19
106,100	27,139	Apr. 23,1872	U	71,000	71,000	70,114	886	20
50,000	2,500	May 2.1872	V	45,000	45,000	44,545	455	21
250,000	....	Dec. 12,1872	B	135,000	135,000	134,675	325	22
175,000	17,000	Dec. 31,1872	B	118,900	118,900	117,725	1,175	23
500,000	3,045	Mar. 18,1873	M	450,000	450,000	447,970	2,030	24
300,000	56,000	Apr. 28,1873	A	100,000	100,000	98,840	1,160	25
500,000	108,000	Sept.19,1873	M	450,000	450,000	442,854	7,146	26
750,000	56,027	Sept.22,1873	V	234,000	234,000	230,819	3,181	27
400,000	18,502	Sept.25,1873	R	360,000	360,000	356,520	3,480	28
200,000	11,801	...do	R	179,200	179,200	177,015	2,185	29
100,000	16,000	Oct 18,1873	P	90,000	90,000	88,927	1,073	30
600,000	14,161	Oct. 23,1873	W	360,000	360,000	356,000	4,000	31
50,000	25,000	Oct. 24,1873	U	45,000	45,000	44,435	565	32
50,000	23,839	Nov. 23,1873	P	45,000	45,000	44,203	707	33
100,000	7,000	Dec. 16.1873	P	90,000	90,000	88,914	1,086	34
100,000	3,000	June 3,1874	G	95,000	95,000	93,610	1,390	35
50,000	1,000	Nov. 28,1874	X	43,800	43,800	43,480	320	36
150,000	18,719	Dec. 10,1874	V	118,191	118,191	117,149	1,042	37
500,000	80,000	Feb. 1,1875	V	285,100	285,100	283,193	1,907	38
100,000	20,000	Oct. 22,1875	E	45,000	45,000	43,995	1,005	39
200,000	22.254	Oct. 28,1875	U	146,585	146,585	144,470	2,115	40
150,000	968	Jan. 24,1876	V	45,000	45,000	44,620	380	41
200,000	....	Feb. 1,1876	V	85,700	85,700	82,891	2,809	42
30,000	....	..do	N	27,000	27,000	26,740	260	43

NATIONAL BANKS WHICH HAVE BEEN PLACED IN THE HANDS OF RECEIVERS,

	Name and location of bank.	Charter number.	Organization.			Total dividends paid during existence as a national banking association.	
			Date.	Capital.	Surplus.	Amount.	Per cent.
44	First National Bank, Osceola, Iowa...	1776	Jan. 26, 1871	$50,000	....	$23,500	46.1
45	First National Bank, Duluth, Minn...	1954	Apr. 6, 1872	50,000	....	25,000	50
46	First National Bank, La Crosse, Wis..	1313	June 20, 1865	50,000	....	31,500	63
47	City National Bank, Chicago, Ill......	818	Feb. 18, 1865	250,000	....	182,500	73
48	Watkins National Bank, Watkins. N. Y	456	June 2, 1864	75,000	....	85,450	113.9
49	First National Bank, Wichita, Kans..	1913	Jan. 2, 1872	50,000	....	36,975	73.9
50	First National Bank. Greenfield, Ohio*	101	Oct. 7, 1863	50,000	....	80,300	160.6
51	National Bank of Fishkill, N. Y	971	Apr. 1, 1865	200,000	$36,205	143,000	71.5
52	First National Bank, Franklin, Ind...	50	Aug. 5, 1863	60,000	....	222,319	370.5
53	Northumberland County National Bank, Shamokin, Pa.	689	Jan. 9, 1865	67,000	2,976	670,000	1000
54	First National Bank, Winchester, Ill .	1484	July 25, 1865	50,000	....	71,750	143.5
55	National Exhange Bank, Minneapolis, Minn.	719	Jan. 16, 1865	50,000	....	124,000	248
56	National Bank of the State of Missouri, St. Louis, Mo.	1665	Oct. 30, 1866	3,410,300	....	....	....
57	First National Bank, Delphi, Ind	1949	Mar. 25, 1872	100,000	....	45,000	45
58	First National Bank. Georgetown, Colo	1991	May 31, 1872	50,000	....	....	....
59	Lock Haven National Bank, Lock Haven, Pa.	1273	June 14, 1865	120,000	15,000	153,600	128
60	Third National Bank, Chicago, Ill.....	236	Feb. 5, 1864	120,000	....	1,035,000	862.5
61	Central National Bank. Chicago, Ill...	2047	Sept. 18, 1872	200,000	....	38,000	19
62	First National Bank, Kansas City, Mo.	1612	Nov. 23, 1865	100,000	1,000	540,500	540.5
63	Commercial National Bank, Kansas City. Mo.	1995	June 3, 1872	100,000	7,214	25,000	25
64	First National Bank, Ashland, Pa.*...	403	Apr. 27, 1864	60,000	....	187,131	311.9
65	First National Bank. Tarrytown, N. Y*	364	Apr. 5, 1864	50,000	....	132,250	264.5
66	First National Bank. Allentown. Pa.*.	161	Dec. 16, 1863	100,000	....	....	....
67	First National Bank, Waynesburg, Pa.*	305	Mar. 5, 1864	100,000	222	86,692	86.7
68	Washington County National Bank, Greenwich, N. Y.	1266	June 13, 1865	200,000	....	205,940	102.9
69	First National Bank, Dallas, Tex......	2157	July 16, 1874	100,000	....	45,750	45.7
70	People's National Bank, Helena, Mont.	2105	May 13, 1873	100,000	....	10,000	10
71	First National Bank, Bozeman, Mont..	2027	Aug. 14, 1872	50,000	....	20,000	40
72	Merchants' National Bank, Fort Scott, Kans.*	1927	Jan. 20, 1872	50,000	....	34,731	69.5
73	Farmers' National Bank, Platte City, Mo.	2356	May 5, 1877	50,000	....	4,000	8
74	First National Bank, Warrensburg, Mo.	1856	July 31, 1871	50,000	....	57,750	115.5
75	German American National Bank, Washington, D. C.	2358	May 14, 1877	130,000	2,000	....	....
76	German National Bank, Chicago, Ill.*.	1734	Nov. 15, 1870	250,000	....	....	....
77	Commercial National Bank, Saratoga Springs. N. Y.	1227	June 6, 1865	100,000	11,872	113,000	113
78	Second National Bank, Scranton, Pa.*.	49	Aug. 5, 1863	100,000	....	392,125	392.1
79	National Bank of Poultney, Vt.......	1200	May 31, 1865	100,000	....	92,000	92
80	First National Bank, Monticello, Ind..	2208	Dec. 3, 1874	50,000	....	7,400	14.8
81	First National Bank, Butler, Pa......	309	Mar. 11, 1864	50,000	....	139,000	278
82	First National Bank, Meadville, Pa ...	115	Oct. 27, 1863	70,000	....	248,400	354.8
83	First National Bank, Newark. N. J....	52	Aug. 7, 1863	125,000	....	605,250	484.2
84	First National Bank, Brattleboro, Vt..	470	June 30, 1864	100,000	....	387,000	387
85	Mechanics' National Bank, Newark, N. J.	1251	June 9, 1865	500,000	251,802	1,198,000	239.6
86	First National Bank. Buffalo, N. Y....	235	Feb. 5, 1864	100,000	....	287,500	287.5
87	Pacific National Bank, Boston. Mass..	2373	Nov. 9, 1877	250,000	....	75,000	30
88	First National Bank of Union Mills, Union City. Pa.	110	Oct. 23, 1863	50,000	....	91,955	183.9
89	Vermont National Bank, St. Albans, Vt.	1583	Oct. 11, 1865	200,000	....	186,000	93
90	First National Bank, Leadville. Colo ..	2420	Mar. 19, 1879	60,000	....	63,000	105
91	City National Bank, Lawrenceburg, Ind.*	2889	Feb. 24, 1883	100,000	....	3,000	3
92	First National Bank, St. Albans, Vt...	269	Feb. 20, 1864	100,000	....	197,000	197
93	First National Bank, Monmouth, Ill ..	2751	July 7, 1882	75,000	....	15,000	20
94	Marine National Bank, New York, N. Y.	1215	June 3, 1865	400,000	....	659,613	164.9
95	Hot Springs National Bank, Hot Springs, Ark.	2887	Feb. 17, 1883	50,000	2,000	3,000	6
96	Richmond National Bank, Richmond, Ind.	2090	Mar. 5, 1873	270,000	....	274,000	101.5

* Formerly in voluntary liquidation.

TOGETHER WITH CAPITAL AND SURPLUS, ETC.—Continued.

Failures				Lawful money deposited.	Circulation.			
Capital.	Surplus.	Receiver appointed.	Cause of failure.		Issued.	Redeemed.	Outstanding.	
$50,000	$10,000	Feb. 25,1876	V	$45,000	$45,000	$44,523	$477	44
100,000	....	Mar. 13,1876	P	45,000	45,000	44,483	517	45
50,000	25,000	Apr. 11,1876	P	45,000	45,000	44,193	807	46
250,000	130,000	May 17,1876	V	137,209	137,209	133,960	3,249	47
75,000	3,000	July 12,1876	G	67,500	67,500	65,960	1,540	48
60,000	12,000	Sept. 23,1876	B	43,200	43,200	42,636	564	49
50,000	10,000	Dec. 12,1876	U	29,662	29,662	28,607	1,055	50
200,000	30,000	Jan. 27,1877	B	177,200	177,200	174,418	2,782	51
132,000	28,538	Feb. 13,1877	B	92,092	92,092	89,802	2,290	52
67,000	....	Mar. 12,1877	M	60,300	60,300	59,135	1,165	53
50,000	17,135	Mar. 16,1877	W	45,000	45,000	44,120	880	54
100,000	20,000	May 24,1877	M	90,000	90,000	88,180	1,820	55
2,500,000	248,775	June 23,1877	O	296,274	296,274	277,104	19,170	56
50,000	20,000	July 20,1877	W	45,000	45,000	44,108	892	57
75,000	65,000	Aug. 18,1877	U	45,000	45,000	44,495	505	58
120,000	8,000	Aug. 20,1877	V	71,200	71,200	69,748	1,452	59
750,000	200,000	Nov. 24,1877	V	597,840	597,840	580,078	17,762	60
200,000	10,000	Dec. 1,1877	V	45,000	45,000	44,243	757	61
500,000	25,000	Feb. 11,1878	X	44,940	44,940	42,260	2,680	62
100,000	6,392	....do	V	44,500	44,500	43,394	1,106	63
112,500	19,000	Feb. 28,1878	V	75,554	75,554	72,544	3,010	64
100,000	25,000	Mar. 23,1878	V	89,200	89,200	86,871	2,329	65
250,000	220,000	Apr. 15,1878	N	78,641	78,641	75,377	3,264	66
100,000	....	May 15,1878	V	7,002	7,002	6,202	800	67
200,000	24,000	June 8,1878	P	114,220	114,220	111,668	2,552	68
50,000	5,000	....do	V	29,800	29,800	29,230	570	69
100,000	8,000	Sept. 13,1878	Q	89,300	89,300	88,360	940	70
50,000	7,000	Sept. 14,1878	Q	44,400	44,400	43,705	695	71
50,000	13,500	Sept. 25,1878	X	35,328	35,328	34,588	740	72
50,000	....	Oct. 1,1878	N	27,000	27,000	26,700	300	73
100,000	10,600	Nov. 1,1878	X	45,000	45,000	44,012	988	74
130,000	2,000	....do	P	62,500	62,500	62,050	450	75
500,000	125,000	Dec. 20,1878	B	42,795	42,795	38,845	3,950	76
100,000	40,476	Feb. 11,1879	X	86,900	86,900	84,905	1,995	77
200,000	70,000	Mar. 15,1879	X	91,465	91,465	87,553	3,912	78
100,000	4,000	Apr. 7,1879	X	90,000	90,000	87,382	2,618	79
50,000	2,008	July 18,1879	N	27,000	27,000	26,446	554	80
50,000	10,000	July 23,1879	E	71,165	71,165	67,820	3,345	81
100,000	20,000	June 9,1880	R	89,500	89,500	86,064	3,436	82
300,000	62,584	June 14,1880	F	326,643	326,643	315,243	11,400	83
300,000	57,000	June 19,1880	N	90,000	90,000	84,663	5,337	84
500,000	400,000	Nov. 2,1881	C	449,900	449,900	430,854	19,046	85
100,000	50,000	Apr. 22,1882	P	99,500	99,500	96,535	2,965	86
961,300	....	May 22,1882	S	450,000	450,000	444,765	5,235	87
50,000	13,455	Mar. 24,1883	S	43,000	43,000	41,420	1,580	88
200,000	25,000	Aug. 9,1883	V	65,200	65,200	60,383	4,517	89
60,000	15,000	Jan. 24,1884	B	53,000	53,000	51,665	1,335	90
100,000	....	Mar. 11,1884	G	77,000	77,000	75,280	1,720	91
100,000	40,000	Apr. 22,1884	P	89,980	89,980	85,668	4,312	92
75,000	15,000	....do	B	27,000	27,000	26,030	970	93
400,000	225,000	May 13,1884	T	260,000	260,000	248,775	11,225	94
50,000	180	June 2,1884	E	40,850	40,850	38,820	2,030	95
250,000	33,000	July 23,1884	H	158,900	158,900	146,900	12,090	96

NATIONAL BANKS WHICH HAVE BEEN PLACED IN THE HANDS OF RECEIVERS,

	Name and location of bank.	Char-ter num-ber.	Organization.			Total dividends paid during existence as a national banking association.	
			Date.	Capital.	Sur-plus.	Amount.	Per cent.
97	First National Bank, Livingston, Mont.	3000	July 16, 1883	$50,000			
98	First National Bank, Albion, N. Y.	166	Dec. 22, 1863	50,030		$170,500	341
99	First National Bank, Jamestown, N. Dak.	2578	Oct. 25, 1881	50,000			
100	Logan National Bank, West Liberty, Ohio.	2942	May 7, 1883	50,000		4,000	8
101	Middletown National Bank, Middle-town, N. Y.	1276	June 14, 1865	200,000	$23,128	356,000	178
102	Farmers' National Bank, Bushnell, Ill.	1791	Feb. 18, 1871	50,000		38,500	77
103	Schoharie County National Bank, Schoharie, N. Y.	1510	Aug. 9, 1865	100,000			
104	Exchange National Bank, Norfolk, Va.	1137	May 13, 1865	100,000		337,500	337.5
105	First National Bank, Lake City, Minn.	1740	Nov. 29, 1870	50,000		30,142	
106	Lancaster National Bank, Clinton, Mass.	583	Nov. 22, 1864	200,000	32,894	285,000	142.5
107	First National Bank, Sioux Falls, S. Dak.	2465	Mar. 15, 1880	50,000		10,000	20
108	First National Bank, Wahpeton, N. Dak.	2624	Feb. 2, 1882	50,000		12,000	24
109	First National Bank, Angelica, N. Y.	564	Nov. 3, 1864	100,000		186,000	186
110	City National Bank, Williamsport, Pa.	2139	Mar. 17, 1874	100,000		38,500	38.5
111	Abington National Bank, Abington, Mass.*	1386	July 1, 1865	150,000	15,000	307,382	204.9
112	First National Bank, Blair, Nebr.	2724	June 7, 1882	50,000		23,000	46
113	First National Bank, Pine Bluff, Ark.	2776	Sept. 18, 1882	50,000			
114	Palatka National Bank, Palatka, Fla.	3266	Nov. 20, 1884	50,000			
115	Fidelity National Bank, Cincinnati, Ohio.	3461	Feb. 27, 1886	1,000,000		2,784	.3
116	Henrietta National Bank, Henrietta, Tex.	3022	Aug. 8, 1883	50,000		12,250	24.5
117	National Bank of Sumter, N. C.	3082	Nov. 26, 1883	50,000		13,500	27
118	First National Bank, Dansville, N. Y.	75	Sept. 4, 1863	50,000		75,825	151.6
119	First National Bank, Corry, Pa.	605	Dec. 6, 1864	100,000		168,500	168.5
120	Stafford National Bank, Stafford Springs, Conn.	686		150,000	10,000	306,000	204
121	Fifth National Bank, St. Louis, Mo.	2635	Dec. 12, 1882	200,000		75,000	37.5
122	Metropolitan National Bank of Cin-cinnati, Ohio.	2542	July 12, 1881	500,000		215,000	43
123	First National Bank, Auburn, N. Y.	231	Feb. 4, 1864	100,000		266,000	266
124	Commercial National Bank, Dubuque, Iowa.	1801	Mar. 11, 1871	100,000		146,806	146.8
125	State National Bank, Raleigh, N. C.	1682	June 17, 1868	100,000			
126	Second National Bank, Xenia, Ohio.	277	Feb. 24, 1861	60,000		278,000	463.3
127	Madison National Bank, Madison, S. Dak.	3597	Dec. 7, 1886	50,000		5,000	10
128	Lowell National Bank, Lowell, Mich.	1280	June 14, 1865	50,000		159,494	318.9
129	California National Bank, San Fran-cisco, Cal.	3592	Oct. 20, 1886	200,000			
130	First National Bank, Anoka, Minn.	2890	Sept. 14, 1882	50,000		18,000	36
131	National Bank of Shelbyville, Tenn.	2198	Oct. 29, 1874	50,000		81,265	163.2
132	First National Bank, Sheffield, Ala.	3617	Jan. 14, 1887	100,000			
133	Third National Bank, Malone, N. Y.	3366	July 15, 1885	50,000		2,000	4
134	First National Bank, Abilene, Kans.	2127	June 23, 1879	50,000		75,350	150.6
135	Harpers National Bank, Harpers, Kans.	3431	Jan. 6, 1886	50,000	1,000	10,000	20
136	Gloucester City National Bank, Glou-cester City, N. J.	3936	Oct. 26, 1888	50,000			
137	Park National Bank, Chicago, Ill.	3502	May 11, 1886	200,000		24,000	12
138	State National Bank, Wellington, Kans.	3564	Oct. 1, 1886	50,000		5,000	10
139	Kingman National Bank, Kingman, Kans.	3550	Sept. 16, 1886	75,000		20,500	27.3
140	First National Bank, Alma, Kans.	3769	Aug. 3, 1887	50,000		14,000	28
141	First National Bank, Belleville, Kans.	3386	Aug. 28, 1885	50,000		17,500	35
142	First National Bank, Meade Center, Kans.	3695	May 5, 1887	50,000		8,857	17.7
143	American National Bank, Arkansas City, Kans.	3992	Mar. 15, 1889	100,000		28,000	28
144	City National Bank, Hastings, Nebr.	3099	Dec. 27, 1883	50,000		44,547	89.1
145	People's National Bank, Fayetteville, N. C.	2003	June 27, 1872	75,000		182,500	243.3

* Restored to solvency.

TOGETHER WITH CAPITAL AND SURPLUS, ETC.—Continued.

	Failures.			Lawful money deposited.	Circulation.			
Capital.	Surplus.	Receiver appointed.	Cause of failure.		Issued.	Redeemed.	Outstanding.	
$50,000	....	Aug. 25, 1884	X	$11,240	$11,240	$10,995	$245	97
100,000	$20,000	Aug. 26, 1884	B	90,000	90,000	84,875	5,125	98
50,000	12,500	Sept. 13, 1884	E	18,650	18,650	18,277	373	99
50,000	1,000	Oct. 18, 1884	P	23,400	23,400	22,750	650	100
200,000	40,000	Nov. 29, 1884	I	176,000	176,000	167,423	8,577	101
50,000	7,500	Dec. 17, 1884	L	44,000	44,000	42,200	1,800	102
50,000	15,000	Mar. 23, 1885	B	38,350	38,350	35,360	2,900	103
300,000	150,000	Apr. 9, 1885	O	228,200	228,200	213,266	14,934	104
50,000	10,000	Jan. 4, 1886	E	44,420	44,420	42,380	2,040	105
100,000	20,000	Jan. 20, 1886	B	72,360	72,360	65,929	6,431	106
50,000	30,447	Mar. 11, 1886	J	10,740	10,740	10,160	580	107
50,000	4,000	Apr. 8, 1886	J	17,120	17,120	16,310	810	108
100,000	20,100	Apr 19, 1886	A	89,000	89,000	82,821	6,179	109
100,000	12,500	May 4, 1886	D	43,140	43,140	39,545	5,505	110
130,000	25,300	Aug. 2, 1886	L	25,425	25,425	25,425	....	111
50,000	11,000	Sept. 8, 1886	U	26,180	26,180	25,315	865	112
50,000	20,000	Nov. 20, 1886	V	26,280	26,280	25,360	920	113
50,000	....	June 3, 1887	V	19,210	19,210	18,335	875	114
1,000,000	50,000	June 27, 1887	B	90,000	90,000	86,587	3,413	115
50,600	8,000	Aug. 17, 1887	K	11,250	11,250	10,770	480	116
50,000	10,000	Aug. 24, 1887	A	11,250	11,250	10,230	1,020	117
50,000	15,000	Sept. 8, 1887	B	15,730	15,730	13,850	1,880	118
100,000	10,183	Oct. 11, 1887	V	73,820	73,820	65,211	8,618	119
200,000	24,000	Oct. 17, 1887	B	139,048	139,048	124,747	14,301	120
300,000	30,000	Nov. 15, 1887	F	44,430	44,430	39,610	4,820	121
1,000,000	180,000	Feb. 10, 1888	V	277,745	277,745	245,070	32,675	122
150,000	....	Feb. 20, 1888	R	63,446	63,446	54,126	9,320	123
100,000	20,000	Apr. 2, 1888	V	62,170	62,170	57,373	4,797	124
100,000	....	Apr. 11, 1888	B	22,500	22,500	18,785	3,715	125
150,000	14,000	May 9, 1888	V	48,470	48,470	40,875	7,595	126
50,000	3,000	June 23, 1888	S	11,250	11,250	10,925	325	127
50,000	10,000	Sept. 19, 1888	W	27,800	27,800	24,305	3,495	128
200,000	10,000	Jan. 14, 1889	Q	45,000	45,000	40,090	4,910	129
50,000	4,300	Apr. 22, 1889	B	11,250	11,250	10,112	1,138	130
50,000	25,000	Dec. 13, 1889	Q	16,710	16,710	12,805	3,815	131
100,000	....	Dec. 23, 1889	V	22,500	22,500	19,060	3,440	132
50,000	400	Dec. 30, 1889	W	10,750	10,750	9,160	1,590	133
100,000	17,600	Jan. 21, 1890	F	21,240	21,240	18,290	2,950	134
50,000	....	Feb. 10, 1890	F	10,750	10,750	8,680	2,070	135
50,000	....	June 12, 1890	F	11,250	11,250	9,870	1,380	136
200,000	21,000	July 14, 1890	F	45,000	45,000	33,300	11,700	137
50,000	3,915	Sept. 25, 1890	W	11,250	11,250	8,410	2,840	138
100,000	1,000	Oct. 2, 1890	X	22,000	22,000	17,805	4,195	139
75,000	1,603	Nov. 21, 1890	H	16,875	16,875	14,013	2,862	140
50,000	5,000	Dec. 12, 1890	G	11,250	11,250	9,295	1,955	141
50,000	4,000	Dec. 24, 1890	V	10,750	10,750	8,725	2,025	142
300,000	24,000	Dec. 26, 1890	G	45,000	45,000	27,880	17,120	143
100,000	....	Jan. 14, 1891	J	22,500	22,500	15,150	7,350	144
125,000	32,000	Jan. 20, 1891	R	28,800	28,800	19,538	9,262	145

NATIONAL BANKS WHICH HAVE BEEN PLACED IN THE HANDS OF RECEIVERS

Name and location of bank.	Organization.				Total dividends paid during existence as a national banking association.	
	Charter number.	Date.	Capital.	Surplus.	Amount.	Per cent.
146 Spokane National Bank, Spokane Falls, Wash.	3838	Jan. 24, 1888	$60,000			
147 First National Bank, Ellsworth, Kans.	3249	Sept. 11, 1884	50,000		$54,500	109
148 Second National Bank, McPherson, Kans.	3791	Sept. 16, 1887	50,000		8,500	17
149 Pratt County National Bank, Pratt, Kans.	3787	Sept. 8, 1887	50,000			
150 Keystone National Bank, Philadelphia, Pa.	2291	July 30, 1875	200,000		122,730	61.4
151 Spring Garden National Bank, Philadelphia, Pa.	3468	Mar. 13, 1886	500,000		122,198	24.4
152 National City Bank, Marshall, Mich..	2023	July 29, 1872	100,000		162.500	162.5
153 Red Cloud National Bank, Red Cloud, Nebr.	3181	May 10, 1884	50,000		23,275	46.5
154 Asbury Park National Bank, Asbury Park, N. J.	3792	Sept. 17, 1887	100,000			
155 Ninth National Bank, Dallas, Tex	4415	Sept. 12, 1890	300,000		18,000	6
156 First National Bank, Red Cloud, Nebr.	2811	Nov. 8, 1882	50,000		57,250	114.5
157 Central Nebraska National Bank, Broken Bow, Nebr.	3927	Sept. 28, 1888	60,000		8,400	14
158 Florence National Bank, Florence, Ala.	4135	Oct. 3, 1889	50,000			
159 First National Bank, Palatka, Fla....	3223	July 15, 1884	50,000		50.000	100.0
160 First National Bank, Kansas City, Kans.	3706	May 17, 1887	100,000		25,000	25
161 Rio Grande National Bank, Laredo, Tex.	4146	Oct. 28, 1889	100,000			
162 First National Bank, Clearfield, Pa...	768	Jan. 30, 1865	100,000		209,000	209
163 Farley National Bank, Montgomery, Ala.*	4180	Dec. 18, 1889	100,000			
164 First National Bank, Coldwater, Kans.	3703	May 9, 1887	52,000		2,080	4
165 Maverick National Bank, Boston, Mass.	677	Dec. 31, 1864	400,000	$61,390	084,000	241
166 Corry National Bank, Corry, Pa.......	569	Nov. 12, 1864	100,000		198,000	198
167 Cheyenne National Bank, Cheyenne, Wyo.	3416	Dec. 2, 1885	100,000		26,000	26
168 California National Bank, San Diego, Cal.	3828	Dec. 29, 1887	150,000		70,000	52.7
169 First National Bank, Wilmington, N. C.	1656	July 25, 1866	250,000		290,710	116.3
170 Huron National Bank, Huron, S. Dak.	3267	Nov. 21, 1884	50,000		27,750	55.5
171 First National Bank, Downs, Kans ...	3569	Oct. 12, 1886	50,000		17,693	35.4
172 First National Bank, Muncy, Pa......	837	Feb. 23, 1865	100,000		212,988	213
173 Bell County National Bank, Temple, Tex.	4404	Aug. 25, 1890	50,000		2,500	5
174 First National Bank, Deming, N. Mex.	3160	Apr. 22, 1884	50,000		56,250	112.5
175 First National Bank, Silver City, N. Mex.	3554	Sept. 17, 1886	50,000		30,000	60
176 Lima National Bank, Lima, Ohio......	2850	Jan. 16, 1883	100,000		87,500	87.5
177 National Bank of Guthrie, Okla	4383	July 31, 1890	100,000		2,500	2.5
178 Cherryvale National Bank, Cherryvale, Kans.	4288	Apr. 16, 1890	50,000		3,500	7
179 First National Bank, Erie, Kans......	3963	Jan. 15, 1889	50,000		5,954	11.9
180 First National Bank, Rockwell, Tex..	3890	May 29, 1888	50,000		15,000	30
181 Vincennes National Bank, Vincennes, Ind.	1454	July 17, 1865	100,000		441,000	441
182 First National Bank, Del Norte, Colo.	4264	Mar. 18, 1890	50,000		3,500	7
183 Newton National Bank, Newton, Kans.	3207	Jan. 28, 1885	65,000		58,500	90
184 Capital National Bank, Lincoln, Nebr.	2088	June 29, 1883	100,000		272,500	272.5
185 Bankers and Merchants' National Bank, Dallas, Tex.	4213	Jan. 21, 1890	500,000		35,000	7
186 First National Bank, Little Rock, Ark.	1648	Apr. 12, 1866	150,000		554,250	369.5
187 Commercial National Bank, Nashville, Tenn.	3228	July 22, 1884	200,000		232,500	116.25
188 Alabama National Bank, Mobile, Ala.	1817	May 13, 1871	300,000		255,830	85.02
189 First National Bank, Ponca, Nebr	3627	Jan. 28, 1887	50,000		24,000	48
190 Second National Bank, Columbia, Tenn.	2568	Oct. 3, 1881	50,000		64,400	128.8
191 Columbia National Bank, Chicago, Ill.	3677	Apr. 23, 1887	200,000		30,000	15

* Restored to solvency.

TOGETHER WITH CAPITAL AND SURPLUS, ETC.—Continued.

Failures.				Lawful money deposited.	Circulation.			
Capital.	Surplus.	Receiver appointed.	Cause of failure.		Issued.	Redeemed.	Outstanding.	
$100,000	$25,000	Feb. 3,1891	H	$21,700	$21,700	$17,515	$4,155	146
50,000	10,000	Feb. 11,1891	F	10,753	10.750	7,480	3,270	147
50,000	7,500	Mar. 25,1891	Q	11,250	11.250	7,890	3,360	148
50,000	3,000	Apr. 7,1891	H	10,750	10,750	7,350	3,400	149
500,000	100,000	May 9,1891	O	41,180	41,180	30,760	10,420	150
750,000	132,500	May 21,1891	Q	45,000	45,000	31,760	13,240	151
100,000	20,000	June 22,1891	D	44,000	44,000	25,413	18,587	152
75,000	3,000	July 1,1891	V		16,875		16,875	153
100,000	3,500	July 2,1891	G	20,700	20,700	14,860	5,840	154
300,000	4,600	July 16,1891	Q		45,000		45,000	155
75,000	9,000	...do...	Q		16,225		16,225	156
60,000	4,600	July 21,1891	G	13,500	13,500	10,123	3,377	157
60,000	500	July 23,1891	O	12,900	12,900	6,550	6,350	158
150,000	23,600	Aug. 7,1891	H	33,250	33,250	22,940	10,310	159
150,000	10,500	Aug.17,1891	G	22,500	33,750	28,190	5,560	160
100,000		Oct. 3,1891	V	22,500	22,500	16,200	6,300	161
100,000	46,000	Oct. 7,1891	S	95,597	95,597	54,447	41,150	162
100,000	8,000	...do...	V		22,500		22,500	163
52,000	790	Oct. 14,1891	H		11,200		11,200	164
400,000	800,000	Nov. 2,1891	F	78,894	78,894	46,470	32,424	165
100,000	17,000	Nov. 21,1891	R	96,180	96,180	57,195	38,985	166
150,000	15,000	Dec. 5,1891	O	24,750	33,750	17,070	10,680	167
500,000	100,000	Dec. 18,1891	O		45,000		45,000	168
250,000	17,512	Dec. 21,1891	B	7,880	52,880	7,880	45,000	169
75,000		Jan. 7,1892	U	18,000	18.000	10,470	7,530	170
50,000		Feb. 6,1892	V	10,750	10.750	5,820	4,930	171
100,000	15,958	Feb. 9,1892	S	94,899	94,899	51,617	43,282	172
50,000	2,500	Feb. 19,1892	B		11,250		11,250	173
100,000	13,500	Feb. 25,1892	P	11,250	22,500	11,250	11,250	174
50,000	4,000	...do...	P		11,250		11,250	175
200,000	44,000	Mar. 21,1892	G	45,000	45,000	22,438	22,562	176
100,000	2,000	June 22,1892	Q	21,800	21,800	6,890	14,910	177
50,000	1,000	July 2,1892	O		11,250		11,250	178
50,000	1,500	...do...	V	11,250	11,250	4,920	6,330	179
125,000	17,500	July 20,1892	Q		26,720		26,720	180
100,000	40,000	July 22,1892	R	41,320	41,320	20,320	21,000	181
50,000	4,800	Jan. 14,1893	G		11,250		11,250	182
100,000		Jan. 16,1893	Y	48.740	48,740	17,630	31,110	183
300,000	6,000	Feb. 6,1893	B		43,700		43,700	184
500,000	10,000	...do...	O	44,000	44,000	10,560	33,440	185
500,000	100,000	...do...	T	63,495	63,495	14,631	48,864	186
500,000	100,000	Apr. 6,1893	Q	45,000	45,000	11,700	33,300	187
150,000		Apr. 17,1893	V	42,800	42,800	800	42,000	188
50,000	3,400	May 13,1893	Q		11,250		11,250	189
100,000	18,500	May 19,1893	T		22,500		22,500	190
1,000,000	50,000	May 22,1893	Q		45,000		45,000	191

NATIONAL BANKS WHICH HAVE BEEN PLACED IN THE HANDS OF RECEIVERS,

	Name and location of bank.	Organization.				Total dividends paid during existence as a national banking association.	
		Charter number.	Date.	Capital.	Surplus.	Amount.	Per cent.
192	Elmira National Bank, Elmira, N. Y.	4105	Aug. 30, 1889	$200,000	....	$11,000	5.5
193	National Bank of North Dakota, Fargo, N. Dak.	4256	Mar. 12, 1890	250,000	....	52,500	21
194	Evanston National Bank, Evanston, Ill.	4767	June 29, 1892	100,000	....	2,000	2
195	National Bank of Deposit of the City of New York.	3771	Aug. 5, 1887	300,000	....	36,000	12
196	Oglethorpo National Bank, Brunswick, Ga.	3753	July 16, 1887	100,000	....	34,500	34.5
197	First National Bank, Lakota, N. Dak.	4143	Oct. 23, 1889	50,000	....	12,000	24
198	First National Bank, Cedar Falls, Iowa.	2177	Sept. 1, 1874	50,000	....	102,600	205.2
199	First National Bank, Brady, Tex	4198	Jan. 7, 1890	50,000	....	15,000	30
200	First National Bank, Arkansas City, Kans.	3360	June 30, 1885	50,000	....	62,000	124
201	Citizens' National Bank, Hillsboro, Ohio.	2039	Sept. 4, 1872	100,000	....	199,156	199.1
202	First National Bank, Brunswick, Ga.	3116	Feb. 2, 1884	55,000	....	56,200	102.2
203	City National Bank, Brownwood, Tex.	4344	June 17, 1890	75,000	....	58,000	77.3
204	Merchants' National Bank, Tacoma, Wash.	3172	May 2, 1884	50,000	....	110,000	220
205	City National Bank, Greenville, Mich.	3243	Aug. 28, 1884	50,000	....	32,250	64.5
206	First National Bank, Whatcom, Wash.	4090	Aug. 26, 1889	50,000	....	5,000	10
207	Columbia National Bank, New Whatcom, Wash.	4351	June 28, 1890	100,000	....	4,000	4
208	Citizens' National Bank, Spokane, Wash.	4185	Apr. 8, 1889	150,000	....	....	....
209	First National Bank, Philipsburg, Mont.	4658	Dec. 5, 1891	50,000	....	....	....
210	Linn County National Bank, Albany, Oregon.	4326	May 31, 1890	100,000	....	10,000	10
211	Nebraska National Bank, Beatrice, Nebr.	4185	Dec. 21, 1889	100,000	....	19.362	19.3
212	Gulf National Bank, Tampa, Fla	4478	Dec. 2, 1890	50,000	....	....	....
213	Livingston National Bank, Livingston, Mont.	4117	Sept. 11, 1889	50,000	....	4,000	8
214	Chemical National Bank, Chicago, Ill.	4666	Dec. 15, 1891	1,000,000	....	....	....
215	Bozeman National Bank, Bozeman, Mont. *	2803	Oct. 23, 1882	50,000	....	49,500	99
216	Consolidated National Bank, San Diego, Cal.	3056	Sept. 22, 1883	250,000	....	180,000	72
217	First National Bank, Cedartown, Ga.	4075	July 16, 1889	75,000	....	11,250	15
218	Merchants' National Bank, Great Falls, Mont.	4434	Oct. 7, 1890	100,000	....	....	....
219	State National Bank, Knoxville, Tenn	4102	Aug. 28, 1889	100,000	....	....	....
220	Montana National Bank, Helena, Mont	2813	Nov. 11, 1882	50,000	....	260,000	104
221	Indianapolis National Bank, Indianapolis, Ind.	581	Nov. 21, 1864	300,000	....	1,249,000	416.3
222	Northern National Bank, Big Rapids, Mich.	1832	June 5, 1871*	90,000	....	183,053	203.4
223	First National Bank, Great Falls, Mont.	3525	July 1, 1886	250,000	....	122,250	48.8
224	First National Bank, Kankakee, Ill.*.	1793	Feb. 20, 1871	50,000	....	140,500	280.9
225	National Bank of the Commonwealth, Manchester, N. H.	4692	Feb. 9, 1892	100,000	....	....	....
226	First National Bank, Starkville, Miss	3688	Apr. 30, 1887	50,000	....	16,500	33
227	Stock-Growers' National Bank, Miles City, Mont.	3275	Dec. 20, 1884	100,000	....	23,000	23
228	Texas National Bank, San Antonio, Tex.	3298	Jan. 31, 1885	100,000	....	26,000	26
229	Albuquerque National Bank, Albuquerque, N. Mex.	3222	July 14, 1884	50,000	....	69,750	133.5
230	First National Bank, Vernon, Tex ..	4033	May 13, 1889	50,000	....	39,000	78
231	First National Bank, Middlesboro, Ky.	4201	Jan. 8, 1890	50,000	....	....	....
232	First National Bank, Orlando, Fla...	3469	Mar. 16, 1886	50,000	....	27,500	45
233	Citizens' National Bank, Muncie, Ind*	2234	Mar. 15, 1875	100,000	....	196,902	196.9
234	First National Bank, Hot Springs, S. Dak.	4370	July 15, 1890	50,000	....	....	....

* Resumed since October 31, 1893.

TOGETHER WITH CAPITAL AND SURPLUS, ETC.—Continued.

Capital.	Surplus.	Receiver appointed.	Cause of failure.	Lawful money deposited.	Issued.	Redeemed.	Outstanding.	
						Circulation.		
$200,000	$16,009	May 26,1893	O	$43,000	$43,000	$4,460	$38,540	192
250,000	7,797	June 6,1893	Q	....	44,250	....	44,250	193
100,000	245	June 7,1893	T	....	22,500	....	22,500	194
300,000	60,000	June 9.1893	F	....	45,000	....	45,000	195
150,000	35,000	June 12,1893	Y	....	32,900	....	32,900	196
50,000	1,931	June 13.1893	U	....	11,250	....	11,250	197
50,000	25,000	....do......	L	....	11,250	....	11,250	198
50,000	3,000	....do......	T	....	10,800	....	10,800	199
125,000	25,000	June 15,1893	G	....	27,520	....	27,520	200
100,000	50,000	June 16.1893	Q	24,550	24,550	....	24,550	201
200,000	50,000	June 17,1893	V	....	44,000	....	44,000	202
150,000	6,000	June 20,1893	F	....	33,750	....	33,750	203
250,000	75,000	June 23,1893	Y	22,500	45,000	7,980	37,020	204
50,000	6,064	June 27,1893	Q	....	11,250	....	11,250	205
50,000	3,000	....do......	Y	....	11,250	....	11,250	206
100,000	1,000	....do......	Y	....	22,500	....	22,500	207
150,000	....	July 1,1893	Y	....	33,000	....	33,000	208
50,000	....	July 8,1893	Y	....	....	....	....	209
100,000	15,000	July 10,1893	V	21.700	21,700	....	21,700	210
100,000	7.500	July 12,1893	Y	....	21,780	....	21,780	211
50,000	....	July 14,1893	Y	....	11,250	....	11,250	212
50,000	10,000	July 20,1893	Y	....	10,750	....	10,750	213
1,000,000	....	July 21,1893	T	45,000	45,000	....	45,000	214
50,000	10,000	July 22,1893	Y	....	11,250	....	11,250	215
250,000	50,000	July 24,1893	Y	....	55,390	....	55,300	216
75,000	8,470	July 26,1893	V	....	16,370	....	16,370	217
100,000	....	July 29,1893	Y	....	22,500	....	22,500	218
100,000	7,000	....do......	Y	21,800	21,800	....	21,800	219
500,000	100,000	Aug. 2.1893	B	....	45,000	....	45,000	220
300,000	60,000	Aug. 3.1893	B	57,212	57,212	....	57,212	221
100,000	....	Aug. 5,1893	T	....	33,250	....	33,250	222
250,000	95,000	....do......	Y	....	45,000	....	45,000	223
50,000	22,000	....do......	....	....	11,250	....	11,250	224
200,000	5,000	Aug.12,1893	O	67,500	67,500	....	67,500	225
60,000	3,782	Aug. 9,1893	O	....	13,500	....	13,500	226
75,000	10,000	....do......	O	....	17,100	....	17,100	227
100,000	20,000	Aug.10.1893	Y	....	22,500	....	22,500	228
175,000	38,000	Aug.11,1893	V	....	45,000	850	44,150	229
100,000	10,000	Aug.12,1893	V	22,500	22,500	1,170	21,330	230
50,000	2,000	....do......	V	....	11,250	....	11,250	231
100,000	....	Aug.14,1893	Y	....	33,750	....	33,750	232
200,000	55,000	....do......	Y	....	45,000	....	45,000	233
50,000	10,000	Aug.17,1893	Y	....	11,250	....	11,250	234

NATIONAL BANKS WHICH HAVE BEEN PLACED IN THE HANDS OF RECEIVERS,

	Name and location of bank.	Organization.				Total dividends paid during existence as a national banking association	
		Charter number.	Date.	Capital.	Surplus.	Amount.	Per cent.
235	First National Bank, Marion, Kans..	3018	July 28, 1883	$75,000	....	$72,682	96.9
236	Washington National Bank, Tacoma, Wash.	4018	Apr. 23, 1889	100,000	....	44,000	44
237	El Paso National Bank, El Paso, Tex.	3608	Dec. 22, 1886	150,000	....	54,000	36
238	Lloyd's National Bank, Jamestown, N. Dak.	4561	May 4, 1891	100,000	....	6,000	6
239	National Granite State Bank, Exeter, N. H.	1147	May 15, 1865	100,000	....	240,500	240.5
240	Chamberlain National Bank, Chamberlain, S. Dak.	4282	Apr. 8, 1890	50,000	....	4,500	9
241	Port Townsend National Bank, Port Townsend, Wash.	4290	Apr. 18, 1890	100,000	....	....	.....
242	First National Bank, Port Angeles, Wash.	4315	May 19, 1890	50,000	....	....	.....
243	First National Bank, Sundance, Wyo.	4343	June 16, 1890	50,000	....	10,000	20
244	First National Bank, North Manchester, Ind.	2903	Mar. 17, 1883	50,000	....	38,673	77.3
245	Commercial National Bank, Denver, Colo.	4113	Sept. 6, 1889	250,000	....	....	.....
246	First National Bank, Dayton, Tenn..	4362	July 10, 1890	50,000	....	8,500	17
	Total			35,465,400	$547,080	25,681,555	70.2

A Defalcation of officers.
B Defalcation of officers and fraudulent management.
C Defalcation of officers and excessive loans to others.
D Defalcation of officers and depreciation of securities.
E Depreciation of securities.
F Excessive loans to others, injudicious banking, and depreciation of securities.
G Excessive loans to officers and directors and depreciation of securities.
H Excessive loans to officers and directors and investments in real estate and mortgages.
I Excessive loans to others and depreciation of securities.
J Excessive loans to others and investments in real estate and mortgages.
K Excessive loans and failure of large debtors.
L Excessive loans to officers and directors.
M Failure of large debtors.

TOGETHER WITH CAPITAL AND SURPLUS, ETC.—Continued.

	Failures.			Lawful money deposited.	Circulation.			
Capital.	Surplus.	Receivor appointed.	Cause of failure.		Issued.	Redeemed.	Outstanding.	
$75,000	....	Aug. 22, 1893	Y	....	$21,900	....	$21,900	235
100,000	$5,600	Aug. 26, 1893	Y	....	43,500	....	43,500	236
150,000	60,000	Sept. 2, 1893	F	....	33,750	....	33,750	237
100,000	10,000	Sept. 14, 1893	O	....	22,500	....	22,500	238
50,000	10,000	Sept. 23, 1893	Y	$18,637	41,137	$760	40,377	239
50,000	1,000	Sept. 30, 1893	V	....	11,250	....	11,250	240
100,000	....	Oct. 3, 1893	O	....	22,500	....	22,500	241
50,000	....	Oct. 5, 1893	Y	....	10,750	....	10,750	242
50,000	5,000	Oct. 11, 1893	T	....	11,250	....	11,250	243
50,000	10,000	Oct. 16, 1893	F	....	27,000	....	27,000	244
250,000	40,000	Oct. 24, 1893	Y	....	45,000	....	45,000	245
50,000	5,000	Oct. 25, 1893	Y	....	11,250	....	11,250	246
43,915,900	7,070,314	....	....	15,756,161	17,333,551	14,407,883	2,925,668	

N Fraudulent management.
O Fraudulent management, excessive loans to officers and directors, and depreciation of securities.
P Fraudulent management and depreciation of securities.
Q Fraudulent management and injudicious banking.
R Fraudulent management, defalcation of officers, and depreciation of securities.
S Fraudulent management, injudicious banking, investments in real estate and mortgages, and depreciation of securities.
T Fraudulent management, excessive loans to officers and directors, and excessive loans to others.
U Injudicious banking.
V Injudicious banking and depreciation of securities.
W Injudicious banking and failure of large debtors.
X Investments in real estate and mortgages and depreciation of securities.
Y General stringency of the money market, shrinkage in values, and imprudent methods of banking.

STATEMENT SHOWING THE NATIONAL BANKS WHICH FAILED DURING THE YEAR ENDED OCTOBER 31, 1893, WITH CAPITAL, SURPLUS AND LIABILITIES, OBTAINED FROM LAST REPORT OF CONDITION.

Name and location of bank.	Date of authority to commence business.	Date of failure.	Receiver appointed.	As shown at date of last report of condition.			
				Capital.	Surplus and undivided profits.	Other liabilities. *	Date of last report of condition.
First National Bank, Del Norte, Colo.....	Mar. 18, 1890	1892. Dec. 19	1893. Jan. 14	$50,000	$5,055.19	$128,066.97	1892. Dec. 9
Newton National Bank, Newton, Kans..............	Jan. 28, 1885	Dec. 15	Jan. 16	100,000	693.93	118,430.74	Dec. 9
Capital National Bank, Lincoln, Nebr..............	June 29, 1883	1893. Jan. 21	Feb. 6	300,000	27,180.75	702,686.62	Dec. 9
Bankers and Merchants National Bank, Dallas, Tex..	Jan. 21, 1890	Jan.. 23	Feb. 6	500,000	37,743.84	146,628.33	Dec. 9
First National Bank, Little Rock, Ark...	Apr. 12, 1866	Feb. 1	Feb. 6	500,000	137,661.60	620,936.14	Dec. 9
Commercial National Bank, Nashville, Tenn................	July 22, 1884	Mar. 25	Apr. 6	500,000	195,052.77	1,715,029.05	1893. Mar. 6
Alabama National Bank, Mobile, Ala..	May 13, 1871	Mar. 14	Apr. 17	150,000	1,654.54	105,680.55	Mar. 6
First National Bank, Ponca, Nobr........	Jan. 28, 1887	Apr. 26	May 13	50,000	4,186.96	143,616.77	Mar. 6
Second National Bank, Columbia, Tenn................	Oct. 3, 1881	Apr. 28	May 19	100,000	20,767.09	286,717.93	Mar. 6
Columbia National Bank, Chicago, Ill..	Apr. 23, 1887	May 11	May 22	1,000,000	98,406.55	1,811,934.58	1892. Dec. 9
Elmira National Bank, Elmira. N. Y.	Aug. 30, 1889	May 23	May 26	200,000	30,627.82	785,138.17	1893. May 4
National Bank North Dakota, Fargo, N. Dak...............	Mar. 12, 1890	May 29	June 6	250,000	36,934.75	63,525.23	May 4
Evanston National Bank, Evanston. Ill.	June 29, 1892	May 18	June 7	100,000	5,434.34	134,694.70	May 4
National Bank of Deposit, New York, N. Y....	Aug. 5. 1887	May 22	June 9	300,000	85,328.03	1,311,883.84	Mar. 6
Oglethorpe National Bank, Brunswick, Ga	July 16, 1887	May 18	June 12	150,000	49,609.41	258,676.53	May 4
First National Bank, Dakota, N. Dak	Oct. 23, 1889	May 27	June 13	50,000	7,851.56	25,620.23	May 4
First National Bank, Cedar Falls, Iowa..	Sept. 1. 1874	May 16	June 13	50,000	29,293.57	134,225.23	May 4
First National Bank, Brady, Tex	Jan. 7, 1890	May 26	June 13	50,000	5,440.94	63,661.93	May 4
First National Bank, Arkansas City, Kans..............	June 30, 1885	June 15	June 15	120,000	18,662.57	524,775.91	May 4
Citizens National Bank, Hillsboro, Ohio..............	Sept. 4, 1872	June 8	June 16	100,000	70,767.63	360,609.84	May 4
First National Bank, Brunswick, Ga.....	Feb. 2, 1884	May 18	June 17	200,000	67,189.07	369,043.01	May 4
City National Bank, Brownwood Tex...	June 17, 1890	June 16	June 20	150,000	15,517.74	203,354.29	May 4
Merchants' National Bank, Tacoma, Wash..............	May 2, 1884	June 1	June 23	250,000	107,376.81	808,745.00	May 4
City National Bank, Greenville, Mich..	Aug. 28, 1884	June 22	June 27	50,000	16,094.75	265,840.97	May 4
First National Bank, Whatcom, Wash...	Aug. 26, 1889	June 22	June 27	50,000	21,056.44	74,416.03	May 4
Columbia National Bank, New Whatcom, Wash	June 28, 1890	June 23	June 27	100,000	9,712.40	118,870.27	May 4
Citizens National Bank, Spokane, Wash..............	Apr. 8, 1889	June 6	July 1	150,000	51,470.33	401,498.07	May 4
First National Bank, Phillipsburg, Mont.	Dec. 5, 1891	July 1	July 8	50,000	14,086.14	180,661.30	May 4
Linn County National Bank, Albany, Oregon......	May 31, 1890	June 19	July 10	100,000	20,105.22	234,666.14	May 4

* Total, as per report, except capital, surplus, circulation, undivided profits, and unpaid dividends.

STATEMENT SHOWING THE NATIONAL BANKS WHICH FAILED DURING THE YEAR ENDED OCTOBER 31, 1893—Continued.

Name and location of bank.	Date of authority to commence business.	Date of failure.	Receiver appointed.	As shown at date of last report of condition.				Date of last report of condition.
				Capital.	Surplus and undivided profits.	Other liabilities.		
Nebraska National Bank, Beatrice, Nebr	Dec. 21, 1889	June 30	July 12	$100,000	$13,908.70	$250,970.62	May 4
Gulf National Bauk, Tampa, Fla	Dec. 2, 1890	May 29	July 14	50,000	5,095.93	159,662.54	May 4
Livingston National Bank, Livingston, Mont*	Sept. 11, 1889	July 7	July 20	50,000	16,693.20	125,513.34	May 4
Chemical National Bauk, Chicago, Ill	Dec. 15, 1891	May 9	July 21	1,000,000	71,982.50	1,039,878.40	Mar. 6
Bozeman National Bank, Bozeman, Mont	Oct. 23, 1882	July 19	July 22	50,000	14,860.87	187,351.47	July 12
Consolidated National Bank, San Diego, Cal	Sept. 22, 1883	June 21	July 24	250,000	74,587.01	808,924.85	May 4
First National Bank, Cedartown, Ga	July 16, 1889	July 17	July 26	75,000	6,837.12	82,664.01	July 12
Merchants' National Bank, Great Falls, Mont	Oct. 7, 1890	July 24	July 29	100,000	11,015.57	178,230.58	July 13
State National Bank, Knoxville, Tenn	Aug. 28, 1889	July 22	July 29	100,000	14,459.56	152,983.33	July 12
Montana National Bank, Helena, Mont	Nov. 11, 1882	July 27	Aug. 2	500,000	210,290.55	1,189,516.08	July 13
Indianapolis National Bank, Indianapolis, Ind	Nov. 21, 1864	July 25	Aug. 3	300,000	144,448.48	1,823,705.08	July 12
Northern National Bank, Big Rapids, Mich	June 5, 1871	July 8	Aug. 5	100,000	4,164.90	334,270.54	May 4
First National Bank, Great Falls, Mont	July 1, 1886	July 28	Aug. 5	250,000	121,738.04	886,886.97	July 12
First National Bank, Kankakee, Ill.*	Feb. 20, 1871	July 29	Aug. 5	50,000	31,516.97	181,083.15	July 12
National Bank of the Commonwealth, Manchester, N.H	Feb. 9, 1892	July 25	Aug. 12	200,000	21,589.49	335,520.71	July 12
First National Bank, Starkville, Miss	Apr. 30, 1887	July 14	Aug. 9	60,000	9,772.44	49,400.72	July 12
Stock Growers National Bank, Miles City, Mont	Dec. 20, 1884	July 29	Aug. 9	75,000	29,123.91	205,192.21	July 12
Texas National Bank, San Antonio Tex	Jan. 31, 1885	Aug. 4	Aug. 10	100,000	26,620.84	113,373.87	July 12
Albuquerque National Bank, Albuquerque, N. Mex.	July 14, 1884	July 3	Aug. 11	175,000	46,353.03	433,559.43	May 4
First National Bauk, Vernon, Tex	May 13, 1889	July 22	Aug. 12	100,000	12,617.58	141,753.54	July 12
First National Bank, Middlesboro.Ky	Jan. 8, 1890	July 27	Aug. 12	50,000	4,178.57	37,305.53	July 12
First National Bank, Orlando, Fla	Mar. 16, 1886	July 24	Aug. 14	150,000	4,789.88	444,514.13	May 4
Citizens' National Bank, Muncie, Ind*.	Mar. 15, 1875	Aug. 4	Aug. 14	200,000	98,922.96	297,150.19	July 12
First National Bank, Hot Springs, S.Dak.	July 15, 1890	July 7	Aug. 17	50,000	13,944.85	83,108.91	May 4
First National Bank, Marion, Kans	July 28, 1883	Aug. 16	Aug. 22	50,000	1,248.01	82,017.54	July 12
Washington National Bank, Tacoma, Wash	Apr. 23, 1889	Aug. 24	Aug. 26	100,000	6,389.40	119,781.87	July 12
El Paso National Bank, El Paso, Tex.	Dec. 22, 1886	Aug. 1	Sept. 2	150,000	78,652.61	289,391.69	July 12
Lloyds National Bank. Jamestown, N. Dak	May 4, 1891	July 10	Sept. 14	100,000	25,221.65	164,409.40	May 4
National Granite State Bank, Exeter, N.H	May 15, 1865	July 27	Sept. 23	50,000	10,000.00	138,355.40	July 12

*Resumed since October 31.

STATEMENT SHOWING THE NATIONAL BANKS WHICH FAILED DURING THE YEAR ENDED OCTOBER 31, 1893—Continued.

Name and location of bank.	Date of authority to commence business.	Date of failure.	Receiver appointed.	As shown at date of last report of condition.			
				Capital.	Surplus and undivided profits.	Other liabilities.*	Date of last report of condition.
Chamberlain National Bank, Chamberlain, S. Dak	Apr. 8, 1890	1892. July 28	1893. Sept. 30	$50,000	$6,361.46	$31,410.51	1892. July 12
Port Townsend National Bank, Port Townsend, Wash...	Apr. 18, 1890	Sept. 18	Oct. 3	100,000	3,832.85	13,375.67	July 12
First National Bank, Port Angeles, Wash	May 19, 1890	June 26	Oct. 5	50,000	4,493.74	130,976.92	May 4
First National Bank, Sundance, Wyo	June 10, 1890	Oct. 3	Oct. 11	50,000	8,463.54	67,943.70	July 12
First National Bank, North Manchester, Ind	Mar. 17, 1883	Oct. 4	Oct. 16	50,000	16,696.47	104,256.41	Oct. 3
Commercial National Bank, Denver, Colo.	Sept. 6, 1889	July 18	Oct. 24	250,000	66,741.80	463,216.11	July 12
First National Bank, Dayton, Tenn	July 10, 1890	Oct. 21	Oct. 25	50,000	2,371.77	51,488.90	Oct. 3
Total...........				10,935,000	2,431,952.21	24,049,466.75	

STATEMENT GIVING THE TITLE OF THE FIVE NATIONAL BANKS THE AFFAIRS OF WHICH WERE CLOSED DURING THE YEAR ENDED OCTOBER 31, 1893, WITH DATE OF APPOINTMENT OF RECEIVER, TOTAL DIVIDENDS ON PRINCIPAL OF CLAIMS, AND PROPORTION OF INTEREST PAID.

Name and location of bank.	Date of appointment of receiver.	Total dividends on principal.	Proportion of interest paid.
		Per cent.	Per cent.
First National Bank, Albion, N. Y	Aug. 26, 1884	35	....
Middletown National Bank, Middletown, N. Y	Nov. 29, 1884	100	21.6
First National Bank, Erie, Kans................................	July 2, 1892	100	....
Pacific National Bank, Boston, Mass	May 22, 1892	65.3	....
First National Bank, Union Mills, Union City, Pa..............	Mar. 24, 1883	70	....

DIVIDENDS, FIFTY-NINE IN NUMBER, PAID TO THE CREDITORS OF INSOLVENT NATIONAL BANKS DURING THE PAST YEAR, WITH THE TOTAL DIVIDENDS IN EACH CASE UP TO NOVEMBER 1, 1893.

Name and location of bank.	Date of appointment of receiver.	Dividends paid during the year.			Total dividends paid depositors.	Proportion of interest paid depositors.
		Date.	Amount.	Per cent.		
				Per cent.	*Per cent.*	
First National Bank, Union Mills, Union City, Pa	Mar. 24, 1883	Apr. 15, 1893	$1, 642. 08	.90	70. 90	
First National Bank, Albion, N. Y	Aug. 26, 1884	Apr. 19, 1893	26, 649. 76	6. 50	35	
Middletown National Bank, Middletown, N. Y	Nov. 29, 1884	May 29, 1893	29, 911. 15	4. 6	100	21. 16
First National Bank, Abilene, Kans	Jan. 21, 1890	Apr. 21, 1893	7, 563. 30	10	80	
First National Bank, Belleville, Kaus	Dec. 12, 1890	Mar. 28, 1893	7, 629. 02	25	95	
Do	...do	Oct. 31, 1893	1, 526. 31	5	100	
People's National Bank, Fayetteville, N. C	Jan. 20, 1891	Aug. 25, 1893	20, 246. 81	15	50	
Second National Bank, McPherson, Kans	Mar. 25, 1891	Jan. 24, 1893	8, 459. 86	20	40	
Do	...do	Oct. 27. 1893	4, 428. 32	10. 3	50. 3	
National City Bank, Marshall, Mich	June 22, 1891	Sept.26, 1893	15, 504. 80	10	95	
Ninth National Bank, Dallas, Tex	July 16, 1891	Oct. 11, 1893	19, 620. 00	20	35	
Florence National Bank, Florence, Ala	July 23, 1891	Aug. 1, 1893	8, 255. 48	25	25	
First National Bank, Palatka, Fla	Aug. 7, 1891	May 17, 1893	27, 430. 34	10	45	
First National Bank, Clearfield, Pa	Oct. 7, 1891	Jan. 21, 1893	39, 756. 50	25	75	
Do	...do	June 16, 1893	37, 424. 46	25	100	
First National Bank, Coldwater, Kaus	Oct. 14, 1891	July 1, 1893	8, 502. 91	25	50	
Corry National Bank, Corry, Pa	Nov.21, 1891	May 26, 1893	56, 795. 15	10	60	
Cheyenne National Bank, Cheyenne, Wyo	Dec. 5, 1891	Apr. 29, 1893	28, 115. 77	10	50	
Do	...do	Dec. 22, 1892	42, 124. 66	15	40	
First National Bank, Wilmington, N. C	Dec. 21, 1891	June 5, 1893	53, 070. 91	10	40	
Huron National Bank, Huron, S. Dak	Jan. 7, 1892	Apr. 5, 1893	2, 827. 36	20	40	
First National Bank, Dowus, Kans	Feb. 6. 1892	Aug. 28, 1893	12, 615. 81	35	60	
Bell County National Bank, Temple, Tex	Feb. 19, 1892	Fob. 10, 1893	7, 732. 17	30	60	
First National Bank, Deming, N. Mex	Feb. 29, 1892	Oct. 11, 1893	20, 294. 94	15	40	
First National Bank, Silver City, N. Mex	...do	...do	16, 901. 14	20	40	
Lima National Bank, Lima, Ohio	Mar. 21, 1892	Nov. 30, 1892	5, 322. 60		100	100
Cherryvale National Bauk, Cherryvale, Kans	July 2, 1892	Feb. 4, 1893	3, 115. 96	20	20	
First National Bank, Erie, Kaus	July 2, 1892	Feb. 14, 1893	11, 725. 18	30	100	
First National Bank, Rockwall. Tex	July 20, 1892	Oct. 23, 1893	15, 900. 00	35	35	
Vincennes National Bank, Vincennes, Iud	July 22, 1892	Jan. 23, 1893	22, 432. 28	10	40	
Do	...do	Apr. 15, 1893	67, 371. 97	30	70	
Do	...do	June 9, 1893	22, 443. 02	10	80	
First National Bank, Del Norte, Colo	Jan. 14, 1893	Aug. 30, 1893	7, 714. 14	10	10	
Newton National Bank, Newton, Kans	Jan. 16, 1893	July 1, 1893	25. 892. 88	30	30	
Do	...do	Oct. 2, 1893	18. 277. 09	20	50	
Capital National Bauk, Lincoln, Nebr	Feb. 6, 1893	Aug. 25, 1893	81, 282. 42	10	10	
Bankers and Merchants' National Bank, Dallas, Tex	...do	Oct. 11, 1893	52, 528. 56	50	50	
Commercial National Bank, Nashville, Tenn	Apr. 6. 1893	July 1, 1893	376, 321. 95	30	30	
Do	...do	Oct. 7, 1893	138, 516. 19	10	40	
Alahama National Bank, Mobile, Ala	Apr. 18, 1893	July 25, 1893	33, 099. 22	50	50	
Evanston National Bank, Evanston, Ill	June 7, 1893	Aug. 10, 1893	14, 950. 80	30	30	

DIVIDENDS, FIFTY-NINE IN NUMBER, PAID TO THE CREDITORS OF INSOLVENT
NATIONAL BANKS DURING THE PAST YEAR, ETC.—Continued.

Name and location of bank.	Date of appointment of receiver.	Dividends paid during the year.			Total dividends paid depositors.	Proportion of interest paid depositors.
		Date.	Amount.	Per cent.		
					Per cent.	*Per cent.*
National Bank of Deposit, New York, N. Y	June 9, 1893	Aug. 5, 1893	$204,630.17	40	40	....
Do	....do	Oct. 24, 1893	109,860.00	35	75	....
First National Bank, Brady, Tex	June 13, 1893	Sept. 25, 1893	12,308.08	40	40	....
Citizens' National Bank, Hillsboro, Ohio	June 16, 1893	....do	81,112.60	25	25	....
Chemical National Bank, Chicago, Ill	July 21, 1893	Sept. 30, 1893	597,032.77	50	50	....
Northern National Bank, Big Rapids, Mich	Aug. 3, 1893	Oct. 31, 1893	56,606.56	25	25	....
Third National Bank, Malone, N. Y	Dec. 30, 1889	Dec. 31, 1892	11,192.92	19.25	99.25	....
Maverick National Bank, Boston, Mass	Nov. 2, 1891	Oct. 31, 1893	189,838.33	2.5	87.5	....
First National Bank, Ponca, Nebr	May 13, 1893	....do	14,771.50	20	20	....
State National Bank, Knoxville, Tenn	July 22, 1893	....do	20,893.75	25	25	....
Consolidated National Bank, San Diego, Cal	July 24, 1893	....do	134,450.73	25	25	....
Chamberlain National Bank, Chamberlain, S. Dak	Sept. 30, 1893	....do	7,712.04	50	50	....
Red Cloud National Bank, Red Cloud, Nebr	July 1, 1891	July 26, 1893	15,053.75	17.5	80	....
First National Bank, Red Cloud, Nebr	July 16, 1891	July 29, 1893	5,709.16	10	50	....
Do	....do	Dec. 1, 1892	10,348.01	20	40	....
First National Bank, Kansas City, Kans	Aug. 17, 1891	June 26, 1893	15,255.74	15	40	....
Pacific National Bank, Boston, Mass	May 22, 1882	July 5, 1893	31,961.73	1.3	65.3	....
Commercial National Bank, Dubuque, Iowa	Apr. 2, 1888	Nov. 18, 1892	30,472.38	7	57	....
Total	....	....	3,041,134.90	....	....	....

STATEMENT SHOWING RECEIVERSHIPS IN AN INACTIVE CONDITION.

Name and location of bank.	Date of appointment of receiver.	Dividends paid.
		Per cent.
First National Bank, Anderson, Ind	Nov. 23, 1873	43
German-American National Bank, Washington, D. C	Nov. 1, 1878	66.7
Third National Bank, Chicago, Ill	Nov. 24, 1877	*100
Mechanics' National Bank, Newark, N. J	Nov. 2, 1881	67.405
First National Bank, Livingston, Mont	Aug. 25, 1884	95
First National Bank, Pine Bluff, Ark	Nov. 20, 1886	45
First National Bank, Leadville, Colo	Jan. 34, 1884	40
First National Bank, St. Albans, Vt	Apr. 22, 1884	25
Fifth National Bank, St. Louis, Mo	Nov. 15, 1887	96
First National Bank, Sioux Falls, S. Dak	Mar. 11, 1886	40
Gloucester City National Bank, Gloucester City, N. J	June 10, 1890	40
First National Bank, Sheffield, Ala	Dec. 23, 1889	15
Harper National Bank, Harper, Kans	Feb. 10, 1890	80
City National Bank, Hastings, Nebr	Jan. 14, 1891	30
Pratt County National Bank, Pratt, Kans	Apr. 7, 1891	70
Florence National Bank, Florence, Ala	Aug. 17, 1891	25

* And interest.

INSOLVENT NATIONAL BANKS, DATES OF ORGANIZATION, APPOINTMENT OF RE
TEM, WITH AMOUNTS OF NOMINAL AND ADDITIONAL ASSETS, AMOUNTS COLLECT
ASSETS, EXPENSES OF RECEIVERSHIP, CLAIMS PROVED, DIVIDENDS PAID AND

	Name and location of bank.	Date of organization.	Capital stock.	Receiver appointed.
1	First National Bank, Attica, N. Y.	Jan. 14, 1864	$50,000	Apr. 14, 1865
2	Venango National Bank, Franklin, Pa.	May 20, 1865	300,000	May 1, 1866
3	Merchants' National Bank, Washington, D. C.	Dec. 14, 1864	200,000	May 8, 1866
4	First National Bank, Medina, N. Y.	Feb. 3, 1864	50,000	Mar. 13, 1867
5	Tennessee National Bank, Memphis, Tenn.	June 5, 1865	100,000	Mar. 21, 1867
6	First National Bank, Selma, Ala	Aug. 24, 1865	100,000	Apr. 30, 1867
7	First National Bank, New Orleans, La.	Dec. 18, 1863	500,000	May 20, 1867
8	National Unadilla Bank, Unadilla, N. Y	July 17, 1865	120,000	Aug. 20, 1867
9	Farmers and Citizens' National Bank, Brooklyn, N. Y.	June 5, 1865	300,000	Sept. 6, 1867
10	Croton National Bank, New York, N. Y.	Sept. 9, 1865	200,000	Oct. 1, 1867
11	First National Bank, Bethel, Conn	May 15, 1865	60,000	Feb. 28, 1868
12	First National Bank, Keokuk, Iowa	Sept. 9, 1863	100,000	Mar. 3, 1868
13	National Bank of Vicksburg, Miss	Feb. 14, 1865	50,000	Apr. 24, 1868
14	First National Bank, Rockford, Ill	May 20, 1864	50,000	Mar. 15, 1869
15	First National Bank of Nevada, Austin, Nev	June 23, 1865	250,000	Oct. 14, 1869
16	Ocean National Bank, New York, N. Y	June 6, 1865	1,000,000	Dec. 13, 1871
17	Union Square National Bank, New York, N. Y	Mar. 30, 1865	200,000	Dec. 15, 1871
18	Eighth National Bank, New York. N. Y.	Apr. 6, 1864	250,000	...do ....
19	Fourth National Bank, Philadelphia, Pa	Feb. 26, 1864	200,000	Dec. 20, 1871
20	Waverly National Bank, Waverly, N. Y.	May 29, 1865	106,100	Apr. 23, 1872
21	First National Bank, Fort Smith, Ark	Feb. 6, 1866	50,000	May 2, 1872
22	Scandinavian National Bank, Chicago, Ill	May 7, 1872	250,000	Dec. 12, 1872
23	Wallkill National Bank, Middletown, N. Y.	July 24, 1865	175,000	Dec. 31, 1872
24	Crescent City National Bank, New Orleans, La	Feb. 15, 1872	500,000	Mar. 18, 1873
25	Atlantic National Bank, New York, N. Y.	July 1, 1865	300,000	Apr. 28, 1873
26	First National Bank, Washington, D. C.	July 16, 1863	500,000	Sept. 19, 1873
27	National Bank of the Commonwealth, New York, N. Y.	July 1, 1865	750,000	Sept. 22, 1873
28	Merchants' National Bank, Petersburg, Va	Sept. 1, 1865	400,000	Sept. 25, 1873
29	First National Bank, Petersburg, Va.	July 1, 1865	200,000	...do ....
30	First National Bank, Mansfield, Ohio	May 24, 1864	100,000	Oct. 18, 1873
31	New Orleans National Banking Association, New Orleans, La.	May 27, 1871	600,000	Oct. 23, 1873
32	First National Bank, Carlisle, Pa	July 7, 1863	50,000	Oct. 24, 1873
33	First National Bank, Anderson, Ind	July 31, 1863	50,000	Nov. 24, 1873
34	First National Bank, Topeka, Kans	Aug. 23, 1866	100,000	Dec. 16, 1873
35	First National Bank, Norfolk, Va	Feb. 23, 1864	100,000	June 3, 1874
36	Gibson County National Bank, Princeton, Ind	Nov. 30, 1872	50,000	Nov. 28, 1874
37	First National Bank of Utah, Salt Lake City, Utah	Nov. 15, 1869	150,000	Dec. 10, 1874
38	Cook County National Bank, Chicago, Ill	July 8, 1871	500,000	Feb. 1, 1875
39	First National Bank, Tiffin, Ohio	Mar. 16, 1865	100,000	Oct. 22, 1875
40	Charlottesville National Bank, Charlottesville, Va	July 19, 1865	200,000	Oct. 28, 1875
41	Miners' National Bank, Georgetown, Colo	Oct. 30, 1874	150,000	Jan. 24, 1876
42	Fourth National Bank, Chicago, Ill.*	Feb. 24, 1865	200,000	Feb. 1, 1876
43	First National Bank, Bedford, Iowa	Sept. 18, 1875	30,000	...do ....
44	First National Bank, Osceola, Iowa	Jan. 26, 1871	50,000	Feb. 26, 1876
45	First National Bank, Duluth, Minn	Apr. 6, 1872	100,000	Mar. 13, 1876
46	First National Bank, La Crosse, Wis	June 20, 1865	50,000	Apr. 11, 1876
47	City National Bank, Chicago, Ill	Feb. 18, 1865	250,000	May 17, 1876
48	Watkins National Bank, Watkins, N. Y	June 2, 1864	75,000	July 12, 1876
49	First National Bank, Wichita, Kans	Jan. 2, 1872	60,000	Sept. 23, 1876
50	First National Bank, Greenfield, Ohio *	Oct. 7, 1863	50,000	Dec. 12, 1876
51	National Bank of Fishkill, N. Y	Apr. 1, 1865	200,000	Jan. 27, 1877
52	First National Bank, Franklin, Ind	Aug. 5, 1863	132,000	Feb. 13, 1877
53	Northumberland County National Bank, Shamokin, Pa.	Jan. 9, 1865	67,000	Mar. 12, 1877
54	First National Bank, Winchester, Ill	July 25, 1865	50,000	Mar. 16, 1877
55	National Exchange Bank, Minneapolis, Minn	Jan. 16, 1865	100,000	May 24, 1877
56	National Bank of the State of Missouri, St. Louis, Mo.	Oct. 30, 1866	2,500,000	June 21, 1877
57	First National Bank, Delhi, Ind	Mar. 25, 1872	50,000	July 20, 1877
58	First National Bank, Georgetown, Colo	May 31, 1872	75,000	Aug. 18, 1877
59	Lock Haven National Bank, Lock Haven, Pa	June 14, 1865	120,000	Aug. 20, 1877
60	Third National Bank, Chicago, Ill	Feb. 5, 1864	750,000	Nov. 24, 1877
61	Central National Bank, Chicago, Ill	Sept. 18, 1872	200,000	Dec. 1, 1877
62	First National Bank, Kansas City, Mo	Nov. 23, 1865	500,000	Feb. 11, 1878
63	Commercial National Bank, Kansas City, Mo	June 3, 1872	100,000	...do ....
64	First National Bank, Ashland, Pa. *	Apr. 27, 1864	112,500	Feb. 28, 1878
65	First National Bank, Tarrytown. N. Y.	Apr. 5, 1864	100,000	Mar. 23, 1878
66	First National Bank, Allentown, Pa. *	Dec. 16, 1863	250,000	Apr. 15, 1878
67	First National Bank, Waynesburg. Pa. *	Mar. 5, 1864	100,000	May 15, 1878
68	Washington County National Bank, Greenwich, N. Y.	June 30, 1865	200,000	June 8, 1878
69	First National Bank. Dallas, Tex	July 16, 1874	50,000	...do ....
70	People's National Bank, Helena, Mont	May 13, 1873	100,000	Sept. 13, 1878
71	First National Bank, Bozeman, Mont	Aug. 14, 1873	50,000	Sept. 14, 1878
72	Merchants' National Bank, Fort Scott, Kans.*	Jan. 20, 1872	50,000	Sept. 15, 1878

* Formerly in voluntary liquidation.

CEIVER AND CLOSING, SINCE THE ORGANIZATION OF THE NATIONAL BANKING SYSTEM FROM ALL SOURCES, LOANS PAID AND OTHER DISBURSEMENTS, LOSSES ON REMAINING ASSETS RETURNED TO STOCKHOLDERS.

Nominal assets at date of suspension.			Additional assets received since date of suspension.	Total assets.	Offsets allowed and settled.	Loss on assets compounded or sold under order of court.	Nominal value of assets returned to stockholders.	
Estimated good.	Estimated doubtful.	Estimated worthless.						
$50,823	$28,053	$115,538	$13,692	$208,106	$18,661	$114,236		1
83,713	57,029	818,154	27,741	986,637	69,445	796,197		2
	860,929			860,929		686,665		3
18,424	2,029	101,072	5,400	126,925		93,688		4
50,000	395,412		26,579	471,991		380,383		5
116,422	96,556	78,415	57,732	349,125	6,815	179,894		6
853,148	276,400	701,116	156,575	1,987,239	58,615	920,289		7
36,748	69,857	86,856	19,449	212,910		152,806		8
1,175,656	121,683	272,757	121,017	1,691,113	55,342	400,943		9
255,235	144,903	65,361	21,572	487,071	30,641	187,586		10
39,486	4,809	83,830	12,212	140,337	1,570	70,122		11
98,240	79,652	125,057	13,426	316,375	33,454	123,409		12
21,584	49,959	22,569		94,112	4,608	57,938		13
7,000	811		30,371	38,182		274		14
129,721	497,292	91,412	42,236	760,661	317,742	219,750		15
1,867,641		942,283	124,832	2,934,756	285,736	1,254,358		16
364,973		91,355	11,895	468,223	101,719		$89,855	17
229,617	736,997	165,442	49,409	1,181,465	38,911	379,794		18
653,658				653,658	303,504			19
86,493	40,000	37,494	32,517	196,504	15,780	56,011		20
15,800	14,174	25,000	6,537	61,511		37,629		21
100,000	100,000	168,100	24,866	392,966	6,211	224,703		22
127,769	50,000	25,000	25,102	227,871	30,378	22,084		23
379,020	110,450	148,920	168,603	800,993	8,949	285,346		24
336,833	58,852	283,550	128,337	807,572	98,460	161,013		25
1,000,000	1,277,600		215,724	2,493,414	280,055	765,356		26
1,435,113	473,372	453,593	404,431	2,766,509	368,992	589,213		27
342,260	252,250	321,722	103,609	1,019,841	103,842	616,642		28
100,000	50,000	79,409	43,225	272,634	3,225	146,764		29
94,483	173,378	7,954	21,095	296,910	5,735	182,231		30
300,000	100,000	376,870	654,185	1,431,055	8,964	715,584		31
28,077	55,386	29,267	2,574	115,304	7,068	51,294		32
50,000	80,000	103,057	100,607	333,664	10,410	235,127		33
25,000	85,000	78,857	14,241	203,038	26,051	118,083		34
77,723	56,350	80,297	3,542	217,912	2,191	55,917		35
51,296	32,011	29,055	12,816	125,178	3,595	54,332		36
6,300	204,600	3,274	15,258	220,432	2,860	196,211		37
619,836	1,250,163	151,439	678,349	2,699,787	452,053	1,948,095		38
140,000	120,000	63,620	18,439	342,059	60,447	84,709		39
169,520	105,218	257,655	30,606	564,089	24,882	58,715		40
20,000	190,069		27,287	237,356	8,761	186,254		41
27,123	131,227	65,802	3,084	227,236	2,100	6,266		42
29,752	26,858	9,359	9,635	75,604	3,510	49,929		43
74,376	19,938	5,737	15,162	115,213	3,043	30,319	33,363	44
18,093	118,300	35,855	13,816	186,064	1,139	111,780		45
35,000	25,000	65,097	44,815	169,912	4,296	85,019		46
453,037	478,917	85,805	86,248	1,104,007	48,381	470,908		47
86,014	44,582	9,105	21,738	161,439	3,151	18,635	53,473	48
59,226	18,387	67,531	3,681	148,825	17,409	67,345		49
	57,675		376	58,051		44,344		50
194,665	262,900	51,403	49,441	558,418	13,192	223,375		51
86,492	68,188	200,909	24,217	360,806	60,311	203,792		52
67,216	112,026	25,941	14,770	219,083	8,487	99,588		53
67,541	66,025	79,101	14,270	226,937	6,537	117,173		54
135,231	90,704	124,371	18,411	368,717	21,498	139,309		55
935,099	2,818,066	633,744	433,400	4,822,109	166,831	1,771,699	36,957	56
175,254	6,250	6,590	13,478	201,578	62,774	1,310	34,259	57
34,368	52,627	629,113	30,398	746,506	36,508	606,580		58
220,481	150,850	24,990	34,350	430,471	41,324	143,664		59
1,330,215	631,797	330,704	97,047	2,389,763	59,322	310,813		60
157,438	161,441	170,712	16,680	506,271	7,245	287,682		61
1,118,118	313,726	405,000	19,817	1,856,661	1,482,725	22,550		62
52,349	74,724	51,175	6,723	184,971	22,962	67,396		63
107,318	41,584	19,070	8,859	176,831	16,072		112,818	64
100,994		153,467	20,289	274,750	164,949			65
19,879	132,445	185,220	2,171	339,715	20,608	268,000		66
	15,869	42,284	1,861	60,014	714	47,239		67
311,324	27,894	236,971	13,749	589,938	18,541	6,972	279,987	68
48,149	36,245	67,423	4,305	150,122	30,088	106,292		69
32,550	95,251	166,151	67,942	361,903	12,492	32,372		70
9,010	76,046	333	21,090	136,479	7,700	20,141		71
21,225	15,543	46,588	1,892	85,248	178	65,804		72

INSOLVENT NATIONAL BANKS, DATES OF ORGANIZATION, APPOINTMENT OF RE
SYSTEM, WITH AMOUNTS OF NOMINAL AND ADDITIONAL ASSETS,

	Name and location of bank.	Date of organization.	Capital stock.	Receiver appointed.
73	Farmers' National Bank, Platte City, Mo	May 5, 1877	$50,000	Oct. 1, 1878
74	First National Bank, Warrensburg, Mo	July 31, 1871	100,000	Nov. 1, 1878
75	German-American National Bank, Washington, D. C ..	May 14, 1887	130,000	....do ......
76	German National Bank, Chicago, Ill. *	Nov. 15, 1870	500,000	Dec. 20, 1878
77	Commercial National Bank, Saratoga Springs, N. Y....	June 6, 1865	100,000	Feb. 11, 1879
78	Second National Bank, Scranton, Pa. *	Aug. 5, 1863	200,000	Mar. 15, 1879
79	National Bank of Poultney, Vt	May 31, 1865	100,000	Apr. 7, 1879
80	First National Bank, Monticello, Ind	Dec. 3, 1874	50,000	July 18, 1879
81	First National Bank, Butler, Pa	Mar. 11, 1864	50,000	July 23, 1879
82	First National Bank, Meadville, Pa	Oct. 27, 1863	100,000	June 9, 1880
83	First National Bank, Newark, N. J	Aug. 7, 1863	300,000	June 14, 1880
84	First National Bank, Brattleboro, Vt	June 30, 1864	300,000	June 19, 1880
85	Mechanics' National Bank, Newark, N. J	June 9, 1865	500,000	Mar. 2, 1881
86	First National Bank, Buffalo, N. Y	Feb. 5, 1864	100,000	Apr. 22, 1882
87	Pacific National Bank, Boston, Mass.	Nov. 9, 1877	961,300	May 22, 1882
88	First National Bank of Union Mills, Union City, Pa...	Oct. 23, 1865	50,000	Mar. 24, 1883
89	Vermont National Bank, St. Albans, Vt	Oct. 11, 1865	200,000	Aug. 9, 1883
90	First National Bank, Leadville, Colo	Mar. 19, 1879	60,000	Jan. 24, 1884
91	City National Bank, Lawrenceburg, Ind. *	Feb. 24, 1883	100,000	Mar. 11, 1884
92	First National Bank, St. Albans, Vt	Feb. 20, 1864	100,000	Apr. 22, 1884
93	First National Bank, Monmouth, Ill	July 7, 1882	75,000	....do ......
94	Marine National Bank, New York, N. Y.	July 7, 1882	400,000	May 13, 1884
95	Hot Springs National Bank, Hot Springs, Ark	Feb. 17, 1883	50,000	June 2, 1884
96	Richmond National Bank, Richmond, Ind	Mar. 5, 1873	250,000	July 23, 1884
97	First National Bank, Livingston, Mont	July 16, 1883	50,000	Aug. 25, 1884
98	First National Bank, Albion, N. Y	Dec. 22, 1863	100,000	Aug. 26, 1884
99	First National Bank, Jamestown, N. Dak	Oct. 25, 1881	50,000	Sept. 13, 1884
100	Logan National Bank, West Liberty, Ohio	May 7, 1884	50,000	Oct. 18, 1884
101	Middletown National Bank, Middletown, N. Y	June 14, 1865	200,000	Nov. 29, 1884
102	Farmers' National Bank, Bushnell, Ill	Feb. 18, 1871	50,000	Dec. 17, 1884
103	Schoharie County National Bank, Schoharie, N. Y	Aug. 9, 1865	50,000	Mar. 23, 1885
104	Exchange National Bank, Norfolk, Va	May 13, 1865	300,000	Apr. 9, 1885
105	First National Bank, Lake City, Minn	Nov. 29, 1870	50,000	Jan. 4, 1886
106	Lancaster National Bank, Clinton, Mass	Nov. 22, 1864	100,000	Jan. 20, 1886
107	First National Bank, Sioux Falls, S. Dak	Mar. 15, 1880	50,000	Mar. 11, 1886
108	First National Bank, Wahpeton, N. Dak	Feb. 2, 1882	50,000	Apr. 8, 1886
109	First National Bank, Angelica, N. Y	Nov. 3, 1864	100,000	Apr. 19, 1886
110	City National Bank, Williamsport, Pa	Mar. 17, 1874	100,000	May 4, 1886
111	Abington National Bank, Abington, Mass.†	July 1, 1865	150,000	Aug. 2, 1886
112	First National Bank, Blair, Nebr	June 7, 1882	50,000	Sept. 8, 1886
113	First National Bank, Pine Bluff, Ark	Sept. 18, 1882	50,000	Nov. 20, 1886
114	Palatka National Bank, Palatka, Fla	Nov. 20, 1884	50,000	June 3, 1887
115	Fidelity National Bank, Cincinnati, Ohio	Feb. 27, 1886	1,000,000	June 27, 1887
116	Henrietta National Bank, Henrietta, Tex	Aug. 8, 1883	50,000	Aug. 17, 1887
117	National Bank of Sumter, S. C	Nov. 26, 1883	50,000	Aug. 24, 1887
118	First National Bank, Danville, N. Y	Sept. 4, 1863	50,000	Sept. 8, 1887
119	First National Bank, Corry, Pa	Dec. 6, 1864	100,000	Oct. 11, 1887
120	Stafford National Bank, Stafford Springs, Conn	Jan. 7, 1865	200,000	Oct. 17, 1887
121	Fifth National Bank, St. Louis, Mo	Dec. 6, 1882	300,000	Nov. 15, 1887
122	Metropolitan National Bank, Cincinnati, Ohio	June 23, 1881	1,000,000	Feb. 10, 1888
123	First National Bank, Auburn, N. Y	Jan. 13, 1864	150,000	Feb. 20, 1888
124	Commercial National Bank, Dubuque, Iowa	Mar. 4, 1871	100,000	Apr. 2, 1888
125	State National Bank, Raleigh, N. C	June 2, 1868	100,000	Mar. 31, 1888
126	Second National Bank, Xenia, Ohio	Jan. 1, 1864	150,000	May 9, 1888
127	Madison National Bank, Madison, S. Dak	Nov. 29, 1886	50,000	June 23, 1888
128	Lowell National Bank, Lowell, Mich	June 14, 1865	50,000	Sept. 19, 1888
129	California National Bank, San Francisco, Cal	Oct. 20, 1886	200,000	Jan. 14, 1889
130	First National Bank, Anoka, Minn	Sept. 14, 1882	50,000	Apr. 22, 1889
131	National Bank of Shelbyville, Tenn	Oct. 29, 1874	50,000	Dec. 13, 1889
132	First National Bank, Sheffield, Ala	Jan. 14, 1887	100,000	Dec. 23, 1889
133	Third National Bank, Malone, N. Y	July 15, 1885	50,000	Dec. 30, 1889
134	First National Bank, Abilene, Kans	June 23, 1879	100,000	Jan. 21, 1890
135	Harper National Bank, Harper, Kaus	Jan. 6, 1886	50,000	Feb. 10, 1890
136	Gloucester City National Bank, Gloucester City, N. J	Oct. 26, 1888	50,000	June 12, 1890
137	Park National Bank, Chicago, Ill	May 11, 1886	200,000	July 14, 1890
138	State National Bank, Wellington, Kans	Oct. 1, 1886	50,000	Sept. 25, 1890
139	Kingman National Bank, Kingman, Kans	Sept. 16, 1886	100,000	Oct. 2, 1890
140	First National Bank, Alma, Kans	Aug. 3, 1887	75,000	Nov. 21, 1890
141	First National Bank, Belleville, Kans	Aug. 28, 1885	50,000	Dec. 12, 1890
142	First National Bank, Meade Center, Kans	May 5, 1887	50,000	Dec. 24, 1890
143	American National Bank, Arkansas City, Kans	Mar. 15, 1889	300,000	Dec. 26, 1890
144	City National Bank, Hastings, Nebr	Dec. 27, 1883	100,000	Jan. 6, 1891
145	People's National Bank, Fayetteville, N. C	June 27, 1872	125,000	Jan. 20, 1891
146	Spokane National Bank, Spokane Falls, Wash	Jan. 24, 1888	100,000	Feb. 3, 1891
147	First National Bank, Ellsworth, Kans	Sept. 11, 1884	50,000	Feb. 11, 1891

* Formerly in voluntary liquidation.   † Restored to solvency.

CEIVED AND CLOSING, SINCE THE ORGANIZATION OF THE NATIONAL BANKING
AMOUNTS COLLECTED FROM ALL SOURCES, ETC.—Continued.

Nominal assets at date of suspension.			Additional assets received since date of suspension.	Total assets.	Offsets allowed and settled.	Loss on assets compounded or sold under order of court.	Nominal value of assets returned to stockholders.	
Estimated good.	Estimated doubtful.	Estimated worthless.						
$9,561	$18,601	$42,296	$1,944	$72,492	$10,947	$8,207		73
90,053	191,457	11,578	33,375	330,363	55,255	118,507		74
256,286	139,514	37,023	61,147	494,870	165,846	92,833		75
104,866	101,971	475,052	29,881	711,870	6,170	521,783		76
133,169	167,503	28,969	17,085	346,726	17,475	101,810	$69,659	77
264,008	101,178	104,858	47,591	518,535	36,737	203,982	72,754	78
68,078	97,257	18,384	19,560	203,279	3,353	25,729	77,592	79
23,646	6,734	4,374	15,017	49,771	8,411	64		80
12,647	134,716	34,737	27,503	209,603	11,920	106,562		81
115,012	22,545	12,863	19,198	169,618	3,345	26,043	26,439	82
418,951	64,041	55,895	41,173	580,060	154,945	86,953		83
51,574	....	302,654	43,895	398,123	4,902	891	302,654	84
1,114,503	185,002	78,286	231,058	608,849	73,925	66,364		85
488,892	65,526	696,987	36,916	1,288,321	172,063	650,736		86
648,710	1,416,793	1,397,334	425,859	3,884,696	73,925	66,364		87
161,699	46,829	16,309	23,640	248,477	4,376	89,925		88
124,114	520,917	118,618	20,617	784,266	19,171	483,834		89
72,197	56,042	102,112	52,069	282,420	8,970	124,948		90
13,993	14,500	2,554	1,599	32,646	52	16,017		91
217,314	96,875	49,951	77,584	441,724	9,888	152,038		92
172,940	90,543	9,088	32,854	312,025	5,320	11,671		93
3,496,495	816,916	1,568,940	712,681	6,595,032	904,558	118,244		94
31,058	27,774	27,190	6,407	92,429	5,381	31,402	18,517	95
367,109	72,356	171,319	124,054	734,838	32,233	348,492		96
33,543	15,304	22,255	867	71,969	84	23,118		97
55,763	44,446	113,329	212,500	426,038	42,269	144,070		98
7,519	29,826	29,352	3,312	70,009	5	49,155		99
60,096	22,695	....	56,057	138,848	11,140	75,679		100
600,810	53,692	167,075	127,451	949,082	22,189	300,526		101
13,170	3,874	62,229	11,899	91,172	3,411	350	41,079	102
96,981	39,593	28,010	4,809	169,303	508	89,506		103
1,273,711	1,441,378	938,916	60,858	3,714,863	197,261	461,520		104
57,487	91,996	7,291	57,994	214,768	584		65,573	105
144,850	138,707	8,004	69,961	361,615	18,833	36,030	60,998	106
48,510	137,859	3,821	5,700	195,890	54,116	21,268		107
20,505	66,965	44,909	4,138	136,517	1,168	106,872		108
59,810	28,450	70,458	7,798	166,525	1,284	10,211	77,725	109
154,870	26,825	24,398	35,202	241,304	4,104	816	70,715	110
122,551	168,164	5,462	21,653	317,810	3,721	76,659	38,917	111
235,474	8,000	6,834	5,439	255,747	5,645	2,358	43,697	112
50,793	82,612	4,909	4,404	142,718	127	76,736		113
15,646	32,092	8,791	1,790	58,319	....		44,068	114
2,461,079	915,577	2,494,511	1,481,980	7,358,147	641,630	1,001,138		115
74,171	35,999	12,995	25,696	148,861	6,594		37,585	116
66,081	....	150	17,769	84,009	883	1,057		117
17,449	8,397	37,572	56,220	119,638	19,806	68,034		118
156,586	20,230	66,710	29,501	273,036	8,971	124,580		119
208,243	119,869	60,869	29,177	418,158	10,556	10,146	133,585	120
580,321	920,388	61,622	88,879	1,660,210	164,276	582,000		121
1,608,952	787,598	125,236	7,111	2,588,897	17,528	16,000	1,164,063	122
268,961	100,617	510,790	253,888	1,194,256	52,010	309,000		123
333,506	324,872	15,112	20,221	1,702,711	71,172	121,369		124
152,390	176,652	137,561	8,398	475,001	67,849	220,176		125
181,870	214,560	78,406	60,652	544,578	13,275	39,557	161,275	126
17,136	91,153	20,025	34,152	162,466	2,001	109,773		127
55,535	71,124	1,316	40,811	174,786	1,840	33,240	39,557	128
400,003	61,519	216,704	95,050	773,276	21,019	128,879		129
83,776	44,698	17,225	18,077	163,776	2,196	22,360		130
1,898	98,099	44,592	6,092	150,681	....	122,751		131
153,262	117,240	72,568	3,067	346,237	3,019	232,147		132
74,662	31,442	33,827	2,383	142,314	1,416	25,354		133
38,896	92,995	81,807	1,641	215,429	1,733	157,695		134
23,775	21,224	19,074	2,868	69,541	5,600	9,164		135
6,675	12,317	56,237	7,266	82,495	281	6,812		136
342,921	256,395	142,551	41,536	786,403	76,124	23,600		137
23,319	77,765	11,646	9,953	122,683	801	8,034		138
11,416	101,635	64,792	5,592	183,435	1,541	32,791		139
9,233	27,273	40,700	13,795	91,010	....	516		140
10,794	50,866	22,426	745	84,831	274	5,000		141
6,201	42,808	21,564	358	70,931	200	8,191		142
206,303	376,977	55,732	108,294	747,306	4,047	7,645		143
48,128	59,642	110,400	15,717	233,887	288	171,877		144
181,878	24,882	124,504	22,626	273,890	8,143	11,543		145
314,354	190,090	9,060	141,626	655,130	67,577	....		146
102,952	46,213	43,981	1,066	194,212	2,420	1,802		147

INSOLVENT NATIONAL BANKS, DATES OF ORGANIZATION, APPOINTMENT OF RE
SYSTEM, WITH AMOUNTS OF NOMINAL AND ADDITIONAL ASSETS,

	Name and location of bank.	Date of organization.	Capital stock.	Receiver appointed.
148	Second National Bank, McPherson, Kans	Sept. 16, 1887	$50,000	Mar. 25, 1891
149	Pratt County National Bank, Pratt, Kans	Sept. 8, 1887	50,000	Apr. 7, 1891
150	Keystone National Bank, Philadelphia, Pa	July 30, 1875	500,000	May 9, 1891
151	Spring Garden National Bank, Philadelphia, Pa	Mar. 13, 1886	750.000	May 21, 1891
152	National City Bank, Marshall, Mich	July 29, 1872	100,000	June 22, 1891
153	Red Cloud National Bank, Red Cloud, Nebr	May 19, 1884	75,000	July 1, 1891
154	Asbury Park National Bank, Asbury Park, N. J	Sept. 17, 1887	100,000	July 2, 1891
155	Ninth National Bank, Dallas, Tex	Sept. 12, 1890	300,000	July 16, 1891
156	First National Bank, Red Cloud, Nebr	Nov. 8, 1882	75,000	....do......
157	Central Nebraska National Bank, Broken Bow, Nebr	Sept. 28, 1888	60,000	July 21, 1891
158	Florence National Bank, Florence, Ala	Oct. 3, 1889	60,000	July 23, 1891
159	First National Bank, Palatka, Fla	July 15, 1884	150,000	Aug. 7, 1891
160	First National Bank, Kansas City, Kans	May 17, 1887	150,000	Aug. 17, 1891
161	Rio Grande National Bank, Laredo, Tex	Oct. 28, 1889	100,000	Oct. 3, 1891
162	First National Bank, Clearfield, Pa	Jan. 30, 1865	100,000	Oct. 7, 1891
163	Farley National Bank, Montgomery, Ala.*	Dec. 18, 1889	100,000	....do......
164	First National Bank, Coldwater, Kans	May 9, 1887	52,000	Oct. 14, 1891
165	Maverick National Bank, Boston, Mass	Dec. 31, 1864	400,000	Nov. 2, 1891
166	Corry National Bank, Corry, Pa	Nov. 12, 1864	100,000	Nov. 21, 1891
167	Cheyenne National Bank, Cheyenne, Wyo	Dec. 2, 1885	150,000	Dec. 5, 1891
168	California National Bank, San Diego, Cal	Dec. 29, 1887	500,000	Dec. 18, 1891
169	First National Bank, Wilmington, N. C	July 25, 1866	250,000	Dec. 21, 1891
170	Huron National Bank, Huron, S. Dak	Nov. 21, 1884	75,000	Jan. 7, 1892
171	First National Bank, Downs, Kans	Oct. 12, 1886	50,000	Feb. 6, 1892
172	First National Bank, Muncy, Pa	Feb. 23, 1865	100,000	Feb. 9, 1892
173	Bell County National Bank, Temple, Tex	Aug. 25, 1890	50,000	Feb. 19, 1892
174	First National Bank, Deming, N. Mex	Apr. 22, 1884	100,000	Feb. 29, 1892
175	First National Bank, Silver City, N. Mex	Sept. 17, 1884	50,000	....do......
176	Lima National Bank, Lima, Ohio	Jan. 16, 1883	200,000	Mar. 21, 1892
177	National Bank of Guthrie, Okla	July 31, 1890	100,000	June 22, 1892
178	Cherryvale National Bank, Cherryvale, Kans	Apr. 16, 1890	50,000	July 2, 1892
179	First National Bank, Erie, Kans	Jan. 15, 1889	50,000	....do......
180	First National Bank, Rockwall, Tex	May 29, 1888	125,000	July 20, 1892
181	Vincennes National Bank, Vincennes, Ind	July 17, 1865	100,000	July 22, 1892
182	First National Bank, Del Norte, Colo	Mar. 18, 1890	50,000	Jan. 14, 1893
183	Newton National Bank, Newton, Kans	Jan. 28, 1885	100,000	Jan. 16, 1893
184	Capital National Bank, Lincoln, Nebr	June 29, 1883	300,000	Feb. 6, 1893
185	Bankers and Merchants' National Bank, Dallas, Tex	Jan. 21, 1890	500,000	....do......
186	First National Bank, Little Rock, Ark	Apr. 12, 1866	500,000	....do......
187	Commercial National Bank, Nashville, Tenn	July 22, 1884	500,000	Apr. 6, 1893
188	Alabama National Bank, Mobile, Ala	May 13, 1871	150,000	Apr. 17, 1893
189	First National Bank, Ponca, Nebr	Jan. 28, 1887	50,000	May 13, 1893
190	Second National Bank, Columbia, Tenn	Oct. 3, 1881	100,000	May 19, 1893
191	Columbia National Bank, Chicago, Ill	Apr. 23, 1887	1,000.000	May 22, 1893
192	Elmira National Bank, Elmira, N. Y	Aug. 30, 1889	200,000	May 26, 1893
193	National Bank of North Dakota, Fargo, N. Dak	Mar. 12, 1890	250,000	June 6, 1893
194	Evanston National Bank, Evanston, Ill	June 29, 1892	100,000	June 7, 1893
195	National Bank of Deposit, New York, N. Y	Aug. 5, 1887	300,000	June 9, 1893
196	Oglethorpe National Bank, Brunswick, Ga	July 16, 1887	150,000	June 12, 1893
197	First National Bank, Lakota, N. Dak	Oct. 23, 1889	50,000	June 13, 1893
198	First National Bank, Cedar Falls, Iowa	Sept. 1, 1874	50,000	....do......
199	First National Bank, Brady, Tex	Jan. 7, 1890	50,000	....do......
200	First National Bank, Arkansas City, Kans	June 30, 1885	125,000	June 15, 1893
201	Citizens' National Bank, Hillsboro, Ohio	Sept. 4, 1872	100,000	June 16, 1893
202	First National Bank, Brunswick, Ga	Feb. 2, 1884	200,000	June 17, 1893
203	City National Bank, Brownwood, Tex	June 17, 1890	150,000	June 20, 1893
204	Merchants' National Bank, Tacoma, Wash	May 2, 1883	250,000	June 23, 1893
205	City National Bank, Greenville, Mich	Aug. 28, 1881	50,000	June 27, 1893
206	First National Bank, Whatcom, Wash	Aug. 26, 1889	50,000	....do......
207	Columbia National Bank, New Whatcom, Wash	June 28, 1890	100,000	....do......
208	Citizens' National Bank, Spokane Falls, Wash	Apr. 8, 1889	150,000	July 1, 1893
209	First National Bank, Phillipsburg, Mont	Dec. 5, 1891	50,000	July 8, 1893
210	Linn County National Bank, Albany, Oregon	May 31, 1890	100,000	July 10, 1893
211	Nebraska National Bank, Beatrice, Nebr	Dec. 21, 1889	100,000	July 12, 1893
212	Gulf National Bank, Tampa, Fla	Dec. 2, 1890	50,000	July 14, 1893
213	Livingston National Bank, Livingston, Mont	Sept. 11, 1889	50,000	July 20, 1893
214	Chemical National Bank, Chicago, Ill	Dec. 15, 1891	1,000,000	July 21, 1893
215	Bozeman National Bank, Bozeman, Mont.*	Oct. 23, 1883	50,000	July 22, 1893
216	Consolidated National Bank, San Diego, Cal	Sept. 22, 1883	250,000	July 24, 1893
217	First National Bank, Cedartown, Ga	July 16, 1889	75,000	July 26, 1893
218	Merchants' National Bank, Great Falls, Mont	Oct. 7, 1890	100,000	July 29, 1893
219	State National Bank, Knoxville, Tenn	Aug. 28, 1889	100,000	....do......
220	Montana National Bank, Helena, Mont	Nov. 11, 1882	600,000	Aug. 2, 1893

* Restored to solvency.

CEIVER, AND CLOSING, SINCE THE ORGANIZATION OF THE NATIONAL BANKING
AMOUNTS COLLECTED FROM ALL SOURCES, ETC.—Continued.

Nominal assets at date of suspension.			Additional assets received since date of suspension.	Total assets.	Offsets allowed and settled.	Loss on assets compounded or sold under order of court.	Nominal value of assets returned to stockholders.	
Estimated good.	Estimated doubtful.	Estimated worthless.						
$7,537	$85,858	$29,718	$43,849	$166,962	$3,610	$107,360		148
24,983	56,756	17,106	4,551	103,456		1,563		149
575,606	966,992	153,913	625,472	2,351,983	72,698	16,540		150
280,592	555,430	1,485,688	219,720	2,541,430	116,892	18,629		151
157,652	38,725	641	2,749	199,767	4,198	2,606		152
33,823	118,383	13,635	13,807	179,598	3,119	20,221		153
24,089	32,015	56,240	23,462	135,806	330	92,652		154
123,895	229,056	218,928	10,363	583,142	14,500	36,700		155
34,040	41,226	82,117	5,167	162,550	803	9,365		156
37,214	91,674	9,321	82	138,291		360		157
27,436	80,860	15,460		123,756	7,328	5,402		158
157,630	214,991	112,844	1,096	486,561	28,719	93,925		159
86,050	87,605	118,023	13,652	305,390	5,281	15,190		160
42,152	27,181	101,848	4,352	175,533	218	1,808		161
74,758	51,564	142,122	51,397	319,841	3,324	213		162
								163
16,121	50,064	19,455	2,909	88,548	2,813	3,850		164
4,170,649	4,747,445	772,597	415,617	10,106,338	1,111,427	147,481		165
429,340	152,513	61,480	36,638	679,971	18,816	10,422		166
130,365	298,762	31,617	62,199	522,943	9,012	18,530		167
541,363	535,479	360,716	165,840	1,603,398	39,325	111,740		168
140,808	369,140	181,995	24,428	716,371	15,385	43,520		169
41,221	17,778	39,147	1,289	99,435	129	4,726		170
17,570	60,938	39,621	1,427	119,556	128	13,927		171
62,381	106,718	9,696	27,100	205,895	7,093		$74,869	172
68,264	65,727	2,650	393	137,034	28,650	18,653		173
24,715	209,549	32,215	2,065	268,544	4,549			174
63,241	86,124	5,048	2,677	157,090	3,127	168		175
124,113	276,990	58,257	19,401	478,761	32,869	2,206		176
								177
15,583	31,110	53,933	26	100,652	7,953	3,740		178
60,369	5,111	30,953	1,549	97,982	1,286			179
31,523	79,936	109,651		221,110	5,254	51		180
106,351	109,297	149,159	26,882	391,089	7,163	592		181
68,135	63,761	26,341	88	178,325	1,878	7		182
30,329	27,959	145,461	6,015	209,764	11,465	71		183
335,352	174,852	413,862	47,827	971,893	10,217	1,500		184
34,142	157,453	437,285	6,005	634,885	2,069	5,029		185
300,549	272,803	477,405	4,952	1,055,709	9,831	24,844		186
1,085,328	365,918	1,000,504	42,157	2,493,907	61,365			187
50,839	131,069	34,910		216,818	2,043	99		188
28,700	121,847	58,679	152	209,378	94			189
81,751	141,672	128,851	485	352,959	1,609			190
831,565	1,097,119	608,148	19,071	2,555,903	243,889			191
158,187	378,953	386,867	25,000	949,007	44,130	2,000		192
19,956	296,498	3,201	779	320,434	149			193
48,169	90,902	53,163	6,728	198,962	2,147	4,843		194
				1,230,986	131,405			195
72,758	267,992	97,917	1,920	440,587	8,116			196
7,968	32,874	1,455	7,613	49,910	10			197
63,781	101,494	39,291	606	205,172	6,465			198
54,586	13,195	41,179	708	109,668	11,717			199
290,157	326,622	106,793	50,625	774,197	4,450	7,750		200
221,171	80,835	252,321	100,550	654,877	10,197	80		201
193,192	387,344	36,388						202
96,328	106,190	88,870	25,803	317,191	7,005			203
371,884	569,688	90,355	13,413	1,015,340	27,998	8,667		204
125,823	159,710	36,245		321,778				205
38,067	65,807	19,564	595	124,033	828			206
115,530	105,146	4,563	150	225,389	1,230			207
422,813	51,149	13,444	4,838	492,244	18,205			208
114,297	62,478	732	510	178,017	6,313			209
149,100	122,381	53,766	2,830	328,177	12,015			210
107,446	156,577	18,026	144	282,193	5,569			211
118,550	16,201	16,684		151,435	7,974	163		212
48,019	50,534	73,431	2,454	174,438	13,388			213
1,245,767	804,337	603,144	73,022	2,726,270	305,102	3,226		214
								215
250,796	437,556	418,910	47,332	1,154,554	22,972	36		216
85,199	60,104	15,848	250	161,401				217
74,026	85,905	117,614	1,804	279,343				218
175,810	44,380	11,323	1,121	232,640	622			219
1,506,255	104,111	118,738	61,573	1,790,677	47,240			220

INSOLVENT NATIONAL BANKS, DATES OF ORGANIZATION, APPOINTMENT OF RE
SYSTEM, WITH AMOUNTS OF NOMINAL AND ADDITIONAL ASSETS,

	Name and location of bank.	Date of organization.	Capital stock.	Receiver appointed.
221	Indianapolis National Bank, Indianapolis, Ind	Nov. 21, 1864	$300,000	Aug. 3, 1893
222	Northern National Bank, Big Rapids, Mich	June 5, 1871	100,000,	Aug. 5, 1893
223	First National Bank, Great Falls. Mont	July 1, 1886	250,000	....do ......
224	First National Bank, Kaukakee, Ill.*	Feb. 20, 1871	50,000	....do ......
225	National Bank of the Commonwealth, Manchester, N. H.	Feb. 9, 1892	200,000	Aug. 12, 1893
226	First National Bank, Starkville, Miss	Apr. 30, 1887	60,000	Aug. 9, 1893
227	Stock Growers' National Bank, Miles City, Mont	Dec. 20, 1884	75,000	....do ......
228	Texas National Bank, San Antonio, Tex	Jan. 31, 1885	100,000	Aug. 10, 1893
229	Albuquerque National Bank, Albuquerque, N. Mex	July 14, 1884	175,000	Aug. 11, 1893
230	First National Bank, Vernon, Tex	May 13, 1889	100,000	Aug. 12, 1893
231	First National Bank, Middlesboro, Ky	Jan. 8, 1890	50,000	....do ......
232	First National Bank, Orlando, Fla	Mar. 16, 1886	100,000	Aug. 14, 1893
233	Citizens' National Bank, Muncie, Ind.*	Mar. 15, 1875	200,000	....do ......
234	First National Bank, Hot Springs, S. Dak	July 15, 1890	50,000	Aug. 17, 1893
235	First National Bank, Marion, Kans	July 28, 1883	75,000	Aug. 22, 1893
236	Washington National Bank, Tacoma, Wash	Apr. 23, 1889	100,000	Aug. 26, 1893
237	El Paso National Bank, El Paso, Tex	Dec. 22, 1886	150,000	Sept. 2, 1893
238	Lloyd's National Bank, Jamestown, N. Dak	May 4, 1891	100,000	Sept. 14, 1893
239	National Granite State Bank Exeter, N. H	June 16, 1890	50,000	Sept. 23, 1893
240	Chamberlain National Bank, Chamberlain, S. Dak	Apr. 8, 1890	50,000	Sept. 30, 1893
241	Port Townsend National Bank, Port Townsend, Wash.	Apr. 18, 1890	100,000	Oct. 3, 1893
242	First National Bank, Port Angeles, Wash	May 19, 1890	50,000	Oct. 5, 1893
243	First National Bank, Sundance, Wyo	June 16, 1890	50,000	Oct. 11, 1893
244	First National Bank, North Manchester, Ind	Mar. 17, 1883	50,000	Oct. 16, 1893
245	Commercial National Bank, Denver, Colo	Sept. 6, 1889	250,000	Oct. 24, 1893
246	First National Bank, Dayton, Tenn	July 10, 1890	50,000	Oct. 25, 1893

* Restored to solvency.

CEIVER, AND CLOSING, SINCE THE ORGANIZATION OF THE NATIONAL BANKING AMOUNTS COLLECTED FROM ALL SOURCES, ETC.—Continued.

Nominal assets at date of suspension.			Additional assets received since date of suspension.	Total assets.	Offsets allowed and settled.	Loss on assets compounded or sold under order of court.	Nominal value of assets returned to stockholders.	
Estimated good.	Estimated doubtful.	Estimated worthless.						
$878,946	$521,577	$697,745	$29,938	$2,128,206	$64,267			221
100,087	233,958	2,378	9,437	346,760	4,234			222
614,780	430,519	31,623	83,453	1,160,375	80,263			223
92,856	118,464	17,507	5,895	234,722	1,406			224
355,823	88,037	53,470	11,203	508,533	2,833			225
31,582	36,726	40,169	774	109,251	1,956			226
52,159	163,247	120,428	257	335,891	5,369			227
78,892	118,193	22,566	3,120	222,780	454			228
224,430	255,910	26,403						229
48,562	178,182	6,840	9,525	243,109	3,294			230
37,602	44,630	1,896	735	84,863	1,236	$58		231
130,065	192,472	101,710		425,147				232
441,072	31,105	167	433	473,767	18,951			233
58,500	71,012	1,814	231	107,558	1,242			234
57,065	47,902	5,331	95	104,393	677			235
55,146	105,596	57,374	367,480	585,596				236
144,470	326,170	9,713	2,000	482,353	1,088			237
130,177	181,527	62,375		374,079				238
68,315	99,600	26,227		194,232				239
								240
13,037	60,828	33,545		107,410				241
103,342	45,056	8,604	870	157,962	1,441			242
9,607	83,387	14,593		107,677				243
104,650	68,238	235		173,123				244
								245
								246

INSOLVENT NATIONAL BANKS, DATES OF ORGANIZATION, APPOINTMENT OF RE-
SYSTEM, WITH AMOUNTS OF NOMINAL AND ADDITIONAL ASSETS,

No.	Nominal value of remaining assets.	Collected from assets.	Collected from assessment upon shareholders.	Total collections from all sources.	Loans paid and other disbursements.	Dividends paid.	Legal expenses.	Receiver's salary and other expenses.
1		$75,209	$1,164	$76,373		$70,811		$5,562
2		120,095	1,245	122,240		101,387		14,390
3		174,264	16,488	190,752	$275	165,769	$6.463	13,427
4		33,287	4,000	37,287	816	32,305	11,281	2,908
5		91,608		91,608	935	65,335	1,258	19,156
6		162,386	7,500	169,886	507	132,608	6,182	24,524
7		999,305	38,224	1,037,529	17,477	884,429	12,247	92,440
8	$200	79,004	2,125	82,029	7,054	58,661	43,183	9,442
9		1,234,868		1,234,868	18,655	1,138,870	6,673	48,666
10		268,844		268,844	72,399	143.307	28,677	35,983
11		68,645	28,935	97,580	208	86,737	17,134	5,320
12		150,512	8,936	168,448	15,507	134,929	5,315	14,008
13		31,566		31,566	3,786	16,654	3,977	9,353
14		37,908		37,908	2,926	29,277	1,773	3,000
15		223,169		223,169	4,932	163,982	2,705	45,164
16		1,394,662	348,961	1,743,623	203,170	1,326.487	9,001	137,318
17		276.649		276,649	72,365	175,920	76,648	16,713
18		762,760	136,172	898,932	596,665	263,065	10,437	29,766
19		350,154		350,154		342,054	9,436	8,100
20		124,713		124,713	2,296	77,568		8,264
21		23,882		23,882		15,142	3,085	1,878
22		162,052	10,079	172,131	1,300	143,209	362	21.564
23		175.409	42,795	218,204	6,248	175,430	6,037	19.817
24		512,698	109,707	622,405	18,964	549,427	16,709	28,638
25		548,099	228,580	776,679	35,839	661,816	25,376	51.445
26		1,447,103	5,200	1,452,303	16,393	1,374,339	27,330	37,128
27		1,808,304		1,808,304	746,153	747,428	24,241	53,287
28		299,357		299,357	20,315	259,487	13,637	18,827
29		122,645	19,675	142,320	4,545	125,667	728	11,858
30		108,944	11,400	120,344		107,258	250	11,362
31		706,507	303,813	1,010,320	3,630	802,263	1,270	70,858
32		56,942		56,942	4,350	46,634	67,569	4,691
33	8,639	79.488		79,488		62,032	1,267	12.391
34		58.064	2,250	60,314	14,289	31,668	4,718	8,278
35	67,835	91,969	37,597	129,566	550	101,545	6,075	19,230
36		67,251		67,251	206	62,646	8,232	4,309
37		30,332		30,332		19,002		10,164
38		298,739	66,535	365,274	56,921	228,412	1,106	37,874
39		196,903		196,903	74,896	108,318	42,067	13,080
40	291,357	188,135	93,619	281,754	2,300	226,308	13,080	31,642
41		42,341	106,451	148,792	445	135,797	21,495	8,604
42	196,790	22,080	11,269	33,349		18,258	3,946	10,348
43		22,165	1,100	23,265		12,624	4,731	9,274
44		48,488		48,488	3,928	34,530	1,367	7,035
45		73,145	42,212	115,357	3,616	88,697	2,077	10,005
46		80,597	4,510	85,107	5,385	65,783	8,804	8,879
47		584,718	58,826	643,544	63,475	545,503	5,060	19,880
48		86,180		80,180	1,579	60,647	13,803	13,874
49		64,071	15,552	79,623	16,773	59,121	592	1,520
50		13,707	2,664	16,371		9,450	2,200	4,164
51		321,851	122,127	443,978	5,000	388,850	2,751	25,082
52		105,703	91,930	197,633	520	173,512	25,040	9,716
53		111,908	43,232	155,140	4,797	136,474	5,146	12,903
54		103,227	8,044	111,271	8,805	89,715	966	10,669
55		207,910	9,540	217,450	753	202,753	2,082	12,046
56		2,846,622	245,108	3,001,730	658,784	2,165,388	1,898	161,036
57		103,295		103,295	4,059	81,941	79,802	10,910
58		103,328		103,328		73,890	2,690	17,251
59		245,483	47,949	293,432	7,846	251,647	11,987	24,271
60	795,384	1,535,260		1,535,260	249,050	1,138,150	6,663	77,802
61	53,800	157,544	65,132	222,676		193,941	15,935	15,601
62		351,377		351,377	1,791	316,828	13,104	27,314
63		94,613		94,613	3,048	52,514	5,444	1,601
64		47,041		47,041		33,105	576	5,013
65		109,801	16,455	126,256		107,575	3,974	13,135
66		51,107	54,536	105,643	1,576	79,725	5,516	13,336
67		12,061	16,447	28,508		21,710	11,006	4,483
68		284,438	123,430	407,868	114,220	262,887	2,315	4,050
69		19,742	16,500	36,242		29,377	10,129	6,040
70	250,854	66,185	23,622	89,807	9,762	66,810	1,352	11,883
71	$30,065	$78,573	$1,810	$80,383	$2,125	$09,437	$634	$8,187
72		19,266	2,880	22,146	272	16,670	1,488	3,716
73	32,519	20,819		20,819	1,633	11,803		3,005
74		156,601	16,277	172,878	47,315	100,870	3,838	8,176
75	150,605	126,536	72,576	199,112	53,898	105,703	15,827	23,051
76		183,917	80,257	264,174	49,466	182,572		32,130
77		157,782		157,782	2,021	137,428	5,385	12,119

CEIVER, AND CLOSING, SINCE THE ORGANIZATION OF THE NATIONAL BANKING AMOUNTS COLLECTED FROM ALL SOURCES, ETC.—Continued.

Balance in hands of Comptroller or receiver.	Amount returned to shareholders in cash.	Amount of assessment upon shareholders.	Amount of claims proved.	Dividends, per cent.	Interest dividends, per cent.	Finally closed.	
		$50,000	$122,089	58		Jan. 2, 1867	1
		300,000	434,531	23.37		Feb. 2, 1885	2
		200,000	669,513	24.70		May 14, 1883	3
		50,000	82,338	39.15		July 28, 1870	4
			376,392	17.333		Feb. 4, 1870	5
		100,000	289,467	46.60		Nov. 25, 1882	6
		500,000	1,119,313	79		Sept. 28, 1882	7
$109		120,000	127,801	45.90		Dec. 19, 1874	8
			1,191,500	96		Nov. 18, 1874	9
21		26,000	170,752	88.50		Aug. 15, 1872	10
		39,300	68,986	100	64	Apr. 7, 1881	11
27		100,000	205,256	68.33		Nov. 30, 1872	12
		34,870		49.20		Nov. 25, 1882	13
		69,874		41.90		Dec. 4, 1875	14
		170,012		92.70		May 16, 1884	15
		400,000	1,282,254	100	46	Apr. 20, 1882	16
	$1,214		157,120	100		Nov. 16, 1874	17
		135,000	378,722	100		Sept. 1, 1875	18
			645,558	100		Feb. 13, 1872	19
	33,500		79,864	100		Oct. 2, 1877	20
	6,500		15,142	100		Jan. 3, 1876	21
21		125,000	254,901	57.46		Feb. 15, 1886	22
		52,500	171,468	100	30	Jan. 8, 1880	23
		350,000	657,020	84.83		June 1, 1881	24
249		300,000	597,885	100	50	Apr. 29, 1884	25
202		300,000	1,619,965	100		July 24, 1876	26
	247,790		796,995	100	100	Mar. 31, 1883	27
		400,000	992,636	34		May 1, 1876	28
		50,000	167,285	76		May 15, 1876	29
454		100,000	175,081	57.50		Nov. 30, 1883	30
		600,000	1,429,595	62		Mar. 21, 1887	31
			87,292	73.50		Dec. 6, 1882	32
							33
347		50,000	144,606	43		Sept. 11, 1878	34
4		45,000	55,372	58.30		June 2, 1883	35
		100,000	176,601	57.50		Sept. 18, 1876	36
			62,646	100		May 14, 1879	37
			93,021	24.391		Nov. 20, 1883	38
		500,000	1,795,992	14.941		Mar. 19, 1879	39
			237,824	66		Apr. 5, 1886	40
		200,000	376,756	62.56		June 2, 1884	41
12		150,000	177,512	76.50		Mar. 4, 1886	42
		34,000	35,801	51		Mar. 28, 1883	43
		50,000	56,457	22.50		Feb. 28, 1878	44
	12		34,535	100		Jan. 31, 1881	45
50	4,185	75,000	91,801	100	100	July 20, 1882	46
704		50,000	135,952	48.40		Feb. 28, 1885	47
		250,000	703,658	77.512		May 23, 1888	48
	9,488		59,226	100	100	July 14, 1880	49
		60,000	97,464	70		Nov. 25, 1882	50
		30,000	35,023	27		Aug. 11, 1884	51
		140,000	352,062	100	28.50	Sept. 14, 1881	52
	8,739	132,000	185,760	100	100	Jan. 18, 1883	53
		67,000	175,952	81.59		July 23, 1881	54
		50,000	140,735	63.60		June 10, 1880	55
		53,000	227,355	89.179		Mar. 26, 1888	56
	26,720	625,000	1,035,721	100	100	Oct. 15, 1881	57
200	3,626		133,112	100	100	Oct. 5, 1885	58
			196,356	37.6483		Mar. 3, 1882	59
54,320		72,000	254,647	100			60
30		200,000	1,061,598	100	100	Feb. 23, 1892	61
			298,324	65.57		July 6, 1881	62
	36,871		392,394	100	100	Mar. 9, 1882	63
	5,849		75,175	100	100	Aug. 5, 1879	64
		35,000	29,204	90.50		June 20, 1882	65
		125,000	118,371	88		Mar. 9, 1885	66
		36,000	90,421	60		Sept. 7, 1885	67
	15,662	100,000	36,100	100		July 5, 1879	68
		50,000	201,887	38.10		Mar. 24, 1885	69
		100,000	77,104	40.7285		Feb. 12, 1889	70
		$21,500	168,048	98.925		Feb. 12, 1889	71
		17,000	$70,191	60		Apr. 8, 1881	72
$108	$3,420		27,801	100	100	Oct. 19, 1879	73
	12,679		32,449	100	100	Mar. 15, 1881	74
		50,000	156,260	68.70			75
		130,000	282,370	100	42.30	Mar. 1, 1884	76
	829	121,750	197,353	100	100	Jan. 17, 1881	77

INSOLVENT NATIONAL BANKS, DATES OF ORGANIZATION, APPOINTMENT OF RE SYSTEM, WITH AMOUNTS OF NOMINAL AND ADDITIONAL ASSETS,

	Nominal value of remaining assets.	Collected from assets.	Collected from assessment upon shareholders.	Total collections from all sources.	Loans paid and other disbursements.	Dividends paid.	Legal expenses.	Receiver's salary and other expenses.
78		$205,062	$54,950	$260,012	$57,745	$166,587	$10,245	$24,551
79		96,605		96,605	53	88,176		7,517
80	$11,877	29,419	4,677	34,096	10	20,998	1,792	11,296
81		91,121	23,001	114,122	8,420	82,060	7,167	16,475
82		113,791		113,791		96,176	3,225	6,739
83		338,162	267,311	605,473	10,037	528,305	19,338	22,690
84		89,766	64,655	154,421		99,847	2,973	10,832
85	101,952	1,366,608	495,550	1,802,158		1,790,932	46,755	24,392
86	8,250	457,272	13,450	470,722	1,910	389,222	45,449	34,141
87	1,760,962	1,191,340	734,724	1,926,064	194,579	1,566,122	80,310	111,237
88	4,157	150,019	8,321	158,340		127,863	8,911	18,873
89		281,261	123,919	405,180	247	321,870	24,279	58,784
90		152,842	12,010	164,852	5,099	83,787	12,054	28,287
91		16,577	23,732	40,309	3,392	26,809	2,223	7,885
92	136,320	143,478	12,892	156,370	17,502	72,657	9,657	24,531
93	33,959	261,075	64,650	325,725	17,527	260,191	10,446	20,031
94	1,478,855	4,242,577	272,474	4,515,051	472,827	3,615,540	110,474	178,642
95		37,129	19,169	56,298		39,812	4,745	11,029
96	59,334	294,779	76,936	371,715	64,035	275,684	5,168	26,828
97	26,023	22,744	18,869	41,613		25,006	2,602	13,178
98	155,259	84,440	94,200	178,640	6,359	143,938	28,750	13,386
99		20,849		20,849	6,515	8,807	52	5,475
100		52,029	23,503	75,532	1,893	59,057	5,012	9,440
101		626,313	159,087	785,400	17,243	681,177	53,425	33,555
102		46,332	50,000	96,332		86,263	1,825	8,244
103		79,289	1,400	80,689		59,461	5,010	16,215
104	983,775	2,282,527	167,438	2,449,965	174,137	2,028,060	95,626	89,349
105		148,611		148,611	231	131,024	192	2,314
106		245,704	58,304	304,008	82,472	188,482	2,855	22,713
107	64,968	60,839	15,730	76,569	16,664	22,558	5,730	15,724
108		28,477	36,700	65,177	625	52,402	1,840	10,299
109		77,305		77,305		66,394	1,155	6,607
110		165,669		165,669	16,177	135,574	1,425	7,321
111		198,513		198,513		117,878	198	5,208
112		204,047		204,047	106,424	82,946	324	4,279
113	3,300	62,871	1,180	65,553		50,597		11,762
114		14,251		14,251	82	9,492		1,348
115	2,911,545	2,929,223	301,669	3,231,252	85,249	2,163,946	111,113	70,595
116		104,682		104,682		86,442	1,990	8,461
117		82,069	18,135	100,204		80,120	7,152	4,802
118		31,798	34,002	65,800	777	46,546	7,746	10,731
119		139,485	34,656	174,141	519	161,497	2,280	9,845
120		263,871		263,871	1,017	255,495	882	3,988
121		920,599	250,028	1,170,627	17,606	1,084,638	28,035	30,518
122		1,391,306		1,391,306	782,390	400,998	630	11,572
123	332,702	453,335	72,577	525,912	5,150	412,784	37,062	31,998
124	285,470	224,700	37,900	262,600	5,810	248,132	3,703	14,053
125		186,976		186,976	1,083	172,909	2,988	9,096
126		330,471		330,471	1,169	318,554	1,810	4,622
127	19,318	35,670	20,400	55,570	7,284	14,874	1,931	13,293
128		100,149		100,149	1,466	93,051	1,923	3,348
129	116,132	507,246	59,645	566,891	59,535	482,013	4,690	13,910
130	49,598	94,681	32,500	127,181	26,881	86,914	3,282	10,469
131		27,930	26,707	54,637	1,177	43,289	5,032	5,139
132	11,803	105,043	19,798	124,841	58,647	23,443	7,755	14,487
133	24,305	91,239		91,239	31,303	57,567	2,089	5,250
134	9,970	53,380	42,408	95,788	20,086	60,510	1,934	8,492
135	37,051	19,508	10,153	29,661	2,522	17,926	660	6,330
136	56,264	19,902	720	20,622	3,404	12,226	140	2,561
137	171,588	511,995		511,995	41,906	452,017	4,455	12,781
138	56,460	56,488	21,240	77,728	10,875	60,824	250	5,417
139	121,488	29,596	34,510	64,106	1,592	51,599	2,601	7,345
140	81,258	10,405	7,437	17,842	4,373		2,695	3,437
141	47,646	35,207	4,770	39,977	6,234	30,516	664	3,809
142	51,896	11,879	3,600	15,479	1,833	5,617	1,203	3,832
143	422,295	330,733		330,733	190,493	118,323	5,578	15,907
144	22,229	41,571	27,450	69,021	17,018	29,482	4,901	5,027
145	105,732	61,581	16,900	78,481	1,049	60,270	2,316	8,809
146	201,057	464,135		464,135	60,648	349,994	0,218	20,183
147	118,157	76,043	7,524	83,567	27,004	44,791	648	6,774
148		58,361	780	59,141	32,132	21,366	934	4,068
149	58,035	47,793	1,058	48,851	8,481	27,603	3,198	4,010
150	1,889,830	380,608	149,634	530,242	4,614	235,860	14,518	30,742
151	2,151,991	259,769	240,087	499,856	64,355	347,243	11,730	27,675
152	48,263	161,995		161,995	8,779	147,205	141	4,930
153	101,983	59,765	22,750	82,515	3,035	68,817	728	3,685
154		42,815		42,815	32,214	8,753	18	1,830

CEIVER, AND CLOSING, SINCE THE ORGANIZATION OF THE NATIONAL BANKING AMOUNTS COLLECTED FROM ALL SOURCES, ETC.—Continued.

Balance in hands of Comptroller or receiver.	Amount returned to shareholders in cash.	Amount of assessment upon shareholders.	Amount of claims proved.	Dividends, per cent.	Interest dividends, per cent.	Finally closed.	
	$884	$160,000	$132,461	100	100	Apr. 24, 1886	78
	850		81,801	100	100	Aug. 1, 1881	79
		10,000	21,182	99.133		Feb. 6, 1883	80
		50,000	108,385	81		Aug. 6, 1887	81
	7,651		93,625	100	100	Feb. 4, 1882	82
	25,103	300,000	580,592	100	100	Feb. 18, 1885	83
	40,709	75,000	104,749	100	100	Oct. 12, 1885	84
		100,000	2,654,000	67.405			85
		100,000	894,767	43.50		Apr. 30, 1892	86
$6,500		961,300	2,397,129	65.3		June 30, 1893	87
		50,000	186,998	70.90		Apr. 15, 1893	88
		200,000	422,772	80.25		June 6, 1892	89
35,624		60,000	206,991	40			90
		50,000	46,441	81.10		Oct. 25, 1880	91
		100,000	204,521	33			92
		75,000	241,521	100			93
137,564		400,000	4,531,375	80			94
	712	25,000	36,526	100	100	Sept. 25, 1889	95
		250,000	365,931	75.25		Sept. 30, 1890	96
827		32,500	26,322	95			97
		100,000	409,030	35		Apr. 19, 1893	98
			8,131	100	100	Oct. 29, 1885	99
130		50,000	84,978	69, 50		Jan. 22, 1890	100
		200,000	651,274	100	21.6	May 29, 1893	101
		50,000	80,238	100	100	Feb. 10, 1888	102
3		50,000	140,333	42.37		Sept. 30, 1890	103
62,790		300,000	2,888,483	70			104
	14,850		127,524	100	100	June 1, 1886	105
	7,486	100,000	171,581	100	100	Sept. 14, 1891	106
15,893		50,000	62,162	40			107
11		50,000	112,135	47		Mar. 20, 1890	108
	3,149		63,609	100	100	Mar. 2, 1888	109
	5,172		130,772	100	100	Aug. 18, 1887	110
	75,229		110,626	100	100	Feb. 17, 1887	111
	10,074		80,452	100	100	Apr. 30, 1887	112
3,193		50,000	108,175	45			113
	3,329		9,379	100	100	Oct. 17, 1887	114
498,678		1,000,000	4,328,084	50			115
	7,787		82,150	100	100	July 11, 1889	116
	8,130	19,500	75,343	100	100	Mar. 5, 1891	117
		50,000	210,074	22.1568		May 13, 1892	118
		60,000	174,120	92.75		Apr. 25, 1892	119
	2,489		247,920	100	100	Oct. 29, 1888	120
9,740		300,000	1,120,984	9.6			121
	195,716		398,236	100	100	June 27, 1883	122
38,916		150,000	825,553	50			123
		100,000	435,319	57		Nov. 11, 1892	124
		100,000	326,222	53		Jan. 15, 1891	125
			311,028	100		Jan. 29, 1889	126
18,233		50,000	49,819	30			127
	361		90,136	100	100	Apr. 24, 1890	128
		75,000	456,667	100	100		129
		50,000	108.127	75			130
		50,000	143,454	30.177		Apr. 26, 1892	131
20,507		100,000	163,082	15			132
		10,000	58,743	90.25			133
4.764		65,000	75,638	80			134
2,213		12,500	22,408	80			135
2,164		20,000	30,566	40			136
		24,000	465,760	100			137
		40,000	56,072	100		Mar. 29, 1893	138
967		80,000	83,980	62.5			139
7,335		33,000	25,163				140
289		11,000	30,516	100			141
2,991		12,000	18,807	30			142
1,331			236,740	50			143
12,692		100,000	98,274	30			144
6,040		62,500	120,547	50			145
15,090			388,882	90			146
4,358		38,000	111,190	40			147
640		39,000	42,962	50.3			148
5,465		4,000	39,325	70			149
98,252		500,000	2,308,100	10			150
48,853		750,000	1,736,252	20			151
847			155,048	95			152
6,251		37,500	86,973				153
			8,753	100		June 30, 1892	154

INSOLVENT NATIONAL BANKS, DATES OF ORGANIZATION, APPOINTMENT OF RE
SYSTEM, WITH AMOUNTS OF NOMINAL AND ADDITIONAL ASSETS,

	Nominal value of remaining assets.	Collected from assets.	Collected from assessment upon shareholders.	Total collections from all sources.	Loans paid and other disbursements.	Dividends paid.	Legal expenses.	Receiver's salary and other expenses.
155	$424,972	$110,202	$3,880	$134,082	$80,974	$34,965	$2,066	$9,157
156	113,902	40,503	20,306	60,800	14,837	28,129	2,324	3,770
157	126,550	15,822	22,970	18,792	8,337		341	3,634
158	70,713	34,816	3,375	38,191	21,436	9,079	2,143	4,164
159	295,102	73,139	83,100	156,230	17,653	123,621	724	6,636
160	213,778	80,539	27,613	108,152	23,871	40,995	2,042	6,282
161	129,786	44,970	6,560	51,530	35,941		543	2,592
162	171,550	166,004		166,004	3,011	149,699	6,395	6,014
163								
164	66,010	17,555	5,215	22,770	1,280	17,006	636	3,567
165	2,267,875	6,636,285	136,890	6,773,175	76,548	6,644,340	30,175	50,072
166	344,142	327,838	23,664	351,502	9,176	326,803	140	6,967
167	312,990	186,174	28,420	214,594	52,814	140,446	2,671	7,243
168	1,192,182	272,066	206,340	478,406	100,935	264,903	16,235	11,300
169	472,558	193,030	103,454	296,484	45,551	218,663	5,654	9,046
170	53,892	43,487		43,487	31,023	5,654	419	3,073
171	72,956	38,141	3,926	42,067	12,913	21,627	1,257	3,143
172		123,933		123,933	11,946	80,636		2,655
173	55,730	35,404	4,136	39,540	6,515	26,565	2,638	4,565
174	255,731	15,659	41,558	57,217	1,531	54,076	395	4,231
175	126,099	29,228	12,123	41,351	4,800	33,482	562	4,482
176	346,520	97,166		97,166	784	85,532	550	
177								
178	61,352	28,513		28,513	20,710	3,141	1,582	2,245
179	67,902	28,794		28,794	4,432	35,146	97	326
180	208,359	8,475	10,266	18,741	425	15,900	69	1,644
181	245,554	143,878	44,362	188,240	706	180,430	290	2,880
182	149,341	28,442		28,442	14,841	7,714	719	2,005
183	182,268	15,691	36,722	52,413	2,865	45,488	577	1,884
184	746,682	214,624	54,451	269,075	141,695	81,282	1,293	3,592
185	597,778	36,800	32,960	69,760	1,971	52,528	2,431	3,108
186	702,621	276,373		276,373	214,687		823	6,391
187	2,000,132	441,426	191,512	632,938	24,690	551,706	50	11,771
188	164,232	56,807		56,807	13,633	33,099	36	2,280
189	190,003	19,690	10,250	29,940	14,509	14,771	10	1,086
190	323,998	28,417	15,862	44,279	33,098			1,905
191	2,035,211	278,576		278,576	147,858		8,592	3,509
192	782,845	125,477		125,477	398		1,362	2,902
193	215,237	6,011		6,011	1,584			2,579
194	139,049	53,143		53,143	14,543	18,309	441	1,683
195	717,132	773,780		773,780	277,318	404,490	200	4,892
196	426,302	6,578	25,162	31,740	547			1,343
197	47,745	2,392		2,392	483			1,255
198	183,255	16,060	500	16,560	729			1,421
199	79,817	18,299		18,299	199	12,308	64	1,109
200	684,168	78,746		78,746	44,027		275	1,039
201	568,495	36,787	50,350	87,137	383	81,112	60	1,700
202								
203	290,865	25,829		25,829	304			1,820
204	988,564	21,501		21,501	1,035			1,175
205	303,779	16,983		16,983	638			1,026
206	121,377	1,831		1,841	100		30	890
207	218,098	6,281		6,281	2,017		293	870
208	401,575	75,158		75,158	11,649		22	2,354
209	134,222	38,391		38,391	185		20	1,987
210	270,965	46,283		46,283	1,040		180	1,020
211	207,194	9,563		9,563	2,197		10	614
212	92,174	51,412		51,412	21,170		135	1,752
213	151,878	9,436		9,436	279		40	1,008
214	1,635,422	793,225		793,225	67,036	507,032	5,544	2,233
215								
216	1,008,182	130,380		130,380	3,601	134,450	22	1,979
217	160,015	1,386		1,386	214		6	175
218	274,248	2,083		2,083	150		99	945
219	205,788	26,390		26,390	6,197	20,891	8	919
220	1,634,746	120,918		120,918	39,139		270	2,484
221	1,882,431	181,712		181,712	75,980			3,085
222	299,364	45,214		45,214	5,531	56,606	20	1,022
223	1,013,892	75,912		75,912	49,040		373	1,370
224	177,345	56,258		56,258	11,326			655
225	453,284	52,540		52,540	23,383			1,610
226	106,935	432		432	318			55
227	307,668	23,468		23,468	4,956		85	930
228	215,388	7,151		7,151	944		9	730
229								
230	226,443	13,658		13,658	216			857
231	82,747	1,251		1,251	1,256			340

CEIVER, AND CLOSING, SINCE THE ORGANIZATION OF THE NATIONAL BANKING
AMOUNTS COLLECTED FROM ALL SOURCES, ETC.—Continued.

Balance in hands of Comptroller or receiver.	Amount returned to shareholders in cash.	Amount of assessment upon shareholders.	Amount of claims proved.	Dividends, per cent.	Interest dividends, per cent.	Finally closed.	
$7,329		$180,000	$122,256	35			155
11,747		47,000	59,391	50			156
6,478		54,000	71,969				157
1,368		45,000	36,018	25			158
7,603		150,000	277,119	45			159
34,060		120,000	102,488	40			160
12,454		41,000	9,274				161
882			149,699	100			162
						Feb. 15, 1892	163
279		18,000	34,013	50			164
		400,000	7,593,533	87.5			165
8,414		100,600	544,669	60			166
11,418		150,000	280,915	50			167
85,132		500,000	882,361	30			168
17,568		250,000	546,175	40			169
3,314			15,891	40			170
3,126		9,500	36,045	60			171
	$28,696		79,330	100	100	Oct. 12, 1892	172
1,544		21,000	44,020	60			173
		82,000	135,305	40			174
14,926		25,000	84,507	40			175
			171,065	50			176
							177
833		17,500	15,796	20			178
			33,457	100		Apr. 6, 1893	179
702		36,250	45,564	35			180
3,874		75,000	224,430	80			181
3,162			77,141	10			182
1,597		75,000	90,911	45			183
41,811		300,000	830,490	10			184
9,720		80,000	105,010	50			185
54,461			95,000				186
44,720		500,000	1,379,265	40			187
7,747			66,760	50			188
		50,000	79,684	20			189
9,275		100,000	85,777				190
118,034			753,361				191
120,813		200,000	236,629				192
1,816			12,007				193
18,291			69,411	30			194
			570,589	75			195
29,850		112,500	39,578				196
648			6,314				197
14,417		50,000	126,182				198
4,616			30,771	40			199
33,403			245,482				200
3,862		100,000	324,460	25			201
							202
17,735			142,516				203
19,191			686,010				204
15,317			219,639				205
935			14,257				206
3,099			58,069				207
61,111			227,270				208
37,008			71,322				209
44,039			125,502				210
6,741			65,427				211
28,384			42,938				212
10,562			43,050				213
121,357			1,194,069	50			214
							215
		250,000	537,813	25			216
990			7,375				217
888			170,458				218
			9,114	25			219
79,055			1,000,181				220
102,640		300,000	314,444				221
			174,706	25			222
25,118			69,486				223
44,275			133,551				224
27,545							225
58							226
17,496			117,287				227
7,970			55,531				228
							229
12,584			1,673				230
656			19,862				231

INSOLVENT NATIONAL BANKS, DATES OF ORGANIZATION, APPOINTMENT OF RE
SYSTEM, WITH AMOUNTS OF NOMINAL AND ADDITIONAL ASSETS,

	Nominal value of remaining assets.	Collected from assets.	Collected from assessment upon shareholders.	Total collections from all sources.	Loans paid and other disbursements.	Dividends paid.	Legal expenses.	Receiver's salary and other expenses.
232								
233	$366,053	$89,054		$89,054	$17,700		$5	$985
234	102,532	2,626		2,626	674			590
235	98,786	5,091		5,091	3,401		125	72
236	582,433	3,536		3,536	200			305
237	412,110	76,226		76,226	46,344			136
238								
239								
240								
241								
242	150,680	4,787		4,787	870			1,573
243								
244								
245								
246								

CEIVER, AND CLOSING, SINCE THE ORGANIZATION OF THE NATIONAL BANKING
AMOUNTS COLLECTED FROM ALL SOURCES, ETC.—Continued.

Balance in hands of Comptroller or receiver.	Amount returned to shareholders in cash.	Amount of assessment upon shareholders.	Amount of claims proved.	Dividends, per cent.	Interest dividends, per cent.	Finally closed.	
							232
$70,363			$319,593				233
2,450			37,118				234
1,953			21,538				235
2,940			1,068				236
29,742			29,923				237
							238
							239
							240
							241
2,545							242
							243
							244
							245
							246

COMPARATIVE STATEMENT FOR TWO YEARS OF THE TRANSACTIONS OF THE NEW YORK CLEARING HOUSE, SHOWING AGGREGATE AMOUNT OF CLEARINGS, AGGREGATE BALANCES, AND THE KINDS AND AMOUNTS OF MONEY PASSING IN SETTLEMENT OF THESE BALANCES.

Year ended—	Aggregate clearings.	Aggregate balances.	U. S. gold certificates.	U. S. Treasury notes.*
Oct. 1, 1892	$36, 279, 905, 236	$1, 861, 500, 575	$791, 022, 000	$357, 971, 000
Oct. 1, 1893	34, 421, 380, 870	1, 696, 207, 176	168, 628, 000	584, 613, 000
Increase				226, 642, 000
Decrease	1, 858, 524, 366	165, 293, 399	622, 394, 000	

Year ended—	Treasury certificates for legal tenders. Sec. 5193.	Legal tenders and minor coin.	Loan certificates.	Percentage to balances.		
				Gold certificates.	Legal tenders.	Loan certificates.
Oct. 1, 1892	$483, 350, 000	$229, 157, 000		42. 5	57. 5	
Oct. 1, 1893	188, 120, 000	525, 063, 000	229, 783, 000	38.	49.	13
Increase		295, 906, 000	229, 783, 000			
Decrease	295, 230, 000					

*United States Treasury notes are issued in pursuance of the provisions of the act of Congress directing the purchase of silver bullion and the issue of Treasury notes thereon, approved July 14, 1890. They are payable on demand in coin.

STATEMENT SHOWING BY COMPARISON THE TRANSACTIONS OF THE NEW YORK CLEARING HOUSE FOR FORTY YEARS, AND FOR EACH YEAR, THE NUMBER OF BANKS, AGGREGATE CAPITAL, CLEARINGS, BALANCES, AVERAGE OF THE DAILY CLEARINGS AND BALANCES, AND THE PERCENTAGE OF BALANCES TO CLEARINGS.

Year.	No. of banks.	Capital.*	Clearings.	Balances paid in money.	Average daily clearings.	Average daily balances paid in money.	Balances to clearings.
							Per ct.
1854	50	$47,044,900	$5,750,455,987	$297,411,494	$19,104,505	$988,078	5.2
1855	48	48,884,180	5,362,912,098	289,694,137	17,412,052	940,565	5.4
1856	50	52,883,700	6,906,213,328	334,714,489	22,278,108	1,079,724	4.8
1857	50	64,420,200	8,333,226,718	365,313,902	26,968,371	1,182,246	4.4
1858	46	67,146,018	4,756,004,386	314,238,911	15,393,736	1,016,954	6.6
1859	47	67,921,714	6,448,005,956	363,984,683	20,807,333	1,177,941	5.6
1860	50	69,907,435	7,231,143,957	380,693,458	23,401,757	1,232,018	5.3
1861	50	68,900,605	5,915,742,758	353,383,944	19,269,520	1,151,088	6
1862	50	68,375,820	6,871,443,591	415,530,331	22,237,682	1,344,758	6
1863	50	68,972,508	14,867,597,849	677,626,483	48,428,657	2,207,252	4.6
1864	49	68,586,763	24,097,196,656	885,719,205	77,984,455	2,866,405	3.7
1865	55	80,363,013	26,032,384,342	1,035,765,108	84,796,040	3,373,828	4
1866	58	82,370,200	28,717,146,914	1,066,135,106	93,541,195	3,472,753	3.7
1867	58	81,770,200	28,675,156,472	1,144,963,451	93,101,167	3,717,414	4
1868	59	82,270,200	28,484,288,637	1,125,455,237	92,182,164	3,612,250	4
1869	59	82,720,200	37,407,028,987	1,120,318,308	121,451,393	3,637,397	3
1870	61	83,620,200	27,804,539,406	1,036,484,822	90,274,479	3,365,210	3.7
1871	62	84,420,200	29,300,986,682	1,209,721,029	95,133,074	3,927,666	4.1
1872	61	84,420,200	33,844,369,568	1,428,582,707	109,884,317	4,636,632	4.2
1873	59	83,370,200	35,461,052,826	1,474,508,025	115,885,794	4,818,654	4.1
1874	59	81,635,200	22,855,927,636	1,286,753,176	74,692,574	4,205,070	5.7
1875	59	80,435,200	25,061,237,902	1,408,608,777	81,899,470	4,603,207	5.6
1876	59	81,731,200	21,597,274,247	1,295,042,029	70,349,428	4,218,378	5.9
1877	58	71,085,200	23,289,243,701	1,373,996,302	76,358,176	4,504,906	5.9
1878	57	63,611,500	22,508,438,442	1,307,843,857	73,555,988	4,274,000	5.8
1879	59	60,800,200	25,178,770,691	1,400,411,063	82,015,540	4,560,622	5.6
1880	57	60,475,200	37,182,128,621	1,516,538,631	121,510,224	4,956,009	4.1
1881	60	61,162,700	48,465,818,212	1,776,018,162	159,232,191	5,823,010	3.5
1882	61	60,962,700	46,552,846,161	1,595,000,245	151,637,935	5,195,440	3.4
1883	63	61,162,700	40,293,165,258	1,568,983,196	132,543,807	5,161,120	3.9
1884	61	60,412,700	34,092,037,338	1,524,930,994	111,048,982	4,967,202	4.5
1885	64	58,612,700	25,250,791,440	1,295,355,252	82,789,480	4,247,069	5.1
1886	63	59,312,700	33,374,082,216	1,510,565,385	109,067,589	4,965,900	4.5
1887	64	60,862,700	34,872,848,786	1,569,626,325	114,337,209	5,146,316	4.5
1888	63	60,762,700	30,863,686,609	1,570,198,528	101,192,445	5,148,192	5.1
1889	63	60,762,700	34,706,405,529	1,757,637,473	114,839,820	5,800,784	5
1890	61	60,812,700	37,660,686,572	1,753,040,145	123,074,130	5,728,889	4.7
1891	63	60,772,700	34,053,698,770	1,584,635,600	111,651,471	5,195,526	4.6
1892	64	60,422,700	36,270,905,236	1,861,500,575	118,561,782	6,083,395	5.1
1893	64	60,922,700	34,421,380,870	1,696,207,170	133,978,082	5,616,580	4.9
Total		†68,127,200	‡1,021,018,193,454	‡45,981,837,600	†83,246,522	†3,749,029	4.5

* The capital is for various dates, the amounts at a uniform date in each year not being obtainable.
† Yearly average for forty years.
‡ Totals for forty years.

STATEMENT SHOWING CLEARING HOUSE TRANSACTIONS OF THE ASSISTANT TREASURER OF THE UNITED STATES, AT NEW YORK, FOR THE YEAR ENDED OCTOBER 1, 1893.

Exchanges received from clearing house $311,667,362.84
Exchanges delivered to clearing house.. 114,840,233.88

Balances paid to clearing house... 199,486,783.98

The balances paid to the clearing houses consisted of—

United States gold coin... $22,810,000.00
United States gold certificates... 9,376,000.00
United States Treasury notes.. 80,938,000.00
Legal tenders and change.. 86,362,783.98

                                                                                     199,486,783.98

STATEMENT SHOWING BY COMPARISON THE EXCHANGES OF THE CLEARING HOUSES OF THE UNITED STATES FOR OCTOBER, 1893, AND 1892.

Clearing house at—	Exchanges for month ended Oct. 31—		Comparisons.	
	1893.	1892.	Increase.	Decrease.
New York	$2,229,354,959	$3,078,486,836		$849,131,877
Boston	353,699,586	456,632,613		102,933,027
Chicago	387,274,811	465,469,612		78,194,801
Philadelphia	247,861,456	345,878,910		98,017,454
St. Louis	86,439,652	106,929,580		20,489,928
San Francisco	57,469,133	76,149,857		18,680,724
Baltimore	52,741,161	67,102,981		14,361,820
Pittsburg	48,792,809	67,453,887		18,663,078
Cincinnati	50,619,900	72,135,800		21,515,900
Galveston	17,892,240	19,042,990		1,150,750
Kansas City	39,260,243	50,116,415		10,856,172
New Orleans	41,349,241	106,929,580		65,580,339
Minneapolis	32,011,154	49,243,286		17,232,132
Buffalo	34,597,008	39,245,547		4,648,539
Milwaukee	20,408,160	36,604,539		16,196,379
Detroit	23,795,581	34,673,510		10,877,929
Louisville	24,861,518	35,244,430		10,382,912
Houston	15,858,939	14,425,053	$1,433,886	
Providence	23,732,700	28,961,400		5,228,700
St. Paul	15,077,798	25,645,860		10,568,062
Cleveland	19,278,928	26,889,161		7,610,233
Denver	10,359,628	21,645,860		11,286,222
Omaha	22,300,000	27,941,513		5,641,513
Indianapolis	5,135,825	5,224,217		88,392
Memphis	6,771,474	9,339,621		2,568,147
Columbus	12,533,800	17,086,100		4,552,300
Dallas	4,464,455	3,978,752	485,703	
Nashville	2,816,738	8,453,404		5,636,666
Hartford	9,150,785	9,667,288		516,503
Portland, Oregon	5,680,515	11,301,793		5,621,278
Fort Worth	2,034,990	2,425,303		390,313
Duluth	8,132,059	9,836,301		1,704,242
Peoria	6,970,882	8,802,115		1,831,233
Washington, D. C.	6,405,186	9,981,491		3,576,305
St. Joseph	6,488,681	8,810,255		2,321,574
New Haven	6,182,836	6,869,702		686,866
Salt Lake	3,300,000	7,818,726		4,518,726
Rochester	6,188,076	7,262,523		1,074,447
Toledo	No report	No report		
Springfield	5,444,161	6,410,110		965,949
Worcester	4,782,936	6,127,397		1,344,461
Portland, Me	5,668,060	6,203,940		535,880
Norfolk	5,188,888	4,613,392	575,496	
Tacoma	2,274,135	5,789,716		3,515,581
Lowell	2,805,380	3,460,764		655,384
Grand Rapids	3,443,872	4,877,645		1,433,773
Sioux City	2,313,307	5,560,237		3,246,930
Syracuse	4,116,784	4,405,380		288,596
Seattle	2,071,209	4,614,845		2,543,636
Los Angeles	3,403,163	3,182,882	220,281	
Wilmington	3,256,450	4,380,090		1,123,640
Lincoln	1,979,334	3,095,803		1,116,469
Des Moines	3,780,623	5,410,147		1,629,524
Chattanooga	813,766	1,523,600		709,834
Wichita	1,400,000	2,288,083		888,083
New Bedford	2,775,070	2,940,015		164,945
Lexington	1,372,246	2,264,656		892,410
Topeka	1,494,904	1,948,667		453,763
Waco	4,249,735	3,419,884	829,851	
Birmingham	471,928	2,268,505		1,796,577
Binghamton	1,420,500	1,284,500	136,000	
Saginaw	1,268,181	1,773,878		505,697
Canton	621,522	816,030		194,508
Great Falls	700,000	1,286,202		586,202
Fremont	392,914	516,704		123,790
Richmond	8,259,114	10,449,433		2,190,319
Savannah	15,476,422	13,456,678	2,019,744	
Atlanta	5,673,151	7,823,958		2,150,807
Total	4,044,210,062	5,501,901,952	5,700,961	1,463,392,251
Decrease		1,457,691,290		1,457,691,290

STATEMENT SHOWING THE EXCHANGES OF THE CLEARING HOUSES OF THE UNITED
STATES FOR WEEKS ENDED OCTOBER 28, 1893, AND OCTOBER 29, 1892.

Clearing house at—	Exchanges for week ended—		Comparisons.	
	October 28, 1893.	October 29, 1892.	Increase.	Decrease.
New York	$545,371,946	$760,238,112		$214,866,166
Boston	79,632,849	107,151,050		27,518,201
Chicago	88,027,220	110,073,508		22,016,288
Philadelphia	57,991,433	86,062,551		28,071,118
St. Louis	17,659,066	25,236,256		7,577,190
San Francisco	10,908,651	17,812,109		6,903,458
Baltimore	12,071,694	14,820,845		2,719,151
Pittsburg	11,297,856	16,426,617		5,128,761
Cincinnati	11,041,650	15,613,000		4,571,350
Galveston	4,636,988	4,585,060		548,172
Kansas City	9,345,640	12,373,461		3,027,821
New Orleans	10,034,505	9,518,234	$510,271	
Minneapolis	7,226,145	10,215,840		2,989,695
Buffalo	8,214,397	8,165,882	48,515	
Milwaukee	4,388,452	9,306,432		4,917,980
Detroit	5,161,180	7,435,151		2,273,971
Louisville	5,769,505	7,872,767		2,103,262
Houston	4,559,916	3,709,155	850,761	
Providence	5,761,890	7,057,190		1,295,300
St. Paul	3,453,270	6,212,999		2,759,729
Cleveland	4,312,266	6,284,120		1,971,854
Denver	2,102,510	5,176,751		3,074,241
Omaha	4,886,733	7,165,480		2,278,747
Indianapolis	1,045,934	1,171,639		125,705
Memphis	1,784,112	2,597,806		813,694
Columbus	2,957,800	3,937,300		979,500
Dallas	1,095,850	1,000,000	95,850	
Nashville	615,256	1,957,683		1,342,427
Hartford	1,643,067	2,208,747		565,680
Portland, Oregon	1,400,000	2,441,339		1,041,339
Fort Worth	650,000	584,843	65,157	
Duluth	1,962,574	2,100,000		137,426
Peoria	1,712,082	2,126,766		414,684
Washington, D. C	1,331,239	2,381,918		1,050,679
St. Joseph	1,437,430	1,946,281		508,851
New Haven	1,317,502	1,478,499		160,997
Salt Lake	No report.	1,676,950		1,676,950
Rochester	1,253,679	1,894,367		640,688
Springfield	1,033,919	1,403,353		369,434
Worcester	1,119,128	1,371,974		252,846
Portland, Me	1,220,706	1,467,735		247,029
Norfolk	1,229,417	992,059	237,358	
Tacoma	558,218	1,478,576		920,358
Lowell	632,796	826,429		193,633
Grand Rapids	708,901	1,035,827		326,920
Sioux City	545,133	1,336,907		791,774
Syracuse	798,924	939,800		140,876
Seattle	430,584	1,097,084		666,500
Los Angeles	670,276	652,892	17,384	
Wilmington	712,504	1,039,665		327,161
Lincoln	484,556	680,000		195,444
Des Moines	968,931	887,453	81,478	
Chattanooga	161,398	474,200		312,802
Wichita	314,407	499,933		185,526
New Bedford	488,345	474,757	13,588	
Lexington	278,851	431,654		152,803
Topeka	288,158	418,204		130,046
Waco	900,240	834,947	65,293	
Birmingham	126,299	553,082		426,783
Binghamton	280,400	334,300		53,900
Total	947,414,898	1,307,247,549	1,991,655	361,824,316
Decrease		359,832,661		359,832,661

STATEMENT SHOWING BY COMPARISON THE EXCHANGES OF THE CLEARING HOUSES OF THE UNITED STATES FOR YEARS ENDED SEPTEMBER 30, 1893, AND SEPTEMBER 30, 1892.

Clearing house at—	Exchanges for years ended September 30—		Comparisons.	
	1893.	1892.	Increase.	Decrease.
New York	$34,421,379,870	$36,279,905,236		$1,858,525,366
Boston	4,864,779,750	4,901,096,976		36,317,226
Chicago	4,970,913,387	4,959,861,142	$11,052,245	
Philadelphia	3,656,677,140	3,671,149,047		14,471,907
St. Louis	1,188,378,457	1,211,370,719		22,992,262
San Francisco	752,949,766	833,617,126		80,667,360
Baltimore	737,568,241	772,435,133		34,866,892
Pittsburg	711,547,291	743,635,356		32,088,065
Cincinnati	679,051,000	728,711,350		49,660,350
Galveston	152,848,438	141,985,866		123,404,057
Kansas City	507,454,919	494,906,132	12,548,787	
New Orleans	523,996,645	488,931,005	35,065,640	
Minneapolis	377,785,380	427,287,201		49,501,821
Buffalo	415,229,127	409,405,192	5,823,935	
Milwaukee	377,740,215	353,849,753	23,890,462	
Detroit	353,558,369	347,737,532	5,820,837	
Louisville	356,361,823	368,698,812		12,336,989
Houston	130,136,394	102,715,466	27,420,928	
Providence	305,593,800	280,637,800	24,956,000	
St. Paul	237,137,633	271,350,612		34,212,979
Cleveland	291,500,368	287,324,716	4,175,652	
Denver	221,784,526	259,519,344		37,734,818
Omaha	315,244,799	271,668,937	43,575,862	
Indianapolis	64,111,531	118,616,627		54,505,096
Memphis	98,939,078	140,387,378		41,448,300
Columbus	171,069,700	177,384,700		6,315,000
Dallas	51,440,379	49,298,231	2,142,148	
Nashville	81,973,258	96,295,409		14,322,151
Hartford	117,542,969	109,746,541	7,796,428	
Portland, Oregon	90,561,073	*108,903,862		18,342,789
Fort Worth	29,850,748	28,841,335	1,009,413	
Duluth	103,447,519	93,413,428	10,034,091	
Peoria	88,318,395	95,873,112		7,554,717
Washington, D. C	104,721,162	98,005,354	6,715,808	
St. Joseph	93,918,878	89,814,345	4,104,533	
New Haven	77,502,994	74,492,129	3,010,865	
Salt Lake	70,692,022	89,463,682		18,771,660
Rochester	81,662,500	77,594,997	4,067,512	
Toledo	No report.	No report.		
Springfield	72,405,148	68,875,781	3,529,367	
Worcester	68,814,169	64,732,396	4,081,773	
Portland, Mo	67,649,613	62,605,687	5,043,326	
Norfolk	47,112,879	52,409,229		5,296,350
Tacoma	42,521,796	47,154,237		4,632,441
Lowell	36,918,580	42,736,155		5,817,575
Grand Rapids	49,344,223	48,622,342	721,881	
Sioux City	50,675,522	54,367,936		3,692,414
Syracuse	50,762,983	47,687,537	3,075,446	
Seattle	48,236,447	52,386,734		4,150,287
Los Angeles	45,239,721	40,027,896	5,211,825	
Wilmington	46,904,288	44,573,069	2,331,219	
Lincoln	29,010,186	32,235,901		3,225,715
Des Moines	50,334,184	49,972,363	361,821	
Chattanooga	19,326,230	*22,681,000		3,354,770
Wichita	24,909,142	27,566,186		2,657,044
New Bedford	25,470,286	24,138,424	1,331,859	
Lexington	20,392,202	*24,352,938		3,060,736
Topeka	19,951,288	20,512,044		560,756
Richmond	119,978,116	No report.	119,978,116	
Waco	32,197,057	No report.	32,197,057	
Birmingham	22,273,145	No report.	22,273,145	
Binghamton	14,883,300	No report.	14,883,300	
Total	58,880,682,455	60,883,572,438	448,231,281	2,585,387,893
		58,880,682,455		448,231,281
Decrease		2,002,889,083		2,137,156,612

*For nine months.

ABSTRACT OF REPORTS OF CONDITION

OF

State Banks, Loan and Trust Companies, Savings and Private Banks,

1892-'93.

ARRANGED BY STATES, TERRITORIES, AND GEOGRAPHICAL DIVISIONS.

NOTE.—Reference marks in the tables following indicate the character of the source of information from which reports were received.

TABLE I.

ABSTRACT OF REPORTS OF CONDITION OF STATE

States, etc.	Date of report.	No. of banks.	RESOURCES.			
			Loans on real estate.	Loans on collateral security other than real estate.	Other loans and discounts.	Overdrafts.
New Hampshire	June 30, 1893	(*1)				
Rhode Island	Nov. 17, 1892	6			$1,603,590	
Connecticut	Oct. 1, 1892	8			5,138,607	$11,430
Total Eastern States		14			6,742,197	11,430
New York	June 1, 1893	201			188,585,572	306,990
New Jersey	June 24, 1893	22	$85,497		8,510,749	12,746
Pennsylvania	Nov. 30, 1892	85	4,505,389	$10,479,878	21,099,502	114,924
Delaware*	June 30, 1893	4	301,453	133,355	1,373,354	
Maryland*	....do	6	38,843	204,490	2,128,698	
Total Middle States		318	4,931,182	10,817,723	221,697,875	434,660
Virginia	July 12, 1893	90			17,896,543	132,526
West Virginia	Sept. 30, 1892	45			8,898,805	50,241
North Carolina	July 12, 1893	33	485,301		3,451,584	66,765
South Carolina*	June 30, 1893	21	51,153	66,342	2,020,244	5,678
Georgia†	....do	87			19,349,456	143,932
Florida	Dec. 31, 1892	11			701,865	26,552
Alabama*	June 30, 1893	18	121,690	590,383	634,911	13,590
Mississippi	July 12, 1893	63			6,304,167	492,949
Louisiana†	June 30, 1893	18	109,099	383,831	7,899,010	85,637
Texas	....do	4			819,902	17,544
Arkansas*	....do	34	109,451	1,604,537	1,517,414	167,144
Kentucky	Sept. 23, 1893	164			33,294,152	
Tennessee*	June 30, 1893	63	159,406	713,186	5,503,590	58,856
Total Southern States		651	1,096,100	3,358,279	108,291,643	1,261,414
Missouri	Apr. 22, 1893	455	7,040,049		67,627,559	1,342,669
Ohio	Oct. 3, 1892	86	7,979,848		20,705,545	80,152
Indiana	July 15, 1893	86			9,404,858	121,278
Illinois	July 25, 1893	89			20,806,717	152,632
Michigan	Oct. 3, 1893	159			33,033,573	163,683
Wisconsin	July 3, 1893	118			34,005,058	163,414
Iowa	June 30, 1893	177			20,534,832	303,983
Minnesota	July 12, 1893	133			28,231,221	166,565
Kansas*	June 30, 1893	255	1,135,297	6,957,043	4,594,384	246,765
Kansas a	Oct. 3, 1893	276	1,047,092		12,460,817	256,053
Nebraska‡	Mar. 6, 1893	522			30,744,628	692,079
Total Western States		2,080	10,155,194	6,957,043	270,288,375	3,433,240
Oregon*	June 30, 1893	12	24,290	327,976	410,943	10,347
Colorado	....do	29			3,473,218	29,021
Utah	....do	5			900,075	85,916
Idaho*	....do	5	7,900	120,783	83,234	4,853
Montana*	....do	4	164	948	796,538	10,792
Wyoming	June 8, 1893	5			165,136	4,212
New Mexico	Jan. 30 and July 3, 1893	2			284,243	
North Dakota‡	July 22, 1893	72			2,579,238	24,305
South Dakota‡	June 12, 1893	135			4,310,649	134,794
Washington	May 31, 1893	64	2,099,332		5,833,011	19,200
Arizona*	June 30, 1893	5	181,701	236,924	117,907	17,990
California	July 1, 1893	173	18,695,198	17,101,891	49,176,228	
Oklahoma*	June 30, 1893	5	42,815	171,409	25,782	456
Total Pacific States, etc.		516	21,051,400	17,959,931	68,216,202	347,886
Total United States		3,579	43,233,876	39,092,976	675,236,292	5,488,630

*Unofficial.   † Semiofficial, and all others official.   ‡ Includes private banks.
(*1 One, included with L. and Tr. Co.'s.)   a Received too late to be included in totals.

TABLE I.

			RESOURCES.					
United States bonds.	State, county, munici-pal, etc., bonds.	Railroad bonds and stocks.	Bank stocks.	All other bonds and stocks.	Due from other banks and bankers.	Real es-tate, fur-niture, and fixtures.	Current expenses and taxes paid.	States.
				$120,695	$122,878	$169,983	$9,270	N. H.
				1,393,656	1,215,363	182,264	15,967	R. I.
								Conn.
				1,520,351	1,338,241	352.252	25,237	
				11,269,839	21,988,013	6,230,890	964,724	N. Y.
				857,102	835.782	290,615	46,224	N. J.
				11,124,536	6,043,942	2,560,801	228,256	Pa.
		$9,450	$6,814	28,840	209,095	180,338	6,599	Del.
$3,495	$86,400	115,500	25,000	217,010	213,651	168,771	1,273	Md.
3,495	66,400	124,950	31.814	23,497,327	29,290,463	9,440.415	1,247,076	
4,000				1,687,717	1,862,817	656,247	84,305	Va.
	312,145	156,375	35,205	416,187	1,582,116	561,645	59,164	W. Va.
	25,667			72.912	424,266	178,844	32,540	N. C.
	23,091	20,000		53,830	135,126	110,056	18,831	S. C.
				1,163,381	2,872,683	1,144,058	256,828	Ga.
				71,174	263,739	79,722	15,328	Fla.
	9,000			45,945	174,436	95,904	23,936	Ala.
				498,969	1,077,016	562,805	103,929	Miss.
	111,356			209,668	172,534	378,833	90,589	La.
						90.761	5,646	Tex.
	87,284			45,503	681,371	202,731	50,095	Ark.
					4,368,010			Ky.
	32.249			284,623	920,727	314,158	84,552	Tenn.
4,000	600,792	176,375	35.205	4,549,909	14,534,841	4.375,764	825,743	
63,826				6,180,166	11,004,655	3,489,531		Mo.
103,125	515,300			2,940,870	4,051,474	1,354,546	223,636	Ohio.
126,458				512.846	1,395.541	446.483	89,352	Ind.
1,650				985,216	3,816.353	606,378	74,707	Ill.
				25,015,335	7,635,961	2,059,180	266,552	Mich.
				1,986,899	5,714,948	1,246,842	68,290	Wis.
					2,126.090	1,286,278		Iowa.
100				468,814	3,262.527	1,975,322	105,538	Minn.
	85,043		31,934	225,690	2,112,253	1.614,876	204,525	Kaus.
				494,918	2,155,792	1,911,385	295,180	Kans.
50,000				961,072	5,282,330	2,183,409	499,035	Nebr.
405,159	606,343		31.934	39,276,908	46,432,132	16,262,845	1,641,575	
	54,639			100	26,734	90,010	21,286	Oregon.
	34,158			275,990	611,888	202,026	35,646	Colo.
				3,179	116,561	136,300	12,482	Utah.
				2,634	20,035	34,515	3,771	Idaho.
	15,289			1,280	53,035	15,429	15,003	Mont.
				55,832	25,219	31,053	2,485	Wyo.
					67,276	2,430		N. Mex.
				48,113	351.773	226,970	82,722	N. Dak.
	125,742			83,850	501,552	572,207	124,922	S. Dak.
	948,024			448,586	728,614	1,121.886	185,116	Wash.
				5,993	65.093	61,325	6,230	Ariz.
				3,480,288	9,432.382	5,647,628		Cal.
	22,871			15,816	103,790	27,080	12,870	Okla.
	1,200,723			4,430,691	12,194,552	8,169,149	502,533	
412,654	2,468,258	301,325	98,953	73,275,186	103,790,249	38,600,425	4,242,164	

TABLE I.

ABSTRACT OF REPORTS OF CONDITION OF STATE BANKS

States, etc.	RESOURCES.			LIABILITIES.
	Cash and cash items.	Other resources.	Total.	Capital stock.
New Hampshire				
Rhode Island	$92,241	$90,076	$2,214,738	$916,675
Connecticut	539,362	....	8,496,649	2,340,000
Total Eastern States	631,603	90,076	10,711,387	3,256,675
New York	56,995,625	608,056	286,949,709	33,559,200
New Jersey	497,710	13,817	11,159,242	1,780,460
Pennsylvania	3,242,330	669,998	60,069,556	8,819,697
Delaware	84,090	6,226	2,339,614	680,000
Maryland	411,835	....	3,594,966	1,128,450
Total Middle States	61,231,590	1,298,097	364,113,087	45,767,807
Virginia	1,558,508	170,885	24,053,348	6,388,588
West Virginia	1,029,587	235	13,101,705	2,421,676
North Carolina	437,742	....	5,175,621	1,913,530
South Carolina	146,083	870	2,651,304	1,123,024
Georgia	2,548,541	60,559	27,539,438	9,363,036
Florida	177,050	....	1,335,430	335,000
Alabama	117,766	2,597	1,830,158	900,910
Mississippi	940,599	....	9,980,434	3,260,925
Louisiana	3,035,690	15,092	12,551,339	2,755,447
Texas	320,755	....	1,254,608	450,000
Arkansas	514,742	3,659	4,983,931	1,675,995
Kentucky	4,443,712	965,021	43,070,895	15,855,430
Tennessee	1,553,744	70,418	9,695,509	5,346,435
Total Southern States	16,824,319	1,289,336	157,223,720	49,789,926
Missouri	10,922,693	....	107,671,168	19,837,105
Ohio	2,817,377	66,959	40,898,832	7,618,325
Indiana	1,602,336	....	13,699,152	4,504,500
Illinois	3,082,954	34,116	30,190,723	7,065,500
Michigan	4,856,906	....	73,631,190	12,102,955
Wisconsin	6,132,989	....	49,338,380	6,806,900
Iowa	1,869,683	....	26,120,866	8,074,420
Minnesota	3,839,740	54,250	38,194,077	9,189,000
Kansas	2,047,797	45,179	19,300,786	5,959,915
Kansas	2,267,311	....	20,888,578	7,740,223
Nebraska	2,435,444	119,008	42,067,005	11,418,995
Total Western States	40,207,919	319,512	442,013,179	92,587,615
Oregon	101,649	3,315	1,071,289	553,800
Colorado	540,618	23,723	5,226,288	1,740,000
Utah	99,500	5,110	1,419,123	750,000
Idaho	17,127	....	295,482	157,500
Montana	76,220	1,285	901,983	365,000
Wyoming	14,112	....	208,049	94,500
New Mexico	79,426	....	133,375	113,800
North Dakota	263,225	....	3,576,346	1,092,340
South Dakota	571,608	68,037	6,583,421	1,987,053
Washington	1,150,859	364,288	12,698,946	4,263,555
Arizona	52,172	52,500	797,835	240,200
California	15,080,785	4,142,618	122,746,218	47,848,938
Oklahoma	103,920	....	526,839	159,000
Total Pacific States, etc	18,131,221	4,460,876	156,665,164	59,365,686
Total United States	137,026,652	7,457,897	1,130,725,537	250,767,709

TABLE I.

IN THE UNITED STATES, 1892-'93—Continued.

	LIABILITIES.						States.
Surplus.	Other undivided profits.	State-bank notes.	Dividends unpaid.	Deposits.	Due to other banks.	Other liabilities.	
....	$176,116	$974	$7,650	$909,777	$177,825	$25,721	N. H.
$809,145	96,913	....	3,194	4,792,373	655,024	....	R. I.
							Conn.
609,145	273,029	974	10,844	5,702,150	832,849	25,721	
10,325,202	12,027,487	....	....	198,013,253	23,051,925	4,172,632	N. Y.
816,178	323,474	....	3,777	7,267,300	527,703	610,341	N. J.
4,115,409	1,492,240	....	40,561	41,737,284	772,073	92,292	Pa.
382,219	25,293	....	9,080	1,090,446	110,576	36,000	Del.
241,000	95,526	....	24,109	2,080,620	24,840	421	Md.
21,910,008	13,964,030	....	77,527	253,194,912	24,287,117	4,911,686	
1,825,602	601,565	....	26,701	13,746,018	475,536	980,338	Va.
688,686	235,526	....	8,564	8,065,828	608,024	173,401	W. Va.
223,002	150,894	....	5,138	2,446,621	90,979	345,457	N. C.
125,365	177,843	....	18,135	671,450	43,568	491,914	S. C.
1,049,856	1,126,117	....	153,930	11,186,277	1,782,083	1,968,139	Ga.
18,434	37,785	....	21	874,751	13,777	55,662	Fla.
53,249	153,489	....	....	542,731	31,377	148,402	Ala.
357,454	451,964	....	....	4,950,993	105,081	854,017	Miss.
531,500	759,205	8,560	66,835	8,338,644	13,304	77,844	La.
135,026	54,872	....	....	577,219	7,491	30,000	Texas.
338,501	176,811	....	....	2,401,054	158,242	230,498	Ark.
5,451,715	....	....	....	21,763,750	....	....	Ky.
512,732	318,582	....	16,667	5,216,275	113,694	171,124	Tenn.
11,911,122	4,256,658	8,560	295,991	81,082,511	3,443,156	5,535,796	
8,723,876	....	....	....	74,037,097	3,263,873	1,809,217	Mo.
1,111,717	898,435	....	14,574	30,308,570	617,673	329,538	Ohio.
643,794	368,027	....	17,542	7,838,886	76,682	249,721	Ind.
1,968,910	801,015	....	8,400	18,523,537	1,424,719	398,642	Ill.
2,375,830	2,234,447	....	23,174	54,737,226	1,183,703	973,855	Mich.
2,826,254	....	....	....	37,826,560	1,826,395	52,271	Wis.
867,451	876,968	....	....	15,725,403	576,624	....	Iowa.
935,618	1,793,888	....	36,973	24,313,059	1,311,781	1,613,758	Minn.
735,719	707,691	....	24,903	11,240,759	212,402	409,397	Kans.
765,127	774,946	....	30,502	10,793,710	41,617	733,448	Kans.
1,001,864	1,398,616	....	6,989	27,396,520	218,667	1,525,354	Nebr.
21,191,033	9,079,087	....	132,555	300,947,617	10,712,519	7,361,753	
20,864	29,441	....	....	429,726	37,089	369	Oregon.
125,849	175,445	....	1,001	3,063,499	24,978	95,516	Colo.
51,500	34,872	....	....	503,599	67,509	11,583	Utah.
1,948	4,185	....	....	128,190	3,653	....	Idaho.
39,575	52,176	....	....	482,297	7,470	45,465	Mont.
....	9,668	....	....	156,000	1,020	36,855	Wyo.
10,402	....	....	4,826	304,347	....	....	N. Mex.
92,844	180,081	....	2,758	1,848,005	29,265	321,553	N. Dak.
212,296	325,181	....	....	3,480,688	75,460	502,743	S. Dak.
217,290	466,575	....	....	6,902,113	584,871	264,512	Wash.
27,793	14,501	....	....	470,203	23,280	21,856	Ariz.
17,810,935	....	....	....	46,934,167	8,128,535	2,024,643	Cal.
5,000	25,801	....	....	336,607	431	....	Okla.
18,616,293	1,327,426	....	8,585	65,038,453	8,983,621	3,325,095	
74,237,606	28,900,230	9,534	525,502	706,865,643	48,259,262	21,160,051	

TABLE II.

ABSTRACT OF REPORTS OF CONDITION OF LOAN AND

States.	Date of report.	No. of companies.	RESOURCES.			
			Loans on real estate.	Loans on collateral security other than real estate.	Other loans and discounts.	Overdrafts.
Maine	Sept. to Nov., 1892.	13	$735,219	$168,936	$1,990,944	
New Hampshire	June 30, 1893	*13	5,349,015	674,251	2,951,345	
Massachusetts	Oct. 31,1892	20	13,028,220	35,055,220	16,889,798	
Rhode Island	Nov. 17,1892	7	2,570,582	2,302,070	8,546,475	
Connecticut	Oct. 1,1892	10			3,786,347	$7,289
Total Eastern States		63	21,683,336	39,100,477	34,175,909	7,289
New York	Jan. 1,1893	34	15,062,290	196,321,422	19,698,925	
New Jersey	...do...	19	2,497,192	4,359,037	1,784,946	829
Pennsylvania	Nov.30,1892	75	19,370,144	61,483,263	3,616,332	65,626
Delaware †	June 30,1893	1	365,112	416,139	305,367	
Maryland †	...do...	2	51,156	950,655		
District of Columbia	July 12,1893	3	3,333,113	2,744,825	1,725	1,107
Total Middle States		134	40,679,007	266,275,941	25,407,295	67,562
West Virginia.—Total Southern States.	Sept. 30,1892	3			128,304	706
Missouri †	June 30,1893	3	2,358,094	1,351,270	19,027	3,295
Illinois	July 25,1893	7			12,356,312	9,926
Iowa †	June30,1893	8	14,891,611	442,707	433,524	
Minnesota	July 31,1893	10	1,676,925		1,749,858	5,139
Total Western States		28	18,926,630	1,793,977	14,558,721	18,360
Total United States		228	81,288,973	307,170,395	74,270,229	93,917

States.	RESOURCES.			LIABILITIES.
	Cash and cash items.	Other resources.	Total.	Capital stock.
Maine	$107,592	$300,488	$4,889,690	$1,060,800
New Hampshire	350,216		11,109,116	1,455,000
Massachusetts	1,730,652	152,371	95,343,442	8,975,000
Rhode Island	1,909,799	37,761	22,414,452	2,557,900
Connecticut	246,625		6,450,872	1,161,600
Total Eastern States	4,347,884	490,620	140,207,572	15,219,300
New York	9,089,687	5,187,311	335,707,780	25,950,000
New Jersey	399,507	328,641	12,898,701	1,695,000
Pennsylvania	4,423,654	25,382,025	175,885,991	36,003,744
Delaware †	11,909	24,417	1,743,972	500,000
Maryland †	176,325	18,073	2,920,884	1,000,000
District of Columbia	331,717		9,077,978	3,250,000
Total Middle States	14,433,009	30,940,467	538,235,306	68,398,744
West Virginia.—Total Southern States	16,184	5,318	227,643	111,490
Missouri †	150,172	99,236	4,642,506	1,050,000
Illinois	2,766,902	3,259	17,436,835	3,460,000
Iowa †	131,223	529,645	18,053,738	2,176,603
Minnesota	371,075	149,241	7,860,906	4,451,131
Total Western States	3,419,372	781,381	47,993,985	11,137,734
Total United States	22,216,539	32,217,786	726,664,506	94,867,268

* Includes one State bank.   † Unofficial; all others official.

TABLE II.

TRUST COMPANIES IN THE UNITED STATES, 1892–'93.

			RESOURCES.					
United States bonds.	State, county, municipal, etc., bonds.	Railroad bonds and stocks.	Bank stocks.	All other bonds and stocks.	Due from other banks and bankers.	Real estate, furniture, and fixtures.	Current expenses and taxes paid.	States.
....	$108,950	$204,486	$66,369	$626,678	$408,607	$152,612	$9,809	Mo.
				1,545,479	238,810	....	....	N. H.
$2,160,496	3,864,612	8,056,727	500,679	1,435,564	9,624,508	1,713,315	228,280	Mass.
500,000	1,366,058	2,928,674	85,200	1,243,738	253,000	644,060	26,735	R. I.
....	....	....	....	1,478,903	614,109	301,116	14,483	Conn.
2,660,496	5,339,620	11,189,887	652,248	6,330,362	11,130,034	2,811,103	279,307	
13,772,540	....	....	....	41,413,109	25,949,229	7,213,267	....	N. Y.
....	....	....	....	1,840,908	1,066,667	620,434	....	N. J.
....	....	....	....	38,419,632	12,177,813	10,536,825	410,377	Pa.
....	161,900	256,001	....	12,030	101,489	82,699	6,840	Del.
....	196,919	193,382	....	906,461	....	396,492	31,421	Md.
50,100	....	....	....	124,082	811,020	1,669,170	11,113	D. C.
15,822,640	358,819	449,443	....	82,716,222	40,106,158	20,518,893	459,760	
....	....	....	....	....	7,199	58,968	10,964	W. Va.
....	9,305	....	9,000	137,938	426,612	70,267	8,200	Mo.
3,500	....	....	....	773,632	1,466,365	28,169	28,770	Ill.
....	134,919	....	7,222	530,806	206,703	627,867	111,511	Iowa.
....	....	....	....	1,692,752	....	2,130,251	85,665	Minn.
3,500	144,314	....	16,222	3,141,128	2,099,680	2,856,554	234,146	
18,486,036	5,842,753	11,639,330	668,470	92,187,712	53,352,071	26,245,518	984,177	

			LIABILITIES.				
Surplus.	Other undivided profits.	Debenture bonds outstanding.	Dividends unpaid.	Deposits subject to check.	Due to other banks.	Other liabilities.	
$79,600	$142,487	$186,300	$2,026	$3,013,880	$9,491	$386,106	Me.
160,471	151,691	4,421,106	....	3,724,279	....	1,196,569	N. H.
4,028,006	2,447,300	....	....	71,485,089	....	8,408,047	Mass.
104,877	699,648	....	282	18,602,034	449,711	....	R. I.
339,555	274,504	....	5,016	4,576,197	....	94,000	Conn.
4,712,509	3,715,630	4,607,406	7,324	101,401,479	459,202	10,084,722	
35,764,529	4,973,153	....	....	264,245,048	....	6,725,050	N. Y.
244,358	459,111	....	....	9,752,510	82,751	665,971	N. J.
9,267,760	9,104,7e5	....	34,751	89,223,195	651,517	31,600,239	Pa.
85,000	37,201	....	....	831,499	....	290,272	Del.
377,056	155,550	....	....	701,780	....	686,498	Md.
250,000	177,098	747,900	938	4,646,704	5,338	....	D. C.
43,987,703	14,906,858	747,900	35,689	369,450,736	739,606	39,968,030	
....	2,453	....	15	113,685	....	....	W. Va.
86,809	63,003	....	21,418	2,145,286	28,336	1,247,654	Mo.
1,111,600	890,597	....	2,512	10,620,340	1,351,7e6	....	Ill.
255,574	413,982	13,071.836	....	665,922	107,900	1,361,921	Iowa.
249,226	375,493	62,400	427	1,846,631	3,646	871,952	Minn.
1,703,209	1,743,075	13,134,236	24,357	15,278,179	1,491,668	3,481,527	
50,403,421	20,368,056	18,489,542	67,385	486,244,079	2,690,476	53,534,279	

TABLE III.

ABSTRACT OF REPORTS OF CONDITION OF THE MUTUAL AND

States, etc.	Date of reports.	No. of banks.	RESOURCES.			
			Loans on real estate.	Loans on collateral security other than real estate.	Other loans and discounts.	Overdrafts.
MUTUAL SAVINGS BANKS.						
Maine	Oct. 31, 1892	53	$7,197,644	....	$7,014,690	....
New Hampshire	June 30, 1893	70	29,677,608	$7,628,425	7,367,399	....
Vermont	June 30, 1893	22	11,695,097	722,226	1,426,084	....
Massachusetts	Oct. 31, 1892	184	165,854,636	14,750,734	94,194,577	....
Rhode Island	Nov. 17, 1892	38	27,468,776	3,350,763	6,099,901	....
Connecticut	Oct. 1, 1892	87	51,891,336	8,680,662	3,569,804	....
Total Eastern States		454	293,785,757	35,141,830	119,672,455	....
New York	Jan. 1, 1893	124	203,971,249	3,209,730	....	....
New Jersey	...do	24	15,671,371	1,705,363	....	....
Pennsylvania	Nov. 30, 1892	14	17,707,170	6,679,270	....	....
Delaware*	June 30, 1893	2	3,122,790	221,796	34,820	....
Maryland*	...do	19	5,423,144	1,977,133	622,909	....
Total Middle States		183	335,955,724	13,793,292	657,729	....
West Virginia—Total Southern States.	Sept. 30, 1892	2	180,719	6,300	7,401	....
Ohio	Oct. 3, 1892	4	8,159,342	2,691,650	7,307	....
Indiana	Oct. 31, 1892	5	....	....	2,932,984	....
Wisconsin	July 3, 1893	1	....	....	166,846	....
Total Western States		10	8,159,842	2,691,650	3,107,137	....
Total mutual savings banks		640	638,081,542	51,633,072	123,444,722	....
STOCK SAVINGS BANKS.						
Vermont—Total Eastern States.	June 30, 1893	17	3,603,912	613,528	1,481,979	....
Maryland*	...do	6	323,743	153,920	274,921	....
District of Columbia*	...do	1	63,044	32,065	....	....
Total Middle States		7	386,787	185,985	274,921	....
North Carolina	July 12, 1893	4	122,721	....	162,943	$154
South Carolina *	June 30, 1893	20	659,550	1,693,881	2,830,679	300
Georgia †	...do	14	....	....	2,292,553	8,939
Florida †	Jan. 1 and June 30, 1893	4	45,205	....	238,344	727
Alabama *	June 30, 1892	4	36,313	553,513	70,100	8,490
Louisiana	July 11, 1893	1	....	....	1,068,366	....
Texas *	June 30, 1893	2	100,072	364,750	230,100	4,343
Arkansas	...do	4	27,910	67,363	136,937	15,050
Tennessee *	...do	8	269,529	484,008	910,915	1,301
Total Southern States		67	1,261,300	3,103,515	8,850,537	39,304
Ohio*	June 30, 1893	12	3,876,789	4,224,704	2,283,956	5,041
Illinois	July 25, 1893	29	....	....	33,438,930	50,008
Iowa	June 30, 1893	148	....	....	29,360,994	173,675
Minnesota	Dec. —, 1892	15	5,095,870	....	2,112,290	342
Total Western States		204	8,972,659	4,224,704	67,205,170	229,069
Oregon *	June 30, 1893	5	346,475	1,203,194	350,026	16,259
Colorado	...do	5	1,050,204	200,610	1,051,429	....
Utah	March to June, 1893	18	....	....	4,812,003	205,853
Montana *	June 30, 1893	2	316,641	23,786	133,436	5,296
New Mexico *	Jan. 25 and July 1, 1893	2	....	....	286,284	....
California	July 1, 1893	60	109,560,205	12,931,483	1,124,328	....
Total Pacific States, etc.		92	111,273,785	14,359,073	7,757,506	227,408
Total stock savings banks.		381	125,498,443	22,546,805	85,570,113	495,781
Total all savings banks		1,030	763,579,985	74,179,877	209,014,835	495,781

* Unofficial; † semiofficial; all others official.

TABLE III.

STOCK SAVINGS BANKS IN THE UNITED STATES, 1892-'93.

| | RESOURCES. | | | | | | |
United States bonds.	State, county, municipal, etc., bonds.	Railroad bonds and stocks.	Bank stocks.	All other bonds and stocks.	Due from other banks and bankers.	Real estate, furniture, and fixtures.	States.
$602,750	$17,274,030	$15,475,712	$2,885,102	$4,258,460		$991,323	Me.
	10,741,172	10,452,118	2,632,225	8,954,938		1,631,466	N. H.
110,750	5,889,862		235,810		$586,345	268,324	Vt.
1,210,600	52,807,003	38,921,448	28,072,054		13,000,580	4,534,864	Mass.
2,326,100	10,937,612	11,484,776	2,621,168	5,169,227		1,727,476	R. I.
726,400	32,269,167	27,193,270	6,573,132			3,340,847	Conn.
4,976,600	130,008,846	103,527,324	43,919,491	18,382,025	13,586,925	12,514,300	
109,373,460	238,773,348				47,325,589	10,519,327	N. Y.
5,717,220	7,841,330	5,281,591		336,959	1,075,363	1,258,120	N. J.
				44,045,916	2,902,975	1,103,087	Pa.
	71,000	339,465	50,831	116,119		202,938	Del.
7,083,000	16,627,269	11,393,399	211,686	632,281	443,285	682,725	Md.
122,177,680	263,312,917	17,014,455	262,517	45,131,275	51,746,812	13,766,197	
	3,677			15,500		14,850	9,948	W. Va.
2,025,000	272,664			10,936,599	1,331,342	928,905	Ohio.
127,410	240,235		3,000	100,000		172,290	Ind.
				7,050		11,620	3,559	Wis.
2,152,410	512,899		3,000	11,043,649	1,342,962	1,104,754	
129,306,090	393,838,369	120,541,779	44,185,008	74,573,049	66,691,549	27,395,199	
1,150	2,046,749		153,199		319,612	109,412	Vt.
	112,400	177,000	19,130	88,564	60,837	32,847	Md.
24,296				2,000	5,673	979	D. C.
24,296	112,400	177,000	19,130	90,564	66,510	33,826	
	12,481			43,726	29,247	7,138	N. C.
10,000	1,302,069	476,860	48,194	491,991	194,902	207,775	S. C.
				269,737	143,344	140,376	Ga.
				209,271	62,752	15,565	Fla.
	1,025		2,000	11,296	78,486	114,382	Ala.
						750	La.
				1,000	26,515	55,857	Tex.
	3,112		269	8,835	67,424	31,828	Ark.
	21,598		58,925	361,014	77,381	158,871	Tenn.
10,000	1,340,285	476,860	109,388	1,396,870	680,051	732,542	
225,000	1,023,896	223,432		30,000	1,448,980	155,991	Ohio.
43,647				8,101,769	6,214,571	282,714	Ill.
					2,675,539	892,642	Iowa.
				2,248,677	1,877,214	370,588	Minn.
268,647	1,023,896	223,432		10,380,446	11,716,304	1,701,935	
	62,725	100,000		1,400	110,964	57,349	Oregon.
					492,326	12,200	Colo.
				29,955	435,612	637,187	Utah.
	181,874			1,277	34,394	8,172	Mont.
				21,659	8,939		N. Mex.
				18,674,379	2,450,847	3,927,537	Cal.
	244,599	100,000		18,728,670	3,533,082	4,642,445	
304,093	4,767,929	977,292	281,717	30,596,550	16,315,559	7,220,160	
129,610,783	398,606,298	121,519,071	44,466,725	105,169,599	83,007,108	34,615,359	

TABLE III.

ABSTRACT OF REPORTS OF CONDITION OF THE MUTUAL AND STOCK

State, etc.	RESOURCES				LIABILITIES	
	Curr't expenses and taxes paid.	Cash and cash items.	Other resources.	Total.	Capital stock.	Surplus.
MUTUAL SAVINGS BANKS.						
Maine		$1, 050, 053	$88, 500	$56. 838, 264		$2, 233, 401
New Hampshire		1, 582, 183		80. 667, 594		5, 131, 675
Vermont		293, 340	41, 994	21. 290, 432		
Massachusetts		955, 132	606, 531	415, 898, 159		14, 545, 655
Rhode Island		1, 628, 373	1, 035, 021	73, 858, 193		
Connecticut		3, 803, 672	551, 003	138, 659, 913		4, 877, 114
Total Eastern States		9, 372, 753	2, 323, 649	787, 212, 555		26, 787, 905
New York		7, 380, 830	7, 890, 129	718, 454, 662		88, 752, 443
New Jersey		326, 450	563, 020	39, 776, 787		3 155, 339
Pennsylvania	$261, 387	1, 997, 721	94, 739	74, 851, 865		6, 116, 328
Delaware	1, 739	32, 739	58, 590	4, 252, 827		487, 670
Maryland	155, 478	577, 446	198, 633	46, 030, 388		1, 235, 112
Total Middle States	418, 604	10, 324, 186	8, 805, 111	883, 366, 529		99, 746, 892
West Virginia—Total Southern States.	1, 778	1, 285		241, 458		2, 405
Ohio	19, 866	602, 709	12, 620	26. 988, 004		
Indiana	14, 586	923, 193		4, 513, 698		330, 809
Wisconsin	451	1, 249		190, 775		
Total Western States	34, 903	1, 527, 151	12, 620	31, 692, 477		330, 809
Total mutual savings banks.	455, 285	21, 225, 375	11, 141, 380	1,792,513,019		126,868,011
STOCK SAVINGS BANKS.						
Vermont—Total Eastern States.		162, 811	57, 302	8, 549, 654	$787,500	
Maryland	3, 679	28, 017	447	1, 273. 505	223, 040	58, 091
District of Columbia	11, 767	2, 671		142, 495	50, 675	
Total Middle States	15, 446	30, 688	447	1, 418, 000	273, 715	58, 091
North Carolina	1, 166	5. 126		384, 702	40. 000	9, 602
South Carolina	25, 931	1, 076, 640	68, 795	9, 096, 567	1, 253, 126	293, 781
Georgia	35, 759	360, 913	49, 908	3, 301, 559	1, 027, 354	145, 059
Florida	6, 204	59, 081		628, 149	210, 000	
Alabama	13, 120	124. 905		1, 013, 936	305, 000	38, 000
Louisiana		300, 902		2, 270, 018	100, 000	
Texas	5, 525	91, 580		880, 051	139, 486	103. 281
Arkansas	15, 038	50, 073		423, 830	123, 157	1, 400
Tennessee	24, 432	452, 303	7, 531	2, 827, 808	555, 000	124, 575
Total Southern States	127, 181	2, 512, 562	126, 234	20, 826, 629	3, 753, 123	715. 678
Ohio	15. 300	203. 154	13, 672	13, 730. 008	1, 860, 000	1, 085, 000
Illinois	29, 203	6, 014, 502	10, 693	54, 186, 037	7, 972, 000	2, 280, 500
Iowa		1, 622, 126		34, 733, 970	6, 409, 700	677. 710
Minnesota	43, 716	139, 792	8, 027	11, 396, 518	225, 000	183, 000
Total Western States	88, 309	7, 979, 574	32, 392	114, 046, 537	16, 466, 700	4, 226, 210
Oregon	9, 427	341. 916	158. 600	2, 758, 335	800, 450	69, 450
Colorado	4, 925	114, 427	1. 277	2, 227, 458	450, 000	36, 004
Utah	33, 114	181, 035	68, 040	6, 403, 699	1, 731, 100	408. 750
Montana	9, 943	155, 213	360	870, 592	200. 000	28, 500
New Mexico	4, 802	11, 568		333, 252	80, 000	13, 625
California		4, 241, 655	217, 538	153, 127. 072	8, 886, 600	5, 031, 807
Tot'l Pac. States, etc	62, 211	5, 045, 814	446, 715	166. 421, 308	12. 148, 150	5, 588, 136
Tot'l stock sav'gs b'ks	293, 147	15, 731, 449	663, 090	311, 262, 128	33, 429, 188	10, 588, 115
Tot'l all sav'gs banks	748, 432	36, 956, 824	11, 804, 470	2,013,775,147	33, 429, 188	137,456,126

TABLE III.

SAVINGS BANKS IN THE UNITED STATES, 1892-'93—Continued.

Other undivided profits.	Dividends unpaid.	Deposits subject to check.	Savings deposits.	Due to other banks.	Other liabilities.	No. of depositors.	Average deposit.	States.
			LIABILITIES.					
$1,138,960			$53,397,950		$67,893	155,323	$343.76	Me.
966,142			74,377,279		192,498	174,654	425.85	N. H.
1,183,266			19,947,166		160,000	63,925	312.04	Vt.
8,044,117			393,019,862		288,525	1,189,936	330.29	Mass.
3,899,810			69,906,903	10,990	40,400	142,492	490.60	R. I.
2,991,630			130,686,729		104,440	331,061	394.75	Conn.
18,223,025			741,335,979	10,990	853,756	2,057,401	360.33	
			629,358,274		343,945	1,593,804	394.88	N. Y.
			36,488,246		133,202	140,772	259.20	N. J.
2,293,385			66,417,794		24,348	252,980	262.54	Pa.
25,673			3,739,484			18,613	200.90	Ill.
731,254			44,038,181	20,670	5,171	145,301	303.08	Md.
3,050,322			780,041,979	20,670	506,666	2,151,470	362.56	
1,346			237,707			5,149	46.16	W. Va.
315,095			24,946,909	76,000	1,650,000	59,401	419.97	Ohio.
104,527			4,073,131		5,231	16,127	252.56	Ind.
5,994			184,698		83	1,164	158.67	Wis.
425,616			29,204,738	76,000	1,655,314	76,692	380.81	
21,701,209			1,550,820,403	107,660	3,015,736	4,290,712	301.43	
307,437			7,315,764		138,953	25,190	290.42	Vt.
24,995	$1,090	$504,742	456,947	5,907	1,683	2,161	211.45	Md.
13,344		3,747	74,729			1,400	53.38	D. C.
37,340	1,090	508,489	531,676	5,907	1,683	3,561	149.26	
7,995	685		301,244	701	24,485	6,112	49.28	N. C.
403,819	4,829	744,102	5,913,130	77,822	405,949	24,422	242.12	S. C.
139,031	1,739	854,649	1,004,765	5,835	123,147	8,404	118.29	Ga.
16,646		181,513	219,448	542		1,321	166.12	Fla.
36,957		595,133	73,032	12,725	13,080	1,848	39.52	Ala.
166,004	160		2,009,854			6,507	307.95	La.
101,951		168,030	356,553	10,750		2,583	138.04	Tex.
32,105		140,810	123,451	2,416	500	844	146.27	Ark.
109,404		229,578	1,778,174	7,821	23,256	14,126	125.88	Tenn.
1,013,912	7,413	2,853,815	11,773,650	118,612	590,426	66,257	177.69	
354,129	10,442	660,949	9,659,304	27,800	72,384	26,213	368.49	Ohio.
1,528,081	1,362	17,577,671	23,498,504	1,208,582	119,337	84,861	276.90	Ill.
682,683			26,426,031	537,852		73,108	361.46	Iowa.
131,173	132,490		10,658,564		66,289	42,212	252.50	Minn.
2,696,066	144,294	18,238,620	70,242,403	1,774,234	258,010	226,394	310.27	
34,965	7,500	944,457	683,620	216,302	1,591	2,461	277.78	Oreg.
40,064		147,898	2,217,547	4,000	31,925	11,639	190.52	Colo.
127,406		795,647	2,935,849	52,726	352,221	22,815	128.68	Utah.
58,465		160,379	423,248			1,736	243.80	Mont
154			186,923		52,550	885	211.21	N. Mex
			138,019,874	70,927	1,118,764	178,949	771.28	Cal.
261,074	7,500	2,048,381	144,467,061	343,955	1,557,051	218,485	661.22	
4,315,838	160,297	23,649,305	234,330,554	2,212,708	2,540,123	539,887	434.04	
26,017,047	160,297	23,649,305	1,785,150,957	2,350,368	5,561,859	4,830,599	369.55	

TABLE IV.

States, etc.	Date of report.	No. of banks.	RESOURCES.		
			Loans on real estate.	Loans on collateral security other than real estate.	Other loans and discounts.
New York	June 30, 1893	22	$158,281	$19,874	$2,567,180
Pennsylvania	....do	33	867,352	502,794	6,638,899
Maryland	....do	4	16,000	15,000	302,975
Total Middle States		59	1,041,633	567,668	9,509,054
Virginia	June 30, 1893	2			57,451
North Carolina*	July 12, 1893	15	77,400		609,026
Georgia	June 30, 1893	5			302,372
Florida	....do	4	3,641	43,956	27,872
Alabama	....do	6	63,814	110,500	252,455
Texas	....do	22	924,729	942,971	2,239,133
Total Southern States		54	1,069,584	1,097,427	3,488,309
Missouri*	April 22, 1893	87	707,581		4,623,113
Ohio	June 30, 1893	86	1,111,497	1,020,017	8,243,072
Indiana	....do	46	357,361	179,033	5,172,285
Illinois	....do	123	1,744,260	3,130,456	6,049,197
Michigan	....do	44	584,359	507,509	1,424,712
Wisconsin*	July 3, 1893	102			4,903,909
Iowa	June 30, 1893	147	1,553,809	1,096,681	7,590,805
Minnesota	....do	46	304,489	564,566	1,355,064
Kansas†	Oct. 3, 1893	112	338,349		3,886,608
Total Western States		681	6,363,356	6,498,262	39,452,217
Nevada	June 30, 1893	2			120,000
Oregon	....do	2		10,000	111,175
Colorado	....do	14	12,849	163,060	487,878
Utah	....do	1	9,105		26,235
Idaho	....do	4	25,100	21,168	131,752
Montana	....do	5	83,250	138,340	68,954
Wyoming	....do	4	142,729	202,730	252,258
New Mexico	....do	3	2,700	4,100	48,539
Washington	....do	4	35,000	122,531	138,352
California*	July 1, 1893	15	987,338	60,090	1,045,152
Total Pacific States, etc		54	1,298,071	722,019	2,430,275
Total United States		848	9,772,644	8,885,376	54,879,855

* Official; all others unofficial.   † Received too late to be included in the totals.

TABLE IV.

Private Banks in the United States, 1893.

			RESOURCES.					
Overdrafts.	United States bonds.	State, county, municipal, etc., bonds.	Railroad bonds and stocks.	Bank stocks.	All other bonds and stocks.	Due from other banks and bankers.	Real estate, furniture, and fixtures.	State.
$10,563	$112.108	$5.500	$128,631	$7,300	$190,018	$397,415	$199,696	N. Y.
9,603	284,100	17,987	102,997	55,389	220,020	993,896	231,622	Pa.
1,292	4,900	5,160	5,856	11.140	24,845	26,520	68,084	Md.
21,458	401,908	28,587	237,484	73,829	444,783	1,417,840	499,402	
619		2,560			1,200	18,677	1,690	Va.
18,227					13,593	191,895	68,707	N. C.
17,895					55,660	31,678	224,290	Ga.
1,186					8,692	7,915	29,336	Fla.
11,502	50	81,500		5,000	101,800	101,750	109,525	Ala.
310,925		21,025	13,000	28,625	181,792	574,690	485,179	Tex.
360,384	50	105,085	13,000	33,625	362,755	926,805	918,637	
208,043	50,484				110,267	952,357	330,648	Mo.
102,508	139,663	252,762	13,021	76,300	84,563	1,349,599	710,012	Ohio.
20,225	834,682	35,355		2,500	15,175	625,261	276,485	Ind.
209,303	39,361	244,049	4,000	75,005	190,967	1,855,261	747,608	Ill.
20,465		11,980	2,000	46,850	16,025	438,434	292,785	Mich.
66,231					187,352	850,837	740,289	Wis.
358,918	6,000	49,143		199,257	17,831	1,351,086	1,060,074	Iowa.
38,944		31,295		3,000	13,016	350,077	182,262	Minn.
153,142	5,000				156,645	881,389	1,021,549	Kan.
1,053,667	1,070,190	624,534	19,021	402,912	635,196	7,781,922	4,340,163	
26,002					3,683	6,298	12,508	Nev.
7,000					95,100	26,276	31,200	Oreg.
7,162		2,616			475	89,999	59,005	Colo.
						9,172	1,375	Utah.
1,387		21,861		7,500		22,052	3,846	Idaho.
10,201		4,200				45,351	10,488	Mont.
13,074					95,129	91,929	65,530	Wyo.
1,742					135	26,242	23,388	N. Mex.
7,359		5,769				29,137	10,970	Wash.
					160,970	78,268	472,637	Cal.
73,927		34,446		7,500	355,692	424,724	690,947	
1,509,436	1,472,148	792,652	269,505	517,866	1,798,426	10,551,291	6,449,149	

TABLE IV.

ABSTRACT OF REPORTS OF CONDITION OF THE PRIVATE

States, etc.	RESOURCES.			
	Current expenses and taxes paid.	Cash and cash items.	Other resources.	Total.
New York................................	$8,492	$317,795	$45,706	$4,208,459
Pennsylvania............................	29.522	628,374	11,484	10,594,839
Maryland................................	3,212	21,334	....	506,267
Total Middle States....................	41,226	967,503	57,190	15,309,565
Virginia................................	3,474	4,606	....	90,277
North Carolina*.........................	6,606	78,042	....	1,063,496
Georgia.................................	750	33,892	851	667,507
Florida.................................	1,320	9,732	....	133,650
Alabama	12,846	156,021	36,802	1,043,604
Texas...................................	34,102	578.188	55,350	6,389,709
Total Southern States	59,188	860,481	93,003	9,388,333
Missouri*...............................	....	542,842	....	7,525,335
Ohio....................................	87,085	1,407,505	48,837	14,647,341
Indiana.................................	25,443	1,386,518	216,794	9,158,117
Illinois................................	74,313	1,379,906	149,302	15,892,968
Michigan................................	15,347	339,599	22,991	3,723,006
Wisconsin *.............................	34,340	769,434	108,954	7,780,346
Iowa	123,555	918,551	38,834	14,364,644
Minnesota...............................	40,702	231,924	47,183	3,162,522
Kansas †................................	100,212	897,092	....	7,439,986
Total Western States...................	401,685	6,978,279	632,895	76,254,290
Nevada..................................	4,655	51,626	436	225,408
Oregon	2,088	8,789	9,500	301,128
Colorado................................	6,877	69,992	3,521	993,434
Utah	....	2,776	....	48,663
Idaho...................................	3,777	24,686	186	263,295
Montana.................................	4,010	52,408	7,000	424,202
Wyoming	2,540	100,259	985	967,163
New Mexico..............................	....	9,852	14,500	131,198
Washington..............................	1,719	42,408	723	394,058
California*.............................	....	276,039	152,103	3,232,597
Total Pacific States, etc	25,666	638,925	188,954	6,891,146
Total United States	527,765	9,445,188	972,042	107,843,343

* Official; all others unofficial.   † Received too late to be included in the totals.

TABLE IV.

BANKS IN THE UNITED STATES, 1893—Continued.

			LIABILITIES.			
Capital.	Surplus.	Other undivided profits.	Individual deposits.	Due to banks.	Other liabilities.	States.
$759,400	$212,115	$349,888	$2,839,343	$24,556	$23,157	N. Y.
1,377,429	930,186	278,210	7,847,896	149,364	11,754	Pa.
166,517	5,141	6,793	293,497	29,484	13,835	Md.
2,303,346	1,147,442	634,891	10,980,736	194,404	48,746	
32,500	....	4,550	50,888	330	2,000	Va.
287,443	129,237	43,157	512,333	19,472	71,854	N. C.
338,000	51,342	1,993	218,800	2,703	54,750	Ga.
49,226	6,078	6,800	66,914	315	4,317	Fla.
430,000	49,000	72,025	425,259	22,516	44,804	Ala.
2,796,800	63,259	83,171	3,146,973	150,137	149,457	Tex.
3,933,969	298,916	211,606	4,421,178	195,482	327,182	
1,178,860	407,839	....	5,623,115	116,720	203,801	Mo.
3,021,549	711,759	306,833	10,173,840	256,392	176,968	Ohio.
2,448,148	318,641	121,235	5,870,498	263,170	136,425	Ind.
3,769,308	1,023,730	337,396	10,481,511	101,913	177,130	Ill.
996,579	201,960	54,576	2,417,364	22,500	30,027	Mich.
1,177,742	....	769,553	5,066,104	133,751	33,196	Wis.
4,328,619	877,560	666,722	8,081,895	196,490	213,358	Iowa.
870,495	76,919	135,245	1,889,633	14,721	175,509	Minn.
2,337,793	266,502	409,618	4,111,172	59,298	255,598	Kans.
17,786,300	3,620,408	2,391,560	50,203,960	1,105,657	1,146,414	
70,000	17,651	....	71,784	....	65,973	Nev.
98,395	27,000	4,825	108,070	....	63,338	Oreg.
467,248	22,900	32,836	372,255	1,227	6,968	Colo.
25,000	....	....	23,663	....	....	Utah.
111,500	2,120	8,381	122,619	18,675	....	Idaho.
190,000	10,826	10,375	187,882	21,306	3,813	Mont.
235,400	11,000	13,091	605,981	6,254	65,437	Wyo.
50,000	10,632	848	41,466	1,062	27,190	N. Mex.
111,403	2,181	27,295	230,139	420	13,701	Wash.
1,560,514	317,607	....	1,143,963	125,862	84,651	Cal.
2,919,460	421,917	97,061	2,946,822	174,815	331,071	
26,943,075	5,488,683	3,335,118	68,552,696	1,670,358	1,853,413	

TABLE V.

ABSTRACT OF REPORTS OF CONDITION OF STATE BANKS, 1872-'73 TO 1892-'93.

	1872-'73.*	1873-'74.	1874-'75.	1875-'76.	1876-'77.	1877-'78.	1878-'79.	1879-'80.	1880-'81.	1881-'82.
	—banks.	—banks.	551 banks.	633 banks.	592 banks.	475 banks.	616 banks.	620 banks.	652 banks.	672 banks.
Resources:										
Loans, etc.	$119,332,341	$154,377,672	$176,308,919	$178,087,496	$266,585,314	$169,391,427	$191,444,093	$206,821,194	$250,819,420	$272,520,217
Overdrafts	237,104	212,772	377,297	348,604	516,565	319,959	447,302	528,543	1,335,310	1,190,360
U. S. bonds	1,544,290	1,961,417	344,984	869,144	924,260	2,150,880	7,739,203	7,142,532	12,046,452	8,740,172
Other stocks, etc.	9,617,667	16,437,515	25,667,950	19,364,450	23,299,670	19,308,287	21,916,024	17,117,117	24,904,903	19,780,527
Due from banks	12,005,100	19,050,046	19,651,146	23,096,812	25,201,782	23,107,119	22,169,065	36,180,433	46,657,328	49,919,183
Real estate, etc	3,209,253	5,372,186	9,005,657	8,561,224	12,609,160	11,082,118	14,264,835	14,227,927	13,914,238	13,037,930
Other resources	944,073	1,164,909	4,909,190	6,863,083	6,442,710	10,694,370	9,221,760	5,801,796	10,512,266	12,306,578
Expenses	889,348	1,284,344	1,353,066	1,350,404	1,211,416	914,720	801,005	878,096	965,327	999,944
Cash items	18,977,321	10,434,018	8,624,086	9,059,547	9,816,456	7,320,845	8,767,391	11,176,374	10,900,325	18,546,073
Specie	3,020,139	1,980,083	1,156,456	1,926,100	2,319,659	3,041,670	1,979,701	6,201,617	17,071,445	17,201,489
Legal tenders, etc.	8,447,776	25,126,706	26,740,215	27,623,988	34,415,712	28,480,374	37,088,961	48,828,255	23,797,046	24,586,682
Total	178,681,407	237,402,068	272,338,996	278,255,852	383,257,704	277,911,831	315,839,340	354,904,486	418,950,060	438,834,173
Liabilities:										
Capital	42,705,834	50,305,512	69,081,980	80,425,634	110,949,515	95,193,292	104,124,871	90,816,575	92,922,525	91,808,213
Circulation	174,714	153,432	177,653	388,397	387,601	388,298	389,512	283,308	274,941	286,391
Surplus	2,109,732	2,942,707	6,797,167	7,027,817	5,605,854	7,981,990	16,667,574	18,816,496	20,976,167	23,148,050
Other profits	10,027,668	12,363,205	9,002,133	10,457,346	18,283,567	11,695,064	5,666,221	6,721,615	7,943,466	8,902,579
Div'ds unpaid	33,492	327,290	85,722	393,410	335,904	324,176	501,831	474,567	567,171	481,858
Deposits	110,734,034	137,594,961	105,871,939	157,958,658	226,654,538	142,764,491	166,968,229	208,731,611	261,362,303	281,835,496
Due to banks	8,858,355	14,241,604	10,530,844	13,307,398	9,412,876	10,348,911	13,093,069	18,462,707	18,870,466	18,262,172
Other liabilities	4,277,578	10,463,357	10,791,058	8,327,183	11,567,789	9,215,603	8,438,003	10,577,607	16,039,021	14,100,414
Total	178,681,407	237,402,068	272,338,996	278,255,852	383,257,704	277,911,831	315,839,340	354,904,486	418,956,060	438,834,173

* In compliance with House resolution, making it one of the duties of the Comptroller of the Currency, the Annual Report for 1873 contained the first report of State and savings banks made to this office, and was the first call of that character ever made upon State by Federal officer.

ABSTRACT OF REPORTS OF CONDITION OF STATE BANKS, 1872-'73 TO 1892-'93—Continued.

TABLE V.

	1882-'83. 754 banks.	1883-'84. 817 banks.	1884-'85. 975 banks.	1885-'86. 849 banks.	1886-'87. 1,413 banks.	1887-'88. 1,403 banks.	1888-'89. 1,671 banks.	1889-'90. 2,101 banks.	1890-'91. 2,572 banks.	1891-'92. 3,191 banks.	1892-'93. 3,570 banks.
Resources:											
Loans on r. estate							$31,128,369	$34,266,559	$37,247,244	$45,025,576	$43,233,876
Loans, coll. sec.							97,561,192	77,806,917	78,349,210	42,903,635	39,082,978
Loans, other	$322,358,227	$331,049,510	$347,880,520	$331,183,626	$436,854,364	$432,002,663	376,623,827	469,397,745	567,161,243	611,759,855	675,226,292
Overdrafts	1,302,261	1,262,725	1,349,098	1,709,388	2,295,610	2,001,781	3,071,724	5,063,263	4,944,702	4,815,017	5,458,630
U.S. bonds	6,287,606	2,337,705	2,994,806	4,392,421	2,530,156	2,007,634	3,051,722	1,313,757	1,100,307	912,123	4,2,661
State, etc., bonds							983,802	2,417,030	2,156,065	2,313,266	2,464,258
R.R. bonds, etc.							329,422	675,414	595,572	450,612	301,325
Bank stocks							310,668	482,987	426,850	901,895	94,953
Other bonds, etc.	22,083,304	31,452,019	32,644,859	27,194,693	30,544,699	34,737,037	33,709,278	35,020,906	37,529,429	45,505,385	73,275,185
Due from banks	68,703,510	48,836,669	59,062,406	49,747,429	64,774,981	58,778,206	79,819,380	86,910,062	82,521,530	104,029,312	103,700,210
Real estate, etc.	13,592,791	15,058,411	15,673,312	14,695,853	20,475,102	20,246,654	25,255,457	27,189,097	28,791,441	32,037,310	38,660,425
Other resources	9,043,706	7,671,876	5,791,111	8,234,886	15,237,143	14,710,227	3,910,628	7,760,635	15,281,560	16,329,044	7,457,897
Expenses	918,403	1,025,237	1,130,833	1,047,782	2,123,672	1,768,158	2,026,800	2,602,607	2,865,063	3,278,395	4,212,164
Cash items	35,113,379	28,219,414	25,972,922	51,698,218	110,845,718	105,314,947	133,210,164	120,765,422	107,453,889	129,745,578	137,026,652
Specie	17,429,817	25,376,565	29,866,724	24,734,684							
Legal tenders	25,302,316	28,787,615	30,994,221	14,726,910							
Total	512,137,026	521,077,766	553,562,761	528,095,920	684,781,815	671,707,317	796,055,613	870,812,131	965,994,142	1,040,697,731	1,130,725,537
Liabilities:											
Capital stock	102,454,461	110,020,351	125,258,240	109,611,596	141,000,377	154,931,868	166,651,582	188,737,307	208,561,811	233,751,171	250,767,709
Circulation	187,978	177,554	98,120	103,430	228,936	148,434	120,161	120,148	110,534	137,232	9,534
Surplus	25,762,738	31,483,912	30,669,575	27,813,508	38,513,720	41,574,468	48,020,464	51,937,077	60,006,623	66,725,191	71,257,646
Other profits	11,287,623	12,718,894	11,574,736	14,095,760	14,482,490	15,510,620	10,762,838	21,825,841	21,109,910	23,672,989	28,900,230
Div'ds unpaid	442,652	473,735	491,926	430,699	749,740	1,045,439		781,819	709,830	756,905	525,502
Deposits	334,995,702	325,365,669	344,307,996	342,682,767	446,560,022	410,047,842	507,084,181	553,634,384	556,637,012	648,513,809	706,965,643
Due to banks	20,651,030	27,125,108	29,930,453	27,600,280	32,415,414	34,358,942	43,167,631	37,016,371	38,826,003	48,590,672	48,359,762
Other liabilities	16,353,542	13,712,513	11,209,706	0,957,890	10,825,117	14,109,684	13,408,483	17,341,281	20,029,369	18,583,762	21,140,651
Total	512,137,026	521,077,766	553,562,761	528,095,920	684,781,815	671,707,317	796,035,613	870,812,131	905,994,142	1,040,697,731	1,130,725,537

TABLE VI.

AGGREGATE RESOURCES AND LIABILITIES OF LOAN AND TRUST COMPANIES FROM 1888-'89 TO 1892-'93.

Resources and liabilities.	1888-'89. 120 banks.	1889-'90. 149 banks.	1890-'91. 171 banks.	1891-'92. 168 banks.	1892-'93. 228 banks.
Resources.					
Loans on real estate................	$53,340,045	$56,669,834	$65,072,641	$55,008,822	$81,288,973
Loans on pers'l and collat'l security.	193,610,054	209,617,297	225,012,238	256,413,894	307,170,395
Other loans and discounts..........	44,491,208	61,595,409	66,791,541	73,760,832	74,270,229
Overdrafts.........................	83,957	91,362	105,608	155,999	93,017
United States bonds................	27,193,201	24,921,203	16,057,015	18,059,578	18,486,636
State, county, and municipal bonds.	3,765,747	2,993,365	3,828,397	6,404,311	5,842,753
Railroad bonds and stocks.........	19,352,398	26,102,410	29,771,125	27,617,700	11,639,330
Bank stocks.......................	737,312	1,230,642	1,159,776	1,008,344	668,470
Other stocks, bonds, and mortgages.	25,676,359	40,459,876	43,157,008	52,516,815	92,187,712
Due from other banks and bankers.	25,084,040	33,307,028	39,948,373	54,975,325	53,352,071
Real estate, furniture, and fixtures..	14,455,406	16,845,480	17,357,290	22,617,764	26,245,518
Current expenses and taxes paid...	438,018	568,924	743,684	648,269	984,177
Cash and cash items...............	25,236,526	19,861,137	16,482,207	22,600,045	22,216,539
Other resources	7,795,152	9,537,369	11,141,299	7,767,180	32,217,786
Total......................	441,268,483	503,801,336	536,628,202	600,244,908	726,664,506
Liabilities.					
Capital stock......................	59,445,937	70,676,247	79,292,889	80,645,972	94,867,268
Surplus fund......................	25,583,905	34,594,751	38,412,197	45,824,747	50,403,421
Other undivided profits............	13,199,209	12,234,252	17,091,648	15,943,401	20,368,056
Debenture bonds	16,902,812	19,565,215	18,907,553	11,305,280	18,489,542
Dividends unpaid	271,981	203,460	83,396	108,479	67,385
Individual deposits	299,612,899	336,456,492	355,330,180	411,653,996	486,244,079
Due to other banks and bankers....	3,013,572	2,863,248	2,210,772	3,771,165	2,690,476
Other liabilities	23,238,168	27,298,671	25,299,670	30,925,568	53,534,279
Total......................	441,268,483	503,801,336	536,628,202	600,244,908	726,664,506

TABLE VII.

AGGREGATE RESOURCES AND LIABILITIES OF SAVINGS BANKS FROM 1888-'89 TO 1892-'93.

Resources and liabilities.	1888-'89. 849 banks.	1889-'90. 921 banks.	1890-'91. 1,011 banks.	1891-'92. 1,059 banks.	1892-'93. 1,030 banks.
Resources.					
Loans on real estate................	$567,373,144	$634,229,417	$687,583,977	$714,832,576	$763,579,985
Loans on personal, etc., security....	160,816,153	70,227,806	93,670,153	79,173,174	74,179,877
Other loans and discounts..........	74,551,588	182,091,574	198,134,045	229,711,725	209,014,835
Overdrafts.........................	813,211	303,916	286,254	328,763	495,781
United States bonds................	158,923,630	148,532,828	139,267,015	133,344,150	129,610,783
State, county, and municipal bonds.	289,139,464	303,919,560	320,278,708	393,190,240	398,606,298
Railroad bonds and stocks.........	101,443,381	110,405,678	115,991,821	131,215,829	121,519,071
Bank stocks.......................	42,263,654	43,735,762	45,038,830	43,688,739	44,405,725
Other stocks, bonds, and mortgages.	101,819,419	111,575,177	107,963,932	71,096,738	105,169,590
Due from other banks and bankers.	61,554,576	65,126,477	70,660,882	81,576,253	83,007,108
Real estate, furniture, and fixtures..	29,652,572	30,211,272	30,438,232	33,097,998	34,615,359
Current expenses and taxes paid...	593,924	753,963	971,206	832,059	748,432
Cash and cash items...............	29,928,532	30,147,978	29,720,473	33,208,271	36,056,824
Other resources	12,758,967	11,356,193	14,502,451	18,748,207	11,804,470
Total......................	1,622,612,215	1,742,617,001	1,854,517,069	1,964,044,861	2,013,775,147
Liabilities.					
Capital stock......................	24,311,848	26,401,035	32,106,127	37,407,475	33,429,188
Surplus fund......................	127,225,533	133,762,883	130,042,098	132,880,724	137,456,126
Other undivided profits............	19,845,228	22,774,766	26,815,395	27,448,960	26,017,047
Dividends unpaid	44,696	123,298	19,364	41,412	160,297
Individual deposits (savings)......	1,425,230,349	1,524,844,506	1,623,079,749	1,712,760,026	1,785,150,957
Individual deposits (not savings) ..	19,160,976	25,179,450	31,746,393	45,560,592	23,649,305
Due to other banks and bankers....	992,323	1,996,161	2,766,225	3,593,717	2,350,368
Other liabilities	6,801,262	7,534,902	8,941,718	4,342,955	5,561,859
Total......................	1,622,612,215	1,742,617,001	1,854,517,069	1,964,044,861	2,013,775,147

TABLE VIII.

TABLE SHOWING, BY STATES, THE AGGREGATE SAVINGS DEPOSITS OF SAVINGS BANKS, WITH THE NUMBER OF THE DEPOSITORS AND THE AVERAGE AMOUNT DUE TO EACH, IN 1891-'92 AND 1892-'93.

States.	1891-'92.			1892-'93.		
	Number of depositors.	Amount of deposits.	Average to each depositor.	Number of depositors.	Amount of deposits.	Average to each depositor.
Maine	146,668	$50,278,452	$342.80	155,333	$53,397,950	$343.76
New Hampshire	169,949	72,430,060	426.24	174,654	74,377,279	425.85
Vermont	80,740	24,674,742	305.60	89,115	27,262,930	305.93
Massachusetts	1,131,203	369,526,386	326.67	1,189,926	393,019,862	330.29
Rhode Island	136,648	66,276,157	485.01	142,492	69,906,993	490.60
Connecticut	317,925	122,582,160	385.57	331,061	130,686,729	394.75
Total Eastern States	1,983,133	705,777,557	355.89	2,082,591	748,651,743	359.48
New York	1,516,289	588,425,421	388.07	1,593,804	629,358,274	349.88
New Jersey	131,739	33,807,634	256.62	140,772	36,488,246	259.20
Pennsylvania	248,471	65,233,993	262.54	252,980	66,417,794	262.54
Delaware	17,318	3,626,319	209.30	18,613	3,739,484	200.90
Maryland	142,135	41,977,868	205.34	147,462	44,495,128	301.74
District of Columbia	1,303	60,178	46.18	1,400	74,729	53.38
Total Middle States	2,057,255	733,131,413	356.36	2,155,031	780,573,655	362.21
West Virginia	8,428	473,848	56.22	*5,149	237.707	46.16
North Carolina	6,247	282,425	45.21	6.112	301,234	49.28
South Carolina	21,397	4,225,459	197.48	24,422	5,913,139	242.12
Georgia	4,569	572,523	125.30	*8,494	1,004,765	118.29
Florida	170	31,012	187.73	*1,321	219,418	166.12
Alabama	1,698	220,046	129.59	1,848	73.032	39.52
Louisiana	5,557	1,605,732	305.15	6,507	2,003,854	307.95
Texas	1,950	279,783	143.48	2,583	356.553	138.04
Arkansas	258	51,854	200.10	844	123,451	146.27
Tennessee	*16,392	1,292.913	78.87	*14,126	1,778,174	125.88
Total Southern States	66,666	9,126,495	136.89	71,406	12,011,357	168.21
Ohio	84,779	33,895,078	399.80	85,614	34.606,213	404.21
Indiana	15,418	3,754,622	243.52	16,127	4,073,131	252.56
Illinois	*73,872	21,106,369	285.72	*84,861	23,498,504	276.90
Michigan	180,391	36,959,573	204.88			
Wisconsin	948	138,926	146.59	1,164	184,698	158.67
Iowa	*71,687	26,115,384	364.29	*73,108	26,426,031	361.46
Minnesota	35,123	8,786,879	250.17	42,212	10,658,564	252.50
Total Western States	462,218	130,756,831	282.89	303,086	99,447,141	328.11
Oregon				*2,461	683.620	277.78
Colorado	*21,215	2,893,276	136.38	*11,639	2,217,547	190.52
Utah	*13,596	2,427,950	178.58	22,815	2,935,849	128.68
Montana				1,736	423.248	243.80
New Mexico	900	149,449	166.05	885	186,923	211.21
Washington	*8,955	1,193,907	133.33			
California	*107,667	127,312,083	759.32	*178,949	138,019,874	771.28
Total Pacific States and Territories	212,333	133,976,730	630.97	218,485	144,467,061	661.22
Total United States	4,781,605	1,712,769,026	358.20	4,830,599	1,785,150,957	369.55

* Partially estimated.

TABLE IX.

TABLE SHOWING THE NUMBER OF SAVINGS BANKS IN THE UNITED STATES, NUMBER OF DEPOSITORS, AMOUNT OF SAVINGS DEPOSITS, AVERAGE AMOUNT DUE EACH DEPOSITOR IN THE YEARS 1820, 1825, 1830, 1835, 1840, AND 1845 to 1893, AND AVERAGE PER CAPITA IN THE UNITED STATES IN THE YEARS GIVEN.

Year.	Number of banks.	Number of depositors.	Deposits.	Average due each depositor.	Average per capita in the United States.
1820	10	8,635	$1,138,576	$131.86	$0.12
1825	15	16,931	2,537,082	149.84	
1830	36	38,085	6,973,304	183.00	.54
1835	52	60,058	10,613,726	176.72	
1840	61	78,701	14,051,520	178.54	.82
1845	70	145,206	24,506,677	168.77	
1846	74	158,709	27,374,325	172.48	
1847	76	187,739	31,627,479	168.40	
1848	83	199,764	33,087,488	165.63	
1849	90	217,318	36,073,924	165.99	
1850	108	251,354	43,431,130	172.78	1.87
1851	128	277,148	50,457,913	182.06	
1852	141	308,803	50,467,453	192.54	
1853	159	365,538	72,313,696	197.82	
1854	190	396,173	77,823,906	196.44	
1855	215	431,602	84,290,076	195.29	
1856	222	487,986	95,598,230	195.90	
1857	231	490,428	98,512,968	200.87	
1858	245	538,840	108,438,287	201.24	
1859	259	622,556	128,657,901	206.66	
1860	278	693,870	149,277,504	215.13	4.75
1861	285	694,487	146,729,882	211.27	
1862	289	787,943	169,434,540	216.03	
1863	293	887,096	200,235,202	232.48	
1864	305	976,025	236,280,401	242.08	
1865	317	980,844	242,619,382	247.35	
1866	336	1,067,061	282,455,794	264.70	
1867	371	1,188,202	337,009,452	283.63	
1868	406	1,310,144	392,781,813	299.80	
1869	476	1,466,684	457,675,050	312.04	
1870	517	1,630,846	549,874,358	337.17	14.26
1871	577	1,902,047	650,745,442	342.13	
1872	647	1,992,925	735,046,805	368.82	
1873	669	2,185,832	802,863,609	367.07	
1874	693	2,293,401	864,556,902	376.98	
1875	771	2,359,864	924,037,304	391.66	
1876	781	2,368,630	941,350,255	397.42	
1877	675	2,395,314	866,218,306	361.63	
1878	663	2,400,785	879,897,425	366.50	
1879	639	2,268,707	802,490,298	353.72	16.33
1880	629	2,335,582	819,106,973	350.71	
1881	629	2,528,749	891,961,142	352.73	
1882	629	2,710,354	966,797,081	356.70	
1883	630	2,876,438	1,024,856,787	356.29	
1884	636	3,015,151	1,073,294,955	355.96	
1885	646	3,071,495	1,095,172,147	356.56	
1886	638	3,158,950	1,141,580,578	361.86	
1887	684	3,418,013	1,235,247,271	361.39	
1888	801	3,838,291	1,364,196,550	355.41	
1889	849	4,021,523	1,425,230,349	354.40	
1890	921	4,258,893	1,524,844,506	358.04	24.35
1891	1,011	4,533,217	1,622,079,749	358.04	25.29
1892	1,059	4,781,605	1,712,769,026	358.20	26.11
1893	1,030	4,830,599	1,785,150,957	369.55	26.63

TABLE X.

PRIVATE BANKS.

AGGREGATE RESOURCES AND LIABILITIES OF PRIVATE BANKS IN 1889, 1890, 1891, 1892, AND 1893.

Resources and liabilities.	1889. 1,324 banks.	1890. 1,344 banks.	1891. 1,235 banks.	1892. 1,161 banks.	1893. 848 banks.
Resources.					
Loans on real estate	$8,386,735	$10,678,574	$15,997,251	$13,782,512	$9,772,644
Loans on personal, etc., security	17,121,720	21,363,819	16,788,321	10,250,256	8,885,376
Other loans and discounts	65,480,534	72,922,802	68,180,783	69,051,435	54,879,855
Overdrafts	1,733,213	2,437,105	2,475,025	2,067,627	1,509,436
United States bonds	1,421,537	1,643,560	1,509,155	1,709,495	1,472,148
State bonds	814,683	930,491	908,983	1,316,540	792,652
Railroad bonds and stocks	470,627	536,068	737,230	404,178	269,595
Bank stocks	514,770	866,787	634,140	703,932	517,866
Other stocks, bonds, etc	3,216,823	3,951,600	1,883,192	3,268,242	1,798,426
Due from banks and bankers	19,753,173	21,726,466	19,380,059	20,007,069	10,551,291
Real estate, furniture, etc	9,474,378	9,812,101	9,217,951	9,317,287	6,449,149
Current expenses, etc	815,829	960,400	797,326	846,197	527,765
Cash and cash items	11,911,866	14,479,550	11,977,512	12,235,490	9,445,188
Other resources	1,845,449	1,705,499	1,209,081	1,601,813	972,042
Total	142,961,337	164,020,822	151,646,018	146,661,673	107,843,343
Liabilities.					
Capital	38,038,690	41,042,018	36,785,458	34,590,227	26,913,075
Surplus fund	8,266,516	9,741,183	8,993,987	7,730,587	5,488,683
Other undivided profits	3,555,590	4,677,667	3,152,635	3,528,577	3,335,118
Dividends unpaid	67,326				
Individual deposits	83,183,718	99,521,667	94,050,727	93,091,118	68,552,696
State, county, etc., deposits	693,969	902,481			
Deposits of State, etc., officers	563,025	586,210			
Due to banks and bankers	3,432,360	3,812,799	2,240,371	1,745,695	1,670,358
Other liabilities	5,160,143	3,736,797	5,513,840	5,975,429	1,853,413
Total	142,961,337	164,020,822	151,646,018	146,661,673	107,843,343

TABLE XI.

	State banks.	Loan and trust companies.	Savings banks.	Private banks.	Total.
	3,579 banks.	228 companies.	1,030 banks.	848 banks.	5,685 banks.
RESOURCES.					
Loans on real estate	$43,233,876	$81,288,973	$763,579,985	$9,772,644	$697,875,478
Loans on collateral security other than real estate	39,092,976	307,170,395	74,179,877	8,885,376	429,328,624
Other loans and discounts	675,236,292	74,270,229	209,014,835	54,879,855	1,013,401,211
Overdrafts	5,488,630	93,917	495,781	1,509,436	7,587,764
United States bonds	412,654	18,486,636	129,610,783	1,472,148	149,982,221
State, county, and municipal bonds	2,468,258	5,842,753	398,606,298	792,652	407,709,961
Railroad bonds and stocks	301,325	11,639,330	121,519,071	269,505	133,729,231
Bank stocks	98,953	663,470	44,466,725	517,866	45,752,014
Other stocks and bonds	73,275,186	92,187,712	105,169,599	1,796,426	272,430,923
Due from other banks and bankers	103,790,249	53,352,071	83,007,108	10,551,291	250,700,719
Real estate, furniture, and fixtures	38,600,425	26,245,518	34,615,359	6,449,149	105,910,451
Current expenses and taxes paid	4,242,164	984,177	748,432	527,765	6,502,538
Cash and cash items	137,026,652	22,216,539	36,956,824	9,445,188	205,645,203
Other resources	7,457,897	32,217,786	11,804,470	972,042	52,452,195
Total	1,130,725,537	726,664,506	2,013,775,147	107,843,343	3,979,008,533
LIABILITIES.					
Capital stock	250,767,709	94,867,268	33,429,188	26,943,075	406,007,240
Surplus fund	74,237,606	50,403,421	137,456,126	5,488,683	267,585,836
Other undivided profits	28,900,230	20,368,056	26,017,047	3,335,118	78,620,451
State bank notes outstanding	9,534				9,534
Debenture bonds		18,489,542			18,489,542
Dividends unpaid	525,502	67,385	160,297		753,184
Individual deposits	706,865,643	486,244,079	23,649,305	68,552,696	1,285,311,723
Savings deposits			1,785,150,957		1,785,150,957
Due to other banks and bankers	48,259,262	2,090,476	2,350,368	1,670,358	54,970,464
Other liabilities	21,160,051	53,534,279	5,561,839	1,853,413	82,109,602
Total	1,130,725,537	726,664,506	2,013,775,147	107,843,343	3,979,008,533

TABLE XII.

STATEMENT SHOWING THE AMOUNT OF GOLD, ETC., HELD BY NATIONAL BANKS ON JULY 12, 1893, AND BY OTHER BANKING INSTITUTIONS ON OR ABOUT THE SAME DATE.

Classification.	National banks (3807).	All other banks (5085).	Total all banks (9492).
Gold coin	$95,799,862	$7,618,014	$103,417,876
Gold Treasury certificates	50,550,100		50,550,100
Gold (clearing-house) certificates	4,285,000		4,285,000
Silver, dollars	7,389,457	} 1,815,624	15,315,056
Silver, fractional	6,119,575		
Silver, Treasury certificates	22,626,180		22,626,180
National-bank notes	20,135,051		20,135,051
Legal-tender notes	95,833,677	*64,512,344	160,346,021
United States certificates for legal tenders	6,669,000		6,669,000
Fractional currency	952,632		952,632
Specie, not classified		15,093,221	15,093,221
Cash not classified		116,606,000	116,606,000
Total	310,342,537	203,645,203	515,987,740

*Includes coin certificates and national-bank notes.

TABLE XIII.

TABLE SHOWING, BY STATES AND TERRITORIES, THE CAPITAL OF THE NATIONAL BANKS ON JULY 12, 1893, AND OF THE STATE, STOCK SAVINGS, AND PRIVATE BANKS AND LOAN AND TRUST COMPANIES AT DATE OF LATEST REPORTS TO THIS BUREAU.

States and Territories.	National banks.	State banks.	Stock savings banks.	Private banks.	Loan and trust companies.	Total.	Average per capital of population.
Maine	$11,214,196				$1,069,800	$12,283,996	$18.50
New Hampshire	6,380,000				1,455,000	7,835,000	20.35
Vermont	7,010,000		$787,500			7,797,500	23.41
Massachusetts	99,217,500				8,975,000	108,102,500	43.95
Rhode Island	20,277,050	$916,675			2,557,000	23,751,625	64.72
Connecticut	22,999,370	2,340,000			1,161,600	26,500,970	33.50
Total Eastern States.	167,098,116	3,256,675	787,500		15,219,300	186,361,591	37.25
New York	87,235,366	33,359,200		$759,400	25,950,000	147,303,966	23.34
New Jersey	14,603,350	1,780,460			1,695,000	18,078,810	11.61
Pennsylvania	73,143,213	8,819,697		1,377,429	36,003,744	119,344.083	21.31
Delaware	2,133,985	680,000			500,000	3,313,985	18.94
Maryland	16,935,289	1,128,450	223,040	166,517	1,000,000	19,453,296	18.20
District of Columbia	2,827,000		50,675		3,250,000	6,127,675	22.78
Total Middle States.	196,878,203	45,767,807	273,715	2,303,346	68,398,744	313,621,815	20.03
Virginia	4,796,300	6,388,583		32,500		11,217,388	6.61
West Virginia	2,951,000	2,421,676			111,490	5,484,166	6.85
North Carolina	2,476,000	1,913,530	40,000	287,443		4,716,973	2.83
South Carolina	1,748,000	1,127,024	1,253,126			4,124,150	3.46
Georgia	4,091,000	9,363,036	1,027,354	338,000		14,819,390	7.73
Florida	1,450,000	335,000	210,000	49,226		2,044,226	4.68
Alabama	3,844,000	900,910	305,000	430,000		5,479,910	3.46
Mississippi	1,115,000	3,260,925				4,375,925	3.28
Louisiana	3,935,000	2,755,447	100,000			6,790,447	5.85
Texas	25,540,500	450,000	139,480	2,796,800		28,926,786	12.12
Arkansas	1,100,000	1,675,925	123,157			2,899,082	2.37
Kentucky	15,009,400	15,855,430				30,864,830	16.20
Tennessee	9,648,620	3,346,435	555,000			13,550,055	7.44
Total Southern States.	77,704,820	49,789,926	3,753,123	3,933,969	111,490	135,203,328	7.08
Missouri	23,865,000	19,837,105		1,173,860	1,050,000	45,925,965	16.14
Ohio	45,694,300	7,618,325	1,860,000	3,021,549		58,194,174	15.29
Indiana	14,171,000	4,504,500		2,448,148		21,123,648	9.39
Illinois	38,218,850	7,065,500	7,972,000	3,769,308	3,460,000	60,485,658	14.68
Michigan	14,684,000	12,102,955		996,579		27,783,534	12.42
Wisconsin	9,235,000	6,896,900		1,177,742		17,219,642	9.43
Iowa	14,615,000	8,074,420	6,409,700	4,328,619	2,176,603	35,604,342	17.96
Minnesota	16,245,230	9,189,000	225,000	870,495	4,451,131	30,980,856	20.68
Kansas	11,902,100	*5,069,915				17,872,015	11.79
Nebraska	12,698,100	*11,418,995				24,117,095	18.48
Total Western States.	201,328,580	92,587,615	16,466,700	17,786,300	11,137,734	339,306,029	14.51
Nevada	282,000			70,000		352,000	7.65
Oregon	3,795,000	553,800	800,450	98,395		5,247,645	14.07
Colorado	8,510,000	1,740,000	450,000	467,248		11,167,248	22.56
Utah	2,550,000	750,000	1,731,100	25,000		5,056,100	21.98
Idaho	825,000	157,500		111,500		1,094,000	10.13
Montana	4,725,000	365,000	200,000	190,000		5,480,000	30.61
Wyoming	1,210,000	94,500		235,400		1,539,900	19.99
New Mexico	750,000	113,800	80,000	50,000		993,800	6.02
North Dakota	2,215,000	*1,092,340				3,307,340	13.07
South Dakota	2,550,000	*1,987,053				4,537,053	10.55
Washington	6,830,000	4,263,555		111,403		11,204,958	23.10
Arizona	400,000	240,200				640,200	10.00
California	7,475,000	47,848,938	8,886,600	1,560,514		65,771,052	49.94
Oklahoma Territory	300,000	159,000				459,000	3.53
Indian Territory	360,000					360,000	1.85
Total Pacific States and Territories	42,777,000	59,365,686	12,148,150	2,919,460		117,210,296	25.77
Total United States	685,786,719	250,767,709	33,429,188	26,943,075	94,867,268	1,091,793,959	16.20

* Capital of banks other than national.

10665 CUR——16

TABLE XIV.

TABLE SHOWING, BY STATES AND TERRITORIES, THE POPULATION OF EACH ON JUNE 1, 1893, AND THE AGGREGATE CAPITAL, SURPLUS, UNDIVIDED PROFITS, AND INDIVIDUAL DEPOSITS OF NATIONAL AND STATE BANKS, LOAN AND TRUST COMPANIES, SAVINGS AND PRIVATE BANKS IN THE UNITED STATES ON OR ABOUT JUNE 30, 1893; THE AVERAGE OF THESE PER CAPITA OF POPULATION, AND THE PER CAPITA AVERAGES OF SUCH RESOURCES IN EACH CLASS OF BANKS AND IN ALL BANKS.

States and Territories.	Population June 1, 1893.*	All banks.		National banks.	State banks.	Loan and trust companies.	Savings banks.	Private banks.
		Capital, etc.	Average per capita.	Average per capita.	Average per captia.	Average per capita.	Average per capita.	Average per capita.
Maine	664,000	$89,707,745	$135.10	$43.14		$0.48	$85.48	
New Hampshire	385,000	102,646,545	266.60	43.32		14.26	209.02	
Vermont	333,000	47,883,258	143.79	55.08			88.71	
Massachusetts	2,462,000	803,901,450	326.52	122.40		35.31	168.81	
Rhode Island	367,000	142,298,067	387.73	121.29	$5.48	59.85	201.11	
Connecticut	791,000	218,071,008	275.69	82.57	9.91	8.04	175.17	
New York	6,311,000	1,839,989,879	291.55	83.82	41.15	52.13	113.79	$0.66
New Jersey	1,557,000	136,829,792	87.88	48.05	6.56	7.80	25.47	
Pennsylvania	5,600,000	635,096,309	113.40	61.96	10.57	25.65	13.36	1.86
Delaware	175,000	15,630,358	89.31	44.17	12.53	8.31	24.30	
Maryland	1,069,000	110,397,805	103.27	53.18	3.34	2.09	44.22	.44
District of Columbia	269,000	22,364,276	83.14	51.66		30.95	.53	
Virginia	1,696,000	44,329,571	26.13	12.76	13.72			.05
West Virginia	800,000	22,621,943	28.28	12.30	15.40	.28	.30	
North Carolina	1,668,000	13,167,178	7.89	4.25	2.84		.22	.58
South Carolina	1,184,000	19,010,617	16.06	6.99	1.79		7.28	
Georgia	1,917,000	38,014,463	19.83	5.45	12.41		1.65	.72
Florida	437,000	8,624,906	19.74	15.11	2.89		1.44	.30
Alabama	1,582,000	14,144,814	8.94	6.66	1.04		.62	.62
Mississippi	1,332,600	12,162,893	9.13	2.36	6.77			
Louisiana	1,160,000	38,032,893	32.78	20.09	10.73		1.96	
Texas	2,386,000	73,245,261	30.70	27.27	.51		.37	2.53
Arkansas	1,222,000	8,357,230	6.83	2.73	3.76		.34	
Kentucky	1,905,000	78,873,841	41.40	18.79	22.61			
Tennessee	1,820,000	37,523,635	20.62	13.91	5.17		1.54	
Missouri	2,845,000	176,600,771	62.07	22.29	36.06	1.18		2.54
Ohio	3,804,000	246,557,236	64.81	40.35	10.50		10.23	3.73
Indiana	2,256,000	78,951,829	35.09	29.25	5.95		2.00	3.89
Illinois	4,119,000	285,184,145	69.23	41.82	6.89	3.90	12.83	3.79
Michigan	2,237,000	130,848,877	58.50	24.99	131.95			1.65
Wisconsin	1,826,000	97,715,823	53.51	23.24	26.00		.10	4.17
Iowa	1,982,000	123,873,045	62.49	15.57	12.88	1.77	17.26	7.04
Minnesota	1,498,000	110,295,433	73.62	35.92	23.55	4.62	7.57	1.96
Kansas	1,516,000	52,457,761	34.63	22.31	12.32			
Nebraska	1,305,000	81,135,798	62.17	30.58	31.59			
Nevada	46,000	1,074,641	23.36	19.89				3.47
Oregon	373,000	17,962,442	48.15	37.93	2.77		6.81	.64
Colorado	495,000	39,446,851	79.69	61.72	10.32		5.84	1.81
Utah	230,000	14,040,602	61.04	28.93	5.82		26.08	.21
Idaho	108,000	3,348,828	31.01	26.04	2.70			2.27
Montana	179,000	23,577,740	131.72	119.37	5.25		4.87	2.23
Wyoming	77,000	4,598,610	59.72	44.71	3.38			11.63
New Mexico	165,000	3,386,024	20.52	15.57	2.63		1.70	.62
North Dakota	253,000	10,885,193	43.02	30.27	12.75			
South Dakota	430,000	13,499,311	31.39	17.43	13.96			
Washington	485,000	30,715,357	63.33	38.12	24.43			.78
Arizona	64,000	1,814,601	28.35	16.59	11.76			
California	1,317,000	289,584,676	219.88	16.73	85.49		115.37	2.29
Oklahoma Territory	130,000	1,523,792	11.72	7.67	4.05			
Indian Territory	195,000	891,822	4.57	4.57				
Total United States	67,021,000	6,412,939,954	95.68	38.64	15.83	9.73	29.93	1.55

* Estimated by Mr. Joseph S. McCoy, Government actuary.
†Includes savings banks and loan-trust companies.
‡Includes private banks.

TABLE XV.

TABLE SHOWING, BY STATES AND GEOGRAPHICAL DIVISIONS, THE NUMBER, ASSETS, NIES, AND PRIVATE BANKS IN THE UNITED STATES WHICH WERE COMPELLED TO DAR YEAR.

[From reports to the

States, etc.	State banks.			Savings banks.			Trust companies.		
	No.	Assets.	Liabilities.	No.	Assets.	Liabilities.	No.	Assets.	Liabilities.
Now Hampshire				3	$795,000	$1,150,000	3	$6,225,000	$7,413,000
Vermont									
Rhode Island	1	$250,000	$225,000						
Total Eastern States.	1	250,000	225,000	3	795,000	1,150,000	3	6,225,000	7,413,000
New York	6	6,225,544	5,639,234	1	124,350	122,996			
New Jersey	1	180,000	220,000						
Pennsylvania	2	137,000	275,000						
Delaware									
District of Columbia									
Total Middle States.	9	6,542,544	6,134,234	1	124,350	122,996			
Virginia	5	775,800	597,000	1	40,000	60,000			
West Virginia	1	1,250,000	950,000						
North Carolina	2	525,000	695,000						
South Carolina	1	136,940	133,539	1	3,000	30,000			
Georgia	3	506,000	322,000				1	35,000	15,000
Florida	2	227,225	157,847	1	5,000	15,000			
Alabama	1	140,000	125,000						
Louisiana	1	150,000	70,000						
Texas							1	500,000	760,000
Arkansas	2	5,000	35,000						
Kentucky	2	850,575	554,000						
Tennessee	5	249,000	222,000	4	664,750	645,000			
Total Southern States	25	4,815,540	3,861,386	7	712,750	750,000	2	535,000	775,000
Missouri	8	724,654	584,613	6	1,990,000	2,528,000	2	225,000	311,000
Ohio	3	307,544	212,400	5	2,523,000	1,725,000			
Indiana	12	1,286,000	850,000						
Illinois									
Michigan	1	30,000	40,000	2	1,252,000	1,214,000			
Wisconsin	13	12,094,851	12,123,343	3	252,000	290,643			
Iowa	4	793,041	577,198	3	313,878	231,120	2	2,200,000	6,350,000
Minnesota	15	3,204,250	2,604,941	1	9,000	9,000	2	3,650,000	6,415,000
Kansas	25	1,387,500	1,624,100	1	25,000	35,000			
Nebraska	10	749,961	528,280	3	647,000	713,000	1	1,200,000	800,000
Total Western States	91	20,577,801	19,144,875	24	7,011,878	6,745,763	7	7,275,000	13,876,000
Oregon	4	1,029,047	747,569	3	3,241,905	2,600,000			
Colorado	9	824,000	552,000	4	2,514,000	2,514,000			
Utah	1	60,000	188,000						
Idaho	3	227,729	214,179						
Montana	3	140,000	78,000						
Wyoming	1	45,000	20,000						
Now Mexico				1	220,000	189,216			
North Dakota*	1	15,000	16,000						
South Dakota†									
Washington	4	1,699,897	641,300	2	386,000	219,000	1	302,500	290,000
Arizona	1	88,000	45,000						
California	10	4,967,290	5,035,723	2	2,668,055	2,539,804			
Oklahoma Territory									
Total Pacific States and Territories	40	9,095,963	7,537,771	12	9,029,960	8,062,050	1	302,500	290,000
Total United States	172	41,281,848	36,903,266	47	17,073,938	16,830,809	13	14,337,500	22,354,000

*Incomplete.   †No information.

TABLE XV.

AND LIABILITIES OF STATE AND SAVINGS BANKS, TRUST AND MORTGAGE COMPA-
SUSPEND BUSINESS DURING THE FIRST EIGHT MONTHS OF THE CURRENT CALEN-

Bradstreet Agency.]

Mortgage and investment companies			Private banks.			Total all banks.			States.
No.	Assets.	Liabilities.	No.	Assets.	Liabilities.	No.	Assets.	Liabilities.	
			6			6	$7,020,000	$8,503,000	N. H.
2	$200,000	$750,000	1	$142,875		3	342,875	750,000	Vt.
			1			1	250,000	225,000	R. I.
2	200,000	750,000	1	142,875		10	7,612,875	9,538,000	
			8	531,595	$699,271	15	6,861,489	6,461,501	N. Y.
						1	180,000	220,000	N. J.
			6	1,072,795	1,403,478	8	1,209,795	1,678,478	Pa.
			1	204,000	360,000	1	204,000	360,000	Del.
			‡2						D. C.
			15	1,806,390	2,462,749	25	8,475,284	8,719,979	
			2	180,000	250,000	8	995,800	907,000	Va.
			1	150,000	150,000	2	1,400,000	2,100,000	W. Va.
			2			2	525,000	695,000	N. C.
			2			2	139,940	163,539	S. C.
			2	275,000	95,000	6	816,000	432,000	Ga.
			3	177,598	111,647	6	409,823	284,494	Fla.
			3	2,917,000	1,741,000	4	3,057,000	1,866,000	Ala.
						1	150,000	70,000	La.
			11	483,000	736,000	12	983,000	1,496,000	Tex.
			1	5,000	15,000	3	10,000	50,000	Ark.
			2	990,000	450,000	4	1,840,575	1,001,000	Ky.
			1	15,000	10,000	10	928,750	877,000	Tenn.
			27	5,192,598	3,558,047	61	11,255,888	8,945,033	
			5	360,000	282,000	21	3,299,654	3,705,613	Mo.
			19	1,446,587	1,430,375	27	4,277,131	3,367,775	Ohio.
			11	864,000	565,000	23	2,149,000	1,415,000	Ind.
1	50,000	70,000	23	4,041,027	5,056,813	24	4,091,027	5,126,813	Ill.
			8	174,295	234,547	11	1,456,295	1,488,547	Mich.
			14	1,051,000	1,360,992	30	13,397,851	13,774,978	Wis.
1	150,000	200,000	12	781,700	997,500	22	4,238,619	8,355,818	Iowa.
			8	713,000	438,800	26	7,576,250	9,467,741	Minn.
1	340,803	700,000	5	415,000	638,000	32	2,168,303	2,097,100	Kans.
			2	22,000	37,000	16	2,618,961	2,078,280	Nebr.
3	540,803	970,000	107	9,867,609	11,041,027	232	45,273,091	51,777,665	*
			6	478,533	552,348	13	4,749,485	3,899,917	Oregon.
			7	194,000	236,000	20	3,532,000	3,302,000	Colo.
						1	60,000	188,000	Utah.
			1	4,000	900	4	231,729	215,079	Idaho.
			5	1,375,000	543,000	8	1,515,000	621,000	Mont.
			2	305,000	250,000	3	350,000	270,000	Wyo.
						1	220,000	189,246	N. Mex.
1	20,000	70,000	1	100,000	75,000	3	135,000	161,000	N. Dak.
									S. Dak.
			4	594,254	495,784	11	2,982,651	1,646,084	Wash.
						1	88,000	45,000	Ariz.
						21	7,635,345	7,575,527	Cal.
			1	175,000	100,000	1	175,000	100,000	Okla.
1	20,000	70,000	27	3,225,787	2,253,032	87	21,674,210	18,212,853	
6	760,803	1,790,000	177	20,237,259	19,315,455	415	94,291,348	97,193,530	

‡Not included in returns to Bradstreet.

TABLE XVI.

TABLE SHOWING, BY STATES, TERRITORIES, AND GEOGRAPHICAL DIVISIONS, THE NUMBER, ASSETS, AND LIABILITIES OF SUSPENDED STATE, SAVINGS, AND PRIVATE BANKS, AND LOAN AND TRUST COMPANIES WHICH RESUMED BUSINESS DURING THE FIRST EIGHT MONTHS OF THE CURRENT CALENDAR YEAR.

[From reports to the Bradstreet Agency.]

States, etc.	No. of banks.	State banks. Assets.	State banks. Liabilities.	Savings banks. No.	Savings banks. Assets.	Savings banks. Liabilities.	Loan and trust companies. No.	Loan and trust companies. Assets.	Loan and trust companies. Liabilities.	Private banks. No.	Private banks. Assets.	Private banks. Liabilities.	Total. No.	Total. Assets.	Total. Liabilities.	States.
Vermont—Total Eastern States.											$142,875	$142,875	1	$142,875		Vt.
New York—Total Middle States.	2	$2,646,377	$1,809,055	1	$124,350	$122,990							3	2,772,727	$1,932,051	N. Y.
West Virginia	1	1,250,000	950,000							1	150,000	$150,000	2	1,400,000	1,100,000	W. Va.
South Carolina	1	136,940	133,539										1	136,940	133,539	S. C.
Georgia										1	75,000	45,000	1	75,000	45,000	Ga.
Florida	1	41,117	25,678										1	41,117	25,678	Fla.
Alabama										1	2,837,000	1,641,000	1	2,837,000	1,641,000	Ala.
Louisiana	1	150,000	70,000										1	150,000	70,000	La.
Texas										1	12,000	8,000	1	12,000	6,000	Tex.
Total Southern States	4	1,578,057	1,179,217							4	3,074,000	1,844,000	8	4,652,057	3,023,217	
Missouri	2	360,654	234,613	2	460,000	275,000				1	75,000	40,000	5	901,654	549,613	Mo.
Ohio	1	130,000	70,000	2	1,425,000	865,000				3	240,000	178,000	6	1,795,000	1,113,000	Ohio.
Indiana	2	570,000	245,000							3	245,000	125,000	5	815,000	370,000	Ind.
Michigan										3	80,000	70,000	3	80,000	70,000	Mich.
Wisconsin	4	760,000	458,000							2	145,000	84,500	6	905,000	542,500	Wis.
Iowa	2	397,000	235,000	2	248,000	180,000				2	380,000	398,900	6	1,025,000	813,900	Iowa.
Minnesota	6	1,146,000	633,000				1	$650,000	$415,000	3	178,000	80,800	10	1,974,000	1,128,800	Minn.
Kansas	4	295,000	353,000										4	205,000	355,000	Kans.
Nebraska				1	327,000	420,000	1	1,200,000	800,000				2	1,527,000	1,220,000	Nebr.
Total Western States	21	3,664,654	2,230,613	7	2,460,000	1,740,000	2	1,850,000	1,215,000	16	1,343,000	977,200	46	9,317,654	6,162,813	
Colorado	4	620,000	368,000	1	156,000	105,000				2	121,000	82,000	7	897,000	555,000	Colo.
Montana	1	65,000	28,000										1	65,000	28,000	Mont.
California	12	2,252,000	1,641,000	1	916,663	573,940							13	3,168,663	2,214,940	Cal.
Total Pacific States and Territories.	17	2,937,000	2,037,000	2	1,072,663	678,940				2	121,000	82,000	21	4,130,663	2,797,940	
Total United States	44	10,828,088	7,255,685	10	3,657,013	2,541,936	2	1,850,000	1,215,000	23	4,680,875	2,903,200	70	21,015,976	13,916,021	

TABLE XVII.

REPORT OF THE CONDITION OF THE NATIONAL SAVINGS BANK OF THE DISTRICT OF COLUMBIA, AT WASHINGTON, D. C., AT THE CLOSE OF BUSINESS ON THE 3D DAY OF OCTOBER, 1893.

Dr.   CR.

RESOURCES.		LIABILITIES.	
Loans and discounts, less amount upon which officers and directors are liable (see schedule)............	$23,160.00	Undivided profits..................	$7,642.82
Due from other national banks, subject to check	104,205.43	Individual deposits subject to check	120,139.28
Current expenses and taxes paid ...	416.67		
Total	127,782.10	Total	127,782.10

SCHEDULE.

Loans and discounts.

On demand, secured by stocks, bonds, and other personal securities............................. $23,160

The highest rate of interest paid by the bank on deposits is 2 per cent.

I. Benjamin P. Snyder, president of the National Savings Bank of the District of Columbia, do solemnly swear that the above statement is true, and that the schedules on back of the report fully and correctly represents the true state of the several matters therein contained to the best of my knowledge and belief.

BENJAMIN P. SNYDER, *President.*

Correct. Attest:

LEWIS CLEPHANE,
M. G. EMERY,   } *Directors.*
ALBERT L. STURTEVANT,

DISTRICT OF COLUMBIA, *County of Washington:*

Sworn to and subscribed before me this 6th day of October, 1893.
[SEAL.]   WILLARD H. MYERS, *Notary Public.*

REPORT OF THE CONDITION OF THE NATIONAL SAFE DEPOSIT, SAVINGS, AND TRUST COMPANY OF THE DISTRICT OF COLUMBIA, AT WASHINGTON, D. C., AT THE CLOSE OF BUSINESS ON THE 3D DAY OF OCTOBER, 1893.

Dr.   CR.

RESOURCES.		LIABILITIES.	
Loans and discounts, less amount upon which officers and directors are liable (see schedule)...........	$1,330,470.07	Capital stock paid in	$1,000,000.00
Stock securities, etc. (see schedule).	46,900.00	Undivided profits..................	71,458.92
Due from other national banks, subject to check....................	48,313.58	Individual deposits...............	1,241,491.97
Due from State and private banks and bankers, subject to check....	51,091.99		
Banking house......... $662,789.43			
Furniture and fixtures. 112,210.57	775,000.00		
Current expenses and taxes paid ...	6,565.89		
Premium on bonds for circulation ..	1,938.76		
Checks and other cash items (see schedule)........................	4,079.83		
Bills of other banks	220.00		
Fractional paper currency, nickels, and cents	10.77		
Specie, etc., viz:			
Gold coin $16,000.00			
Gold Treasury certificates............... 3,550.00			
Silver dollars 10.00			
Silver Treasury certificates 8,600.00			
Fractional silver coin 100.00	28,260.00		
Legal-tender notes..................	20,000.00		
Total......................	2,313,450.89	Total	2,313,450.89

SCHEDULES.

Loans and discounts.

On demand, secured by stocks, bonds, and other personal securities...................... $206,798.73
On time, secured by stocks, bonds, and other personal securities........................ 458,124.62
On time, on mortgages or other real estate security (see schedule)..................... 665,546.72

Total 1,330,470.07

Stocks, securities, etc.

District of Columbia 3-05s $23,400.00
Chesapeake and Potomac Telephone Company 5s... 16,000.00
U. S. Electric Light Company 6s... 6,000.00
Washington Market Company 6s.. 1,000.00
Masonic Hall Association 6s... 500.00

Total 46,900.00

The highest rate of interest paid by the bank on deposits is 2 per cent.

I. Benjamin P. Snyder, president of the National Safe Deposit, Savings, and Trust Company, of the District of Columbia, do solemnly swear that the above statement is true, and that the schedules on the back of the report fully and correctly represent the true state of the several matters therein contained to the best of my knowledge and belief.

BENJAMIN P. SNYDER, *President.*

JAMES M. JOHNSTON,
ANDREW WYLIE,   } *Directors.*
M. G. EMERY,
JOHN G. PARKE,

DISTRICT OF COLUMBIA, *County of Washington:*

Sworn to and subscribed before me this 5th day of October, 1893.
[SEAL.]
WILLARD H. MYERS, *Notary Public.*

Correct. Attest:

REPORT OF THE CONDITION OF THE WASHINGTON LOAN AND TRUST COMPANY, AT WASHINGTON, IN THE DISTRICT OF COLUMBIA, AT THE CLOSE OF BUSINESS ON THE 3D DAY OF OCTOBER, 1893.

DR.   CR.

RESOURCES.		LIABILITIES.	
Loans and discounts, less amount upon which officers and directors are liable (see schedule)	$1,617,723.88	Capital stock paid in	$1,000,000.00
Loans and discounts upon which officers and directors are liable (see schedule)	207,582.21	Surplus fund	100,000.00
		Undivided profits	66,187.23
		Dividends unpaid	3,765.59
Overdrafts, unsecured (see schedule)	165.26	Interest on real estate trust bonds unpaid	652.50
Stocks, securities, etc. (see schedule)	28,292.50		
Due from national banks, subject to check..............................	180,605.47	Individual deposits subject to check.... $740,316.11	
Due from State and private banks and bankers and trust companies, subject to check...................	4,906.83	Demand certificates of deposit 5,000.00	
Banking house $560,587.53		Time certificates of deposit 687,709.64	
Furniture and fixtures, vault and safe work.. 41,069.34		Certified checks 13,952.15	
	601,656.87		1,446,977.90
Current expenses and taxes paid ..	1,037.20	Due to national banks, subject to check..............................	5,338.34
Checks and other cash items (see schedule)	8,317.96	Bills payable, including certificates of deposit representing money borrowed................	60,000.00
Fractional paper currency, nickels, and cents.....................	27.35	Real-estate trust bonds............	128,500.00
Specie, viz:			
Gold coin $19,812.50			
Silver dollars........ 100.00			
Silver Treasury certificates............. 10,329.00			
Fractional silver coin 44.50			
	30,286.00		
Legal-tender notes..................	31,820.00		
Total	2,811,421.56	Total	2,811,421.56

SCHEDULES.

Loans and discounts.

On demand, secured by stocks, bonds, and other personal securities.	$554,276.24
On time, paper with two or more individual or firm names.	855.00
On time, secured by stocks, bonds, and other personal securities.	538,348.73
On time, on mortgages or other real-estate security (see schedule).	821,826.15
Total	1,915,306.12
Included in the above are—	
Other suspended and overdue paper	141,495.19
Liabilities of directors (individual and firm) as payers	164,373.42

Stocks, securities, etc.

Enter number shares of stock or face value of bonds.	Name of corporation issuing stock, bonds, etc.	Amount at which carried on books.	Estimated actual market value.
65	Washington Loan and Trust Company	$10,092.50	$7,800
2	Ohio National Bank	200.00	200
8,500	Eckington and Soldiers' Home Railroad	8,500.00	8,500
9,500	Edison Electric Illuminating Company	9,500.00	9,500

Checks and other cash items.

Checks and drafts on banks, etc., in this city	$8,317.96

Average reserve and interest.

The highest rate of interest paid by the bank on deposits is 4 per cent; on bills payable is 4 per cent; real-estate trust bonds 5 per cent.

Overdrafts—unsecured.

Temporary	$165.26

I, Brainard H. Warner, president of the Washington Loan and Trust Company, do solemnly swear that the above statement is true, and that the schedules on back of the report fully and correctly represent the true state of the several matters therein contained to the best of my knowledge and belief.

BRAINARD H. WARNER, President.

DISTRICT OF COLUMBIA, *County of Washington:*

Sworn to and subscribed before me this 6th day of October, 1893.
[SEAL.]

TENNY ROSS, Notary Public.

Correct. Attest:

JNO. R. CARMODY, ISADORE SAKS, W. H. SHEA, F. C. STEVENS, THEODORE W. NOYES, JNO. JOY EDSON, J. S. SWORMSTEDT, ALBERT F. FOX, LOUIS D. WINE, T. W. WOODWARD, W. E. BARKER, JOHN B. LARNER,	Directors.

REPORT OF THE CONDITION OF THE AMERICAN SECURITY AND TRUST COMPANY, AT WASHINGTON, IN THE DISTRICT OF COLUMBIA, AT THE CLOSE OF BUSINESS ON THE 3D DAY OF OCTOBER, 1893.

DR.   **CR.**

RESOURCES.		LIABILITIES.	
Loans and discounts, less amount upon which officers and directors are liable (see schedule)	$1,973,158.03	Capital stock paid in	$1,250,000.00
Loans and discounts upon which officers and directors are liable (see schedule)	209,681.15	Surplus fund	150,000.00
Overdrafts, unsecured (see schedule)	109.92	Undivided profits	38,401.42
Stocks, securities, etc. (see schedule)	46,245.00	Individual deposits, subject to check.... $612,441.46	
Due from other national banks, subject to check	42,476.46	Time certificates of deposit............. 96,746.68	
Due from State and private banks and bankers and trust companies, subject to check	51,391.42	Certified checks....... 1,751.14	710,939.28
Banking house........ $152,172.89		Debenture bonds	609,650.00
Furniture and fixtures. 7,939.57	160,112.46		
Other real estate and mortgages owned (see schedule)	133,188.60		
Current expenses and taxes paid	2,666.10		
Checks and other cash items (see schedule)	12,427.87		
Bills of other banks	200.00		
Fractional paper currency, nickels, and cents	49.69		
Specie, viz:			
Gold coin.......... $42,384.00			
Gold Treasury certificates.......... 26,550.00			
Silver dollars 355.00			
Silver Treasury certificates.......... 23,574.00			
Fractional silver coin.............. 189.20	93,052.00		
Legal-tender notes	34,142.00		
Total	2,758,990.70	Total	2,758,990.70

SCHEDULES

Loans and discounts.

On demand, paper with one or more individual or firm names	$393,415.42
On time, secured by stocks, bonds, and other personal securities	148,049.00
On time, on mortgages or other real-estate security (see schedule)	1,641,344.76
Total	2,182,839.18

Included in the above are--
Liabilities of directors (individual and firm) as payers.................... 142,833.33

Stocks, securities, etc.

Enter number of shares of stock or face value of bonds.	Name of corporation issuing stock, bonds, etc.	Amount at which carried on books.	Estimated actual market value.	State whether taken for "debts previously contracted," or otherwise.
$5,000	Bonds of Choptank Steamboat Company...	$4,750	$5,000	For investment.
43,000	Bonds of Chesapeake and Potomac Telephone Company......................	41,495	43,000	Do.

Checks and other cash items.

Checks and drafts on banks, etc., in this city $10,341.84
Checks and drafts on other banks 2,080.03

Overdrafts unsecured.

Temporary... $199.92

I, J. W. Whelpley, cashier of the American Security and Trust Company, do solemnly swear that the above statement is true, and that the schedules on back of the report fully and correctly represent the true state of the several matters therein contained to the best of my knowledge and belief.

J. W. WHELPLEY, *Cashier.*

DISTRICT OF COLUMBIA, *City of Washington:*

Sworn to and subscribed before me this 5th day of October, 1893.

[SEAL.]

HOWARD S. REESIDE, *Notary Public.*

Correct. Attest:

> A. T. BRITTON,
> W. S. THOMPSON,
> H. A. WILLARD,
> M. G. EMERY,
> MYRON M. PARKER, } *Directors.*
> JOHN E. HERRELL,
> M. W. BEVERIDGE,
> JAMES E. FITCH,
> HENRY F. BLOUNT,

TABLE XVIII.

CANADIAN BANKS.

SUMMARY OF THE CONDITION OF THE THIRTY-NINE CHARTERED BANKS OF THE DOMINION OF CANADA, ON AUGUST 31, 1893.

RESOURCES.		LIABILITIES.	
Mortgages on real estate	$660,395	Capital stock......................	$62,029,038
Loans on bonds and stocks..........	14,398,606	Reserve fund	26,062,576
Current loans	205,956,200	Notes in circulation	33,308,967
Loans to Dominion and Provinces..	1,426,480	Due Dominion Government........	2,476,608
Overdue debts.....................	2,964,099	Due provincial governments.......	3,769,284
Deposits to secure circulation	1,818,448	Demand deposits	61,437,993
Dominion debentures..............	3,188,572	Time deposits	105,015,710
Canadian municipal, etc., securities	9,398,221	Due to other banks and agencies...	8,661,289
Railway securities.................	5,979,906	Other liabilities	250,002
Due from banks and agencies......	20,264,956		
Real estate and bank premises......	5,827,520		
Notes and checks on other banks...	6,519,072		
Specie	7,706,937		
Dominion notes....................	12,749,809		
Other resources...................	1,901,035		
Excess of liabilities	2,149,551		
Total	303,011,467	Total	303,011,467

AGGREGATE RESOURCES AND LIABILITIES

OF

THE NATIONAL BANKS

FROM

OCTOBER, 1863, TO OCTOBER, 1893.

AGGREGATE RESOURCES AND LIABILITIES OF THE NATIONAL

1863.

Resources.	JANUARY.	APRIL.	JULY.	OCTOBER 5.
				66 banks.
Loans and discounts....				$5,466,088.33
U. S. bonds and securities....				5,662,600.00
Other items......				196,009.12
Due from nat'l and other b'ks.				2,625,597.05
Real estate, furniture, etc ...				177,565.69
Current expenses..........				53,808.92
Premiums paid				2,503.69
Checks and other cash items.				402,138.58
Bills of nat'l and other banks.				764,725.00
Specie and other lawful mon'y				1,446,607.62
Total......				16,797,644.00

1864.

	JANUARY 4.	APRIL 4.	JULY 4.	OCTOBER 3.
	139 banks.	307 banks.	467 banks	508 banks.
Loans and discounts	$10,666,005.60	$31,593,943.43	$70,740,513.33	$93,238,657.92
U. S. bonds and securities....	15,112,250.00	41,175,150.00	92,530,500.00	108,694,400.00
Other items...................	74,571.48	432,059.95	842,017.73	1,434,739.76
Due from national banks	....	4,600,479.56	15,935,730.13	19,965,720.47
Due from other b'ks and b'krs.	*4,786,124.58	8,537,908.64	17,337,558.66	14,051,390.31
Real estate, furniture, etc....	381,144.00	755,196.41	1,694,049.46	2,202,318.20
Current expenses............	118,854.43	352,720.77	502,341.31	1,021,569.02
Checks and other cash items.	577,507.92	2,651,916.96	5,057,122.90	7,640,169.14
Bills of nat'l and other banks.	895,521.00	1,660,000.00	5,344,172.00	4,687,727.00
Specie and other lawful mon'y	5,018,622.57	22,961,411.64	42,283,798.23	44,801,497.48
Total...................	37,630,691.58	114,820,287.66	252,273,803.75	297,108,195.30

1865.

	JANUARY 2.	APRIL 3.	JULY 3.	OCTOBER 2.
	638 banks.	907 banks.	1,294 banks.	1,513 banks.
Loans and discounts........	$166,448,718.00	$252,404,208.07	$302,442,743.08	$487,170,136.29
U .S bonds and securities ..	176,578,750.00	277,619,900.00	391,744,850.00	427,731,300.00
Other items................	3,294,883.27	4,275,769.51	12,569,120.38	10,048,513.15
Due from national banks.....	30,820,175.44	40,963,243.47	76,977,539.59	83,978,960.55
Due from other b'ks and b'krs.	19,836,072.83	22,554,636.57	26,078,028.01	17,393,232.25
Real estate, furniture, etc....	4,083,220.12	6,525,118.80	11,231,557.28	14,703,281.77
Current expenses............	1,053,725.34	2,298,025.65	2,358,775.56	4,549,525.11
Premiums paid	1,323,023.56	1,823,291.84	2,243,210.31	2,885,501.06
Checks and other cash items	17,837,406.77	29,681,391.13	41,314,904.50	72,309,854.44
Bills of nat'l and other banks.	14,275,153.00	13,710,370.00	21,651,826.00	16,217,241.00
Specie.................... ...	4,481,937.68	6,659,660.47	9,437,069.40	18,072,012.59
Legal tenders and frac'l cur'y	72,535,504.67	112,099,320.50	168,426,166.55	180,988,496.28
Total	512,508,660.08	771,514,939.10	1,120,455,481.66	1,359,768,074.49

* Including amount due from national banks.

BANKS FROM OCTOBER, 1863, TO OCTOBER. 1893.

1863.

Liabilities.	JANUARY.	APRIL.	JULY.	OCTOBER 5. 66 banks.
Capital stock				$7, 188, 393. 00
Undivided profits...............				128, 030. 06
Individual and other deposits.				8, 497, 681. 84
Due to nat'l and other banks⁴.				981, 178. 59
Other items..................				2, 360. 51
Total................				16, 797, 644. 00

1864.

	JANUARY 4. 139 banks.	APRIL 4. 307 banks.	JULY 4. 467 banks.	OCTOBER 3. 508 banks.
Capital stock	$14, 740, 522. 00	$42, 204, 474. 00	$75, 213, 945. 00	$86, 782, 802. 00
Surplus fund			1, 129, 910. 22	2, 010, 286. 10
Undivided profits...........	432, 827. 21	1, 625, 656. 87	3, 094, 330. 11	5, 982, 392. 22
National b'k notes outstanding	30, 155. 00	9, 797, 975. 00	25, 825, 665. 00	45, 260, 504. 00
Individual and other deposits.	19, 450, 492. 53	51, 274, 914. 01	119, 414, 239 03	122, 166, 536. 40
Due to nat'l and other banks⁴.	2, 153, 779. 38	6, 814, 930. 40	27, 382, 006. 37	34, 862, 384. 81
Other items	822, 014. 86	3, 102, 337. 38	213, 708. 02	43, 289. 77
Total	37, 630, 691. 58	114, 820, 287. 66	252, 273, 603. 75	297, 108, 195. 30

1865.

	JANUARY 2. 638 banks.	APRIL 3. 907 banks.	JULY 3. 1,294 banks.	OCTOBER 2. 1,513 banks.
Capital stock	$135, 618, 874. 00	$215, 326, 023. 00	$325, 834, 558. 00	$393, 157, 206. 00
Surplus fund	8, 663, 311. 22	17, 318, 942. 65	31, 303, 565. 64	38, 713, 380. 72
Undivided profits...........	12, 283, 812. 65	17, 809, 307. 14	23, 159, 408. 17	32, 330, 278. 19
National b'k notes outstanding	66, 769, 375. 00	98, 896, 488. 00	131, 452, 158. 00	171, 321, 903. 00
Individual and other deposits.	183, 479, 636. 98	262, 961, 473. 13	398, 357, 559. 59	500, 910, 573. 22
United States deposits.......	37, 764, 729. 77	57, 630, 141. 01	58, 032, 720. 67	48, 170, 381. 31
Due to national banks	30, 619, 175. 57	41, 301, 031. 16	78, 261, 045. 64	90, 044, 837. 08
Due to other b'ks and bankers⁴	37, 104, 130. 62	50, 692, 581. 64	79, 591, 594. 03	84, 155, 161. 27
Other items..................	265, 620. 87	578, 951. 37	462, 871. 02	944, 053. 70
Total	512, 568, 666. 68	771, 514, 930. 10	1, 126, 455, 481. 66	1, 359, 708, 074. 40

* Including State bank circulation outstanding.

AGGREGATE RESOURCES AND LIABILITIES OF THE NATIONAL

1866.

Resources.	JANUARY 1. 1,582 banks.	APRIL 2. 1,612 banks.	JULY 2. 1,634 banks.	OCTOBER 1. 1,644 banks.
Loans and discounts	$500,650,100.10	$528,080,526.70	$550,353,004.17	$603,314,704.83
U. S. b'ds dep'd to secure circ'n	298,376,850.00	315,850,300.00	326,483,350.00	331,843,200.00
Other U. S. b'ds and securities	142,003,500.00	125,625,750.00	121,152,950.00	94,974,650.00
Oth'r stocks, b'ds, and mortg's	17,483,753.18	17,379,738.92	17,505,911.46	15,887,490.06
Due from national banks	93,254,551.02	87,564,329.71	96,696,482.66	107,656,174.18
Due from other b'ks and b'k'rs	14,658,229.87	13,682,345.12	13,982,613.23	15,211,117.16
Real estate, furniture, etc	15,436,296.16	15,895,564.46	16,730,923.62	17,134,602.58
Current expenses	3,193,717.78	4,927,599.79	3,032,716.27	5,311,253.35
Premiums paid	2,423,918.02	2,423,516.31	2,398,872.26	2,493,773.47
Checks and other cash items	89,837,684.50	105,490,619.36	96,077,134.53	103,684,249.21
Bills of national and other b'ks	20,406,442.00	18,279,816.00	17,866,742.00	17,437,779.00
Specie	19,205,018.75	19,205,018.75	12,020,576.30	9,226,831.82
Legal tenders and fract'l cur'y	187,846,548.82	189,807,852.52	201,425,041.63	203,793,578.76
Total	1,404,776,619.29	1,442,407,737.31	1,476,395,208.13	1,526,962,804.42

1867.

	JANUARY 7. 1,648 banks.	APRIL 1. 1,642 banks.	JULY 1. 1,636 banks.	OCTOBER 7. 1,642 banks.
Loans and discounts	$608,771,799.61	$597,648,286.53	$583,450,396.12	$609,675,214.61
U. S. b'ds dep'd to secure circ'n	339,570,700.00	338,803,650.00	337,681,250.00	338,610,150.00
U. S. b'ds dep'd to sec're redep'ts	36,185,950.00	38,465,800.00	38,368,950.00	37,862,100.00
U. S. b'ds and sec'ties on hand	52,949,300.00	46,639,400.00	45,633,700.00	42,460,800.00
Oth'r stocks, b'ds, and mortg's	15,073,737.45	20,104,875.21	21,452,615.43	21,507,881.42
Due from national banks	92,552,206.29	94,121,186.21	92,308,911.87	95,217,610.14
Due from other b'ks and b'k'rs	12,996,157.40	10,737,392.90	9,663,322.82	8,389,226.47
Real estate, furniture, etc	18,925,315.51	19,625,893.81	19,800,905.86	20,630,708.23
Current expenses	2,822,675.18	5,693,784.17	3,249,153.31	5,297,494.13
Premiums paid	2,860,398.85	3,411,325.56	3,338,600.37	2,764,186.35
Checks and other cash items	101,430,220.18	87,951,405.13	128,312,177.79	134,603,231.51
Bills of national banks	19,263,718.00	12,873,785.00	16,138,769.00	11,841,104.00
Bills of other banks	1,176,142.00	825,748.00	531,267.00	313,209.00
Specie	19,726,043.20	11,444,529.15	11,128,672.98	12,798,044.40
Legal tenders and fract'l cur'y	104,872,371.04	92,861,254.17	102,534,613.46	100,550,819.91
Compound-interest notes	82,047,250.00	84,065,790.00	75,488,220.00	56,888,250.00
Total	1,511,222,985.40	1,465,451,105.84	1,404,084,526.01	1,499,469,060.17

1868.

	JANUARY 6. 1,642 banks.	APRIL 6. 1,643 banks.	JULY 6. 1,640 banks.	OCTOBER 5. 1,643 banks.
Loans and discounts	$616,603,479.89	$628,029,347.65	$655,729,546.42	$657,668,847.83
U. S. b'ds dep'd to secure circ'n	339,061,200.00	339,686,650.00	339,569,100.00	340,487,050.00
U. S. b'ds dep'd to sec're redep't's	37,315,750.00	37,446,600.00	37,853,150.00	37,360,150.00
U. S. b'ds and sec'ties on hand	44,164,500.00	45,958,550.00	43,068,350.00	36,817,600.00
Oth'r stocks, b'ds, and mortg's	19,365,864.77	19,874,381.33	20,007,327.42	20,693,406.40
Due from national banks	99,311,446.60	95,900,606.35	114,434,097.93	102,278,547.77
Due from other b'ks and b'k'rs	8,480,199.74	7,074,297.44	8,642,456.72	7,818,822.24
Real estate, furniture, etc	21,125,665.68	22,082,570.25	22,090,829.70	22,747,875.18
Current expenses	2,986,893.86	5,428,460.25	2,038,519.01	5,278,911.22
Premiums paid	2,464,536.06	2,660,105.00	2,432,074.37	1,819,815.50
Checks and other cash items	100,390,266.37	114,093,036.23	124,076,097.71	143,241,394.99
Bills of national banks	16,055,572.00	12,573,514.00	13,210,179.00	11,842,974.00
Bills of other banks	261,209.00	196,106.00	312,550.00	222,668.00
Fractional currency	1,927,876.78	1,825,640.16	1,853,358.91	2,262,791.97
Specie	20,981,601.45	18,373,013.22	20,755,919.04	13,003,715.04
Legal-tender notes	111,306,491.00	84,390,219.00	100,166,100.00	92,453,475.00
Compound-interest notes	39,697,030.00	38,917,490.00	19,473,420.00	4,513,730.00
Three per cent. certificates	8,245,000.00	24,255,000.00	44,905,000.00	59,080,000.00
Total	1,502,647,644.10	1,499,668,920.97	1,572,167,076.26	1,559,621,773.49

BANKS FROM OCTOBER, 1863, TO OCTOBER, 1893—Continued.

1866.

Liabilities.	JANUARY 1. 1,582 banks.	APRIL 2. 1,612 banks.	JULY 2. 1,634 banks.	OCTOBER 1. 1,644 banks.
Capital stock	$403,357,346.00	$409,273,534.00	$414,270,493.00	$415,472,369.00
Surplus fund	43,000,370.78	44,687,810.54	50,151,991.77	53,359,277.64
Undivided profits	26,972,493.70	36,964,422.73	29,286,175.45	32,593,486.60
National b'k notes outstand'g	213,239,530.00	248,886,282.00	267,798,678.00	280,253,818.00
State bank notes outstanding	45,449,155.00	33,800,865.00	10,096,163.00	9,748,025.00
Individual deposits	522,507,829.27	534,734,950.33	593,338,174.25	504,616,777.64
U.S. deposits	29,747,230.15	29,150,720.82	36,038,185.03	30,420,819.80
Dep'ts of U.S. disb'sing officers			3,066,892.22	2,870,953.77
Due to national banks	94,700,074.15	89,007,501.54	96,496,726.42	110,531,957.31
Due to other b'ks and bankers	23,793,584.24	21,841,641.35	25,951,728.99	26,986,317.57
Total	1,404,776,619.29	1,442,407,737.31	1,476,395,208.13	1,526,962,804.42

1867.

	JANUARY 7. 1,648 banks.	APRIL 1. 1,642 banks.	JULY 1. 1,636 banks.	OCTOBER 7. 1,642 banks.
Capital stock	$420,229,739.00	$419,399,484.00	$418,558,148.00	$420,073,415.00
Surplus fund	59,992,874.57	60,200,013.58	63,232,811.12	66,695,587.01
Undivided profits	26,961,382.60	31,131,034.39	30,656,222.84	33,751,446.21
National b'k notes outstand'g	291,436,749.00	292,788,572.00	291,769,553.00	293,887,041.00
State bank notes outstanding	6,961,499.00	5,460,312.00	4,484,112.00	4,092,153.00
Individual deposits	558,699,768.06	512,046,182.47	539,593,076.11	540,797,837.51
U.S. deposits	27,284,876.93	27,473,005.66	29,838,391.53	23,062,119.92
Dep'ts of U.S. disb'sing officers	2,477,500.48	2,650,081.39	3,474,192.74	4,352,379.43
Due to national banks	92,761,908.43	91,156,800.89	89,821,751.60	93,311,240.80
Due to other b'ks and bankers	24,416,588.33	23,138,620.46	22,659,267.08	19,644,910.20
Total	1,511,222,985.40	1,465,451,105.84	1,494,084,520.01	1,490,469,000.17

1868.

	JANUARY 6. 1,642 banks.	APRIL 6. 1,643 banks.	JULY 6. 1,640 banks.	OCTOBER 5. 1,643 banks.
Capital stock	$420,260,790.00	$420,676,210.00	$420,105,011.00	$420,034,511.00
Surplus fund	70,586,125.70	72,349,119.60	75,810,118.01	77,995,701.40
Undivided profits	31,399,877.57	32,861,597.08	33,543,223.35	36,095,883.98
National b'k notes outstand'g	294,377,390.00	295,336,044.00	294,906,264.00	295,769,489.00
State bank notes outstanding	3,792,013.00	3,310,177.00	3,163,771.00	2,906,352.00
Individual deposits	534,704,709.00	532,011,480.36	575,842,070.12	580,940,820.85
U.S. deposits	24,305,638.02	22,750,342.77	24,603,676.06	17,573,250.64
Dep'ts of U.S. disb'sing officers	3,208,783.03	4,670,682.31	3,499,389.99	4,570,478.10
Due to national banks	98,144,669.61	94,073,631.25	113,306,346.34	99,414,307.28
Due to other b'ks and bankers	21,867,048.17	21,323,636.60	27,355,204.56	23,720,829.18
Total	1,502,647,644.10	1,499,668,920.97	1,572,167,070.26	1,559,021,773.49

10665 CUR——17

AGGREGATE RESOURCES AND LIABILITIES OF THE NATIONAL

1869.

Resources.	JANUARY 4. 1,628 banks.	APRIL 17. 1,620 banks.	JUNE 12. 1,619 banks.	OCTOBER 9. 1,617 banks.
Loans and discounts	$644,945,039.53	$662,084,813.47	$686,347,755.81	$682,883,106.97
U.S. bonds to secure circ'lat'n	338,539,050.00	338,379,250.00	338,609,750.00	339,480,100.00
U.S. bonds to secure deposits	34,538,350.00	20,721,350.00	27,625,350.00	18,701,000.00
U.S. b'ds and sec'ties on hand	35,010,600.00	30,226,550.00	27,476,650.00	25,903,950.00
Oth'r stocks, b'ds,and mortg's	20,127,732.96	20,074,435.69	20,777,560.53	22,250,697.14
Due from redeeming agents	65,727,070.80	57,654,382.55	62,912,636.82	56,669,562.84
Due from other national b'nks	36,067,316.84	30,620,527.89	35,556,504.53	35,393,563.47
Due from State b'ks and b'k'rs	7,715,719.34	8,075,505.60	9,140,019.24	8,790,418.57
Real estate, furniture, etc	23,289,838.28	23,798,188.13	23,850,271.17	25,169,188.95
Current expenses	3,265,990.81	5,641,195.01	5,820,577.87	5,646,382.96
Premiums paid	1,654,352.70	1,716,210.13	1,809,070.01	2,092,304.85
Checks and other cash items	142,605,984.92	154,137,191.23	161,014,852.66	108,809,817.37
Bills of other national banks	14,684,799.03	11,725,239.00	11,524,447.00	10,776,023.00
Fractional currency	2,289,471.06	2,088,545.18	1,804,855.53	2,093,727.38
Specie	29,626,750.26	9,941,532.15	18,435,090.48	23,002,405.83
Legal tender notes	88,239,300.00	80,875,161.00	80,934,119.00	83,719,295.00
Three per cent. certificates	52,075,000.00	51,190,000.00	49,815,000.00	45,845,000.00
Total	1,540,394,266.50	1,517,753,167.03	1,564,174,410.65	1,497,226,601.33

1870.

	JANUARY 22. 1,615 banks.	MARCH 24. 1,615 banks.	JUNE 9. 1,612 banks.	OCTOBER 8. 1,615 banks.	DECEMBER 28. 1,648 banks.
Loans and discounts	$688,875,203.70	$710,848,609.39	$719,341,186.06	$715,028,079.81	$725,515,538.49
Bonds for circulation	339,350,750.00	339,251,350.00	338,845,950.00	340,457,450.00	344,104,200.00
Bonds for deposits	17,592,000.00	16,102,000.00	15,704,000.00	15,381,500.00	15,189,500.00
U.S. bonds on hand	24,677,100.00	27,292,150.00	28,276,600.00	22,323,800.00	23,893,300.00
Other stocks and bd's	21,082,412.00	20,524,294.55	23,300,681.87	23,614,731.25	22,686,358.59
Due from red'g ag'nts	71,641,486.05	73,435,117.98	74,635,475.61	66,275,668.92	64,805,062.88
Due from nat'l banks	31,994,609.26	29,510,688.11	36,128,759.66	33,948,805.65	37,478,166.49
Due from State banks	9,319,560.54	10,248,219.85	10,430,781.32	9,202,496.71	9,821,144.18
Real estate, etc	26,002,713.01	26,330,701.21	26,393,357.00	27,470,746.97	28,021,637.44
Current expenses	3,469,588.60	6,684,189.54	6,324,955.47	5,871,750.02	6,905,073.32
Premiums paid	2,439,501.41	2,080,882.39	3,076,456.74	2,491,222.11	3,251,648.72
Cash items	111,624,822.00	11,267,703.12	11,497,534.13	12,536,613.57	13,229,403.34
Cl'r'g-house exch'gs		75,317,992.22	83,936,515.64	79,089,688.39	76,204,707.00
National bank notes	15,840,669.00	14,226,417.00	16,342,582.00	12,512,927.00	17,001,846.00
Fractional currency	2,476,966.75	2,245,430.02	2,181,714.39	2,078,178.05	2,150,522.89
Specie	48,345,383.72	37,006,543.44	31,099,437.78	18,460,011.47	26,307,251.50
Legal-tender notes	87,708,592.00	82,485,078.00	94,573,761.00	79,324,577.00	80,580,745.00
Three per cent. certfs	43,820,000.00	43,570,000.00	43,465,000.00	43,345,000.00	41,845,000.00
Total	1,546,261,367.44	1,520,147,735.85	1,565,756,909.67	1,510,713,236.92	1,538,998,105.93

1871.

	MARCH 18. 1,688 banks.	APRIL 29. 1,707 banks.	JUNE 10. 1,723 banks.	OCTOBER 2. 1,767 banks.	DECEMBER 16. 1,790 banks.
Loans and discounts	$767,858,490.50	$779,321,828.11	$789,416,568.13	$831,552,210.00	$848,996,311.74
Bonds for circulation	351,556,700.00	354,427,200.00	357,388,950.00	364,475,800.00	366,810,200.00
Bonds for deposits	15,231,500.00	15,236,500.00	15,250,500.00	28,087,500.00	23,153,150.00
U.S. bonds on hand	22,911,350.00	22,487,950.00	24,200,300.00	17,733,650.00	17,675,503.00
Other stocks and b'ds	22,763,809.20	22,414,649.05	23,132,871.05	24,517,069.35	23,061,181.30
Due from red'g ag'nts	83,890,188.02	85,061,016.31	92,369,246.71	86,878,608.84	77,965,600.53
Due from nat'l banks	39,201,110.99	38,332,670.74	39,656,579.35	43,525,362.05	43,313,344.58
Due from State banks	10,271,605.34	11,478,174.71	11,853,308.60	12,772,069.83	13,069,301.40
Real estate, etc	28,805,814.79	29,242,762.79	20,637,996.30	30,189,783.85	30,670,339.57
Current expenses	6,691,014.17	6,764,150.73	6,295,699.46	6,153,370.29	7,330,424.12
Premiums paid	3,939,995.20	4,144,755.40	5,026,385.97	5,500,890.17	5,956,073.74
Cash items	11,642,644.74	12,749,289.84	13,101,197.95	14,058,268.86	13,784,424.76
Cl'r'g-house exch'gs	100,693,917.54	130,855,698.15	102,991,311.75	101,165,854.52	114,538,539.93
National bank notes	13,137,006.00	16,432,201.00	19,101,389.00	14,197,653.00	13,055,904.00
Fractional currency	2,103,298.16	2,135,763.09	2,160,713.22	2,095,485.79	2,061,600.89
Specie	25,760,196.64	22,732,627.02	19,593,365.10	13,232,998.17	20,505,290.56
Legal-tender notes	91,072,349.00	106,219,126.40	122,137,660.00	109,414,735.00	83,042,707.00
Three per cent. cert'fs	37,570,000.00	33,935,000.00	30,690,000.00	25,075,000.00	21,400,000.00
Total	1,627,032,030.28	1,691,440,912.04	1,703,415,335.65	1,730,566,899.72	1,715,861,897.22

1869.

Liabilities.	JANUARY 4.	APRIL 17.	JUNE 12.	OCTOBER 9.
	1,628 banks.	1,620 banks.	1,619 banks.	1,617 banks.
Capital stock	$419,040,931.00	$420,818,721.00	$422,059,260.00	$420,390,151.00
Surplus fund	81,169,936.52	82,053,989.10	82,218,570.47	86,165,334.32
Undivided profits	35,318,273.71	37,489,314.82	43,812,898.70	40,687,300.92
Nat'l bank notes outstanding	294,476,702.00	292,457,008.00	292,753,286.00	293,593,645.00
State bank notes outstanding	2,734,669.00	2,615,387.00	2,558,874.00	2,454,607.00
Individual deposits	568,530,934.11	547,922,174.91	574,307,382.77	511,400,106.63
U. S. deposits	13,211,850.10	10,114,328.32	10,301,907.71	7,112,646.07
Dep't's U. S. disburs'g officers	3,472,884.90	3,665,131.01	2,454,048.99	4,516,648.12
Due to national banks	95,453,139.33	92,662,648.49	100,033,910.03	95,067,892.83
Due to State banks and b'k'rs.	26,984,945.74	23,018,610.62	24,046,771.30	23,849,371.62
Notes and bills re-discounted		2,464,849.81	2,392,265.61	3,839,357.10
Bills payable		1,870,913.20	1,735,289.07	2,140,363.12
Total	1,540,394,266.50	1,517,753,167.03	1,564,174,410.65	1,497,226,604.33

1870.

	JANUARY 22.	MARCH 24.	JUNE 9.	OCTOBER 8.	DECEMBER 28.
	1,615 banks.	1,615 banks.	1,612 banks.	1,615 banks.	1,648 banks.
Capital stock	$426,074,951.00	$427,504,247.00	$427,235,701.00	$430,399,301.00	$435,356,004.00
Surplus fund	90,174,281.14	90,229,954.59	91,689,834.12	94,001,438.95	91,705,740.34
Undivided profits	34,300,430.80	43,109,471.02	42,861,712.59	38,006,018.91	46,050,428.55
Nat'l bank circulat'n	292,838,935.00	292,509,149.00	291,183,614.00	291,798,640.00	296,205,446.00
State bank circulat'n	2,351,993.00	2,279,469.00	2,222,793.00	2,138,548.00	2,091,799.00
Dividends unpaid	2,299,296.27	1,483,416.15	1,517,595.18	2,462,591.31	2,212,556.49
Individual deposits	546,236,881.57	516,058,085.26	542,201,503.18	501,407,586.90	507,368,618.67
U. S. deposits	6,750,139.19	6,424,421.25	10,677,873.92	6,807,978.49	6,074,407.90
Dep'ts U. S. dis. offic's	2,592,001.21	4,778,225.93	2,592,967.54	4,550,142.08	4,155,304.25
Due to national banks	108,351,300.33	109,667,715.95	115,456,491.84	100,348,292.45	106,090,414.53
Due to State banks	28,901,849.14	29,767,575.21	33,012,162.78	29,093,910.80	29,200,587.20
Notes re-discounted	3,812,542.30	2,462,047.49	2,741,843.53	3,843,577.67	4,612,131.08
Bills payable	1,543,753.49	2,873,357.40	2,302,756.99	4,592,009.76	4,838,667.83
Total	1,546,261,357.44	1,529,147,735.85	1,565,756,909.67	1,510,713,236.92	1,538,998,105.93

1871.

	MARCH 18.	APRIL 29.	JUNE 10.	OCTOBER 2.	DECEMBER 16.
	1,688 banks.	1,707 banks.	1,723 banks.	1,767 banks.	1,790 banks.
Capital stock	$144,232,771.00	$446,925,493.00	$450,330,841.00	$458,255,096.00	$460,225,800.00
Surplus funds	96,862,081.06	97,020,099.28	98,322,203.80	101,112,071.91	101,573,153.02
Undivided profits	43,883,857.04	44,776,030.71	45,535,227.79	42,908,714.38	48,630,925.81
Nat'l bank circulat'n	301,713,460.00	306,131,393.00	307,793,880.00	315,519,117.00	318,265,481.00
State bank circulat'n	2,035,800.00	1,982,580.00	1,908,058.00	1,921,056.00	1,886,538.00
Dividends unpaid	1,263,767.70	2,235,248.46	1,408,028.25	4,540,194.61	1,393,427.98
Individual deposits	561,190,830.41	611,025,174.10	602,110,758.16	600,868,480.55	596,580,487.51
U. S. deposits	6,314,957.81	6,521,572.02	6,205,107.94	20,511,935.98	14,820,525.65
Dep't's U. S. dis. offic's	4,813,016.06	3,757,873.84	4,895,907.23	5,393,598.89	5,399,108.34
Due to national b'nks	118,904,865.58	128,037,469.17	135,167,847.60	131,730,713.04	118,057,014.16
Due to State banks	37,311,519.13	36,113,290.67	41,219,802.06	40,211,971.07	38,110,950.07
Notes re-discounted	3,256,696.42	3,573,723.02	3,120,039.09	3,964,552.57	4,022,455.78
Bills payable	5,248,206.01	5,740,064.77	5,278,973.72	4,528,191.12	5,374,362.67
Total	1,627,032,030.28	1,694,440,912.04	1,703,415,335.65	1,730,566,899.72	1,715,861,897.12

AGGREGATE RESOURCES AND LIABILITIES OF THE NATIONAL

1872.

Resources.	FEBRUARY 27.	APRIL 19.	JUNE 10.	OCTOBER 3.	DECEMBER 27.
	1,814 banks.	1,843 banks.	1,853 banks.	1,919 banks.	1,940 banks.
Loans and discounts.	$839,665,077.91	$814,902,253.49	$871,531,448.67	$877,197,923.47	$885,653,449.62
Bonds for circulation	370,924,700.00	374,428,450.00	377,029,700.00	382,046,400.60	384,458,500.00
Bonds for deposits...	15,870,000.00	15,169,000.00	15,409,050.00	15,479,750.00	16,304,750.00
U. S. bonds on hand..	21,323,150.00	19,292,100.00	16,458,250.00	12,142,500.00	10,306,100.00
Other stocks and b'ds	22,838,388.80	21,528,914.06	22,270,610.47	23,533,151.73	23,160,557.29
Due from red'g ag'nts	89,518,329.93	82,120,017.24	91,561,269.53	80,717,071.30	86,401,459.44
Due from na'tl banks	38,282,905.86	36,697,592.81	39,468,323.39	34,486,593.87	42,707,613.54
Due from State banks	12,269,822.68	12,299,716.94	13,014,265.26	12,976,878.01	12,008,843.54
Real estate, etc......	30,637,676.75	30,800,274.98	31,123,843.21	32,276,498.17	33,014,796.83
Current expenses....	6,205,655.13	7,026,041.23	6,719,794.90	6,310,428.79	8,454,803.97
Premiums paid......	6,308,821.86	6,544,279.20	6,616,174.75	6,646,848.52	7,097,847.86
Cash items..........	12,143,403.12	12,461,171.40	13,458,753.80	14,910,784.34	13,696,723.85
Clear'g-house exch'gs	93,151,319.74	114,195,966.36	88,592,800.16	110,086,315.37	90,145,482.72
National-bank notes.	15,552,087.00	18,492,832.00	16,253,560.00	15,787,296.00	19,070,322.00
Fractional currency.	2,278,143.21	2,143,249.29	2,069,464.12	2,151,747.88	2,270,576.32
Specie..............	25,507,825.32	24,433,899.46	24,256,614.14	10,229,756.79	19,047,336.45
Legal-tender notes ..	97,865,400.00	105,732,455.00	122,994,417.00	105,121,104.00	102,922,369.00
U.S. cert'fs of deposit				6,710,000.00	12,650,000.00
Three per cent.cort'fs	18,980,000.00	15,365,000.00	12,005,000.00	7,140,000.00	4,185,000.00
Total.........	1,719,415,057.34	1,743,652,213.55	1,770,837,269.40	1,755,857,098.24	1,773,556,532.43

1873.

	FEBRUARY 28.	APRIL 25.	JUNE 13.	SEPTEMBER 12.	DECEMBER 26.
	1,947 banks.	1,962 banks.	1,968 banks.	1,976 banks.	1,976 banks.
Loans and discounts.	$913,205,189.67	$912,064,267.31	$925,557,682.42	$944,220,116.34	$856,816,555.05
Bonds for circulation	384,675,050.00	386,763,800.00	388,080,300.00	388,330,400.00	389,384,400.00
Bonds for deposits ..	15,035,000.00	16,235,000.00	15,935,000.00	14,805,000.00	14,815,200.00
U. S. bonds on hand..	10,436,950.00	9,613,550.00	9,789,400.00	8,824,850.00	8,630,850.00
Other stocks and b'ds	22,063,366.20	22,449,146.04	22,912,415.63	23,709,031.53	24,358,125.06
Due from red'g ag'nts	95,773,077.16	88,815,557.80	97,143,326.94	96,134,120.66	73,032,046.87
Due from nat'l banks	30,483,700.09	38,671,088.63	43,328,792.29	41,413,680.06	40,404,757.97
Due from State banks	13,595,679.17	12,883,353.37	14,073,287.77	12,022,873.41	11,185,253.68
Real estate, etc......	34,023,057.77	34,216,878.07	34,820,562.77	34,661,823.21	35,556,746.48
Current expenses.....	6,977,831.35	7,410,045.87	7,154,211.69	6,985,436.99	8,678,270.30
Premiums paid......	7,205,250.67	7,550,987.67	7,800,962.14	7,752,843.87	7,987,107.14
Cash items..........	11,761,711.50	11,425,209.00	13,036,482.58	11,433,913.22	12,321,972.80
Clear'g-house exch'gs	131,383,860.15	94,132,125.24	91,918,526.59	88,926,003.53	62,881,342.16
National-bank notes.	15,908,779.00	19,310,202.00	20,394,772.00	16,103,842.00	21,403,179.00
Fractional currency	2,289,680.21	2,198,973.37	2,197,559.84	2,302,775.26	2,287,454.03
Specie..............	17,777,673.53	16,868,808.74	27,950,088.72	19,868,409.45	26,907,037.58
Legal-tender notes ..	97,141,009.00	100,605,287.00	106,381,491.00	92,522,663.00	108,719,506.00
U.S.cert'fs of deposit	18,460,000.00	18,370,000.00	22,305,000.00	20,610,000.00	24,010,000.00
Three per cent.cort'fs	1,805,000.00	710,000.00	305,000.00		
Total.........	1,839,152,715.21	1,800,303,280.11	1,851,234,860.38	1,830,627,845.53	1,729,380,303.01

1874.

	FEBRUARY 27.	MAY 1.	JUNE 26.	OCTOBER 2.	DECEMBER 31.
	1,975 banks.	1,978 banks.	1,983 banks.	2,004 banks.	2,027 banks.
Loans and discounts.	$897,850,600.46	$923,347,030.79	$926,195,671.70	$954,394,791.59	$955,862,580.51
Bonds for circulation	389,614,700.00	389,249,100.00	390,281,700.00	383,251,600.00	382,976,200.00
Bonds for deposits...	14,600,200.00	14,890,200.00	14,890,200.00	14,691,700.00	14,714,000.00
U.S. bonds on hand..	11,013,400.00	10,152,000.00	10,456,000.00	13,313,550.00	15,290,300.00
Other stocks and b'ds	25,305,736.24	25,466,460.20	27,010,727.48	27,807,826.92	28,313,473.12
Due from res've ag'ts	101,502,861.58	94,017,603.31	97,871,517.06	83,885,126.94	80,488,831.45
Due from nat'l banks	36,624,001.39	41,291,015.24	45,770,715.59	30,695,309.47	48,100,842.02
Due from State banks	11,406,711.47	12,374,391.28	12,469,502.33	11,196,611.73	11,635,573.07
Real estate, etc......	36,043,741.50	36,708,066.39	37,276,676.51	38,112,926.52	39,106,681.04
Current expenses ...	6,968,875.75	7,547,203.05	7,550,125.20	7,658,738.82	5,510,568.47
Premiums paid......	8,741,028.77	8,680,370.81	8,563,262.27	8,376,659.07	8,626,112.16
Cash items..........	10,260,955.50	11,949,026.71	10,496,257.00	12,296,416.77	14,005,517.33
Clear'g-house exch'gs	62,768,110.19	91,877,796.52	93,896,271.31	97,383,687.11	112,995,317.55
National-bank notes.	20,003,251.00	20,073,452.00	23,527,991.00	18,450,013.00	22,532,336.00
Fractional currency.	2,309,910.73	2,187,186.69	2,283,808.92	2,224,943.12	2,302,068.74
Specie..............	33,365,863.58	32,569,969.26	22,326,207.27	21,240,945.23	22,436,701.84
Legal-tender notes..	102,717,561.00	101,692,930.00	103,168,350.00	80,021,946.00	82,604,791.00
U.S. cert'fs of deposit	37,235,000.00	40,135,000.00	47,780,000.00	42,825,000.00	33,670,000.00
Dep. with U.S. Treas			91,250.00	20,349,950.15	21,043,084.36
Total.........	1,808,500,529.16	1,867,802,796.28	1,851,840,913.64	1,877,180,042.44	1,902,409,638.48

BANKS FROM OCTOBER, 1863, to OCTOBER, 1893—Continued.

1872.

Liabilities.	FEBRUARY 27.	APRIL 10.	JUNE 10.	OCTOBER 3.	DECEMBER 27.
	1,814 banks.	1,843 banks.	1,853 banks.	1,919 banks.	1,940 banks.
Capital stock	$464,081,744.00	$467,924,318.00	$470,543,301.00	$479,629,174.00	$482,606,252.00
Surplus fund	103,787,082.62	104,312,525.81	105,181,943.28	110,257,516.45	111,410,248.98
Undivided profits	43,310,344,46	46,428,590.90	50,234,298.32	46,623,784.50	56,762,411.89
Nat'l bank circulation	321,634,675.00	325,305,752.00	327,092,752.00	333,495,027.00	336,289,285.00
State bank circulation	1,830,563.00	1,763,685.00	1,700,935.00	1,567,143.00	1,511,396.00
Dividends unpaid	1,451,746.29	1,561,914.45	1,454,044.06	3,149,749.61	1,356,934.48
Individual deposits	593,645,666.16	620,775,265.78	618,801,610.49	613,290,671.43	598,114,679.26
U. S. deposits	7,114,893.47	6,355,722.95	6,993,014.77	7,853,772.41	7,863,894.93
Dep'ts U.S.dis.officers	5,024,609.44	3,416,371.16	5,463,953.48	4,563,833.79	5,136,597.74
Due to national banks	128,627,494.44	120,755,565.86	132,804,924.02	110,047,347.67	124,218,392.83
Due to State banks	39,025,165.44	35,005,127.84	39,878,826.42	33,789,083.82	34,794,963.37
Notes rediscounted	3,818,686.91	4,225,022.04	4,745,178.22	5,549,431.88	6,545,059.78
Bills payable	6,002,806.91	5,821,551.76	5,942,470.34	6,040,562.66	6,940,416.17
Total	1,719,415,657.34	1,743,652,213.55	1,770,837,269.40	1,755,857,098.24	1,773,556,532.43

1873.

	FEBRUARY 28.	APRIL 25.	JUNE 13.	SEPTEMBER 12.	DECEMBER 26.
	1,947 banks.	1,962 banks.	1,968 banks.	1,976 banks.	1,976 banks.
Capital stock	$484,551,811.00	$487,891,251.00	$490,109,831.00	$491,072,616.00	$490,266,611.00
Surplus fund	114,681,048.73	115,805,574.57	116,847,454.62	120,314,409.20	120,961,267.91
Undivided profits	48,578,045.28	52,415,348.46	55,300,154.60	51,515,131.76	58,375,169.43
Nat'l bank circulation	336,292,459.00	338,163,804.00	338,788,504.00	330,081,799.00	341,320,256.00
State bank circulation	1,308,271.00	1,280,208.00	1,224,470.00	1,188,853.00	1,130,585.00
Dividends unpaid	1,465,993.60	1,462,330.77	1,400,491.90	1,402,547.89	1,209,474.74
Individual deposits	656,187,551.61	616,848,358.25	641,121,775.27	622,685,563.20	540,510,602.78
U. S. Deposits	7,041,848.34	7,880,057.73	8,601,091.95	7,829,327.73	7,680,375.26
Dep'ts U.S.dis.officers	5,835,696.60	4,425,760.14	6,416,275.10	8,098,560.13	4,705,593.36
Due to national banks	134,231,842.95	126,831,026.24	137,856,085.67	133,672,732.94	114,996,666.54
Due to State banks	38,124,803.85	35,036,433.18	40,741,788.47	30,298,148.14	36,598,076.29
Notes rediscounted	5,117,810.50	5,403,043.38	5,515,900.67	5,987,512.36	3,811,487.89
Bills payable	5,672,532.75	7,059,128.39	7,215,157.04	5,480,554.09	7,754,137.41
Total	1,839,152,715.21	1,800,303,280.11	1,851,204,860.38	1,830,627,845.53	1,729,380,303.61

1874.

	FEBRUARY 27.	MAY 1.	JUNE 26.	OCTOBER 2.	DECEMBER 31.
	1,975 banks.	1,978 banks.	1,983 banks.	2,004 banks.	2,027 banks.
Capital stock	$490,859,101.00	$490,077,001.00	$491,003,711.00	$193,765,121.00	$495,802,481.00
Surplus fund	123,497,347.20	125,561,081.23	126,239,308.41	128,958,106.84	130,485,641.37
Undivided profits	50,226,019.88	54,331,713.13	53,332,065.71	51,481,437.92	51,477,628.33
Nat'l bank circulation	339,602,955.00	340,267,049.00	338,538,743.00	333,225,298.00	331,193,159.60
State bank circulation	1,078,088.00	1,049,286.00	1,009,021.00	864,567.00	860,417.00
Dividends unpaid	1,291,055.63	2,259,129.91	1,242,474.81	3,516,276.99	6,088,845.01
Individual deposits	595,350,334.90	649,286,208.95	622,863,154.44	669,068,995.88	682,846,607.15
U. S. deposits	7,276,959.87	7,994,422.37	7,322,830.85	7,302,153.58	7,492,307.78
Dep'ts U.S.dis.officers	5,034,624.46	3,297,089.24	3,238,633.20	3,027,828.27	3,579,722.94
Due to national banks	138,435,378.39	135,640,418.24	143,033,822.25	125,192,049.93	129,188,671.42
Due to State banks	48,112,223.40	48,683,924.34	50,227,426.18	50,718,007.87	51,629,002.56
Notes rediscounted	3,448,828.92	4,581,420.38	4,436,256.22	4,197,372.25	6,365,652.97
Bills payable	4,275,002.51	4,772,662.59	4,352,560.57	4,050,727.51	5,398,900.83
Total	1,808,500,529.16	1,867,802,796.28	1,851,840,913.64	1,877,180,942.44	1,902,409,638.46

AGGREGATE RESOURCES AND LIABILITIES OF THE NATIONAL

1875.

Resources.	MARCH 1. 2,029 banks.	MAY 1. 2,046 banks.	JUNE 30. 2,076 banks.	OCTOBER 1. 2,088 banks.	DECEMBER 17. 2,086 banks.
Loans and discounts	$956,485,939.35	$971,835,298.74	$972,926,532.14	$984,601,434.40	$962,571,807.70
Bonds for circulation	380,682,650.00	378,026,000.00	375,127,900.00	370,321,700.00	363,618,100.00
Bonds for deposits...	14,492,200.00	14,372,200.00	14,147,200.00	14,697,200.00	13,981,500.00
U.S. bonds on hand..	18,062,150.00	14,207,650.00	12,753,000.00	13,949,950.00	16,000,550.00
Other stocks and b'ds	28,268,841.69	29,102,197.10	32,010,316.18	33,505,015.15	31,657,960.52
Due from res've ag'ts	89,991,175.34	80,620,878.75	80,788,903.73	85,701,259.82	81,462,682.27
Due from nat'l banks	44,720,394.11	46,039,597.57	48,513,385.86	47,028,709.18	44,831,891.48
Due from State banks	12,724,243.97	12,094,086.39	11,625,647.15	11,963,768.90	11,895,551.08
Real estate, etc......	39,430,952.12	40,312,285.99	40,909,020.49	42,366,617.65	41,583,311.94
Current expenses ...	7,790,581.86	7,706,700.42	4,992,011.34	7,841,213.05	9,218,455.47
Premiums paid......	9,006,880.92	8,434,453.14	8,742,303.83	8,670,091.18	9,442,801.54
Cash items.........	11,734,762.42	13,122,145.88	12,433,100.43	12,758,872.63	11,238,725.72
Clear'g-houseexch'gs	81,127,796.39	56,970,819.05	88,924,025.93	75,142,803.45	67,886,967.04
Bills of other banks.	18,909,397.00	19,501,640.00	24,261,961.00	18,528,837.00	17,166,190.00
Fractional currency	3,008,592.12	2,702,326.44	2,620,504.26	2,595,651.78	2,901,023.10
Specie.............	16,667,106.17	10,620,361.64	18,9 9,582.50	8,050,329.73	17,070,905.90
Legal-tender notes ..	78,508,170.00	84,015,928.00	87,492,605.00	76,458,734.00	70,725,077.00
U.S. cert'fs of deposit	37,200,000.00	38,615,000.00	47,310,000.00	48,810,000.00	31,005,000.00
Due from U.S. Treas	21,007,919.76	21,454,422.29	19,640,785.52	19,686,960.30	19,202,256.68
Total............	1,869,819,753.22	1,909,847,891.40	1,913,239,201.16	1,882,209,307.62	1,823,469,752.44

1876.

	MARCH 10. 2,091 banks.	MAY 12. 2,089 banks.	JUNE 30. 2,091 banks.	OCTOBER 2. 2,089 banks.	DECEMBER 22. 2,082 banks.
Loans and discounts.	$950,205,555.62	$939,803,085.34	$933,686,530.45	$931,304,714.06	$929,066,408.42
Bonds for circulation	354,547,750.00	344,537,350.00	341,751,750.00	337,170,400.00	336,705,300.00
Bonds for deposits...	14,216,500.00	14,128,000.00	14,328,000.00	14,698,000.00	14,757,000.00
U.S. bonds on hand..	25,910,650.00	26,577,000.00	30,842,300.00	33,142,150.00	31,937,950.00
Other stocks and b'ds	30,425,430.43	30,905,193.82	32,482,805.75	34,445,157.16	31,565,914.50
Due from res've ag'ts	90,068,300.53	86,769,083.97	87,989,900.90	87,326,950.48	83,789,174.65
Due from nat'l banks	42,341,542.67	44,328,609.46	47,417,020.03	47,525,089.08	44,011,664.97
Due from State banks	11,180,562.15	11,262,193.96	10,989,507.95	12,061,283.08	12,415,841.97
Real estate, etc......	41,937,617.25	42,183,958.78	42,722,415.27	43,121,942.01	43,498,445.49
Current expenses ...	8,296,207.85	6,820,573.35	5,025,549.38	6,087,644.46	9,818,422.88
Premiums paid......	10,946,713.15	10,414,347.28	10,621,634.03	10,715,251.16	10,300,066
Cash items.........	9,517,868.86	9,693,186.37	11,724,592.67	12,043,139.68	10,658,709.26
Clear'g-houseexch'gs	58,863,182.43	56,590,632.63	75,328,878.84	87,870,817.06	68,027,016.40
Bills of other banks.	18,536,502.00	20,347,964.00	20,398,422.00	15,910,315.00	17,521,663.00
Fractional currency	3,215,594.30	2,771,886.26	1,987,807.44	1,417,203.66	1,146,741.94
Specie.............	29,077,345.85	21,714,594.36	25,218,469.92	21,360,767.42	32,990,647.89
Legal-tender notes ..	70,768,446.00	79,858,661.00	90,836,870.00	84,250,847.00	66,221,400.00
U.S. cert'fs of deposit	30,805,000.00	27,380,000.00	27,955,000.00	29,170,000.00	26,095,000.00
Due from U.S. Treas	18,479,112.79	16,911,680.20	17,063,407.65	16,743,695.40	16,350,491.73
Total.........	1,834,369,941.70	1,793,306,002.78	1,825,760,907.28	1,827,265,307.61	1,787,407,093.76

1877.

	JANUARY 20. 2,083 banks.	APRIL 14. 2,073 banks.	JUNE 22. 2,078 banks.	OCTOBER 1. 2,080 banks.	DECEMBER 28. 2,074 banks.
Loans and discounts.	$920,561,018.65	$911,946,833.88	$901,731,416.03	$891,920,593.54	$881,856,744.87
Bonds for circulation	337,590,700.00	339,658,100.00	337,754,100.00	336,810,950.00	343,869,550.00
Bonds for deposits ..	14,782,000.00	15,084,000.00	14,971,000.00	14,903,000.00	13,538,000.00
U.S. bonds on hand..	31,988,650.00	32,664,250.00	32,344,050.00	30,068,700.00	28,479,800.00
Other stocks and b'ds	31,819,930.20	32,554,594.44	35,655,755.29	34,435,995.21	32,169,491.03
Due from res've ag'ts	88,698,308.85	81,942,718.41	83,122,099.96	73,284,133.12	75,660,087.27
Due from nat'l banks	41,844,616.88	42,027,778.81	44,567,303.63	45,217,246.82	44,123,924.97
Due from State banks	13,680,990.81	11,911,437.36	11,240,349.70	11,415,761.60	11,471,945.65
Real estate, etc......	43,704,355.47	44,736,549.09	44,818,722.07	45,229,983.25	45,511,932.25
Current expenses ...	4,131,516.48	7,842,296.86	7,910,881.84	6,915,792.50	8,958,903.00
Premiums paid......	10,991,714.50	10,494,565.12	10,300,674.34	9,219,174.62	8,841,939.09
Cash items.........	10,295,401.19	10,410,623.87	10,099,988.40	11,674,587.50	10,265,059.49
Clear'g-houseexch'gs	51,117,889.04	55,159,422.74	57,861,481.13	74,525,215.89	61,304,015.40
Bills of other banks.	18,418,727.00	17,042,693.00	20,182,948.00	15,531,467.00	20,312,692.00
Fractional currency	1,238,228.68	1,114,820.26	1,055,123.61	900,805.47	778,084.78
Specie.............	49,700,267.55	27,070,037.78	21,335,996.06	22,658,820.31	32,907,750.70
Legal-tender notes ..	72,669,990.81	72,351,573.00	90,836,870.00	66,920,684.00	70,568,248.00
U.S. cert'fs of deposit	25,470,000.00	32,100,000.00	44,430,000.00	32,410,000.00	36,515,000.00
Due from U.S. Treas	16,441,509.98	16,291,040.84	17,932,574.00	16,021,753.01	16,493,577.08
Total.........	1,818,174,517.68	1,796,603,275.20	1,774,352,833.81	1,741,084,663.84	1,737,295,145.79

Banks from October, 1863, to October, 1893—Continued.

1875.

Liabilities.	MARCH 1. 2,029 banks.	MAY 1. 2,046 banks.	JUNE 30. 2,076 banks.	OCTOBER 1. 2,086 banks.	DECEMBER 17. 2,086 banks.
Capital stock	$496,272,901.00	$498,717,143.00	$501,568,563.50	$504,829,769.00	$505,485,865.00
Surplus fund	131,249,079.47	131,604,608.66	133,169,094.79	134,356,076.41	133,085,422.30
Undivided profits	51,650,243.62	55,907,619.95	52,160,101.68	52,961,953.50	50,204,957.81
Nat'l bank circulation	324,525,319.00	323,321,230.00	318,148,406.00	318,350,379.00	311,979,451.00
State bank circulation	824,876.00	815,220.00	786,844.00	772,348.00	752,722.00
Dividends unpaid	1,601,255.48	2,501,742.39	6,105,519.34	4,003,534.90	1,353,396.80
Individual deposits	617,735,879.69	695,347,677.70	686,478,630.48	664,579,619.39	618,517,215.74
U. S. deposits	7,971,932.75	6,797,972.00	6,714,328.70	6,507,531.59	6,652,556.07
Dep't's U.S.dis.officers	5,330,414.16	2,766,387.41	3,459,061.80	4,271,195.19	4,232,550.87
Due to nat'onal banks	137,735,121.44	127,280,034.62	138,914,828.39	129,810,681.60	119,843,665.44
Due to State banks	55,294,063.84	53,037,582.89	55,714,055.18	49,918,530.95	47,048,174.56
Notes re-discounted	4,841,600.20	5,671,031.44	4,261,464.45	5,254,453.66	5,257,160.61
Bills payable	4,780,436.57	6,070,632.94	5,758,299.85	6,590,231.43	7,056,583.64
Total	1,869,819,753.22	1,909,847,891.40	1,913,239,201.16	1,852,209,307.62	1,823,469,752.44

1876.

	MARCH 10. 2,091 banks.	MAY 12. 2,089 banks.	JUNE 30. 2,091 banks.	OCTOBER 2. 2,089 banks.	DECEMBER 22. 2,082 banks.
Capital stock	$504,818,666.00	$500,982,006.00	$500,393,796.00	$499,802,232.00	$497,482,016.00
Surplus fund	133,091,739.50	131,795,199.91	131,897,197.21	132,202,282.00	131,390,664.07
Undivided profits	51,177,031.26	49,039,278.75	46,609,341.51	46,445,215.59	52,327,715.08
Nat'l bank circulation	307,476,155.00	300,252,085.00	294,444,678.00	291,544,020.00	292,011,575.00
State bank circulation	714,539.00	667,000.00	658,938.00	628,847.00	608,548.00
Dividends unpaid	1,405,829.06	2,325,523.51	6,116,679.30	3,848,705.64	1,286,540.28
Individual deposits	620,674,211.05	612,355,096.59	641,432,896.08	651,385,210.19	619,350,221.00
U. S. deposits	6,606,394.90	8,493,878.18	7,667,722.97	7,256,801.42	6,727,155.14
Dep't's U.S.dis.officers	4,313,915.45	2,505,273.30	3,392,969.48	3,746,781.58	4,749,615.39
Due to national banks	139,407,880.06	127,880,045.04	131,702,164.87	131,535,969.04	122,351,818.09
Due to State banks	54,002,131.54	46,706,969.52	51,403,995.59	48,250,111.63	48,685,392.11
Notes re-discounted	4,631,882.57	4,653,460.08	3,867,622.24	4,461,407.31	4,553,158.70
Bills payable	6,049,566.31	5,650,126.87	6,173,006.03	6,154,784.21	5,882,672.15
Total	1,834,369,941.70	1,793,306,002.78	1,825,760,967.28	1,827,265,367.61	1,787,407,003.70

1877.

	JANUARY 20. 2,083 banks.	APRIL 14. 2,073 banks.	JUNE 22. 2,078 banks.	OCTOBER 1. 2,080 banks.	DECEMBER 28. 2,074 banks.
Capital stock	$493,634,611.00	$489,684,645.00	$481,044,771.00	$479,467,771.00	$477,128,771.00
Surplus fund	130,224,169.02	127,793,320.52	124,714,072.03	122,776,121.24	121,618,455.32
Undivided profits	37,456,530.32	45,009,418.27	50,508,351.70	44,572,678.72	51,530,910.18
Nat'l bank circulation	292,851,351.00	294,710,313.00	290,002,057.00	291,874,236.00	299,240,475.00
State bank circulation	581,242.00	535,963.00	521,611.00	481,738.00	470,540.00
Dividends unpaid	2,448,909.70	1,853,974.79	1,398,101.52	3,623,703.43	1,404,178.34
Individual deposits	659,891,969.76	641,772,526.08	636,267,529.20	616,400,987.12	604,512,514.52
U. S. deposits	7,234,686.96	7,584,267.72	7,187,431.67	7,972,714.75	6,529,031.00
Dep't's U.S.dis.officers	3,108,316.55	3,076,878.70	3,710,167.20	2,376,983.02	3,780,759.43
Due to national banks	130,293,566.36	125,422,444.43	121,413,601.23	115,028,954.38	115,773,660.58
Due to State banks	49,965,770.27	48,604,820.09	48,352,583.90	46,577,439.83	44,807,958.79
Notes re-discounted	4,000,063.82	3,995,459.75	2,959,128.58	3,791,219.47	4,654,764.11
Bills payable	6,453,320.92	5,969,241.94	6,249,426.88	6,137,116.83	5,843,107.03
Total	1,818,174,517.68	1,796,603,275.29	1,774,352,833.81	1,741,084,663.84	1,737,295,145.70

AGGREGATE RESOURCES AND LIABILITIES OF THE NATIONAL

1878.

Resources.	MARCH 15. 2,063 banks.	MAY 1. 2,059 banks.	JUNE 29. 2,056 banks.	OCTOBER 1. 2,053 banks.	DECEMBER 6. 2,055 banks.
Loans and discounts	$854,750,708.87	$847,620,392.49	$835,078,133.13	$833,088,450.59	$826,017,451.87
Bonds for circulation	343,871,350.00	345,256,350.00	347,332,100.00	347,556,650.00	347,812,300.00
Bonds for deposits	13,820,000.00	19,536,000.00	26,371,000.00	47,936,850.00	49,110,800.00
U. S. bonds on hand	34,881,600.00	33,615,700.00	40,479,900.00	46,785,600.00	44,255,850.00
Other stocks and b'ds	34,674,307.21	34,607,320.53	36,604,996.24	36,859,534.82	35,816,810.47
Due from res've agt's	86,016,990.78	71,331,219.27	78,875,055.92	85,083,418.51	81,733,137.00
Due from nat'l banks	39,692,105.87	40,545,522.72	41,897,858.89	41,492,918.75	43,144,220.68
Due from State banks	11,683,050.17	12,413,570.10	12,232,316.30	12,314,698.11	12,259,856.09
Real estate, etc	45,792,363.73	45,901,536.93	46,153,409.35	46,702,476.26	46,728,147.36
Current expenses	7,786,572.42	7,239,365.78	4,718,618.66	6,272,506.73	7,608,128.83
Premiums paid	7,806,252.00	7,574,255.95	7,335,454.49	7,134,735.68	6,978,708.71
Cash items	10,107,583.76	10,989,440.78	11,525,376.07	10,982,432.89	9,985,004.21
Clear'g-house exch'gs	66,408,965.23	95,525,134.28	87,494,287.82	82,372,537.88	61,998,286.11
Bills of other banks	16,250,560.00	18,363,335.00	17,063,576.00	16,920,721.00	10,392,281.00
Fractional currency	607,398.86	661,044.69	610,084.25	515,661.04	496,804.34
Specie	54,729,553.02	46,023,756.06	29,251,469.77	30,688,606.59	34,355,250.36
Legal-tender notes	64,034,972.00	67,245,075.00	71,643,402.00	61,428,600.00	64,672,762.00
U. S. cert'fs of deposit	20,605,000.00	20,995,000.00	36,905,000.00	32,690,000.00	32,520,000.00
Due from U. S. Treas	16,257,608.98	16,364,030.47	16,798,667.62	16,543,674.36	17,040,018.34
Total	1,729,465,956.90	1,741,898,959.05	1,750,464,766.51	1,767,279,133.21	1,742,826,837.37

1879.

	JANUARY 1. 2,051 banks.	APRIL 4. 2,048 banks.	JUNE 14. 2,048 banks.	OCTOBER 2. 2,048 banks.	DECEMBER 12. 2,052 banks.
Loans and discounts	$823,906,765.68	$814,653,422.69	$835,875,012.36	$878,503,097.45	$933,543,661.93
Bonds for circulation	347,118,300.00	348,487,700.00	352,208,000.00	357,313,300.00	364,272,700.00
Bonds for deposits	66,507,350.00	309,348,450.00	257,638,200.00	18,204,650.00	14,788,800.00
U. S. bonds on hand	44,287,250.00	54,601,750.00	62,160,300.00	52,942,100.00	40,677,500.00
Other stocks and b'ds	35,569,400.93	36,747,129.40	37,617,015.13	39,671,916.50	38,836,369.80
Due from res've ag'ts	77,025,068.68	74,003,830.40	93,443,463.95	107,023,546.81	102,742,452.54
Due from nat'l banks	44,161,948.46	39,143,3+8.90	48,192,531.93	46,692,994.78	55,352,459.82
Due from State banks	11,892,540.26	10,535,252.99	11,258,526.45	13,630,772.63	14,425,072.00
Real estate, etc	47,091,964.70	47,461,614.54	47,796,108.26	47,817,169.36	47,992,332.99
Current expenses	4,033,024.67	6,693,668.43	6,913,430.46	6,111,256.56	7,474,0+2.10
Premiums paid	6,366,048.85	6,609,390.80	5,674,497.80	4,332,419.63	4,150,836.17
Cash items	13,564,550.26	10,911,294.64	10,209,982.43	11,306,132.48	10,777,272.77
Clear'g-house exch'gs	100,035,237.82	63,712,445.55	83,152,359.40	12,964,064.25	112,172,677.95
Bills of other banks	19,535,588.00	17,668,505.00	16,685,484.00	16,707,550.00	16,406,218.00
Fractional currency	475,538.56	467,177.47	446,217.26	396,065.06	374,227.02
Specie	41,499,757.32	41,148,563.41	42,333,287.44	42,173,731.23	79,913,041.59
Legal-tender notes	70,561,233.00	64,461,231.00	67,059,552.00	69,190,696.00	54,715,096.00
U. S. cert'fs of deposit	28,915,000.00	21,885,000.00	25,180,000.00	26,770,000.00	10,860,000.00
Due from U. S. Treas	17,175,435.13	17,029,121.31	16,620,986.20	17,020,063.45	17,054,816.40
Total	1,800,592,002.25	1,984,068,936.53	2,019,884,549.16	1,868,787,428.19	1,925,2 29,017.08

1880.

	FEBRUARY 21. 2,061 banks.	APRIL 23. 2,075 banks.	JUNE 11. 2,076 banks.	OCTOBER 1. 2,090 banks.	DECEMBER 31. 2,095 banks.
Loans and discounts	$974,205,360.70	$992,070,823.10	$994,712,646.41	$1,040,077,267.53	$1,071,356,141.79
Bonds for circulation	361,901,700.00	361,274,650.00	359,512,050.00	357,789,350.00	358,042,550.00
Bonds for deposits	14,917,000.00	14,722,000.00	14,727,000.00	14,827,000.00	14,726,500.00
U. S. bonds on hand	36,798,600.00	29,509,600.00	28,695,800.00	28,793,400.00	25,016,400.00
Other stocks and b'ds	41,223,583.33	42,494,927.73	44,047,345.75	48,863,150.22	48,628,372.77
Due from res've agt's	117,791,386.81	103,064,220.84	115,035,668.27	134,562,778.79	120,155,014.40
Due from nat'l banks	53,230,034.03	54,493,465.09	56,578,441.60	63,023,796.84	69,079,326.15
Due from State banks	14,501,152.51	13,293,775.94	13,861,562.39	15,881,197.74	17,111,241.03
Real estate, etc	47,845,915.77	47,808,207.09	47,979,244.53	48,615,832.51	47,784,46.47
Current expenses	6,404,743.54	7,007,404.19	6,778,829.19	6,386,182.01	4,442,440.02
Premiums paid	3,008,059.27	3,791,703.33	5,702,354.60	3,488,470.11	3,288,602.63
Cash items	10,320,274.51	9,857,045.34	9,080,179.32	12,720,002.19	14,713,920.02
Clear'g-house exch'gs	166,736,402.64	99,357,056.41	122,300,409.45	121,005,249.72	229,733,904.59
Bills of other banks	15,360,257.00	21,064,504.00	21,908,103.00	18,210,043.00	21,549,367.00
Fractional currency	397,187.23	395,747.67	387,226.13	367,171.73	389,921.75
Specie	89,442,051.75	86,420,732.21	99,506,565.26	100,346,069.49	107,172,900.92
Legal-tender notes	55,229,408.00	61,048,941.00	64,470,717.00	56,610,458.00	59,216,034.00
U. S. cert'fs of deposit	19,760,060.00	7,890,000.00	12,510,000.00	7,655,000.00	6,150,000.00
Due from U. S. Treas	16,994,381.37	17,226,060.01	16,999,083.78	17,103,860.00	17,125,822.37
Total	2,038,066,408.46	1,974,600,473.95	2,035,493,280.15	2,105,786,625.82	2,241,688,829.91

BANKS FROM OCTOBER, 1863, TO OCTOBER, 1893—Continued.

1878.

Liabilities.	MARCH 15.	MAY 1.	JUNE 29.	OCTOBER 1.	DECEMBER 6.
	2,063 banks.	2,059 banks.	2,056 banks.	2,053 banks.	2,055 banks.
Capital stock	$473,952,541.00	$471,971,627.00	$470,893,366.00	$466,147,436.00	$464,874,996.00
Surplus fund	120,870,290.10	119,231,126.13	118,178,530.75	116,897,779.98	116,402,118.84
Undivided profits....	45,040,851,85	43,938,961.98	40,482,522.64	40,936,213.58	44,040,171.84
Nat'l bank circulat'n	300,926,284.00	301,884,704.00	209,621,059.00	301,888,092.00	303,324,733.00
State bank circulat'n	430,339.00	426,504.00	417,808.00	413,913.00	400,715.00
Dividends unpaid....	1,207,472.68	1,930,669.58	5,466,350.52	3,118,389.91	1,473,784.86
Individual deposits..	602,882,585.17	625,479,771.12	621,632,160.06	620,236,176.82	598,805,775.66
U.S. deposits	7,243,253.29	13,811,474.14	22,686,619.67	41,654,812.08	40,209,825.72
Dep's U.S. dis.officers	3,004,064.90	2,392,281.61	2,903,531.09	3,342,794.73	3,451,436.56
Due to national banks	123,239,448.50	109,720,396.70	117,845,495.88	122,496,513.92	120,261,774.54
Due to State banks ..	43,979,239,39	44,006,551,05	43,360,527.86	42,636,703.42	41,767,755.07
Notes re-discounted .	2,465,390.79	2,834,012.00	2,453,839.77	3,007,324.85	3,228,132.03
Bills payable	4,215,196.23	4,270,879.74	5,022,801.27	4,502,082.92	4,525,617.45
Total	1,729,465,956.90	1,741,898,059.05	1,750,464,706.51	1,767,279,733.21	1,742,826,837.37

1879.

	JANUARY 1.	APRIL 4.	JUNE 14.	OCTOBER 2.	DECEMBER 12.
	2,051 banks.	2,048 banks.	2,048 banks.	2,048 banks.	2,052 banks.
Capital stock	$462,031,396.00	$455,611,362.00	$455,244,415.00	$454,667,365.00	$454,498,515.00
Surplus fund	116,200,863.52	114,823,316.40	114,321,375.87	114,786,528.10	115,429,031.93
Undivided profits...	36,836.269.21	40,812,777.59	45,802,815.82	41,300,941.40	47,573,820.73
Nat'l bank circulat'n	303,506,470.00	304,467,189.00	307,328,695.00	313,786,342.00	321,949,154.00
State bank circulat'n	388,368.00	352,452.00	330,927.00	325,954.00	322,502.00
Dividends unpaid....	5,810,348.82	2,158,516.79	1,309,059.13	2,658,337.40	1,305,480.45
Individual deposits..	643,337,745.26	508,822,604.02	648,934,141.42	719,737,568.80	755,459,906.01
U.S. deposits	59,701,222.00	303,463,505.09	248,431,840.25	11,018,862.74	6,923,323.97
Dep's U.S. dis.officers	3,556,801.25	2,689,180.44	3,682,320.67	3,469,600.02	3,893,217.43
Due to national banks	118,311,635.60	110,481,176.98	137,360,091.60	149,200,257.16	152,484,079.44
Due to State banks ..	44,035,787.56	43,709,770.14	50,403,064.54	52,022,453.99	59,232,391.93
Notes re-discounted .	2,926,434.95	2,224,491.91	2,226,396.39	2,205,015.54	2,116,484.47
Bills payable	3,942,659.18	4,452,544.48	4,510,676.47	4,208,201.89	4,041,649.70
Total	1,800,592,002.25	1,984,008,936.53	2,019,884,540.16	1,868,787,428 19	1,925,229,617.08

1880.

	FEBRUARY 21.	APRIL 23.	JUNE 11.	OCTOBER 1.	DECEMBER 31.
	2,061 banks.	2,075 banks.	2,076 banks.	2,090 banks.	2,095 banks.
Capital stock	$454,518,585.00	$456,007,935.00	$455,909,565.00	$457,553,985.00	$458,540,085.00
Surplus fund	117,041,043.03	117,299,350.09	118,102,014.11	120,518,583.43	121,824,629.03
Undivided profits....	42,863,804.95	48,226,087.61	50,443,635,45	46,139,690.24	47,946,741.64
Nat'l bank circulat'n	320,303,874.00	320,759,472.00	318,088,502.00	317,350,036.00	317,484,496.00
State bank circulat'n	303,452.00	299,790.00	290,738.00	271,045.00	258,493.00
Dividends unpaid ...	1,365,001.91	1,542,447.98	1,330,170.85	3,452,504.17	6,108,238.38
Individual deposits..	848,926,509.86	791,555,050.63	833,701,034.20	873,537,637.07	1,006,452,852.82
U.S. deposits	7,856,701.97	7,925,988.37	7,680,905.47	7,548,528.67	7,898,100.94
Dep's U.S.dis.officers	3,069,880.74	3,220,606.64	3,026,757.34	3,344,386.02	3,480,501.01
Due to national banks	170,245,061.08	157,209,759.14	171,402,131.23	192,124,705.10	192,413,295.78
Due to State banks ..	65,430,334.51	63,317,107.96	67,938,795.35	75,735,677.06	71,185,817.08
Notes re discounted .	1,918,788.88	2,616,900.55	2,258,514.72	3,178,232.50	3,354,697.18
Bills payable	4,181,280.53	4,529,067.98	5,266,417.43	5,031,604.96	4,636,876.05
Total	2,038,066,498.46	1,974,600,472.05	2,035,493,280.15	2,105,786,625.82	2,241,681,829.91

AGGREGATE RESOURCES AND LIABILITIES OF THE NATIONAL

1 8 8 1.

Resources.	MARCH 11.	MAY 6,	JUNE 30.	OCTOBER 1.	DECEMBER 31.
	2,094 banks.	2,102 banks.	2,115 banks.	2,132 banks.	2,164 banks.
Loans and discounts.	$1,073,786,749. 70	$1,093,649,382. 18	$1,141,988 049. 45	$1,173,796,083. 09	$1,169,177,567. 16
Bonds for circulation	339,811,950. 00	352,653,500. 00	358,287,500. 00	368,385,500. 00	368,735,700. 00
Bonds for deposits ..	14,851,500. 00	15,240 000 00	15,265,000. 00	15,510,000. 00	15,715,000. 00
U. S. bonds on hand .	46,626,150. 00	44,116 500. 00	48 584,950. 00	40,806,750. 00	31,884,000. 00
Other stocks and b'ds	49,545,154. 92	52,908 123. 90	58,049,292 63	61,952,402. 95	62,663,218. 93
Due from res'vo ag'ts	120,820,691. 09	128,017,627. 03	156,258 637. 05	132 968,183. 12	123,530,465. 75
Due from nat'l banks	62,295,517. 34	63,176,225. 67	75,703,598. 78	78,505,146. 17	77,633,902. 77
Due from State banks	17,032,261. 64	16,038,734. 56	18,850.775. 34	10,306,826 62	17,644,704. 62
Real estate, etc......	47,525,790. 02	47,791 348. 36	47,834,000. 20	47,329,111. 16	47,445,050. 46
Current expenses....	7,810.030. 83	6,056.109. 78	4,235.911. 19	6,731,936. 48	4,647,101. 04
Premiums paid......	3,530,516. 71	4 024,763. 60	4,115 980 01	4,138,485. 71	3,891,728. 72
Cash items.........	10,144.682. 87	11,826,603. 16	13,534.227. 31	14,831 879. 30	17,337,964. 78
Clear'g-house exch'gs	147,761,543. 96	196,673 558. 01	143,960 236. 84	189,222,255. 95	217,214,627. 10
Bills of other banks.	17,733,032. 00	25,120,633. 00	21,631.032. 00	17,732,712. 00	24,190,534. 00
Fractional currency.	386,560. 63	346.950. 21	372,140. 23	373,945. 96	366 861. 52
Specie..............	105,156.195. 24	122,626,502. 05	128,638,927. 50	114,334,786. 12	113,680,639. 60
Legal-tender notes ..	52,156,439. 00	62,516,206. 00	58,728,713. 00	53,158 441. 00	60,104,387. 00
U. S. cert's of deposit.	6,120,000. 00	8,045,000. 00	9,540,000. 00	6,740,000. 00	7 930 000. 00
Due from U. S. Treas.	17,015,269. 83	18,456,600. 14	17,251,868. 22	17,472,593. 96	18,097,923. 40
Total..........	2,140,110,944. 78	2,270,226,817. 76	2,325,832,700. 75	2,358,387,391. 59	2,381,890,866. 85

1 8 8 2.

	MARCH 11.	MAY 19.	JULY 1.	OCTOBER 3.	DECEMBER 30.
	2,187 banks.	2,224 banks.	2,239 banks.	2,269 banks.	2,308 banks.
Loans and discounts.	$1,182,661,609. 53	$1,189,094,830. 35	$1,208,932 655. 92	$1,243,203,210. 08	$1,230,456,213. 97
Bonds for circulation	367,333,700. 00	360,153,800. 00	355,789 550. 00	357,631,750. 00	357,047,550. 00
Bonds for deposits ..	16,093,000. 00	15,920,000. 00	15,920 000. 00	16,111,000. 00	16,344,060. 00
U. S. bonds on hand.	28,523,450. 00	20,662,700. 00	27,242 550. 00	21,314,750. 00	15,492 150. 00
Other stocks and b'ds	64,430,686. 18	65,274,999. 32	66,601,399. 56	66,168,916. 64	66,998,620. 36
Due from res've ag't	117,452,719. 75	124,189,945. 23	118,455,012. 38	113,277,227. 87	122,046,108. 75
Due from nat'l banks	68,301,645. 12	66,883,512. 75	75,366,970. 74	68,516,841. 06	76,073,227. 76
Due from State banks	15,921,432. 07	16,890,174. 92	16,344,688. 66	17,105,468. 44	18,405,748. 49
Real estate, etc......	47,073,247. 45	46,956,574. 28	46,425,331. 40	46,537,068. 41	46,993,408 41
Current expenses ...	8,494,036. 21	6,774,571. 86	3,030,464. 69	7,238,270. 17	5,130,505. 53
Premiums paid......	3,762,382. 59	5,062,311. 52	5,494,724. 35	6,515,155. 03	6,472,585. 84
Cash items	13,368,120. 70	12,295,256. 96	20,166,927. 35	14,784,025. 21	16,281,315. 67
Clear'g-house exch'gs	162,088,077. 94	107,270,091. 71	150,114,220. 08	208,306,540. 08	155,951,191. 81
Bills of other banks.	19,440,089. 00	25,226,186. 00	21,405,758. 00	20,689,425. 00	25,344,775. 00
Fractional currency.	389,508. 67	390,236. 36	373,725. 83	396 367. 64	401,314. 70
Specie.............	100,984,111. 01	112,415,306. 73	111,604,262. 54	102,857,778. 27	106,427,150. 40
Legal-tender notes .	56,635,579. 00	65,969 622. 00	64,019 518. 00	63,313,517. 00	68,478,421. 00
U.S. cert's of deposit.	9,445 000. 00	16,395,000. 00	11,045,000. 00	8,645,000. 00	8,475,000. 00
Due from U. S. Treas.	17,720,701. 67	17,099,385. 14	16,830,407. 40	17,161,367. 94	17,954,069. 42
Total..........	2,309,057,088. 72	2,277,024,011. 13	2,344,342,686. 90	2,399,833,676. 84	2,360,793,467. 09

1 8 8 3.

	MARCH 13.	MAY 1.	JUNE 22.	OCTOBER 2.	DECEMBER 31.
	2,343 banks.	2,375 banks.	2,417 banks.	2,501 banks.	2,529 banks.
Loans and discounts	$1,249,114,879. 43	$1,262,339,981. 87	$1,285,591,002. 19	$1,309,244,781. 64	$1,307,491,250. 34
Bonds for circulation	354,746,000. 00	354,480,250. 00	354,002,000. 00	351 412,850. 00	345,595,800. 00
Bonds for deposits ..	16,799,000. 00	16,949,000. 00	17,116,000. 00	17,081,000. 00	16,846,000. 00
U. S. bonds on hand .	17,850,160. 00	17,850,250. 00	16,078,150. 00	13,593 050. 00	13,151,250. 00
Other stocks and b'ds	68,428,685. 67	68,340,590. 79	68,552,073. 03	71,114,031. 11	71,609,421. 62
Due from res've ag't	121,024 154. 60	100,306,823. 23	126,646 954. 24	124,918,7:8. 71	126,999,606. 92
Due from nat'l banks	67,263,503. 86	68,477,918. 62	66,164 638. 21	65,714,229. 44	77,902,785. 07
Due from State banks	16 993,341. 72	19,582,129. 33	19,451,498. 10	18,266,275. 05	19,402,047. 12
Real estate, etc......	47,063,205. 68	47,155,909. 80	47,502,563. 52	48,337,605. 02	49,510,760. 35
Current expenses ...	8,949,615. 28	7,754,058. 86	8,829,278. 26	6,808,327. 30	4,878,318. 44
Premiums paid......	7,420,939. 84	7,798,445. 04	8,079,726. 01	8,061,073. 00	8,642,252. 98
Cash Items.........	11,360,731. 07	15,461,050. 16	11,100,701. 18	13,581,049. 94	17,491,804. 43
Clear'g-house exch'gs	107,790,065. 17	145,990,998. 18	90 792,075. 68	66,353,211. 76	134,545,273. 98
Bills of other banks.	19,739,526. 00	22,655,833. 00	26,279,856. 00	22,675,447. 00	28,809,699. 00
Fractional currency.	431,931. 15	444,489. 94	456,447. 00	443,031. 12	444,304. 00
Specie..............	97,062,366. 34	103,607,264. 32	115,354,384. 62	107,817,083. 53	114,276,158. 04
Legal-tender notes .	60,844 648. 00	68,256,468. 00	73,832,458. 00	70,672,197. 00	80,559,736. 00
U. S. cert's of deposit.	8,405,000. 00	8,420,000. 00	10,085,000. 00	9,970,000. 00	18,840,000. 00
Due from U. S. Treas.	16,726,151. 30	17,407,694. 31	17,407,900. 20	16,586,712. 60	18,865,948. 85
Total..........	2,298,918,165. 11	2,360,192,235. 85	2,364,893,122. 44	2,372,656,901. 87	2,415,880,917. 49

BANKS FROM OCTOBER, 1863, TO OCTOBER, 1893—Continued.

1881.

Liabilities.	MARCH 11. 2,094 banks.	MAY 6. 2,102 banks.	JUNE 30. 2,115 banks.	OCTOBER 1. 2,132 banks.	DECEMBER 31. 2,104 banks.
Capital stock	$458,254,935.00	$459,039,205.00	$460,227,835.00	$463,621,985.00	$465,859,835.00
Surplus fund	122,470,986.73	124,405,926.91	126,679,517.07	128,140,617.75	129,867,493.92
Undivided profits	54,072,225.49	54,906,690.47	54,684,137.16	56,372,190.92	54,221,816.10
Nat'l bank circulation	298,590,802.00	309,737,193.00	312,223,352.00	320,200,069.00	325,018,161.00
State bank circulat'n	252,763.00	252,647.00	242,967.00	244,399.00	241,701.00
Dividends unpaid	1,402,118.43	2,617,134.37	5,871,595.59	3,836,445.84	6,372,737.13
Individual deposits	933,392,430.75	1,027,040,514.10	1,031,731,643.42	1,070,997,431.71	1,102,679,163.71
U. S. deposits	7,381,149.25	9,504,081.25	8,971,826.73	8,476,689.74	8,796,078.73
Dep's U. S. dis. officers	3,839,324.77	3,371,512.48	3,272,610.45	3,631,603.41	3,595,726.83
Due to national banks	181,677,285.37	191,250,091.90	223,503,034.19	205,802,945.80	197,252,326.01
Due to State banks	71,579,477.47	80,700,506.00	91,035,599.65	89,047,471.00	79,380,429.38
Notes re-discounted	2,616,203.05	2,908,370.45	2,220,053.02	3,091,165.30	4,122,472.79
Bills payable	4,581,231.47	4,493,544.77	5,109,128.57	4,664,077.12	4,482,325.25
Total	2,140,110,914.78	2,270,226,817.76	2,325,832,700.75	2,356,387,301.59	2,381,690,866.85

1882.

	MARCH 11. 2,187 banks.	MAY 19. 2,224 banks.	JULY 1. 2,239 banks.	OCTOBER 3. 2,269 banks.	DECEMBER 30. 2,308 banks.
Capital stock	$469,390,232.00	$473,819,124.00	$477,184,390.00	$483,104,213.00	$484,883,492.00
Surplus fund	130,924,139.66	129,233,358.24	131,079,251.16	131,077,450.77	135,930,969.31
Undivided profits	60,475,764.98	62,345,199.19	52,128,817.73	61,180,310.53	55,343,916.94
Nat'l bank circulation	323,651,577.00	315,671,236.00	308,921,898.00	314,721,215.00	315,230,925.00
State bank circulat'n	241,527.00	241,319.00	235,173.00	221,177.00	207,273.00
Dividends unpaid	1,418,119.12	1,950,554.88	6,034,372.20	3,153,836.30	6,805,057.82
Individual deposits	1,036,595,098.20	1,001,687,693.74	1,066,707,248.75	1,122,472,682.46	1,066,901,719.85
U. S. deposits	8,853,242.16	9,741,183.36	9,817,224.44	8,817,411.21	9,622,303.50
Dep's U. S. dis. officers	3,372,363.96	3,493,252.88	2,807,385.63	3,627,846.72	3,786,262.20
Due to national banks	187,433,824.90	192,067,865.26	194,868,025.46	180,075,749.77	194,491,266.60
Due to State banks	78,359,675.85	78,911,787.20	84,066,023.60	79,885,652.22	77,031,165.82
Notes re-discounted	3,912,962.38	3,754,044.38	4,195,210.99	5,747,614.68	6,703,164.45
Bills payable	4,428,531.51	5,008,343.00	5,037,605.88	4,818,517.18	3,856,056.54
Total	2,309,057,088.72	2,277,924,911.13	2,344,342,680.90	2,399,833,676.84	2,300,793,467.09

1883.

	MARCH 13. 2,343 banks.	MAY 1. 2,375 banks.	JUNE 22. 2,417 banks.	OCTOBER 2. 2,501 banks.	DECEMBER 31. 2,529 banks.
Capital stock	$490,456,932.00	$493,963,069.00	$500,298,312.00	$509,699,787.00	$511,837,575.00
Surplus fund	136,922,884.44	137,775,004.39	138,331,902.06	141,991,789.18	144,800,252.13
Undivided profits	59,340,913.64	60,739,878.85	68,354,157.15	61,560,652.04	58,787,945.91
Nat'l bank circulation	312,778,053.00	313,549,993.00	311,063,330.00	310,517,857.00	304,944,131.00
State bank circulat'n	206,779.00	198,162.00	189,253.00	184,357.00	181,121.00
Dividends unpaid	1,389,092.96	2,849,629.87	1,454,232.01	3,229,226.31	7,082,682.58
Individual deposits	1,001,111,400.55	1,067,962,238.35	1,043,137,763.11	1,049,437,700.57	1,106,453,608.23
U. S. deposits	9,613,873.33	11,624,864.77	10,130,757.88	10,183,190.95	10,026,777.79
Dep's U. S. dis. officers	3,787,225.31	3,618,114.79	3,743,326.56	3,980,259.28	3,768,862.04
Due to national banks	191,296,859.14	180,445,876.92	194,150,676.43	186,828,676.27	200,807,280.06
Due to State banks	80,251,968.26	78,544,128.82	84,741,666.35	83,602,073.01	84,776,421.60
Notes re-discounted	5,101,458.69	5,657,183.69	5,197,514.12	7,387,537.40	8,248,562.67
Bills payable	3,660,724.79	3,361,061.60	3,137,259.77	4,053,252.81	4,106,297.78
Total	2,298,918,165.11	2,360,192,235.85	2,364,833,122.44	2,372,656,364.82	2,445,880,917.49

AGGREGATE RESOURCES AND LIABILITIES OF THE NATIONAL

1884.

Resources.	MARCH 7. 2,563 banks.	APRIL 24. 2,589 banks.	JUNE 20. 2,625 banks.	SEPTEMBER 30. 2,664 banks.	DECEMBER 30. 2,664 banks.
Loans and discounts	$1,321,548,289.82	$1,333,433,230.54	$1,269,862,935.90	$1,215,294,093.37	$1,234,202,226.44
Bonds for circulation	339,816,150.00	337,342,900.00	334,346,350.00	327,435,000.00	317,586,050.00
Bonds for deposits ..	16,850,000.00	17,135,000.00	17,000,000.00	16,840,000.00	16,749,000.00
U. S. bonds on hand..	18,672,250.00	15,560,400.00	14,143,000.00	13,570,600.00	12,305,990.30
Other stocks and b'ds	73,155,084.60	73,424,815.97	72,572,306.93	71,363,477.46	73,449,352.07
Due from res've ag'ts	138,705,012.74	122,491,957.08	95,247,152.62	111,993,019.65	121,161,976.80
Due from nat'l banks	64,638,322.58	68,031,209.90	64,891,670.13	66,335,544.57	69,459,884.45
Due from State banks	17,937,076.35	18,145,827.61	16,306,500.91	15,833,082.98	18,329,912.01
Real estate, etc	49,418,805.02	49,667,126.87	50,149,083.90	49,900,886.91	49,889,936.06
Current expenses....	7,813,880.56	8,054,290.82	8,866,558.09	6,913,508.85	9,070,990.14
Premiums paid......	9,742,601.42	9,826,386.76	10,605,343.49	11,632,631.68	11,923,447.15
Cash items..........	11,383,792.57	11,237,075.71	11,382,292.69	13,103,098.55	11,924,152.80
Cl'g-house loan cert's	....	....	10,335,000.00	1,690,000.00	1,870,000.00
Clear'g-house exc'gs	68,403,373.30	83,531,472.58	69,498,913.13	66,257,118.15	75,196,955.95
Bills of other banks	23,485,124.00	26,525,120.00	23,386,695.00	23,258,854.00	22,377,985.00
Fractional currency.	491,067.76	489,802.51	473,046.66	469,023.89	456,778.26
Specie...............	122,080,127.33	114,744,707.09	109,661,682.11	128,609,474.73	139,747,079.53
Legal-tender notes ..	75,847,095.00	77,712,628.00	76,917,212.00	77,044,500.00	76,309,555.00
U. S. cert's of deposit	14,045,000.00	11,900,000.00	9,870,000.00	14,200,000.00	19,040,000.00
Due from U. S.Treas.	16,465,785.66	17,468,976.58	17,022,999.34	17,730,906.28	15,442,300.52
Total..........	2,390,500,638.51	2,396,813,834.92	2,282,598,742.96	2,279,493,880.07	2,297,143,474.27

1885.

	MARCH 10. 2,671 banks.	MAY 6. 2,678 banks.	JULY 1. 2,689 banks.	OCTOBER 1. 2,714 banks.	DECEMBER 24. 2,732 banks.
Loans and discounts	$1,232,327,453.69	$1,241,450,649.70	$1,257,655,547.92	$1,306,143,990.46	$1,343,517,559.96
Bonds for circulation	313,106,200.00	312,168,500.00	310,102,200.00	307,657,050.00	304,776,750.00
Bonds for deposits ..	16,815,000.00	16,740,000.00	17,007,000.00	17,457,000.00	18,012,000.00
U. S. bonds on hand..	14,607,650.00	14,769,250.00	14,588,800.00	14,320,400.00	12,665,750.00
Other stocks and b'ds	75,152,919.35	75,019,208.99	77,249,159.42	77,495,220.25	77,533,841.38
Due from res've ag'ts	136,402,273.36	130,903,103.77	132,733,901.34	138,378,515.15	139,239,444.82
Due from nat'l banks	66,442,054.87	67,866,656.57	77,220,072.29	78,967,607.86	79,452,309.67
Due from State banks	17,572,822.65	17,348,938.11	17,180,008.46	17,987,891.44	18,553,946.46
Real estate, etc	49,699,501.42	49,886,378.87	50,729,896.08	51,203,801.16	51,963,082.01
Current expenses....	7,877,320.27	7,090,298.06	3,533,759.49	6,853,392.72	9,416,971.01
Premiums paid......	12,330,437.60	12,358,982.70	12,690,663.41	12,511,333.41	11,802,199.86
Cash items..........	11,228,856.82	11,276,626.48	17,214,373.52	14,347,570.53	12,810,187.64
Cl'g-house loan cert's	1,530,000.00	1,430,000.00	1,380,000.00	1,110,000.00	630,000.00
Clear'g-house exc'gs	59,085,781.99	72,259,129.39	113,158,675.32	84,926,730.78	92,351,296.77
Bills of other banks	22,013,314.00	26,217,171.00	23,465,388.00	23,052,765.00	23,178,052.00
Fractional currency	519,529.96	513,200.12	489,927.18	477,055.17	415,082.64
Trade dollars.......	....	....	....	1,605,763.69	1,670,961.77
Specie...............	167,115,873.67	177,433,119.30	177,612,492.02	174,872,572.54	165,354,352.37
Legal-tender notes ..	71,017,322.20	77,336,909.00	79,701,352.00	69,738,119.00	67,585,466.00
U. S. cert's of deposit	22,760,000.00	19,135,000.00	22,020,000.00	18,800,000.00	11,765,000.00
Due from U. S.Treas.	15,079,935.80	15,473,270.84	14,617,897.02	14,897,114.24	14,981,021.79
Total..........	2,312,744,247.35	2,346,682,452.99	2,421,852,016.47	2,432,913,002.38	2,457,675,250.13

1886.

	MARCH 1. 2,708 banks.	JUNE 3. 2,809 banks.	AUGUST 27. 2,849 banks.	OCTOBER 7. 2,852 banks.	DECEMBER 28. 2,875 banks.
Loans and discounts.	$1,367,705,252.80	$1,398,552,009.71	$1,421,547,199.22	$1,450,957,054.93	$1,470,157,681.13
Bonds for circulation	206,661,400.00	270,414,400.00	270,315,850.00	258,498,950.00	228,384,350.00
Bonds for deposits ..	18,637,000.00	18,810,000.00	19,984,900.00	20,105,900.00	21,040,900.00
U. S. bonds on hand..	16,580,050.00	12,535,500.00	14,308,850.00	12,326,500.00	10,576,200.00
Other stocks and b'ds	80,227,388.98	83,347,119.93	82,439,901.54	81,825,260.40	81,431,000.66
Due from res've ag'ts	142,805,686.01	133,027,136.53	143,715,221.45	140,764,570.01	142,117,979.28
Due from nat'l banks	76,933,579.67	77,642,198.47	78,091,411.58	80,526,615.77	88,271,697.96
Due from State banks	18,834,245.58	17,730,924.26	18,387,215.76	20,140,256.27	21,465,427.08
Real estate, etc	52,262,718.07	53,117,564.42	53,834,583.58	54,090,070.94	54,763,530.37
Current expenses....	7,705,850.57	8,684,672.33	5,837,175.21	7,438,741.12	10,283,007.79
Premiums paid......	12,237,689.15	13,298,269.23	13,641,463.72	14,303,529.55	15,160,621.67
Cash items..........	15,135,538.48	12,181,455.80	10,408,981.58	13,277,169.64	13,218,973.44
Cl'g-house loan cert's	565,000.00	205,000.00	85,000.00	....	....
Clear'g-house exc'gs	99,023,656.84	70,140,339.60	62,474,665.80	95,530,941.15	70,525,126.02
Bills of other banks	20,503,303.00	25,129,638.00	21,062,661.00	22,734,085.00	20,132,330.00
Fractional currency.	470,175.18	452,361.34	451,308.89	434,220.93	447,833.09
Trade dollars.......	1,681,580.00	1,713,384.35	1,857,011.50	1,880,704.55	1,827,364.20
Specie...............	171,615,919.39	157,459,870.49	149,000,492.10	156,387,090.00	166,983,556.01
Legal-tender notes ..	67,014,880.00	79,656,788.00	64,939,751.00	62,812,322.00	67,739,819.90
U. S. cert's of deposit	12,430,000.00	11,850,000.00	8,115,000.00	5,855,000.00	6,105,000.00
5 % fund with Treas	12,953,248.20	12,105,526.43	11,865,912.52	11,358,014.97	10,056,128.39
Due from U. S.Treas.	1,513,019.07	1,416,892.00	1,509,303.36	2,592,042.94	975,370.96
Total..........	2,494,337,129.44	2,474,514,481.89	2,453,666,630.07	2,513,854,751.17	2,507,753,912.93

BANKS FROM OCTOBER, 1863, TO OCTOBER, 1893—Continued.

1884.

Liabilities.	MARCH 7. 2,763 banks.	APRIL 24. 2,589 banks.	JUNE 20. 2,625 banks.	SEPTEMBER 30. 2,664 banks.	DECEMBER 20. 2,664 banks.
Capital stock	$515,725,005.00	$518,471,844.00	$522,515,996.00	$524,271,345.00	$524,089,065.00
Surplus fund	145,741,679.90	146,047,958.07	145,763,416.17	147,055,037.85	146,867,119.06
Undivided profits	63,044,861.56	67,450,459.00	70,597,487.21	63,234,237.62	70,711,309.95
Nat'l bank circulati'n	298,791,610.00	297,506,243.00	295,175,334.00	289,775,123.00	280,197,043.00
State bank circulati'n	180,589.00	180,576.00	179,666.00	179,653.00	174,645.00
Dividends unpaid	1,422,901.91	1,415,889.58	1,384,686.71	3,086,160.33	1,331,421.54
Individual deposits	1,046,050,167.90	1,060,776,388.06	979,020,349.63	975,243,795.14	987,649,055.68
U.S. deposits	9,956,875.24	11,233,495.77	10,530,759.44	10,367,909.92	10,655,803.72
Dep's U.S. dis. offic'rs	3,856,461.66	3,588,980.50	3,664,326.13	3,703,804.34	3,749,900.85
Due to national banks	207,461,179.63	192,868,942.31	155,785,354.44	173,979,149.80	187,296,348.30
Due to State banks	88,466,363.89	86,778,138.85	70,480,617.11	72,408,200.85	72,572,384.43
Notes re-discounted	6,234,202.32	7,299,284.58	11,343,505.55	11,008,595.07	8,433,724.67
Bills payable	2,068,740.50	3,193,035.20	4,262,244.57	4,580,862.15	3,415,524.07
Cl'g-house loan cert's			11,893,000.00		
Total	2,390,500,638.51	2,396,813,834.92	2,282,598,742.96	2,279,493,880.07	2,297,143,474.27

1885.

Liabilities.	MARCH 10. 2,671 banks.	MAY 6. 2,678 banks.	JULY 1. 2,689 banks.	OCTOBER 1. 2,714 banks.	DECEMBER 24. 2,732 banks.
Capital stock	$524,255,151.00	$525,195,577.00	$526,273,002.00	$527,524,410.00	$529,360,725.00
Surplus fund	145,907,800.02	145,103,770.01	146,523,790.94	146,624,642.06	150,155,549.52
Undivided profits	60,200,452.56	60,184,358.12	52,229,946.61	59,335,519.11	69,229,645.82
Nat'l bank circulati'n	274,054,157.00	273,703,047.00	269,147,690.00	268,860,597.00	267,430,837.00
State bank circulati'n	162,581.00	144,490.00	144,489.00	136,898.00	133,932.00
Dividends unpaid	1,301,937.73	2,577,236.08	6,414,263.98	3,508,325.38	1,360,077.27
Individua. deposits	996,501,647.40	1,035,802,188.56	1,106,376,516.80	1,102,372,450.35	1,111,429,914.08
U.S. deposits	11,006,919.47	11,690,707.52	10,995,974.68	11,552,621.98	12,058,768.36
Dep's U.S. dis. offic'rs	3,039,646.40	3,330,522.70	3,027,218.02	2,714,399.37	3,005,783.11
Due to national banks	205,877,203.09	199,081,104.40	203,932,800.05	213,634,005.08	216,564,533.06
Due to State banks	82,190,567.43	81,966,092.25	88,847,454.78	86,115,061.25	85,060,162.27
Notes re-discounted	6,299,722.15	5,736,012.02	5,864,000.85	8,432,702.64	9,932,828.24
Bills payable	1,850,462.10	2,167,333.33	2,074,259.76	2,191,380.16	1,951,598.00
Total	2,312,744,247.35	2,340,682,452.99	2,421,852,016.47	2,432,013,002.38	2,457,675,256.13

1886.

Liabilities.	MARCH 1. 2,768 banks.	JUNE 3. 2,809 banks.	AUGUST 27. 2,849 banks.	OCTOBER 7. 2,852 banks.	DECEMBER 28. 2,875 banks.
Capital stock	$533,360,615.00	$539,109,291.72	$545,522,508.00	$548,240,730.00	$550,608,675.00
Surplus fund	152,872,349.01	153,642,934.89	157,003,875.60	157,249,190.87	159,573,479.21
Undivided profits	59,376,381.80	67,602,886.02	62,211,565.63	66,563,494.72	79,298,286.13
Nat'l bank circulati'n	256,972,138.00	244,893,097.00	238,273,685.00	228,672,610.00	202,078,287.00
State bank circulati'n	133,931.00	132,470.00	128,336.00	125,002.00	115,352.00
Dividends unpaid	1,534,905.58	1,526,776.66	1,863,303.62	2,227,810.59	1,590,345.06
Individual deposits	1,152,660,402.00	1,146,240,911.43	1,113,459,187.35	1,172,008,308.61	1,169,716,413.13
U.S. deposits	12,414,566.52	13,670,721.76	14,295,927.74	13,842,023.69	13,705,700.73
Dep's U.S. dis. offic'rs	3,019,018.72	2,702,841.55	2,884,865.62	2,721,276.77	4,276,257.85
Due to national banks	219,778,171.80	204,405,273.11	218,327,437.33	218,395,950.54	223,842,279.46
Due to State banks	92,663,570.46	90,591,102.81	90,366,354.90	90,246,483.31	91,254,533.23
Notes re-discounted	8,376,095.20	8,718,911.71	7,948,698.27	10,594,176.56	9,159,345.79
Bills payable	1,174,874.29	1,145,240.26	1,381,095.01	2,067,693.48	2,444,958.36
Total	2,494,337,129.44	2,474,514,481.89	2,453,666,930.07	2,513,854,751.17	2,507,753,912.95

AGGREGATE RESOURCES AND LIABILITIES OF THE NATIONAL

1887.

Resources.	MARCH 4. 2,909 banks.	MAY 13. 2,955 banks.	AUGUST 1. 3,014 banks.	OCTOBER 5. 3,049 banks.	DECEMBER 7. 3,070 banks.
Loans and discounts	$1,515,534,674.07	$1,560,291,810.73	$1,560,371,741.05	$1,587,549,133.76	$1,583,941,484.96
Bonds for circulation	211,537,150.00	200,452,300.00	183,632,050.00	189,083,100.00	186,431,900.00
Bonds for deposits	22,976,000.00	24,990,500.00	26,492,000.00	27,757,000.00	42,203,000.00
U. S. bonds on hand	9,721,450.00	8,157,250.00	7,808,000.00	6,014,350.00	6,988,550.00
Other stocks and b'ds	87,441,034.86	88,031,124.15	83,374,837.99	88,831,009.90	90,775,413.31
Due from res'v'e ag't's	163,161,181.57	148,067,874.43	140,270,155.75	140,873,587.98	132,959,765.34
Due from nat'l banks	86,460,829.09	105,576,841.99	299,487,767.80	93,302,413.94	98,227,065.30
Due from State banks	21,725,805.99	22,746,190.43	30,952,187.86	22,103,677.18	21,995,356.41
Real estate, etc	55,128,600.78	55,729,098.76	56,954,622.58	57,968,150.71	58,825,108.16
Current expenses	8,064,292.40	7,781,151.97	5,166,940.86	8,253,890.72	10,600,817.35
Premiums paid	15,537,721.22	16,806,431.83	17,353,130.17	17,288,771.35	18,797,203.70
Cash items	13,308,520.04	13,065,063.79	16,914,070.02	14,691,373.38	13,326,455.77
Clear'g-house exc'gs	89,239,194.59	86,829,363.73	128,211,628.48	88,775,457.99	85,097,380.41
Bills of other banks	22,295,206.00	25,188,137.00	22,962,737.00	21,937,884.00	23,447,294.00
Fractional currency	577,878.03	650,186.75	564,266.72	540,594.50	554,906.55
Trade dollars	1,803,661.40	184,203.08	63,671.97	509.25	328.00
Specie	171,678,906.15	167,315,665.02	165,104,210.28	165,085,454.38	159,240,643.48
Legal-tender notes	60,228,158.00	79,595,088.00	74,477,342.00	73,751,215.00	75,361,975.00
U. S. cert's of deposit	7,645,000.00	8,025,000.00	7,810,000.00	7,810,000.00	6,165,000.00
5% fund with Treas	9,280,755.33	8,810,585.35	8,341,988.77	8,190,000.00	8,168,503.20
Due from U.S.Treas	1,856,195.13	1,113,554.81	660,818.42	985,410.14	1,068,117.43
Total	2,581,143,115.05	2,620,314,022.42	2,637,276,167.72	2,620,193,475.59	2,624,186,330.55

1888.

Resources.	FEBRUARY 14. 3,077 banks.	APRIL 30. 3,098 banks.	JUNE 30. 3,120 banks.	OCTOBER 4. 3,140 banks.	DECEMBER 12. 3,150 banks.
Loans and discounts	$1,540,170,370.51	$1,606,397,923.95	$1,628,124,561.83	$1,684,180,624.27	$1,676,554,863.67
Bonds for circulation	181,845,450.00	181,042,950.00	177,543,900.00	171,867,200.00	162,820,650.00
Bonds for deposits	56,864,000.00	56,643,000.00	55,786,000.00	54,208,000.00	48,949,000.00
U. S. bonds on hand	6,450,500.00	7,639,350.00	7,830,150.00	6,507,050.00	6,374,400.00
Other stocks and bd's	94,153,688.97	95,296,917.07	96,265,812.31	99,752,403.73	102,276,898.17
Due from res've ag'ts	155,341,246.86	146,477,902.83	158,133,598.31	170,458,593.83	156,587,109.27
Due from nat'l banks	92,840,682.48	95,819,102.26	101,689,774.90	99,821,000.57	107,175,402.59
Due from State banks	21,880,060.60	22,709,703.01	22,714,258.27	23,767,260.53	24,217,165.51
Real estate, etc	59,366,247.85	60,111,356.86	61,101,833.19	62,634,791.74	63,436,066.74
Current expenses	6,531,217.71	9,843,637.81	5,685,313.21	8,498,758.28	11,342,102.45
Premiums paid	10,779,498.56	10,501,481.06	18,903,434.54	17,615,808.02	16,681,256.56
Cash items	12,255,978.69	14,644,675.77	16,855,801.15	15,071,024.30	14,140,858.12
Clear'g-house exc'gs	73,418,037.20	117,270,706.86	74,229,763.69	102,439,751.67	91,765,292.99
Bills of other banks	23,145,206.00	24,434,212.00	21,343,405.00	21,600,818.00	21,728,238.00
Fractional currency	683,148.93	602,722.27	632,602.42	684,268.41	628,387.42
Trade dollars	437.59	351.15	371.76	419.05	763.56
Specie	173,830,614.62	172,074,011.10	181,292,276.70	178,097,816.64	172,734,278.50
Legal-tender notes	82,317,670.00	83,574,210.00	81,995,643.00	81,099,461.00	82,353,060.00
U. S. cert's of deposit	10,120,000.00	9,330,000.00	12,315,000.00	8,055,000.00	9,220,000.00
5% fund with Treas	7,993,189.22	7,887,959.36	7,765,837.16	7,535,401.72	7,141,434.41
Due from U.S.Treas	1,240,035.56	1,361,033.74	1,236,675.66	935,799.31	1,216,391.04
Total	2,664,366,304.44	2,732,420,108.19	2,731,448,016.16	2,815,751,341.07	2,777,575,799.00

1889.

Resources.	FEBRUARY 26. 3,170 banks.	MAY 13. 3,206 banks.	JULY 12. 3,239 banks.	SEPTEMBER 30. 3,290 banks.	DECEMBER 11. 3,326 banks.
Loans and discounts	$1,704,067,489.39	$1,730,651,934.67	$1,779,054,527.66	$1,817,257,703.17	$1,811,646,891.57
Bonds for circulation	156,728,200.00	155,520,850.00	147,502,200.00	164,471,700.00	143,434,700.00
Bonds for deposit	46,384,000.00	44,882,000.00	44,832,000.00	44,063,000.00	41,951,000.00
U. S. bonds on hand	6,395,000.00	6,690,800.00	6,810,100.00	4,438,200.00	3,740,350.00
Other stocks and b'ds	102,215,096.01	103,030,575.31	106,712,474.80	109,313,635.01	111,341,480.32
Due from res've ag'ts	192,702,196.35	187,372,205.47	192,500,073.84	189,136,281.01	161,889,765.16
Due from nat'l banks	101,327,319.18	107,091,577.44	108,992,878.96	117,860,749.37	118,206,354.91
Due from State banks	24,651,712.33	26,924,218.24	25,956,516.98	28,417,511.26	28,113,681.33
Real estate, etc	66,248,183.93	66,855,303.68	67,377,183.12	69,377,173.73	70,604,191.37
Current expenses	7,418,190.08	8,984,846.65	3,760,961.17	8,525,924.84	11,902,368.22
Premiums paid	16,729,244.88	17,658,275.41	17,126,726.31	16,613,917.93	15,847,602.85
Cash items	15,049,325.16	15,049,325.16	14,350,763.37	17,059,786.57	15,134,700.19
Clear'g house exc'gs	84,111,547.63	101,452,588.54	101,552,062.37	85,783,162.26	104,719,453.43
Bills of other banks	22,411,826.00	23,722,720.00	24,761,487.00	20,875,528.00	20,388,807.00
Fractional currency	717,823.63	698,369.91	719,273.63	682,034.93	720,402.37
Specie	182,281,803.00	185,176,450.86	175,003,868.08	184,320,448.84	171,080,458.10
Legal-tender notes	88,624,860.00	97,638,385.00	97,452,820.06	86,752,693.00	84,490,894.00
U. S. cert's of deposit	13,785,000.00	13,355,000.00	14,890,000.00	12,945,000.00	0,045,000.00
5% fund with Treas	6,860,148.44	6,565,205.97	6,457,820.06	6,403,658.18	6,276,650.40
Due from U.S.Treas	1,066,950.97	1,601,795.11	1,161,617.26	976,737.81	1,230,667.11
Total	2,837,466,213.93	2,901,922,517.45	2,937,976,370.24	2,908,290,645.91	2,933,670,687.23

Banks from October, 1863, to October. 1893—Continued.

1887.

Liabilities.	MARCH 4. 2,609 banks.	MAY 13. 2,955 banks.	AUGUST 1. 3,014 banks.	OCTOBER 5. 3,019 banks.	DECEMBER 7. 3,070 banks.
Capital stock	$555, 351, 765. 00	$565, 629, 008. 45	$571, 648, 611. 00	$578, 462, 765. 00	$580, 733, 094. 42
Surplus fund..	161, 337, 152. 72	167, 411, 521. 03	172, 348, 398. 99	173, 913, 440. 07	175, 246, 408. 26
Undivided profits...	67, 248, 949. 16	70, 153, 368. 11	62, 294, 634. 02	71, 451, 167. 02	79, 899, 218. 96
Nat'l·bank circulat'n	180, 231, 498. 00	176, 771, 539. 00	166, 625, 658. 00	167, 283, 343. 00	104, 904, 094. 00
State-bank circulat'n	106, 100. 00	98, 716. 00	98, 607. 00	98, 699. 00	= 98, 676. 50
Dividends unpaid...	1, 441, 628. 17	1, 977, 314. 40	2, 239, 929. 46	2, 495, 127. 83	1, 343, 963. 98
Individual deposits	1, 224 925, 698. 26	1, 266, 570, 537. 67	1, 285, 070, 978. 68	1, 249, 477, 126. 95	1, 235, 757, 041. 59
U. S. deposits	15, 233. 599. 91	17, 556, 485. 93	19, 186, 712. 77	20, 392, 284. 03	38, 416. 276. 87
Dep's U.S.dis.offic'rs	4, 277, 187. 61	3, 779, 735. 14	4, 074, 003. 62	4, 831, 066. 14	4, 515, 024. 05
Due to national ba'ks	240, 337, 482. 40	244, 575, 545. 12	235, 966, 622. 46	227, 491, 984. 15	223, 088, 927. 85
Due to State banks.	103, 012, 552. 48	102, 089, 438. 63	103, 603, 598. 14	102, 094, 625. 08	98, 809, 344. 00
Notes rediscounted .	7, 556, 837. 10	10. 132, 799. 64	11, 125, 236. 08	17, 312, 806. 39	10, 268, 247. 74
Bills payable	2, 082, 374. 21	2, 567, 953. 30	2, 985, 987. 60	4, 888, 439. 43	5, 165, 112. 57
Total	2, 581, 143, 115. 03	2, 029, 314, 022. 42	2, 637, 276, 167. 72	2, 020, 193, 475. 59	2, 624, 180, 330. 55

1888.

Liabilities.	FEBRUARY 14. 3,077 banks.	APRIL 30. 3,098 banks.	JUNE 30. 3,120 banks.	OCTOBER 4. 3,140 banks.	DECEMBER 12. 3,150 banks.
Capital stock	$582, 194, 263. 75	$585, 449, 487. 75	$588, 384, 018. 25	$592, 621, 656. 04	$593, 848, 247. 29
Surplus fund.......	179, 533, 475. 38	180, 053, 507. 27	183, 106, 435. 70	185, 520, 564. 68	187, 202, 460. 97
Undivided profits...	66, 606, 930. 87	78, 196, 708. 9.	70, 296, 173. 67	77, 434, 426. 23	88, 302, 639. 01
Nat'l bank circulat'n	150, 750, 193. 50	158, 697, 572. 00	155, 313, 353. 50	151, 702, 809. 50	143, 549, 296. 50
Statebank circulat'n	98, 652. 50	91, 878. 50	82, 372. 50	82, 354. 50	82, 351. 50
Dividends unpaid...	1, 534, 314. 51	1, 766, 496. 41	7, 381, 894. 42	2, 378, 275. 70	1, 267, 930. 19
Individual deposits	1, 251. 957, 844. 42	1, 309, 731, 015. 16	1, 292, 342, 471. 28	1, 350, 320, 861. 11	1, 331, 265, 617. 08
U. S. deposits. ..	55, 193, 899. 19	51, 691, 454. 69	54, 679, 643. 93	52, 140, 562. 97	46, 707, 010. 38
Dep's U.S dis.offic'rs	4, 255, 362. 02	4, 789, 093. 63	3, 690, 652. 65	3, 993, 900. 51	4, 415, 668. 41
Due to national ba'ks	241, 038, 499. 93	237, 056, 910. 91	248, 248, 440. 03	250, 607, 968. 60	252, 201, 134. 80
Due to State banks.	105, 539, 405. 53	104, 502, 668. 21	109, 871, 372. 41	114, 936, 397. 15	108, 001, 696. 40
Notes rediscounted .	12, 866, 722. 85	12, 721, 238. 71	13, 096, 119. 55	17, 305, 750. 61	14, 841, 303. 00
Bills payable.......	3, 796, 739. 99	4, 469, 076. 04	4, 955, 068. 27	6, 615, 813. 47	5, 707, 581. 41
Total	2, 661, 366, 304. 44	2, 732, 423, 198. 19	2, 731, 418, 016. 16	2, 815, 751, 341. 07	2, 777, 504, 700. 00

1889.

Liabilities.	FEBRUARY 26. 3,170 banks.	MAY 13. 3,206 banks.	JULY 12. 3,239 banks.	SEPTEMBER 30. 3,290 banks.	DECEMBER 11. 3,326 banks.
Capital stock	$596, 569, 330. 70	$599, 472, 742. 88	$605, 831, 640. 50	$612, 584, 095. 00	$617, 840, 161. 67
Surplus fund	192, 458, 759. 90	193, 746, 169. 52	196, 911, 605. 90	197, 394, 760. 55	198, 508, 794. 14
Undivided profits...	76, 901, 041. 65	83, 956, 827. 81	72, 532, 950. 94	84, 866, 899. 13	97, 050, 091. 86
Nat'l bank circulat'n	137, 216, 136. 50	131, 128, 137. 00	128, 807, 425. 00	128, 450, 600. 00	126, 039, 541. 30
State-bank circulat'n	82, 347. 50	81, 899. 50	81, 008. 50	80, 410. 50	81, 006. 50
Dividends unpaid...	1, 338, 706. 37	2, 007, 667. 72	3, 517, 506. 07	3, 600, 054. 96	1, 289, 651. 13
Individual deposits	1, 354, 973, 525. 80	1, 422, 042, 136. 92	1, 412, 137, 979. 08	1, 475, 407, 560. 37	1, 436, 402, 685. 65
U.S. deposits	43, 554, 480. 27	42, 963, 811. 22	43, 297, 861. 17	41, 588, 613. 71	39, 224, 588. 51
Dep's U.S.dis.offic'rs	4, 541, 501. 55	4, 136, 285. 33	3, 451, 180. 34	4, 936, 644. 66	4, 672. 950. 14
Due to national ba'ks	289, 753, 579. 16	286, 204, 670. 61	295, 841, 107. 17	293, 015, 192. 86	267, 150, 449. 09
Due to State banks .	127, 751, 135. 48	124, 755, 971. 73	131, 383, 466. 80	132, 327, 094. 47	123, 713, 409. 48
Notes rediscounted .	9, 249, 531. 33	10, 310, 502. 04	10, 133, 196. 24	10, 782, 511. 36	15, 723, 378. 11
Bills payable	3, 013, 127. 72	4, 683, 695. 11	4, 019, 334. 53	7, 196, 238. 34	5, 970, 976. 65
Total	2, 837, 406, 213. 93	2, 901, 922, 517. 43	2, 937, 976, 370. 24	2, 998, 290, 645. 91	2, 933, 076, 687. 23

AGGREGATE RESOURCES AND LIABILITIES OF THE NATIONAL
1890.

Resources.	FEBRUARY 28.	MAY 17.	JULY 18.	OCTOBER 2.	DECEMBER 19.
	3,383 banks.	3,438 banks.	3,484 banks.	3,540 banks.	3,573 banks.
Loans and discounts	$1,844,078,433.06	$1,904,167,351.00	$1,933,509,332.80	$1,980,058,320.13	$1,932,393,206.08
Bonds for circulation	142,531,500.00	143,790,900.00	144,624,750.00	139,969,050.00	139,088,150.00
Bonds for deposits	31,620,000.00	29,893,000.00	29,663,000.00	28,386,500.00	27,858,500.00
U. S. bonds on hand	5,870,550.00	5,591,800.00	5,624,350.00	2,297,500.00	2,075,600.00
Other stocks and b'ds	116,848,501.23	117,051,244.07	116,469,536.45	115,528,951.02	116,609,301.46
Due from res've ag'ts	188,064,131.03	183,206,306.36	185,821,768.04	189,451,786.49	160,220,682.79
Due from nat'l banks	114,379,065.00	113,600,039.35	112,207,068.35	118,289,612.46	111,573,147.08
Due from State banks	28,800,812.21	28,345,930.67	27,311,955.07	28,485,223.32	28,434,882.79
Real estate, etc	72,566,724.91	74,211,949.99	75,657,886.82	76,835,316.02	78,060,490.13
Current expenses	9,038,138.73	9,916,955.10	4,257,508.27	9,099,402.20	13,434,642.44
Premiums paid	14,735,693.95	14,430,752.21	14,316,075.03	14,248,483.10	14,568,760.03
Cash items	15,187,240.17	15,443,751.05	13,875,200.34	17,201,810.17	15,057,481.84
Clear'g-house exch'gs	112,613,788.35	68,428,149.94	88,237,944.43	106,767,176.06	88,818,299.11
C'lg-house loan cert's	......	......	......	......	13,395,249.00
Bills of other banks	21,318,480.00	19,813,670.00	21,184,428.00	18,492,392.00	18,832,221.00
Fractional currency	807,162.57	746,199.91	793,646.45	766,846.68	755,021.82
Specie	181,546,137.80	178,165,494.43	178,604,063.56	195,908,858.84	190,063,006.20
Legal-tender notes	86,551,602.00	88,088,992.00	92,480,409.00	80,604,731.00	82,177,126.00
U. S. cert's of deposit	8,830,000.00	8,135,000.00	9,825,000.00	6,155,000.00	5,760,000.00
5% fund with Treas.	6,191,888.87	6,301,510.51	6,305,121.98	6,123,597.88	6,009,110.84
Due from U. S. Treas.	855,119.70	867,223.14	1,001,631.02	810,923.48	1,093,947.04
Total	3,003,334,970.28	3,010,216,220.33	3,061,770,825.70	3,141,487,491.85	3,016,938,825.59

1891.

Resources.	FEBRUARY 26.	MAY 4.	JULY 9.	SEPTEMBER 25.	DECEMBER 2.
	3,601 banks.	3,633 banks.	3,652 banks.	3,677 banks.	3,692 banks.
Loans and discounts	$1,927,654,550.80	$1,969,846,379.67	$1,963,704,948.07	$2,005,463,205.03	$2,001,032,625.05
Bonds for circulation	140,181,450.00	140,498,400.00	142,886,400.00	150,035,600.00	153,834,200.00
Bonds for deposits	27,904,500.00	27,954,500.00	25,150,500.00	20,432,500.00	19,186,500.00
U. S. bonds on hand	3,466,250.00	3,768,850.00	4,063,650.00	4,439,450.00	4,279,750.00
Other stocks and b'ds	121,099,034.59	122,333,707.66	122,347,244.98	125,179,076.40	128,440,959.39
Due from res've ag'ts	182,645,602.94	180,004,721.63	175,591,085.51	103,990,323.44	104,319,537.81
Due from nat'l banks	110,850,874.53	112,500,098.73	114,471,893.70	115,196,682.26	124,827,315.25
Due from State banks	27,955,862.77	28,172,653.23	27,742,727.64	29,471,898.65	32,425,379.39
Real estate, etc	79,096,556.48	80,874,913.58	81,910,491.00	83,270,122.08	84,386,316.90
Current expenses	8,396,041.93	11,405,934.04	4,624,889.19	9,879,231.42	13,279,136.79
Premiums paid	14,491,627.05	14,960,592.48	14,351,727.16	14,705,700.70	14,695,279.96
Cash items	13,349,231.06	17,602,457.69	16,073,092.99	13,272,545.10	17,939,023.04
Clear'g-house exch'gs	77,828,113.56	126,447,381.31	80,305,873.21	122,039,882.10	108,243,483.92
C'lg-house loan cert's	610,000.00	120,000.00	......	......	......
Bills of other banks	19,076,085.00	20,456,257.00	21,418,977.00	19,991,167.00	20,255,014.00
Fractional currency	864,742.88	830,198.62	863,181.74	867,462.37	837,175.54
Specie	201,240,362.82	194,939,411.31	190,769,537.46	183,515,075.91	207,896,034.75
Legal-tender notes	89,400,399.00	96,375,249.00	100,399,811.00	97,615,608.00	93,854,354.00
U. S. cert's of deposit	11,655,000.00	11,515,000.00	18,815,000.00	15,720,000.00	8,765,000.00
5% fund with Treas.	6,133,544.12	6,158,960.87	6,129,840.09	6,536,931.51	6,682,280.18
Due from U. S. Treas	1,100,310.17	729,226.35	1,155,473.05	1,457,807.85	1,047,684.18
Total	3,065,002,152.30	3,167,404,901.17	3,113,415,253.79	3,213,080,271.02	3,237,866,210.07

1892.

Resources.	MARCH 1.	MAY 17.	JULY 12.	SEPTEMBER 30.	DECEMBER 9.
	3,711 banks.	3,734 banks.	3,759 banks.	3,773 banks.	3,781 banks.
Loans and discounts	$2,058,925,167.12	$2,108,360,340.54	$2,127,757,191.30	$2,171,044,086.11	$2,166,615,720.22
Bonds for circulation	158,109,300.09	160,634,550.00	161,639,800.00	163,275,300.00	166,419,250.00
Bonds for deposits	17,416,500.00	16,386,000.00	15,447,000.00	15,282,000.00	15,321,000.00
U. S. bonds on hand	4,638,100.00	5,412,002.00	4,851,600.00	4,882,250.00	4,148,600.00
Other stocks and b'ds	138,055,947.09	144,058,842.17	151,125,823.17	154,555,514.54	153,648,160.17
Due from res've ag'ts	256,750,998.13	250,249,071.26	252,473,640.18	236,414,330.89	204,948,159.79
Due from nat'l banks	131,258,888.45	130,124,053.23	137,125,158.05	140,516,353.09	142,623,106.03
Due from State banks	32,171,053.96	32,006,102.99	33,497,034.87	32,572,735.51	34,403,231.75
Real estate, etc	85,126,961.74	84,562,679.31	86,678,315.56	87,861,911.86	85,052,032.25
Current expenses	10,340,571.29	11,574,071.41	4,567,100.02	10,317,128.23	14,204,970.25
Premiums paid	14,405,799.74	14,390,888.43	13,997,560.54	12,409,616.43	13,913,289.71
Cash items	17,644,105.99	15,036,575.86	16,819,439.46	17,705,561.31	110,522,668.49
Clear'g-house exch'gs	129,515,655.31	99,954,483.17	90,364,300.19	105,522,711.81	110,522,668.49
Bills of other banks	19,765,178.00	21,014,241.00	21,325,840.00	19,537,474.00	20,488,781.00
Fractional currency	924,866.86	924,375.50	930,382.87	934,648.37	503,909.82
Specie	230,147,068.28	239,044,108.15	229,320,480.41	209,116,378.69	200,256,850.70
Legal-tender notes	99,445,735.00	107,981,402.00	113,915,016.00	101,267,945.00	102,276,335.00
U. S. cert's of deposit	21,080,000.00	26,445,000.00	23,115,000.00	13,995,000.00	6,470,000.00
5% fund with Treas	6,898,132.04	6,990,517.09	7,092,591.94	7,139,561.69	7,282,413.90
Due from U. S. Treas	1,051,330.53	926,158.95	1,409,312.15	1,106,987.93	1,268,405.03
Total	3,436,672,358.56	3,479,035,128.44	3,493,791,586.71	3,510,094,897.40	3,480,349,667.19

BANKS FROM OCTOBER, 1863, TO OCTOBER, 1893—Continued.

1890.

Liabilities.	FEBRUARY 28. 3,383 banks.	MAY 17. 3,438 banks.	JULY 18. 3,484 banks.	OCTOBER 2. 3,540 banks.	DECEMBER 19. 3,573 banks.
Capital stock	$626,598,200.00	$635,055,276.00	$642,073,076.00	$650,447,235.00	$657,877,225.00
Surplus fund	204,433,604.10	207,136,196.13	212,614,661.01	213,563,895.78	214,965,633.67
Undivided profits	85,753,976.34	94,049,477.44	78,854,737.58	97,006,635.71	111,772,985.42
Nat'l bank circul'n	123,862,282.00	125,791,940.00	126,323,880.00	122,928,084.50	123,038,785.50
State-bank circul'n	81,003.50	77,352.50	77,335.50	77,333.50	77,328.50
Dividends unpaid	1,612,499.50	1,766,523.94	2,844,708.73	2,876,836.34	1,167,262.71
Individual deposits	1,479,986,027.48	1,480,474,472.32	1,521,745,665.23	1,564,845,174.67	1,485,095,855.70
U.S. deposits	28,194,911.44	27,047,519.80	27,023,610.38	25,118,559.39	24,922,263.36
Dep's U.S. offic's	4,277,638.17	3,672,054.34	3,552,392.28	4,229,511.42	4,456,472.43
Due to nat'l banks	297,098,933.41	281,994,358.12	288,296,836.21	285,081,259.25	253,082,126.32
Due to State banks	137,067,285.29	132,465,337.41	135,305,641.11	141,350,726.21	121,438,255.50
Notes and bills rediscounted	10,371,343.20	13,419,992.95	15,027,632.53	23,660,329.51	25,598,405.72
Bills payable	3,997,265.67	7,265,719.29	7,028,049.14	10,301,913.51	11,561,225.76
Cl'g-house loan c't's					11,945,000.00
Total	3,003,334,970.28	3,010,216,220.33	3,061,770,825.70	3,141,487,494.85	3,046,938,825.59

1891.

Liabilities.	FEBRUARY 26. 3,601 banks.	MAY 4. 3,633 banks.	JULY 9. 3,652 banks.	SEPTEMBER 25. 3,677 banks.	DECEMBER 2. 3,692 banks.
Capital stock	$662,818,459.15	$667,787,406.15	$672,903,597.45	$677,426,870.25	$677,356,927.00
Surplus fund	220,515,678.70	222,491,983.46	227,199,041.46	227,576,485.91	228,221,530.31
Undivided profits	95,972,506.90	101,502,054.06	87,448,472.14	103,284,673.73	108,116,263.56
Nat'l-bank circul'n	123,112,529.00	123,447,633.00	123,915,643.00	131,323,301.50	134,792,873.25
State-bank circul'n	76,700.50	74,117.50	74,138.50	74,118.50	74,118.50
Dividends unpaid	1,338,745.25	2,104,185.98	4,645,261.20	1,453,735.58	1,503,539.69
Individual deposits	1,483,450,033.17	1,575,506,099.18	1,535,058,563.73	1,588,318,081.37	1,602,652,766.59
U.S. deposits	24,923,462.24	24,411,606.10	21,523,185.64	15,700,672.40	14,478,542.91
Dep's U.S. dis.offic's	4,323,323.50	4,781,045.75	4,387,991.88	4,566,660.39	3,955,227.37
Due to nat'l banks	286,514,008.37	277,560,322.78	270,744,474.60	288,576,703.96	292,480,956.07
Due to State banks	142,324,866.04	142,455,768.77	137,727,372.05	142,018,070.06	149,334,721.20
Notes and bills rediscounted	17,330,630.55	16,604,735.21	19,719,695.08	21,981,952.56	16,325,642.89
Bills payable	7,456,781.57	8,482,342.63	8,067,812.86	10,778,944.87	7,994,514.30
Liabilities other than those above stated					1,178,586.43
Cl'g-house loan c't's	1,144,416.46	285,000.00			
Total	3,065,002,152.30	3,167,494,901.17	3,113,415,253.79	3,213,080,271.02	3,237,866,210.07

1892.

Liabilities.	MARCH 1. 3,711 banks.	MAY 17. 3,734 banks.	JULY 12. 3,759 banks.	SEPTEMBER 30. 3,773 banks.	DECEMBER 9. 3,784 banks.
Capital stock	$679,970,110.00	$682,232,158.00	$684,678,203.25	$686,573,015.00	$689,698,017.50
Surplus fund	234,009,984.34	235,192,004.95	238,230,970.94	238,871,424.84	239,931,932.08
Undivided profits	96,574,522.85	103,376,029.20	88,227,388.88	101,652,754.66	114,603,884.52
Nat'l-bank circulat'n	137,627,107.25	140,052,343.50	141,061,533.00	143,423,298.00	145,669,499.00
State-bank circulat'n	75,097.50	71,507.50	75,070.50	75,076.50	74,176.50
Dividends unpaid	1,470,937.98	1,657,310.34	3,904,292.83	3,888,865.78	1,308,137.97
Individual deposits	1,702,240,957.6-	1,743,787,545.10	1,753,309,079.86	1,705,422,983.68	1,764,456,177.11
U.S. deposits	12,757,046.94	11,911,030.77	10,823,973.08	9,828,144.24	9,673,349.92
Dep's U.S. dis.offic'rs	3,806,323.51	3,025,107.19	3,356,091.88	4,044,734.04	4,034,240.37
Due to national banks	372,985,405.11	361,503,119.66	367,143,324.53	352,046,184.05	323,339,449.03
Due to State banks	181,688,074.58	181,538,222.87	188,683,254.94	178,607,018.34	160,778,117.18
Notes and bills rediscounted	8,517,205.36	9,090,680.27	9,181,650.14	17,132,487.71	15,775,618.63
Bills payable	3,870,404.20	3,816,163.49	4,581,163.01	6,549,163.65	9,318,249.82
Liabilities other than those above stated	1,013,181.26	1,092,506.20	498,983.87	1,079,740.07	1,688,817.56
Total	3,430,672,358.56	3,470,035,128.44	3,493,794,586.71	3,510,094,897.46	3,480,349,607.10

AGGREGATE RESOURCES AND LIABILITIES OF THE NATIONAL

1893.

Resources.	MARCH 6. 3,806 banks.	MAY 4. 3,830 banks.	JULY 12. 3,807 banks.	OCTOBER 3. 3.781 banks.
Loans and discounts	$2,159,614,092.48	$2,162,401,858.59	$2,020,483,671.04	$1,843,634,167.51
Bonds for circulation	170,096,550.00	172,412,550.00	176,588,050.00	206,463,850.00
Bonds for deposit	15,351,000.00	15,261,000.00	15,256,000.00	14,816,000.00
U. S. bonds on hand	4,372,600.00	3,519,550.00	3,078,050.00	2,760,950.00
Other stocks and bonds	153,420,770.06	150,747,862.86	149,690,701.61	148,569,950.46
Due from reserve agents	202,612,051.30	174,312,119.44	159,352,677.33	158,499,644.28
Due from national banks	124,381,881.35	121,673,794.24	111,956,506.81	91,740,014.97
Due from State banks	30,126,300.21	32,681,708.90	27,211,234.32	24,229,106.82
Real estate, etc	89,710,408.54	90,033,775.48	90,383,276.28	89,151,776.08
Current expenses	10,992,932.60	11,746,470.23	4,892,772.88	11,071,996.65
Premiums paid	13,270,691.10	12,935,077.74	11,933,004.69	13,981,867.44
Cash items	18,755,010.52	17,546,973.03	16,707,680.61	15,359,764.56
Clearing-house exchanges	125,142,839.74	114,977,271.06	107,765,890.44	106,181,394.59
Bills of other banks	18,248,706.00	20,085,688.00	20,135,051.00	22,402,611.00
Fractional currency	945,532.50	952,810.90	952,632.48	1,026,813.90
Specie	208,341,816.42	207,222,141.81	186,761,173.31	224,703,860.07
Legal-tender notes	90,935,774,00	103,511,163.00	95,833,677.00	114,709,352.00
U. S. certificates of deposit	14,675,000.00	12,130,000.00	6,660,000.00	7,030,000.00
5% fund with Treasurer	7,401,630.74	7,467,989.77	7,600,604.72	8,977,414.18
Due from U. S. Treasurer	1,322,444.60	1,556,891.28	1,019,074.42	1,262,749.85
Total	3,459,721,235.78	3,432,176,697.25	3,213,261,731.94	3,109,563,284.36

BANKS FROM OCTOBER, 1863, TO OCTOBER, 1893—Continued.

1893.

Liabilities.	MARCH 6.	MAY 4.	JULY 12.	OCTOBER 3.
	3,806 banks.	3,830 banks.	3,807 banks.	3,781 banks.
Capital stock	$688,612,876.00	$688,701,200.00	$685,786,718.56	$678,540,338.93
Surplus fund	245,478,362.77	246,139,183.32	249,138,300.30	246,750,781.32
Undivided profits	103,067,550.15	106,966,733.57	93,944,649.73	103,474,662.87
National-bank circulation	149,124,818.00	151,604,110.00	155,070,821.50	182,959,725.90
State-bank circulation	75,075.50	75,075.50	75,072.50	75,069.50
Dividends unpaid	1,350,392.10	2,579,556.38	3,879,673.50	2,874,697.59
Individual deposits	1,751,439,374.14	1,749,930,817.51	1,556,761,230.17	1,451,124,330.55
U. S. deposits	9,813,762.17	9,657,243.49	10,379,842.66	10,546,135.51
Deposits U. S. disbursing officer	3,927,760.44	4,293,739.93	3,321,271.84	3,776,438.21
Due to national banks	304,785,336.02	275,127,220.28	238,913,573.51	226,423,979.06
Due to State banks	166,901,054.78	153,500,023.9	125,970,422.16	122,591,098.21
Notes and bills rediscounted	14,021,596.43	18,953,306.08	20,940,438.56	21,096,797.01
Bills payable	16,180,228.71	21,506,247.53	31,381,451.27	27,426,937.54
Liabilities other than those above stated	2,913,047.88	3,051,379.82	28,689,265.68	31,632,352.16
Total	3,459,721,235.68	3,492,176,697.25	3,213,261,731.94	3,109,563,284.36

A SUMMARY

OF THE

STATE AND CONDITION

OF

THE NATIONAL BANKS

ON

DECEMBER 9, 1892, MARCH 6, MAY 4, JULY 12, AND OCTOBER 3, 1893.

Arranged by States, Territories, and Reserve Cities.

NOTE.—The abstract of each State is exclusive of any reserve city therein.

ABSTRACT OF REPORTS SINCE SEPTEMBER 30, 1892,

MAINE.

Resources.	DECEMBER 9	MARCH 6.	MAY 4.	JULY 12.	OCTOBER 3.
	81 banks.	83 banks.	83 banks.	83 banks.	83 banks.
Loans and discounts.	$22,012,128.22	$21,860,437.70	$22,633,020.24	$22,539,567.26	$21,342,008.40
Bonds for circulation.	3,848,900.00	3,951,400.00	3,951,400.00	3,971,400.00	4,246,900.00
Bonds for deposits...	180,000.00	190,000.00	190,000.00	190,000.00	190,000.00
U. S. bonds on hand..	500.00	500.00	500.00	500.00	500.00
Other stocks and b'ds	1,894,193.58	1,903,756.77	1,940,766.24	1,934,114.05	1,937,355.23
Due from res've ag't's	2,348,028.03	2,154,210.89	2,077,297.09	2,372,052.55	2,483,624.70
Due from nat'l banks	787,773.16	759,352.86	712,694.25	773,854.92	721,097.13
Due from State banks	54,696.62	48,456.13	76,558.24	90,889.63	112,288.85
Banking house, etc...	501,379.93	603,499.40	609,030.26	598,984.33	597,019.38
Real estate, etc	31,893.96	32,393.96	35,693.96	33,338.31	33,425.71
Current expenses....	94,396.41	63,455.98	74,266.86	25,897.30	68,388.41
Premiums paid	122,969.63	124,161.02	118,701.19	116,857.49	139,385.57
Cash items	198,365.97	201,353.99	194,552.58	238,804.92	220,340.08
Clear'g-house exch'gs	100,976.81	97,570.73	77,597.89	122,470.16	109,798.56
Bills of other banks..	312,257.00	282,396.00	299,540.00	332,430.00	420,930.00
Fractional currency..	5,807.77	7,431.88	7,959.91	7,493.31	7,654.40
Specie.............	990,634.56	995,778.85	1,055,580.79	1,029,235.82	1,114,389.13
Legal-tender notes...	275,050.00	292,330.00	300,282.00	355,393.00	360,330.00
U. S. cert's of deposit.					
5 % fund with Treas.	171,770.25	173,237.25	165,812.75	177,312.75	187,655.25
Due from U. S. Treas	5,840.00	5,000.00	11,430.00	4,190.00	3,800.00
Total..........	34,027,471.90	33,749,753.41	34,532,684.25	34,914,786.70	34,306,880.80

NEW HAMPSHIRE.

	54 banks.	54 banks.	54 banks.	53 banks.	51 banks.
Loans and discounts.	$12,589,651.00	$12,260,699.52	$12,250,523.45	$11,898,167.79	$10,918,692.54
Bonds for circulation.	2,938,000.00	3,231,000.00	3,271,000.00	3,397,500.00	3,689,000.00
Bonds for deposits...	175,000.00	175,000.00	175,000.00	175,000.00	175,000.00
U. S. bonds on hand.	15,100.00	15,100.00	15,100.00	75,100.00	100.00
Other stocks and b'ds	2,317,490.14	2,377,301.34	2,357,483.49	2,355,342.24	2,182,259.82
Due from res've ag't's	1,619,468.60	1,298,899.18	1,257,009.41	1,589,666.21	1,702,967.55
Due from nat'l banks.	363,031.62	219,768.88	203,796.02	267,194.51	157,885.13
Due from State banks	40,202.71	11,630.08	16,594.84	29,041.82	143,362.87
Banking house, etc..	263,896.05	261,836.94	266,797.34	263,903.45	253,720.23
Real estate, etc......	33,665.99	51,112.96	52,138.58	52,003.71	78,156.84
Current expenses....	78,891.47	70,636.79	71,502.51	42,048.40	57,417.37
Premiums paid	127,931.22	142,973.26	145,612.14	151,539.39	166,876.89
Cash items	157,335.78	121,284.46	130,925.82	164,672.12	156,015.20
Clear'g-house exch'gs					
Bills of other banks..	232,076.00	186,284.00	220,351.00	267,997.00	336,261.00
Fractional currency..	7,638.30	6,894.99	7,320.52	7,476.42	9,008.15
Specie.............	532,762.44	509,109.08	534,453.60	548,637.64	585,050.84
Legal-tender notes...	200,905.00	196,036.00	190,555.00	183,512.00	283,749.00
U. S. cert's of deposit					
5 % fund with Treas.	132,210.00	139,629.00	145,060.00	147,830.00	166,005.00
Due from U. S. Treas.	40.00	3,520.00	120.70	3,060.00	1,999.50
Total	21,825,203.98	21,278,716.48	21,310,383.33	21,619,112.70	21,063,527.93

VERMONT.

Resources.	49 banks.	49 banks.	49 banks.	48 banks.	48 banks.
Loans and discounts.	$14,836,897.76	$14,640,877.67	$14,845,905.48	$14,082,356.87	$13,354,330.59
Bonds for circulation.	3,050,000.00	3,044,000.00	3,054,000.00	3,147,500.00	3,445,000.00
Bonds for deposits...	50,000.00	50,000.00	50,000.00	50,000.00	50,000.00
U. S. bonds on hand..	123,200.00	124,600.00	123,300.00	123,100.00	133,600.00
Other stocks and b'ds	906,616.39	942,732.08	929,106.27	928,513.77	1,078,403.32
Due from res've ag't's	1,333,157.05	1,230,298.12	1,667,235.51	1,621,206.14	1,358,560.32
Due from nat'l banks.	302,735.37	281,012.19	309,021.91	325,635.70	174,260.01
Due from State banks	62,160.24	25,822.06	46,542.88	59,962.67	28,127.06
Banking house, etc...	211,609.85	210,175.72	210,175.72	210,490.50	220,088.31
Real estate, etc......	45,711.01	39,327.06	39,263.15	48,882.02	47,405.81
Current expenses....	73,370.72	30,854.27	62,382.72	9,877.62	46,289.56
Premiums paid	110,161.65	100,055.87	101,674.74	110,481.16	124,049.60
Cash items	84,471.85	79,202.90	95,785.05	119,307.00	102,001.47
Clear'g-house exch'gs					
Bills of other banks..	96,797.00	86,759.00	96,900.00	105,645.00	113,267.00
Fractional currency.	6,538.24	7,559.17	7,531.52	6,572.58	6,755.47
Specie.............	500,709.33	507,336.71	546,682.63	587,493.08	643,991.41
Legal-tender notes...	308,888.00	205,563.00	223,016.00	359,625.00	436,767.00
U. S. cert's of deposit					
5 % fund with Treas.	120,182.40	109,380.00	122,272.50	126,482.50	131,412.50
Due from U.S. Treas.	1,650.00	1,412.50	4,810.00	4,800.00	1,175.00
Total	22,230,322.86	21,717,897.93	21,955,636.10	22,029,997.70	21,396,370.43

ARRANGED BY STATES AND RESERVE CITIES.

MAINE.

Liabilities.	DECEMBER 9.	MARCH 6.	MAY 4.	JULY 12.	OCTOBER 3.
	81 banks.	83 banks.	83 banks.	83 banks.	83 banks.
Capital stock	$11,110,000.00	$11,197,000.00	$11,202,000.00	$11,214,195.56	$11,220,600.00
Surplus fund	2,602,003.60	2,706,920.00	2,709,306.87	2,712,441.87	2,699,427.00
Undivided profits	1,751,367.50	1,576,501.58	1,675,388.99	1,456,866.08	1,610,528.37
Nat'l-bank circulation	3,399,393.00	3,481,515.50	3,498,669.50	3,521,746.50	3,754,400.50
State-bank circulation					
Dividends unpaid	33,368.74	43,269.80	61,539.46	112,417.98	76,936.91
Individual deposits	13,002,413.00	12,873,408.79	12,970,392.20	13,133,657.83	12,889,665.46
U. S. deposits	69,073.92	72,936.86	81,392.43	83,994.50	78,605.41
Dep'ts U.S.dis.officers	83,470.87	96,364.00	81,339.21	79,386.81	105,878.38
Due to national banks	922,134.54	547,044.21	718,060.45	725,984.97	559,982.25
Due to State banks	217,601.70	294,414.28	279,330.46	338,696.22	295,495.88
Notes rediscounted	69,415.83	50,603.88	142,732.97	396,393.23	350,399.08
Bills payable	652,345.05	772,087.21	994,858.89	1,092,503.05	661,060.56
Other liabilities	24,674.15	37,537.30	118,243.82	46,307.20	
Total	34,027,471.90	33,749,753.41	34,532,684.25	34,914,786.70	34,306,880.80

NEW HAMPSHIRE.

	54 banks.	54 banks.	54 banks.	53 banks.	51 banks.
Capital stock	$6,200,000.00	$6,430,000.00	$6,430,000.00	$6,380,000.00	$6,130,000.00
Surplus fund	1,572,916.78	1,581,671.45	1,580,571.45	1,570,409.83	1,547,840.28
Undivided profits	902,247.27	784,784.32	823,300.50	711,444.61	768,829.08
Nat'l-bank circulation	2,580,310.00	2,829,940.00	2,907,275.00	3,002,637.50	3,255,457.50
State-bank circulation	6,828.00	6,828.00	6,828.00	6,828.00	6,828.00
Dividends unpaid	18,352.52	19,383.50	29,597.70	54,730.36	32,562.08
Individual deposits	8,633,312.90	7,833,717.82	7,642,477.28	7,963,414.03	7,930,699.28
U. S. deposits	98,571.08	106,926.50	86,049.51	130,011.31	99,111.58
Dep'ts U.S.dis.officers	78,390.27	62,430.94	90,962.78	50,800.79	78,015.70
Due to national banks	1,068,733.54	490,569.20	1,032,860.64	1,014,618.67	688,780.43
Due to State banks	442,189.51	752,052.42	395,802.11	367,297.79	349,173.82
Notes rediscounted	102,641.08	152,003.33	183,458.72	152,015.21	99,300.18
Bills payable	20,671.03	227,500.00	101,184.64	212,790.60	76,200.00
Other liabilities				905.00	100.00
Total	21,825,203.98	21,278,710.48	21,310,383.33	21,619,112.70	21,063,527.93

VERMONT.

	49 banks.	49 banks.	49 banks.	48 banks.	48 banks.
Capital stock	$7,160,000.00	$7,060,000.00	$7,060,000.00	$7,010,000.00	$6,985,000.00
Surplus fund	1,861,175.00	1,855,175.00	1,853,975.00	1,826,200.00	1,819,750.00
Undivided profits	1,074,188.09	847,840.66	989,839.67	778,433.10	805,491.07
Nat'l-bank circulation	2,690,510.00	2,682,585.00	2,710,585.00	2,758,415.00	3,030,100.00
State-bank circulation					
Dividends unpaid	9,070.16	11,318.45	7,348.53	59,655.68	9,284.10
Individual deposits	8,619,234.79	8,429,042.85	8,330,424.45	8,667,836.14	7,956,147.50
U. S. deposits	41,187.55	40,998.89	40,087.86	42,812.86	42,184.17
Dep'ts U.S.dis.officers	3,237.04	2,909.85	3,579.70	1,404.49	7,018.34
Due to national banks	502,458.96	518,495.59	612,017.35	433,780.10	307,627.50
Due to State banks	148,391.73	112,321.06	127,600.41	150,380.87	158,593.67
Notes rediscounted	20,866.54	40,423.61	85,083.13	98,200.64	68,924.08
Bills payable	10,000.00	110,786.97	135,295.00	195,448.24	116,250.00
Other liabilities				1,400.58	
Total	22,230,322.86	21,717,807.93	21,955,626.10	22,029,997.70	21,396,370.43

ABSTRACT OF REPORTS SINCE SEPTEMBER 30, 1892, ARRANGED

MASSACHUSETTS.

Resources.	DECEMBER 9. 213 banks.	MARCH 6. 213 banks.	MAY 4. 213 banks.	JULY 12. 214 banks.	OCTOBER 3. 214 banks.
Loans and discounts	$113,429,207.57	$113,713,084.07	$113,712,442.55	$100,017,758.75	$102,385,129.29
Bonds for circulation	16,733,950.60	16,887,950.00	17,195,450.00	17,554,950.00	19,977,100.00
Bonds for deposits	100,000.00	100,000.00	100,000.00	100,000.00	100,000.00
U.S. bonds on hand	33,300.00	15,300.00	12,800.00	200,700.00	33,200.00
Other stocks and b'ds	6,856,105.38	6,546,282.61	6,325,360.48	6,501,450.32	6,601,913.54
Due from res've ag'ts	10,241,750.14	8,672,453.78	8,471,801.13	10,105,627.94	11,314,881.22
Due from nat'l banks	1,562,650.87	1,227,281.94	1,029,768.49	1,106,605.47	912,653.28
Due from State banks	142,595.24	80,599.85	175,138.46	218,304.28	117,261.71
Banking house, etc	3,031,447.90	3,097,330.96	3,193,551.13	3,214,919.12	3,246,854.08
Real estate, etc	208,369.16	226,455.27	203,393.40	210,750.90	269,232.08
Current expenses	650,394.45	633,042.21	268,541.31	297,721.50	292,089.88
Premiums paid	941,821.32	932,551.95	914,315.75	891,729.72	1,019,195.18
Cash items	783,010.50	832,792.27	929,572.93	804,575.74	924,522.24
Clear'g house exch'gs	95,216.95	104,582.61	90,022.90	155,680.73	162,256.45
Bills of other banks	879,303.15	855,511.00	860,614.00	1,107,195.00	1,006,464.00
Fractional currency	53,108.69	56,585.64	52,434.92	54,215.81	66,170.19
Specie	4,121,003.15	4,145,201.70	4,273,616.72	4,445,283.73	4,520,952.43
Legal-tender notes	1,875,428.00	1,886,075.00	1,929,980.00	2,228,778.00	2,157,719.00
U.S. cert's of deposit	175,000.00	175,000.00	165,000.00	165,000.00	125,000.00
5 % fund with Treas.	726,297.75	739,582.75	766,572.25	776,405.25	881,364.75
Due from U.S. Treas.	54,030.00	20,630.00	45,600.00	12,260.00	14,890.00
Total	162,677,062.07	160,966,204.71	160,716,187.02	159,160,471.26	156,158,850.22

CITY OF BOSTON.

	55 banks.	55 banks.	55 banks.	55 banks.	55 banks.
Loans and discounts	$150,644,052.30	$146,201,894.53	$142,975,348.30	$137,484,411.80	$136,798,614.88
Bonds for circulation	5,910,000.00	6,595,000.00	6,935,000.00	7,505,000.00	10,565,000.00
Bonds for deposits	265,000.00	265,000.00	265,000.00	265,000.00	265,000.00
U.S. bonds on hand	100,800.00	100,800.00	100,800.00	210,800.00	115,000.00
Other stocks and b'ds	5,697,095.03	5,197,284.02	5,219,828.18	5,256,577.30	5,442,157.96
Due from res've ag'ts	20,536,331.09	17,712,418.65	17,104,700.24	15,704,363.79	18,194,793.43
Due from nat'l banks	16,160,779.20	15,270,837.70	15,116,859.56	16,968,628.90	14,592,880.50
Due from State banks	806,016.67	474,709.04	786,115.78	1,135,439.03	684,901.85
Banking house, etc	2,739,433.21	2,736,960.31	2,735,821.45	2,740,125.04	2,734,020.49
Real estate, etc	210,221.99	210,306.27	230,107.07	303,321.87	368,612.00
Current expenses	546,825.86	1,219,532.65	216,114.46	581,581.01	30,083.90
Premiums paid	632,472.14	683,653.14	604,287.39	735,504.95	901,466.09
Cash items	376,412.57	327,234.33	344,188.23	398,920.07	456,168.43
Clear'g house exch'gs	9,688,835.09	9,236,845.08	10,589,906.46	11,088,603.37	12,285,296.63
Bills of other banks	834,782.00	586,816.00	728,602.00	785,306.00	911,327.00
Fractional currency	17,173.82	17,250.83	18,784.17	19,788.24	22,825.55
Specie	11,077,782.41	10,524,436.80	6,857,478.31	7,300,644.88	9,952,788.60
Legal-tender notes	5,204,428.00	3,485,604.00	7,222,102.00	5,398,907.00	5,527,750.00
U.S. cert's of deposit	645,000.00	455,000.00	305,000.00	170,000.00	880,000.00
5% fund with Treas.	265,947.50	288,450.00	312,075.00	326,025.00	474,605.00
Due from U.S. Treas	157,000.00	86,150.00	167,684.00	92,550.00	50,600.00
Total	232,530,398.88	221,673,414.25	219,226,054.60	214,564,888.34	221,262,039.40

RHODE ISLAND.

	59 banks.	59 banks.	59 banks.	59 banks.	59 banks.
Loans and discounts	$36,726,317.46	$37,407,890.12	$37,150,849.42	$35,809,758.33	$34,001,268.34
Bonds for circulation	6,492,250.00	6,656,750.00	6,749,750.00	7,116,750.00	7,721,250.00
Bonds for deposits	100,000.00	100,000.00	100,000.00	100,000.00	100,000.00
U.S. bonds on hand	50.00	50.00	11,050.00	9,050.00	50.00
Other stocks and b'ds	2,426,619.10	2,422,458.54	2,450,310.94	2,503,948.65	2,388,380.39
Due from res've ag'ts	2,667,207.37	2,598,308.66	2,397,901.42	3,538,707.35	3,429,881.40
Due from nat'l banks	1,200,118.25	853,218.29	1,220,628.87	1,070,254.82	958,259.91
Due from State banks	45,923.80	58,204.41	76,375.42	171,637.08	57,527.32
Banking house, etc	919,012.44	969,304.86	1,014,167.61	1,017,334.13	1,021,985.42
Real estate, etc	273,999.14	267,556.51	202,922.80	200,083.97	200,343.36
Current expenses	144,571.06	119,698.23	117,302.25	68,079.63	108,410.26
Premiums paid	668,940.43	643,149.55	676,133.21	641,247.41	700,157.32
Cash items	197,083.65	154,821.83	145,491.92	160,484.82	156,980.73
Clear'g house exch'gs	617,817.87	450,168.41	309,557.81	273,243.78	295,011.94
Bills of other banks	362,282.00	239,880.00	302,074.00	325,017.00	254,871.00
Fractional currency	13,002.90	13,023.91	14,635.46	14,965.23	27,278.22
Specie	1,016,103.00	1,031,205.43	1,036,034.43	1,052,084.80	1,195,466.80
Legal-tender notes	665,280.00	546,228.00	521,319.00	599,978.00	565,790.00
U.S. cert's of deposit					
5% fund with Treas	283,426.10	287,583.25	296,313.75	316,438.75	344,761.25
Due from U.S. Treas	42,482.50	21,584.85	24,262.50	28,634.60	23,524.00
Total	54,883,686.53	54,932,209.88	51,817,581.20	55,017,707.85	53,611,203.66

BY STATES AND RESERVE CITIES—Continued.

MASSACHUSETTS.

Liabilities.	DECEMBER 9. 213 banks.	MARCH 6. 213 banks.	MAY 4. 213 banks.	JULY 12. 214 banks.	OCTOBER 3. 214 banks.
Capital stock	$46,165,420.00	$46,117,500.00	$45,917,500.00	$46,117,500.00	$46,117,500.00
Surplus fund	15,529,645.67	15,571,597.71	15,572,666.66	15,641,457.66	15,672,564.58
Undivided profits	5,919,808.91	6,456,532.03	5,547,865.97	6,019,892.57	5,479,755.11
Nat'l-bank circulation	14,776,144.50	14,918,819.50	15,208,339.50	15,515,652.00	17,738,309.50
State-bank circulation					
Dividends unpaid	95,131.33	73,756.91	171,067.53	169,691.26	565,909.49
Individual deposits	74,818,404.89	72,814,836.98	72,976,727.10	69,478,723.96	65,918,322.47
U. S. deposits	81,262.43	80,535.55	78,920.29	84,133.23	98,752.60
Dep'ts U.S.dis.officers	2,518.60	2,791.54	5,530.39	1,509.00	339.41
Due to national banks	4,085,386.29	2,619,471.75	3,116,086.94	2,670,011.82	2,059,514.12
Due to State banks	311,661.60	336,607.49	227,663.73	402,410.87	248,652.53
Notes rediscounted	580,966.45	524,369.40	470,081.11	1,137,884.43	862,426.38
Bills payable	301,120.45	1,420,074.86	1,373,728.62	1,810,271.46	1,325,819.30
Other liabilities	599.95		50,030.18	120,000.00	51,000.73
Total	162,677,602.07	160,966,204.71	160,716,187.02	159,169,471.26	156,158,850.23

CITY OF PHILADELPHIA.

	41 banks.	41 banks.	41 banks.	41 banks.	41 banks.
Capital stock	$22,465,000.00	$22,765,000.00	$22,765,000.00	$22,765,000.00	$22,765,000.00
Surplus fund	14,066,303.08	14,106,303.08	14,281,303.08	14,301,303.08	14,281,303.08
Undivided profits	2,396,689.52	3,128,611.85	2,230,532.88	2,633,501.88	3,719,579.98
Nat'l-bank circulation	3,704,480.00	3,699,410.00	3,684,480.00	3,007,510.00	6,011,390.00
State-bank circulation					
Dividends unpaid	72,287.96	41,207.51	393,220.81	93,806.56	38,885.81
Individual deposits	94,660,991.37	90,303,722.39	95,449,471.35	89,042,094.90	84,688,009.64
J. S. deposits	174,002.24	176,452.75	163,714.40	182,353.53	191,115.00
Dep'ts U.S.dis.officers					
Due to national banks	18,271,060.04	17,714,191.60	17,951,864.49	17,962,259.80	17,707,233.75
Due to State banks	5,979,112.68	5,356,861.03	4,839,740.67	4,278,876.16	4,436,724.70
Notes rediscounted	200,000.00			50,000.00	
Bills payable		350,000.00	410,000.00	335,000.00	125,000.00
Other liabilities	100,000.00	100,000.00	100,000.00	5,485,000.00	6,160,000.00
Total	162,088,926.89	157,744,880.21	162,318,336.68	161,036,705.91	160,124,241.96

CITY OF PITTSBURGH.

	50 banks.	50 banks.	50 banks.	50 banks.	50 banks.
Capital stock	$20,277,050.00	$20,277,050.00	$20,277,050.00	$20,277,050.00	$20,277,050.00
Surplus fund	4,698,192.64	4,810,996.45	4,822,567.05	5,090,833.43	5,140,129.03
Undivided profits	2,007,152.08	1,852,423.12	1,871,551.89	1,508,029.58	1,620,283.05
Nat'l-bank circulation	5,581,062.00	5,891,307.50	5,978,542.50	6,303,070.00	6,893,120.00
State-bank circulation					
Dividends unpaid	79,711.09	80,214.44	124,113.39	141,075.99	130,788.67
Individual deposits	17,344,977.86	18,438,061.15	17,718,694.88	17,499,315.72	16,780,164.97
U. S. deposits	27,895.41	36,397.92	61,264.85	61,503.83	51,746.40
Dep'ts U.S.dis.officers	50,193.60	29,833.52	21,091.61	13,086.09	30,337.00
Due to national banks	3,071,317.72	1,710,141.34	1,874,139.12	1,934,870.30	1,293,815.84
Due to State banks	1,652,134.13	1,420,784.44	1,756,754.48	2,047,120.87	1,200,290.64
Notes rediscounted	10,000.00		10,000.00		164,978.06
Bills payable		100,000.00	153,000.00	125,000.00	17,500.00
Other liabilities	80,000.60	285,000.00	148,808.43	18,662.04	
Total	54,883,686.53	54,932,209.88	54,817,581.20	55,017,707.85	53,611,203.66

ABSTRACT OF REPORTS SINCE SEPTEMBER 30, 1892, ARRANGED

CONNECTICUT.

Resources.	DECEMBER 9. 84 banks.	MARCH 6. 84 banks.	MAY 4. 84 banks.	JULY 12. 84 banks.	OCTOBER 3. 84 banks.
Loans and discounts	$50,338,350.44	$51,495,792.25	$50,880,357.09	$46,909,224.87	$43,569,640.19
Bonds for circulation	6,523,000.00	6,683,000.00	6,823,000.00	7,040,500.00	7,845,500.00
Bonds for deposits	250,000.00	250,000.00	250,000.00	250,000.00	250,000.00
U. S. bonds on hand	50,200.00	100,000.00		50,000.00	70,000.00
Other stocks and b'ds	4,943,310.24	5,189,866.63	5,072,510.90	5,026,093.41	5,044,479.52
Due from res've ag'ts	6,034,610.65	5,514,114.31	5,072,116.50	6,467,629.31	5,289,977.13
Due from nat'l banks	3,162,270.56	2,378,973.49	2,098,934.70	2,592,938.59	1,237,361.06
Due from State banks	437,189.76	304,190.18	329,050.61	365,432.23	282,581.81
Banking house, etc	1,610,189.41	1,618,450.67	1,638,437.61	1,666,825.79	1,695,163.64
Real estate, etc	186,202.31	182,298.43	197,203.43	285,276.36	252,273.59
Current expenses	299,065.21	155,898.65	258,301.55	69,497.55	216,988.60
Premiums paid	499,628.85	457,792.71	448,517.54	430,175.21	488,970.93
Cash items	343,182.00	361,916.20	361,303.94	413,413.06	365,274.51
Clear'g house exch'gs	403,293.63	367,476.68	300,018.64	328,056.99	272,384.79
Bills of other banks	637,318.00	463,711.00	523,336.00	578,156.00	532,711.00
Fractional currency	24,042.22	25,006.85	25,219.04	25,910.00	24,613.41
Specie	2,628,201.48	2,625,099.63	2,772,269.19	2,827,476.36	2,806,699.23
Legal-tender notes	903,675.00	769,028.00	834,111.00	1,056,403.00	1,093,548.00
U. S. cert's of deposit					
5 % fund with Treas	290,637.01	291,160.00	278,260.00	312,710.00	345,316.00
Due from U. S. Treas	52,000.00	36,425.00	39,460.00	55,610.00	14,892.00
Total	79,616,966.77	79,273,200.68	78,222,446.14	76,750,329.33	72,088,375.42

CITY OF BOSTON.

	55 banks.	55 banks.	55 banks.	55 banks.	55 banks.
Loans and discounts	$150,644,052.30	$146,261,894.53	$142,975,348.30	$137,484,411.89	$136,708,614.88
Bonds for circulation	5,910,000.00	6,535,000.00	6,935,000.00	7,595,000.00	10,565,000.00
Bonds for deposits	265,000.00	265,000.00	265,000.00	265,000.00	265,000.00
U. S. bonds on hand	100,800.00	100,800.00	100,800.00	210,800.00	115,000.00
Other stocks and b'ds	5,697,095.03	5,197,284.02	5,219,828.18	5,256,577.39	5,442,157.96
Due from res've ag'ts	20,536,331.09	17,712,418.65	17,604,709.24	15,704,363.79	18,194,703.43
Due from nat'l banks	16,180,779.20	15,270,837.70	15,416,859.56	16,968,628.90	14,592,589.50
Due from State banks	806,016.67	474,709.94	786,115.78	1,135,439.03	684,991.85
Banking house, etc	2,739,433.21	2,736,690.31	2,755,824.45	2,740,125.04	2,734,029.46
Real estate, etc	210,221.99	210,306.27	230,197.07	303,321.87	368,612.09
Current expenses	546,825.86	1,210,532.65	216,114.46	584,581.01	30,683.00
Premiums paid	632,472.14	683,633.14	694,287.39	735,594.95	601,466.09
Cash items	370,412.57	327,244.33	344,184.23	398,920.07	456,168.43
Clear'g house exch'gs	9,688,835.09	9,236,845.08	10,589,966.46	11,088,003.37	12,285,296.63
Bills of other banks	834,782.00	586,816.00	728,692.00	785,306.00	911,327.00
Fractional currency	17,173.82	17,250.83	18,784.17	19,788.24	22,825.55
Specie	11,077,782.41	10,524,436.80	6,857,178.31	7,300,644.88	9,952,788.60
Legal-tender notes	5,204,428.00	3,483,404.00	7,222,102.00	5,398,007.00	5,527,759.00
U S cert's of deposit	645,000.00	455,000.00	305,000.00	170,000.00	880,000.00
5% fund with Treas	265,047.50	288,150.00	312,075.00	326,925.00	474,605.00
Due from U. S. Treas	157,000.00	86,150.00	167,681.00	92,530.00	59,600.00
Total	232,530,398.88	221,673,414.25	219,226,054.60	214,564,888.34	221,262,939.40

RHODE ISLAND.

	59 banks.	59 banks.	59 banks.	59 banks.	59 banks.
Loans and discounts	$30,726,317.46	$37,497,890.12	$37,150,849.42	$35,809,738.33	$34,061,368.34
Bonds for circulation	6,402,250.00	6,656,750.00	6,740,750.00	7,116,750.00	7,721,250.00
Bonds for deposits	100,000.00	100,000.00	100,000.00	100,000.00	100,000.00
U. S. bonds on hand	50.00	50.00	11,050.00	9,050.00	
Other stocks and b'ds	2,426,619.10	2,422,458.54	2,450,310.94	2,503,948.05	2,388,380.39
Due from res've ag'ts	2,667,207.37	2,598,308.66	2,397,901.42	3,538,707.35	3,429,881.40
Due from nat'l banks	1,200,118.25	853,218.29	1,220,628.87	1,079,254.82	958,259.91
Due from State banks	45,923.80	58,201.41	76,375.82	171,637.08	57,527.32
Banking house, etc	919,012.44	960,391.86	1,014,167.61	1,017,334.13	1,021,085.42
Real estate, etc	273,999.14	267,556.51	202,922.89	200,083.97	204,343.36
Current expenses	144,571.06	119,698.23	117,362.25	68,079.63	108,416.26
Premiums paid	668,940.43	643,149.55	676,133.21	641,247.41	709,157.32
Cash items	197,083.65	154,821.83	145,901.92	160,484.82	156,980.73
Clear'g house exch'gs	617,817.87	450,168.44	509,557.81	273,243.78	295,011.91
Bills of other banks	382,282.00	239,880.00	302,074.00	325,047.00	254,871.00
Fractional currency	13,002.90	13,083.01	14,635.46	14,965.23	27,278.22
Specie	1,016,093.46	1,031,205.43	1,036,634.33	1,052,084.90	1,195,466.80
Legal-tender notes	605,289.00	546,228.00	521,319.00	590,978.00	565,790.00
U. S. cert's of deposit					
5% fund with Treas	283,426.10	287,583.25	296,313.75	316,438.75	344,761.25
Due from U. S. Treas	42,482.50	21,584.85	24,202.50	28,631.60	23,524.00
Total	54,883,686.53	54,932,209.88	51,817,581.20	55,017,707.85	53,611,203.66

PENNSYLVANIA.

Liabilities.	DECEMBER 9.	MARCH 6	MAY 4.	JULY 12.	OCTOBER 3.
	308 banks.	313 banks.	318 banks.	325 banks.	326 banks.
Capital stock	$37,822,300.00	$38,088,390.00	$38,503,390.00	$38,918,213.00	$39,103,900.00
Surplus fund	16,657,456.05	17,080,381.81	17,268,980.16	17,590,069.87	17,566,355.86
Undivided profits	5,101,488.32	4,919,372.34	5,094,641.24	4,261,671.76	5,553,923.50
Nat'l-bank circulation	10,874,220.00	11,063,267.50	11,262,855.00	11,753,150.00	13,426,260.00
State-bank circulation	643.00	1,543.00	1,543.00	1,543.00	1,543.00
Dividends unpaid	210,318.53	169,944.47	460,085.96	387,414.33	159,811.39
Individual deposits	108,154,546.17	109,859,317.65	113,772,281.83	105,935,847.86	99,037,065.94
U. S. deposits	261,618.77	261,572.46	261,098.24	267,445.05	282,020.61
Dep'ts U.S.dis.officers	9,035.54	8,238.53	10,320.24	7,195.76	15,481.48
Due to national banks	4,683,398.09	3,036,379.50	3,403,186.14	4,167,646.60	2,051,747.60
Due to State banks	660,609.05	614,381.34	619,758.85	683,295.22	576,571.67
Notes rediscounted	207,377.34	205,461.27	255,810.25	963,093.61	987,188.65
Bills payable	205,890.28	407,662.96	588,576.30	690,533.00	639,551.92
Other liabilities	46,930.61	98,174.25	97,712.98	38,712.27	91,795.77
Total	184,896,911.79	185,013,087.08	191,600,240.19	185,665,830.73	179,493,877.39

CITY OF PHILADELPHIA.

	41 banks.	41 banks.	41 banks.	41 banks.	41 banks.
Capital stock	$22,465,000.00	$22,765,000.00	$22,765,000.00	$22,765,000.00	$22,765,000.00
Surplus fund	14,060,303.08	14,100,303.08	14,281,303.08	14,301,303.08	14,281,303.08
Undivided profits	2,396,689.52	3,128,611.85	2,239,632.88	2,633,501.88	3,719,579.98
Nat'l-bank circulation	3,704,480.00	3,699,440.00	3,684,480.00	3,907,510.00	6,011,390.00
State-bank circulation					
Dividends unpaid	72,287.96	41,297.51	393,220.81	93,806.56	38,885.81
Individual deposits	94,660,991.37	90,303,722.33	95,400,471.35	89,042,091.90	84,688,009.64
U. S. deposits	174,002.24	179,452.75	163,714.40	182,353.53	191,115.00
Dep'ts U.S.dis.officers					
Due to national banks	18,271,060.04	17,714,191.60	17,951,864.49	17,962,259.80	17,707,233.75
Due to State banks	5,979,112.68	5,356,861.03	4,839,749.67	4,278,876.16	4,436,724.70
Notes rediscounted	200,000.00			50,000.00	
Bills payable		350,000.00	410,000.00	335,000.00	125,000.00
Other liabilities	100,000.00	100,000.00	100,000.00	5,485,000.00	6,160,000.00
Total	162,088,926.89	157,744,880.21	162,318,336.68	161,036,795.91	160,124,241.96

CITY OF PITTSBURGH.

	59 banks.	59 banks.	59 banks.	59 banks.	59 banks.
Capital stock	$20,277,050.00	$20,277,050.00	$20,277,050.00	$20,277,050.00	$20,277,050.00
Surplus fund	4,698,192.64	4,810,996.45	4,822,567.05	5,090,833.43	5,140,120.03
Undivided profits	2,007,152.08	1,852,423.12	1,871,551.89	1,508,029.58	1,620,283.05
Nat'l-bank circulation	5,581,062.00	5,891,307.50	5,978,542.50	6,303,070.00	6,893,120.00
State-bank circulation					
Dividends unpaid	79,711.09	80,214.44	124,113.39	141,075.99	130,788.67
Individual deposits	17,344,977.80	18,438,061.15	17,718,691.88	17,499,316.72	16,780,164.97
U. S. deposits	22,895.41	36,397.92	61,264.85	61,593.83	51,746.40
Dep'ts U.S.dis.officers	59,193.60	20,843.52	21,094.61	13,086.09	39,337.00
Due to national banks	3,071,317.72	1,710,141.34	1,874,139.12	1,931,879.30	1,295,815.84
Due to State banks	1,652,134.13	1,420,784.44	1,756,754.48	2,047,120.87	1,200,290.64
Notes rediscounted	10,000.00		10,000.00		164,978.06
Bills payable		100,000.00	153,000.00	127,000.00	17,500.00
Other liabilities	80,000.00	285,000.00	148,808.43	18,662.04	
Total	54,883,686.53	54,632,209.88	54,817,581.20	55,017,707.85	53,611,203.66

ABSTRACT OF REPORTS SINCE SEPTEMBER 30, 1892, ARRANGED

DELAWARE.

Resources.	DECEMBER 9. 18 banks.	MARCH 6. 18 banks.	MAY 4. 18 banks.	JULY 12. 18 banks.	OCTOBER 3. 18 banks.
Loans and discounts.	$5,997,006.19	$5,863,652.60	$5,823,030.24	$5,488,511.92	$5,436,125.41
Bonds for circulation	740,000.00	740,000.00	760,000.00	770,000.00	926,000.00
Bonds for deposits ..	50,000.00	50,000.00	50,000.00	50,000.00	50,000.00
U. S. bonds on hand .		20,000.00			6,000.00
Other stocks and b'ds	509,800.37	491,847.12	502,857.12	478,826.26	450,994.46
Due from res've ag'ts	711,519.28	649,013.30	528,205.84	673,673.06	738,344.47
Due from nat'l banks	211,677.43	140,792.72	107,270.82	152,112.74	158,404.74
Due from State banks	02,873.04	47,644.10	57,946.10	85,422.26	66,742.39
Banking house, otc..	322,839.18	321,839.18	321,839.18	319,839.18	318,839.18
Real estate, etc	51,015.13	52,417.20	53,180.26	48,667.96	52,987.98
Current expenses ...	47,707.88	25,684.82	36,415.74	9,973.56	35,915.70
Premiums paid......	59,864.00	57,686.98	57,561.98	55,230.98	68,690.00
Cash items	43,113.27	60,227.46	60,454.54	60,511.17	39,226.87
Clear'g house exch'gs	33,378.93	40,601.52	34,461.47	73,506.47	69,716.11
Bills of other banks .	38,412.00	28,997.00	31,191.00	30,278.00	42,719.00
Fractional currency .	4,686.90	5,955.72	6,874.32	6,143.09	6,106.92
Specie	308,982.86	326,817.14	353,874.60	313,690.73	415,170.77
Legal-tender notes ..	162,341.00	152,945.00	142,546.00	155,616.00	202,615.00
U. S. cert's of deposit.					
5 % fund with Treas.	33,203.42	32,650.00	33,100.00	33,760.00	41,620.00
Due from U. S. Treas.	16,500.00	2,050.00	13,000.00		2,170.00
Total............	9,435,820.58	9,123,211.05	8,974,109.21	8,823,778.38	9,137,389.00

MARYLAND.

	44 banks.	44 banks.	44 banks.	46 banks.	46 banks.
Loans and discounts	$10,077,269.94	$10,157,258.77	$10,550,613.12	$10,575,262.90	$10,186,9.0.42
Bonds for circulation	1,561,000.00	1,561,000.00	1,561,000.00	1,608,500.00	1,710,500.00
Bonds for deposits ..	50,000.00	50,000.00	50,000.00	50,000.00	50,000.00
U. S. bonds on hand..	10,500.00	10,500.00	10,500.00	10,500.00	5,500.00
Other stocks and b'ds	1,509,250.90	1,505,554.26	1,505,356.43	1,482,432.81	1,470,516.19
Due from res'vo ag'ts	1,248,004.72	1,292,772.46	974,561.97	1,088,603.89	1,215,004.37
Due from nat'l banks	410,058.16	371,240.49	346,452.58	441,593.45	405,029.71
Due from State banks	107,145.14	108,900.12	85,563.12	74,342.24	54,775.21
Banking house, etc..	541,606.03	523,308.29	528,147.96	531,558.18	538,962.03
Real estate, otc	40,514.28	51,463.19	51,963.19	52,463.19	52,563.19
Current expenses....	97,118.26	52,227.31	81,195.42	32,570.26	91,463.64
Premiums paid	147,998.14	137,282.56	130,977.31	124,581.03	140,453.53
Cash items	60,180.15	62,532.12	55,787.65	80,361.64	71,432.50
Clear'g house exch'gs					
Bills of other banks..	44,510.00	48,680.00	51,120.00	52,764.60	65,893.00
Fractional currency.	6,896.84	9,067.87	7,301.78	9,011.50	7,984.74
Specie	702,049.26	683,758.70	675,062.99	659,172.96	715,875.77
Legal-tender notes ..	320,573.00	329,782.00	370,978.00	411,832.00	539,341.00
U. S. cert's of deposit.					
5 % fund with Treas.	66,411.16	68,133.43	66,527.25	66,272.25	72,095.93
Due from U. S. Treas.	3,220.00	11,070.00	4,046.18	1,406.18	1,160.00
Total..........	17,094,305.98	10,944,531.57	17,113,154.95	17,353,228.48	17,393,471.23

NEW PORT CITY.

Loans and discounts	48 banks.	48 banks.	49 banks.	49 banks.	49 banks.
Loans and discounts	$323,790,791.96	$323,445,104.33	$307,372,242.62	$308,646,934.40	$281,320,466.46
Bonds for circulation	7,015,000.00	7,170,000.00	7,220,050.00	7,904,000.00	18,148,500.00
Bonds for deposits ..	1,100,000.00	1,100,000.00	1,100,000.00	1,100,000.00	900,000.00
U. S. bonds on hand..	715,800.00	923,450.00	721,850.00	129,450.00	79,450.00
Other stocks and b'ds	27,531,053.76	29,400,137.46	28,813,211.92	28,188,857.47	28,349,305.68
Due from res've ag'ts					
Due from nat'l banks	36,530,655.94	28,020,315.56	30,571,378.64	27,647,998.09	23,845,425.11
Due from State banks	5,795,091.72	4,312,667.03	5,543,318.80	4,842,975.75	3,699,143.22
Banking house, etc..	11,410,726.14	11,391,405.58	11,365,822.70	11,400,789.57	11,444,322.52
Real estate, etc......	990,988.02	992,493.08	717,280.03	737,685.92	756,548.88
Current expenses....	1,856,741.71	772,038.17	1,211,479.61	200,702.05	1,360,021.04
Premiums paid......	586,255.70	615,300.00	547,718.68	431,088.13	1,144,421.01
Cash items	2,813,610.29	2,705,513.75	2,929,291.61	2,790,857.81	2,742,847.46
Clear'g-house exch'gs	69,831,089.87	85,931,623.71	74,391,728.84	65,403,779.13	57,499,566.72
Bills of other banks..	1,157,205.00	1,054,108.00	1,224,785.00	1,101,600.00	1,468,723.60
Fractional currency.	41,786.07	45,775.87	45,536.56	45,017.97	41,034.90
Specie	65,775,020.98	61,577,139.58	63,570,493.50	55,008,276.31	75,703,063.60
Legal-tender notes ..	28,587,057.00	24,282,810.00	29,336,199.00	19,741,077.00	31,082,821.00
U. S. cert's of deposit	2,520,000.00	8,655,000.00	5,180,000.00	1,970,000.00	1,420,000.00
5 % fund with Treas.	301,060.00	312,650.00	313,650.00	312,870.00	811,112.00
Due from U. S. Treas.	331,404.56	463,408.10	582,224.64	353,777.09	654,882.68
Total..........	589,021,851.72	593,323,917.37	572,758,212.24	538,037,745.09	512,531,655.01

DELAWARE.

Liabilities.	DECEMBER 9. 18 banks.	MARCH 6. 18 banks.	MAY 4. 18 banks.	JULY 12. 18 banks.	OCTOBER 3. 18 banks.
Capital stock	$2,133,985.00	$2,133,985.00	$2,133,985.00	$2,133,985.00	$2,133,985.00
Surplus fund	963,600.47	947,150.47	947,100.47	953,050.47	953,050.47
Undivided profits	339,071.90	245,614.00	281,080.23	216,657.35	279,356.94
Nat'l-bank circulation	657,172.50	655,302.50	674,052.50	686,882.50	822,992.50
State-bank circulation	570.50	570.50	570.50	567.50	567.50
Dividends unpaid	8,573.22	11,721.69	14,064.05	28,829.66	6,977.18
Individual deposits	4,738,203.41	4,640,077.44	4,496,819.09	4,397,371.36	4,602,939.10
U. S. deposits	27,274.23	28,430.49	20,516.49	24,317.67	25,516.42
Dep'ts U.S.dis.officers	11,776.64	10,492.68	17,067.73	15,585.23	19,188.88
Due to national banks	466,459.16	318,707.64	301,411.04	290,610.56	223,099.51
Due to State banks	62,913.10	6,888.01	13,100.94	9,081.73	9,014.50
Notes rediscounted	16,220.75	16,994.46	39,291.17	25,939.36	4,800.00
Bills payable	10,000.00	105,000.00	35,000.00	40,000.00	53,000.00
Other liabilities		2,277.07			
Total	9,435,820.88	9,123,211.05	8,974,109.21	8,823,778.38	9,137,389.00

MARYLAND.

	41 banks.	44 banks.	44 banks.	46 banks.	46 banks.
Capital stock	$3,596,700.00	$3,611,700.00	$3,611,700.00	$3,692,029.00	$3,724,320.00
Surplus fund	1,315,126.98	1,345,771.98	1,345,771.98	1,377,050.00	1,377,350.00
Undivided profits	516,665.87	424,353.68	520,455.84	374,711.73	490,344.52
Nat'l-bank circulation	1,329,100.00	1,317,995.00	1,323,900.00	1,365,920.00	1,474,480.00
State-bank circulation					
Dividends unpaid	26,068.56	18,658.60	18,877.93	47,751.95	26,107.81
Individual deposits	9,688,737.19	9,702,681.61	9,623,598.90	9,553,629.37	9,602,618.33
U. S. deposits	40,000.00	40,000.00	40,000.00	40,000.00	50,000.00
Dep'ts U.S.dis.officers					
Due to national banks	428,352.71	324,584.73	328,182.84	516,339.38	411,727.97
Due to State banks	55,056.68	57,720.67	63,086.61	54,200.82	76,393.19
Notes rediscounted	63,137.99	71,065.30	112,5o0.85	112,097.23	67,919.13
Bills payable	35,000.00	30,000.00	95,000.00	219,500.00	62,000.00
Other liabilities					120.28
Total	17,094,305.98	16,944,531.57	17,113,154.95	17,353,228.48	17,393,471.13

NEW YORK CITY.

	48 banks.	48 banks.	49 banks.	49 banks.	49 banks.
Capital stock	$49,650,000.00	$49,650,000.00	$49,810,000.00	$50,733,500.00	$51,250,000.00
Surplus fund	40,547,592.52	40,931,961.14	41,272,839.14	41,493,774.61	41,533,247.45
Undivided profits	17,952,257.39	17,355,332.59	18,675,919.62	16,859,915.51	18,784,747.55
Nat'l-bank circulation	5,870,920.00	6,007,230.00	6,070,115.00	6,468,467.50	15,818,057.50
State-bank circulation	21,328.00	24,328.00	24,328.00	24,328.00	24,325.00
Dividends unpaid	140,205.16	175,022.45	223,383.24	330,983.20	230,591.22
Individual deposits	284,145,409.91	284,898,689.33	286,985,310.15	246,736,850.53	249,606,107.06
U. S. deposits	686,899.91	685,893.40	589,694.03	586,068.17	690,687.58
Dept's U.S.dis.officers	302,200.13	178,462.02	463,917.01	346,547.43	100,216.41
Due to national banks	133,221,649.46	137,046,455.27	114,634,512.25	106,882,507.91	100,751,310.93
Due to State banks	56,474,380.24	56,371,164.17	53,849,193.80	48,624,710.50	45,105,498.72
Notes rediscounted			100,000.00		
Bills payable			50,000.00		
Other liabilities				18,041,032.70	18,636,865.59
Total	589,021,851.72	593,323,047.37	572,758,212.24	538,037,745.09	542,531,655.01

ABSTRACT OF REPORTS SINCE SEPTEMBER 30, 1892, ARRANGED

DISTRICT OF COLUMBIA.

Resources.	DECEMBER 9. 1 bank.	MARCH 6. 1 bank.	MAY 4. 1 bank.	JULY 12. 1 bank.	OCTOBER 3. 1 bank.
Loans and discounts	$700,585.66	$655,352.07	$640,058.71	$685,799.43	$524,290.04
Bonds for circulation	250,000.00	250,000.00	250,000.00	250,000.00	250,000.00
Bonds for deposits					
U. S. bonds on hand	1,200.00	1,200.00	1,200.00	1,200.00	1,200.00
Other stocks and b'ds	199,292.50	199,292.50	199,292.50	199,292.50	199,292.50
Due from res've ag'ts	48,313.68	139,331.17	49,578.78	71,981.76	79,305.91
Due from nat'l banks	31,052.73	19,962.65	24,105.59	9,077.93	18,885.70
Due from State banks	393.85		2.25	311.76	
Banking house, etc	23,000.00	23,000.00	23,000.00	23,000.00	23,000.00
Real estate, etc					
Current expenses	7,756.47	3,974.96	6,842.62	155.88	4,521.33
Premiums paid	9,000.00	4,000.00	4,000.00		
Cash items	11,525.01	8,882.09	11,756.11	8,393.38	11,385.79
Clear'g-house exch'gs					
Bills of other banks	2,285.00	5,000.00	4,000.00	770.00	1,400.00
Fractional currency	47.14	107.11	76.73	181.67	143.71
Specie	256,162.00	242,068.50	298,026.25	237,431.70	237,627.50
Legal-tender notes	16,010.00	58,494.00	35,561.00	31,790.00	53,253.00
U. S. cert's of deposit					
5 % fund with Treas.	11,250.00	11,250.00	11,250.00	11,250.00	11,250.00
Due from U. S. Treas					
Total	1,569,874.04	1,621,915.05	1,558,750.54	1,530,635.31	1,415,645.48

CITY OF WASHINGTON.

	12 banks.	12 banks.	12 banks.	12 banks.	12 banks.
Loans and discounts	$8,153,131.70	$7,691,356.88	$7,036,111.23	$7,316,524.04	$6,027,825.53
Bonds for circulation	650,000.00	650,000.00	650,000.00	705,400.00	905,400.00
Bonds for deposits	100,000.00	100,000.00	100,000.00	100,000.00	100,000.00
U. S. bonds on hand	266,600.00	261,900.00	274,700.00	140,350.00	118,350.00
Other stocks and b'ds	755,895.09	745,021.72	860,773.83	805,573.37	791,241.26
Due from res've ag'ts	767,488.53	1,347,321.99	745,122.92	656,475.92	453,079.07
Due from nat'l banks	553,069.88	632,164.26	683,556.92	345,622.25	290,145.67
Due from State banks	20,271.78	30,280.30	21,216.76	17,411.23	24,700.34
Banking house, etc	1,005,676.32	1,003,060.67	1,063,748.04	1,061,821.54	1,061,821.54
Real estate, etc	8,300.00	7,900.00	7,950.00	7,300.00	17,100.00
Current expenses	102,225.87	49,820.62	86,496.83	14,057.68	57,347.79
Premiums paid	64,485.51	111,552.98	59,189.92	109,518.40	52,428.01
Cash items	101,107.07	253,857.10	182,723.89	138,282.12	133,857.36
Clear'g-house exch'gs	188,073.78	218,874.10	303,371.54	156,420.12	151,753.83
Bills of other banks	37,533.00	51,337.00	23,885.00	26,155.00	38,386.00
Fractional currency	11,216.70	8,199.52	9,350.77	8,502.73	7,886.58
Specie	1,575,831.30	1,835,255.30	1,896,677.10	1,518,656.50	1,393,848.40
Legal-tender notes	749,742.00	870,826.00	833,995.00	359,497.00	965,029.00
U.S. cert's of deposit		10,000.00	100,000.00	190,000.00	260,000.00
5 % fund with Treas.	27,000.00	26,000.00	27,000.00	26,500.00	38,489.50
Due from U. S. Treas.	2,362.00	4,780.00	1,501.00	1,672.00	4,591.52
Total	15,290,014.03	15,960,508.44	15,867,364.74	13,609,440.89	12,921,323.40

NEW JERSEY.

	98 banks.	98 banks.	99 banks.	99 banks.	99 banks.
Loans and discounts	$53,290,539.17	$52,888,382.31	$54,550,825.97	$51,475,570.04	$47,341,415.30
Bonds for circulation	4,319,750.00	4,369,750.00	4,382,250.00	4,797,250.00	5,237,250.00
Bonds for deposits	275,000.00	275,000.00	275,000.00	275,000.00	275,000.00
U. S. bonds on hand	51,300.00	51,000.00	51,000.00	21,000.00	1,000.00
Other stocks and b'ds	7,034,821.17	7,695,207.66	7,409,905.72	7,333,628.69	7,702,811.73
Due from res've ag'ts	7,907,122.45	8,100,293.07	6,851,372.53	6,858,141.77	8,252,903.23
Due from nat'l banks	2,380,052.87	2,023,968.78	2,269,286.84	2,386,550.17	1,707,111.42
Due from State banks	515,968.84	408,792.71	398,612.87	485,212.65	397,054.27
Banking house, etc	2,541,933.19	2,551,903.95	2,556,576.21	2,574,557.72	2,598,828.94
Real estate, etc	360,071.33	383,053.21	381,311.38	374,813.18	360,208.93
Current expenses	388,261.01	242,815.96	286,313.22	112,702.93	222,083.17
Premiums paid	332,882.71	311,902.87	300,536.87	205,985.93	321,022.25
Cash items	1,055,988.05	1,822,462.25	1,062,930.34	1,448,350.51	712,360.69
Clear'g-house exch'gs					417,918.59
Bills of other banks	361,937.00	377,311.00	406,555.00	376,785.00	431,652.00
Fractional currency	37,739.91	40,055.12	38,351.68	37,568.90	42,465.83
Specie	2,550,477.46	2,595,775.06	2,826,960.13	2,818,283.04	3,229,653.65
Legal-tender notes	2,360,870.00	2,395,671.00	2,440,128.00	2,583,961.00	2,400,670.00
U.S. cert's of deposit	10,000.00	10,000.00	10,000.00	10,000.00	10,000.00
5 % fund with Treas.	187,969.36	193,476.25	189,128.25	200,463.03	229,260.03
Due from U.S. Treas	24,220.00	23,579.78	17,359.78	17,310.00	8,820.50
Total	86,018,091.05	86,760,550.98	86,704,224.69	84,513,224.56	82,049,490.53

BY STATES AND RESERVE CITIES—Continued.

DISTRICT OF COLUMBIA.

Liabilities.	DECEMBER 9. 1 bank.	MARCH 6. 1 bank.	MAY 4. 1 bank.	JULY 12. 1 bank.	OCTOBER 3. 1 bank.
Capital stock	$252,000.00	$252,000.00	$252,000.00	$252,000.00	$252,000.00
Surplus fund	100,000 00	100,000.00	100,000.00	100,000.00	100,000.00
Undivided profits	78,441.47	68,911.38	81,496.45	68,564.31	70,309.76
Nat'l-bank circulation	197,800.00	182,200.00	179,750.00	192,200.00	223,500.00
State-bank circulation					
Dividends unpaid	3,740.00	4,136.00	4,000.00	5,348.00	4,272.00
Individual deposits	926,769.85	691,355.58	932,590.38	889,146.83	742,192.20
U. S. deposits					
Dep'ts U.S.dis.officers					
Due to national banks	11,122.72	22,519.89	9,003.71	23,376.17	14,268.04
Due to State banks		792.20			103.48
Notes rediscounted					
Bills payable					
Other liabilities					
Total	1,569,874.04	1,621,915.05	1,558,750.54	1,530,635.31	1,415,645.48

CITY OF WASHINGTON.

	12 banks.	12 banks.	12 banks.	12 banks.	12 banks.
Capital stock	$2,575,000.00	$2,575,000.00	$2,575,000.00	$2,575,000.00	$2,575,000.00
Surplus fund	1,192,000.00	1,285,000.00	1,285,000.00	1,295,000.00	1,305,000.00
Undivided profits	341,435.98	186,356.20	275,980.19	189,071.12	235,568.88
Nat'l-bank circulation	524,675.00	522,855.00	512,695.00	535,275.00	703,765.00
State-bank circulation					
Dividends unpaid	2,909.50	3,390.50	2,603.00	8,051.50	4,608.00
Individual deposits	10,148,679.54	10,909,229.26	10,722,476.73	8,514,860.89	7,431,693.42
U. S. deposits	77,102.55	85,654.69	89,014.56	75,975.39	90,119.71
Dep'ts U.S.dis.officers					
Due to national banks	336,048.58	293,766.21	314,596.98	321,127.71	316,926.02
Due to State banks	52,162.88	68,256.58	54,098.28	44,671.48	95,979.77
Notes rediscounted				105,407.80	11,630.00
Bills payable	40,000.00	40,000.00	35,000.00	35,000.00	85,000.00
Other liabilities					
Total	15,290,014.03	15,969,508.44	15,867,364.74	13,699,440.80	12,921,323.40

NEW JERSEY.

	98 banks.	98 banks.	99 banks.	99 banks.	99 banks.
Capital stock	$14,568,350.00	$14,568,350.00	$14,588,350.00	$14,603,350.00	$14,608,350.00
Surplus fund	7,083,150.00	7,243,238.00	7,285,096.61	7,421,766.61	7,417,266.61
Undivided profits	3,990,427.22	3,578,062.79	3,787,617.30	3,407,431.34	3,585,766.99
Nat'l-bank circulation	3,825,367.00	3,849,192.00	3,872,274.50	4,224,669.50	4,598,549.50
State-bank circulation	7,827.00	7,827.00	7,827.00	7,827.00	7,827.00
Dividends unpaid	39,541.63	49,936.24	48,871.11	132,123.78	123,645.43
Individual deposits	51,560,849.80	52,934,412.30	51,761,098.49	49,250,358.26	47,375,320.49
U. S. deposits	159,623.28	140,779.32	166,892.04	172,253.01	231,021.06
Dep't's U.S.dis.officers	77,660.39	85,508.60	73,346.03	68,745.18	43,565.77
Due to national banks	4,290,399.17	3,330,272.38	3,856,081.66	3,771,541.64	2,920,597.48
Due to State banks	684,961.55	569,741.37	742,667.71	535,720.49	418,794.42
Notes rediscounted	306,937.01	117,140.98	229,102.24	323,360.98	128,785.78
Bills payable	313,000.00	276,000.00	275,000.00	582,015.62	560,000.00
Other liabilities	10,000.00	10,000.00	10,000.00	11,152.16	
Total	86,918,094.05	86,760,650.98	86,704,221.09	84,513,224.56	82,049,400.53

ABSTRACT OF REPORTS SINCE SEPTEMBER 30, 1892, ARRANGED

DELAWARE.

Resources.	DECEMBER 9. 18 banks.	MARCH 6. 18 banks.	MAY 4. 18 banks.	JULY 12. 18 banks.	OCTOBER 3. 18 banks.
Loans and discounts.	$5,997,006.19	$5,863,652.60	$5,823,030.24	$5,488,511.92	$5,436,125.41
Bonds for circulation	740,000.00	740,000.00	760,000.00	770,000.00	926,000.00
Bonds for deposits ..	50,000.00	50,000.00	50,000.00	50,000.00	50,000.00
U. S. bonds on hand		20,000.00			6,000.00
Other stocks and b'ds	509,800.37	491,847.12	602,857.12	478,820.26	459,994.46
Due from res've ag'ts	711,519.28	649,013.30	528,205.84	673,673.06	738,344 47
Due from nat'l banks	211,677.43	140,792.72	107,270.82	152,112.74	158,404 74
Due from State banks	92,873.04	47,644.10	57,946.10	85,422.26	66,742.39
Banking house, etc..	322,839.18	321,839.18	321,839.18	319,839.18	318,839.18
Real estate, etc......	51,915 13	52,417.29	53,180.26	48,667.96	52,987.98
Current expenses ...	47,707.88	25,684.82	36,415.74	9,973.56	35,915.70
Premiums paid......	59,864.00	57,686.98	57,561.98	55,236.98	68,690.00
Cash items	43,113.27	69,227.46	60,454.54	69,511.17	39,226.87
Clear'g house exch'gs	33,378.93	40,991.52	34,461.47	73,506.47	69,716.11
Bills of other banks .	38,412.00	28,997.00	31,191.00	39,278.00	42,719.00
Fractional currency .	4,686.90	3,955.72	6,874.32	6,143.09	6,106.92
Specie	308,982.86	326,817.14	353,874.60	313,609.73	415,170.77
Legal-tender notes ..	162,341.00	152,045.00	142,546.00	155,616.00	202,615.00
U. S. cert's of deposit.					
5 % fund with Treas.	33,203.43	32,650.00	33,100.00	33,760.00	41,620.00
Due from U. S. Treas.	16,500.00	2,050.00	13,000.00		2,170.00
Total.............	9,435,820.88	9,123.211.95	8,974,109.21	8,823,778.38	9,137,389.00

MARYLAND.

	44 banks.	44 banks.	44 banks.	46 banks.	46 banks.
Loans and discounts	$10,077,269.94	$10,157,218.77	$10,550,613.12	$10,575,262.90	$10,186,9'0.42
Bonds for circulation	1,561,000.00	1,561,000.00	1,561,000.00	1,608,500.00	1,710,500.00
Bonds for deposits ..	50,000.00	50,000.00	50,000.00	50,000.00	50,000.00
U. S. bonds on band..	10,500.00	10,500.00	10,500.00	10,500.00	5,500.00
Other stocks and b'ds	1,599,250.90	1,505,554.26	1,505,356.43	1,482,432.81	1,470,516.19
Due from res've ag'ts	1,248,004.72	1,202,772.46	974,561.97	1,084,003.89	1,215,004.37
Due from nat'l banks	410,058.16	371,240.49	346,452.58	441,593.45	405,020.71
Due from State banks	107,145.14	108,900.12	85,563.12	74,342.24	54,775.21
Banking house, etc..	541,606.03	523,308.29	528,147.96	531,558.18	538,962.03
Real estate, etc......	40,514.28	51,463.19	51,963.19	52,463.19	52,563.19
Current expenses....	97,118.26	52,227.31	81,195.42	32,570.26	91,463.64
Premiums paid......	147,998.14	137,982.56	136,977.31	124,581.03	140,453.83
Cash items	60,180.15	62,582.12	55,787.65	80,361.64	71,432.50
Clear'g house oxcb'gs					
Bills of other banks..	44,510.00	48,680.00	51,120.00	52,764.00	62,893.00
Fractional currency.	6,896.84	9,067.87	7,301.78	9,011.50	7,084.74
Specie	702,040.26	683,758.70	675,062.99	639,172.96	715,875.77
Legal-tender notes ..	320,573.00	329,782.00	370,978.00	411,832.00	539,341.00
U. S. cert's of deposit.					
5 % fund with Treas.	66,411.16	68,133.43	66,527.25	66,272.25	72,095.93
Due from U. S. Treas.	3,220.00	11,070.00	4,046.18	1,406.18	1,160.00
Total............	17,094,305.98	16,944,531.57	17,113,154.96	17,353,228.48	17,393,471.23

CITY OF BALTIMORE.

	26 banks.	26 banks.	27 banks.	29 banks.	29 banks.
Loans and discounts	$40,333,196.26	$38,780,251.60	$41,561,952.06	$39,924,226.27	$35,966,478.37
Bonds for circulation	1,780,000.00	1,780,000.00	2,188,500.00	2,588,500.00	3,226,500.00
Bonds for deposits ..	250,000.00	250,000.00	250,000.00	250,000.00	250,000.00
U. S. bonds on hand..	150.00			1,500.00	5,500.00
Other stocks and b'ds	2,067,571.95	1,770,678.32	1,685,143.72	1,473,970.42	1,392,428.48
Due from res've ag'ts	3,151,428.36	4,279,722.01	3,090,237.40	2,673,827.15	2,474,891.37
Due from nat'l banks.	1,251,286.64	1,303,477.47	1,576,211.01	1,383,735.36	1,408,420.19
Due from State banks	297,419.48	285,513.08	301,851.80	327,512.87	230,383.18
Banking house, etc..	2,636,730.16	2,660,648.26	2,732,375.48	2,801,350.81	2,881,520.19
Real estate, etc......	907,556.72	958,401.71	923,675.63	936,249.13	910,069.85
Current expenses....	178,487.53	207,586.81	170,210.36	71,226.75	252,874.25
Premiums paid	166,444.62	151,181.76	197,574.26	206,310.26	262,542.91
Cash items	185,094.75	176,044.30	201,256.60	247,843.07	189,366.62
Clear'g-house exch'gs	1,640,022.04	1,478,421.24	2,075,533.11	1,571,775.76	2,330,832.83
Bills of other banks..	282,476.00	182,995.00	256,001.00	208,035.00	233,216.00
Fractional currency .	16,437.67	17,592.77	17,141.97	16,180.89	23,320.11
Specie	3,703,144.75	4,207,670.52	4,178,872.41	3,629,098.04	4,012,840.34
Legal-tender notes ..	2,340,583.00	1,897,853.00	2,558,376.00	1,624,904.00	1,933,206.00
U. S. cert's of deposit.					
5 % fund with Treas.	80,075.00	80,675.00	91,320.00	91,917.50	134,342.43
Due from U. S. Treas.	11,000.00	18,050.00	21,000.00	15,150.00	1,245.00
Total............	61,279,104.93	60,486,165.85	64,083,232.90	60,043,320.28	58,209,990.12

DELAWARE.

Liabilities.	DECEMBER 9. 18 banks.	MARCH 6. 18 banks.	MAY 4. 18 banks.	JULY 12. 18 banks.	OCTOBER 3. 18 banks.
Capital stock	$2, 133, 985. 00	$2, 133, 985. 00	$2, 133, 985. 00	$2, 133, 985. 00	$2, 133, 985. 00
Surplus fund.........	963, 600. 47	947, 150. 47	947, 160. 47	953, 950. 47	953, 950. 47
Undivided profits....	339, 071. 90	245, 614. 00	281, 080. 23	216, 657. 35	279, 356. 94
Nat'l-bank circulation	657, 172. 50	655, 302. 50	674. 052. 50	686, 882. 50	822, 992. 50
State-bank circulation,	570. 50	570. 50	570. 50	567. 50	567. 50
Dividends unpaid....	8, 573. 22	11, 721. 69	14, 064. 05	28, 820. 66	6, 977. 18
Individual deposits ..	4, 738, 203. 41	4, 640, 077. 44	4, 496, 819. 09	4, 397, 371. 36	4, 602, 939. 10
U. S. deposits	27, 274. 23	28, 430. 49	20, 516. 40	24, 317. 67	25, 516. 42
Dep'ts U.S.dis.officers	11, 776. 64	10, 492. 68	17, 067. 73	15, 585. 23	10, 188, 18
Due to national banks	466, 459. 16	318, 707. 64	301, 411. 04	290, 610. 56	223, 699. 51
Due to State banks...	62, 913. 10	6, 888. 01	13, 100. 94	9, 081. 72	9, 014. 70
Notes rediscounted ..	16, 220. 75	16, 994. 46	39, 291. 17	25, 939. 36	4, 800. 00
Bills payable	10, 000. 00	105, 000. 00	35, 000. 00	40, 000. 00	55, 000. 00
Other liabilities......		2, 277. 07			
Total............	9, 435, 820. 88	9, 123, 211. 95	8, 974, 109. 21	8, 823, 778. 36	9, 137, 389. 00

MARYLAND.

	44 banks.	44 banks.	44 banks.	46 banks.	46 banks.
Capital stock	$3, 596, 700. 00	$3, 611, 700. 00	$3, 611, 700. 00	$3, 692, 029. 00	$3, 724, 320. 00
Surplus fund	1, 315, 126. 98	1, 345, 771. 98	1, 345, 771. 98	1, 377, 050. 00	1, 377, 350. 00
Undivided profits....	516, 695. 87	424, 353. 68	520, 455. 84	374, 711. 73	400, 344. 52
Nat'l-bank circulation	1, 329, 160. 00	1, 317, 995. 00	1, 323, 900. 00	1, 363, 920. 00	1, 474, 480. 00
State-bank circulation					
Dividends unpaid....	26, 068. 56	18, 658. 60	18, 677. 93	47, 751. 95	26, 197. 81
Individual deposits ..	9, 688, 737. 10	9, 702, 681. 61	9, 623, 598. 90	9, 553, 629. 37	9, 602, 618. 33
U. S. deposits........	40, 000. 00	40, 000. 00	40, 000. 00	40, 000. 00	50, 000. 00
Dep'ts U.S.dis.officers					
Due to national banks	428, 232. 71	324, 584 73	328, 182. 84	516, 338. 38	411, 727. 97
Due to State banks...	55, 056. 68	57, 720. 67	63, 086. 61	54, 200. 82	76, 393. 19
Notes rediscounted ..	63, 137. 99	71, 065. 30	112, 580. 85	112, 097. 23	67, 919. 13
Bills payable.........	35, 000. 00	30, 000. 00	95, 000. 00	219, 500. 00	62, 000. 00
Other liabilities......					120. 28
Total	17, 094, 305. 98	16, 944, 531. 57	17, 113, 154. 03	17, 353, 228. 48	17, 393, 471. 13

CITY OF BALTIMORE.

	26 banks.	26 banks.	27 banks.	29 banks.	29 banks.
Capital stock	$10, 900, 000. 00	$10, 900, 000. 00	$11, 100, 000. 00	$11, 460, 000. 00	$11, 640, 000. 00
Surplus fund.........	6, 653, 612. 19	7, 045, 612. 19	7, 165, 612. 19	7, 271, 330. 59	7, 287, 550. 50
Undivided profits....	1, 578, 504. 17	1, 283, 275. 31	1, 369, 102. 54	1, 176, 801. 46	1, 555, 053. 09
Nat'l-bank circulation	1, 547, 560. 00	1, 575, 310. 00	1, 955, 080. 00	2, 320, 340. 00	2, 897, 567. 50
State-bank circulation					
Dividends unpaid....	71, 969. 13	59, 874. 13	153, 781. 89	150, 510. 88	79, 045. 88
Individual deposits ..	33, 675, 222. 81	32, 622, 414. 92	35, 381, 954. 40	31, 008, 069. 40	29, 049, 573. 90
U. S. deposits........	182, 700. 76	228, 802. 17	235, 255. 91	190, 153. 23	132, 851. 03
Dep'ts U.S.dis.officers	77, 820. 39	39, 253. 19	33. 844. 99	72, 569. 66	202, 006. 25
Due to national banks	4, 336, 771. 74	4, 470, 058. 07	4, 423, 929. 70	3, 578, 111. 54	2, 948, 014. 38
Due to State banks...	2, 198, 437. 74	2, 237, 565. 87	2, 137, 989. 64	1, 426, 681. 62	1, 191, 432. 98
Notes rediscounted ..	56, 500. 00		101, 003. 56	1, 329, 742. 90	555, 974. 52
Bills payable.........		30, 000. 00	25, 000. 00	60, 000. 00	185, 000. 00
Other liabilities......					485, 000. 00
Total	61, 279, 104. 93	60, 486, 165. 85	64, 083, 232 00	60, 043, 320. 28	58, 209, 990. 12

ABSTRACT OF REPORTS SINCE SEPTEMBER 30, 1892, ARRANGED

DISTRICT OF COLUMBIA.

Resources.	DECEMBER 9. 1 bank.	MARCH 6. 1 bank.	MAY 4. 1 bank.	JULY 12. 1 bank.	OCTOBER 3. 1 bank.
Loans and discounts	$700,585.66	$655,352.07	$640,058.71	$685,799.43	$524,200.04
Bonds for circulation	250,000.00	250,000.00	250,000.00	250,000.00	250,000.00
Bonds for deposits					
U. S. bonds on hand..	1,200.00	1,200.00	1,200.00	1,200.00	1,200.00
Other stocks and b'ds	199,292.50	199,292.50	199,292.50	199,292.50	199,292.50
Due from res'v'e ag'ts	48,313.68	139,331.17	49,578.78	71,081.76	79,305.91
Due from nat'l banks	31,052.73	10,962.65	24,105.59	9,077.03	18,885.70
Due from State banks	393.85		2.25	311.76	
Banking house, etc..	23,000.60	23,000.00	23,000.00	23,000.00	23,000.00
Real estate, etc					
Current expenses....	7,756.47	3,974.96	6,842.62	155.88	4,521.33
Premiums paid	9,000.00	4,000.00	4,000.00		
Cash items	11,525.01	8,882.09	11,756.11	8,393.58	11,385.79
Clear'g house exch'gs					
Bills of other banks..	2,285.00	5,000.00	4,000.00	770.00	1,400.00
Fractional currency.	47.14	107.11	76.73	181.67	143.71
Specie	256,162.00	242,068.50	298,026.25	237,431.70	237,627.50
Legal-tender notes ..	18,010.00	58,494.00	35,561.00	31,790.00	53,253.00
U. S. cert's of deposit					
5% fund with Treas.	11,250.00	11,250.00	11,250.00	11,250.00	11,250.00
Due from U. S. Treas					
Total	1,569,874.04	1,621,915.05	1,558,750.54	1,530,635.31	1,415,645.48

CITY OF WASHINGTON.

	12 banks.	12 banks.	12 banks.	12 banks.	12 banks.
Loans and discounts.	$8,153,131.70	$7,691,356.68	$7,936,111.23	$7,316,524.04	$6,027,825.53
Bonds for circulation	650,000.00	650,000.00	650,000.00	705,400.00	905,400.00
Bonds for deposits...	100,000.00	100,000.00	100,000.00	100,000.00	100,000.00
U. S. bonds on hand..	266,600.00	261,900.00	274,700.00	140,350.00	118,350.00
Other stocks and b'ds	755,895.99	745,021.72	860,773.83	805,573.37	791,211.26
Due from res've ag'ts	767,488.53	1,347,321.99	745,122.92	650,475.92	453,079.07
Due from nat'l banks	553,060.88	632,164.26	683,556.92	345,022.25	200,145.67
Due from State banks	20,271.78	30,280.30	21,216.76	17,411.23	24,700.34
Banking house, etc.	1,005,676.32	1,063,060.67	1,063,748.04	1,061,821.54	1,061,821.54
Real estate, etc	8,300.00	7,900.40	7,950.00	7,300.00	17,100.00
Current expenses ...	102,225.87	49,840.62	86,496.82	14,057.68	57,387.70
Premiums paid	64,485.51	111,552.98	59,183.92	109,518.49	52,428.01
Cash items	191,107.67	253,857.10	182,723.80	138,282.12	153,857.36
Clear'g house exch'gs	188,673.78	218,874.10	303,371.54	156,420.12	151,753.83
Bills of other banks..	37,533.00	51,337.00	23,885.00	26,155.00	38,386.00
Fractional currency.	11,216.70	8,199.52	9,350.77	8,892.73	7,886.58
Specie	1,575,833.30	1,835,255.30	1,896,677.10	1,518,656.50	1,398,848.40
Legal-tender notes...	740,742.00	870,826.00	833,995.00	359,407.00	905,020.00
U.S. cert's of deposit		10,000.00	100,000.00	190,000.00	260,000.00
5% fund with Treas.	27,000.00	26,000.00	27,000.00	26,590.00	38,489.50
Due from U. S. Treas.	2,362.00	4,780.00	1,501.00	1,672.00	4,591.52
Total	15,290,014.03	15,969,508.44	15,867,364.74	13,699,440.89	12,921,323.40

	22 banks.	22 banks.	22 banks.	22 banks.	22 banks.
Loans and discounts.	$31,592,801.53	$32,590,017.96	$32,780,822.92	$30,352,144.76	$30,202,291.94
Bonds for circulation	1,300,000.00	1,300,000.00	1,300,000.00	1,300,000.00	2,020,000.00
Bonds for deposits...	150,000.00	150,000.00	150,000.00	150,000.00	150,000.00
U. S. bonds on hand					
Other stocks and b'ds	1,937,952.99	1,974,798.85	1,871,079.35	1,727,607.51	1,655,288.43
Due from res've ag'ts	3,787,017.09	1,422,353.67	2,438,256.15	2,433,398.87	1,536,793.58
Due from nat'l banks	2,498,632.30	1,691,145.69	1,768,270.52	2,285,020.46	1,683,476.91
Due from State banks	306,038.25	354,440.20	449,865.37	371,419.42	331,733.04
Banking-house, etc..	1,341,231.39	1,350,037.81	1,365,942.45	1,386,544.87	1,408,261.18
Real estate, etc	267,375.81	265,952.07	262,302.07	260,081.08	283,304.44
Current expenses....	232,045.88	126,310.32	194,160.10	56,600.02	100,154.25
Premiums paid	77,149.35	72,225.72	60,477.09	60,326.37	89,513.87
Cash items	65,918.68	46,664.88	60,147.15	86,522.49	68,782.46
Clear'g house exch'gs	1,739,426.48	1,454,496.87	1,424,812.65	1,976,553.76	2,485,957.60
Bills of other banks..	120,704.00	141,538.00	108,381.00	156,398.00	144,476.00
Fractional currency.	15,248.58	11,124.06	12,574.87	8,958.89	15,403.38
Specie	3,054,514.52	2,868,168.95	3,251,231.45	2,828,466.03	2,940,801.70
Legal-tender notes ..	1,369,316.00	859,509.60	1,072,787.00	1,790,861.00	1,246,853.00
U.S. cert's of deposit	625,000.00	570,000.00	630,000.00	570,000.00	680,000.60
5% fund with Treas.	57,150.00	58,500.00	58,450.00	58,500.00	85,680.00
Due from U. S. Treas.	1,000.00	12,150.00	17,420.00	3,137.88	17,600.00
Total	50,628,551.75	48,319,434.07	49,344,080.23	47,871,544.41	47,236,391.87

BY STATES AND RESERVE CITIES—Continued.

DISTRICT OF COLUMBIA.

Liabilities.	DECEMBER 9. 1 bank.	MARCH 6. 1 bank.	MAY 4. 1 bank.	JULY 12. 1 bank.	OCTOBER 3. 1 bank.
Capital stock	$252,000.00	$252,000.00	$252,000.00	$252,000.00	$252,000.00
Surplus fund	100,000 00	100,000.00	100,000.00	100,000.00	100,000.00
Undivided profits	78,441.47	68,011.38	81,496.45	68,564.31	79,309.70
Nat'l-bank circulation	107,800.00	182,200.00	170,759.00	192,200.00	223,500.00
State-bank circulation					
Dividends unpaid	3,740.00	4,136.00	4,000.00	5,318.00	4,272.00
Individual deposits	920,769.85	691,355.58	932,590.38	880,146.83	742,192.20
U. S. deposits					
Dep'ts U.S.dis.officers					
Due to national banks	11,122.72	22,519.89	9,003.71	23,376.17	14,268.04
Due to State banks		792.20			103.48
Notes rediscounted					
Bills payable					
Other liabilities					
Total	1,569,874.04	1,621,915.05	1,558,750.54	1,530,635.31	1,415,645.48

CITY OF WASHINGTON.

	12 banks.	12 banks.	12 banks.	12 banks.	12 banks.
Capital stock	$2,575,060.00	$2,575,000.00	$2,575,000.00	$2,575,000.00	$2,575,000.00
Surplus fund	1,192,000.00	1,285,000.00	1,285,000.00	1,295,000.00	1,305,000.00
Undivided profits	341,435.98	186,356.20	275,980.19	189,071.12	235,568.88
Nat'l-bank circulation	524,675.00	522,855.00	512,695.00	535,275.00	763,765.00
State-bank circulation					
Dividends unpaid	2,909.50	3,390.50	2,603.00	8,051.50	4,608.00
Individual deposits	10,148,679.54	10,909,229.26	10,722,476.73	8,514,800.89	7,431,693.42
U. S. deposits	77,102.55	85,654.69	89,914.56	75,075.39	90,149.71
Dep'ts U.S.dis.officers					
Due to national banks	336,048.58	293,766.21	314,596.98	321,127.71	316,928.62
Due to State banks	52,102.88	68,256.58	54,098.28	44,671.48	95,970.77
Notes rediscounted				105,407.80	11,630.00
Bills payable	40,000.00	40,000.00	35,000.00	35,000.00	85,000.00
Other liabilities					
Total	15,290,014.03	15,969,508.44	15,867,364.74	13,699,440.89	12,921,323.40

	22 banks.	22 banks.	22 banks.	22 banks.	22 banks.
Capital stock	$13,243,260.00	$13,243,260.00	$13,243,260.00	$13,243,260.00	$13,243,260.00
Surplus fund	4,477,900.00	4,526,900.00	3,973,000.00	4,505,312.60	4,505,312.60
Undivided profits	1,502,263.48	1,276,913.40	2,072,075.66	1,056,970.57	1,406,596.45
Nat'l-bank circulation	1,097,465.00	1,093,150.00	1,102,310.00	1,108,960.00	1,798,150.00
State-bank circulation	4,790.00	4,789.00	4,789.00	4,789.00	4,789.00
Dividends unpaid	51,846.80	60,175.73	47,130.55	211,332.85	52,982.14
Individual deposits	24,826,269.31	22,521,710.83	23,298,972.82	22,787,256.80	20,951,366.50
U. S. deposits	166,109.87	161,436.12	182,089.27	170,950.82	162,913.59
Dep'ts U.S.dis.officers					
Due to national banks	4,303,679.83	4,323,019.37	4,032,905.92	3,387,126.36	3,420,809.70
Due to State banks	954,663.51	928,090.62	762,357.01	720,624.43	815,211.70
Notes rediscounted			165,000.00	105,960.80	
Bills payable		160,600.00	455,000.00	345,060.00	190,000.00
Other liabilities	98.89			125,000.00	625,000.00
Total	50,628,551.75	48,319,434.07	49,344,980.23	47,871,544.41	47,296,391.87

ABSTRACT OF REPORTS SINCE SEPTEMBER 30, 1892, ARRANGED

WEST VIRGINIA.

Resources.	DECEMBER 9.	MARCH 6.	MAY 4.	JULY 12.	OCTOBER 3.
	29 banks.	30 banks.	30 banks.	30 banks.	30 banks.
Loans and discounts	$7,553,166.92	$7,832,913.08	$8,015,718.90	$7,539,958.98	$6,900,842.90
Bonds for circulation	816,250.00	828,750 00	853,750.00	853,750.00	962,500.00
Bonds for deposits...	50,000.00	50,000.00	50,000.00	50,000.00	50,000.00
U. S. bonds on hand..	7,000.00	7,000.00	2,500.00	2,500.00	2,600.00
Other stocks and b'ds	254,316.16	313,642.06	314,877.01	309,480.76	319,486.40
Due from res've ag'ts	811,613.45	714,117.98	595,291.14	305,273.21	572,044.78
Due from nat'l banks.	453,502.95	402,113.55	333,357.19	250,481.41	262,850.16
Due from State banks	155,136.79	136,673.22	121,436.54	103,568.04	92,822.82
Banking house, etc ..	334,163.22	336,656.94	340,091.93	343,587.47	357,107.37
Real estate, etc	31,795.90	31,705.90	34,795.90	34,795.90	37,556.90
Current expenses ...	84,956.97	39,746.03	68,238.02	11,609.99	46,003.03
Premiums paid	60,158.51	51,243.50	54,694.50	46,387.00	54,966.92
Cash items	62,125.64	59,300.21	38,144.87	39,447.94	40,154.94
Clear'g house exch'gs					1,330.60
Bills of other banks..	71,940.00	65,436.00	77,035.00	78,209.00	94,152.00
Fractional currency.	5,919.62	5,454.53	6,363.81	6,309.43	6,887.09
Specie	473,442.06	459,705.36	497,984.71	535,317.32	592,983.60
Legal-tender notes ..	442,036.00	376,893.00	368,859.00	448,799.00	511,384.00
U. S. cert's of deposit					
5 % fund with Treas.	25,370.75	35,091.60	37,037.25	35,847.10	40,756.67
Due from U. S. Treas.	2,476.45	4,262.95	5,297.15	3,493.80	2,702.98
Total	11,734,780.99	11,750,349.91	11,815,472.92	11,097,845.35	10,949,194.15

NORTH CAROLINA.

	23 banks.	23 banks.	24 banks.	23 banks.	24 banks.
Loans and discounts	$6,176,193.09	$6,378,723.92	$6,553,095.37	$5,664,525.40	$5,740,271.33
Bonds for circulation	709,000.00	709,000.00	781,500.00	731,500.00	867,600.00
Bonds for deposits ..	100,000.00	100,000.00	100,000.00	100,000.00	100,000.00
U. S. bonds on hand..					
Other stocks and b'ds	210,660.76	257,018.06	206,466.08	201,309.36	216,979.05
Due from res've ag'ts	511,248.92	586,879.71	461,330.19	401,725.00	297,359.19
Due from nat'l banks	335,666.59	373,787.86	220,138.32	190,842.10	203,946.95
Due from State banks	202,322.81	162,590.12	149,962.49	102,036.65	111,524.92
Banking-house, etc ..	261,451.02	263,961.30	303,997.71	282,740.05	307,802.16
Real estate, etc	73,566.74	81,905.52	97,815.65	87,920.50	99,590.27
Current expenses....	71,908.73	28,987.60	55,209.31	7,506.48	40,531.31
Premiums paid	64,165.63	60,340.63	52,903.13	48,615.63	59,922.13
Cash items	66,452.46	80,324.16	64,700.77	37,572.21	55,313.44
Clear'g house exch'gs					
Bills of other banks..	108,077.00	71,935.00	65,920.00	67,198.00	106,152.00
Fractional currency .	3,182.80	4,950.64	3,166.50	5,375.97	8,320.01
Specie	315,195.81	379,040.55	400,054.20	403,401.75	373,454.06
Legal-tender notes ..	298,839.00	264,316.00	253,762.00	257,165.00	284,820.00
U. S. cert's of deposit					
5 % fund with Treas	33,202.29	33,554.75	33,184.75	28,767.25	34,113.75
Due from U. S. Treas	1,000.00	1,568.50	7,187.50	77.20	
Total	9,632,053.65	9,808,895.32	9,810,094.12	8,638,338.66	8,907,750.57

SOUTH CAROLINA.

	14 banks.	14 banks.	14 banks.	14 banks.	14 banks.
Loans and discounts	$5,456,762.61	$5,825,537.55	$6,158,129.87	$6,227,129.33	$6,054,973.39
Bonds for circulation	468,750.00	474,750.00	474,750.00	474,750.00	474,750.00
Bonds for deposits ..	150,000.00	150,000.00	150,000.00	150,000.00	150,000.00
U. S. bonds on hand..	100.00	100.00	100.00	100.00	100.00
Other stocks and b'ds	516,876.57	483,907.67	575,906.81	739,009.91	598,323.82
Due from res've ag'ts	417,796.48	270,253.17	89,393.25	909,156.19	156,057.63
Due from nat'l banks..	201,267.58	137,869.03	150,321.71	446,625.87	132,382.78
Due from State banks	276,357.99	201,210.82	121,979.18	174,310.40	181,338.92
Banking house, etc ..	123,968.12	118,792.99	118,760.74	116,213.44	116,647.14
Real estate, etc	19,000.21	22,786.57	24,502.57	19,771.99	19,771.99
Current expenses....	92,104.44	36,615.29	81,950.56	4,018.34	45,185.91
Premiums paid	12,250.00	11,640.00	10,640.00	7,750.00	7,750.00
Cash items	79,527.38	37,706.46	36,796.78	61,928.17	84,300.04
Clear'g house exch'gs					3,653.00
Bills of other banks..	68,006.00	30,401.00	33,492.00	36,879.00	62,125.00
Fractional currency .	7,641.80	7,858.64	8,304.95	9,960.25	5,203.05
Specie	230,648.60	264,209.85	285,348.60	258,110.70	263,083.90
Legal-tender notes ..	394,435.00	237,846.00	194,791.00	672,381.00	240,374.00
U. S. cert's of deposit					
5 % fund with Treas	21,093.75	21,363.75	21,013.75	21,252.95	19,313.25
Due from U. S. Treas.	10,313.12	7,250.50	12,721.50		1,000.00
Total	8,546,949.65	8,340,308.29	8,548,884.27	10,330,256.63	8,615,783.82

BY STATES AND RESERVE CITIES -Continued.

WEST VIRGINIA.

Liabilities.	DECEMBER 9. 20 banks.	MARCH 6. 30 banks.	MAY 4. 30 banks.	JULY 12. 30 banks.	OCTOBER 3. 30 banks.
Capital stock	$2,871,000.00	$2,936,000.00	$2,946,000.00	$2,951,000.00	$2,961,000.00
Surplus fund	661,996.91	726,915.40	726,915.46	730,672.88	764,672.88
Undivided profits	376,044.78	235,417.61	325,844.71	208,420.43	286,354.52
Nat'l-bank circulation	609,400.00	729,905.00	757,865.00	756,820.00	863,615.00
State-bank circulation					
Dividends unpaid	7,260.58	11,676.58	8,107.08	43,231.58	10,657.58
Individual deposits	6,573,601.27	6,623,860.42	6,603,773.61	5,875,256.74	5,622,970.59
U. S. deposits	43,723.35	35,639.68	36,400.85	39,819.21	42,913.69
Dop'ts U.S.dis.officers	1,276.65	9,360.32	8,599.15	4,532.98	6,982.31
Due to national banks	330,218.28	231,737.48	246,946.49	195,080.19	161,739.69
Due to State banks	106,713.00	144,197.65	123,114.81	100,120.37	100,145.17
Notes rediscounted	63,606.08	65,629.77	44,905.82	168,610.97	100,542.73
Bills payable			11,000.00		22,500.00
Other liabilities					
Total	11,734,780.99	11,750,349.91	11,845,472.92	11,097,845.35	10,949,194.15

NORTH CAROLINA.

	23 banks.	23 banks.	24 banks.	23 banks.	24 banks.
Capital stock	$2,626,000.00	$2,626,000.00	$2,676,000.00	$2,476,000.00	$2,676,000.00
Surplus fund	738,065.63	766,127.31	766,127.31	728,959.38	729,559.38
Undivided profits	404,176.62	358,660.21	438,567.28	328,393.56	413,898.00
Nat'l-bank circulation	641,675.00	641,195.00	639,915.00	606,715.00	749,605.00
State-bank circulation					
Dividends unpaid	260.00	498.00	141.00	8,484.00	512.00
Individual deposits	4,235,352.70	4,582,572.98	4,404,724.92	3,551,470.20	3,392,824.16
U. S. deposits	54,831.72	55,855.03	54,268.33	62,702.06	61,433.80
Dep'ts U.S.dis.officers	40,168.28	39,144.97	40,205.07	32,297.04	38,566.20
Due to national banks	257,593.06	230,795.82	178,997.96	143,655.26	30,999.66
Due to State banks	129,364.48	101,727.70	88,451.30	65,591.60	109,343.14
Notes rediscounted	407,572.07	349,446.60	450,701.65	494,282.78	78,257.58
Bills payable	34,000.00	141,471.70	72,894.30	131,686.88	487,657.66
Other liabilities				5,100.00	199,093.30
Total	9,632,053.65	9,898,855.32	9,810,991.12	8,638,338.66	8,907,750.57

SOUTH CAROLINA.

	14 banks.	14 banks.	14 banks.	14 banks.	14 banks.
Capital stock	$1,623,000.00	$1,648,000.00	$1,748,000.00	$1,748,000.00	$1,748,000.00
Surplus fund	887,600.00	834,100.00	834,100.00	840,600.00	840,600.00
Undivided profits	910,936.28	780,289.22	773,609.72	630,474.40	890,127.94
Nat'l-bank circulation	409,165.00	390,599.00	394,610.00	412,255.00	417,565.00
State-bank circulation					
Dividends unpaid	9,706.00	12,466.50	10,078.00	21,373.90	11,902.50
Individual deposits	3,586,074.36	3,659,955.10	3,630,890.28	5,011,550.66	3,058,352.50
U. S. deposits	115,290.22	112,327.31	108,402.38	123,722.19	129,627.93
Dep'ts U.S.dis.officers	34,087.16	38,750.72	41,612.23	29,720.10	25,219.04
Due to national banks	181,790.25	93,384.65	233,714.45	142,352.65	97,989.84
Due to State banks	537,090.13	433,180.01	419,572.59	583,413.19	401,588.27
Notes rediscounted	166,310.25	216,864.78	198,804.62	403,551.14	526,525.67
Bills payable	85,000.00	120,400.00	155,400.00	353,243.40	664,910.07
Other liabilities					3,975.00
Total	8,546,949.65	8,340,308.29	8,548,864.27	10,330,256.63	8,615,783.82

GEORGIA.

Resources.	DECEMBER 0. 32 banks.	MARCH 6. 30 banks.	MAY 4. 30 banks.	JULY 12. 29 banks.	OCTOBER 3. 27 banks.
Loans and discounts.	$10,700,569.16	$9,953,531.35	$9,946,599.99	$8,800,450.95	$8,018,122.57
Bonds for circulation	1,080,250.00	1,011,250.00	1,011.230.00	073,750.00	1,005,000.00
Bonds for deposits ..	100,000.00	100,000.00	100,000.00	159,000.00	100,000.00
U. S. bonds on hand ..					
Other stocks and b'ds	429,260.43	498,846.34	487,703.10	461,391.51	510,417.52
Due from res'v eng'ts	845 222.38	408,562.63	325,127.97	266,252.21	387,777.51
Due from nat'l banks	345,458.95	223,399.38	295,931.11	193,378.86	232,863.49
Due from State banks	248,575.79	141,545.07	172,356.64	118,813.56	170,200.59
Banking house, etc..	484,983.70	365,526.20	375,872.99	308,006.33	332,896 99
Real estate, etc......	100,072.95	86,696.81	87,258.95	86,736.42	87,343.22
Current expenses....	154,533.63	64,930.50	111,154.00	43,658.73	87,258.64
Premiums paid	112,525.36	94,722.30	97,775.36	99,525.36	92,650.36
Cash items	206,624.09	184,616.92	190,937.85	108,850.29	119,525.47
Clear'g-house exch'gs					52,462.95
Bills of other banks..	191,524.00	203,029.00	146,095.00	95,608.00	173,566.00
Fractional currency.	10,109.61	9,479.16	8,750.77	9,054.17	8,110.24
Specie	517,680.16	639,742.26	678,252.30	549,541.07	467,897.15
Legal-tender notes ..	499,159.00	554,064.00	414,950.00	329,255.00	361,401.00
U. S. cert's of deposit					
5 % fund with Treas.	47,058.50	40,400.80	42,503.71	41,477.70	39,679.96
Due from U. S. Treas.	12,622.16	8,228.35	10,437.15	11,625.76	1,253.85
Total	16,098,835.87	14,580,671.19	14,503,036.95	12,639,375.92	12,248,459.51

FLORIDA.

	19 banks.	20 banks.	19 banks.	18 banks.	17 banks.
Loans and discounts.	$4,561,122.70	$4,751,633.23	$4,976,591.59	$4,527,054.93	$3,501,085.14
Bonds for circulation	392,500.00	417,500.00	417,500.00	403,000.00	367,500.00
Bonds for deposits...	75,000.00	75,000.00	75,000.00	75,000.00	75,000.00
U. S. bonds on hand..					
Other stocks and b'ds	281,661.93	335,247.25	302,027.14	403,100.54	390,233.87
Due from res'v eng'ts	601,505.37	843,437.02	902,448.28	606,128.28	354,090.84
Due from nat'l banks	426,730.71	557,676.50	603,687.29	348,563.27	192,612.29
Due from State banks	153,699.93	222,056.66	189,203.31	124,710.57	74,834.92
Banking house, etc..	196,716.13	221,643.15	235,756.44	222,570.44	218,495.71
Real estate, etc.....	60,414.06	75,482.06	74,732.06	78,438.44	68,728.81
Current expenses....	72,339.53	52,371.23	70,735.83	35,064.42	62,028.29
Premiums paid	57,580.12	60,280.12	58,180.12	51,184.10	46,934.10
Cash items	80,029.64	107,005.08	93,097.61	66,546.08	29,800.89
Clear'g-house exch'gs					30,674.24
Bills of other banks..	138,214.00	173,033.00	163,467.00	108,676.00	106,675.00
Fractional currency .	3,211.99	3,512.98	2,821.28	3,145.06	3,228.07
Specie	191,080.44	207,049.92	220,139.70	267,364.87	253,297.25
Legal-tender notes ..	245,823.00	353,152.00	329,395.00	303,352.00	311,466.00
U. S. cert's of deposit					
5 % fund with Treas	16,930.00	17,602.50	16,747.00	17,445.00	16,537.50
Due from U. S. Treas.	1,670.00	1,559.50		2,447.50	1,037.50
Total..........	7,556,229.55	8,476,202.20	8,851,520.65	7,643,852.10	6,099,880.42

ALABAMA.

	29 banks.	30 banks.	20 banks.	29 banks.	28 banks.
Loans and discounts	$7,410,624.63	$7,631,400.32	$7,724,166.18	$7,618,317.71	$6,067,796.15
Bonds for circulation	1,152,900.00	1,171,500.00	1,133,500.00	1,133,500.00	1,083,500.00
Bonds for deposits ..	100,000.00	100,000.00	100,000.00	100,000.00	50,000.00
U. S. bonds on hand..		3,000.00			
Other stocks and b'ds	1,160,315.88	1,290,291.90	1,246,090.10	1,249,123.56	1,068,029.07
Due from res'v eng'ts	630,410.08	443,926.10	412,226.33	415,535.42	300,884.54
Due from nat'l banks	620,020.35	709,260.61	678,487.04	302,354.11	182,413.56
Due from State banks	238,451.94	246,214.67	223,473.85	147,487.16	92,052.06
Banking house, etc..	451,233.34	415,741.49	444,051.57	448,856.43	361,877.52
Real estate, etc	132,290.40	143,838.89	173,926.61	180,707.88	183,123.28
Current expenses....	147,263.53	73,183.78	111,969.28	45,653.49	78,797.85
Premiums paid	138,424.79	131,262.92	124,422.92	117,438.54	109,313.54
Cash items	56,531.25	72,491.53	48,906.50	51,906.14	25,476.27
Clear'g-house exch'gs	20,406.37	49,306.31	38,723.30	19,523.74	51,887.52
Bills of other banks..	134,352.00	105,991.00	115,876.00	66,576.00	92,028.00
Fractional currency.	4,091.62	5,160.67	6,659.32	4,913.18	5,418.67
Specie	504,098.31	569,324.71	596,884 15	510,506.68	495,235.95
Legal-tender notes ..	387,750.00	290,471.00	308,050.00	292,556.00	283,021.00
U. S. cert's of deposit					
5 % fund with Treas.	51,340.00	51,687.50	47,907.50	46,920.50	40,100 50
Due from U. S. Treas.	6,484.79	8,660.00	10,720.00	1,200.00	3,650.00
Total..........	13,349,170.28	13,602,718.40	13,547,000.05	12,783,076.54	10,577,970.48

GEORGIA.

Liabilities.	DECEMBER 9. 32 banks.	MARCH 6. 30 banks.	MAY 4. 30 banks.	JULY 12. 29 banks.	OCTOBER 3. 27 banks.
Capital stock	$4,541,600.00	$4,191,000.00	$4,191,000.00	$4,091,000.00	$3,766,000.00
Surplus fund	1,193,016.98	1,160,557.61	1,174,757.61	1,005,448.12	1,090,653.12
Undivided profits	952,551.04	771,679.91	869,866.71	676,708.20	752,411.37
Nat'l-bank circulation	950,725.00	869,305.00	856,015.00	841,735.00	879,085.00
State-bank circulation					
Dividends unpaid	4,618.50	3,849.00	3,007.00	23,465.50	3,165.00
Individual deposits	6,742,230.16	6,041,587.54	5,930,930.16	4,555,405.01	4,182,989.98
U. S. deposits	24,709.42	21,896.94	17,572.25	66,324.04	53,071.45
Dep'ts U.S.dis.officers	52,959.59	51,937.21	62,026.25	61,951.66	62,964.68
Due to national banks	492,319.86	258,838.07	440,709.32	171,123.20	87,469.38
Due to State banks	325,247.59	342,555.58	188,186.05	144,019.82	139,011.44
Notes rediscounted	647,467.83	627,465.83	566,936.57	687,229.48	791,489.75
Bills payable	172,000.00	207,600.00	202,000.00	209,851.91	425,711.34
Other liabilities		12,031.50		14,518.89	13,507.00
Total	10,098,895.87	14,580,671.19	14,503,036.95	12,639,375.92	12,218,459.51

FLORIDA.

	19 banks.	20 banks.	19 banks.	18 banks.	17 banks.
Capital stock	$1,400,000.00	$1,400,600.00	$1,480,400.00	$1,450,000.00	$1,300,000.00
Surplus fund	264,870.00	293,700.00	273,200.00	287,200.00	288,411.00
Undivided profits	276,502.80	256,285.69	260,759.10	243,391.88	266,663.31
Nat'l-bank circulation	334,670.00	365,130.00	365,570.00	355,210.00	324,560.00
State-bank circulation					
Dividends unpaid	1,376.00	1,679.00	2,091.00	3,950.00	2,503.00
Individual deposits	4,542,736.61	5,473,147.34	5,780,092.78	4,617,747.50	3,217,392.37
U. S. deposits	55,839.85	49,218.74	24,416.22	36,878.39	29,690.00
Dep'ts U.S.dis.officers	19,978.18	16,148.00	51,040.63	38,752.02	46,667.44
Due to national banks	213,122.34	251,064.57	274,331.58	193,048.10	150,097.67
Due to State banks	191,732.48	214,893.97	196,177.04	192,768.50	92,216.44
Notes rediscounted	167,401.20	66,833.99	86,521.30	120,875.56	190,677.10
Bills payable	55,000.00	27,500.00	17,000.00	95,000.00	191,000.00
Other liabilities					
Total	7,556,220.55	8,476,202.20	8,851,529.65	7,643,852.10	6,099,880.42

ALABAMA.

	29 banks.	30 banks.	29 banks.	29 banks.	28 banks.
Capital stock	$3,919,000.00	$3,994,600.00	$3,844,000.00	$3,844,000.00	$3,504,000.00
Surplus fund	982,267.73	1,016,793.96	1,017,703.96	1,021,457.30	832,437.50
Undivided profits	707,774.11	691,970.79	706,129.57	563,504.41	575,905.29
Nat'l-bank circulation	1,031,807.00	1,013,897.50	992,447.50	1,017,717.50	975,147.50
State-bank circulation					
Dividends unpaid	5,730.60	16,605.40	7,383.40	47,265.40	25,449.40
Individual deposits	5,570,612.59	6,068,268.78	6,043,931.54	5,053,800.33	3,356,197.04
U. S. deposits	66,552.21	61,368.96	80,874.79	82,688.90	393,375.33
Dep'ts U.S.dis.officers	13,917.40	7,236.09	7,197.12	7,295.85	16,624.68
Due to national banks	204,638.16	248,914.40	192,962.78	180,703.30	101,332.34
Due to State banks	168,350.27	94,239.50	66,532.86	50,661.88	83,834.38
Notes rediscounted	527,921.21	358,645.75	489,019.49	596,750.93	542,981.15
Bills payable	60,500.00	87,777.27	93,560.00	318,194.74	410,624.87
Other liabilities			5,307.04		40,050.00
Total	13,349,170.28	13,602,718.40	13,517,090.95	12,783,076.54	10,577,979.48

ABSTRACT OF REPORTS SINCE SEPTEMBER 30, 1892, ARRANGED

MISSISSIPPI.

Resources.	DECEMBER 9.	MARCH 6.	MAY 4.	JULY 12.	OCTOBER 3.
	13 banks.	13 banks.	13 banks.	13 banks.	12 banks.
Loans and discounts.	$3,068,038.10	$2,800,763.81	$2,722,470.40	$2,479,660.94	$2,357,725.26
Bonds for circulation	353,750.00	353,750.00	353,750.00	353,750.00	338,750.00
Bonds for deposits...					
U. S. bonds on hand..		40,000.00	40,000.00		
Other stocks and b'ds	258,113.58	201,095.33	178,651.60	166,917.00	177,686.59
Due from res've ag'ts	214,236.38	225,442.36	156,394.76	141,801.52	108,853.85
Due from nat'l banks	74,003.67	94,996.97	115,305.61	45,849.10	60,990.80
Due from State banks	123,911.91	36,105.38	42,637.90	37,115.56	16,580.97
Banking house, etc..	112,660.34	112,154.66	113,020.17	113,109.42	108,507.91
Real estate, etc......	60,557.94	74,361.29	82,226.53	79,784.53	79,618.03
Current expenses....	48,419.32	24,941.93	29,643.67	14,523.49	30,255.23
Premiums paid......	32,847.20	27,464.37	27,464.37	20,564.37	20,150.00
Cash items.........	20,195.82	18,462.09	16,456.58	11,426.90	23,588.05
Clear'g-house exch'gs					
Bills of other banks.	14,094.00	15,491.00	15,593.00	12,973.00	10,025.00
Fractional currency.	2,112.91	2,265.01	3,705.52	3,819.54	4,536.53
Specie.............	93,625.90	171,452.95	156,617.19	169,511.45	138,963.13
Legal-tender notes ..	208,030.00	180,049.00	142,412.00	169,146.00	165,729.00
U. S. cert's of deposit					
5% fund with Treas.	15,874.33	15,450.52	15,510.22	15,919.50	13,662.20
Due from U. S. Treas.	1,100.00	2,006.80	17,200.00	2,500.00	1,000.00
Total.........	4,706,547.40	4,486,156.47	4,229,281.52	3,838,462.32	3,710,013.55

LOUISIANA.

	11 banks.	11 banks.	11 banks.	11 banks.	11 banks.
Loans and discounts	$2,344,473.79	$2,452,059.30	$2,474,908.31	$2,430,949.91	$2,350,160.97
Bonds for circulation	252,500.00	252,500.00	252,500.00	252,500.00	252,500.00
Bonds for deposits..					
U. S. bonds on hand..					
Other stocks and b'ds	50,569.24	25,982.83	35,600.54	48,566.79	48,066.79
Due from res've ag'ts	373,851.60	373,777.67	366,742.07	106,130.61	156,771.21
Due from nat'l banks.	54,143.58	69,589.47	61,013.80	39,211.19	14,608.44
Due from State banks	14,018.89	21,349.92	9,634.53	4,956.55	10,257.05
Banking house, etc..	44,474.00	44,658.40	44,846.84	44,737.11	44,777.61
Real estate, etc......	4,700.00	17,692.26	21,010.57	21,720.33	21,778.83
Current expenses....	33,872.78	20,484.11	32,722.55	4,671.35	18,730.13
Premiums paid......	15,325.63	13,435.00	13,435.00	11,810.00	11,685.00
Cash items	50,786.73	24,742.17	24,650.88	14,964.76	27,960.47
Clear'g-house exch'gs					
Bills of other banks..	13,150.00	42,240.00	34,760.00	32,400.00	16,805.00
Fractional currency.	619.48	1,485.68	1,679.18	2,924.85	1,809.69
Specie.............	168,085.30	227,719.35	207,954.55	203,108.55	133,797.85
Legal-tender notes ..	71,976.00	97,064.00	101,928.00	90,473.00	58,535.00
U. S. cert's of deposit.					
5% fund with Treas.	11,362.50	11,362.50	11,362.50	11,362.50	11,362.50
Due from U. S. Treas.				900.00	
Total.........	3,510,842.52	3,696,142.86	3,696,310.22	3,330,387.50	3,180,360.54

CITY OF NEW ORLEANS.

	10 banks.	10 banks.	10 banks.	9 banks.	9 banks.
Loans and discounts	$16,267,819.86	$15,830,184.24	$14,860,894.12	$13,938,133.08	$14,240,554.38
Bonds for circulation	950,000.00	950,000.00	950,000.00	900,000.00	900,000.00
Bonds for deposits ..					
U. S. bonds on hand..	201,900.00	203,600.00	206,800.00	201,500.00	
Other stocks and b'ds	3,593,810.38	3,096,103.54	3,066,034.75	2,705,284.04	2,619,316.23
Due from res've ag'ts	1,401,827.69	1,337,469.23	1,149,168.11	1,061,371.81	537,996.76
Due from nat'l banks	514,681.70	347,713.85	325,505.83	290,703.01	256,846.98
Due from State banks	678,984.58	602,122.24	480,180.95	192,560.38	208,548.99
Banking house, etc..	570,397.94	582,226.64	597,820.58	609,980.92	634,258.06
Real estate, etc......	32,003.13	31,288.13	31,288.13	50,913.03	61,365.06
Current expenses....	224,017.75	90,469.16	170,131.09	16,820.18	134,110.80
Premiums paid......	146,701.40	127,091.25	126,267.55	92,560.00	75,062.50
Cash items	8,244.98	26,650.18	10,919.07	32,503.84	456,215.50
Clear'g-house exch'gs	1,810,789.82	2,186,245.76	1,554,223.42	799,288.69	940,334.79
Bills of other banks..	93,042.00	90,390.00	77,407.00	83,715.00	48,385.00
Fractional currency.	11,591.13	9,739.42	6,716.24	10,615.49	10,080.23
Specie	1,742,567.65	2,037,717.10	2,090,671.40	1,732,550.02	1,179,603.21
Legal-tender notes ..	1,106,826.00	1,717,467.00	1,828,471.00	1,361,326.00	816,554.00
U. S. cert's of deposit					
5% fund with Treas	42,750.00	42,750.00	42,750.00	40,500.00	40,500.00
Due from U. S. Treas		4,200.00		2,740.00	
Total.........	29,395,355.32	29,317,866.71	27,484,679.44	24,125,017.09	23,252,731.49

MISSISSIPPI.

Liabilities.	DECEMBER 9. 13 banks.	MARCH 6. 13 banks.	MAY 4. 13 banks.	JULY 12. 13 banks.	OCTOBER 3. 12 banks.
Capital stock	$1,165,000.00	$1,115,000.00	$1,115,000.00	$1,115,000.00	$1,055,000.00
Surplus fund	428,707.58	459,732.58	459,732.58	460,532.58	456,750.00
Undivided profits	199,948.67	128,303.38	147,568.34	93,072.23	106,853.75
Nat'l-bank circulation	316,950.00	312,770.00	314,350.00	317,600.00	304,850.00
State-bank circulation					
Dividends unpaid	5,095.00	660.00	9,320.00	10,143.00	4,041.90
Individual deposits	2,014,125.43	2,160,960.73	1,908,546.56	1,462,803.76	1,221,100.43
U. S. deposits					
Dep'ts U.S.dis.officers					
Due to national banks	163,772.78	107,884.49	77,031.49	36,446.49	26,207.44
Due to State banks	14,449.11	22,025.22	17,189.88	8,703.99	11,044.80
Notes rediscounted	297,998.83	79,320.07	78,542.17	181,402.90	302,858.53
Bills payable	100,500.00	70,500.00	102,000.00	152,000.00	224,242.00
Other liabilities		29,000.00		752.37	2,762.00
Total	4,706,547.40	4,486,156.47	4,229,281.52	3,838,462.32	3,716,013.55

LOUISIANA.

	11 banks.	11 banks.	11 banks.	11 banks.	11 banks.
Capital stock	$810,000.00	$810,000.00	$810,000.00	$810,000.00	$810,000.00
Surplus fund	238,752.42	260,000.92	260,600.92	289,943.72	289,943.72
Undivided profits	196,504.93	162,208.15	205,998.68	148,662.96	166,078.88
Nat'l-bank circulation	225,400.00	220,420.00	221,920.00	224,250.00	220,350.00
State-bank circulation					
Dividends unpaid	544.00	2,189.33	1,236.66	13,764.00	5,357.33
Individual deposits	1,823,541.98	2,072,330.36	2,050,260.94	1,647,932.07	1,248,276.64
U. S. deposits					
Dep'ts U.S.dis.officers					
Due to national banks	81,076.63	65,404.74	30,156.33	13,941.15	19,739.22
Due to State banks	1,578.19	6,601.23	3,398.77	1,640.98	643.81
Notes rediscounted	89,944.37	30,388.13	34,737.92	73,252.62	186,576.94
Bills payable	43,500.00	66,000.00	60,000.00	107,000.00	226,500.00
Other liabilities					
Total	3,510,842.52	3,696,142.80	3,696,310.22	3,330,387.50	3,180,366.54

CITY OF NEW ORLEANS.

	10 banks.	10 banks.	10 banks.	9 banks.	9 banks.
Capital stock	$3,625,000.00	$3,625,000.00	$3,625,000.00	$3,125,000.00	$3,125,000.00
Surplus fund	1,009,107.96	2,088,985.81	2,088,985.81	2,206,000.00	2,206,000.00
Undivided profits	832,439.49	503,477.02	710,498.50	333,329.22	506,182.54
Nat'l-bank circulation	841,242.00	837,192.50	836,692.50	798,392.50	807,802.50
State-bank circulation					
Dividends unpaid	14,667.19	17,414.82	12,535.82	53,810.82	26,736.07
Individual deposits	18,274,701.54	18,784,007.48	17,509,329.62	14,682,795.28	12,301,072.01
U. S. deposits					
Dep'ts U.S.dis.officers					
Due to national banks	1,215,961.03	1,638,197.55	1,225,803.51	664,272.20	829,502.46
Due to State banks	1,396,302.04	1,421,755.78	1,329,841.50	1,151,184.05	1,138,012.90
Notes rediscounted	580,874.07	182,667.46	120,932.18	428,151.72	897,278.14
Bills payable	705,000.00	170,000.00	25,000.00	550,465.40	810,000.00
Other liabilities		49,167.60		131,309.90	574,954.87
Total	29,395,355.32	29,317,866.71	27,484,679.44	24,125,017.09	23,252,731.49

ABSTRACT OF REPORTS SINCE SEPTEMBER 30, 1892, ARRANGED

TEXAS.

Resources.	DECEMBER 9. 223 banks.	MARCH 6. 223 banks.	MAY 4. 227 banks.	JULY 12. 228 banks.	OCTOBER 3. 222 banks.
Loans and discounts.	$52,381,323.00	$49,808,610.02	$51,876,432.85	$49,801,727.40	$44,827,908.40
Bonds for circulation	5,266,850.00	5,296,900.00	5,334,400.00	5,315,600.00	5,180,600.00
Bonds for deposits ..	398,000.00	368,000.00	368,000.00	318,000.00	268,000.00
U.S. bonds on hand..	....	10,000.00	47,500.00	15,000.00	100,000.00
Other stocks and b'ds	1,841,417.37	1,755,137.07	2,036,590.81	2,108,261.85	1,743,944.68
Due from res've ag'ts	5,887,252.35	6,714,968.38	5,126,370.16	3,273,789.46	2,264,867.92
Due from nat'l banks	4,359,966.23	4,971,333.68	4,335,838.20	2,867,362.96	2,045,903.13
Due from State banks	1,195,605.10	1,847,895.99	1,038,806.35	738,850.69	795,974.79
Banking house, etc ..	2,426,877.67	2,420,245.80	2,441,104.57	2,427,924.05	2,365,655.23
Real estate, etc	654,843.68	1,052,138.45	838,923.03	865,813.89	633,672.49
Current expenses....	760,961.36	434,032.70	728,518.20	224,791.06	483,522.20
Premiums paid	587,820.80	504,216.92	490,806.77	406,775.11	388,019.67
Cash items..........	334,939.99	342,237.27	273,618.92	279,185.37	311,495.07
Clear'g-house exch'gs	194,528.64	218,911.05	180,699.04	95,308.04	172,386.20
Bills of other banks..	1,089,527.00	1,137,077.00	737,237.00	599,810.00	639,715.00
Fractional currency .	21,014.51	26,328.35	30,985.22	36,688.03	28,790.33
Specie..............	2,980,735.73	3,654,643.55	3,427,651.82	3,614,613.76	3,408,077.26
Legal-tender notes...	4,202,369.00	4,268,044.00	3,231,402.00	2,824,354.00	2,564,734.00
U.S. cert's of deposit.					
5% fund with Treas.	213,961.50	230,295.00	230,438.00	228,438.00	224,666.50
Due from U.S. Treas	7,871.11	19,362.61	25,069.00	7,617.40	6,243.00
Total..........	84,765,865.22	84,260,407.86	82,800,392.24	76,049,943.16	68,545,255.78

ARKANSAS.

	10 banks.	9 banks.	9 banks.	9 banks.	9 banks.
Loans and discounts.	$3,749,957.94	$2,771,350.41	$2,723,659.73	$2,529,895.93	$2,194,009.01
Bonds for circulation	310,000.00	250,000.00	250,000.00	250,000.00	250,000.00
Bonds for deposits...	75,000.00				
U.S. bonds on hand..	100.00				
Other stocks and b'ds	91,887.80	68,524.23	62,867.31	61,105.57	82,027.62
Due from res've ag'ts	150,596.93	227,816.83	227,028.74	244,061.43	124,466.70
Due from nat'l banks.	100,822.54	106,868.66	153,297.17	60,361.31	61,987.29
Due from State banks.	76,474.12	36,119.14	61,179.38	44,831.27	8,905.78
Banking house, etc ..	67,604.24	50,266.86	50,215.31	49,964.11	50,642.11
Real estate, etc	71,083.96	49,141.92	63,305.04	63,430.96	63,551.65
Current expenses....	40,983.26	20,465.61	33,760.64	19,334.71	27,166.43
Premiums paid	43,966.50	22,193.25	21,693.25	10,318.25	17,403.25
Cash items	61,731.27	77,553.84	58,437.16	33,401.22	23,265.78
Clear'g-house exch'gs					10,232.78
Bills of other banks..	20,144.00	33,788.00	38,616.00	31,897.00	22,665.00
Fractional currency.	1,172.62	1,023.07	1,094.15	2,036.83	1,665.13
Specie..............	128,590.70	158,671.45	213,453.00	160,903.35	210,503.60
Legal-tender notes ..	124,701.00	131,927.00	133,713.00	181,440.00	143,095.00
U.S. cert's of deposit.					
5% fund with Treas.	13,950.00	10,150.00	10,450.00	11,250.00	9,300.00
Due from U.S. Treas.	900.00			1,000.00	
Total..........	5,147,666.88	4,015,860.27	4,103,669.88	3,764,916.94	3,309,077.13

KENTUCKY.

	72 banks.	72 banks.	72 banks.	71 banks.	71 banks.
Loans and discounts	$21,685,924.79	$21,843,244.60	$22,336,493.36	$20,946,742.52	$19,059,907.48
Bonds for circulation	3,482,500.00	3,245,000.60	3,265,000.00	3,282,500.00	3,405,500.00
Bonds for deposits ..	525,000.00	525,000.00	525,000.00	525,000.00	525,000.00
U.S. bonds on hand..	6,000.00	1,000.00			41,200.00
Other stocks and b'ds	816,385.24	754,748.41	732,201.91	770,710.69	742,818.15
Due from res've ag'ts.	2,595,980.64	2,147,423.84	1,441,184.18	1,160,212.74	1,186,381.69
Due from nat'l banks.	630,438.10	603,826.42	424,936.96	380,807.99	396,216.33
Due from State banks	294,552.02	281,092.83	211,599.69	241,683.21	149,114.76
Banking house, etc ..	614,906.15	577,591.14	575,931.52	557,187.05	584,280.22
Real estate, etc	82,451.00	84,517.57	85,044.78	82,130.85	75,676.61
Current expenses....	107,120.78	107,651.60	159,639.42	40,343.39	152,143.42
Premiums paid	304,640.74	244,729.25	246,361.69	212,471.44	230,256.58
Cash items	90,501.51	104,535.33	151,082.92	136,876.56	102,398.85
Clear'g-house exch'gs		13,138.67		3,259.97	
Bills of other banks..	190,857.00	212,516.00	170,480.00	174,322.00	212,879.00
Fractional currency.	7,938.04	6,096.74	6,972.69	7,358.05	8,562.46
Specie..............	716,347.37	715,250.61	727,078.78	751,380.28	784,353.70
Legal-tender notes ..	592,835.00	574,915.00	653,312.00	609,593.00	647,706.00
U.S. cert's of deposit.					
5% fund with Treas.	153,647.53	138,114.49	140,738.71	140,438.21	144,302.00
Due from U.S. Treas.	3,095.78	2,400.00	26,810.00	1,000.00	1,078.44
Total..........	33,005,223.89	32,184,532.55	31,804,855.60	30,033,023.94	28,449,062.16

TEXAS.

Liabilities.	DECEMBER 9. 223 banks.	MARCH 6. 223 banks.	MAY 4. 227 banks.	JULY 12. 228 banks.	OCTOBER 3. 222 banks.
Capital stock	$26,337,782.50	$26,030,000.00	$26,170,000.00	$25,510,500.00	$24,506,175.00
Surplus fund	4,572,461.70	4,942,406.70	4,871,308.76	5,015,898.69	4,936,379.64
Undivided profits	3,226,483.26	1,041,288.36	2,688,075.26	1,918,589.71	2,331,550.54
Nat'l-bank circulation	4,690,500.00	4,619,275.00	4,652,220.00	4,661,100.00	4,611,475.00
State-bank circulation					
Dividends unpaid	4,898.12	32,169.78	10,976.80	129,965.57	42,817.98
Individual deposits	38,128,665.48	39,352,756.63	37,680,171.07	32,463,783.39	25,747,560.91
U. S. deposits	168,622.23	147,652.25	196,568.26	244,120.46	175,526.48
Dep'ts U.S.dis.officers	117,606.46	152,581.65	103,189.27	35,564.76	95,231.09
Due to national banks	3,820,296.68	4,055,385.13	3,458,065.72	2,098,206.64	1,659,473.91
Due to State banks	966,037.58	1,205,701.02	1,036,813.03	580,412.21	594,076.28
Notes rediscounted	1,712,562.08	1,007,100.31	1,373,004.48	2,510,594.99	6,251,491.49
Bills payable	825,766.33	712,550.28	565,999.59	821,625.91	1,481,597.04
Other liabilities	17,182.80	1,540.66		6,080.83	16,691.11
Total	84,765,865.22	84,260,407.86	82,800,392.24	76,040,043.16	68,545,255.78

ARKANSAS.

	10 banks.	9 banks.	9 banks.	9 banks.	9 banks.
Capital stock	$1,600,000.00	$1,100,000.00	$1,100,000.00	$1,100,000.00	$1,100,000.00
Surplus fund	472,000.00	378,250.00	378,250.00	380,250.00	380,250.00
Undivided profits	156,303.73	65,456.22	98,901.57	76,828.09	100,591.10
Nat'l-bank circulation	279,000.00	224,500.00	225,000.00	225,000.00	225,000.00
State bank circulation					
Dividends unpaid	400.00	1,565.00	160.00	23,570.00	16,580.00
Individual deposits	2,050,534.28	1,087,959.25	2,116,467.21	1,700,468.24	1,266,608.53
U. S. deposits	43,230.58				
Dep'ts U.S.dis.officers	34,791.40				
Due to national banks	33,224.09	16,058.03	20,310.39	16,276.30	7,302.76
Due to State banks	107,952.21	134,744.67	129,050.71	83,120.19	51,279.91
Notes rediscounted	352,730.49	82,327.10	10,500.00	96,495.29	127,864.81
Bills payable	18,500.00	25,000.00	25,000.00		34,500.00
Other liabilities				2,903.83	
Total	5,147,666.88	4,015,860.27	4,103,669.88	3,761,916.94	3,309,977.13

KENTUCKY.

	72 banks.	72 banks.	72 banks.	71 banks.	71 banks.
Capital stock	$10,507,900.00	$10,157,900.00	$10,157,900.00	$10,107,900.00	$10,061,400.00
Surplus fund	2,814,178.59	2,807,501.12	2,809,489.69	2,828,018.84	2,815,418.64
Undivided profits	1,111,221.26	806,113.03	992,118.19	641,911.03	875,153.21
Nat'l-bank circulation	3,119,147.50	2,891,805.00	2,944,842.50	2,913,897.50	3,054,607.00
State-bank circulation					
Dividends unpaid	21,678.00	20,261.50	19,486.50	73,296.50	18,377.50
Individual deposits	13,220,568.05	13,587,970.68	13,014,492.66	11,555,578.78	10,092,702.30
U. S. deposits	505,498.88	500,955.18	496,931.63	506,270.22	506,409.56
Dep'ts U.S.dis.officers	21,009.37	24,265.87	28,698.65	18,747.01	19,50.322
Due to national banks	559,928.64	625,071.14	561,387.48	464,975.58	229,754.16
Due to State banks	879,865.55	494,129.61	322,307.82	301,586.53	215,636.61
Notes rediscounted	181,068.41	243,408.70	313,285.12	327,919.95	266,386.50
Bills payable	23,000.00	25,388.75	135,101.75	259,759.35	288,953.42
Other liabilities	10,159.64	3,101.07	8,813.61	3,762.85	5,359.98
Total	33,005,223.89	32,184,532.55	31,804,855.60	30,033,623.94	28,449,662.16

ABSTRACT OF REPORTS SINCE SEPTEMBER 30, 1892, ARRANGED

CITY OF LOUISVILLE.

Resources.	DECEMBER 9. 10 banks.	MARCH 6. 10 banks.	MAY 4. 10 banks.	JULY 12. 10 banks.	OCTOBER 3. 10 banks.
Loans and discounts.	$12, 828, 537. 15	$12, 697, 604. 57	$12, 406, 098. 46	$10, 691, 769. 13	$8, 826, 961. 67
Bonds for circulation	500, 000. 60	500, 000. 00	500, 000. 00	500, 000. 00	555, 000. 00
Bonds for deposits...	300, 000. 00	300, 000. 00	300, 000. 00	300, 000. 00	800, 000. 00
U. S. bonds on hand..					
Other stocks and b'ds	199, 527. 13	260, 034. 48	305, 093. 30	415, 793. 10	351, 716. 28
Due from res've ag'ts	1, 041, 451. 73	1, 151, 151. 58	785, 448. 76	464, 395. 08	559, 109. 91
Due from nat'l banks	726, 599. 78	619, 998. 75	679, 770. 73	442, 721. 06	264. 066. 00
Due from State banks	409, 348. 71	330, 168. 82	280, 935. 00	274, 187. 53	175, 121. 38
Banking house, etc..	324, 494. 58	324, 793. 01	324, 960. 61	324, 960. 01	270, 277. 95
Real estate, etc	121, 712. 97	98, 521. 80	97, 275. 55	106, 063. 55	111, 094. 98
Current expenses....	67, 945. 33	82, 389. 10	48, 695. 84	• 47, 237. 27	74, 752. 03
Premiums paid	102, 500. 00	98, .00. 00	93, 500. 00	89, 000. 00	133, 978. 12
Cash items	31, 476. 89	53, 141. 92	41, 939. 00	31, 838. 16	16, 217. 53
Clear'g-house exch'gs	97, 920. 03	93, 473. 67	112, 620. 67	48, 008. 81	43, 317. 42
Bills of other banks..	54, 983. 50	55, 455. 00	56, 167. 00	55, 965. 00	65, 245. 00
Fractional currency.	4, 243. 34	3, 499. 77	2, 672. 66	4, 836. 38	3, 106. 87
Specie	400, 633 68	387, 774. 14	409, 804. 79	205, 291. 55	576, 062. 86
Legal-tender notes ..	585, 897. 00	638, 138. 00	525, 768. 00	811, 982. 00	617, 689. 00
U. S. cert's of deposit					
5 % fund with Treas.	22, 500. 00	22, 500. 60	22, 500. 00	22, 500. 00	24, 750. 00
Due from U. S. Treas	5, 580. 00	4, 350. 00	4, 500. 00	3, 450. 00	200. 00
Total	17, 829, 360. 92	17, 729, 894. 61	17, 066, 750. 37	14, 930, 039. 23	13, 798, 704. 00

TENNESSEE.

	55 banks.	56 banks.	54 banks.	54 banks.	52 banks.
Loans and discounts	$24, 882, 490. 05	$24, 487, 770. 39	$22, 472, 479. 36	$20, 624. 030 41	$18, 335, 554. 84
Bonds for circulation	1, 479, 000. 00	1, 494, 000. 00	1, 419, 000. 00	1, 419, 000. 00	1, 364, 000. 00
Bonds for deposits...	300, 000. 00	300, 000. 00	300, 000. 60	300, 000. 00	300, 000. 00
U. S. bonds on hand..				20, 000. 00	
Other stocks and b'ds	753, 894. 08	798, 938. 62	701, 350. 45	600, 459. 24	711, 432. 14
Due from res've ag'ts.	1, 862. 418. 02	2, 255, 442. 72	1, 672, 974. 02	1, 311, 649. 29	1, 093, 999. 19
Due from nat'l banks	1, 248, 566. 57	1, 491, 873. 82	1, 210, 029. 28	641, 071 70	631, 780. 16
Due from State banks	521, 947. 94	633, 841. 71	314, 286. 23	274, 616. 93	179, 759. 66
Banking house, etc ..	695, 912. 23	726. 038. 10	725, 658. 93	792, 463. 33	782, 718. 53
Real estate, etc	304, 097. 48	304, 295. 96	290, 478. 13	308, 751. 10	336, 968. 08
Current expenses....	239, 491. .0	203, 670. 99	212, 331, 07	93, 800. 15	135, 084. 13
Premiums paid	190, 195. 85	169, 781. 27	159, 881, 27	126, 850. 00	112, 350. 00
Cash items	258, 242. 20	324, 980. 94	238, 015. 97	133, 003. 85	183, 372. 65
Clear'g-house exch'gs	302, 780. 55	231, 227. 07	253, 349. 65	134, 534. 97	110, 276. 47
Bills of other banks	235. 930. 00	283, 631. 00	263, 224. 00	409, 608. 00	319, 211. 00
Fractional currency.	17, 270. 08	13, 081. 00	14, 144. 58	14, 538. 99	17, 407. 07
Specie	840, 388. 10	880, 821. 40	1, 169, 819. 29	1, 200, 812. 86	1, 474, 964. 70
Legal-tender notes ..	965, 477. 00	944, 113. 00	1, 225, 307. 00	1, 326, 454. 00	1, 198, 802. 00
U. S. cert's of deposit					
5 % fund with Treas	63, 933. 90	63, 279. 75	62, 479. 75	61, 720. 75	• 59, 852. 25
Due from U. S. Treas	19, 715. 50	17, 401, 41	13, 590. 70	6, 402. 50	1, 157. 20
Total	35, 181, 782. 04	35, 560, 180. 05	32, 817, 828. 67	30, 089, 777. 07	27, 348, 670. 07

OHIO.

	215 banks.	217 banks.	219 banks.	219 banks.	218 banks.
Loans and discounts.	$73, 677, 870. 64	$75, 300, 694. 15	$76. 938, 433. 97	$71, 054, 153, 01	$64, 712, 083. 20
Bonds for circulation	8, 793, 500. 00	9, 061, 750. 00	9, 144, 750. 00	9, 287, 150. 00	10, 078, 750. 00
Bonds for deposits ..	478, 000. 00	528, 000. 00	528, 000. 00	528, 000. 00	528, 000. 00
U. S. bonds on hand..	322, 200. 00	323, 100. 00	277. 050. 00	204, 000. 00	215, 300. 00
Other stocks and b'ds	4, 850, 268. 97	4, 713, 236. 39	4, 683, 026. 05	4, 706, 336. 84	4, 842. 911. 70
Due from res've ag'ts	8, 768, 439. 10	8, 037, 152. 65	5, 933, 303. 74	5, 910, 889. 93	5, 767, 700. 10
Due from nat'l banks	1, 603, 139. 43	1, 787, 047. 84	1, 460, 037. 85	1, 386, 597. 25	1, 339, 005. 94
Due from State banks	565, 191. 66	577, 571. 89	468, 657. 59	443, 251. 22	411, 257. 40
Banking house, etc..	1, 818, 627. 59	1, 848, 581. 73	1, 867, 891. 69	1, 878. 687, 50	1, 870, 712. 98
Real estate, etc	404. 173. 20	474, 314. 54	487, 192. 68	491, 906. 44	490, 432. 14
Current expenses....	371, 354. 90	569, 428. 14	279, 868, 89	255, 684. 41	622, 799. 20
Premiums paid	639, 578. 68	649, 591. 24	606, 793. 71	556, 204. 28	601, 254. 42
Cash items	598, 661. 40	722, 906. 21	554, 486. 77	595, 458. 82	507, 410. 06
Clear'g-house exch'gs	116, 824. 46	70, 287. 46	114. 855. 28	57, 716. 07	101, 147. 90
Bills of other banks..	1, 320, 055. 00	1, 269, 398. 00	1, 281, 957. 00	1, 318, 725. 00	1, 258, 651. 00
Fractional currency.	39, 635. 40	40, 617. 91	39, 601. 00	39, 602. 77	44, 530. 98
Specie	4, 117, 671. 19	4, 204, 311. 63	4, 454, 897. 05	4, 314, 278. 59	4, 810, 757. 27
Legal-tender notes ..	3, 501, 140. 00	3, 206, 107. 00	3, 295, 300. 00	4, 011, 982. 00	3, 775, 732. 00
U. S. cert's of deposit					
5 % fund with Treas	376, 624. 96	377, 507. 70	379, 478. 75	407, 838. 22	422, 070. 47
Due from U. S. Treas	28, 005. 56	41, 976. 33	500, 619 20	37, 061. 23	14, 203. 99
Total	112, 393, 071. 23	113, 803, 793. 21	112, 848, 261. 31	107, 475, 510. 18	102, 480, 030. 84

CITY OF LOUISVILLE.

Liabilities.	DECEMBER 9. 10 banks.	MARCH 6. 10 banks.	MAY 4. 10 banks.	JULY 12. 10 banks.	OCTOBER 3. 10 banks.
Capital stock	$4,901,500.00	$4,901,500.00	$4,901,500.00	$4,901,500.00	$4,401,500.00
Surplus fund	1,019,800.00	1,023,800.00	1,027,300.00	1,010,300.00	916,945.03
Undivided profits	416,631.65	462,623.64	392,869.75	328,017.00	368,850.79
Nat'l-bank circulation	449,940.00	449,940.00	449,000.00	449,940.00	494,950.00
State-bank circulation					
Dividends unpaid	9,001.00	6,953.00	39,702.00	20,732.00	8,907.00
Individual deposits	5,499,619.12	5,430,219.47	5,483,096.65	4,335,692.28	4,530,957.72
U.S. deposits	124,951.02	152,587.91	168,490.50	191,731.83	820,225.57
Dep'ts U.S.dis.officers	205,045.98	177,412.06	161,5 0.50	138,268.17	45,518.73
Due to national banks	2,437,885.75	2,201,725.52	1,740,936.44	1,254,329.40	964,983.58
Due to State banks	2,317,715.62	2,026,663.00	1,572,829.70	1,192,203.40	909,622.14
Notes rediscounted	206,367.78	471,460.98	781,515.83	818,508.67	212,772.38
Bills payable	210,000.00	425,000.00	348,000.00	288,816.48	109,471.06
Other liabilities					14,000.00
Total	17,829,360.92	17,723,894.61	17,066,750.37	14,930,039.23	13,798,704.00

TENNESSEE.

	55 banks.	56 banks.	54 banks.	54 banks.	52 banks.
Capital stock	$10,187,729.00	$9,480,150 00	$9,643,360.00	$9,643,620.00	$9,400,000.00
Surplus fund	2,245,305.14	2,222,859.19	2,105,359.19	2,117,962.95	2,109,302.95
Undivided profits	1,330,969.28	1,177,504.77	1,167,238.93	950,702.79	1,048,165.16
Nat'l-bank circulation	1,323,655.00	1,326,235.00	1,274,785.00	1,274,205.00	1,224,035.00
State-bank circulation					
Dividends unpaid	2,316.00	2 480.00	1,637.00	19,394.50	3,777.75
Individual deposits	15,011,950.48	16,810,058.24	15,026,363.85	12,579,532.76	10,453,984.33
U.S. deposits	160,956.67	174,161.45	164,621.66	225,941.27	178,087.87
Dep'ts U.S.dis.officers	96,200.75	107,281.14	116,382.91	72,149.30	112,555.07
Due to national banks	2,242,739.51	1,434,160.81	1,226,639.93	947,758.15	504,803.43
Due to State banks	1,410,771.77	1,962,916.98	1,271,247.30	900,972.54	635,162.22
Notes rediscounted	944,287.80	405,632.26	502,457.55	1,027,112.18	1,072,713.70
Bills payable	234,900.64	462,431.47	257,735.35	325,422.57	514,022.60
Other liabilities		299.74			
Total	35,181,782.04	35,566,180.05	32,817,828.67	30,089,777.07	27,348,670.07

OHIO.

	215 banks.	217 banks.	219 banks.	219 banks.	216 banks.
Capital stock	$26,965,600.00	$27,156,590.00	$27,356,345.00	$27,544,300.00	$27,495,100.00
Surplus fund	7,385,010.74	7,478,547.90	7,501,745.65	7,613,139.32	7,572,254.32
Undivided profits	2,594,774.62	2,825,900.55	2,256,981.11	2,250,304.08	2,919,844.09
Nat'l-bank circulation	7,734,937.50	7,972,202.50	8,073,932.50	8,230,472.50	8,012,692.50
State bank circulation	688.00	688.00	688.00	688.00	688.00
Dividends unpaid	35,189.52	22,483.00	103,962.50	95,918.35	52,420.15
Individual deposits	63,692,644.44	63,992,803.62	62,574,881.37	56,617,175.82	51,793,100.21
U.S. deposits	255,086.02	247,466.21	257,996.00	250,114.76	386,388.60
Dep'ts U.S.dis.officers	168,131.41	192,805.89	274,974.66	276,113.92	142,159.99
Due to national banks	1,987,297.63	1,809,754.91	1,916,299.11	1,460,722.49	1,120,184.18
Due to State banks	812,673.53	811,457.79	858,194.08	632,293.89	677,588.21
Notes rediscounted	305,327.81	662,829.35	939,203.74	1,577,576.35	620,449.25
Bills payable	447,747.56	624,736.97	660,146.77	843,740.67	722,104.17
Other liabilities	18,862.43	5,457.02	72,910.73	82,949.03	65,627.17
Total	112,393,971.23	113,803,793.21	112,848,261.31	107,475,516.08	102,489,650.84

ABSTRACT OF REPORTS SINCE SEPTEMBER 30, 1892, ARRANGED

CITY OF CINCINNATI.

Resources.	DECEMBER 9. 13 banks.	MARCH 0. 13 banks.	MAY 4. 13 banks.	JULY 12. 13 banks.	OCTOBER 3. 13 banks.
Loans and discounts.	$29,478,859.33	$28,390,782.12	$27,376,524 99	$23,599,986.17	$22,085,400.23
Bonds for circulation.	2,767,000.00	2,932,000.00	3,092,000.00	3,092,000.00	4,175,000.00
Bonds for deposits ..	850,990.00	850,000.00	850,000.00	850,000.00	850,000.00
U. S. bonds on hand..	95,400.00	257,750.00	84,400.00	89,950.00	85,250.00
Other stocks and b'ds	3,048,269.81	2,889,120.65	2,866,861.05	2,812,576.86	2,827,217.42
Due from res've ag'ts	3,625,296.43	3,110,878.43	2,634,980.29	2,718,546.64	2,294,688.06
Due from nat'l banks.	2,546,012.73	2,393,025.90	2,056,237.43	1,680,282.76	1,595,091.64
Due from State banks	1,094,538.50	883,607.56	966,099.38	632,856.22	601,494.18
Banking house, etc..	416,463.07	400,745.07	373,745.07	373,745.07	378,050.82
Real estate, etc	30,066.61	30,966.61	33,158.61	58,724.17	53,417.78
Current expenses....	93,323.83	208,086.78	62,704.99	141,751.80	251,137.67
Premiums paid	445,331.86	419,983.95	307,887.72	356,699.48	502,732.57
Cash items	112,906.02	133,597.17	109,506.20	46,522.17	44,133.23
Clear'g-house oxch'gs	265,146.00	242,636.03	229,967.92	237,800.16	256,125.95
Bills of other banks..	191,023.00	253,931.00	339,890.00	405,310.00	412,571.00
Fractional currency.	4,010.86	4,192.07	4,372.35	4,805.98	5,173.94
Specie	1,950,434.85	1,865,743.20	1,167,830.46	1,377,824.91	1,640,406.90
Legal-tender notes ..	1,942,488.00	1,778,814.00	2,517,243.00	2,223,912.00	2,828,228.00
U. S. cert's of deposit.	710,000.00	740,000.00	870,000.00	550,000.00	805,000.00
5 % fund with Treas.	124,514.00	125,204.60	124,750.00	139,139.00	187,875.00
Due from U. S. Treas	....	1,000.00	20,160.00	....	74,460.00
Total.........	40,792,887.96	47,918,070.54	46,178,329.36	41,468,493.39	41,957,354.39

CITY OF CLEVELAND.

	11 banks.	11 banks.	11 banks.	11 banks.	11 banks.
Loans and discounts	$25,483,888.90	$26,694,183.69	$27,330,275.27	$26,419,892.51	$24,212,861.06
Bonds for circulation	775,000.00	815,000.00	815,000.00	1,015,000.00	1,465,000.00
Bonds for deposits ...	60,000.00	60,000.00	60,000.00	60,000.00	60,000.00
U. S. bonds on band..	....	....	....	....	....
Other stocks and b'ds	139,313.11	114.238.11	126,163.11	195,838.48	365,988.48
Due from res've ag'ts	2,654,059.52	2,747,652.29	1,299,282.81	2,283,527.17	1,985,570.77
Due from nat'l banks.	1,820,435.10	1,616,798.17	1,679,747.89	1,499,319.26	1,352,028.92
Due from State banks	557,998.56	428,967.61	436,381.15	467,042.75	352,361.75
Banking house, etc..	409,603.06	516,465.63	511,169.74	511,544.12	512,015.12
Real estate, etc	144,235.03	194,713.29	111,296.62	60,818.36	60,818.36
Current expenses....	29,381.90	198,464.03	1,549.18	64,863.07	217,247.01
Premiums paid	11,000.00	11,000.00	11,000.00	11,000.00	57,070.00
Cash items	61,188.36	64,711.84	64,932.48	102,518.29	94,996.46
Clear'g-house exch'gs	223,797.35	236,404.01	224,831.21	308,825.25	258,767.95
Bills of other banks..	195,609.00	102,420.00	120,811.00	143,338.00	138,816.00
Fractional currency	4,446.56	7,228.75	5,245.57	4,412.96	3,959.06
Specie	1,532,354.25	1,730,199.06	1,688,914.50	1,589,491.50	1,692,028.50
Legal-tender notes ..	1,489,621.00	1,039,358.00	942,000.00	848,212.00	1,230,000.00
U. S. cert's of deposit.	....	....	....	....	....
5 % fund with Treas.	32,233.23	36,315.00	36,175.00	35,485.00	56,612.50
Due from U. S. Treas	....	6,000.00	5,340.00	10,699.95	5,850.00
Total.........	35,714,361.03	36,620,140.48	35,470,115.53	35,631,828.67	34,152,030.94

INDIANA.

	109 banks.	113 banks.	116 banks.	116 banks.	115 banks.
Loans and discounts .	$40,153,183.00	$40,288,416.20	$41,591,134.51	$37,970,151.99	$31,109,512.66
Bonds for circulation.	4,576,050.00	4,838,550.00	4,888,550.00	4,803,550.00	5,072,050.00
Bonds for deposits ..	525,000.00	525,000.00	525,000.00	525,000.00	200,000.00
U. S. bonds on hand..	227,500.00	236,500.00	213,250.00	263,600.00	172,950.00
Other stocks and b'ds	2,095,502.46	2,239,856.85	2,089,228.02	2,138,400.39	2,257,451.75
Due from res've ag'ts	6,141,156.57	5,438,939.81	4,616,099.35	3,174,886.99	2,591,842.60
Due from nat'l banks.	3,030,109.11	2,440,575.60	2,517,709.67	1,319,202.62	1,309,713.79
Due from State banks	609,727.11	577,888.54	590,326.34	422,393.98	389,118.65
Banking house, etc..	1,171,116.59	1,190,004.80	1,193,497.88	1,203,007.54	1,227,866.05
Real estate, etc	303,461.12	302,111.47	313,998.26	332,675.52	343,488.57
Current expenses....	358,008.11	170,734.93	338,307.13	103,997.44	259,360.89
Premiums paid	292,654.58	267,008.16	261,058.25	246,664.22	254,089.43
Cash items	285,107.03	369,911.94	329,668.58	319,956.75	325,838.78
Clear'g-house exch'gs	105,422.07	144,979.90	131,652.55	96,380.04	76,765.48
Bills of other banks..	1,374,772.00	1,151,633.00	1,353,757.00	1,169,382.00	1,339,212.00
Fractional currency.	31,920.30	35,244.55	33,073.90	31,121.33	30,440.06
Specie	3,936,404.12	4,031,450.47	3,943,490.92	4,018,745.86	4,335,884.01
Legal-tender notes ..	2,240,505.00	1,963,608.00	2,122,132.00	2,153,630.00	2,389,678.00
U. S. cert's of deposit.	....	....	....	....	....
5 % fund with Treas.	196,803.17	200,173.07	207,187.77	203,805.57	212,766.00
Due from U. S. Treas.	18,487.54	10,101.90	11,056.65	11,081.60	6,645.35
Total.........	67,673,550.57	66,138,777.79	67,210,208.78	60,508,722.84	54,994,075.03

CITY OF CINCINNATI.

Liabilities.	DECEMBER 9. 13 banks.	MARCH 6. 13 banks.	MAY 4. 13 banks.	JULY 12. 13 banks.	OCTOBER 3. 13 banks.
Capital stock	$9,100,000.00	$9,100,000.00	$9,100,000.00	$9,100,000.00	$9,100,000.00
Surplus fund	2,700,000.00	2,700,000.00	2,745,000.00	2,745,000.00	2,745,000.00
Undivided profits	1,158,809.37	1,312,162.03	877,010.05	1,073,938.08	1,380,197.16
Nat'l-bank circulation	2,366,510.00	2,591,230.00	2,756,360.00	2,782,860.00	3,654,910.00
State-bank circulation					
Dividends unpaid	4,289.00	3,452.00	96,551.00	8,402.00	9,364.60
Individual deposits	22,317,237.50	20,849,768.22	20,790,800.19	18,393,221.49	16,889,946.75
U. S. deposits	717,076.15	745,532.22	711,735.35	714,008.35	704,280.30
Dep'ts U.S.dis.officers					
Due to national banks	7,730,806.51	6,409,570.96	5,458,221.00	3,879,524.20	4,548,684.19
Due to State banks	3,422,859.43	3,443,755.11	2,611,498.77	2,032,199.18	2,192,451.99
Notes rediscounted					
Bills payable		175,000.00	420,000.00	160,000.00	43,320.00
Other liabilities	269,300.00	587,000.00	581,150.00	573,400.00	599,200.00
Total	49,792,887.96	47,918,070.54	46,178,329.36	41,468,493.39	41,957,354.39

CITY OF CLEVELAND.

	11 banks.	11 banks.	11 banks.	11 banks.	11 banks.
Capital stock	$9,050,000.00	$9,050,000.00	$9,050,000.00	$9,050,000.00	$9,050,000.00
Surplus fund	1,777,500.60	1,777,500.00	1,800,000.00	1,800,000.00	1,800,000.00
Undivided profits	636,985.39	910,646.65	569,556.08	764,691.50	981,447.00
Nat'l-bank circulation	664,100.00	735,500.00	731,900.00	817,550.00	1,313,450.00
State-bank circulation					
Dividends unpaid	1,378.00	951.00	74,601.75	2,748.00	790.00
Individual deposits	17,234,237.78	18,233,672.56	16,212,007.76	16,440,965.09	15,756,601.07
U. S. deposits	48,850.73	53,777.45	47,429.99	54,315.13	24,606.02
Dep'ts U.S.dis.officers	9,698.31	8,596.93	9,639.93	8,277.12	33,684.28
Due to national banks	2,352,934.87	2,372,020.58	1,901,440.98	1,521,473.44	1,351,721.79
Due to State banks	1,452,906.96	1,431,607.75	1,510,599.25	1,058,000.86	960,886.18
Notes rediscounted	139,656.35		388,437.61	752,119.61	254,863.52
Bills payable	1,810,000.00	1,440,500.00	2,595,185.62	2,585,476.25	1,815,000.00
Other liabilities	536,316.56	601,316.56	576,316.56	776,178.58	766,891.08
Total	35,714,564.95	36,620,149.48	35,470,115.53	35,631,828.67	34,152,030.94

INDIANA.

	109 banks.	113 banks.	116 banks.	116 banks.	115 banks.
Capital stock	$13,722,060.00	$13,924,100.00	$14,106,300.00	$14,171,000.00	$13,777,000.00
Surplus fund	4,591,243.86	4,711,530.80	4,719,230.80	4,851,381.25	4,704,012.77
Undivided profits	2,226,610.83	1,785,335.70	2,119,873.89	1,688,295.87	1,867,075.66
Nat'l-bank circulation	4,088,354.50	4,240,604.00	4,329,254.50	4,316,609.50	4,557,189.00
State-bank circulation					
Dividends unpaid	20,776.03	23,448.76	27,253.50	70,721.52	32,446.52
Individual deposits	38,362,861.35	37,452,120.97	37,580,922.67	31,533,692.31	26,495,725.95
U. S. deposits	275,096.83	264,727.13	231,516.65	321,222.87	53,577.27
Dep'ts U.S.dis.officers	186,012.20	203,220.93	160,869.97	143,798.54	104,905.93
Due to national banks	2,031,957.66	1,659,040.97	1,823,760.33	1,118,329.48	993,790.27
Due to State banks	2,121,028.82	1,742,610.75	1,744,581.19	1,227,961.76	1,008,517.51
Notes rediscounted	102,678.49	390,758.78	304,636.45	592,288.61	274,248.00
Bills payable	20,000.00	51,260.00	39,000.00	470,047.47	125,550.52
Other liabilities	1,240.00		14,008.83	373.66	569.01
Total	67,679,550.57	66,438,777.70	67,210,208.78	60,508,722.84	53,994,675.03

ABSTRACT OF REPORTS SINCE SEPTEMBER 30, 1892, ARRANGED

ILLINOIS.

Resources.	DECEMBER 9.	MARCH 6.	MAY 4.	JULY 12.	OCTOBER 3.
	189 banks.	191 banks.	190 banks.	192 banks.	191 banks.
Loans and discounts.	$56,001,309.92	$56,575,714.60	$56,004.257.02	$50,433,832.06	$43,005,659.75
Bonds for circulation.	5,141,500.00	5,183,000.00	5,176,750.00	5,210,500.00	5,646,000.00
Bonds for deposits ..	920,000.00	920,000.00	980,000.00	955,000.00	955,000.00
U. S. bonds on hand..	265,400.00	263,000.00	268,350.00	276,800.00	189,300.00
Other stocks and b'ds	4,800,396.40	4,840,691.68	4,538,849.27	4,371,901.51	4,235,991.78
Due from res've ag'ts	6,638,003.00	7,058,950.24	6,983,876.67	6,127,830.28	6,046,018.68
Due from nat'l banks	1,191,851.70	1,162,340.04	890,859.36	819,021.77	703,778.63
Due from State banks	318,136.51	3-0,203.06	326,648.22	307,731.71	288,878.24
Banking house, etc ..	1,786,732.43	1,806,762.26	1,840,852.92	1,872,579.15	1,919,170.72
Real estate, etc......	409,789.93	475,707.57	516,772.28	461,705.86	499,914.53
Current expenses....	401,896.96	269,044.83	484,403.36	131,580.07	303,354.35
Premiums paid	425,838.71	388,902.90	390,291.54	358,416.45	377,401.62
Cash items	542,059.90	602,526.38	526,459.91	433,725.65	415,175.18
Clear'g-house exch'gs	117,592.64	123,624.40	80,802.54	73,912.68	101,701.38
Bills of other banks..	898,789.60	1,029,263.00	903,440.00	1,012,222.00	1,015,599.00
Fractional currency	35,263.81	37,854.51	36,115.30	36,892.62	40,394.12
Specie	3,831,033.59	3,023,885.79	4,063,656.33	4,222,167.05	4,176,615.05
Legal-tender notes ..	1,737,317.00	2,015,197.00	1,871,809.00	2,003,322.00	1,976,409.00
U. S. cert's of deposit	10,000.00	....	....	....	....
5 % fund with Treas	228,140.82	228,880.25	227,520.65	230,211.25	247,781.75
Due from U. S. Treas	22,133.71	27,204.90	23,654.03	18,649.20	16,438.70
Total..........	85,726,195.98	88,221,792.41	87,035,459.32	79,418,002.21	72,102,672.48

CITY OF CHICAGO.

	23 banks.	23 banks.	21 banks.	21 banks.	21 banks.
Loans and discounts	$97,956,713.53	$100,414,204.64	$96,824,856.96	$83,420,381.04	$73,516,242.32
Bonds for circulation	1,300,000.00	1,200,000.00	1,200,000.00	1,200,000.00	1,200,000.00
Bonds for deposits ..	300,000.00	300,000.00	300,000.00	300,000.00	300,000.00
U. S. bonds on hand...	380,950.00	357,300.00	45,300.00	56,250.00	261,700.00
Other stocks and b'ds	6,330,636.63	6,327,978.66	6,002,463.39	6,387,770.63	5,444,723.61
Due from res've ag'ts	....	....			
Due from nat'l banks	15,203,879.08	13,898,113.55	12,783,332.74	13,004,854.64	12,226,981.87
Due from State banks	4,002,612.63	3,715,508.56	4,229,959.03	3,231,714.98	4,056,812.41
Banking house, etc..	869,763.68	870,340.87	862,178.29	877,154.05	877,840.89
Real estate, etc......	456,037.11	490,903.23	490,760.85	500,495.86	508,952.30
Current expenses.....	255,391.91	202,566.16	258,556.14	31,037.60	168,374.08
Premiums paid	100,164.44	90,918.87	42,775.52	27,409.63	33,279.63
Cash items	89,794.36	79,613.93	65,274.75	128,920.18	51,215.61
Clear'g-house exch'gs	7,109,944.43	6,363,265.06	6,620,247.33	4,710,709.52	5,808,907.82
Bills of other banks..	1,036,352.00	761,225.00	1,710,257.00	1,265,696.00	3,114,040.00
Fractional currency.	36,759.03	59,052.72	43,493.41	32,939.77	34,878.54
Specie	22,163,893.13	22,422,967.20	21,547,194.60	15,412,970.04	22,771,923.25
Legal-tender notes ..	7,206,821.00	5,046,559.00	7,335,834.00	9,329,412.00	15,641,892.00
U. S. cert's of deposit	670,000.00	180,000.00	390,000.00	120,000.00	520,000.00
5 % fund with Treas	58,500.00	59,400.00	54,000.00	54,000.00	54,000.00
Due from U. S. Treas	96,255.00	91,000.00	58,280.00	103,000.00	192,050.00
Total	165,744,470.06	163,609,917.45	160,861,804.01	139,286,775.94	146,873,914.23

MICHIGAN.

	96 banks.	95 banks.	95 banks.	93 banks.	92 banks.
Loans and discounts	$34,898,669.98	$35,197,858.11	$36,586,558.91	$32,443,096.27	$28,480,685.43
Bonds for circulation	2,883,000.00	3,530,500.00	3,723,000.00	3,673,000.00	3,693,000.00
Bonds for deposits ..	100,000.00	200,000.00	100,000.00	100,000.00	100,000.00
U. S. bonds on hand..	5,600.00	8,950.00	8,450.00	8,450.00	8,450.00
Other stocks and b'ds	788,185.38	727,944.98	735,759.07	814,409.97	1,069,779.53
Due from res've ag'ts	5,571,906.73	4,851,502.74	3,528,037.41	3,660,203.65	3,236,826.09
Due from nat'l banks	825,078.63	560,796.46	379,622.35	391,868.39	262,399.01
Due from State banks	258,674.20	272,133.06	249,031.97	252,334.49	240,025.11
Banking house, etc ..	1,075,527.02	1,056,988.52	1,058,908.18	1,031,634.90	1,035,989.48
Real estate, etc	492,218.70	511,483.82	506,884.63	333,030.66	342,520.22
Current expenses....	270,523.72	138,905.09	219,981.94	52,274.43	196,524.75
Premiums paid	201,932.79	282,352.63	286,868.25	261,184.01	263,633.49
Cash items..........	214,090.86	246,532.39	191,978.11	170,278.91	163,115.27
Clear'g-house exch'gs	87,143.42	97,025.79	53,035.54	44,644.66	68,786.07
Bills of other banks..	518,644.00	375,576.00	521,367.00	562,392.00	482,367.00
Fractional currency.	18,593.95	21,933.80	20,742.78	21,012.53	23,050.56
Specie	1,864,481.20	1,906,168.15	1,960,029.51	2,017,009.38	2,241,172.24
Legal-tender notes ..	899,448.00	770,351.00	906,472.00	1,004,003.00	1,013,086.00
U. S. cert's of deposit.	....	....	....	....	....
5 % fund with Treas	127,569.00	176,267.50	164,945.00	164,285.00	155,286.20
Due from U. S. Treas.	10,107.50	12,698.50	12,579.50	23,393.50	3,317.13
Total	51,122,815.17	50,925,681.14	51,219,251.55	47,119,164.85	43,083,925.59

ILLINOIS.

Liabilities.	DECEMBER 9. 189 banks.	MARCH 6. 191 banks.	MAY 4. 190 banks.	JULY 12. 192 banks.	OCTOBER 3. 191 banks.
Capital stock	$17,131,600.00	$17,285,620.00	$17,253,630.00	$17,318,850.00	$17,295,450.00
Surplus fund	6,121,201.65	6,358,560.69	6,342,324.27	6,419,305.58	6,403,330.08
Undivided profits	3,387,528.57	2,895,610.07	3,235,407.88	2,594,285.16	2,902,885.92
Nat'l-bank circulation	4,553,907.00	4,573,907.00	4,576,614.50	4,627,174.50	4,988,279.50
State-bank circulation					
Dividends unpaid	31,895.45	23,953.21	31,291.24	144,607.11	37,699.11
Individual deposits	51,090,037.62	53,211,363.24	51,884,402.42	44,630,602.59	37,151,607.94
U. S. deposits	811,172.08	812,482.31	800,809.83	831,943.84	943,455.84
Dep'ts U.S.dis.officers	35,949.67	28,504.06	46,857.31	20,484.77	41,599.84
Due to national banks	586,749.77	411,303.19	538,555.62	353,084.97	380,157.34
Due to State banks	1,317,156.33	1,471,730.24	1,292,834.59	1,159,108.61	1,211,660.05
Notes rediscounted	461,007.24	488,040.44	528,731.66	610,755.08	328,363.86
Bills payable	198,000.00	654,000.00	490,000.00	682,500.00	503,776.00
Other liabilities	500.00	6,711.03		25,000.00	4,400.00
Total	85,726,195.98	88,221,792.41	87,035,459.32	79,418,002.21	72,192,672.48

CITY OF CHICAGO.

	23 banks.	23 banks.	21 banks.	21 banks.	21 banks.
Capital stock	$22,900,000.00	$22,900,000.00	$20,900,000.00	$20,900,000.00	$20,900,000.00
Surplus fund	10,055,900.00	11,516,300.00	11,516,700.00	11,522,700.00	11,522,700.00
Undivided profits	4,030,205.58	2,482,399.91	2,596,815.67	2,273,227.57	2,541,590.37
Nat'l-bank circulation	908,300.00	976,760.00	886,500.00	912,090.00	856,010.00
State-bank circulation					
Dividends unpaid	32,177.50	3,763.50	4,120.00	23,326.00	61,188.51
Individual deposits	75,329,920.45	69,552,834.78	75,781,073.65	66,433,366.88	67,681,245.46
U. S. deposits	254,062.74	265,783.64	280,750.90	253,307.45	213,075.59
Dep'ts U.S.dis.officers	17,393.98	33,942.46	5,432.37	37,676.80	45,613.84
Due to national banks	30,818,961.12	31,125,762.26	28,129,410.66	18,769,686.56	24,670,403.16
Due to State banks	21,397,459.29	24,752,370.50	20,727,180.76	18,162,344.68	18,381,487.31
Notes rediscounted			30,000.00		
Bills payable					
Other liabilities			6,800.00	50.00	
Total	165,744,470.96	163,609,917.45	160,864,604.01	139,286,775.94	146,873,914.23

MICHIGAN.

	96 banks.	95 banks.	95 banks.	97 banks.	92 banks.
Capital stock	$10,534,000.00	$10,433,000.00	$10,434,000.00	$10,284,000.00	$10,234,000.00
Surplus fund	3,207,283.29	3,169,657.39	3,191,007.39	3,209,493.11	3,198,273.96
Undivided profits	1,739,418.28	1,255,440.16	1,548,059.28	1,106,163.72	1,376,587.90
Nat'l-bank circulation	2,521,160.00	3,153,170.00	3,320,270.00	3,286,650.00	3,308,545.00
State-bank circulation					
Dividends unpaid	18,175.86	8,173.82	6,291.12	85,063.96	24,003.86
Individual deposits	31,482,235.26	31,102,706.32	30,687,598.58	27,000,691.05	23,345,911.31
U. S. deposits	76,062.75	78,437.12	76,783.71	77,742.64	93,123.22
Dep'ts U.S.dis.officers	4,150.57	1,376.75	2,896.52	1,844.36	6,594.09
Due to national banks	510,851.38	360,534.22	280,086.71	196,731.23	131,605.48
Due to State banks	826,204.80	756,825.77	782,715.18	561,455.84	574,630.58
Notes rediscounted	203,263.98	268,559.50	649,324.51	886,429.74	616,760.43
Bills payable		337,000.00	219,000.00	422,830.50	269,122.38
Other liabilities		800.00	20,318.55	68.70	5,567.38
Total	51,122,815.17	50,925,681.14	51,219,251.55	47,119,164.85	44,083,925.59

ABSTRACT OF REPORTS SINCE SEPTEMBER 30, 1892, ARRANGED

CITY OF DETROIT.

Resources.	DECEMBER 9.	MARCH 6.	MAY 4.	JULY 12.	OCTOBER 3.
	8 banks.	8 banks.	8 banks.	8 banks.	8 banks.
Loans and discounts	$18,145,704.48	$17,648,344.64	$17,298,377.64	$15,070,110,21	$13,487,642.29
Bonds for circulation	950,000.00	1,450,000.00	1,450,000.00	1,450,000.00	1,450,000.00
Bonds for deposits...	300,000.00	300,000.00	300,000.00	300,000.00	300,000.00
U. S. bonds on hand..	500,000.00				
Other stocks and b'ds	86,285.02	65,285.02	55,285.02	54,785.02	78,437.07
Due from res've ag'ts	2,792,190.90	2,035,347,63	1,446,496.66	1,500,360,05	1,456,788.93
Due from nat'l banks	937,245.17	658,426.67	711,764.87	578,101.71	591,655.06
Due from State banks	436,595.23	316,259.55	367,294.37	350,128.38	205,852.76
Banking house, etc..	16,803.50	16,803.50	16,803.50	16,803.50	16,803.50
Real estate, etc	105,214.97	92,721.64	92,721.61	130,694.53	156,938.96
Current expenses....	60,102.60	37,498.60	44,485.15	6,727.78	15,461.60
Premiums paid	214,000.00	220,500.00	218,060.00	189,500.00	187,000.00
Cash items	54,297.54	60,068.17	69,348.64	124,939.87	60,611.01
Clear'g-house exch'gs	332,868.37	310,401.28	363,762.86	254,270.32	421,122.80
Bills of other banks..	123,264.00	119,380.00	133,589.00	101,381.00	79,701.00
Fractional currency.	5,463.29	5,463.29	6,204.59	5,280.63	9,003.73
Specie	1,122,071.67	1,162,107.65	1,161,072.75	961,517.80	971,071.38
Legal-tender notes ..	927,055.00	982,750.00	693,428.00	525,652.00	581,633.00
U.S. cert's of deposit.					
5 % fund with Treas.	34,500.00	65,250.60	65,250.00	65,250.00	65,250.00
Due from U.S. Treas.	29,106.60	3,236.09	10,423.85	23,453.65	16,215.40
Total..........	27,112,870.93	25,579,852.94	24,503,190.54	21,714,945.35	20,160,219.39

WISCONSIN.

	74 banks.	74 banks.	75 banks.	76 banks.	76 banks.
Loans and discounts	$25,768,418.56	$26,847,735.67	$27,710,086.64	$24,154,416.76	$20,118,691.70
Bonds for circulation	1,690,750.00	1,700,750.00	1,714,250.00	1,856,750.00	1,875,250.00
Bonds for deposits...	150,000.00	150,000.00	150,000.00	150,000.00	150,000.00
U. S. bonds on hand..	1,050.00	1,050.00	51,050.00	1,250.00	2,550.00
Other stocks and b'ds	1,143,674.58	1,144,140.90	1,108,117.36	994,234.83	990,828.23
Due from res've ag'ts	3,827,802.73	4,081,661.95	3,196,990.41	3,118,972.62	2,808,280.07
Due from nat'l banks	398,411.41	429,511.37	474,282.86	350,945.56	424,250.22
Due from State banks	178,353.82	204,986.64	159,085.25	176,085.00	118,412.15
Banking house, etc..	769,460.20	779,210.37	790,363.22	800,914.26	798,794.86
Real estate, etc	53,376.67	60,879.66	66,949.12	72,145.95	54,912.04
Current expenses....	177,883.31	105,811.76	171,854.30	37,063.39	132,092.78
Premiums paid	138,676.56	124,757.31	134,188.56	128,442.23	132,843.98
Cash items	170,725.23	171,086.45	193,714.45	165,123.44	126,246.73
Clear'g-house exch'gs					10,511.00
Bills of other banks..	320,905.00	237,150.00	278,138.00	297,767.00	329,850.00
Fractional currency	13,982.08	16,025.52	15,883.33	15,410.49	15,891.02
Specie	1,915,508.71	2,021,085.48	2,249,314.35	2,413,933.93	2,320,637.32
Legal-tender notes ..	653,680.00	602,757.00	736,999.00	911,852.00	832,135.00
U. S. cert's of deposit					
5 % fund with Treas.	73,660.58	75,298.00	75,203.00	81,755.00	81,709.50
Due from U.S. Treas	3,536.72	7,177.99	3,036.10	1,735.39	1,301.49
Total..........	37,464,955.16	38,770,105.36	39,313,406.10	35,727,797.17	31,337,278.15

CITY OF MILWAUKEE.

	5 banks.	5 banks.	5 banks.	5 banks.	5 banks.
Loans and discounts	$7,281,193.55	$8,761,184.62	$8,836,458.80	$7,615,256.58	$6,805,859.13
Bonds for circulation	450,000.00	450,000.00	450,000.00	450,000.00	450,000.00
Bonds for deposits ..	320,000.00	320,000.00	320,000.00	340,000.00	340,000.00
U. S. bonds on hand	8,750.00	7,700.00	1,250.00	1,550.00	1,050.00
Other stocks and b'ds	813,178.13	677,605.14	615,812.90	454,812.90	370,215.40
Due from res've ag'ts	2,172,035.09	2,158,568.24	1,444,916.82	1,023,318.96	1,620,322.27
Due from nat'l banks	420,855.60	298,617.27	289,907.88	292,795.12	260,171.23
Due from State banks	150,461.50	80,146.10	73,250.02	170,144.90	204,004.00
Banking house, etc..	90,642.75	98,458.46	98,470.46	104,282.86	122,628.90
Real estate, etc			19,432.58	19,432.58	19,432.58
Current expenses....	645.61	5,709.39			10,513.18
Premiums paid	50,241.85	54,141.50	50,911.50	43,579.72	42,362.22
Cash items	16,370.93	2,816.36	5,102.95	9,173.65	4,877.38
Clear'g-house exch'gs	250,249.47	262,026.90	352,002.14	180,014.21	272,011.30
Bills of other banks..	46,469.00	49,364.00	34,751.00	68,546.00	56,908.00
Fractional currency.	4,538.75	7,738.40	3,089.64	2,192.14	6,521.50
Specie	1,100,960.00	1,323,368.00	1,335,034.00	1,175,317.31	1,580,857.10
U. S. cert's of deposit.	508,478.00	241,777.00	263,985.00	453,906.00	786,571.00
5 % fund with Treas.	15,745.00	20,250.00	20,250.00	19,620.00	20,250.00
Due from U. S. Treas.		4,000.00	18,557.91	3,000.00	4,000.00
Total..........	13,799,833.23	14,793,621.47	14,263,219.20	12,408,072.94	12,907,516.27

BY STATES AND RESERVE CITIES—Continued.

CITY OF DETROIT.

Liabilities.	DECEMBER 9. 8 banks.	MARCH 6 8 banks.	MAY 4. 8 banks.	JULY 12. 8 banks.	OCTOBER 3. 8 banks.
Capital stock	$4,400,000.00	$4,400,000.00	$4,400,000.00	$4,400,000.00	$4,400,000.00
Surplus fund	651,000.00	666,000.00	669,600.00	677,000.00	681,000.00
Undivided profits	636,121.71	545,284.99	599,140.18	446,438.39	491,612.18
Nat'l-bank circulation	760,140.00	1,282,210.00	1,300,720.00	1,295,250.00	1,291,630.00
State-bank circulation					
Dividends unpaid	36.75	324.69	824.00	4,500.06	11,462.60
Individual deposits	11,026,848.97	10,682,857.77	10,002,795.37	8,401,415.55	8,145,618.18
U. S. deposits	147,008.77	120,849.66	199,954.62	199,376.67	170,223.48
Dep'ts U.S.dis.officers	103,327.59	147,837.03	86,933.08	102,579.03	129,175.95
Due to national banks	3,003,412.60	2,869,602.88	2,440,494.09	1,770,358.23	1,213,319.55
Due to State banks	4,706,155.45	4,520,320.29	3,729,505.35	3,047,914.38	2,606,285.05
Notes rediscounted	262,819.00	110,575.63	308,703.85	314,359.48	180,719.09
Bills payable		125,000.00	375,000.00	915,753.56	814,173.31
Other liabil.ties	516,000.00	100,000.00	300,000.00	50,600.00	25,000.00
Total	27,112,670.03	25,570,852.94	24,503,190.54	21,714,045.35	20,160,210.30

WISCONSIN.

	74 banks.	74 banks.	75 banks.	76 banks.	76 banks.
Capital stock	$6,765,550.00	$6,745,900.00	$7,045,900.00	$7,085,000.00	$7,010,318.97
Surplus fund	1,971,816.01	2,050,314.02	2,055,748.93	2,068,849.02	2,009,099.02
Undivided profits	1,321,760.61	969,090.08	1,193,650.36	954,718.70	1,082,948.41
Nat'l-bank circulation	1,506,166.00	1,520,866.00	1,543,456.00	1,648,766.00	1,682,616.00
State-bank circulation					
Dividends unpaid	546.00	2,016.75	4,279.00	35,273.50	6,042.00
Individual deposits	25,207,353.08	26,794,458.47	26,655,074.52	22,800,186.14	18,872,300.88
U. S. deposits	101,621.19	125,604.87	114,742.46	118,301.60	90,736.84
Dep'ts U.S.dis.officers	31,959.02	8,715.08	16,991.61	7,043.44	27,408.71
Due to national banks	81,634.53	51,703.10	128,038.23	90,768.78	121,893.57
Due to State banks	268,900.53	317,437.45	322,057.01	262,008.53	196,838.60
Notes rediscounted	199,106.02	138,909.08	220,907.95	475,381.46	121,475.10
Bills payable	6,000.00	15,000.00	12,500.60	166,560.00	93,700.00
Other liabilities	141.27				
Total	37,464,955.16	38,770,105.30	39,313,406.10	35,727,797.17	31,337,278.15

CITY OF MILWAUKEE.

	5 banks.	5 banks.	5 banks.	5 banks.	5 banks.
Capital stock	$1,650,000.00	$2,150,000.00	$2,150,000.00	$2,150,000.00	$2,300,000.00
Surplus fund	475,000.00	475,600.00	475,000.00	475,000.00	275,000.00
Undivided profits	363,373.79	383,702.55	426,037.64	410,961.90	343,123.44
Nat'l-bank circulation	314,900.00	388,800.00	405,600.00	404,250.00	405,000.00
State-bank circulation					
Dividends unpaid					
Individual deposits	7,962,780.67	8,438,733.14	8,097,750.13	6,403,030.07	7,592,227.70
U. S. deposits	117,657.76	124,142.34	55,453.03	159,501.10	104,280.58
Dep'ts U.S.dis.officers	183,286.87	189,200.63	269,469.54	171,515.75	149,850.23
Due to national banks	1,960,290.35	1,706,224.93	1,440,575.31	1,322,987.19	1,183,780.67
Due to State banks	599,676.50	833,331.74	701,643.36	465,928.82	404,181.65
Notes rediscounted	232,828.20	104,485,94	233,290.19	230,798.11	
Bills payable				125,000.00	60,000.00
Other liabilities					
Total	13,799,833.23	14,793,621.47	14,263,219.20	12,408,972.94	12,997,516.27

ABSTRACT OF REPORTS SINCE SEPTEMBER 30, 1892, ARRANGED

IOWA.

Resources.	DECEMBER 9. 158 banks.	MARCH 6. 160 banks.	MAY 4. 162 banks.	JULY 12. 163 banks.	OCTOBER 3. 165 banks.
Loans and discounts	$39,686,502.98	$40,364,653.86	$40,559,469.51	$35,647,177.58	$31,839,875.27
Bonds for circulation	3,362,000.00	3,374,500.00	3,374,500.00	3,387,000.00	3,522,500.00
Bonds for deposits..	160,000.00	160,000.00	100,000.00	160,000.00	100,000.00
U. S. bonds on hand..	3,450.00	2,550.00	1,550.00	550.00	3,050.00
Other stocks and b'ds	1,464,248.61	1,677,531.99	1,628,974.61	1,495,651.07	1,346,899.62
Due from res've ag'ts	3,507,901,49	4,603,769.05	3,500,363.45	3,214,116.66	3,927,166.78
Due from nat'l banks	1,489,054.94	1,560,452.57	1,344,313.12	983,157.98	1,033,127.95
Due from State banks	433,142.06	531,762.09	427,047.50	365,203.39	371,988.62
Banking house, etc ..	1,468,248.63	1,504,421.34	1,531,611.84	1,538,212.04	1,557,481.21
Real estate, etc......	287,428.42	306,666.81	291,195.28	260,326.61	277,983.80
Current expenses ...	405,999.48	219,493.41	366,385.78	104,220.08	309,631.17
Premiums paid......	254,860.30	230,811.52	228,426.96	213,025.43	222,957.54
Cash items	358,130.55	366,243.46	254,894.87	240,943.63	313,017.86
Clear'g-house exch'gs	83,526.84	57,175.14	76,836.28	32,583.47	70,272.08
Bills of other banks .	500,688.00	567,450.00	538,954.00	523,021.00	510,662.00
Fractional currency	22,497.14	25,163.81	27,201.74	25,421.20	24,709.54
Specie	2,124,651.87	2,287,837.24	2,436,141.07	2,581,794.00	2,480,183.67
Legal-tender notes .	1,204,019.00	1,258,727.00	1,171,296.00	1,215,283.00	1,208,025.00
U. S. cert's of deposit.					
5 % fund with Treas.	140,029.55	150,020,41	148,343.68	148,472.91	154,920.41
Due from U. S. Treas.	8,847.15	11,713.27	13,902.90	3,710.02	7,387.50
Total..........	56,974,327.01	59,266,942.97	58,184,408.59	52,040,003.07	49,405,840.02

CITY OF DES MOINES.

Resources.	4 banks.	4 banks.	4 banks.	4 banks.	4 banks.
Loans and discounts	$2,803,385.88	$2,710,309.04	$2,765,733.02	$2,314,846.95	$1,960,652.24
Bonds for circulation	150,000.00	150,000.00	150,000.00	150,000.00	175,000.00
Bonds for deposits ..					
U. S. bonds on hand..					
Other stocks and b'ds	252,211.44	202,008.01	193,444.17	143,284.98	175,799.70
Due from res've ag'ts	290,532.04	429,700.08	221,143.22	222,783.02	324,757.18
Due from nat'l banks	183,976.27	205,436.73	127,133.13	96,344.64	82,181.55
Due from State banks	41,596.33	58,954.71	50,571.02	29,416.04	36,081.62
Banking house, etc ..	125,235.64	125,235.64	125,235.64	125,235.64	125,235.64
Real estate, etc	78,719.14	125,912.28	111,877.28	111,841.91	114,783.17
Current expenses....	21,167.73	17,216.00	25,026.91	5,673.74	24,559.31
Premiums paid	10,500.00	10,000.00	9,750.00	9,000.00	11,718.75
Cash items	9,518.51	9,955.78	7,646.50	7,015.30	9,102.98
Clear'g-house exch'gs	77,012.97	99,228.24	70,386.71	62,447.47	60,854.54
Bills of other banks..	23,310.00	38,995.00	45,655.00	29,725.00	40,611.00
Fractional currency	1,852.66	1,515.60	2,170.21	1,914.00	1,935.83
Specie	181,764.95	110,446.15	225,387.45	135,250.53	115,527.75
Legal-tender notes ..	116,964.00	184,596.00	100,953.00	181,233.00	142,084.00
U. S. cert's of deposit					
5 % fund with Treas.	6,750.00	6,750.00	6,750.00	6,750.00	7,213.00
Due from U. S. Treas.	1,000.00	1,000.00	1,000.00	1,000.00	1,000.00
Total..........	4,465,527.56	4,508,299.26	4,239,817.26	3,633,813.12	3,424,092.26

MINNESOTA.

Resources.	60 banks.	63 banks.	64 banks.	64 banks.	65 banks.
Loans and discounts	$19,175,690.07	$18,755,926.58	$18,812,521.80	$17,579,016.21	$15,334,446.26
Bonds for circulation	1,279,800.00	1,317,300.00	1,329,800.00	1,330,800.00	1,355,800.00
Bonds for deposits ..	50,000.00	50,000.00	50,000.00	50,000.00	
U. S. bonds on hand..		11,000.00	11,000.00	2,200.00	2,000.00
Other stocks and b'ds	318,198.12	309,504.11	403,278.34	390,001.40	420,158.73
Due from res've ag'ts	2,313,141.26	2,377,545.80	2,184,690.74	1,053,470.53	1,820,243.17
Due from nat'l banks	223,598.85	298,214.34	246,025.61	305,012.25	338,878.60
Due from State banks	249,426.51	247,774.61	252,828.55	193,406,87	283,456.20
Banking house, etc ..	852,492.78	865,765.95	882,207.31	883,104·58	890,933.66
Real estate, etc	214,770.71	208,053.72	218,531.40	200,783.19	202,445.64
Current expenses....	118,517.16	154,511.43	212,623.34	53,488.60	125,811.53
Premiums paid	106,120.14	96,260.57	81,568.81	76,154.06	70,791.56
Cash items	85,740.95	74,774.29	69,987.83	81,491.30	89,400.66
Clear'g-house exch'gs	104,688.92	75,520.30	74,191.52	34,422.58	55,551.05
Bills of other banks..	117,147.00	94,246.00	111,490.00	128,304.00	103,710.00
Fractional currency	7,707.27	9,811.37	10,389.91	10,777.73	13,288.46
Specie	1,067,491.43	1,126,677.81	1,244,870.32	1,453,238.50	1,428,364.51
Legal-tender notes ..	454,110.00	383,026.00	316,632.00	429,139.00	424,643.00
U. S. cert's of deposit..					
5 % fund with Treas.	57,585.50	57,011.00	56,063.50	55,271.50	59,105.50
Due from U. S. Treas.	3,501.00	3,160.50	9,310.50	1,574.00	2,818.15
Total..........	26,829,070.67	26,540,110.38	26,598,902.48	25,213,740.39	23,023,852.68

BY STATES AND RESERVE CITIES—Continued.

IOWA.

Liabilities.	DECEMBER 9. 158 banks.	MARCH 6. 160 banks.	MAY 4. 162 banks.	JULY 12. 161 banks.	OCTOBER 3. 165 banks.
Capital stock	$13,795,000.00	$13,920,000 00	$13,905,500.00	$13,915,000.00	$14,000,000.00
Surplus fund	2,977,083.96	3,067,708.27	3,050,673.25	3,045,173.78	3,031,005.14
Undivided profits	1,720,431.11	1,424,013.69	1,657,337.66	1,261,310.56	1,479,124.54
Nat'l-bank circulation	2,974,467.00	3,001,412.00	2,983,082.00	3,005,905.03	3,159,965.00
State-bank circulation					
Dividends unpaid	29,137.92	28,291.33	18,898.83	95,526.67	35,530.50
Individual deposits	29,772,605.27	31,488,014.99	30,699,767.78	25,913,397.82	23,588,396.60
U. S. deposits	94,988.60	101,889.40	72,886.33	69,351.20	110,850.25
Dep'ts U.S.dis.officers	28,950.32	32,634.14	61,646.32	41,490.24	34,841.71
Due to national banks	1,020,669.12	1,005,150.87	1,306,102.15	926,003.74	831,327.32
Due to State banks	2,635,061.00	3,270,349.16	2,626,155.16	1,740,666.34	1,941,832.96
Notes rediscounted	982,032.71	655,634.45	946,704.39	1,161,077.72	550,886.30
Bills payable	343,000.00	675,874.07	843,950.16	871,100.00	637,059.70
Other liabilities			3,604.56		5,000.00
Total	56,974,327.01	59,256,942.97	58,184,408.59	52,040,003.07	49,405,810.02

CITY OF DES MOINES.

	4 banks.	4 banks.	4 banks.	4 banks.	4 banks.
Capital stock	$700,000.00	$700,000.00	$700,000.00	$700,000.00	$700,000.00
Surplus fund	311,500.00	325,500.00	343,000.00	334,000.00	334,000.00
Undivided profits	167,972.03	144,845.96	151,537.00	128,099.37	148,219.49
Nat'l-bank circulation	135,000.00	131,800.00	131,900.00	135,600.00	143,310.00
State-bank circulation					
Dividends unpaid	1,139.50	1,296.50	4,193.50	13,376.50	3,322.50
Individual deposits	1,992,428.18	1,785,005.03	1,623,389.46	1,256,917.50	1,036,115.49
U. S. deposits					
Dep'ts U.S.dis.officers					
Due to national banks	324,649.08	393,385.16	331,383.41	211,691.53	306,334.90
Due to State banks	777,347.77	958,456.61	901,413.89	625,728.22	615,193.83
Notes rediscounted	53,500.00	5,000.00		91,000.00	37,696.00
Bills payable		63,000.00	60,000.00	135,000.00	109,000.00
Other liabilities					
Total	4,465,527.56	4,508,289.26	4,239,817.26	3,633,813.12	3,124,092.20

MINNESOTA.

	60 banks.	63 banks.	64 banks.	64 banks.	65 banks.
Capital stock	$5,720,220.00	$5,925,230.00	$5,078,200.00	$5,995,230.00	$6,080,070.00
Surplus fund	1,086,973.12	1,111,890.58	1,063,240.58	1,074,331.56	1,072,096.88
Undivided profits	1,003,634.68	809,347.04	967,684.06	692,831.06	775,601.03
Nat'l-bank circulation	1,145,834.50	1,166,194.50	1,177,252.00	1,171,212.00	1,212,352.00
State-bank circulation					
Dividends unpaid	3,961.87	4,019.20	1,825.37	29,019.70	5,684.00
Individual deposits	16,599,839.64	16,007,253.47	15,836,327.01	14,707,538.98	12,532,543.13
U. S. deposits	3,082.53	13,917.31	28,915.43	10,314.55	
Dep'ts U.S.dis.officers	21,259.83	22,988.32	11,051.57	6,464.51	
Due to national banks	167,460.38	194,702.22	173,593.90	183,595.29	143,555.63
Due to State banks	312,920.90	355,078.55	753,618.63	181,560.03	200,812.48
Notes rediscounted	687,108.83	775,148.45	886,365.54	857,500.40	660,762.14
Bills payable	48,000.00	99,863.45	86,500.00	271,000.00	266,750.60
Other liabilities	2,765.39	470.89	34,295.30	33,115.25	64,565.37
Total	20,829,070.67	26,546,110.38	26,658,902.48	25,213,746.39	23,023,852.68

ABSTRACT OF REPORTS SINCE SEPTEMBER 30, 1892, ARRANGED

CITY OF ST. PAUL.

Resources.	DECEMBER 9.	MARCH 6.	MAY 4.	JULY 12.	OCTOBER 3.
	5 banks.	5 banks.	5 banks.	5 banks.	4 banks.
Loans and discounts.	15,406,364.94	14,895,795.00	15,045,509.30	14,329,700.92	9,647,745.63
Bonds for circulation.	300,000.00	300,000.00	300,000.00	300,000.00	250,000.00
Bonds for deposits..	475,000.00	475,000.00	475,000.00	475,000.00	475,000.00
U. S. bonds on hand					
Other stocks and b'ds	491,169.60	538,581.31	551,548.10	318,054.07	412,753.26
Due from res've ag'ts.	1,246,551.18	1,172,771.21	1,030,598.96	992,131.07	1,049,894.77
Due from nat'l banks.	523,713.14	351,542.12	368,560.30	321,379.32	250,546.65
Due from State banks	338,203.43	273,369.09	228,044.14	147,990.40	70,819.49
Banking house, etc...	842,091.48	827,563.62	842,063.62	842,063.62	399,318.78
Real estate, etc	249,316.83	290,586.90	270,427.35	269,503.28	44,455.75
Current expenses ...	56,619.53	57,589.73	65,906.64	7,608.11	6,031.68
Premiums paid......	51,730.57	47,244.05	6,000.00	6,000.00	6,000.00
Cash items.........	79,822.26	78,143.26	60,466.06	65,169.58	96,843.57
Clear'g house exch'gs	397,462.78	374,361.66	369,187.52	224,243.70	242,616.65
Bills of other banks.	73,237.00	38,082.00	44,000.00	55,582.00	52,841.00
Fractional currency.	5,426.96	4,167.90	3,469.07	5,187.20	4,557.40
Specie.............	2,057,974.34	2,150,834.27	1,940,751.06	1,975,027.49	2,176,790.10
Legal-tender notes..	358,420.00	191,515.00	148,282.00	165,820.00	211,836.00
U. S. cert's of deposit.					
5 % fund with Treas.	13,500.00	13,235.41	13,500.00	13,500.00	11,250.00
Due from U. S. Treas	6,396.01	16,800.00	4,185.11	2,294.81	614.51
Total.........	22,973,699.06	22,106,173.62	21,774,099.23	20,510,345.57	15,418,406.24

CITY OF MINNEAPOLIS.

	7 banks.	7 banks.	7 banks.	7 banks.	7 banks.
Loans and discounts.	$14,162,339.87	$13,348,462.62	$13,945,509.98	$13,141,168.63	$12,320,518.51
Bonds for circulation.	350,000.00	350,000.00	350,000.00	350,000.00	350,000.00
Bonds for deposits...	50,000.00	50,000.00	50,000.00	50,000.00	50,000.00
U. S. bonds on hand...					
Other stocks and b'ds	430,804.53	420,370.90	420,370.90	450,920.61	600,183.32
Due from res've ag'ts	1,036,852.31	1,114,624.61	1,186,631.07	729,830.29	866,276.06
Due from nat'l banks.	800,225.77	508,602.88	493,482.24	473,083.96	407,381.68
Due from State banks	263,875.79	225,168.63	306,515.53	187,749.14	233,070.05
Banking house, etc..	261,640.13	264,237.55	264,237.55	168,239.55	188,239.55
Real estate, etc	130,052.67	260,704.97	199,853.13	278,628.85	372,556.13
Current expenses ...	70,919.76	88,368.85	126,337.60	8,655.17	52,098.91
Premiums paid......	42,375.00	37,625.00	35,125.00	26,125.00	26,125.00
Cash items.........	33,422.04	20,070.57	31,755.60	24,740.10	21,758.87
Clear'g house exch'gs	644,713.06	449,075.72	317,171.75	414,912.71	467,509.27
Bills of other banks..	166,142.00	127,602.00	156,054.00	72,866.00	99,229.00
Fractional currency.	3,187.07	5,103.92	5,613.90	5,741.39	5,913.60
Specie.............	882,491.70	1,048,993.75	1,240,417.15	890,378.25	975,527.65
Legal-tender notes ..	782,517.00	431,237.00	631,673.00	592,770.00	435,000.00
U. S. cert's of deposit.					
5 % fund with Treas.	15,750.00	15,150.00	15,750.00	15,200.00	13,700.00
Due from U. S. Treas.	3,000.00	10,780.00	1,100.00	2,480.00	127.70
Total	20,130,308.70	18,717,078.97	19,777,598.40	17,003,489.65	17,485,345.30

MISSOURI.

	58 banks.	58 banks.	58 banks.	57 banks.	57 banks.
Loans and discounts	$10,353,712.36	$10,734,065.95	$10,627,385.02	$9,720,211.24	$8,553,430.05
Bonds for circulation	1,208,800.00	1,207,800.00	1,207,800.00	1,195,300.00	1,195,300.00
Bonds for deposits..					
U. S. bonds on hand..	4,150.00	4,150.00	3,500.00	350.00	350.00
Other stocks and b'ds	775,234.58	808,688.61	702,606.69	752,662.23	725,161.83
Due from res've ag'ts.	1,334,897.73	1,617,247.20	1,389,598.05	891,442.13	898,063.88
Due from nat'l banks	108,330.80	207,174.69	226,186.45	154,301.87	152,656.82
Due from State banks	142,725.71	202,736.61	161,046.64	63,363.03	69,937.57
Banking house, etc..	498,219.99	501,276.61	502,370.23	501,609.81	502,788.99
Real estate, etc	124,056.69	131,578.35	140,661.21	138,607.47	158,328.99
Current expenses.....	120,789.02	96,465.19	131,140.97	41,021.17	81,121.01
Premiums paid......	117,315.62	108,974.99	98,716.59	87,318.74	84,610.34
Cash items.........	82,583.65	118,358.05	121,530.00	63,345.51	81,482.82
Clear'g house exch'gs					9,426.68
Bills of other banks..	192,656.00	172,325.00	169,566.00	183,757.00	196,803.00
Fractional currency.	3,895.88	4,332.20	3,956.72	4,068.50	3,768.16
Specie.............	468,764.63	516,893.04	521,634.56	531,218.63	522,209.10
Legal-tender notes ..	353,691.00	370,500.00	347,431.00	318,889.00	363,166.00
U. S. cert's of deposit.					
5 % fund with Treas.	52,321.21	53,751.00	53,451.00	51,798.50	52,488.50
Due from U. S. Treas	452.50	1,077.50	1,222.50	502.50	960.00
Total.........	15,951,598.87	16,857,395.11	16,470,705.83	14,700,657.33	13,652,030.04

CITY OF ST. PAUL.

Liabilities.	DECEMBER 9.	MARCH 6.	MAY 4.	JULY 12.	OCTOBER 3.
	5 banks.	5 banks.	5 banks.	5 banks.	4 banks.
Capital stock	$4,800,000.00	$4,800,000.00	$4,800,000.00	$4,800,000.00	$2,800,000.00
Surplus fund	1,298,000.00	1,326,000.00	1,326,000.00	1,328,000.00	1,103,000.00
Undivided profits	1,444,268.69	1,260,716.48	1,154,081.07	1,030,436.12	1,003,960.85
Nat'l-bank circulation	269,220.00	266,020.00	269,000.00	269,370.00	223,780.00
State-bank circulation					
Dividends unpaid	1,840.50	2,732.50	2,409.00	17,401.00	11,072.00
Individual deposits	10,530,904.85	9,908,618.25	9,714,651.56	9,390,272.17	7,167,602.98
U. S. deposits	248,711.54	252,265.55	160,721.13	285,177.54	167,477.17
Dep'ts U.S.dis.officers	249,139.03	203,145.04	293,927.50	194,124.36	275,812.33
Due to national banks	2,686,675.70	2,005,597.78	1,814,469.17	1,410,923.78	1,550,789.87
Due to State banks	1,460,248.73	1,530,078.02	1,408,060.35	773,119.06	733,800.30
Notes rediscounted	5,000.00	351,000.00	571,779.45	717,578.54	81,020.65
Bills payable					
Other liabilities		200,000.00	200,000.00	300,000.00	300,000.00
Total	22,973,039.06	22,106,173.62	21,774,099.23	20,516,313.57	15,418,406.24

CITY OF MINNEAPOLIS.

	7 banks.	7 banks.	7 banks.	7 banks.	7 banks.
Capital stock	$5,450,000.00	$5,450,000.00	$5,450,000.00	$5,450,000.00	$5,450,000.00
Surplus fund	639,000.00	650,000.00	650,000.00	674,000.00	674,000.00
Undivided profits	900,526.60	738,274.01	848,598.28	705,813.17	783,012.93
Nat'l-bank circulation	288,727.00	283,767.50	284,147.50	313,995.00	314,497.50
State-bank circulation					
Dividends unpaid	505.50	2,202.00	1,010.00	47,343.00	604.00
Individual deposits	8,999,857.30	8,560,778.72	8,929,716.98	7,859,188.22	7,403,824.39
U. S. deposits	36,862.16	36,851.30	38,222.63	49,882.95	47,945.17
Dep'ts U.S.dis.officers	2,814.53	2,400.35	1,856.30		1,406.99
Due to national banks	1,761,847.33	1,447,018.55	1,506,653.94	815,581.74	1,045,659.67
Due to State banks	1,040,055.63	911,549.90	828,208.61	573,227.81	587,382.18
Notes rediscounted	601,112.60	350,233.55	538,575.16	953,427.76	569,408.53
Bills payable	400,000.00	275,000.00	700,000.00	470,000.00	607,000.00
Other liabilities					
Total	20,130,308.70	18,717,078.97	19,777,598.40	17,903,489.65	17,485,345.30

MISSOURI.

	58 banks.	58 banks.	58 banks.	57 banks.	57 banks.
Capital stock	$4,640,000.00	$4,680,000.00	$4,665,000.00	$4,615,000.00	$4,615,000.00
Surplus fund	752,118.63	793,502.02	792,502.02	788,019.02	797,269.02
Undivided profits	512,717.63	341,950.29	433,392.81	263,308.53	350,019.97
Nat'l-bank circulation	1,062,520.00	1,075,540.00	1,078,760.00	1,069,530.00	1,074,467.90
State-bank circulation					
Dividends unpaid	6,352.50	2,493.00	687.50	22,534.50	15,647.50
Individual deposits	8,479,962.33	9,336,835.18	8,833,153.91	7,256,351.36	6,220,405.97
U. S. deposits					
Dep'ts U.S.dis.officers					
Due to national banks	37,522.11	47,779.19	41,704.49	27,925.23	38,560.53
Due to State banks	65,315.76	180,173.78	123,439.73	73,071.74	66,962.50
Notes rediscounted	221,088.91	239,844.65	346,268.37	335,736.95	235,884.65
Bills payable	171,000.00	150,277.60	156,277.00	246,277.00	237,815.00
Other liabilities			500.00		
Total	15,951,598.87	16,857,395.11	16,470,705.83	14,700,657.33	13,652,030.04

ABSTRACT OF REPORTS SINCE SEPTEMBER 30, 1892, ARRANGED

CITY OF ST. LOUIS.

Resources.	DECEMBER 9. 9 banks.	MARCH 6. 9 banks.	MAY 4. 9 banks.	JULY 12. 9 banks.	OCTOBER 3. 9 banks.
Loans and discounts.	$31,186,432.53	$32,389,183.16	$32,736,801.99	$26,508,101.76	$22,956,175.14
Bonds for circulation.	450,000.00	450,000.00	450,000.00	450,000.00	450,000.00
Bonds for deposits ..	250,000.00	250,000.00	250,000.00	250,000.00	250,000.00
U.S. bonds on hand..					
Other stocks and b'ds	1,893,790.74	1,782,160.44	1,358,144.44	1,501,436.71	1,533,547.06
Due from res'r eag'ts					
Due from nat'l banks.	3,903,065.87	3,961,608.62	2,765,622.94	2,389,053.87	2,244,672.70
Due from State banks	854,958.48	811,731.85	894,375.12	532,343.99	561,382.72
Banking house, etc ..	878,308.05	871,843.51	874,343.51	878,343.51	892,981.16
Real estate, etc	175,048.30	175,048.30	175,048.30	175,048.30	177,320.46
Current expenses....	18,946.13	54,680.86	72,924.63	47,445.08	98,720.88
Premiums paid	85,300.00	75,300.00	74,300.00	62,300.00	59,800.00
Cash items	177,959.76	183,008.34	125,012.50	106,272.92	108,984.09
Clear'g-house exch'gs	1,644,120.92	1,548,238.02	1,492,002.55	1,212,136.43	987,696.43
Bills of other banks..	172,953.00	178,299.00	144,525.00	114,529.00	156,542.00
Fractional currency.	4,063.73	4,320.00	5,406.95	3,285.87	4,823.78
Specie	4,006,481.05	4,818,284.30	3,762,026.70	2,535,019.02	3,639,674.75
Legal-tender notes ..	1,679,550.00	1,934,690.00	2,166,836.00	1,843,208.00	2,051,573.00
U.S. cert's of deposit.	30,000.00			75,000.00	10,000.00
5% fund with Treas.	20,250.00	20,250.00	20,250.00	20,250.00	20,250.00
Due from U.S. Treas.	6,600.00	3,000.00	5,600.00	7,000.00	6,000.00
Total..........	47,527,828.56	49,541,646.40	47,372,229.63	38,730,804.46	36,249,247.73

KANSAS CITY.

	10 banks.	10 banks.	9 banks.	9 banks.	8 banks.
Loans and discounts.	$18,921,646.06	$18,166,563.97	$18,609,948.50	$15,987,379.89	$11,425,110.10
Bonds for circulation.	500,000.00	500,000.00	450,000.00	450,000.00	400,000.00
Bonds for deposits ..	100,000.00	100,000.00	100,000.00	100,000.00	100,000.00
U.S. bonds on hand ..			28,254.00		
Other stocks and b'ds	1,131,134.73	1,396,232.63	1,390,324.23	1,422,986.68	909,141.72
Due from res'r eag'ts	3,075,549.76	3,407,083.76	1,983,112.26	1,152,547.23	1,492,311.85
Due from nat'l banks.	904,420.35	1,016,283.85	860,929.87	822,031.46	869,906.03
Due from State banks	727,723.68	830,493.28	925,420.36	626,620.91	430,337.74
Banking house, etc ..	384,684.42	406,959.42	398,402.92	397,902.92	219,117.62
Real estate, etc	333,652.72	345,211.44	343,211.44	349,938.44	201,943.48
Current expenses....	85,756.76	62,552.50	58,343.19	25,247.61	39,735.23
Premiums paid	79,000.00	67,000.00	58,000.00	53,500.00	47,000.00
Cash items	50,276.59	78,078.29	96,872.07	52,949.90	97,357.09
Clear'g-house exch'gs	583,241.34	763,742.80	591,482.29	248,773.63	535,486.18
Bills of other banks..	301,181.00	310,804.00	196,697.00	232,293.00	290,433.00
Fractional currency.	4,938.31	4,124.28	4,221.53	4,772.37	6,040.74
Specie	1,238,292.75	1,457,540.30	1,580,346.55	746,069.20	1,254,807.60
Legal-tender notes ..	1,347,625.00	1,318,574.00	1,442,552.00	795,037.00	1,003,719.00
U.S. cert's of deposit					
5% fund with Treas.	21,900.00	22,500.00	20,250.00	20,250.00	18,000.00
Due from U.S. Treas.	9,700.00	7,200.00	20,001.00	8,100.00	3,700.00
Total..........	29,800,722.47	30,257,034.61	29,158,375.32	23,491,400.24	19,336,047.73

CITY OF ST. JOSEPH.

	4 banks.	4 banks.	4 banks.	4 banks.	4 banks.
Loans and discounts	$5,706,907.94	$5,683,061.40	$5,891,283.58	$5,019,083.36	$4,490,475.94
Bonds for circulation.	300,000.00	300,000.00	300,000.00	250,000.00	250,000.00
Bonds for deposits...	50,000.00	50,000.00	50,000.00	50,000.00	50,000.00
U.S. bonds on hand..					
Other stocks and b'ds	126,640.32	174,433.35	174,183.75	180,358.55	164,156.94
Due from res'r eag'ts.	513,455.58	644,357.54	464,841.45	518,370.36	841,296.41
Due from nat'l banks	326,540.23	492,195.42	330,356.03	357,240.24	298,954.28
Due from State banks	82,970.66	103,360.88	49,553.36	92,635.07	98,192.67
Banking house, etc ..	128,350.00	126,850.00	126,850.00	120,850.00	120,850.00
Real estate, etc	9,922.73	4,890.06	4,890.06	41,096.06	6,578.70
Current expenses....	18,711.82	10,096.89	13,650.93	2,414.06	9,314.09
Premiums paid	15,500.00	12,500.00	12,500.00	10,500.00	10,500.00
Cash items	87,998.00	100,792.70	73,555.77	44,776.41	47,538.66
Clear'g-house exch'gs	83,860.43	98,271.14	109,751.70	54,924.02	102,132.84
Bills of other banks..	36,295.00	25,920.00	16,970.00	17,714.00	35,843.00
Fractional currency.	637.76	721.25	763.81	979.29	830.75
Specie	338,714.70	340,869.05	318,729.85	314,507.95	445,062.00
Legal-tender notes ..	276,886.00	287,680.00	239,688.00	261,479.00	285,550.00
U.S. cert's of deposit					
5% fund with Treas.	13,500.00	13,500.00	13,500.00	11,250.00	11,250.00
Due from U.S. Treas.	1,150.00	1,400.00	1,700.00	550.00	700.00
Total	8,112,089.17	8,471,808.59	8,180,067.65	7,378,728.37	7,260,346.28

CITY OF ST. LOUIS.

Liabilities.	DECEMBER 9. 9 banks.	MARCH 6. 9 banks.	MAY 4. 9 banks.	JULY 12. 9 banks.	OCTOBER 3. 9 banks.
Capital stock........	$10,700,000.00	$10,700,000.00	$10,700,000.00	$10,700,000.00	$10,700,000.00
Surplus fund.........	1,730,000.00	1,811,000.00	1,951,000.00	2,033,000.00	2,053,700.89
Undivided profits....	898,364.61	956,215.52	920,167.10	830,155.15	930,483.04
Nat'l-bank circulation	402,950.00	405,000.00	401,910.00	405,000.00	405,000.00
State-bank circulation					
Dividends unpaid....	11,827.50	19,502.25	41,489.00	1,919.00	1,275.50
Individual deposits ..	20,896,288.40	20,216,664.47	19,853,231.78	15,606,472.39	13,616,078.19
U. S. deposits........	240,000.00	240,000.00	240,000.00	240,000.00	250,000.00
Dep'ts U.S.dis.officers					
Due to national banks	8,813,686.49	8,225,706.75	6,774,039.93	4,230,771.00	4,291,511.71
Due to State banks...	5,262,721.56	6,780,549.84	6,148,465.63	4,050,978.28	3,696,069.40
Notes rediscounted ..	272,000.00	100,000.00	279,917.19	247,508.64	
Bills payable	390,000.00	80,000.00	60,000.00	365,000.00	250,000.00
Other liabilities......		7,007.57		20,000.00	
Total	47,527,828.56	49,541,646.40	47,372,220.63	38,730,801.46	36,249,247.73

KANSAS CITY.

	10 banks.	10 banks.	9 banks.	9 banks.	8 banks.
Capital stock........	$6,800,000.00	$6,800,000.00	$6,550,000.00	$6,550,000.00	$5,550,000.00
Surplus fund.........	852,000.00	725,600.00	726,000.00	730,700.00	533,789.00
Undivided profits....	393,493.52	231,306.88	237,721.57	183,584.91	183,390.48
Nat'l-bank circulation	450,000.00	450,000.00	405,000.00	405,000.00	360,600.00
State-bank circulation					
Dividends unpaid....	304.50	492.75	992.00	28,080.25	253.25
Individual deposits...	11,308,556.51	11,076,291.12	9,867,065.74	8,312,352.38	6,350,634.49
U. S. deposits........	57,077.42	08,413.91	67,248.26	80,674.03	01,476.01
Dep'ts U.S.dis.officers	27,378.46	22,025.30	17,391.66	8,919.23	19,417.09
Due to national banks	5,208,402.66	5,202,856.96	5,309,144.16	2,432,564.49	2,868,397.17
Due to State banks...	4,643,504.40	5,580,047.09	5,342,811.93	2,794,190.17	2,693,967.24
Notes rediscounted ..			60,000.00	160,821.78	34,500.00
Bills payable........		100,000.00	575,000.00	1,795,500.00	674,287.00
Other liabilities......					
Total	29,800,723.47	30,257,034.61	29,158,375.32	24,491,460.24	19,336,047.73

CITY OF ST. JOSEPH.

	4 banks.	4 banks.	4 banks.	4 banks.	4 banks.
Capital stock........	$2,000,000.00	$2,000,000.00	$2,000,000.00	$2,000,000.00	$2,000,000.00
Surplus fund.........	210,000.00	220,000.00	221,000.00	223,500.00	223,500.00
Undivided profits....	116,386.92	56,993.69	75,599.34	45,818.08	83,549.16
Nat'l-bank circulation	269,000.00	270,000.00	269,000.00	225,000.00	225,000.00
State-bank circulation					
Dividends unpaid....	56.00	556.00	434.00		
Individual deposits...	3,734,107.08	3,674,157.99	3,480,750.87	3,239,659.54	2,941,865.04
U. S. deposits........	43,714.43	44,351.39	43,449.30	41,911.20	49,412.18
Dep'ts U.S.dis.officers	319.30	338.61	525.49	40.10	81.40
Due to national banks	568,032.15	709,127.83	786,837.52	583,001.01	551,665.40
Due to State banks...	1,020,213.22	1,385,925.96	1,200,464.38	937,198.44	1,179,116.95
Notes rediscounted ..	91,260.07	6',297.10	48,866.75	50,000.00	5,156.00
Bills payable........	50,000.00	50,000.00	51,000.00	20,600.00	10,000.00
Other liabilities......					
Total	8,112,089.17	8,471,808.59	8,186,967.65	7,378,728.37	7,269,346.28

ABSTRACT OF REPORTS SINCE SEPTEMBER 30, 1892, ARRANGED

KANSAS.

Resources.	DECEMBER 9. 142 banks.	MARCH 6. 140 banks.	MAY 4. 140 banks.	JULY 12. 138 banks.	OCTOBER 3. 136 banks.
Loans and discounts	$25,416,981.03	$25,255,029.80	$25,387,793.00	$23,300,208.05	$19,065,551.97
Bonds for circulation	2,892,750.00	2,855,250.00	2,830,250.00	2,836,500.00	2,881,500.00
Bonds for deposits	310,000.00	310,000.00	310,000.00	260,000.00	260,000.00
U.S. bonds on hand	9,100.00	16,700.00	16,700.00	21,100.00	2,100.00
Other stocks and b'ds	916,192.22	815,496.89	863,598.31	837,593.57	842,797.24
Due from res've ag'ts	4,218,578.83	5,038,855.76	4,757,258.28	3,393,400.96	3,290,762.31
Due from nat'l banks	753,652.50	816,263.95	964,454.21	659,708.84	747,517.01
Due from State banks	180,793.69	205,545.95	286,611.96	145,641.84	284,341.33
Banking house, etc	1,601,575.44	1,550,793.26	1,562,498.87	1,568,063.21	1,557,299.16
Real estate, etc	742,907.79	746,243.85	777,030.20	739,587.18	765,759.32
Current expenses	339,225.02	173,616.67	278,524.58	108,239.94	212,361.53
Premiums paid	260,386.98	248,579.12	233,817.26	191,904.99	187,493.72
Cash items	333,395.98	460,205.39	573,470.69	397,543.30	260,073.84
Clear'g-house exch'gs	29,080.80	40,477.55	45,336.91	23,755.72	360,824.84
Bills of other banks	486,944.00	583,206.00	582,671.00	708,821.00	708,524.00
Fractional currency	14,519.80	17,540.59	18,541.78	18,099.97	16,655.03
Specie	1,580,038.90	1,763,980.25	1,843,100.39	1,943,060.20	1,806,245.81
Legal-tender notes	954,325.00	907,008.00	925,154.00	905,229.00	980,396.00
U.S. cert's of deposit					
5% fund with Treas	128,201.14	126,221.25	122,398.75	120,715.28	122,772.84
Due from U.S. Treas	5,874.50	18,931.95	18,270.80	2,441.30	505.20
Total	41,183,096.64	41,950,916.23	42,497,529.08	38,104,532.44	35,266,485.02

NEBRASKA.

	126 banks.	126 banks.	123 banks.	122 banks.	121 banks.
Loans and discounts	$21,822,081.24	$24,755,391.73	$20,927,754.91	$18,302,860.09	$16,336,688.20
Bonds for circulation	2,270,000.00	2,232,500.00	2,070,000.00	2,030,000.00	2,042,500.00
Bonds for deposits					
U.S. bonds on hand					
Other stocks and b'ds	395,407.98	407,767.18	339,835.18	322,869.66	347,483.74
Due from res've ag'ts	2,677,854.40	3,388,412.95	2,726,650.21	2,337,072.75	2,230,529.68
Due from nat'l banks	603,989.43	780,223.55	360,758.86	303,910.49	350,775.98
Due from State banks	261,184.82	263,684.60	304,601.73	204,130.74	209,239.53
Banking house, etc	1,368,993.21	1,415,675.31	1,346,524.12	1,302,080.61	1,297,083.50
Real estate, etc	448,279.40	409,100.15	403,450.20	438,121.18	432,390.37
Current expenses	377,531.76	261,512.61	353,609.36	94,661.60	239,142.57
Premiums paid	186,407.94	172,509.95	161,406.20	142,706.08	138,392.60
Cash items	359,830.63	445,766.15	282,237.94	296,947.02	332,683.05
Clear'g-house exch'gs	58,636.01	46,843.06			5,955.74
Bills of other banks	121,298.00	148,205.00	137,752.00	124,814.00	117,500.00
Fractional currency	10,631.97	12,029.11	10,557.64	10,818.70	10,919.32
Specie	1,210,655.46	1,385,379.74	1,166,906.85	1,169,904.83	1,112,188.66
Legal-tender notes	482,030.00	537,667.00	339,497.00	443,350.00	381,821.00
U.S. cert's of deposit					
5% fund with Treas	100,743.65	90,061.50	91,024.50	89,286.50	87,371.50
Due from U.S. Treas	2,912.50	5,495.00	3,805.00	2,545.00	2,481.75
Total	35,760,648.46	36,768,818.65	31,035,029.70	27,018,029.55	25,674,337.49

CITY OF LINCOLN.

	Banks.	Banks.	4 banks.	4 banks.	4 banks.
Loans and discounts			$3,726,056.62	$3,010,062.54	$2,630,497.90
Bonds for circulation			175,000.00	175,000.00	175,000.00
Bonds for deposits					
U.S. bonds on hand					
Other stocks and b'ds			50,137.21	51,157.56	53,748.80
Due from res've ag'ts			332,574.70	238,735.57	148,575.44
Due from nat'l banks			78,687.65	93,652.93	88,570.43
Due from State banks			17,409.08	52,620.72	87,423.74
Banking house, etc			70,935.67	80,242.67	80,382.67
Real estate, etc			31,407.25	33,307.65	48,258.76
Current expenses			55,861.03	26,640.41	49,148.00
Premiums paid			8,900.00	8,650.00	7,650.00
Cash items			38,409.08	149,790.26	50,261.53
Clear'g-house exch'gs			54,621.51	20,689.06	50,731.97
Bills of other banks			12,408.00	7,402.00	5,968.00
Fractional currency			3,356.14	4,000.20	1,958.75
Specie			205,532.67	136,323.25	271,385.41
Legal-tender notes			10,189.00	76,373.00	42,880.00
U.S. cert's of deposit					
5% fund with Treas			7,875.00	7,875.00	7,875.00
Due from U.S. Treas				820.00	
Total			4,898,660.61	4,173,441.82	3,809,115.40

KANSAS.

Liabilities.	DECEMBER 9. 142 banks.	MARCH 6. 140 banks.	MAY 4. 140 banks.	JULY 12. 138 banks.	OCTOBER 3. 136 banks.
Capital stock	$12,412,100.00	$12,087,100.00	$12,092,100.00	$11,902,100.00	$11,047,100.00
Surplus fund	1,755,014.23	1,756,652.25	1,729,261.46	1,752,176.93	1,750,423.54
Undivided profits	1,349,397.05	741,622.10	957,008.73	648,813.34	771,103.22
Nat'l-bank circulation	2,582,490.00	2,540,485.00	2,520,142.50	2,498,100.00	2,583,480.00
State-bank circulation					
Dividends unpaid	1,146.36	7,709.01	45,568.90	51,835.37	32,111.86
Individual deposits	20,974,815.50	22,380,261.06	22,588,540.83	19,463,850.28	16,683,300.59
U. S. deposits	101,484.92	77,776.85	47,040.10	135,216.68	104,151.24
Dep'ts U.S.dis.officers	189,467.23	218,040.32	238,957.01	116,220.25	154,505.02
Due to national banks	431,951.81	557,522.28	894,974.60	446,496.42	416,901.25
Due to State banks	584,665.13	719,116.76	678,471.18	521,881.37	669,626.22
Notes rediscounted	475,660.71	469,330.60	385,393.90	385,067.10	133,094.93
Bills payable	294,978.75	380,679.23	265,750.37	272,260.54	374,680.25
Other liabilities	14.95	5,024.17	15,319.50	455.16	
Total	41,183,096.64	41,950,946.23	42,497,529.08	38,194,532.44	35,266,485.02

NEBRASKA.

	126 banks.	126 banks.	123 banks.	122 banks.	121 banks.
Capital stock	$9,118,100.00	$8,918,100.00	$7,943,100.00	$7,748,100.00	$7,703,170.00
Surplus fund	1,648,942.38	1,709,941.44	1,577,741.44	1,591,850.49	1,572,025.40
Undivided profits	1,121,171.54	774,846.00	940,000.28	562,614.77	732,736.20
Nat'l-bank circulation	2,042,017.50	2,001,022.50	1,851,002.50	1,812,532.50	1,832,700.00
State-bank circulation					
Dividends unpaid	1,008.50	4,382.18	1,109.50	52,124.94	26,694.00
Individual deposits	19,032,339.91	20,181,651.26	16,757,705.05	14,076,988.87	12,119,399.62
U. S. deposits					
Dep'ts U.S.dis.officers					
Due to national banks	509,928.22	607,377.51	319,099.60	303,088.56	266,770.96
Due to State banks	1,050,844.42	1,332,863.66	669,602.57	435,338.47	374,494.76
Notes rediscounted	986,129.02	852,705.74	707,996.21	687,229.49	564,107.16
Bills payable	250,000.00	323,983.93	287,505.78	347,357.52	381,329.23
Other liabilities	166.97	1,914.43	157.77	402.94	10,910.07
Total	35,760,648.46	36,768,818.65	31,055,020.70	27,618,029.55	25,674,337.49

CITY OF LINCOLN.

	Banks.	Banks.	4 banks.	4 banks.	4 banks.
Capital stock			$1,000,000.00	$1,000,000.00	$1,000,000.00
Surplus fund			140,000.00	147,000.00	148,000.00
Undivided profits			103,754.13	98,010.55	124,858.14
Nat'l bank circulation			157,500.00	157,500.00	157,500.00
State-bank circulation					
Dividends unpaid			39.00	3,000.00	3,000.00
Individual deposits			2,491,603.31	1,986,846.38	1,580,576.71
U. S. deposits					
Dep'ts U.S.dis.officers					
Due to national banks			263,733.62	157,550.46	229,391.85
Due to State banks			526,980.55	267,934.43	293,788.70
Notes rediscounted			215,050.00	280,600.00	174,500.00
Bills payable				75,000.00	22,500.00
Other liabilities					75,000.00
Total			4,808,660.61	4,173,441.82	3,809,315.40

ABSTRACT OF REPORTS SINCE SEPTEMBER 30, 1892, ARRANGED

CITY OF OMAHA.

Resources.	DECEMBER 9.	MARCH 6.	MAY 4.	JULY 12.	OCTOBER 3.
	9 banks.	9 banks.	9 banks.	8 banks.	9 banks.
Loans and discounts	$12,379,701.96	$12,636,815.35	$12,471,274.20	$10,181,716.31	$9,362,659.76
Bonds for circulation	730,000.00	730,000.00	730,000.00	730,000.00	780,000.00
Bonds for deposits	475,000.00	475,000.00	475,000.00	475,000.00	475,000.00
U.S. bonds on hand					
Other stocks and b'ds	213,398.92	257,321.89	284,974.39	217,767.31	271,018.67
Due from res've ag'ts	1,666,849.68	1,935,509.13	1,258,154.70	1,236,757.31	1,320,136.32
Due from nat'l banks	1,320,548.67	1,152,618.16	901,739.45	571,684.80	446,790.31
Due from State banks	927,023.57	689,848.99	672,814.85	419,892.68	422,953.52
Banking house, etc	837,656.85	837,264.92	837,264.92	827,760.36	835,800.07
Real estate, etc	132,857.69	163,398.61	165,276.44	196,437.80	243,910.22
Current expenses	90,839.81	81,200.30	77,675.04	50,959.76	79,998.99
Premiums paid	166,521.88	162,521.88	152,146.88	134,046.88	134,546.88
Cash items	270,486.99	461,846.55	552,463.10	377,262.60	173,707.40
Clear'g-house exch'gs	413,182.78	621,635.76	468,217.86	291,646.37	295,988.68
Bills of other banks	127,463.00	127,592.00	125,282.00	114,122.00	138,723.60
Fractional currency	5,748.45	2,195.19	4,785.16	2,492.24	8,345.58
Specie	1,841,445.98	1,812,293.10	1,796,777.60	1,336,006.79	1,700,906.92
Legal-tender notes	581,600.00	608,500.00	586,996.00	502,506.00	527,705.00
U.S. cert's of deposit					
5 % fund with Treas.	31,000.00	32,850.00	30,320.00	31,777.50	35,100.00
Due from U.S. Treas.	9,590.00	1,190.00	1,000.00	5,259.55	16,697.03
Total	22,204,814.23	22,780,590.83	21,592,162.59	17,793,105.26	17,269,778.35

COLORADO.

	53 banks.	53 banks.	53 banks.	47 banks.	51 banks.
Loans and discounts	$24,647,945.01	$26,655,542.41	$26,270,113.66	$23,824,414.43	$22,107,147.17
Bonds for circulation	1,609,250.00	1,609,250.00	1,609,250.00	1,556,750.00	1,642,750.00
Bonds for deposits	500,000.00	500,000.00	500,000.00	500,000.00	450,000.00
U.S. bonds on hand					
Other stocks and b'ds	1,320,304.29	1,443,999.33	1,410,960.53	1,225,521.60	1,317,008.87
Due from res've ag'ts	4,924,393.52	4,572,611.58	3,158,691.82	1,471,477.20	2,173,987.37
Due from nat'l banks	2,767,403.38	2,529,191.30	2,028,786.55	715,177.05	1,141,273.62
Due from State banks	491,365.58	482,471.09	503,157.78	220,402.23	242,182.83
Banking house, etc	1,022,294.25	1,012,439.76	1,015,697.68	908,926.64	998,714.52
Real estate, etc	307,770.70	322,027.28	382,715.03	352,245.63	464,008.52
Current expenses	277,519.40	181,446.80	214,707.28	50,912.88	166,845.75
Premiums paid	222,358.06	197,327.43	190,134.93	167,378.18	154,565.60
Cash items	164,573.08	201,481.24	202,003.03	158,790.08	183,047.81
Clear'g-house exch'gs	580,289.60	691,965.39	618,160.30	429,104.30	343,030.29
Bills of other banks	465,731.00	424,325.00	461,797.00	573,483.00	468,362.00
Fractional currency	8,558.06	10,311.10	9,822.56	8,042.17	10,587.49
Specie	3,026,019.30	3,356,895.52	3,162,009.68	2,187,060.00	2,656,418.68
Legal-tender notes	1,308,036.00	1,095,857.00	1,188,987.00	833,978.00	1,595,752.00
U.S. cert's of deposit					
5% fund with Treas.	75,945.75	74,983.25	76,445.75	69,530.75	71,653.25
Due from U.S. Treas	10,310.00	12,677.50	7,362.50	1,902.50	2.50
Total	47,820,076.17	47,466,802.48	46,089,812.15	35,255,226.63	36,187,538.57

NEVADA.

	2 banks.	2 banks.	2 banks.	2 banks.	2 banks.
Loans and discounts	$763,630.55	$747,588.98	$665,057.66	$678,913.99	$610,459.83
Bonds for circulation	70,500.00	70,500.00	70,500.00	70,500.00	70,500.00
Bonds for deposits					
U.S. bonds on hand					
Other stocks and b'ds	27,088.84	10,314.13	10,091.41	11,437.99	14,922.27
Due from res've ag'ts	62,510.85	42,012.77	45,130.83	60,606.53	26,607.19
Due from nat'l banks	3,606.12	11,069.85	51,712.93	200.58	210.08
Due from State banks	16,361.76	2,403.56	29,361.91	13,777.96	3,256.64
Banking house, etc	42,886.78	42,886.78	42,886.78	42,886.78	42,886.78
Real estate, etc	7,081.35	7,981.35	41,672.80	42,846.87	61,228.31
Current expenses	14,649.15	5,270.76	9,201.40	970.55	6,581.24
Premiums paid	11,050.00	9,650.00	9,650.00	7,150.00	6,350.00
Cash items	1,393.99	1,982.00	681.00	133.28	808.15
Clear'g-house exch'gs					
Bills of other banks	2,325.00	4,640.00	0,430.00	1,570.00	245.00
Fractional currency	133.90	174.91	129.94	122.07	170.66
Specie	52,241.15	56,372.65	50,118.25	75,267.15	53,476.00
Legal-tender notes	1,471.00	4,575.00	11,613.00	332.00	87.00
U.S. cert's of deposit					
5% fund with Treas	3,172.50	3,172.50	3,172.50	3,172.50	3,102.50
Due from U.S. Treas		720.00	1,600.00	480.00	
Total	1,081,002.21	1,021,906.24	1,049,890.41	1,016,428.05	900,001.65

CITY OF OMAHA.

Liabilities.	DECEMBER 9. 9 banks.	MARCH 6. 9 banks.	MAY 4. 9 banks.	JULY 12. 8 banks.	OCTOBER 3. 9 banks.
Capital stock	$4,150,600.00	$4,150,600.00	$4,150,000.00	$3,950,000.00	$4,150,000.00
Surplus fund	470,400.00	478,600.00	483,600.00	471,600.00	476,600.00
Undivided profits	270,236.51	243,321.94	250,167.70	164,598.17	186,632.67
Nat'l-bank circulation	655,345.00	654,195.00	656,985.00	634,145.00	701,995.00
State-bank circulation					
Dividends unpaid		315.00	255.00	1,710.00	210.00
Individual deposits	10,141,498.43	9,728,115.25	9,424,168.06	8,058,301.71	7,572,194.38
U. S. deposits	201,403.65	173,148.79	220,468.88	210,102.79	208,290.44
Dep'ts U.S.dis.officers	203,176.92	227,402.79	156,288.11	159,432.51	245,168.36
Due to national banks	3,459,757.94	3,923,212.02	3,143,044.16	1,682,465.42	1,615,625.97
Due to State banks	2,576,841.11	3,085,160.21	2,988,625.35	1,812,787.99	1,940,641.25
Notes rediscounted	166,174.67	126,699.83	63,500.33	428,801.67	122,352.68
Bills payable			55,000.00	210,000.00	50,000.00
Other liabilities					
Total	22,294,811.23	22,789,590.83	21,592,162.59	17,793,105.26	17,269,778.35

COLORADO.

	53 banks.	53 banks.	53 banks.	47 banks.	51 banks.
Capital stock	$9,075,000.00	$9,050,000.00	$9,060,000.00	$8,510,000.00	$8,775,000.00
Surplus fund	2,267,106.81	2,354,506.81	2,354,883.84	2,014,383.84	2,237,883.84
Undivided profits	2,118,850.33	1,708,405.29	1,937,580.47	1,662,804.85	1,808,242.46
Nat'l-bank circulation	1,522,865.00	1,514,815.00	1,521,915.00	1,398,822.50	1,476,932.50
State-bank circulation					
Dividends unpaid	2,071.00	1,082.00	3,692.00	76,401.00	5,600.00
Individual deposits	27,531,926.36	27,781,022.36	26,706,206.15	18,290,606.12	18,477,482.87
U. S. deposits	305,258.93	330,842.00	306,582.18	368,017.84	246,537.48
Dep'ts U.S.dis.officers	145,875.95	187,671.87	98,460.58	45,107.67	141,325.77
Due to national banks	2,639,758.33	2,205,251.97	1,824,985.15	783,554.14	1,001,509.87
Due to State banks	2,167,153.46	2,356,686.41	2,173,323.19	920,557.73	967,524.32
Notes rediscounted	53,210.00	11,500.00	30,600.00	302,558.00	384,088.88
Bills payable		13,000.00	58,000.00	812,880.10	640,120.58
Other liabilities		2,028.77	13,553.59	412.84	24,000.00
Total	47,829,076.17	47,466,802.48	46,689,812.15	35,255,226.63	36,187,338.57

NEVADA.

	2 banks.	2 banks.	2 banks.	2 banks.	2 banks.
Capital stock	$282,000.00	$282,000.00	$282,000.00	$282,000.00	$282,000.00
Surplus fund	128,000.00	128,000.00	128,000.00	128,000.00	128,000.00
Undivided profits	27,557.97	23,956.66	31,578.23	25,430.77	27,677.40
Nat'l-bank circulation	63,430.00	63,430.00	63,430.00	62,930.00	63,430.00
State-bank circulation					
Dividends unpaid		537.00	162.00	15,000.00	721.50
Individual deposits	520,317.23	468,570.17	522,209.78	464,775.26	363,512.82
U. S. deposits					
Dep'ts U.S.dis.officers					
Due to national banks	28,557.61		5,019.74		
Due to State banks	4,039.43	26,214.69	17,151.19	7,273.03	834.03
Notes rediscounted	18,000.00			15,000.00	8,000.00
Bills payable					20,000.00
Other liabilities		20,197.72	339.47	16,018.99	6,785.90
Total	1,031,902.21	1,021,906.24	1,049,890.41	1,016,428.05	900,961.65

ABSTRACT OF REPORTS SINCE SEPTEMBER 30, 1892, ARRANGED

CALIFORNIA.

Resources.	DECEMBER 0. 34 banks.	MARCH 6. 34 banks.	MAY 4. 36 banks.	JULY 12. 30 banks.	OCTOBER 3. 33 banks.
Loans and discounts	$13,565,795.24	$13,700,574.06	$13,870,153.65	$10,313,813.52	$10,969,647.25
Bonds for circulation	1,306,750.00	1,368,750.00	1,406,250.00	1,193,750.00	1,306,250.00
Bonds for deposits	200,000.00	200,000.00	200,000.00	200,000.00	200,000.00
U.S. bonds on hand	400.00	50,400.00	400.00	400.00	
Other stocks and b'ds	891,354.80	789,440.01	882,000.52	502,687.65	950,881.55
Due from res'veag'ts	1,811,096.06	1,721,596.36	1,792,065.05	332,318.12	430,908.68
Due from nat'l banks	287,083.03	26.,197.68	405,492.55	160,454.92	237,073.54
Due from State banks	008,079.76	649,325.74	876,457.43	519,14'.75	582,179.08
Banking house, etc	1,103,665.07	1,117,988.70	1,122,313.71	700,021.46	928,325.31
Real estate, etc	420,076.85	431,232.26	355,170.68	205,067.13	261,386.14
Current expenses	174,182.61	82,241.02	144,884.52	52,532.91	100,260.55
Premiums paid	156,811.50	15,611.50	138,848.09	121,697.47	121,654.22
Cash items	159,334.15	246,275.51	203,531.63	105,686.10	84,061.07
Clear'g-house exch'gs	27,312.97	46,200.91	27,216.45	7,983.88	89,046.59
Bills of other banks	88,905.00	109,142.00	85,986.00	56,891.00	50,625.00
Fractional currency	2,230.28	2,543.27	3,401.41	2,636.92	2,758.89
Specie	2,053,507.70	1,949,458.05	1,823,751.58	1,834,474.00	1,873,085.16
Legal-tender notes	180,319.00	236,932.00	214,012.00	102,203.00	71,806.00
U.S. cert's of deposit					
5 % fund with Treas	60,873.50	61,593.50	62,781.00	53,118.50	56,831.00
Due from U.S. Treas	1,280.00	7,712.90	5,340.00		1,600.00
Total	23,461,057.53	23,190,305.47	23,620,057.17	16,644,938.93	18,333,163.93

CITY OF SAN FRANCISCO.

	2 banks.	2 banks.	2 banks.	2 banks.	2 banks.
Loans and discounts	$6,357,185.28	$6,582,196.24	$6,733,798.02	$5,910,214.04	$5,901,072.22
Bonds for circulation	100,000.00	100,000.00	100,000.00	100,000.00	100,000.00
Bonds for deposits	100,000.00	100,000.00	100,000.00	100,000.00	100,000.00
U.S. bonds on hand	28,000.00	19,000.00			
Other stocks and b'ds	26,079.80	20,500.00	20,500.00	20,500.00	20,500.00
Due from res'veag'ts	118,867.72	134,579.15	11,411.37	16,593.91	78,089.56
Due from nat'l banks	229,695.45	250,688.62	196,100.63	325,230.00	158,297.36
Due from State banks	283,477.39	255,914.07	220,035.09	281,322.95	286,065.02
Banking house, etc	315,014.80	346,140.37	346,140.37	316,400.77	346,400.77
Real estate, etc					
Current expenses	1,432.50	1,496.30	1,642.85	1,623.35	1,174.35
Premiums paid	31,140.00	28,260.00	26,750.00	22,500.00	21,750.00
Cash items	3,183.37	1,622.92	4,097.05		
Clear'g-house exch'gs	164,497.74	262,351.96	193,014.43	102,571.97	195,432.22
Bills of other banks	4,500.00	3,500.00	5,000.00	8,782.00	1,500.00
Fractional currency	336.43	116.91	122.93	217.59	41.64
Specie	1,659,142.50	1,462,205.00	1,093,586.00	804,960.00	1,082,260.00
Legal-tender notes	9,130.00	9,057.00	31,503,00	171,687.00	22,110.00
U.S. cert's of deposit					
5 % fund with Treas	4,500.00	4,500.00	4,500.00	4,500.00	4,500.00
Due from U.S. Treas					
Total	9,457,182.98	9,582,148.54	9,088,256.64	8,310,112.64	8,319,293.34

OREGON.

	40 banks.	40 banks.	40 banks.	39 banks.	39 banks.
Loans and discounts	$12,048,168.41	$11,864,728.79	$12,557,071.90	$11,041,970.68	$9,892,533.79
Bonds for circulation	801,050.00	801,050.00	801,050.00	776,050.00	776,050.00
Bonds for deposits	450,000.00	450,000.00	450,000.00	450,000.00	450,000.00
U.S. bonds on hand					
Other stocks and b'ds	825,606.55	615,539.02	891,658.52	942,943.71	825,502.86
Due from res'veag'ts	537,307.30	560,080.63	613,861.22	252,784.68	297,306.60
Due from nat'l banks	766,827.22	691,863.64	829,925.57	455,917.67	390,516.63
Due from State banks	553,269.26	573,797.28	561,565.26	353,283.44	222,407.17
Banking house, etc	420,161.98	420,368.95	421,311.91	404,078.05	404,096.07
Real estate, etc	41,265.59	56,560.56	36,825.53	44,694.11	40,609.27
Current expenses	100,662.78	71,381.63	102,505.96	28,144.21	63,281.49
Premiums paid	100,906.75	93,772.21	89,817.21	72,500.00	69,400.00
Cash items	49,933.45	53,418.87	62,802.70	35,837.64	64,824.01
Clear'g-house exch'gs	97,875.27	162,786.06	73,112.56	30,235.59	45,603.50
Bills of other banks	21,937.00	24,056.00	18,867.00	25,121.00	16,631.00
Fractional currency	2,974.52	4,096.86	3,961.75	3,214.16	4,884.63
Specie	1,544,658.60	1,591,598.27	1,570,563.22	1,022,063.71	1,523,649.43
Legal-tender notes	59,904.00	34,810.00	32,242.00	70,848.00	48,163.00
U.S. cert's of deposit					
5 % fund with Treas	35,541.22	31,046.50	35,546.50	33,421.50	33,021.50
Due from U.S. Treas	40.00	4,720.00	500.00	500.00	500.00
Total	18,458,118.90	18,412,605.67	19,153,230.84	16,061,642.15	15,184,130.93

CALIFORNIA.

Liabilities.	DECEMBER 9. 34 banks.	MARCH 6. 34 banks.	MAY 4. 36 banks.	JULY 12. 30 banks.	OCTOBER 3. 33 banks.
Capital stock	$5,675,000.00	$5,675,000.00	$5,800,000.00	$4,975,000.00	$5,625,000.00
Surplus fund	1,153,857.86	1,174,243.00	1,172,743.00	1,075,700.00	1,150,500.00
Undivided profits	1,140,458.63	976,897.73	1,096,557.37	764,116.82	975,170.36
Nat'l-bank circulation	1,195,240.00	1,199,310.00	1,228,820.00	1,058,440.00	1,172,530.00
State-bank circulation					
Dividends unpaid	2,817.75	10,116.54	5,023.73	26,529.70	14,621.61
Individual deposits	13,391,733.64	13,184,939.16	13,385,647.46	7,887,982.73	8,020,272.81
U. S. deposits	38,339.50	6,501.44	18,581.79	76,413.35	65,698.96
Dep'ts U.S.dis.officers	136,047.67	179,721.39	176,315.75	127,630.35	131,550.61
Due to national banks	244,071.23	304,823.13	327,059.41	373,291.92	266,721.12
Due to State banks	462,875.37	339,200.03	385,890.04	228,457.54	179,069.46
Notes rediscounted	8,500.00	33,500.00	8,500.00		17,000.00
Bills payable		15,000.00	19,015.62	89,015.62	115,000.00
Other liabilities	2,215.84	1,020.00	2,100.00	2,354.00	
Total	23,461,057.58	23,190,305.47	23,620,057.17	16,614,938.93	18,333,163.93

CITY OF SAN FRANCISCO.

	2 banks.	2 banks.	2 banks.	2 banks.	2 banks.
Capital stock	$2,500,000.00	$2,500,000.00	$2,500,000.00	$2,500,000.00	$2,500,000.00
Surplus fund	950,000.00	1,075,000.00	1,075,000.00	1,100,000.00	1,100,000.00
Undivided profits	328,511.07	182,707.28	249,760.24	167,571.96	244,855.23
Nat'l-bank circulation	88,950.00	90,000.00	88,100.00	90,000.00	90,000.00
State-bank circulation					
Dividends unpaid	902.00	815.00	430.00	17,905.00	575.00
Individual deposits	3,860,476.00	3,939,470.30	3,743,472.49	3,556,458.53	3,554,567.02
U. S. deposits	112,640.00	111,270.70	100,400.31	104,915.30	123,397.41
Dep'ts U.S.dis.officers					
Due to national banks	745,703.24	866,886.04	638,944.21	565,434.51	352,845.30
Due to State banks	860,909.68	815,969.16	694,050.39	237,827.34	353,053.33
Notes rediscounted					
Bills payable					
Other liabilities					
Total	9,457,182.98	9,582,143.54	9,088,230.64	8,340,112.64	8,310,293.34

OREGON.

	40 banks.	40 banks.	40 banks.	39 banks.	39 banks.
Capital stock	$3,695,000.00	$3,895,000.00	$3,895,000.00	$3,795,000.00	$3,795,000.00
Surplus fund	871,500.00	909,500.00	909,500.00	908,000.00	910,000.00
Undivided profits	1,537,580.60	1,412,393.37	1,450,225.22	1,361,245.81	1,332,072.60
Nat'l-bank circulation	694,150.00	708,130.00	699,700.00	691,220.00	692,190.00
State-bank circulation					
Dividends unpaid	6,028.00	26,054.00	7,042.00	16,826.00	38,977.00
Individual deposits	9,639,357.30	9,197,925.28	9,961,362.67	8,069,306.94	6,915,503.35
U. S. deposits	167,534.02	202,948.68	201,694.77	205,310.92	182,930.87
Dep'ts U.S.dis.officers	250,713.08	242,280.18	234,498.80	136,466.21	248,345.54
Due to national banks	881,010.03	927,572.05	903,911.19	527,213.52	489,343.83
Due to State banks	455,062.35	603,241.42	508,682.72	569,060.80	270,803.68
Notes rediscounted	40,000.00	72,296.55	69,651.61	57,927.14	38,803.00
Bills payable		125,255.14	226,760.08	285,828.06	239,875.71
Other liabilities	20,264.52		25,198.75	38,206.75	21,195.35
Total	18,458,148.09	18,412,605.07	19,153,230.81	16,661,642.15	15,181,130.93

ABSTRACT OF REPORTS SINCE SEPTEMBER 30, 1892, ARRANGED

ARIZONA.

Resources.	DECEMBER 9.	MARCH 6.	MAY 4.	JULY 12.	OCTOBER 3.
	4 banks.	4 banks.	5 banks.	5 banks.	5 banks.
Loans and discounts	$115,980.05	$487,957.92	$559,110.02	$541,731.81	$479,377.95
Bonds for circulation	75,500.00	75,500.00	100,500.00	100,500.00	100,500.00
Bonds for deposits				50,000.00	50,000.00
U.S. bonds on hand			50,000.00		
Other stocks and b'ds	181,111.08	162,916.83	171,890.39	175,185.98	171,797.20
Due from res've ag'ts	113,917.33	104,522.05	97,102.13	58,278.25	58,477.89
Due from nat'l banks	31,379.62	17,962.32	57,699.14	4,850.59	8,031.10
Due from State banks	55,514.01	53,124.02	44,225.96	24,834.60	29,362.32
Banking house, etc	24,671.96	24,610.00	25,731.70	27,762.80	27,743.05
Real estate, etc	1,862.00	1,862.00	1,862.00	1,862.00	1,862.00
Current expenses	18,142.77	6,398.07	25,259.34	16,591.61	14,114.51
Premiums paid	6,802.50	6,412.50	5,506.25	5,116.25	5,116.25
Cash items	2,281.66	1,877.92	3,779.96	6,357.48	6,404.51
Clear'g-house exch'gs					276.07
Bills of other banks	10,272.00	5,558.00	3,145.00	3,520.00	2,649.00
Fractional currency	260.32	163.94	159.91	188.68	152.57
Specie	102,131.25	102,980.45	90,127.75	188,878.10	119,754.40
Legal-tender notes	16,040.00	29,298.00	24,861.00	24,105.00	20,387.00
U.S. cert's of deposit					
5 % fund with Treas	3,397.50	2,947.50	4,522.50	4,172.50	4,172.50
Due from U.S. Treas	450.00		120.00		
Total	1,089,714.05	1,084,100.52	1,265,621.05	1,233,925.05	1,100,178.32

NORTH DAKOTA.

	34 banks.	35 banks.	35 banks.	32 banks.	32 banks.
Loans and discounts	$7,178,917.17	$7,043,489.59	$7,091,698.97	$6,394,409.92	$5,863,784.16
Bonds for circulation	631,500.00	644,000.00	644,000.00	569,000.00	569,000.00
Bonds for deposits	50,000.00	50,000.00	50,000.00	50,000.00	50,000.00
U.S. bonds on hand					
Other stocks and b'ds	421,076.71	443,745.95	438,159.37	344,627.21	286,240.88
Due from res've ag'ts	553,558.98	564,614.25	386,275.27	406,776.33	517,841.48
Due from nat'l banks	109,430.13	73,449.73	36,639.39	85,919.65	94,819.39
Due from State banks	134,775.96	122,306.39	101,069.85	79,893.81	132,745.14
Banking house, etc	511,118.00	520,045.29	521,147.90	398,293.20	428,283.57
Real estate, etc	203,964.82	208,238.44	204,546.50	184,688.91	195,216.54
Current expenses	89,805.69	79,640.93	110,321.83	39,714.76	83,939.01
Premiums paid	41,301.98	42,390.00	40,321.25	34,440.37	33,211.87
Cash items	130,198.86	71,026.61	51,965.76	63,731.89	69,739.68
Clear'g-house exch'gs					11,659.65
Bills of other banks	81,170.00	47,947.00	39,022.00	38,937.00	66,698.00
Fractional currency	4,190.80	5,018.78	4,850.29	5,127.40	4,361.01
Specie	392,407.75	301,787.85	370,773.05	310,962.15	269,268.40
Legal-tender notes	281,975.00	208,827.00	123,458.00	120,249.00	217,084.00
U.S. cert's of deposit					
5 % fund with Treas	24,807.20	27,495.00	26,344.70	24,460.00	23,969.50
Due from U.S. Treas	323.45	3,324.70	1,425.00	806.00	693.50
Total	10,846,821.88	10,518,247.51	10,242,010.13	9,152,035.60	8,910,396.11

SOUTH DAKOTA.

	40 banks.	40 banks.	41 banks.	40 banks.	39 banks.
Loans and discounts	$5,861,930.62	$5,705,816.51	$5,793,781.61	$5,230,330.44	$4,510,816.81
Bonds for circulation	654,750.00	692,250.00	704,750.00	692,250.00	692,250.00
Bonds for deposits	150,000.00	150,000.00	150,000.00	150,000.00	150,000.00
U.S. bonds on hand			20,000.00		
Other stocks and b'ds	704,767.65	700,915.29	681,662.31	626,555.10	633,690.05
Due from res've ag'ts	561,075.71	536,194.58	504,148.92	400,408.38	385,667.61
Due from nat'l banks	589,024.86	565,787.89	435,728.19	305,717.73	342,677.69
Due from State banks	83,494.65	65,405.90	58,486.40	47,707.03	110,455.94
Banking house, etc	361,305.25	357,017.07	359,144.51	367,298.37	371,278.75
Real estate, etc	160,634.72	184,033.97	179,424.73	178,321.44	211,621.24
Current expenses	101,733.58	68,563.12	117,357.16	67,688.70	72,914.35
Premiums paid	75,771.67	77,447.52	73,434.56	63,961.44	61,940.60
Cash items	54,976.67	58,646.29	53,534.25	44,996.58	41,050.34
Clear'g-house exch'gs					5,713.93
Bills of other banks	70,003.00	56,593.00	57,959.00	55,610.00	52,686.00
Fractional currency		3,411.88	3,517.18	3,133.65	3,185.84
Specie	361,204.73	338,633.07	382,762.01	316,902.61	364,604.30
Legal-tender notes	337,001.00	296,373.00	272,663.00	243,392.00	204,056.00
U.S. cert's of deposit					
5 % fund with Treas	28,063.75	28,863.75	29,151.25	29,650.75	28,140.25
Due from U.S. Treas	91.00	3,173.22		520.00	485.00
Total	10,158,019.29	9,909,126.06	9,856,875.08	8,881,347.22	8,251,131.79

BY STATES AND RESERVE CITIES—Continued.

ARIZONA.

Liabilities.	DECEMBER 9.	MARCH 6.	MAY 4.	JULY 12.	OCTOBER 3.
	4 banks.	4 banks.	5 banks.	5 banks.	5 banks.
Capital stock	$300,000.00	$300,000.00	$350,000.00	$400,000.00	$400,000.00
Surplus fund	34,150.00	36,360.89	36,360.89	36,150.00	36,150.00
Undivided profits	72,982 09	62,398.80	76,924.43	70,832.37	75,393.40
Nat'l-bank circulation	67,350.00	67,210.00	89,160.00	90,450.00	90,000.00
State-bank circulation					
Dividends unpaid					
Individual deposits	603,532.44	606,769.29	704,022.15	554,900.43	440,511.10
U. S. deposits				1,010.00	12,050.05
Dep'ts U.S.dis.officers					
Due to national banks	4,932.80	707.60	5,575.60	2,235.15	1,014.72
Due to State banks	0,760.72	10,653.94	3,577.98	70,327.70	12,058.99
Notes rediscounted					
Bills payable				8,000.00	33,000.00
Other liabilities					
Total	1,089,714.05	1,084,100.52	1,265,021.05	1,233,925.05	1,100,178.32

NORTH DAKOTA.

	34 banks.	35 banks.	35 banks.	32 banks.	32 banks.
Capital stock	$2,515,000.00	$2,565,000.00	$2,565,000.00	$2,215,000.00	$2,215,000.00
Surplus fund	409,068.65	550,018.65	512,018.65	487,290.00	488,200.00
Undivided profits	428,804.81	258,939.23	333,256.31	243,423.61	256,760.02
Nat'l-bank circulation	567,330.00	579,590.00	579,425.00	512,075.00	512,090.00
State-bank circulation					
Dividends unpaid	635.00	15,754.32	7 575.00	6,351.00	8,500.00
Individual deposits	6,387,200.93	5,745,559.71	5,359,701.91	4,707,600.09	4,636,294.71
U.S. deposits	41,049.35	15,576.41	13,547.36	13,489.01	20,001.60
Dep'ts U.S.dis.officers	3,329.78	29,951.52	28,093.41	27,114.70	33,250.05
Due to national banks	40,583.10	22,622.50	25,837.39	14,636.63	28,811.68
Due to State banks	169,300,93	122,822.71	91,687.46	38,351.31	82,525.41
Notes rediscounted	87,808.33	281,556.77	395,468.09	369,040.02	210,454.42
Bills payable	96,711.00	330,850.00	330,408.55	511,414.14	427,418.22
Other liabilities	10,000.00	5.00		6,270.00	
Total	10,846,821.88	10,518,247.51	10,242,019.13	9,152,055.60	8,919,396.11

SOUTH DAKOTA.

	40 banks.	40 banks.	41 banks.	40 banks.	30 banks.
Capital stock	$2,010,000.00	$2,560,000.00	$2,590,000.00	$2,550,000.00	$2,510,000.00
Surplus fund	629,175.00	612,125.00	642,125.00	607,375.00	600,375.00
Undivided profits	305,308 60	200,258.17	257,293.61	219,303.98	204,302.70
Nat'l-bank circulation	583,275.00	616,005.00	627,655.00	618,025.00	615,355.00
State-bank circulation					
Dividends unpaid	205.00	1,915.00	1,160.00	14,162.00	8,914.00
Individual deposits	5,177,263.00	5,005,799.74	5,009,073.65	4,103,251.61	3,580,792.46
U. S. deposits	103,362.92	101,170.37	99,390.95	105,028.32	113,245.24
Dep'ts U.S.dis.officers	27,417.74	26,671.99	24,361.40	21,417.30	32,859.46
Due to national banks	225,562.58	214,481.93	1,100.45	156,234.51	140,893.80
Due to State banks	391,409.39	336,503.08	155,778.10	157,203.17	166,723.28
Notes rediscounted	44,900.00	134,335.78	251,318.09	155,890.33	111,773.85
Bills payable	45,050.00	63,800.00	146,313.83	170,450.00	188,900.00
Other liabilities	15,000.00		51,300.00		
Total	10,158,919.20	9,909,126.06	9,850,875.08	8,884,347.22	8,254,134.79

ABSTRACT OF REPORTS SINCE SEPTEMBER 30, 1892, ARRANGED

IDAHO.

Resources.	DECEMBER 9. 11 banks.	MARCH 6. 13 banks.	MAY 4. 13 banks.	JULY 12. 13 banks.	OCTOBER 3. 13 banks.
Loans and discounts.	$1,919,309.65	$2,018,108.35	$2,029,177.35	$1,920,798.26	$1,636,188.73
Bonds for circulation.	181,250.00	206,250.00	206,250.00	206,250.00	206,250.00
Bonds for deposits ..	50,000.00	50,000.00	50,000.00	50,000.00	50,000.00
U. S. bonds on hand .					
Other stocks and b'ds	317,437.23	232,800.95	314,035.59	317,729.23	335,243.73
Due from res'r eag'ts.	111,140.88	71,335.10	50,385.31	49,590.89	56,071.00
Due from nat'l banks	111,706.97	126,566.14	80,259.79	62,831.79	46,632.40
Due from State banks	44,931.25	85,296.51	53,267.51	72,575.59	63,833.35
Banking house, etc ..	181,925.52	173,288.02	172,228.59	171,601.89	170,801.51
Real estate, etc......	54,453.37	47,493.32	45,140.92	45,334.52	49,260.08
Current expenses...	41,014.13	17,971.48	28,826.41	16,115.41	30,897.57
Premiums paid......	17,131.13	14,988.03	14,813.03	13,338.03	12,188.03
Cash items...........	31,531.51	10,633.52	6,029.42	18,519.40	8,375.28
Clear'g-house exch'gs					
Bills of other banks .	26,468.00	35,181.00	22,973.00	16,715.00	16,301.00
Fractional currency .	412.72	449.33	339.36	424.90	396.90
Specie..............	260,423.90	302,296.82	264,990.87	229,088.35	227,930.59
Legal-tender notes ..	85,935.00	72,364.00	48,001.00	50,860.00	51,469.00
U. S. cert's of deposit.					
5 % fund with Treas.	8,155.25	9,279.75	9,280.75	8,780.75	8,780.75
Due from U. S. Treas.		600.00	600.00	500.00	
Total.........	3,446,286.60	3,474,842.32	3,396,607.90	3,251,063.01	2,971,540.92

MONTANA.

	35 banks.	35 banks.	35 banks.	33 banks.	22 banks.
Loans and disc'nts.	$17,749,141.13	$18,037,496.33	$18,348,575.15	$17,403,589.48	$8,486,074.43
Bonds for circulation.	930,850.00	920,850.00	927,100.00	902,100.00	575,600.00
Bonds for deposits...	300,000.00	300,000.00	300,000.00	300,000.00	100,000.00
U. S. bonds on hand..					
Other stocks and b'ds	923,186.50	875,100.87	922,942.83	904,573.60	356,772.92
Due from res've ag'ts.	1,700,398.88	1,280,732.25	1,212,162.43	895,173.24	752,421.64
Due from nat'l banks.	953,950.55	638,468.34	607,799.48	560,552.43	337,480.41
Due from State banks	376,968.12	276,152.21	206,978.35	251,854.65	155,814.87
Banking house, etc..	763,591.79	775,713.66	776,500.82	752,125.20	378,777.81
Real estate, etc......	214,434.71	224,833.83	223,494.18	240,037.26	147,168.77
Current expenses....	250,755.60	97,527.58	160,503.33	42,058.93	66,155.50
Premiums paid......	79,971.70	66,190.90	64,604.53	59,279.53	41,854.53
Cash items...........	242,307.49	120,266.21	105,602.45	78,181.70	32,435.41
Clear'g-house exch'gs					279.83
Bills of other banks..	268,571.00	191,623.00	169,030.00	168,904.00	171,467.00
Fractional currency.	4,633.41	5,900.00	5,746.48	4,873.87	3,300.53
Specie..............	1,190,704.30	1,377,843.55	1,242,704.40	928,500.35	940,607.00
Legal-tender notes..	634,110.00	620,120.00	473,848.00	572,519.00	461,371.00
U. S. cert's of deposit.					
5 % fund with Treas.	40,292.50	40,031.50	40,594.00	38,486.00	25,401.50
Due from U. S. Treas.	18,070.14	37,202.39	7,725.95	1,658.95	
Total	26,648,015.82	25,886,052.62	25,885,912.38	24,194,468.10	13,045,674.05

NEW MEXICO.

	11 banks.	11 banks.	11 banks.	10 banks.	10 banks.
Loans and discounts	$2,292,150.38	$2,446,302.37	$2,512,433.21	$1,883,506.44	$1,673,482.32
Bonds for circulation	315,000.00	315,000.00	315,000.00	265,000.00	265,000.00
Bonds for deposits ..	200,000.00	200,000.00	200,000.00	200,000.00	200,000.00
U. S. bonds on hand ..					
Other stocks and b'ds	74,502.77	80,290.33	86,239.55	110,518.15	121,008.45
Due from res'r o ag'ts.	206,668.22	305,889.76	296,144.89	169,672.47	112,763.63
Due from nat'l banks.	626,153.96	410,195.04	333,207.56	209,306.22	86,138.04
Due from State banks	39,299.49	31,665.12	37,931.40	41,565.81	17,023.24
Banking house, etc..	117,554.16	116,091.16	117,827.87	108,070.93	110,804.48
Real estate, etc......	26,590.38	28,273.29	28,273.29	16,866.20	16,866.20
Current expenses....	55,459.34	23,538.03	42,487.68	48,421.72	26,982.73
Premiums paid......	31,106.25	27,981.25	27,656.25	18,575.00	14,575.00
Cash items...........	43,961.20	26,059.71	30,768.57	14,482.30	13,665.44
Clear'g-house exch'gs					
Bills of other banks..	23,371.00	28,219.00	20,775.00	30,040.00	9,802.06
Fractional currency	951.46	1,174.45	1,509.82	716.02	710.02
Specie..............	226,780.80	215,384.35	227,397.00	166,014.34	191,868.85
Legal-tender notes ..	87,143.00	61,572.00	66,376.00	76,189.00	45,234.00
U. S. cert's of deposit.					
5 % fund with Treas	13,675.00	13,675.00	13,675.00	11,425.00	11,425.00
Due from U. S. Treas.	1,000.00	1,520.00	500.00	1,600.00	
Total.........	4,471,357.41	4,332,839.86	4,358,403.69	3,342,208.60	2,917,846.11

BY STATES AND RESERVE CITIES—Continued.

IDAHO.

Liabilities.	DECEMBER 9. 11 banks.	MARCH 6. 13 banks.	MAY 4. 13 banks.	JULY 12. 13 banks.	OCTOBER 3. 13 banks.
Capital stock	$700,000.00	$803,621.00	$815,000.00	$825,000.00	$825,000.00
Surplus fund	194,000.00	218,000.00	218,000.00	242,983.65	247,000.00
Undivided profits...	186,693.79	138,459.14	178,403.83	162,052.55	170,945.39
Nat'l-bank circulation	162,715.00	185,115.00	184,665.00	185,615.00	185,615.00
State-bank circulation					
Dividends unpaid....				078.00	30.00
Individual deposits..	2,050,635.67	1,935,516.78	1,762,755.59	1,581,663.94	1,302,609.60
U. S. deposits	34,340.93	32,312.58	36,685.90	42,990.16	41,922.51
Dept's U.S.dis.officers	15,137.21	16,491.30	12,583.87	6,737,63	8,021.85
Due to national banks	43,335.70	36,684.30	36,301.22	55,797.84	24,350.58
Due to State banks ..	44,428.30	88,042.20	38,212.49	44,919.24	49,959.24
Notes rediscounted ..	5,000.00	5,000.00	77,000.00	15,625.00	7,586.75
Bills payable	10,000.00	15,000.00	35,000.00	87,000.00	99,500.00
Other liabilities					
Total	3,446,286.60	3,474,842.32	3,396,607.90	3,251,063.01	2,871,540.92

MONTANA.

	35 banks.	35 banks.	35 banks.	33 banks.	22 banks.
Capital stock	$4,840,000.00	$4,800,500.00	$4,825,000.00	$4,725,000.00	$2,775,000.00
Surplus fund........	705,100.00	773,583.90	774,783.90	766,483.90	374,650.00
Undivided profits....	2,753,570.94	2,419,173.33	2,491,623.22	2,414,183.47	1,640,648.59
Nat'l-bank circulation	802,980.00	792,520.00	807,490.00	758,390.00	517,440.00
State-bank circulation					
Dividends unpaid....	35.00	3,315.00	3,220.00	51,040.00	15,535.00
Individual deposits..	13,827,138.35	15,214,794.89	14,900,733.94	13,410,309.88	6,958,461.59
U. S. deposits	149,430.10	171,167.74	187,469.92	217,736.36	38,757.65
Dep'ts U.S.dis.officers	108,694.71	114,621.11	81,987.34	37,290.81	73,184.86
Due to national banks	896,751.80	598,884.65	617,541.92	529,260.10	112,687.83
Due to State banks...	409,650.33	333,933.78	337,981.47	250,283.04	83,269.26
Notes rediscounted ..	124,664.59	405,558.22	448,530.67	517,855.18	229,161.87
Bills payable	30,000.00	235,000.00	235,000.00	477,000.00	226,877.31
Other liabilities......		3,000.00	146,550.00	7,635.45	.09
Total	26,648,015.82	25,886,052.62	25,885,912.38	24,194,468.19	13,045,074.05

NEW MEXICO.

	11 banks.	11 banks.	11 banks.	10 banks.	10 banks.
Capital stock	$925,000.00	$925,000.00	$925,000.00	$750,000.00	$750,000.00
Surplus fund........	193,000.00	225,067.42	225,067.42	188,567.42	169,072.11
Undivided profits....	106,281.84	36,322.55	75,019.59	67,058.69	57,666.99
Nat'l-bank circulation	279,750.00	283,000.00	282,150.00	237,900.00	238,000.00
State-bank circulation					
Dividends unpaid....		25.00		287.50	1,337.50
Individual deposits..	2,457,104.07	2,241,920.80	2,302,540.56	1,563,088.30	1,208,019.40
U. S. deposits	114,626.79	131,498.55	130,772.80	138,115.31	110,783.11
Dep'ts U.S.dis.officers	79,483.51	49,757.70	57,126.53	49,384.69	73,315.07
Due to national banks	153,799.38	184,278.11	172,459.54	125,097.12	21,231.86
Due to State banks...	108,279.82	191,922.08	115,979.40	49,637.79	78,065.93
Notes rediscounted ..	18,030.00	28,000.00	25,500.00	24,555.88	34,663.15
Bills payable	6,000.00	36,047.65	46,787.85	148,515.99	155,690.99
Other liabilities......					
Total	4,471,357.41	4,332,839.86	4,358,403.69	3,342,208.69	2,917,846.11

ABSTRACT OF REPORTS SINCE SEPTEMBER 30, 1892, ARRANGED

UTAH.

RESOURCES.	DECEMBER 9. 14 banks.	MARCH 6 14 banks.	MAY 4. 14 banks.	JULY 12. 11 banks.	OCTOBER 3. 14 banks.
Loans and discounts	$5,520,733.97	$5,304,940.60	$5,487,966.40	$4,506,829.89	$4,554,484.17
Bonds for circulation	485,000.00	475,000.00	475,000.00	460,600.00	475,000.00
Bonds for deposits .	125,000.00	125,000.00	125,000.00	125,000.00	125,000.00
U. S. bonds on hand	51,900.00	51,900.00	51,900.00	1,900.00	1,900.00
Other stocks and b'ds	301,318.77	283,720.29	284,130.30	218,311.51	229,504.30
Due from res've ag'ts	428,685.50	463,570.20	352,961.19	160,541.07	184,452.28
Due from nat'l banks	187,976.33	163,297.06	153,037.29	78,079.66	46,351.67
Due from State banks	175,138.64	170,554.18	232,647.54	205,681.76	192,636.11
Banking house, etc.	455,901.82	453,735.16	453,740.16	427,665.18	471,193.95
Real estate, etc	98,564.76	98,423.35	117,943.10	87,142.48	125,243.73
Current expenses	79,629.70	46,706.14	52,441.85	16,510.00	52,823.50
Premiums paid	47,150.00	38,025.00	37,900.00	28,525.00	28,525.00
Cash items	32,346.63	109,192.02	76,413.82	57,647.96	28,433.90
Clear'g-house exch'gs	82,378.04	90,539.98	101,422.60	57,164.77	46,023.93
Bills of other banks	41,801.00	48,371.00	48,895.00	79,542.00	53,865.00
Fractional currency.	2,982.35	4,653.20	5,019.48	3,201.92	4,979.93
Specie	857,982.45	771,282.25	718,084.20	708,881.68	775,915.45
Legal-tender notes	58,074.00	55,640.00	69,538.00	154,668.00	128,062.00
U. S. cert's of deposit.					
5% fund with Treas.	21,375.00	21,375.00	20,725.00	18,000.00	20,775.00
Due from U. S. Treas.					
Total	9,053,938.96	8,775,925.52	8,864,764.32	7,424,695.88	7,515,259.92

WASHINGTON.

	70 banks.	70 banks.	70 banks.	64 banks.	57 banks.
Loans and discounts.	$17,727,382.13	$17,692,004.21	$18,166,209.80	$14,879,146.32	$12,430,299.05
Bonds for circulation.	1,758,000.00	1,758,000.00	1,745,500.00	1,595,500.00	1,380,500.00
Bonds for deposits	50,000.00	50,000.00	50,000.00	50,000.00	50,000.00
U. S. bonds on hand	25,000.00	35,000.00			
Other stocks and b'ds	824,129.46	833,105.58	818,548.72	628,031.96	682,385.60
Due from res've ag'ts.	1,637,513.91	1,241,687.08	1,026,929.31	483,707.13	318,891.17
Due from nat'l banks.	1,150,104.73	1,055,621.07	975,871.01	443,472.52	422,912.46
Due from State banks	452,115.53	488,872.94	512,932.05	361,839.07	313,939.06
Banking house, etc.	1,022,573.37	1,091,500.03	1,091,512.58	863,324.34	695,760.46
Real estate, etc	412,863.68	399,973.83	412,150.57	436,432.68	350,062.25
Current expenses	304,912.95	160,685.50	275,624.31	123,477.74	178,165.24
Premiums paid	174,813.13	158,474.55	150,321.78	121,096.64	104,209.14
Cash items	147,932.21	136,888.80	190,151.24	84,389.40	70,276.07
Clear'g-house exch'gs	133,091.97	200,811.61	112,543.18	135,517.67	78,952.79
Bills of other banks	118,461.00	99,161.00	86,306.00	96,186.00	43,187.00
Fractional currency.	4,467.69	5,923.78	6,608.35	4,776.24	4,602.36
Specie	2,216,180.05	2,163,196.25	1,787,440.65	1,771,251.77	1,277,366.55
Legal-tender notes	148,199.00	163,191.00	118,619.00	145,092.00	90,018.00
U. S. cert's of deposit.					
5% fund with Treas	79,109.25	73,359.25	75,247.25	65,027.25	58,722.25
Due from U. S. Treas.	500.00	6,360.00	650.60	850.00	3,815.00
Total	28,387,380.06	27,813,907.07	27,603,198.80	22,290,921.73	18,563,185.45

WYOMING.

	13 banks.	13 banks.	13 banks.	13 banks.	13 banks.
Loans and discounts	$3,065,600.00	$2,963,815.61	$2,907,490.15	$2,770,507.62	$2,409,450.15
Bonds for circulation.	302,500.00	302,500.06	302,500.00	302,500.00	302,500.00
Bonds for deposits					
U. S. bonds on hand .					
Other stocks and b'ds	221,807.22	179,676.13	186,403.46	197,930.50	203,257.69
Due from res've ag'ts.	593,291.07	301,924.83	310,831.07	168,552.07	138,047.41
Due from nat'l banks.	156,410.23	71,638.60	80,114.69	45,221.21	34,229.65
Due from State banks	17,066.37	29,862.06	10,054.91	17,630.35	13,021.40
Banking house, etc	139,399.27	141,000.09	143,502.97	141,433.95	141,398.05
Real estate, etc	34,256.29	35,725.85	31,6.9.03	43,408.27	55,367.57
Current expenses	46,258.48	22,721.83	38,849.68	11,838.52	20,529.74
Premiums paid	25,353.91	22,147.66	21,980.16	19,422.66	16,892.66
Cash items	31,723.27	21,004.21	25,925.86	24,460.14	25,127.49
Clear'g-house exch'gs					
Bills of other banks	17,003.00	19,118.00	13,218.00	15,315.00	18,038.00
Fractional currency .	1,788.59	1,847.16	1,623.78	1,680.96	1,869.16
Specie	396,454.25	304,882.65	278,740.10	238,971.85	218,473.05
Legal-tender notes	44,598.00	38,918.00	29,453.00	41,104.00	33,214.00
U. S. cert's of deposit.					
5% fund with Treas	13,012.50	13,612.25	13,612.25	13,112.25	13,112.25
Due from U. S. Treas.	1,429.37		1,700.00		2,000.00
Total	5,047,860.82	4,470,897.93	4,487,608.51	4,053,179.68	3,738,949.17

BY STATES AND RESERVE CITIES—Continued.

UTAH.

LIABILITIES.	DECEMBER 0. 14 banks.	MARCH 6. 14 banks.	MAY 4 14 banks.	JULY 12. 11 banks.	OCTOBER 3. 11 banks.
Capital stock	$2,800,000.00	$2,800,000.00	$2,800,000.00	$2,550,000.00	$2,800,000.00
Surplus fund	956,300.00	952,300.00	952,300.00	915,200.00	936,700.00
Undivided profits....	227,702.00	152,884.69	175,659.28	153,065.20	224,778.51
Nat'l bank circulation	359,740.00	354,000.00	358,190.00	315,000.00	382,500.00
State bank circulation					
Dividends unpaid...	1,465.00	1,664.00	4,987.00	10,281.00	2,870.00
Individual deposits .	4,248,496.22	3,961,897.96	4,142,021.81	3,024,653.36	2,713,180.95
U. S. deposits.......	73,675.21	41,245.29	63,722.48	67,657.80	51,694.11
Dep'ts U.S.dis.officers	46,182.32	78,456.85	52,451.24	47,309.49	71,509.49
Due to national banks	66,051.28	69,054.68	68,381.95	27,292.21	35,717.61
Due to State banks...	233,826.93	248,412.30	162,113.31	144,704.82	123,301.25
Notes rediscounted ..	10,501.00	98,937.75	78,083.75	89,605.00	50,130.00
Bills payable	30,000.00	15,500.00		80.000.00	149,663.54
Other liabilities.			6,853.50		205.46
Total	9,053,938.96	8,775,925.52	8,804,764.32	7,424,695.88	7,545,259.92

WASHINGTON.

	70 banks.	70 banks.	70 banks.	64 banks.	57 banks.
Capital stock	$7,895,000.00	$7,470,000.00	$7,475,000.00	$6,830,000.00	$6,020,600.00
Surplus fund	1,673,380.62	1,789,880.66	1,793,639.66	1,721,439.66	1,658,199.66
Undivided profits....	1,332,753.31	977,026.95	1,177,326.64	910,160.44	800,651.80
Nat'l-bank circulation	1,575,875.00	1,557,455.00	1,540,860.00	1,430,625.00	1,241,945.00
State-bank circulation					
Dividends unpaid ..	4,921.75	15,255.50	5,807.50	26,561.00	33,501.00
Individual deposits ..	14,080,716.95	13,848,182.19	13,499,463.33	8,997,734.86	7,009,614.17
U. S. deposits........	31,297.06	30,740.68	25,619.75	42,403.44	41,203.05
Dep'ts U.S.dis.officers	14,214.10	16,305.64	21,474.43	3,116.80	12,732.71
Due to national banks	800,233.80	801,445.91	678,474.53	448,290.29	303,427.05
Due to State banks..	678,561.44	536,151.80	664,518.69	525,673.79	207,440.60
Notes rediscouuted ..	210,677.93	253,924.64	340,787.43	635,181.11	276,490.31
Bills payable........	23,747.50	407,447.50	335,447.50	645,607.50	923,374.50
Other liabilities......		34,081.60	44,779.34	73,831.84	28,515.00
Total	28,387,380.06	27,813,007.07	27,603,198.80	22,290,921.72	18,563,185.45

WYOMING.

	13 banks.	13 banks.	13 banks.	13 banks.	13 banks.
Capital stock........	$1,210,000.00	$1,210,000.00	$1,210,000.00	$1,210,000.00	$1,210,000.00
Surplus fund........	199,800.00	171,550.00	171,850.00	177,350.00	180,600.00
Undivided profits ...	121,256.89	61,691.02	106,486.09	45,992.54	63,184.04
Nat'l bank circulation	267,445.00	267,395.00	270,315.00	272,245.00	271,625.00
State bank circulation					
Dividends unpaid ...		210.00	310.00	4,490.00	4,000.00
Individual deposits..	3,006,021.95	2,654,520.20	2,541,115.95	2,005,140.29	1,709,406.77
U. S. deposits.......					
Dep's U.S.dis.officers					
Due to national banks	113,152.27	40,371.06	43,560.74	32,695.12	16,684.70
Due to State banks..	22,302.37	17,473.87	16,700.59	13,037.77	25,327.10
Notes rediscounted..	7,182.34	22,505.28	57,261.14	159,728.96	61,621.47
Bills payable........	10,000.00	25,000.00	70,000.00	132,500.00	136,500.00
Other liabilities.....					
Total..........	5,047,860.82	4,470,897.93	4,487,608.51	4,053,179.68	3,738,919.17

ABSTRACT OF REPORTS SINCE SEPTEMBER 30, 1892, ARRANGED

OKLAHOMA TERRITORY.

Resources.	DECEMBER 9. 4 banks.	MARCH 6. 5 banks.	MAY 4. 5 banks.	JULY 12. 6 banks.	OCTOBER 3. 6 banks.
Loans and discounts.	$338,902.65	$366,425.07	$377,315.82	$370,380.83	$338,725.91
Bonds for circulation	50,000.00	62,500.00	62,500.00	75,000.00	75,000.00
Bonds for deposits...					
U.S. bonds on hand..					
Other stocks and b'ds	141,483.24	145,573.61	204,625.81	189,356.97	153,472.85
Due from res've ag'ts	101,439.92	190,618.03	224,406.78	102,728.25	126,132.43
Due from nat'l banks	65,802.27	103,659.43	101,657.56	36,240.97	68,006.84
Due from State banks	28,026.05	13,003.30	11,132.99	20,268.30	9,186.92
Banking house, etc..	63,539.46	77,726.01	92,197.56	103,032.84	111,566.47
Real estate, etc					• 150.00
Current expenses...	11,223.77	7,046.79	15,605.85	919.51	9,379.92
Premiums paid.....	3,863.53	3,750.00	3,625.00	2,987.50	2,737.50
Cash items..........	6,665.19	15,352.70	6,387.44	8,388.68	13,937.75
Clear'g-house exch'gs					
Bills of other banks.	20,766.00	23,194.00	26,318.00	49,724.00	29,679.00
Fractional currency.	332.56	386.13	582.14	534.77	1,275.04
Specie..............	51,632.05	39,056.85	53,087.50	81,408.20	74,321.00
Legal-tender notes..	35,533.00	42,758.00	58,385.00	47,695.00	60,297.00
U.S. cer'ts of deposit.					
5 % fund with Treas.	2,250.00	2,270.00	2,812.50	3,375.00	3,375.00
Due from U.S. Treas.					
Total........	922,059.69	1,093,319.92	1,240,639.95	1,092,100.82	1,077,243.63

INDIAN TERRITORY.

	6 banks.	6 banks.	6 banks.	6 banks.	6 banks.
Loans and discounts.	$582,376.33	$651,709.40	$670,017.71	$604,761.45	$541,123.90
Bonds for circulation	90,000.00	90,000.00	90,000.00	90,000.00	90,000.00
Bonds for deposits...					
U.S. bonds on hand..					
Other stocks and b'ds		1,027.00	1,027.00	1,000.00	1,000.00
Due from res've ag'ts	106,848.49	99,506.50	64,531.88	87,375.82	108,018.34
Due from nat'l banks	69,015.32	26,316.59	30,290.85	40,578.98	29,075.42
Due from State banks	10,452.02	11,412.31	17,292.48	11,419.48	22,530.16
Banking house, etc..	33,383.11	38,788.04	45,169.68	45,501.05	31,784.48
Real estate, etc	5,644.32	4,200.00	4,403.05	4,293.00	2,111.95
Current expenses...	10,848.49	6,896.31	11,986.90	2,630.72	7,453.76
Premiums paid	11,475.00	11,275.00	11,100.00	10,625.00	7,225.00
Cash items..........	6,462.57	6,695.72	2,752.40	3,816.07	6,863.91
Clear'g-house exch'gs					
Bills of other banks.	16,250.00	9,713.00	14,742.00	16,027.00	12,836.00
Fractional currency.	187.77	308.14	381.71	400.33	529.14
Specie	33,647.65	39,860.25	50,672.90	57,640.80	63,541.35
Legal-tender notes..	22,190.00	27,420.00	21,870.00	21,400.00	24,215.00
U.S. cert's of deposit.					
5 % fund with Treas.	4,049.50	4,050.00	4,050.00	4,050.00	4,050.00
Due from U.S. Treas.	250.00	50.00	90.00		140.00
Total	1,003,080.57	1,029,228.26	1,040,378.50	1,001,528.70	952,398.41

BY STATES AND RESERVE CITIES—Continued.

OKLAHOMA TERRITORY.

Liabilities.	DECEMBER 9.	MARCH 6.	MAY 4.	JULY 12.	OCTOBER 3.
	4 banks.	5 banks.	5 banks.	6 banks.	6 banks.
Capital stock	$200,000.00	$235,000.00	$210,000.00	$300,000.00	$300,000.00
Surplus fund	11,000.00	15,000.00	13,000.00	17,000.00	16,000.00
Undivided profits	41,519.07	35,277.40	51,374.28	35,859.38	49,187.28
Nat'l bank circulation	44,500.00	55,750.00	56,250.00	67,500.00	67,500.00
State bank circulation					
Dividends unpaid					
Individual deposits	613,366.80	713,229.90	828,497.25	644,524.87	591,812.09
U. S. deposits					
Dep's U. S.dis. officers					
Due to national banks	7,580.39	14,938.48	20,095.24	14,670.30	5,602.14
Due to State banks	4,083.74	12,124.74	22,823.18	7,546.27	33,421.03
Notes rediscounted					8,661.09
Bills payable		11,999.40		5,000.00	5,000.00
Other liabilities					
Total	922,050.69	1,093,319.92	1,240,659.95	1,092,100.82	1,077,243.03

INDIAN TERRITORY.

	6 banks.	6 banks.	6 banks.	6 banks.	6 banks.
Capital stock	$360,000.00	$360,000.00	$360,000.00	$360,000.00	$360,000.00
Surplus fund	15,700.00	27,100.00	27,100.00	39,700.00	42,200.00
Undivided profits	36,430.02	25,664.22	40,451.55	10,836.62	20,039.26
Nat'l-bank circulation	80,990.00	81,000.00	81,000.00	81,000.00	81,000.00
State-bank circulation					
Dividends unpaid		4,132.00		50.00	
Individual deposits	475,666.25	521,790.17	487,754.71	475,235.46	423,538.22
U. S. deposits					
Dep'ts U.S.dis.officers					
Due to national banks	9,065.85	8,640.21	23,026.65	12,436.61	8,248.38
Due to State banks	227.85	881.66	1,045.65	1,270.01	2,372.55
Notes rediscounted					
Bills payable	25,000.00		20,000.00	10,000.00	15,000.00
Other liabilities				5,000 00	
Total	1,003,080.57	1,029,228.26	1,040,378.56	1,001,528.70	952,398.41

INDEX.

10665 CUR——22

www.ingramcontent.com/pod-product-compliance
Lightning Source LLC
Chambersburg PA
CBHW021115270326
41929CB00009B/896